INSIGHT GUIDES
NEW ZEALAND

APA PUBLICATIONS
Part of the Langenscheidt Publishing Group

※ INSIGHT GUIDE
NEW ZEALAND

Editorial
Managing Editor
Tom Le Bas
Art Director
Ian Spick
Picture Manager
Steven Lawrence
Series Manager
Rachel Fox

Distribution

UK & Ireland
GeoCenter International Ltd
Meridian House, Churchill Way West
Basingstoke, Hampshire RG21 6YR
sales@geocenter.co.uk

United States
Langenscheidt Publishers, Inc.
36–36 33rd Street 4th Floor
Long Island City, NY 11106
orders@langenscheidt.com

Australia
Universal Publishers
1 Waterloo Road
Macquarie Park, NSW 2113
sales@universalpublishers.com.au

New Zealand
Hema Maps New Zealand Ltd (HNZ)
Unit 2, 10 Cryers Road
East Tamaki, Auckland 2013
sales.hema@clear.net.nz

Worldwide
Apa Publications GmbH & Co.
Verlag KG (Singapore branch)
38 Joo Koon Road, Singapore 628990
Tel: (65) 6865 1600
apasin@signet.com.sg

Printing

Insight Print Services (Pte) Ltd
38 Joo Koon Road, Singapore 628990
Tel: (65) 6865 1600. Fax: (65) 6861 6438

©2009 Apa Publications GmbH & Co.
Verlag KG (Singapore branch)
All Rights Reserved

First Edition 1984
Eighth Edition 2009

CONTACTING THE EDITORS
We would appreciate it if readers
would alert us to errors or out-
dated information by writing to:
Insight Guides, P.O. Box 7910,
London SE1 1WE, England.
Fax: (44) 20 7403 0290.
insight@apaguide.co.uk

www.insightguides.com

ABOUT THIS BOOK

The first Insight Guide pioneered
the use of creative full-colour
photography in travel guides in
1970. Since then, we have
expanded our range to cater for our
readers' need not only for reliable
information about their chosen destination but also for a real understanding of the culture and workings
of that destination. Now, when the
internet can supply inexhaustible
(but not always reliable) facts, our
books marry text and pictures to
provide those much more elusive
qualities: knowledge and discern-
ment. To achieve this, they rely
heavily on the authority of locally
based writers and photographers.

Insight Guide: New Zealand is structured to convey an understanding of
the country and its people as well as
to guide readers through its wealth
of attractions:

◆ The **Features** section, indicated by
a pink bar at the top of each page,
covers the natural and cultural history
of New Zealand as well as illuminat-
ing essays on the Maori heritage,
society, culture and daily life, food and
wine, architecture, the arts, the environment and outdoor activities.
◆ The main **Places** section, indicated by a blue bar, is a complete
guide to all the sights and areas
worth visiting across New Zealand.
Places of special interest are coordinated by number with the maps.
◆ The **Travel Tips** listings section,
with a yellow bar, provides full information on transport, hotels, restaurants, activities from culture to
shopping to sports and a detailed list
of outdoor activities, and an A–Z section of essential practical information. An easy-to-find contents list for
Travel Tips is printed on the back flap,
which also serves as a bookmark.

LEFT: high in the Southern Alps.

The contributors

This fully revised and updated edition was managed and edited by **Tom Le Bas** at Insight Guides' London office. The entire book was comprehensively updated by **Donna Blaber**, a travel journalist based in the historical township of Waipu in Northland but spending months each year on the highways and back roads across the country. Donna has also added a new introductory chapter on New Zealand's geography, expanded the content of the Places chapters, written a new photo essay on *The Lord of the Rings* filming locations, and compiled new listings for the A–Z directory at the back of the book.

The eighth incarnation of *Insight New Zealand* builds on the best-selling earlier editions largely written by **Craig Dowling**, who has lived and worked as a journalist in New Zealand's three largest cities, Auckland,

Wellington and Christchurch. Other past contributors include **Denis Welch**, who wrote the chapter on Contemporary Art and Literature. The feature on Performing Arts, Music and Film was written by **Philip Matthews**, while lending her expertise to the info panel on Contemporary Maori Art was **Ngarino Ellis**, a Maori lecturer on art history at the University of Auckland. Cuisine is a subject close to the heart of ex-restaurateur **Lois Daish**, and complementing it is the feature on Wines by **Keith Stewart**, an art and wine critic. The chapter on Outdoor Activities was the work of sports enthusiast **Angie Belcher**. **Michael King** wrote about the Arrival of the Maori and the Modern Maori, **Gordon McLauchlan** described the Voyages of Discovery, Settlement and Colonisation, and **Terence Barrow** wrote about Maori Art.

The Places chapters were originally written by **Peter Calder** (Auckland and Surroundings); **Jack Adlington** (Northland); **Joseph Frahm** (Coromandel; **Colin Taylor** (Rotorua); **Janet Leggett** (The Waikato); **John Harvey** (Taranaki, Wanganui and Manawatu); **Geoff Conly** (Poverty Bay and Hawke's Bay); **David McGill** (Wellington); **William Hobbs** (Nelson and Marlborough); **John Goulter** (Christchurch); **Les Bloxham** (Canterbury, West Coast); **Anne Stark** (Queenstown and Central Otago); **Robin Charteris** (Dunedin); **Clive Lind** (Southland); and **Brian Parkinson** (Stewart Island).

The book was proofread by **Neil Titman** and indexed by **Helen Peters**. The picture editors were **Steven Lawrence** and **Richard Cooke**.

Map Legend

– – – –	Province Boundry
—•—	National Park/Reserve
– – –	Ferry Route
✈ ✈	Airport: International/Regional
🚌	Bus Station
❶	Tourist Information
✝ ✝ ✝	Church/Ruins
∴	Archaeological Site
⌂ ⌂	Castle/Ruins
☾	Mosque
✡	Synagogue
∩	Cave
🯅	Statue/Monument
★	Place of Interest
⚑	Beach
▲	Mountain Peak
🗼	Lighthouse
🚠	Cable Car
⛳	Golf
⛷	Skiing

The main places of interest in the Places section are coordinated by number with a full-colour map (e.g. ❶), and a symbol at the top of every right-hand page tells you where to find the map.

Contents

LEFT: sunrise over the Hauraki Gulf, Auckland.

THE BEST OF NEW ZEALAND: TOP SIGHTS

Discover New Zealand's unique attractions –
breathtaking landscapes, exciting adventure activities,
absorbing museums, indigenous culture... here, at a
glance, are our recommendations

△ **Glacier Walking, Franz Josef or Fox Glacier**
Explore stunning blue glacier ice and crevasses on a
half- or full-day glacier walk, led by knowledgeable and
safety-conscious guides. All the gear, including
crampons, is provided. *Page 269.*

▽ **White Island, Bay of Plenty** See the pure, raw
energy of nature at work on the world's most accessible
marine volcano. Hike across this unique lunar landscape
pockmarked with fumeroles to view its colourful and
ever-changing crater lake. *Page 174.*

◁
Maori culture.
New Zealand's
indigenous culture
can be experienced
by attending a
traditional *kapa haka*
(song and dance show)
performed at venues
nationwide; at a
hangi feast; and on
guided walking tours
of local *marae* (open
courtyards) and
meeting houses.
Pages 135, 153, 182.

△ **Waitomo Caves, the Waikato**
Venture underground on a guided tour to see ancient limestone stalactites and stalagmites. The highlight comes at the end: an awe-inspiring boat ride through enormous caverns, radiantly lit by millions of tiny glow-worms. *Page 165.*

◁ **Wai-O-Tapu Thermal Wonderland, Rotorua**
Visit Rotorua's most vibrant and colourful thermal park to see the eruption of the Lady Knox Geyser and other highlights, including the bubbly Champagne Pool, brilliantly hued silica terraces and Bridal Veil Falls. *Page 188.*

◁ **Waipoua Forest, Northland**
Stroll through the vertiginous canopy of tangled foliage in this mighty Northland kauri forest, where sights such as New Zealand's oldest living kauri tree – the mammoth Tane Mahuta – are, quite simply, unforgettable. *Page 158.*

△ **Dart River Jet, Queenstown**
Hop aboard for a spectacular jet boat adventure up the glacier-fed Dart River, passing glorious beech forests, snow-covered peaks and waterfalls, and on into the pristine environs of the Mount Aspiring National Park. *Page 286.*

△ **Te Papa Tongarewa Museum, Wellington**
Art, artefacts, natural history and hands-on interactive fun for kids, including an earthquake house, make this state-of-the-art museum the best in New Zealand. *Page 215.*

▽ **Rakiura National Park, Stewart Island**
Discover this seldom-explored 170,000ha (420,000-acre) paradise of wondrous beauty – a dense wilderness of podocarp rainforest, granite peaks, freshwater wetlands and deserted beaches which are a refuge for New Zealand's rarest birds. *Page 315.*

△ **New Zealand food and wine, Hawke's Bay and Marlborough** Tempt your tastebuds with cuisine inspired by the freshest of locally gathered produce, perfectly matched to a selection of fine regional wines. *Pages 202 and 236.*

THE BEST OF NEW ZEALAND: EDITOR'S CHOICE

Our selection of the best outdoor experiences and adventures, the top cultural and historical sights, and some handy pointers to help you get the most out of your dollars .

MUST-SEE NATURAL SCENERY

Bay of Islands, Northland A rugged 800-km (500-mile) coastline embracing 144 islands and steeped in history, where beauty knows no bounds. *Page 152.*

Aoraki Mount Cook National Park, Canterbury Admire New Zealand's highest mountain and the mighty Tasman Glacier, in this vastly contrasting landscape of mountains and plains. *Page 262.*

Tongariro National Park There's plenty to do year-round – from hiking the acclaimed Tongariro Crossing, kayaking and mountain biking during the summer months, to skiing in the winter. *Page 190.*

Abel Tasman National Park Paradise on earth for campers, kayakers and hikers. The Coastal Track offers exceptional views. *Page 240.*

Punakaiki, West Coast Remarkable petrified rocks and blowholes complemented by stunning coastal views. *Page 274.*

Fiordland National Park A pristine environment offering a wealth of truly breathtaking scenery. Highlights include Milford Sound, Doubtful Sound and Mitre Peak. *Page 309.*

ABOVE: Lake Pukaki and Mount Cook. **LEFT:** a kakapo parrot. **RIGHT:** a Maori *haka* dance.

BEST ARTS AND CULTURAL EXPERIENCES

Auckland War Memorial Museum Home to the world's finest collection of Maori and Polynesian artefacts, Maori cultural performances, and a great deal more. *Page 135.*

Whakarewarewa Thermal Village See culture in action at the geothermally powered Maori village and the Te Puia Maori Arts and Crafts Institute. *Page 182.*

Waitangi Culture North Show Waitangi's Treaty House comes alive at night with a cleverly choreographed performance of the Bay of Islands history, performed by local Maori. *Page 153.*

Dunedin Public Art Gallery The place to see some of the country's finest displays of national and international art. *Page 292.*

Suter Gallery Central to Nelson's thriving art scene is its public art museum, with a substantial collection of local artworks. *Page 238.*

BEST ADVENTURE / OUTDOOR ACTIVITIES

Diving at the Poor Knight Islands Discover a microcosm of underwater diversity amid dense kelp forests, arches and caverns, including Riko Riko, the world's largest sea cave. *Page 159.*

Tandem Skydiving Free-fall attached to a parachute and a skydiving professional who pulls the cord just in time for the perfect touchdown. *Page 281.*

Bungee Jumping, Queenstown Take the plunge off where it first began, the Kawarau Bridge, home of the bungee, or have a go at the Nevis Highwire or the Ledge. *Pages 285, 286.*

Jet Boating, Queenstown Jump in and hold on tight – jet boat-powered thrills and spills on the Shotover River. *Page 283.*

White-water rafting, Tongariro National Park The fast-flowing Rangitikei River is one of the top white-water rafting destinations in the world. *Page 191.*

Whale Watch Kaikoura Cruise over the edge of the continental shelf to spot sperm whales as they resurface. *Page 237.*

ABOVE: Dunedin has a splendid Victorian heritage.
BELOW LEFT: tandem skydiving.

BEST HISTORICAL SIGHTS

Oamaru, Otago New Zealand's largest collection of protected heritage buildings is found here. Crafted from a creamy textured local limestone, they are a rare sight to behold. *Page 298.*

Dunedin Amble around this southern city and enjoy its unique Scottish Victorian, Edwardian and Art Deco architectural heritage. Don't miss Dunedin Railway Station, the city's most photographed building. *Page 291.*

Russell, Bay of Islands Highlights include the old Duke of Marlborough Hotel, Pompallier and Christ Church. The latter survived the Battle of Kororareka in 1845, and is peppered with musketball holes. *Page 153.*

Arrowtown, Otago Journey back in time along the streets of this picturesque former gold-mining town. Visit its museum and see rusty relics lining the Arrow River. *Page 284.*

Taieri Gorge Railway, Otago Vintage rail at its best, traversing one of the country's greatest historical railway lines through the stunning Southland scenery. *Page 298.*

MONEY-SAVING TIPS

● **Museums, botanic gardens, National Parks** Hours of pleasure to be had for free exploring New Zealand's museums, botanic gardens, and National Parks. Fully one-third of the country is made up of national parkland and reserves, and there is a huge range of walks available ranging from 10 minute strolls to epic hikes.

● **Seniors and students** Special rates apply for seniors and students on many activities, attractions and transport. Carry ID in English. *See page 383.*

● **Kids' holiday specials** Take advantage of cheaper rates for children during the off-peak New Zealand school holiday periods (mid-April, early–mid-July and early October). Real Journeys (www. realjourneys.co.nz), one of the largest operators in the South Island, is one of several companies offering highly discounted travel for children under 10 years of age.

● **Pick up free maps**, information and accommodation guides and advice at i-Site Visitor Centres throughout the country. The Automobile Association (AA) also provides assistance to members. *See page 381.*

● **Beaches/great outdoors** Fabulous beach walks and breathtaking views are free for all.

AOTEAROA

How did New Zealand become home to so many natural marvels? An ancient myth may hold the answer...

New Zealand – called Aotearoa, "land of the long white cloud", by the Maori – is a breathtakingly beautiful land of majestic snow-capped peaks and unexplored rainforests, of pristine lakes swarming with trout and turquoise ocean bays speckled with wooded isles, of glaciers and fiords, geysers and volcanoes. And you don't have to travel far to experience its sensational landscapes – an Alpine peak can be just a short drive from a barren desert, a primeval beach minutes from a busy city. There are kauri forests and kiwi fruit plantations, modern cosmopolitan cities and backcountry sheep stations. This land of plenty produces some of the world's finest food and wine.

All this is ranged across the two similarly sized main islands, North and South, plus Stewart Island off the southern tip, and a scattering of uninhabited islands, some of which are nature reserves. The North Island has the largest population, though there are still large expanses of empty landscapes; the South Island is more spectacular still – the "Middle Earth" of the film version of the *Lord of the Rings* trilogy. It is a combination of a land that time forgot, completely uninhabited until relatively recent times, and a land that is impossible to forget. But first, it was the land of the Maori.

Anthropologists tell of a remarkable migration as the Polynesian ancestors of the Maori moved through the Pacific, arriving here by outrigger canoe from about AD 800. Europeans arrived in the late 18th century, and despite a degree of conflict, New Zealand's past has none of the crimes against indigenous peoples that scar the history of nearby Australia. It is also a nation with a proud tradition of enlightened social policies.

Its natural wonders have made New Zealand a recreational paradise, and New Zealanders love the outdoors – from the rugby fields to the ski fields, from barbecues to bungee-jumping. Active yet reflective, New Zealanders take pride in what they have and what they do. Above all, they are eager to share their marvellous country and its bounty with all visitors. ❏

PRECEDING PAGES: refreshment from a mountain stream on the Copland Track; kayaking on Milford Sound; Maori dance at the Paparoa *marae*, Bay of Plenty.
LEFT: Rotorua's Lady Knox geyser erupts punctually each morning at 10.15.
TOP: Lake Wakatipu. **ABOVE:** sailing off Auckland's North Shore.

THE LAND

An archipelago of more than 700 islands, New Zealand perches atop two tectonic plates, the creators of a landscape filled with wild contrasts and awe-inspiring natural phenomena

O f all the land masses on earth, the islands of New Zealand are the most isolated, surrounded on all sides by great expanses of ocean. But this has not always been the case. For several hundred million years, New Zealand lay on the edge of the supercontinent Gondwana. Finally, some 80 million years ago, during the heyday of the dinosaurs, a huge sliver of land that was to become the North and South islands broke away from Gondwana and headed out into the Pacific. Almost immediately it began to sink and the sea washed further and further inland. Mountains eroded to low hills and waves ate them away. It was only at the "last minute" – geologically speaking – that compressive plate movements came to the rescue, pushing the land up and out of the sea. As these forces continued, hills grew to become jagged mountains, volcanoes erupted, and these were carved by water and ice to form the landscape of today. Around 60 million years ago it reached its present distance from Australia.

The lay of the land

New Zealand extends for some 1,500km (900 miles) from the subtropical Ninety Mile Beach in the far north of the North Island to the sub-Antarctic wilderness of Stewart Island in the stormy southern latitudes. Both the main islands are largely mountainous, although there are also extensive areas of plains and plateaux. One-third of the country is made up of national parkland and reserves, so many of its landscapes remain in a near-pristine state. Travellers who wish to experience a true

LEFT: waterfall at Milford Sound.
RIGHT: boiling mud pools, Rotorua.

"wilderness" will be easily satisfied by a wealth of natural phenomena: sooty volcanoes, ancient glaciers, bubbling mud pools, iridescent lakes and magnificent stands of temperate rainforest. The extreme environment has helped to ensure a relative lack of human impact on the land.

The largely volcanic North Island reaches 2,796 metres (9,173ft) at Mount Ruapehu in the Central Plateau, with range upon range of rolling hills tumbling to the sea. While Rotorua is famous for its gushing geysers and pools of boiling mud, naturally formed hot springs can be found island-wide. Lake Taupo, itself formed by a massive eruption, forms the liquid heart of the North Island and lush farmlands radiate from its epicentre, covering expansive valleys and plains. Although its land area is somewhat smaller than that of the South Island, the North's coastline is longer, thanks to its multitude of deep inlets, mangrove-filled estuaries and sheltered harbours ribboned with sandy beaches. Crashing surf and darker sands predominate in the west, while to the east the coastline is tamer, a seemingly endless string of golden sands punctuated by rocky headlands and offshore islets.

In the South Island the land rises from the Canterbury Plains in the east to the Southern

Alps in the west: the highest peak in the country is Mount Cook at 3,754 metres (12,316ft), but there are numerous majestic snow-capped peaks rising above 3,000 metres (10,000ft). The west coast is marked by plunging cliffs and wild beaches and backed by dense swathes of temperate rainforest. To the east, snow-fed rivers nourish the prosperous farmlands of the Canterbury Plains. In Marlborough at the northernmost point of the South Island lie the drowned sea-valleys of the Marlborough Sounds, which form a unique topography of channels, peninsulas and islands. In the southern regions huge ancient glaciers bulldozed rock to form spectacular lakes, and with over 360 known glaciers in action today, with Franz

Josef and Fox Glaciers recognised as the largest and most readily accessible, the landscape is constantly changing.

New Zealand's third isle, Stewart Island, located some 30km (19 miles) off the southern tip of the South Island, features rugged beaches, swampy valleys, large areas of forest and peaks including Mount Anglem, the island's highest at 980 metres (3,215ft).

For information on the climate of New Zealand see page 378.

Plate tectonics

New Zealand currently sits upon two huge moving "plates", the Indo-Australian plate and the Pacific plate, the former pushing under the latter, causing the land to rise and creating wrenching forces beneath the surface resulting in earthquakes and volcanoes. The South Island's Alps were formed by plate movement over the last 2 million years – a mere blink in geological time – and they continue to rise by several centimetres a year.

During the formation of the Alps, worldwide cooling became extreme and the Ice Age ensued. During its colder intervals huge glaciers appeared flowing down valleys, and this combination of young mountains and huge glaciers has created landscapes rating among the most spectacular to be found on earth. In Fiordland, the rock walls of ancient glacial valleys drop vertically thousands of feet directly into the sea, while on the other side of the Alps, lakes such as Wanaka and Wakatipu are the result of glacial "bulldozing". Further north, the Fox and Franz Josef glaciers plunge towards sea level through the mid-altitude rainforests – a unique sight.

Not all New Zealand's recent history has been one of uplift. In the north of the South

> New Zealand's volcanic nature can be destructive, but overall is a blessing in disguise. Volcanic rocks rejuvenate the landscape, weathering to form the country's richest soils, a fact well recognised by the dairy industry.

Island, the Marlborough Sounds were produced when an extensive river system was drowned. In the North Island the major geological story is of volcanoes, and in a complex situation a whole variety of volcanic types has been produced.

The city of Auckland is built amongst numerous small, perfectly formed, extinct volcanic cones, created by gentle outpourings of lava and ash. As naturally defensive positions, most were terraced and palisaded by Maori to form *pa* (forts). In the Central Plateau a different form of lava produces a very dangerous, explosive type of volcano. About AD 130 – long before any humans arrived on the islands – one of the largest volcanic explosions in historical times formed Lake Taupo. This spread hot ash over a large part of the North Island, flattening huge areas of forest.

Mineral resources

New Zealand's most precious materials are closely tied to the history of the Southern Alps. The Maori's sacred *pounamu* (or greenstone) was formed from exotic rock existing deep below the earth's crust. Altered by heat and pressure during mountain-forming processes, these rocks were pushed to the surface in isolated places on the west coast of the South Island. Its rareness, beauty and material properties in a culture where metal was unknown gave *pounamu* a high value.

Gold also existed in the quartz veins of "schist" rock, the main component of the Alps. As the mountains grew, they also eroded, and as the lighter and softer minerals of the schist washed away, gold, by virtue of its high density, became concentrated in the nooks and crannies of river beds, exploited during several 19th-century gold rushes across the country.

Dinosaurs and other fauna

The most striking aspect of New Zealand's indigenous fauna is its absence of large four-footed land animals, in particular mammals (other than two species of bat that are found nowhere else), as well as its complete lack of snakes. This was originally attributed to the timing of New Zealand's breakaway from Gondwana, but recent discoveries suggest that carnivorous and herbivorous dinosaurs, as well as flying pterosaurs, were living in New Zealand at that time. The only fossil evidence of land-based, four-footed animals since the dinosaurs is a single crocodile jawbone discovered near St Bathans, in Central Otago. Crocodiles,

however, do not exist in New Zealand today.

Mammals, too, may once have been part of a "native" fauna that developed before New Zealand broke away from Australia. The present absence of large land animals – other than birds – is almost certainly a result of extinction over the past 80 million years. With nothing to prey on them, birds proliferated, and some, lacking the need, eventually lost the ability to fly. Of the very distinct New Zealand animals, such as the extinct moa, the kiwi and tuatara (three-eyed centenarian lizards), there is no ancient fossil record. *For more on local wildlife and plants see pages 99–103.* ❑

RAIN AND THE RAINFOREST

When air currents are forced to rise over the Southern Alps of New Zealand, moisture drops, causing considerable rainfall – sometimes over 5,000mm (200 inches) a year – on the west coast. On the other side of the mountains, though, there's a corresponding rainfall shadow, so that only a few kilometres from the wettest parts of New Zealand, the annual rainfall can be as low as 300mm (12 inches). Odd as it sounds, the high rainfall can actually be totally incompatible with the survival of the rainforests, as the soil is rapidly leached of the nutrients it needs to sustain them, resulting in stunted vegetation.

LEFT: admiring the view across Lake Wakatipu near Queenstown. **RIGHT:** volcanic landscape, Rotorua.

DECISIVE DATES

Traders and explorers

c. AD 800–900

The first Polynesians arrive in New Zealand (some scientists believe this occurred later).

1642

Abel Tasman is the first European to sight the country.

1769

Captain James Cook is the first European to explore, and set foot in, New Zealand.

1790s

European seal hunters and whalers move into the region.

1809

First European settlers arrive in Russell.

1817

Anglican Mission established at Bay of Islands.

1818

The Maori "Musket Wars" begin; 12 years of inter-tribal conflict kills 20,000 people.

Colonisation

1830s

Early European settlements grow in size; beginnings of trade with New South Wales.

1840

Maori chiefs sign the Treaty of Waitangi. Auckland becomes the capital. New Zealand Company colonists reach Wellington and establish settlements.

1845

Hone Heke cuts down the flagstaff at Kororareka (Russell); 1,000 Maori take arms against the British.

1848–50

Otago and Canterbury are settled.

1852

Colonisation of Taranaki begins.

1856

New Zealand becomes a self-governing British colony. Gold rush and land struggles.

1860–72

Maori Land Wars (New Zealand Wars); vast tracts of land are confiscated.

1861

Otago gold rush begins.

1865

Wellington becomes New Zealand's capital.

1866

Cook Strait submarine telegraph cable is laid.

1867

Maori are given the vote.

1868

Raids by Titokowaru and Te Kooti throw New Zealand into crisis.

1869

Te Kooti is defeated. Otago University is established.

1870

First rugby

match is played in New Zealand.

1877

Treaty of Waitangi ruled null by Chief Justice Prendergast. Free compulsory education introduced.

1882

The first refrigerated agricultural produce cargo is dispatched to England.

1886

Mount Tarawera erupts.

Social reforms and World Wars

1893

Women are given the vote, 25 years before Britain and the United States.

1896

Maori population drops to 42,000 (from 100,000 in 1769).

1898

World's first old-age pension for men is introduced.

1899–1902

New Zealand troops fight in Boer War.

1907
New Zealand is elevated from a colony to a dominion.

1908
Ernest Rutherford awarded Nobel Prize for Chemistry. Population exceeds 1 million.

1915
New Zealand suffers heavy losses in Gallipoli campaign of World War I.

1918–19
Influenza kills 6,700.

1938
Health care and social security are introduced.

1939
World War II breaks out. New Zealand suffers heavy losses.

An independent nation

1947
New Zealand becomes fully independent.

1951
ANZUS defence alliance with Australia and the United States is signed.

1953
New Zealander Edmund Hillary becomes the first person to successfully climb Mount Everest.

1958
Hillary reaches the South Pole.

1962
Maurice Wilkins shares Nobel Prize in physiology and medicine for discovery of DNA.

1965
New Zealand troops are sent to Vietnam.

1971
New Zealand joins South Pacific Forum.

1975
Parliament passes the Treaty of Waitangi Act, establishing a tribunal to investigate claims.

1981
Anti-apartheid protests during South African rugby team tour creates civil unrest.

1985
Greenpeace protest vessel *Rainbow Warrior* is bombed in Auckland. Government bans visits by ships carrying nuclear weapons.

1987
Maori becomes an official language by law.

1993
Proportional representation election system, MMP (Mixed Member Proportional) introduced.

1995
New Zealand wins the prestigious America's Cup.

1997
The National Party's Jenny Shipley becomes New

Zealand's first woman prime minister.

1999
Labour Party leader Helen Clark elected prime minister.

2003
Population hits 4 million.

2005
Civil Union Act passed.

2007
Sir Edmund Hillary dies.

2008
John Key's National Party voted into power following Helen Clark's nine-year reign.

2009
New Zealand becomes one of the first countries to confirm cases of swine flu.

FAR LEFT TOP: panning for gold in the 1860s. FAR LEFT BELOW: whaling has been important to the economy in the past. ABOVE: John Key celebrates electoral success in 2008. BELOW: Anzac Day.

ARRIVAL OF THE MAORI

Polynesian settlers are thought to have arrived in New Zealand from around AD 800–1000. Having established themselves on the islands, they evolved a sophisticated and highly organised culture

Human habitation on New Zealand only dates back around 1,000 years (recent estimates suggest just 800 years), making this the world's last sizeable land area – outside of the polar regions – to be settled by man. The origin of its first people, the Maori, is the source of much controversy. Nineteenth-century scholars said Maori were wandering Aryans, others believed they were Hindu, and some thought that they were a lost tribe of Israel. Linguistic and archaeological evidence has led to the current consensus that the Maori are a Polynesian people, and that their ancestors (Austronesian people who originated in Southeast Asia) sailed south from the Asian mainland some 2,000 to 3,000 years ago. Some went southwest, ultimately to Madagascar; others journeyed southeast along the Malaysian, Indonesian and Philippine island chains.

The Pacific Austronesians travelled through the Melanesian islands, reaching Fiji by about 1300 BC and Tonga before 1100 BC. It was here that Polynesian culture as recognised today evolved. And it was from East Polynesia that a migration was launched to New Zealand. There is a great deal of controversy over the dates of the southward migration: the Maori traditionally date their earliest encounters with New Zealand at around AD 800; some anthropologists, however, believe that these first migrations may have taken place hundreds of years later – possibly as late as AD 1280.

Whatever the date, the land was unlike anything that Polynesians had hitherto encountered.

LEFT: a Maori chief as depicted by Sydney Parkinson, an artist on one of Captain James Cook's expeditions.
RIGHT: Maori feather box.

It was far larger and more varied than the Pacific islands they had colonised previously. It was temperate rather than tropical and sufficiently cold in much of the South Island to prevent the growing of traditional crops. Other than bats, there were no mammals until rats (*kiore*) and dogs (*kuri*) were brought over by the new colonists.

The ancestors of modern Maori showed great fortitude and adaptability. The lack of meat was compensated for by an abundance of seafood and aquatic mammals. Inland waterways contained additional resources – waterfowl, eel, fish and shellfish – and there were nearly 200 species of bird, many of them palatable. The land provided a staple diet of native fern root and nurtured imported cultivated crops such as taro, kumara, yam, gourds and the paper mulberry. The most coveted food source, however ,was the huge flightless bird, the moa, which offered a plentiful food supply. Some early groups of Maori based their entire economy around moas, until over-hunting led to their extinction *(see page 100)*.

Maori culture

Ethnologists recognise two distinguishable but related phases in Maori civilisation. The first is New Zealand East Polynesian, or Archaic Maori, and the second, Classic Maori, the culture

up in a unified vision in which every aspect of living was related to every other. And the universal acceptance of concepts such as *tapu* (sacredness), *mana* (spiritual authority), *mauri* (life force), *utu* (satisfaction) and a belief in *makutu* (sorcery) regulated all aspects of life.

Maori society was stratified. A few people were born into *rangatira* or chiefly families; all others were *tutua* (commoners). They became slaves if they were captured in warfare. Immediate authority was exercised by the *kaumatua*, the elders. Whole communities, sharing a common ancestor, were under the jurisdiction of the *rangatira* families whose authority was in part

encountered and recorded by the earliest European navigators *(see pages 67–70)*. When James Cook observed New Zealand in 1769, New Zealand Polynesians had settled throughout the land. The language they shared was similar, although dialectal differences were pronounced. While some regional variations were apparent, Maori culture was largely homogeneous throughout the country.

Competitive tribalism, for example, was the basis of Maori life. The family and *hapu* (sub-tribe) were the units of society that determined who married whom, where people lived, where and when they fought other people and why. Tribal ancestors were venerated, as were gods representing the natural elements. Life was bound

hereditary and in part based on past achievement. Occasionally federations of *hapu* and tribes would come together and join forces

> When items of food became scarce in a kainga *(village)* or pa *(fortified settlement)*, the inhabitants had a rahui, *or prohibition, laid on them to conserve precious supplies.*

under an *ariki* (paramount chief) for joint ventures such as waging war against foreign elements, trading or foraging for resources. The most common relationship among even closely related *hapu*, however, was fierce competition.

Communities ranging from a handful of households to those comprised of more than 500 lived in *kainga* (villages). These were usually based on membership of a single *hapu*. The *kainga* would be close to water, food sources and crops. Some settlements, called *pa*, were fortified – many of them elaborately constructed with an interior stronghold, ditches, banks and palisades. More often the *kainga* were adjacent to hilltop *pa*, to which communities could retreat when under attack.

Communal patterns of life in Maori settlements were organised around food gathering, food growing and (in areas where fighting was common) warfare. Cultivation and foraging were carried out by large parties of workers.

Maori warfare

Warfare was an important feature of Maori life in most parts of the country. It was conducted to obtain territory abundant in food or other natural resources; to avenge insults; to obtain satisfaction from *hapu* whose members had transgressed the social code; or to resolve serious disagreements over authority.

Prior to the introduction of the musket with the arrival of the Europeans, most warfare was not totally destructive, with the most common weapons being *taiaha* (long wooden-bladed swords) and short clubs known as *patu* and *mere*. It often involved only individuals or small raiding parties, and ambush or short, sporadic attacks. Even when larger groups fought, the dead rarely amounted to more than a few score. Fighting was rarely carried out far from home except when a migration was under way. (Migrations were seasonal, undertaken by most tribes, and principally related to the harvesting or gathering of food.)

For individual men, as for tribes, *mana* (spiritual authority) was paramount. An individual's *mana* was intensified by victory and diminished by defeat. Courage and combat skills were also essential ingredients in initiation and acceptance, especially in the case of chiefs.

Other aspects of Maori life

In spite of competition, warfare and tribal demarcations among Maori, trading was extensive. South Islanders exported *pounamu* green-

stone, highly valued for carving. Bay of Plenty settlers distributed Mayor Island obsidian; Nelson and D'Urville Island inhabitants traded argillite. Sometimes food such as mutton birds was also preserved and bartered. People travelled long distances for materials and food delicacies. Although the Maori's ocean-going vessels disappeared by the 18th century, canoes were still widely used for transport on New Zealand's waterways.

Medical examination of pre-European remains reveals that few Maori lived beyond the age of 30. From their late 20s, many suffered from arthritis, and infected gums and loss of teeth due

to a diet of fern roots. The healthy-looking "elderly" men whose condition Captain James Cook commented favourably on in 1770 may have been, at the most, around 40 years of age.

The population, probably 100,000 to 120,000 when Cook landed, were so long separated from other cultures they had no concept of nationhood. But they were fiercely assertive of their ancestry and *hapu* membership. To that extent they led a tribal existence, but what they shared strongly, no matter which tribe they were born to, was a deep and profound affinity with the land and its bounty. They called the land Aotearoa: "the land of the long white cloud".

For details of Maori art and more on ancient Maori society, see pages 67–70. ❑

LEFT: idealised view of Maori by Sydney Parkinson.
RIGHT: Sydney Parkinson's portrait of a Maori warrior.

VOYAGES OF DISCOVERY

A Dutchman searching for a "Great Southern Continent"
first stumbled upon New Zealand in 1642, but it was
another 130 years before any European returned

The southern Pacific was the last habitable part of the world to be reached by Europeans. It was then only gradually explored at the end of long-haul routes down the coast of South America on one side and Africa on the other. Once inside the rim of the world's largest ocean, seafarers faced vast areas to be crossed, always hundreds, even thousands of miles away from any familiar territory. So it required not only steady courage to venture into this region but a high degree of navigational skill.

The islands of the South Pacific – tucked away near the bottom of the globe – remained the domain of Polynesian peoples for nearly 150 years after the Europeans first burst into the western Pacific. Furthermore, New Zealand was ignored for another 130 years after its initial 1642 sighting by the Dutchman Abel Janszoon Tasman. It was left to the Englishman James Cook to put the South Pacific firmly on the world map in the latter part of the 18th century.

The Dutch traders

European knowledge of the Pacific Ocean had gradually expanded during the 16th and 17th centuries. This was the era in which Spanish and Portuguese seafarers such as Magellan and Quiros, and England's Francis Drake, made their epic expeditions.

Then, towards the end of the 16th century, the Dutch emerged as the great seafaring and trading nation of the central and western Pacific. They set up a major administrative and trading centre at Batavia (now Jakarta) in Java

early in the 17th century, an operation dominated by the Dutch East India Company. For the ensuing 200 years the Dutch were a major power in the region, though for most of that period the voyages of exploration were incidental to the activities of trade.

The Dutch ships eventually found that by staying south after rounding the tip of Africa at the Cape of Good Hope and catching the consistent westerlies almost as far as the western coast of Australia, they could make the journey to Java more quickly than by adopting the traditional route – sailing up the east coast of Africa and then catching seasonal winds for the journey eastwards. As a result, islands off the

LEFT: Captain James Cook arrives at Golden Bay in 1769. **RIGHT:** 18th-century sketch of Cook's ship *Endeavour*.

west coast of Australia and stretches of the coast of the unknown continent itself began to be noted on charts.

Tasman's visit

An ambitious governor of Batavia, Anthony van Diemen, showed a more imaginative interest in discovering new lands for trade than most of his predecessors. In 1642 he chose Abel Tasman to lead an expedition south, to be accompanied by a highly competent navigator, Frans Visscher. The proposed voyage would take them first to Mauritius, then southwest to between 50° and 55°S in search of the great southern continent,

Terra Australis Incognita. The expedition, aboard the vessels *Heemskerck* and *Zeehaen*, was then to travel eastwards if no land had been found to impede their progress and to sail across to investigate a shorter route to Chile, a rich trading area and the preserve of the Spanish. As it turned out, the expedition ventured only as far as 49°S before turning eastwards, whereupon it made two great South Pacific discoveries – Tasmania (or Van Diemen's Land, as he named it at the time) and New Zealand (which he called Staten Landt).

On 13 December 1642, Tasman and his men saw what was described as "land uplifted high" – the Southern Alps of the South Island – and, in strong winds and heavy seas, sailed northwards up the coast of Westland, before rounding Cape Farewell and entering what is now known as Golden Bay. Tasman's voyage was not immediately regarded as a major success (*see box below*), but ultimately he was given his due for a gallant and well-recorded exploration.

Cook's exploration

Within a year or two, other navigators had established that New Zealand could not be attached to a huge continent which was thought may extend all the way across to South America. The name was therefore changed from Staten Landt (the Dutch name for South America) to New Zealand, after the Dutch province of Zeeland.

Over a century passed before serious exploration resumed in the region. It was primarily to observe the transit of Venus over the disc of the sun in June 1769 that the English Captain James Cook was dispatched to the South Seas in the 373-ton Whitby-built barque, *Endeavour*. He was instructed to sail to Otaheite (Tahiti) for the transit and then to sail southwards as far as 50°S latitude on another search for the great southern continent, charting the positions of any islands he might incidentally discover.

Cook rounded Cape Horn and entered the Pacific Ocean for the first time on 27 January 1769. After observing the transit of Venus and investigating other islands (which he named the Society Islands), he sailed south and then west. On 6 October, a ship's boy, Nicholas Young, sighted the east coast of the North Island where it is today called Young Nick's Head.

Two days after this first sighting of what Cook knew to be the east coast of New Zealand, the land reported by Tasman, the *Endeavour* sailed

TASMAN'S NEAR MISS

Tasman's first and only encounter with the Maori was nothing short of disastrous. When a canoe rammed a small boat that was travelling between the *Zeehaen* and the *Heemskerck*, fighting broke out and there was loss of life on both sides. Tasman called the place Massacre Bay and continued his journey northwards. He did not land again. What Tasman failed to realise was that he had actually been inside the western entrance to the stretch of water separating North and South islands, now known as Cook Strait. A voyage eastwards of only a few kilometres would have revealed this to him, and perhaps it might be known today as the Tasman Strait.

into a bay where smoke could be seen – a clear sign that there were inhabitants. Their first visit ashore ended with violence when a band of Maori attacked four boys left guarding the ship's boat; one of the attackers was shot dead.

It was discovered that a Tahitian chief on board the *Endeavour*, Tupaea, could converse with the Maori, and he was taken ashore with Cook the next morning. But the Maori were in a threatening mood and Cook ordered one of them shot to make them retreat. That afternoon, the firing of a musket over a canoe (merely to attract attention) brought an attack on the boat from which the shot had been fired;

planet Mercury was made there. In Mercury Bay, for the first time, the explorers made friends with the local Maori and traded trinkets for supplies of fish, birds and clean water. They were shown over the Maori settlement and inspected a nearby fortified *pa* which greatly impressed Cook.

The expedition circumnavigated New Zealand and with brilliant accuracy made a chart of the coastline which proved basically reliable for more than 150 years. Cook and his crew spent weeks in Ship Cove, in a long inlet which he called Queen Charlotte Sound, on the northern coast of the South Island, refurbishing the

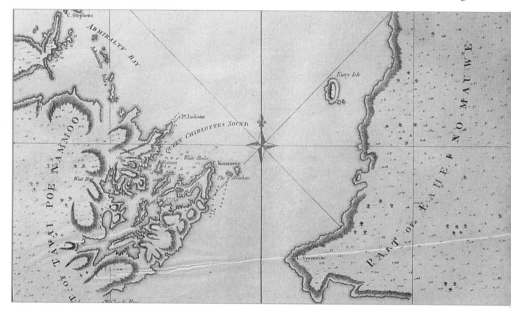

a few more Maori were shot. Cook had quickly learnt that the native population was powerful, aggressive and brave. (Rather than commemorating the bloodshed, the bay was named Poverty Bay to record the fact that the English failed to find the supplies they wanted there.)

First friendly encounter

The *Endeavour* sailed south into Hawke's Bay, and then north again around the top of East Cape. It spent 10 days in Mercury Bay, so called because an observation of the transit of the

ship and gathering supplies. The stay gave the two botanists aboard, Joseph Banks and Daniel Solander, a wonderful opportunity to study

> *James Cook made two major cartographical errors: attaching Stewart Island to the South Island as a peninsula, and mapping Banks Peninsula as an island.*

closely the flora and fauna of the area, and while the ship was being cleaned, the smaller boats undertook detailed survey work.

The *Endeavour* left for home at the end of March 1770, sailing up the east coast of Australia,

LEFT: Abel Tasman. **ABOVE:** map showing the yet-to-be-named Cook Strait, used by Captain Cook on one of his early expeditions.

through the Dutch East Indies and then rounding the Cape of Good Hope to complete a circumnavigation of the world. The expedition was an extraordinary feat of seamanship, putting New Zealand firmly on the map and gathering a huge amount of data. Cook seemed to personify the Great Discoverer as defined by his biographer, Beaglehole: "In every great discoverer there is a dual passion – the passion to see, the passion to report; and in the greatest this duality is fused into one – a passion to see and to report truly." Cook's first voyage was one of the most successful and detailed expeditions of exploration in all history.

Return visits

Cook twice again led expeditions into the Pacific – from 1772 to 1775 and from 1776 to 1780. During the second of these, he twice took his ship south of the Antarctic Circle where no vessel was known to have gone before, but he was unlucky in that he did not become the first person ever to see the Antarctic continent.

It was to Dusky Sound in the South Island fiords that Cook repaired for rest and recovery after the extreme hardships faced by his crew in the southern ocean. During the seven weeks his expedition was there, the crew set up a workshop and an observatory, and restored their

COOK'S CREDENTIALS

The son of a Yorkshire labourer, James Cook was born in 1728. He served as an apprentice seaman on a collier, and then volunteered as an able seaman with the Royal Navy during the Seven Years War. He helped survey Canada's St Lawrence River, an essential preliminary to the capture of Québec by General James Wolfe, and enhanced an already growing reputation as a marine surveyor by charting the St Lawrence and part of the Newfoundland and Nova Scotia coasts. In 1766 he observed an eclipse of the sun; both the Royal Society and the Admiralty were impressed with his report, and this led to his appointment to the South Seas voyage.

health with spruce beer (to defeat scurvy) and the plenitude of fish and birds. They made contact with a single family of Maori in an area which was never thickly populated, then or now. They planted seeds on the shore of the sound, and then sailed for their favourite anchorage in Ship Cove at the other end of the South Island.

On Cook's way home from New Zealand during his second voyage a few years later, he gave pigs, fowl and vegetable seeds to a Maori community near Hawke's Bay, returning again to Ship Cove on his third voyage. By now he had a friendship with some of the local Maori that had lasted nearly 10 years. In his journals, he referred to the Maori as "manly and mild" and wrote that "they have some arts among them which they execute with great judgement and unwearied patience".

By then he had done such a thorough job of charting the coasts of New Zealand that there was little else for explorers to discover without going inland. But a number of navigators followed during the remaining years of the 18th century – Frenchmen Dumont d'Urville (who arrived only two months after Cook first set foot in New Zealand) and, later, Marion du Fresne; an Italian, Don Alessandro Malaspina, who commanded a Spanish expedition; and George Vancouver, who had served with Cook.

Next, in the last years of the 18th century, came the whalers – some of them driven from the Pacific coast of South America because of the dangers brought about by the war between Spain and Britain. Ships from Britain, Australia and the United States hunted the sperm whale in this region, and visits brought their crew members into frequent contact with the Maori of Northland at Kororareka (later renamed Russell).

At first, relations between Europeans and Maori were friendly. But visits were infrequent for a few years after the burning of a vessel called the *Boyd* in 1809 and the massacre of its crew. This was a reprisal against previous pun-

First European settlement

In 10 years, within the decade of the 1770s, Cook and his contemporaries had opened up the Pacific entirely, and, in 1788, Sydney, in Australia, was established as a British convict settlement. The first Europeans to make an impact on New Zealand, however, were the sealers, with the first gang put ashore on the southwest coast of the South Island in 1792. There was a brief boom in the early years of the 19th century, but it wasn't long before the seals were in short supply and the ships had to venture further south to the sub-Antarctic islands.

ishment of high-born Maori seamen by Pakeha (European) skippers.

The inland exploration of New Zealand took place mostly during the early to mid-19th cen-

> Captain Cook was killed in January 1778 in Kealakekua Bay, Hawaii, after a series of thefts from his expedition led to a skirmish with locals.

tury, mainly those parts that were fairly accessible from the coast. Vast areas of the South Island, however, were not successfully explored by Europeans until the 20th century. ❏

LEFT: a 1990s replica of the *Endeavour*.
ABOVE: an English visitor is greeted by native Maori.

SETTLEMENT AND COLONISATION

The colonisation of New Zealand was debated and fought over by Maori, missionaries, politicians, settlers and land speculators

The bleak experiences of Abel Tasman – and the much more successful endeavours of James Cook nearly 130 years later – had no immediate impact on New Zealand. The Dutch were preoccupied with the Indonesian archipelago; the British were consolidating and expanding their trading territories in India. New Zealand, it seemed, had little to offer a colonial power.

Across the Tasman Sea, Australia's Botany Bay was established as a penal settlement in 1788. This was a direct result of America's victory in the War of Independence (previously convicts were sent to America), but the Land of the Long White Cloud was mostly ignored.

Sealskins and whale oil

As the 19th century began, with Europe in the midst of the Napoleonic Wars, demand increased for commodities such as sealskins and whale oil. Seals and whales were plentiful in New Zealand waters, and skippers from Sydney's Port Jackson and Hobart in Van Diemen's Land (Tasmania) wasted no time in putting to sea. Many skippers found a convenient watering hole at Kororareka (now Russell) in the Bay of Islands. The anchorage there was calm and well protected, and there was a ready supply of kauri wood for spars and masts.

Kororareka, with its new European arrivals, rapidly became a lusty, brawling town; the missionaries who arrived there damned it as the "hell-hole of the Pacific". The newcomers carried dangerous baggage which in time completely eradicated some of the Maori tribes, and seriously decimated others: muskets, hard liquor or "grog", prostitutes, and a host of infectious diseases – many of which proved fatal – to

which the Maori had never previously been exposed and therefore had no natural resistance.

Despite all this, contacts between Maori and Europeans were essentially peaceful – although isolated hostilities occurred in the early decades of the 19th century, such as the burning of the brig *Boyd* and the killing and eating of its crew in Whangaroa Harbour in 1809. A barter trade flourished, the Maori trading vegetables and flax for a variety of European trinkets, tools and weapons. The Maori helped cut down giant kauri trees and drag the trunks from bush to beach; they crewed on European sealing and whaling vessels; they were physically strong and vigorous, but also proud – a fact often overlooked by most Europeans.

Colonial law but no colony

In 1817, mainly in response to lawlessness in the Bay of Islands, the laws of the Colony of New South Wales in Australia were extended to include New Zealand. Around this time, the Reverend Samuel Marsden arrived from that fledgling colony across the Tasman Sea. A dedicated evangelist, he believed that missionary tradesmen should not only encourage the conversion of Maori to Christianity but also develop their expertise in carpentry, farming and European technology.

But the missionary-tradesman-teachers in whom Marsden had placed his faith were in fact an ill-assorted bunch who could hardly be regarded as a civilising, evangelising force by the people they had come to convert. With so many of them involved in gun-running, adultery and drunkenness, it is not surprising that 10 years passed before the first Maori baptism. Not until the 1820s did the Maori begin to find Christianity an attractive proposition.

The missionaries did accomplish some good. Thomas Kendall was instrumental in compiling the first grammar and dictionary of the Maori language, and in 1820 accompanied two famous chiefs, Hongi and Waikato, to Britain.

By 1830, Maori were involved in export trading. In that year 28 ships made 56 voyages to New South Wales, carrying substantial cargoes, including tons of Maori-grown potatoes.

The inclusion of New Zealand within the framework of the laws of New South Wales did not, however, make New Zealand a British colony. And, in any case, the legislation did not prove very effective. The governors had no way of proving charges nor of enforcing their authority while a ship was in New Zealand waters, and they had no authority over foreign vessels and their crews.

Perhaps surprisingly, the early missionaries were generally united in wanting to see New Zealand avoid large-scale colonisation. They

> The missionary William Colenso arrived at Paihia in 1834 and set up a printing press that played a major role in the development of Maori literacy. Among his achievements was a translation of the New Testament into Maori.

hoped to be allowed to spread what they saw as the benefits of Christian civilisation among the Maori, leaving them uncorrupted by the depravity introduced to earlier colonies by European

LEFT: Samuel Marsden is credited with introducing Christianity to New Zealand. **ABOVE:** *Kororareka Bay of Islands*, a painting by Charles Heaphy from 1841.

settlers and adventurers. On the other hand, many believed that organised and responsible settlement would be able to avoid the disasters inflicted by Europeans upon indigenous peoples of other countries. The most influential proponent of this view was Edward Gibbon Wakefield *(see page 37)*.

On a less idealistic level, there was also pressure among Britons for new colonies with land for settlement, and the notion that if Britain did not take sovereignty over New Zealand and populate it with European immigrants, some other colonial power – most probably France – would do so.

Land conflict

The issue of formal colonisation was allowed to drift, yet by the 1830s the scramble for land was

> Pakeha, *the Maori term for the white settlers, is a word in common use in contemporary New Zealand; some find it offensive – the original translation is thought to be "white pig" – but for most it is simply a functional term.*

in full swing – a scramble that was to produce tragic results within 20 years.

The Maori had no concept of permanent, private ownership of land. Traditionally tribes would inherit land, and if it were sold a chief's authority was generally strong enough to have a sale accepted by most members of the tribe. Sometimes, however, this process was complicated by conflicting claims of ownership among tribes, and such claims could involve large areas. Many land transfers between the white settlers (known to the Maori as *Pakeha*) and Maori led to conflicts in the 1860s; some of them are still being legally contested today.

There was also the problem of what was being bought. The settlers, and rapacious speculators in Britain, thought they were buying outright freehold land, but in many cases, the Maori believed they were merely leasing their lands for a fee.

The missionaries were not skilled in matters of British law, and certainly not in the area of land conveyancing. The time had finally come for government intervention, however reluctant. In 1833, after the arrival in the Bay of Islands of James Busby as "British Resident", the move was made. The notion of "Resident" was vague. A Resident, in most cases, had the full backing of His or Her Majesty's Government as a diplomat representing British interests in a territory that had not yet been annexed by the Crown. He could advise local chieftains, he could cajole – but he had no real power because no treaty or agreement had yet been reached.

Busby did what he could. He attempted to create unity and overall sovereignty among the disparate Maori by formally establishing a confederation of Maori chiefs. Then, in 1835 he proposed that Britain and the United Tribes of New Zealand, as it was termed, should agree to an arrangement under which the confederation would represent the Maori people and gradually expand its influence as a government while the British government, in the meantime, administered the country in trust.

Busby won personal respect from the Maori. Even so, he keenly felt his own impotence and was well aware that he would never be able to achieve law and order here without the backing of some adequate force.

The Wakefield Scheme

In the course of the 1830s it had become obvious that land buying was going to cause serious trouble. Speculators were gambling on Britain taking over and settling the country, while Busby, the British Resident, was powerless to prevent such "deals" from taking place. Colonisation was inevitable. In 1836, Edward Gibbon Wakefield, a British politician who had been a strong advocate of migration to the new colony of South Australia, told a committee of the House of Commons that Britain was colonising New Zealand already, but "in a most slovenly and scrambling and disgraceful manner".

In 1837, at the behest of the government of New South Wales, Captain William Hobson, commanding HMS *Rattlesnake*, sailed from Sydney to the Bay of Islands to report on the situation. Hobson suggested a formal treaty with the Maori chiefs and the placing of all British subjects in New Zealand under British rule. Hobson's report provoked a response, but it was Wakefield's influence that ensured the outcome.

Wakefield disliked the results of colonisation in the United States, Canada, New South Wales and Tasmania. He believed that if land was sold at "a sufficient price" to "capitalist" settlers, labourers among the immigrants would stay in the new communities working for landowners – at least for a few years – until they could afford to buy land for themselves at the "sufficient price".

Land prices were crucial to Wakefield's system, and New Zealand was his testing ground. Unfortunately he underestimated the aspirations of immigrant labourers and he did not foresee the readiness with which they would move out of the centralised settlements to areas they considered more profitable.

During the late 1830s and early 1840s Wakefield helped establish the New Zealand Company. This became a joint stock company, so that the people involved would bear the costs of establishing the settlements they planned.

The Treaty of Waitangi

Around this time the British government at last responded to the anti-colonial feelings of the missionary groups. Britain decided that the Maori should be consulted on their own future, and that their consent should be obtained before any formal annexation of their country. The result was the Treaty of Waitangi, signed at Waitangi in the Bay of Islands on 6 February 1840 by Hobson (now appointed Lieutenant-Governor)

on behalf of the British government. The treaty was later taken to other parts of the country for signing by most of the Maori chiefs.

Ironically, the famous treaty was never actually ratified. Within a decade the Chief Justice, Sir William Martin, ruled that it had no legal validity because it was not incorporated in New Zealand's statutory law. The date of the original signing of the treaty is now considered to be the "founding day" of New Zealand as a British colony.

The treaty itself, the opposite of what the missionaries had hoped to achieve, remains a bone of contention. The text of the document

was written in English and apparently amended by Hobson after it was first explained to the assembled Maori leaders. A rather loosely translated version in Maori was signed by most of the Maori leaders. The Maori had put much faith in advice from the missionaries, being told that they were signing a solemn pact, under which New Zealand sovereignty was being vested in the British Crown in return for guarantees of certain Maori rights. Many Europeans (and also Maori) genuinely believed this, and for some years the British government upheld the agreement.

It is almost impossible now to regard the treaty objectively. In the context of its time it was an example of enlightened respect for the

LEFT: Tomika Te Mutu, chief of Motuhoa Island.
RIGHT: Hone Heke with his wife and Chief Kawiti.

rights of an indigenous population. But because it was never ratified, and never truly honoured by the land-hungry white settlers, it is easily construed these days as an expedient fraud and is the focus of some civil dissent.

The formal British annexation of New Zealand implicit in the 1840 Treaty of Waitangi was quickly followed by the arrival of ships carrying immigrants organised by Wakefield's New Zealand Company. The *Tory*, despatched prior to the signing of the treaty, arrived early in 1840, carrying immigrants who were to settle in the Wellington area. The Wanganui district received its first settlers shortly after-

Auckland was to be the new capital. Trade from Russell declined and Hone Heke got fractious. He and his warriors demolished the flagpole (the symbol of royal authority) on three occasions, and once sacked the entire town, as British settlers scampered off into the woods or took to boats. George Grey, who arrived as Governor in 1845, called in the army to suppress the rebellion. With the help of Maori dissidents who refused to support Heke, Grey won the day.

Such open conflict did nothing to encourage emigration, and the New Zealand Company went into a terminal decline. It became almost bankrupt in the late 1840s, surrendered its char-

wards, and in 1841 a subsidiary of the Company, based in Plymouth, England, and established New Plymouth.

The South Island was not ignored. Captain Arthur Wakefield, one of Edward's many brothers, arrived at Nelson in 1841 and was followed by some 3,000 settlers in 1842.

Signs of trouble

In the Bay of Islands, Hone Heke, a prominent Maori leader and signatory to the Treaty of Waitangi, quickly became disenchanted with the treaty's implications. Although Kororareka (Russell) had been the de facto "capital" of New Zealand before the signing of the treaty, Lieutenant-Governor Hobson decided that

THE WAIRAU MASSACRE

Despite (or perhaps because of) the Treaty of Waitangi, land claims soon became a matter of bitter dispute. In 1843, Arthur Wakefield (brother of Edward Wakefield) led a party of armed Nelson settlers into the fertile Wairau Valley. It was his contention that the land had been bought by the New Zealand Company from the widow of a European trader, who had previously given the Maori a cannon in exchange for it. The local chief, Te Rauparaha, and his nephew, Rangihaeata, thought otherwise, and when the two sides met violence inevitably broke out. Te Rauparaha's wife was shot and the Maori killed 22 Pakeha, including Wakefield himself.

ter, and handed over to the government some 400,000 hectares (about 1 million acres) of land for which about $500,000 were due; in 1858 the Company was dissolved.

Nonetheless, in its last decade of operation the New Zealand Company remained active, lending its organisational support to members of the Scottish Free Church who established Dunedin in 1848, and to the Anglicans who founded Christchurch in 1850. It helped to open up the pasturelands of the Canterbury Plains, and settlers imported sheep, mostly merinos, from Australia, marking the beginnings of large-scale farming.

In 1852 the colony was granted self-government by Britain with the passing of the New Zealand Constitution Act (the first New Zealand parliament convened in 1854).

Wakefield, who did not set foot in New Zealand until 1852, achieved much, but also lived to see that his ideal of cohesive but expanding communities, complete with "capitalists" and "labourers", was not viable. The immigrants didn't necessarily make the choice for "town life", and many left the fledgling settlements to establish agricultural or pastoral properties well beyond the confines of the towns. However, thanks largely to Wakefield's efforts, the settlement and colonisation of New Zealand were achieved in a more orderly manner than had been the case, several decades earlier, in Canada and Australia.

The New Zealand Wars

The new colony, however, was facing problems. There had been a great deal of speculation in land sales, and many Maori were beginning to realise this: land was being sold for as much as 20 times what they had been paid for it.

A direct result of this injustice was the election in 1858 of a Maori "King" (later called the *Kingitanga* or Maori King Movement) by tribes in the North Island around the Waikato region. There had never been such a title among the Maori, who owed their allegiance to a tribe or sub-tribe, but it was hoped that the *mana* (spiritual authority) of a king, uniting many tribes, would help protect their land against purchase by the Pakeha (white settlers). However, it didn't work out that way.

LEFT: a stagecoach fording a North Island stream.
RIGHT: the NZ Wars were marked by bloody clashes.

In Taranaki, another group of tribes rose up against the government in June 1860 following a blatantly fraudulent land purchase by the colonial administration, the Waitara Land Deal. British regular troops, hastily assembled, were virtually annihilated south of Waitara.

For the next few days, the North Island was ablaze with clashes between Maori and Pakeha. The New Zealand Wars were marked by extraordinary courage on both sides. The conflicts were frequently indecisive, but bloody. On the Pakeha side, the brunt of the early fighting, until 1865, was borne by British regular troops, 14 of whom received Britain's highest battle honour, the Vic-

toria Cross. Between 1865 and 1872, locally raised militia and constabulary forces played an important role – assisted by some Maori tribes who had decided not to join the Maori King's confederation. The "official" end of the conflict came in 1872, with the Maori exhausted by a lack of food and heavy losses, although sporadic fighting continued until formal surrender in 1881.

Despite war, the country's prospects continued to improve. The discovery of gold in the South Island led to a fresh influx of migrants in the early 1860s, and the pursuit of pasture was opening up vast tracts of the country. The increasing importance of the southern lands caused the capital to be moved from Auckland to Wellington in 1865. ❑

A NEW NATION

The 20th century saw a series of unprecedented economic, social and political challenges for the people of New Zealand

Progress towards full independence from Britain began almost as soon as the Maori-Pakeha Land Wars began to settle down. In the 1870s, colonial treasurer Sir Julius Vogel, who borrowed heavily overseas for public works construction, notably railways, sparked an economic boom. A flood of immigrants followed, mainly from Britain but also from Scandinavia and Germany.

But Vogel miscalculated the negative impact of his borrow-to-boom credo. In 1880, New Zealand narrowly averted bankruptcy following steep falls in wool and grain prices. A full-scale depression quickly set in, with unemployment spreading rapidly. In 1888, more than 9,000 settlers left the colony, most of them for Australia, which had remained relatively prosperous.

The years of hardship may have had an impact on the emergence of New Zealand as one of the most socially progressive communities in the world. In 1877 free, compulsory and secular primary school education became law and two years later, every adult man – Maori and Pakeha alike – won the right to vote (*see box, page 42*).

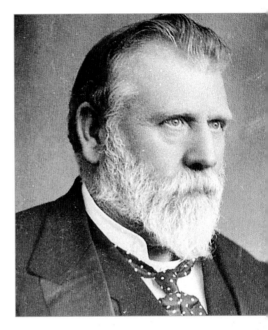

Lamb for the world's tables

There were some other signs of hope, too, with the emergence of a new industry that was set to pave the way in years to come. In 1882, the refrigerated vessel *Dunedin*, loaded with sheep carcasses, made the voyage to England, arriving three months later. The trip was an arduous

one, but the meat arrived safely and profits were much higher than in New Zealand. Farmers subsequently began to breed sheep for meat as well as wool, and the frozen meat industry became an economic staple. This, combined with the expansion of dairy exports in the early 20th century, saw the affluence and influence of farmers grow.

New Zealand politely refused an invitation to become a part of the new Commonwealth of Australia and was subsequently upgraded by the British Empire from "colony" to "dominion" in 1907 (a largely symbolic change of status, but one which would pave the way to full independence within forty years). The new Reform

---

LEFT: modern New Zealand is, by and large, a relaxed and pleasant place to live. **RIGHT:** Richard John Seddon, much-admired prime minister from 1893 to 1906.

Party squeezed into power four years later; the new prime minister, William Massey, a dairy farmer, helped consolidate New Zealand's position as an offshore farm for Britain.

World Wars and depression

War brought a new sense of nationalism to New Zealand, and at the same time reinforced the country's ties to Britain. Between 1914 and 1918, 100,000 men joined the Australia-New Zealand Army Corps (Anzac) forces fighting with the Allies in Africa and Europe.

The Great Depression of the 1930s hit the country hard. Curtailed British demand for meat, wool and dairy products led to severe unemployment and several bloody riots. The new Labour Party swept into power in 1935 and managed to pull the nation out of the doldrums. Under Prime Minister Michael Savage, New Zealand again moved to the forefront of world social change, establishing a full social security system.

Savage also led the country into World War II. This time, nearly 200,000 Kiwis were called to battle, many of them engaged in the Pacific campaign, others in North Africa, Italy and Crete. More than 10,000 died. American writer James A. Michener once claimed that the bravest sol-

AN ENLIGHTENED LIBERAL NATION

New Zealand has a long history of enlightened social innovation. All the way back in 1877, free education became available for all children aged between 7 and 14. Two years later, universal male suffrage became law. In the 1890s under the Liberal Party government headed by John Ballance, sweeping land reforms were introduced, breaking down the large inland estates and providing money for first mortgages to put people on the land. Industrial legislation provided improved conditions for workers as well as the world's first compulsory system of industrial arbitration. Meanwhile, the aged poor were awarded a pension.

The country became the first self-governing nation to grant the right to vote to all adult women in September 1893, when the Governor approved the Electoral Bill passed by Parliament 11 days earlier. This marked the end of an epic struggle by suffragettes, led by Kate Sheppard. During a seven-year campaign, 31,872 signatures were collected, culminating in the 1893 petition for the enfranchisement of women. At the time it was the largest petition ever gathered in Australasia.

The principal minds behind these great social reforms were William Pember Reeves, a New Zealand-born socialist, and Richard John Seddon, who became prime minister when Ballance died in 1893. Seddon's legendary toughness and political judgement gave him enormous power within the party and in the country.

dier in each of the World Wars was a New Zealander – Bernard Freyberg in the first and, in the second, Charles Upham, "a stumpy square-jawed chap" whose "behaviour under fire seems incredible". Upham won the Victoria Cross twice.

Back home, a successful economic stabilisation policy and full employment made the 1940s a decade of relative prosperity, and the country emerged from the war with a stronger sense of nationhood and identity. It was an appropriate time, in 1947, for the government to adopt the Statute of Westminster and formally achieve full independence from Britain.

The Labour Party, however, had by then lost entire social structure – between 1984 and 1990 (*see page 45*).

One of the first actions taken by the unicameral House was the ratification of the ANZUS (Australia–New Zealand–United States) security pact in 1951, sealing the nation's defence requirements.

End of isolation

The first post-war revolution, however, came with the end of isolation. Before mass travel became a possibility, New Zealand's hotels shut at 6pm, restaurants were forbidden to sell liquor and a rigid 40-hour, five-day working week

its vigour, and its defeat in 1949 ended an era. The victors were the National Party, who ran on a platform extolling private enterprise. The 1950s began with a political tremor as this new government abolished the Legislative Council, the upper house of the national Parliament. New Zealand became one of the few democratic nations with a unicameral legislature. This gave inordinate power to the executive – a Cabinet made up of members of the ruling party. The power to change the law dramatically, and within hours, enabled the Labour Party to transform the nation's economy – and its

Left: Anzac Day parade. **Above:** Prime Minister John Key meets Queen Elizabeth on a visit to London in 2008.

New Zealand and World War I

By the time World War I ended, almost 17,000 New Zealanders had lost their lives. Indeed, the casualties were out of all proportion to the country's population, then about a million. The futility was underscored by the debacle that took place on Turkey's Gallipoli Peninsula, from 25 April 1915 (a day now marked in memoriam every year as "Anzac Day") until British naval evacuation some eight months later; the affair cost the lives of 8,587 servicemen from Australia and New Zealand. This heroic tragedy, dramatised some years later in Peter Weir's film *Gallipoli*, gave New Zealand a new identity within the British Empire.

meant shop hours were strictly controlled and most families spent weekends at home. Society remained in that time warp until the 1950s, when passenger ships began their trade again. Thousands of young Kiwis went away for their "OE" (overseas experience), almost always to London, and for the first time could compare their society with others.

Air travel and advances in telecommunications in the 1960s and '70s led to radical changes in this narrow, closed, highly controlled society. By the 1980s, shops were staying open into the evenings and weekends, most restrictions were lifted from hotels and taverns, New Zealand

tion into the European Economic Community (EEC) in 1973 left them in confusion.

Tumultuous times

During the 1970s, New Zealand's sheep population rose past 70 million for the first time as farmers received state payments to boost stock numbers. Primary industry was widely subsidised and manufacturing tightly protected from 1975–84 under Sir Robert Muldoon's National government. Meanwhile, trade barriers imposed on Britain by EEC membership, combined with rocketing oil prices, sent the cost of industrial goods sky high.

SHOULD AULD ACQUAINTANCE BE FORGOT?

wines began to rank among the world's best, and restaurants and cafés made eating out part of the national culture. On the back of such sophistication, tourism boomed.

The transition has not always been smooth. In the early 1970s New Zealand began grappling with the problem of diversifying both its production away from bulk commodities and its markets away from Britain. When oil prices soared, debt began to pile up as both Labour and National administrations borrowed and hoped primary production prices would pick up. It was a matter of marketing. But marketing was something New Zealanders had never needed to do. They had lived well for so long, simply by farming well, that the British transi-

Muldoon's government doubled the tight measures imposed by Labour on immigration, imports and the dollar. A pugnacious man, Muldoon provoked the anger of trade unionists by imposing a wage freeze, but held his line in the face of numerous strikes and demonstrations.

By the end of the 1970s and the beginning of the 1980s, internal inflation was raging so strongly (up to 17 percent) that farm costs skyrocketed and the Muldoon ministry humiliatingly had to bolster subsidies to New Zealand farmers. All the regulation and readjustment caused an agony of doubt about the short-term future of the economy. By 1984, unemployment had reached 130,000 and the national overseas debt stood at NZ$14.3 billion.

When a new Labour government came to power towards the end of 1984, the situation changed rapidly: farm and other production subsidies were withdrawn virtually overnight, import licences abandoned, wage structures dismantled and a broad policy of economic laissez-faire put in place.

On returning to power in 1990, the National Party under Jim Bolger quickly made it clear that they would keep faith with economic deregulation. In the mid-1990s the economy began steadily to recover and the government eased up slightly on its expenditure and its tight monetary policy.

ments with New Zealand. Labour, under Prime Minister David Lange, pledged to set up a nuclear-free zone around the shores of New Zealand, and to renegotiate the 33-year-old ANZUS security pact to force the US to keep nuclear armaments out of New Zealand ports. Division within the Labour government on other issues had grown so wide, however, that Lange resigned in 1989.

Early in the post-war period, New Zealand had realised that its best economic hope for the future was some sort of pact with Australia. In 1965, the New Zealand Australia Free Trade Agreement (NAFTA) was signed. The plan was

Foreign affairs

New Zealand began to assert itself on the international stage during the 1960s, as France stepped up its campaign of nuclear testing in its Polynesian-governed islands. There were several mass demonstrations, and strong anti-nuclear sentiment reached its peak in New Zealand when the Labour government refused nuclear-armed or nuclear-powered US naval vessels entry to New Zealand ports in 1985. The Americans insisted on their right as allies under the ANZUS Pact and broke off all defence arrange-

LEFT: Britain's entry into the EEC in 1973 dealt a serious blow to New Zealand's economy. **ABOVE:** campaigning for a nuclear-free state in the 1960s.

gradually to dismantle trade barriers between the two countries, but progress was slow. In 1983, the two governments signed the CER (Closer Economic Relations) pact, and by the beginning of the 1990s, free trade was virtually in place across the Tasman Sea.

Both New Zealand and Australia have turned their economic attention northwards to the burgeoning Asian economies, and these days more than one-third of New Zealand exports are bound for Asian markets – more than to North America and Europe combined – and over one-third of imports come from Asia. Japan and Singapore have long been trading partners, but

nal to consider these claims, and this process continues today. Many land claims were conceded, particularly land held by the government, and a major fishing concession was awarded to the Maori.

Although there is a consensus that redress is due, some tension has prevailed over particular Waitangi claims. That tension has spilt over on several occasions. The landmark tree on One Tree Hill in Auckland *(see page 138)* was attacked in 1994 and again in 1996; another activist attacked the America's Cup yachting trophy with a sledgehammer, claiming it was a symbol of Pakeha elitism. Progress towards set-

business is also booming with China, Korea, Thailand, Malaysia, Indonesia and Taiwan.

The Maori issue

During the 30 years of social and economic turbulence that began in the 1960s, New Zealand proved to be one of the most stable democracies in the world. But there remained a festering sore beneath the surface, caused by injustices to the Maori over a century before.

The 1984–90 Labour government finally acknowledged the validity of Maori claims for land, fishing grounds and other assets that were illegally taken from them – claims that were based on the 1840 Treaty of Waitangi. The Labour government set up the Waitangi Tribu-

tlement of land claims continues and is high on the political agenda, but whatever progress is made is destined to fail to please everyone. The difficulties, however, are seen by many as the growing pains of a new nation.

Electoral reform

Dissatisfaction with the rapid pace of change and with the performance of recent governments was expressed in a referendum on electoral reform. In 1993, the country voted to scrap traditional first-past-the-post elections in favour of a proportional system called the MMP (Mixed Member Proportional). Many worried that this would further fragment the structure of political parties – and to an extent it has.

In the 1996 elections, the National Party, led by Jim Bolger, won 44 seats in the 120-member house, while the Labour Party won 37. The New Zealand First Party, having won 17 seats, including four Maori seats (areas mainly populated by Maori who had previously voted for Labour), held the balance of power and emerged as the coalition partner in a new government with the National Party. The situation became volatile after 1996, with change becoming a constant theme in politics; in 1997 Prime Minister Bolger resigned.

In December 1997, Jenny Shipley became the country's first female prime minister, replacing Bolger as leader of the National Party. However, weakened by the break-up of her coalition party and a floundering economy, Shipley lost the 1999 elections to a Labour Party-led coalition, helmed by another woman, Helen Clark. Clark's tough-as-nails approach, aided by a strong domestic economy and lower unemployment rate, clinched her and the Labour Party a second term at the 2002 elections and a third term in 2005, albeit by the narrowest of margins. In 2008, the National Party, led by John Key, swept into power, and on the same day, Helen Clark resigned as the leader of the Labour Party.

A new confidence

New Zealand was long dominated by a self-denigrating "cultural cringe" which saw it constantly measuring itself unfavourably against other countries. This accounts in part for the high number of people who have left for what are

> On 31 December 1999, New Zealanders made much of the fact that their country was the first in the world to enter the new millennium. This reflected a growing awareness of the nation's uniqueness and individuality.

perceived as greener pastures. Many, from writer Katherine Mansfield to rock group The Datsuns, were only recognised in their own country after they had achieved overseas success.

LEFT: Maori rights protestors during Queen Elizabeth's 1989 visit. The banner reads "Honour the Treaty of Waitangi". **RIGHT:** a Maori performs a traditional *hongi* greeting.

Although New Zealand has long ceased to be a smaller version of Australia or a pale reflection of the "mother country", England, once New Zealanders had realised what it wasn't, they had to work out what it was. The process of defining this identity was facilitated by several factors, not least among them the institution of the MMP system in 1993, which established a truly representative government. In the elections immediately following its adoption, there were more Maori and women MPs, and the first Pacific Island, Asian and Muslim MPs were elected.

This in turn made it clear that New Zealand was no longer a bicultural, Maori-Pakeha society,

but a multicultural one. And this process was abetted by a generous immigration policy which saw a boom in the number of Asian immigrants, a side-effect of which has been an opportunity for demagogues to incite new racial tensions in the community. *For more on New Zealand's multicultural society, see pages 51–7.*

New Zealand will find its own solutions to these difficulties. Its remoteness may have made its people parochial, but it has also forced them to develop the so-called "No. 8-wire spirit" – after the legend that a Kiwi can fix anything with a piece of No. 8 fencing wire – in which they take much pride. And they will increasingly appreciate who they are and what they have – something which has long been obvious to visitors. ❏

PEOPLE

In multicultural New Zealand, Maori, Pakeha and Pacific Islanders have been joined by a diverse mix of new arrivals, all helping to shape the distinctive New Zealand character

New Zealanders, while numerically rare by global standards, are found the world over, with around a million living overseas. The other 4.3 million live at home in what Kiwis dub "Godzone", one of the most beautiful and least crowded countries on the planet. Yet at the same time New Zealand is also one of the world's most urbanised and suburbanised nations, with fully 86 percent of its residents living in the four main centres, and the rest scattered across the rural spaces in between. The population of Auckland alone exceeds that of the entire South Island, while half the South Island population is to be found in and around Christchurch. You're less likely to run into anyone in Westland, where perhaps more than anywhere else, one can sense that New Zealand has been home to humans for only a very short time – probably, in fact, less than 1,000 years *(see page 25)*. By any standards, this is a very young country.

Despite the overwhelming majority of urbanites, farming remains the backbone of the economy. It is a way of life valued by close-knit rural communities throughout the land. Voluntary activity runs everything, and in the countryside you will also find the warmth, friendly neighbourhood security and community spirit that once set the tone for the nation as a whole. As for the legendary black-singletted, gumboot-clad Fred Dagg-like character (invented by the satirist John Clarke), the doyen of the family farm with a dog at his heel – he's increasingly rare. Chances are, today, the guy working in the cowshed hails from Mumbai or Tokyo.

PRECEDING PAGES: four generations of a Maori *whanau* (family) at a meeting house. **LEFT:** traditional dances survive in local celebrations. **RIGHT:** a Wellington café.

Many an urban office worker may be only one generation away from the farm. Until the 1950s, the rural–urban split was roughly 50/50, but that changed with the post-war drift of job-seekers to the cities where they laid claim to the stock standard quarter-acre (about 1,000 sq. metres) section.

Although New Zealand is still a paradise of sorts, growing crime – the main offenders being drunk and drug-fuelled youth – renders urban areas rather less so today. Meanwhile, the quarter-acre has shrunk to a mere eighth of an acre, and the traditional vegetable plot, a former essential in most Kiwi families, is history. This change in space and lifestyle has come about quickly, and for many New Zealanders, although pricey, the ideal is now lifestyle block living (2–4-hectare/5–10-acre blocks of land located within 1½ hours drive of major city).

Modern Maori

The indigenous people of New Zealand, the Maori or *Tangata Whenua* (people of the land), first settled on the islands at some point between the 9th and 13th centuries AD – although scientists increasingly believe it to be close to the latter stages of that period. Two centuries after the earliest European settlers arrived, the Maori now make up about one-seventh of

the population, with most living in the North Island. The Maori language *(te reo)* is spoken throughout New Zealand and the vast majority of place names are of Maori origin.

If one single person can be credited for the survival of Maori culture into modern times, it must be the great parliamentarian Sir Apirana Ngata (1874–1950). By the late 1920s, knighted and made Minister of Native Affairs, Ngata had devised legislation to develop Maori land, established a school at Rotorua and initiated a work programme for the building of Maori community facilities. Working with Ngata to implement national policy at a local level was a group of community leaders including Princess Te Puea Herangi of Waikato. Te Puea was the force behind the *Kingitanga*, or Maori King Movement, formed in 1858 to unite and strengthen the Maori community and to halt the loss of Maori land *(see page 39)*.

After her death in 1952, Te Puea's great-niece, Te Arikinui Dame Te Atairangikaahu, led the Kingitanga for the next 40 years, during which it grew in stature. It is today seen as the Maoris' single most important political leadership. The five-day *tangi* (funeral service) following Te Ata's death in August 2006 brought Maori together on an unprecedented scale. Her eldest son, Tuheitia Paki, has succeeded as king.

In the 1930s the living standards of Maori rose considerably under the Labour government's welfare programme, ensuring the physical survival of the race, which had been threatened by diseases introduced by European settlers. (Numbers never dropped perilously low, however: the Maori population, estimated

THE HUI, TRADITIONAL MAORI GATHERING

For visitors, the *hui* offers the most revealing glimpse of Maori culture. It will usually be held on a *marae* (the open courtyard in front of the meeting house where formal greetings and discussions take place) under the supervision of the *tangata whenua* or host tribe. Visitors are called on to the *marae* with a *karanga* – a long, wailing call. Answering the call, the visitors enter led by their own women, usually dressed in black. Then follows a pause and a *tangi* (ritual weeping) for the dead. This is succeeded by the *mihi* (speeches) of welcome and reply, made by male elders. At the end of each speech, the orator's companions stand and perform a *waiata* (song), usually a lament. Once these formalities are over, visitors move forward and *hongi* (press noses) with the locals.

The food served on such occasions is special: meat and vegetables are cooked in a *hangi* (earth oven). There will be seafood, with delicacies such as shellfish, *kina* (sea egg), eel and dried shark. Other treats include fermented *kumara* and *titi* (mutton bird, also known as the sooty shearwater), and *Rewena* (a scone-like loaf) will accompany the meal. Far more than in Pakeha society, eating together is a way to communicate goodwill, and acceptance of such hospitality is as important as offering it.

There are many tourist operators in New Zealand, particularly in Rotorua, who can organise *marae* visits which often include a *powhiri* (formal welcome) and a *wero* (challenge).

at around 100,000 when the Europeans arrived, had declined to 42,000 by 1900, and after this date numbers began to recover.)

Following World War II, however, there was a major shift in Maori society. A decline in rural employment and a rapid expansion of secondary industry in urban areas brought Maori into the cities in increasing numbers, and by the 1980s less than 10 percent remained in rural settlements. For the first time, Maori and Pakeha found themselves living alongside one another.

This new relationship brought difficulties. With no ready access or encouragement to further their education, many new urban Maori

has adapted accordingly and *Kohanga Reo* (language nests) have been set up to expose preschool Maori to their language and customs. The current school curriculum reflects the importance of Maori culture, programmes have been established to encourage Maori to study at university, and laws ban discrimination in the workplace. Legal aid and translation facilities are now available in the courts, and Maori is now the country's second official language.

Maori values, too, remain beneath the cloak of Western appearances. Concepts such as *tapu* (sacredness), *noa* (the passing of *tapu* to a person, ie a blessing), *wairua* (things of the spirit) and

became trapped in low-paying jobs. Housing conditions were also poor. That led to stereotyping that further hindered their prospects. It was a harsh and different world, lacking the support network offered by the extended family in the rural environment. Many born in the new environment reacted in a strongly anti-social manner. The Maori crime rate increased, adding further to a negative Maori stereotype.

The problems, however, have been recognised, and since then much progress has been made. The education system in New Zealand

mana (spiritual authority), all persist in modern Maori life. Yet poverty remains a problem in many areas, and Maoris still make up a disproportionate number of the prison population. Some commentators have suggested the social problems are deep-rooted, perhaps going back as far as European colonisation. Regardless of this, the Maori profile is increasing and a more positive image is replacing the old negative stereotype.

Non-Maori increasingly show respect for Maori rituals and for places that are *tapu* (sites of sacred objects, historic events or burials). There are many places throughout New Zealand that are sacred to Maori. Visitors are urged to recognise the cultural significance of these places and treat them with respect.

LEFT: Maoris make up around 15 percent of the population. **ABOVE:** identically dressed participants in a Maori cultural dance performance *(kapa haka).*

Britain in the South Seas

Starting in earnest around 1830, hundreds of years after the arrival of the Maori, the pioneering English, Scottish, Irish and Welsh settlers arrived in New Zealand. The original plan, mooted by the New Zealand Company, was to establish a "Better Britain" or "Britain of the South". Unlike Australia, however, a criminal record did not provide a one-way ticket. Instead, industrious immigrants, respectable, hard-working rural labourers and cultured men of capital were determinedly sought. Prosperity and respectability were promised in exchange for hard work. The idea of owning one's own land, deeply entrenched in the Kiwi psyche, arrived with the settlers for whom it was largely an impossibility back home.

Land issues were a constant source of conflict between the Maori and the Europeans in the early days (see page 36). The Europeans' land-grabbing ways, and later wars between the two groups, did nothing to endear many of the new arrivals to the native population. The greatest conflicts arose over the mutual misunderstanding of what constituted land ownership. Even today, land issues surrounding the 1840 Treaty of Waitangi (see page 37) remain highly contentious.

KIWI INGENUITY

It is popularly said that a New Zealander can fix anything with a length of No. 8 (4mm/¼-inch) fencing wire. New Zealanders' inventiveness and do-it-yourself mentality arrived with the early European settlers, who found themselves in an untamed land, devoid of the trappings (and spare parts) of civilisation. Machinery had to be fixed or redesigned with whatever was available. Necessity has endowed New Zealand with more inventors per capita than anywhere else. Among them are two South Island farmers – Sir William Hamilton, who invented the Hamilton jet boat, and Richard "Mad" Pearse, who designed his own planes and reputedly flew before the Wright brothers.

For the first 50 years of European settlement, almost half the newcomers were English, with significant numbers of Welsh (the original statistics lumped both together). Nowhere in New Zealand does this heritage survive better than in the city of Christchurch, whose founders transplanted a complete cross-section of English Episcopalian society, with an earl and a bishop (both of whom soon fled the privation of the pioneering scene) at the top and the labouring classes at the bottom. The utopian Episcopalian dream might have foundered (see page 35), but Christchurch has prospered and remains about as close to the mother country as it is possible to get outside of England itself.

The Scots made up the second-largest immigrant group, at 24 percent. Their pioneers, a stiff-backed band of Free Kirk (Church) Presbyterians, arrived in 1848, driven by the urge to escape economic depression and the schism that had developed between their Church and the Church of Scotland. This clannish but brave little community possessed the determination and toughness to endure the notoriously bleak winters and the rugged terrain of Otago, where they created a "Scotland of the South". Their main city, Dunedin (the old Gaelic name for Edinburgh), became New Zealand's most populous town for a time in the 19th century.

The pioneers brought with them their Northern Hemisphere traditions, language, festivals, faith and food, some of which have passed unchanged into 21st-century Kiwi culture. With menus intact, some Pakeha continue to enjoy haggis on Burns Night and Hogmanay, and eggs at Easter, as well as roast, fruit mince pies and steamed fruit pudding – traditional winter fare – at Christmas, eaten in the midst of summer. Increasingly, however, many now ignore traditions in favour of a Kiwi institution – the good old New Zealand barbecue.

The gold rushes also brought a host of fortune seekers from many nations flooding into

A sizeable number of Irish immigrants, many of whom were diggers who followed the gold

> 66 *If an English butler and an English nanny sat down to design a country, they would come up with New Zealand.* Anon 99

trail down from California and Australia, arrived in large numbers during the Otago gold rushes of the 1860s.

LEFT: women queue to cast their votes, 1899. New Zealand was the first country in the world to introduce universal suffrage. **ABOVE:** panning for gold in Otago.

the country through Dunedin, the nearest port to the Otago goldfields. Among the newcomers were Germans, Scandinavians, Poles, French, Italians and Chinese. Yet, despite the influx of these new immigrants, as the 19th century progressed the unmistakably British character of New Zealand continued strongly, bolstered by the arrival of another 100,000 Europeans – mostly British – in the 1870s.

Old prejudices also persisted, and were bolstered by a few new ones. In many a Protestant mind, there was a distinctive "us" and "them" mentality – "them" being the Catholic Irish. This prejudice persisted well into the 1950s. And, predictably, most of the European arrivals displayed racial prejudice towards the Maori.

The new New Zealanders

Up to the 1960s, there was little to challenge the original plan of a distinctly British New Zealand. Most immigrants were British, and those who were not, for example the 30,000-strong Dutch community who arrived in the 1950s, were expected to adopt the local ways and get on with it. But with the 1960s came television and cheap air travel, which opened New Zealand to the world and the world to New Zealand like never before. The 1970s saw a severing of traditional ties with Britain after it joined the European Economic Community in 1973, and an end to assisted British immigration. A new wave of immigrants, from Asia and the Pacific, followed. Added to the mix are a growing number of refugees and asylum seekers, attracted by New Zealand's progressive humanitarian stance, liberal politics and world-leading social welfare. Today they continue to arrive from various hot spots around the globe – Afghanistan, Iran, Somalia, South Africa and Zimbabwe. Overall, about 20 percent of New Zealand's residents today were born overseas, with more of these living in Auckland than anywhere else in the country.

While certain Kiwi characteristics prevail, the 21st-century New Zealander is becoming

NOTEWORTHY NEW ZEALANDERS

In 1991 the Reserve Bank of New Zealand announced that new banknotes were required and suggested that the portrait of the Queen on some of the banknotes be replaced by those of notable New Zealanders. This was a significant moment for New Zealand, being seen as a meaningful break with the colonial past (although, to appease the royalists, the Queen's visage was retained on the NZ$20 note). The nation was called upon to nominate worthy candidates. The illustrious Nobel Prize-winning scientist Sir Ernest Rutherford topped the bill. The first to split the atom, he looks pensively from the NZ$100 note that bills him as Lord Rutherford of Nelson. National hero, the late Sir Edmund Hillary polled a close second. Once voted the country's most trusted citizen in a nationwide poll, Hillary was respected as much for his conquest of Mount Everest as for his humanitarian and conservation causes. He looks towards the mountains in the distance on the NZ$5 note.

Kate Sheppard graces the NZ$10 note. An intelligent Christian socialist, Sheppard led the women's movement whose efforts made New Zealand the world's first sovereign state to give women the vote. Maori leader Apirana Ngata adorns the NZ$50 note. The first Maori to obtain a degree, Ngata graduated with a Bachelor of Arts in 1893, and in 1905 entered Parliament as member for Eastern Maori, a seat he held for 38 years. The notes are still the same today, albeit now in plastic rather than paper.

increasingly difficult to define. Statistically speaking, if one were to gather together 100 randomly selected New Zealanders, one would be in the company of roughly 70 Europeans, 15 Maori, seven Pacific Islanders, seven Asians and one person from a minority cultural group. The median age would be 36 years, 12 would be over 65 years old, and 29 would be from Auckland.

While traditional fish and chips remains the favourite for the rest of New Zealand, Asian foods are the takeaway of choice in Auckland, home to the country's largest Asian population. Today, Chinese from China, Taiwan and Hong Kong form the largest Asian immigrant group,

South Auckland, in particular, is home to the largest Pacific Island population in the world. The first Pacific Islanders (other than the Maori) were brought by missionaries to New Zealand for biblical training; after World War II, they mostly came to fill labour shortages.

The majority of the Pacific Islanders today are New Zealand-born. Their contributions to New Zealand culture are considerable, particularly in the fields of sport and music. Former All Blacks Tana Umaga and Jonah Lomu, shot-put champion Beatrice Faumina, Silver Fern netballer Bernice Mene and hip-hop artists Che Fu and Scribe are all Kiwi heroes. The largest group

followed by Indians. Within these groups are families who have been in the country for several generations. The rest of the Asian community come mainly from Korea, Sri Lanka and Japan. Their reasons for coming vary; some came for education, others to invest or transfer their skills, and many to establish their families in a less crowded, cleaner and healthier environment.

Pacific Islanders

Auckland's distinctly multicultural character contrasts markedly with the rest of the country.

LEFT: the All Blacks doing the *haka* warrior dance.
ABOVE: beach barbecue featuring red snapper.
RIGHT: modern Maori mum and child.

among the Pacific Islanders are the Samoans, whose payments to relatives back home provide half of Samoa's foreign exchange. Cook Islands Maori and Tongans make up the next largest groups, followed by Niueans, Fijians and Tokelauans. Indeed, many more Niueans, Cook Islands Maori and Tokelauans are found in New Zealand than in the islands themselves.

Of the many tongues spoken in New Zealand, the most common after the official English and Maori is Samoan, followed by Tongan, Cantonese and Mandarin.

The big OE

New Zealanders have long been ranked among the world's most travelled citizens. A significant proportion of those who emigrate here are likely to spend a large amount of time away from their new home visiting relatives in other countries. And many New Zealanders themselves emigrate: just why 1 million of them live overseas has everything to do with New Zealand's geographical remoteness and the national rite of passage known as the big OE – Overseas Experience.

Lasting anything from a few years to decades, OE was originally a sea journey home to Britain and Europe for the early settlers. It then became an essential cultural escape for New Zealand artists and writers of the 1920s and 1930s, stifled

103,000 New Zealanders moved to Australia and settled there permanently. Today an estimated half a million New Zealanders have relocated to their large neighbour across the Tasman Sea, attracted by higher wages, lower taxes, warmer climate and proximity to home. Another 50,000 Kiwis are overseas in countries other than Australia and Britain. Most, having satisfied their curiosity, return home to bring up their children or to retire. Settling back in has its challenges, though: the more travelled find it less easy to adjust to the limits of their homeland's insular shores, particularly if they are not fans of rugby or the great outdoors.

by the insular, tight-lipped narrow-mindedness of home. From the 1960s onwards, cheaper air travel brought the rest of the world within the

> New Zealand's former prime minister, Robert Muldoon, once remarked that "New Zealanders who leave for Australia raise the IQ of both countries".

reach of more Kiwis who chose to escape and explore their past and the world at large, and pursue lives around the globe.

The main Meccas of Kiwi pilgrimage remain Britain and Australia. Between 1976 and 1982,

The next generation

The first generation, born in a new country, live between two cultures, that of the land of their birth, and that of their parents' homeland. While some stay in touch with their parents' culture and speak their mother tongue at home, others struggle with identity issues. Many first-generation Pacific Island New Zealanders regard the loss of language as the main reason for their generation's lack of confidence and equate fluency in their parents' language as the key to preserving their culture. Yet with each passing generation, cultural anxiety may lessen. The multicultural Kiwi melting pot bubbles on with the healthy addition of increasing mixed parentage and new immigrants. ❏

What Makes a Kiwi

The fact that New Zealand is a small country a very long way from anywhere else has helped to shape the locals' distinctive outlook

New Zealanders are as homogeneous – or as diverse – as the people of any other nation in this age of globalism, the Internet and international air travel. That said, the isolation and insularity of this country have bred some distinct qualities and characteristics.

One that is likely to be noticed early on by visitors is known as the "cultural cringe", the belief that, because New Zealand is so small and remote, anything from another country is automatically superior to the local version. This characteristic indicates a desperate need for approval from foreigners. The first question visitors are likely to be asked is: "How do you like New Zealand?" (The correct answer is: "It's wonderful, I'm thinking of moving here.")

As a consequence of this dependence on overseas approval, the New Zealanders who have succeeded overseas are the ones who are most respected at home – the likes of Sir Edmund Hillary, Sam Neill and Kiri Te Kanawa. There is a suspicion that those people who choose to remain here to climb mountains or act or sing opera do so because "they couldn't make it overseas".

Don't be a "tall poppy"

Another corollary of New Zealand's size is that it is quite easy for an individual to shine. Anyone engaged in any form of endeavour is likely to be among the top five in his or her field simply because there won't be many more than five people engaged in it. This is directly connected to the so-called "tall poppy" syndrome, meaning that anyone who rises above the crowd will be cut down in a frenzy of negative criticism generated by envy. This is much-quoted but simply not true, and the syndrome may well be the invention of an over-sensitive elite who cannot abide any suggestion that they fall short of perfection.

The notion of a tall poppy springs from the fact that, despite the wide gap between rich and poor, New Zealand is still at heart an egalitarian society,

the legacy of the utopians who colonised it. There is a class system, but it is far less rigid and confining than in most other Western democracies.

New Zealanders are a relatively laconic race, so it's paradoxical that when they do speak, they talk very quickly, packing a greater number of words into a breath than most other native English-speakers. At the same time, their conversation labours under a conspicuous drawl. Those who recoil at the length of time it takes a New Zealander to meander through a vowel should be warned that many linguists theorise that the English-speaking world is undergoing a Great Vowel Shift which will eventually see everyone talking like "thus".

A highly active sense of humour is a strong part of the national make-up, though it often goes unnoticed because it is so dry. If a New Zealander says something that sounds absurd, he probably means it to be, but he won't drive it home with series of hearty guffaws and thigh-slapping.

Though overwhelmingly urbanite in number, New Zealanders' heritage has given them many rural values which persist beyond the farm gate diligence, support for others, strong community spirit, practicality (with a concomitant distrust of intellectuals) and a can-do attitude. The phrase "No. 8-wire spirit" holds that a New Zealander can solve any practical problem with a piece of No. 8 fencing wire. New Zealanders are certainly ingenious; they are also diverse, imaginative and entertaining hosts. ❑

LEFT: hands-on learning. **RIGHT:** a Maori woman displays her heritage with traditional bone jewellery.

CONTEMPORARY ART AND LITERATURE

Behind much of New Zealand's art and literature lies a degree of tension between the landscape and the people who inhabit it

Many New Zealanders have always had something of an ambivalent attitude towards the arts. Grants to artists and writers by the state funding agency once regularly aroused derision, as if wastrels and idlers were getting money for nothing. Today philistinism is never far from the surface. But in spite of this – or perhaps precisely because of it – a robust indigenous culture has flourished. The very isolation of artists has forced them to forge their own way, without too much reliance on overseas models or local encouragement.

The practical do-it-yourself tradition of New Zealanders in other fields – notably farming and home renovation – shows through in the work of artists as diverse as the inventive Michael Parekowhai and the masterful Ralph Hotere, whose paintings frequently incorporate materials like corrugated iron and old timber. New Zealand's contribution to the 2003 Venice Biennale, an installation by Michael Stevenson, featured a Trekka (the country's only locally designed vehicle) alongside a Moniac (a water-driven computer that, not surprisingly, never went into production anywhere).

It remains a scandal that there is no national art gallery in New Zealand. The remains of what used to be one have been squeezed into an upstairs space at Te Papa, and although this museum is a must, don't expect to find a truly representative display of New Zealand art here. Instead you should trawl the fine range of city and provincial galleries – notably the superb Christchurch Art Gallery (*see page 247*). The long

wavy line of its glass-and-metal exterior hints at the shape of the *koru*, a stylised fern frond that also decorates the tails of Air New Zealand planes and symbolises growth and harmony. Wellington's City Gallery (*page 217*), the Auckland Art Gallery (*page 133*), the Dunedin Public Art Gallery (*page 292*), the adventurous Govett-Brewster Art Gallery (*page 205*) in New Plymouth and the Eastern Southland Art Gallery in Gore, not to mention the more multicultural Pataka in Porirua, are all stimulating.

Fine art

One of the first artists to be exhibited at the new Christchurch Art Gallery when it opened

LEFT: contemporary Maori ceramics on sale at an Auckland gallery. **RIGHT:** the *koru* spiral symbolises new life and harmony.

in 2003 was W.A. (Bill) Sutton, the long-lived local painter (1917–2002) whose spare, semi-abstract landscapes seem to symbolise the artist's relationship with the land – often perceived in New Zealand art as empty, brooding, even hostile to humans.

The hugely popular realist landscapes of Grahame Sydney, though softer in style, catch some of this mood. Sydney's work has been likened, with good reason, to that of Andrew Wyeth. The godfather of New Zealand art, as it were, is Colin McCahon, whose work moved beyond simple landscapes with religious connotations to vast, dark, mystical incantations whose brood-

ard Killeen, Peter Robinson and the quirky Bill Hammond, of whose surrealist paintings it has been said: "Everything about them is odd."

Sculpture and pottery

Sculpture has always laboured to find its feet in New Zealand. The size of the country and a perception that money spent on art is not money well spent has meant that public commissions are rare and grudging. Sculptors tend to work on a small scale, but there are two who merit particular attention. Terry Stringer's work often playfully exploits the tension between the firmness of bronze, one of his favourite media, and

ing power lay as much in the prayers inscribed upon them as in their massive cubist forms.

But contemporary New Zealand art is not all gloom and doom. McCahon's less tormented successors have been more inclined towards

> The South Island city of Nelson is renowned for its wealth of talented artisans, and the region possesses more working artists per capita than anywhere else in New Zealand.

playfulness and postmodern irony in their work, particularly artists like Joanna Braithwaite, Shane Cotton, Dick Frizzell, Don Driver, Rich-

the softness of his subject matter. Something of a traditionalist, though often with a postmodern edge, Stringer is also an accomplished portrait painter.

Experimentation with light is regarded as the province of the painter, but Neil Dawson creates sculptures in which the shadows cast by the work can be equally as important as the shapes he has moulded out of such favoured materials as aluminium and steel. His dramatic *Ferns* hover above the Civic Square in Wellington, and he has created the monumental *Chalice* to adorn Cathedral Square in his home town of Christchurch.

It's not entirely clear why pottery has long been such a popular creative endeavour in New Zealand. There are two representative currents.

The first is the rough-hewn, hands-on, earth-connecting style. One iconic name in this field is Barry Brickell at Coromandel's Driving Creek Railway and Potteries *(see page 169)*. The other strand is a more "fine art" approach represented by John Parker, who has worked for years producing pottery solely in white, in which an elegant severity of form and line is a major concern.

Outside the mainstream of New Zealand art – and outside the country for much of his life – is Len Lye (1901–80). Lye worked in numerous media but is mainly remembered as a kinetic sculptor and pioneer of direct film, in which he scratched and otherwise worked

Katherine Mansfield, whose delicate short stories have – despite her own gloomy prediction – survived numerous changes of fashion and can be read with as much pleasure today as when they were written, mostly in the 15 years or so before her death in 1923 at the age of 34. New Zealand in the early 20th century was claustrophobic for the young writer, and in 1908 Mansfield left her country, with some eagerness, in pursuit of a career – first in London and later in Switzerland and the south of France. She never returned.

Not until 1985 was another New Zealander as widely read, when the Booker Prize was

directly on film to create entrancing abstract images. These were set to music in a way that has resulted in them being described as proto-music videos. The Govett-Brewster Gallery in New Plymouth *(see page 205)* holds the Len Lye collection and archive, and regularly exhibits his work. His arresting sculpture *Wind Wand* has been installed on the New Plymouth foreshore.

Literature

The first New Zealand writer to attract significant attention outside her own country was

LEFT: Christchurch Art Gallery.
ABOVE: idiosyncratic pottery at Nelson.

BEST SELLER

The best-selling book in New Zealand history is not a volume of verse by one of the country's many fine poets, nor an internationally esteemed novel such as Keri Hulme's Booker Prize-winning *The Bone People*. It is the *Edmonds Cookery Book*, initially published to promote the use of Edmonds Baking Powder ("Sure to Rise"), and first published in 1907. It is determinedly old-fashioned and slow to keep pace with changing tastes in food, though this may have been part of its appeal to traditionalists in New Zealand. Back in 2003, in its 51st edition, it had sold some 4 million copies in a country whose population had only just reached that figure.

awarded to Keri Hulme for *The Bone People*. The book has been translated into some 40 languages and has sold millions of copies worldwide. A difference between the two writers that summarises the development of New Zealand literature is that Mansfield's work, with its lightness of touch, was only marginally concerned with New Zealand issues, while Hulme's monumental work was almost aggressively focused on issues of national identity and biculturalism alongside more universal themes.

Incredibly, it was only as recently as 1972 that the first book by a Maori writer was published in New Zealand – Witi Ihimaera's short-story

collection *Pounamu Pounamu*. Ihimaera went on to become one of the country's leading novelists: his 1987 novel *The Whale Rider* was a hit film in 2002. Another work that was successfully adapted for the big screen was *Once Were Warriors* by Alan Duff, a sensational book – "the first New Zealand novel", according to the *Oxford Companion to New Zealand Literature*, "to deal full on with the actualities of modern urban Maori life" – that took the country by storm in the 1990s.

Novelists to have made their mark since then include Elizabeth Knox, who broke into the international market with *The Vintner's Luck*, a fantasy about a 19th-century Frenchman's encounters with an angel, and the protean

Lloyd Jones, who followed *The Book of Fame* – a remarkable riff on the 1905 All Blacks' rugby tour of Britain – with the completely different *Here at the End of the World We Learn to Dance*.

The field of history and biography has been dominated for many years by the late Michael King, who moved on from pioneering biographies of Maori woman leaders (Te Puea, Whina Cooper) to the lives of two of the country's greatest writers: Frank Sargeson and the late Janet Frame. Historians such as Miles Fairburn, James Belich, Anne Salmond and Philip Temple have helped to move the writing of history away from the recording of purely political and economic matters to more finely shaded explorations of society, culture and Maori–Pakeha relations.

Children's literature is spearheaded by such international successes as Lynley Dodd, famous for the *Hairy Maclary* series for younger children, and Joy Cowley, whose novel *The Silent One* was memorably filmed and whose reading texts are widely used in the field of education the world over. And then there is Margaret Mahy, who was the 2006 winner of the Hans Christian Andersen Author Award, the world's premier prize for children's literature. Through her books and through readings and public appearances, she has virtually achieved national treasure status.

Poetry

Poetry does surprisingly well in New Zealand. Though the average volume of verse sells no more than a few hundred copies, dozens are published every year, while poetry workshops and creative writing courses are booming. When the American poet Billy Collins visited New Zealand, he was mobbed like a rock star. Most major cities have poetry cafés, bars or venues where open readings are regularly held; and a remarkable number of literary festivals have sprung up around the country, some as adjuncts to arts festivals. The biennial Auckland Go-West Writers Festival and the Writers & Readers Week of Wellington's biennial International Arts Festival are the pick of these.

New Zealand does have an unofficial poet laureate, but it is not a position that is widely

LEFT: modern art in the Wellington City Gallery.
RIGHT: Frederick Hundertwasser's whimsical lavatory art at Kawakawa.

recognised. Only one poet has achieved the kind of stature that might be called legendary: the passionately nationalistic James K. Baxter, who was famous for wandering through the country barefoot with long hair and a Jesus-like beard in the last years before his death in 1972 at the age of 46. Since Baxter's death the favoured style has been cooler, more distanced and ironic, less given to big-picture stuff – less given, in fact, to ideas. Bill Manhire would be the leading exponent of this school. The old preoccupation with forging a "New Zealand identity" has long been discarded because New Zealand writers are surer of their place in the world now. Even Allen Curnow, the country's senior poet until his death in 2002, moved a long way from the romantic nationalism of his youth to what one commentator described as a more "vividly colloquial" style: dry and abbreviated and razor-sharp.

Most Maori poets and novelists write in English, but there is a great deal of crossover between the languages. If you read the self-deprecating poems of Colquhoun, for instance, you'd be hard pressed to know if he was Pakeha or Maori. It is more than likely you would conclude that it really doesn't matter much anyway. ❏

LOCAL ARCHITECTURE: STYLE OR KITSCH

With the possible exception of Napier – rebuilt largely in Art Deco style after an earthquake flattened the town in 1931 – no major town or city in New Zealand has achieved any notable architectural unity or harmony. Perhaps the most noteworthy is Dunedin, which retains a certain pre-war charm and is distinctive for its use of the local white Oamaru stone.

While Maori themes have sometimes been incorporated into the design of New Zealand's European-style public buildings, notably Te Papa in Wellington and the Christchurch Art Gallery, they have not influenced architectural thinking to any great degree. Examples of English Gothic may still be seen here and there – in Wellington's splendid Old St Paul's Cathedral for instance – built not with stone but with timber. John Scott's Futuna chapel in suburban Wellington is a highly regarded modernist work; but perhaps the capital's most impressive public building is the postmodernist Wellington Central Library, whose designer, Ian Athfield, pillared the front face with metallic versions of the nikau palm tree. The adjacent Athfield-designed Civic Square is equally striking.

For architectural impact – in terms of just being noticed – the country's two best-known buildings run the gamut from the sublime to the ridiculous. You work out which is which. One is Auckland's Sky City Tower poking out like a giant ice-lolly stick and the other is Frederick Hundertwasser's public toilet in Kawakawa, Northland.

V shape cen

Bands on f
and temples

where
in mo
the eye

ornament
of Tiwhan
corner of

ornamen
between

double
upper p

notch
nose.

double
nostrils

pattern
lip

Born Lip
Ngutu
Pattern

8 Bands f
to chin

stab on the
centre of

SPIRAL on the upper cheeks
KOWIRI —

ANCIENT MAORI ART AND SOCIETY

Maori works of art are not only beautiful to look at,
but also reveal a great deal about their
society's beliefs, history and social structure

The classic art of New Zealand Maori is an unsurpassed Pacific tribal art. Many creative styles and much skilled craftsmanship yielded, and continue to yield, objects of great beauty. To appreciate the achievements of Maori arts and crafts, it is invaluable to have an understanding of the materials used, the techniques of crafts, design and symbolism, and the economic, social and religious requirements that inspired the making of artefacts.

Cultural connections

Traditional Maori artefacts fell into three distinctive categories. The first was communally owned objects, such as *waka* (war canoes). The second category consisted of personal items *(see panel, page 70)*, such as garments, *pounamu* (greenstone) ornaments, combs, musical instruments and indelible skin tattoos, while the last category encompassed artefacts of ritual magic kept under the guardianship of *tohunga* (priests) – godsticks, crop gods and anything else used in ceremonial communication with gods and ancestral spirits.

Periods of Maori art merge, yet there are four distinctive eras: Archaic, Classic, Historic and Modern. The Archaic Maori, immediate descendants of the Polynesians who first settled the land, survived by hunting, fishing and foraging. Their art, including carvings and bone and stone work, is characterised by austere forms that, as pure sculpture, can surpass much of the later work.

In time, the cultivation of the sweet potato *(kumara)* and other crops, along with an advanced ability to exploit all natural resources

of forest and ocean, allowed a settled way of village life. With this came food surpluses, a tightly organised tribal system and territorial boundaries. These were the Classic Maori, and their altered society supported dedicated craftspeople within each community.

The third period of Maori art, the Historic, underwent rapid changes due to the adoption of metal tools, Christianity, Western fabrics, newly introduced crops, muskets and cannon. The fourth phase, the Modern, was under way before 1900, and remains with us. The great rise in interest in Maori culture *(Maoritanga)* in recent decades is in step with a renaissance of Maori culture.

LEFT: sketch of a traditional *moko* (facial tattoo).
RIGHT: carving on a Maori meeting house.

Displaying hierarchy

Society and the arts have always been associated with fighting chiefs who had a hereditary right to control tribal affairs. They were the best dressed, ornamented and accoutred: tribal prestige *(mana)* depended on these leaders.

People dressed according to rank – chiefs *(rangatira)*, nobles *(ariki)*, commoners *(tutua)*, and slaves *(taurekareka)* – yet when engaged in daily routine work both high and low classes used any old garments. Men and women wore a waist wrap, plus a shoulder cloak when weather or ceremony required. Pre-pubescent children usually went about naked.

The special indication of rank was the facial tattoo. Men's faces were marked in painful, deep-grooved cuts made by birdbone chisels dipped

> With no written language, the indigenous Maori relied on sophisticated oral traditions. Considerable mana (prestige) was bestowed on the best orators.

in a sooty pigment, which looked blue under the skin. Northern warriors often had additional tattoos over buttocks and thighs. Women were deeply tattooed on their lips and chin, made blue by the use of comb-type "needles".

This remarkable artwork can still be seen on Maori mummified heads, a process involving steaming, smoking and oiling: heads so treated remained intact and retained hair, skin and teeth. Out of respect for Maori beliefs, such heads are rarely exhibited in New Zealand's museums.

Art for the gods

Religious inspiration in Maori art was based on the prevailing beliefs about gods and ancestral spirits. In pre-Christian times supernatural beings were believed to inhabit natural objects. Rituals and chants were thus necessary to ensure the successful pursuit of any task.

In traditional Maori society the sexes were kept apart in all their craft activities. While men worked the hard materials of wood, bone and stone, women used soft materials *(see page 70)* or prepared flax fibres used in making garments and decorative *taniko* borders. It was believed women were *noa* – non-sacred – and the male, conversely, a *tapu* (sacred or holy) being. This put females in a subservient position which precluded them from high religious practices and from crafts and activities in which high gods and ancestral spirits were directly involved.

Priests used wooden stickgods *(tiki wananga)*, bound with sacred cords and dressed in red feathers to communicate with gods and ancestral spirits to protect the welfare of the tribe. Stone crop gods *(taumata atua)* were placed in or near gardens to promote fertility in growing crops.

Wooden burial chests were used to contain the bones of the deceased. Maori burial practice, at least for persons of rank, required an initial burial, then a recovery of the bones a year or two later when a final, ceremonial burial would take place. Monuments and cenotaphs of various forms were erected in memory of the dead. Some were posts with carvings of stylised humans called *tiki (see below)*, while others took the form of canoes buried in the earth deeply enough to stand vertically.

Symbols and motifs in Maori art

In Maori art the human form, dominant in most compositions, is generally referred to as a *tiki* and represents the first created man of Maori mythology. The *pounamu* (greenstone)

LEFT: elaborate *moko* tattoo. **RIGHT:** carving at the Waitangi Treaty Grounds, Northland.
FAR RIGHT: carved *pounamu* (greenstone) pendant.

hei-tiki pendant is the best known of ornaments. *Tiki* represent ancestors and gods in the sculptural arts, and may be carved in wood, bone or stone. In ceremonial meeting-house architecture, ancestral *tiki* were carved on panels supporting the rafters or on other parts of the structure. They were highly stylised with large heads to fill in areas of posts or panels. This design also stressed the importance of the head in Maori belief – along with the sexual organs, it was the most sacred part of the body.

Sexual organs were often exaggerated in both male and female carved figures; both penis and vulva were regarded as centres of potent magic in promoting fertility and protection. Small birth figures were often placed between the legs or on the bodies of *tiki* representing descending generations. The out-thrust tongue was an expression of defiance and of protective magic.

Often *tiki* figures have slanted, staring eyes, clawed hands with a spur thumb, a beaked mouth and other bird-like features. These motifs probably stemmed from the belief that the souls of the dead and the gods used birds as spirit vehicles.

The *manaia*, another major symbol, is a beaked figure rendered in profile with a body that has arms and legs.

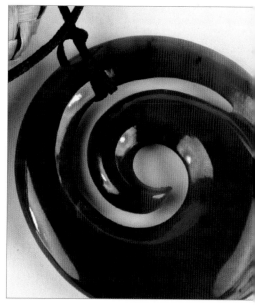

MAORI MEETING HOUSES

During the Historic era, the meeting house *(whare runanga)* increasingly became the focus of Maori social life and of a Maori art revolution. They played a vital role throughout the 19th century, when meetings were held to discuss issues affecting the tribe.

The walls of meeting houses were decorated with *tukutuku* panels or sections of ornamental lattice-work used to cover walls between carvings. Each panel consisted of vertical stakes and horizontal rods (traditionally made of bracken-fern or totara wood), and flexible materials such as flax were used to form a pattern which told a story that would be "read" and passed on by *kaumatuas* (seniors) from one generation to the next.

Many of these ornate meeting houses can still be seen throughout the North Island, including Whare Runanga at Waitangi in the Bay of Islands. They were usually named after an ancestor, and the construction symbolised the actual person; the ridge pole the spine, the rafters were his ribs, and the facade boards, which at times terminated in fingers, were his arms. At the gable peak was the face mask. Some Maori still believe that when they enter a particular house they are entering the protective body of their ancestor.

Many communal houses can be visited, and a fine example is Tama-te-Kapua at Ohinemutu, Rotorua, built in 1878. While others are often on private property, visitors are welcome as long as they get permission beforehand.

Whales *(pakake)* and whale-like creatures appeared on the slanting facades of storehouses. Some fish, dogs and other creatures occurred in carvings, but on the whole they are rare; there was no attempt to depict nature in a naturalistic way. *Marakihau*, fascinating mermen monsters of the *taniwha* class (mythical monsters), appeared on panels and as greenstone ornaments. *Marakihau* were probably ancestral spirits that took to the sea and are depicted on 19th-century house panels with sinuous bodies terminating in curled tails. Their heads have horns, large round eyes and tube tongues, and were occasionally depicted sucking in a fish. _

The *koru*, a well-known symbol based on an emerging fern frond, is today often used as a symbol of New Zealand, including Air New Zealand's company logo; the symbol signifies new life, adventure, an awakening.

Craft tools and materials

The tools and materials of the Maori craftwork were limited to woods, stone, fibres and shells; metal tools did not exist until after the arrival of the Europeans. Adzes, the principal equipment for woodcarvers, were made of stone blades lashed to wooden helves. *Pounamu*, the nephritic jade also known as greenstone, was the most valued blade material and was sacred. Found only on the western coast of South Island, this rare commodity was widely traded. Chisels, stone-pointed rotary drills and various wooden wedges and mallets completed the Maori tool kit.

The introduction of oil-based paints ousted the old red ochre pigment *(kokowai)*, which can be seen today only in traces on older carvings. The later practice of overpainting old carvings with European red paint was unfortunate as it obliterated much patination and often the older ochres, resulting in the loss of the polychrome-painted work of the Historic period.

The iridescent *paua* (abalone) shell was used as inlay in woodcarving, and textile dyes were made from barks. A deep-black dye was obtained by soaking fibres in swamp mud.

Flax plaited into cords provided fine fibre for garments and baskets. As there were no metal nails and the Maori did not use wooden pegs as an alternative, war canoes, houses and food-stores were assembled using flax cord. Weavers fashioned intricate ceremonial clothing from feathers, flax and other materials.

The New Zealand forests contained larger trees than Polynesians would previously have seen. This enabled them to build bigger dugout canoes, and also contributed to the woodcarving tradition. Durable totara and kauri trees, the latter only found in the warm, northern parts of the North Island, were favoured by carvers, and bone was used in many ways. Whalebone was especially favoured for weapons, while Sperm whale teeth made fine ornaments and feathers decorated weapons and cloaks. ❏

PRECIOUS POSSESSIONS

The personal possessions of the Maori demonstrate their most exquisite artwork. Combs, feathered garments, treasure boxes, cloak pins, greenstone ornaments (including *hei-tiki* ancestral pendants) and weapons were often given a "personal touch" to reflect the *mana* (spiritual authority) of their owner. Wooden treasure boxes *(wakahuia)* were made to contain some of the more precious items, such as greenstone ornaments or feathers. These lidded boxes, designed to be hung from house rafters, were ornately carved on all sides, but especially on the underside since they were so frequently looked at from below.

LEFT: traditional arts are taught at the Maori Art School, Lower Hutt, Wellington.

Modern Maori Art

Maori art is an important cultural phenomenon, and is one that embraces modern media and form as well as respecting the past

There are hundreds of Maori artists working in New Zealand today, and their work spans many media, from the newest technologies to the arts of their Maori forefathers. Contemporary Maori art is as diverse as the Maori people themselves, and wherever you travel to in New Zealand, you will easily find exhibitions and galleries that reward exploration.

During the 20th century Maori art formed into two main streams. The first were those arts based in the *whare whakairo* (carved meeting house), such as *whakairo* (carving), *kowhaiwhai* (painting) and *tukutuku* (woven panels). The second stream was that of modern media, such as Western-style painting. Many Maori artists welcomed new artistic movements introduced into New Zealand, such as modernism and postmodernism, and have interacted within these styles in their own particular way, fusing the indigenous with the global.

By the 1960s, Maori were showing their artworks at galleries, both individually and collectively. There have been successive generations of artists, starting with the *kaumatua* (senior citizens) generation of men and women such as Ralph Hotere, Paratene Matchitt, Arnold Manaaki Wilson, Sandy Adsett, Fred Graham and others. Their work showed New Zealand that Maori art deserved to be exhibited in a gallery setting rather than be seen merely as anthropological specimens.

During the 1970s and 1980s a new group emerged, including artists such as Emare Karaka, Robyn Kahukiwa, Kura Te Waru-Rewiri and Shona Rapira-Davies. Much of their art was overtly political, including symbols of protest, bright colours and expressive paint styles. Since then, a further wave of artists has emerged, such as Brett Graham, Michael Parekowhai, Natalie Robertson, Areta Wilkinson and Lisa Reihana, many of whom have been trained in universities. Their work ventures into new territories in terms of media, such as digital/video installation,

RIGHT: Maori meeting houses *(whare runanga)*, traditional focal point for social, cultural and spiritual life.

and in so doing challenges the ideas of what Maori art is in form. Galleries are now opening dedicated solely to Maori art, such as the Mataora Gallery in Parnell Street and Te Taumata Gallery in Upper Symonds Street, both in Auckland.

The traditional Maori house is still an important centre for contemporary arts. Many contemporary *whare whakairo* maintain aspects of the traditional in terms of the basic architectural structure and choice of design elements (carving, painting and woven panels), yet innovate with the range of materials and imagery used. Master carvers, such as Pakaariki Harrison, are highly sought after, and travel the around the globe to talk about their work.

The number of publications about Maori art has increased, and they examine both the tribal arts and the modern. Most notable is the fact that all of these publications are written by Maori, for Maori.

The face of the Maori is also changing, and *moko* (tattooing) is a visible expression of the culture. Traditional sites on the body to *ta moko* (tattoo) are still used, especially the face (full facial for men, lips and chins for women) and thighs and legs of both men and women. *Tohunga ta moko* (tattoo specialists), both men and women, practise around the country. Since the mid-1970s there has been a renaissance of *moko*, and it is not uncommon to see wearers sipping lattes in upmarket cafés. Most use modern gun machines, yet there is a trend towards learning more about traditional tools. ❏

MAORI HANDICRAFTS

The Stone-Age culture of the Maori developed extraordinary skills using the simplest of resources, and traditional crafts are flourishing once again

When the Maori migrated to temperate New Zealand from tropical Polynesia, much of what they found was unfamiliar, but they soon learned to make the best use of the available resources. For example, they used stone adzes to make long, graceful canoes from giant kauri or totara trees, whose wood was ideally suited to carving. To ensure durability, they preserved their sculptures by painting them with a mixture of red clay and shark oil.

PRACTICAL AND RELIGIOUS OBJECTS

Functional everyday items such as eating utensils, tools and weapons were obviously important to the Maori, but away from the prosaic everyday routines, their spiritual outlook produced some beautiful works of art – for example, *marae* meeting-places were dominated by imposing wooden figures of important ancestors. Personal keepsakes, such as the *tiki* good-luck charms, were often superbly crafted items featuring a stylised human figure and made from *pounamu* greenstone or bone; a *hei-tiki* is a pendant worn round the neck.

A RENAISSANCE

As the Maori have grown increasingly aware of their heritage, so traditional crafts have enjoyed a rebirth. The main place where young people learn to carve wood, bone and greenstone is the Maori Arts and Crafts Institute in Rotorua. Recently, there has been increased demand from New Zealanders of European origin for traditional Polynesian crafts. Greenstone carving in particular has become an extraordinarily intricate art, which has nothing in common with the mass-produced items for sale in souvenir shops.

ABOVE: sculptures of monstrous skulls and grimacing faces are typical of Maori art, which has always had a strong spiritual dimension. Originally, such carvings would have been placed on the protecting palisades of a *pa* (fortified village) to frighten off attackers.

LEFT: centuries ago, richly ornamented carvings *(tiki)* were made from moa bones, using sharp stone tools. Now that the huge birds have become extinct, *tiki* are made from the bones of other animals.

COMMUNAL WAR CANOES

War canoes, ornately decorated with both sculpture and painting, were objects of great prestige in a Maori community. Most were painted red, with black and white detailing, and festooned with feathers. The magnificent 35-metre (115ft) war canoe *(pictured above)* at Waitangi was carved from the trunks of two huge kauri trees from the Puketi Forest. It took 27 months to build, and was launched in 1940 to mark the centenary of the Waitangi Treaty.

The streamlined hull is at no point more than 2 metres (7ft) wide, but the canoe was big enough for 160 warriors to sit without treading on one another's feet. Propelled by 80 paddles, the canoe reached an impressive speed in the sheltered waters of the Bay of Islands, and the seafaring skills of the Maori were brought vividly to life for the spectators.

In their quest for a new homeland, the Maori crossed the vast and often turbulent Pacific in handbuilt boats; not slender war canoes like this one, but more stable outriggers with greater space for food and personal belongings. In 1985, a 21-metre (69ft) replica of one of these traditional boats sailed from Rarotonga in the Cook Islands to New Zealand. The 5,000km (3,107-mile) journey took just over five weeks, with the crew steering by the stars, moon and tides, just as the Maori had once done.

ABOVE: as the Maori had no written language, their myths and legends were passed on verbally from generation to generation. Here a grandmother skilfully creates string figures to illustrate her story of the Tongariro and Ruapehu volcanoes, which are believed to personify temperamental nature gods.

LEFT: flax is softened in thermal springs before Maori women weave its fibres into elegant dresses. Maori men traditionally wear cloaks made from flax and bordered with geometric patterns.

RIGHT: wooden figures of important ancestors are traditionally used to protect a tribe against the wrath of the gods and to intercede on the tribe's behalf.

MUSIC, THEATRE AND FILM

Music, theatre and their sister arts have struggled to survive in New Zealand as meagre resourcing stifled creativity, but recently have become more confident and secure

Given New Zealanders' reputation as a laconic, almost self-effacing people, it may seem remarkable that they can be persuaded to engage in any of the performing arts at all. Many New Zealanders have found it necessary to go overseas to find work which is commensurate with their talent, notably Kiri Te Kanawa, Russell Crowe and Sam Neill.

While there is pride in their success, it is the New Zealanders who have remained and continued to strive with, work for and speak to their own people who are most admired. Peter Jackson's insistence that Hollywood had to come to him to make his movies inspired a confidence in the "local product" that resulted in a tremendous upsurge of all kinds of creative activity in the first years of the 21st century.

Classical music

The New Zealand Symphony Orchestra (NZSO), based in Wellington, was formed in 1946 amid a post-war optimism in which the nation's few intellectuals, composers, painters and actors conspired to invent a national culture (such groups as the Royal New Zealand Ballet and the New Zealand Players were born in the same era). Composers including Douglas Lilburn Jack Body, Hirini Melbourne, Gareth Farr and Philip Dadson have created a rich and diverse repertoire, some of it drawing on Maori and Polynesian styles.

But New Zealand's most famous practitioner of classical music remains the soprano Kiri Te Kanawa. A true diva, she seldom performs at

home and, worse, according to New Zealanders, appears to have little affection for it. Still, New Zealand is a prolific producer of good singers, including the sopranos Hayley Westenra and Malvina Major, and the up-and-coming bass Jonathan Lemalu; a performance by the New Zealand Opera (usually at The St James in Wellington or Aotea Centre in Auckland) is a fairly safe bet. The company is often accused of making safe choices, but productions are frequently first-rate. However, anyone hoping to see an opera written by a New Zealander should plan to be in Wellington for its biennial New Zealand Festival, a highlight of the performing arts calendar.

LEFT: Peter Jackson's epic *The Lord of the Rings*, filmed in New Zealand. **RIGHT:** award-winning comedy duo Flight of the Conchords.

Ballet and modern dance

The history of dance in New Zealand is one of struggle and perseverance, writ large. Dance is costly to develop and tour, and it was something of a miracle that the Royal New Zealand Ballet celebrated its 50th anniversary in 2003. It has a reputation for hard work and commitment, but the tutu-and-fairy-dust expectations of audiences often keep it from more groundbreaking work.

New Zealand's two leading modern choreographers, Douglas Wright and Michael Parmenter, emerged from the trail blazed by the influential modern dance troupe Limbs, formed in the 1970s and dissolved in the 1980s. Both have pro-

duced stunning, moving and important work, but have found it increasingly difficult to create works with scant financial resources.

Black Grace, an Auckland-based all-male troupe who combine the physicality of rugby players and the grace of ballet dancers, is renowned for its energetic blend of modern dance and Maori and Polynesian forms. Catch them if you happen to be in Auckland.

Theatre

Richard and Edith Campion, the parents of the film director Jane Campion, inaugurated professional theatre in New Zealand when they formed the New Zealand Players in 1953. Before this, theatre-lovers only had sporadic vis-

its by condescending British companies or community repertory groups. Summarising the suspicion visited upon all arts in those years, playwright Bruce Mason remembers such repertory groups being "ignored, sometimes actively abhorred by the average Kiwi".

The New Zealand Players folded in 1960 but inspired a whole new generation of actors and professional companies. The first was Wellington's Downstage, which survives even though its position as the top theatre in the country's unofficial "theatre capital" was lost to the rival Circa some years ago. Circa has a reliable company of actors who perform international work and local plays, notably those written by Roger Hall.

No history of New Zealand theatre is possible without mentioning Hall, a British emigrant with a style of middle-class, middle-aged and middlebrow comedy that both connects with the audience's fears, desires and interests and reminds them of British TV comedies. More challenging playwrights have emerged since, including Duncan Sarkies, Jo Randerson, Hone Kouka and Briar Grace Smith; the latter two have written about New Zealand history from a Maori perspective.

Professional theatre in New Zealand exists on a diet of the latest intelligent British or American blockbuster, revivals of the classics and, when they're feeling adventurous, new local works. Beyond Downstage and Circa, these theatres are Palmerston North's Centrepoint, Christchurch's Court Theatre and Dunedin's Fortune. The Auckland Theatre Company (ATC) does not have its own theatre, but usually performs at the Aotea Centre's Herald Theatre or

> Auckland's Civic Theatre is an architectural folly built in 1929 featuring Buddhas, elephants, panthers and a replica of the Southern Hemisphere sky.

Auckland University's Maidment. ATC's productions have been criticised as being conservative, but more and more local plays are being staged as the company grows, and it has a large pool of capable actors, most of whom are pleased

LEFT: the Royal New Zealand Ballet, a long-running cultural beacon. **RIGHT:** Polynesian hip-hop group Nesian Mystik.

to get a break from less challenging TV work.

New Zealand's avant-garde theatre scene is less visible, but Auckland's Silo and Wellington's Bats can both feel like tiny pockets of anti-establishment resistance. The work can be patchy but sometimes daring and inspired; one of the few reliable practitioners is the Christchurch multimedia group called The Clinic. Stylistically, the avant-garde theatre scene is pitched somewhere between lively stand-up comedy and the more traditional dramatic fare on offer at places like Silo and Bats. In the 1990s, comedy found a permanent venue at Auckland's Classic, and there's a big comedy festival in March every year. The country's comedy profile has risen with the global popularity of Bret McKenzie and Jemaine Clement, together known as the Flight of the Conchords. The duo have won numerous awards and now have their own series on US television.

Festivals provide opportunities for new works to debut and existing works to tour. The biggest is Wellington's biennial (on even years) New Zealand Festival. Christchurch, New Plymouth, Taupo, Tauranga, Nelson and the Bay of Islands also have their own arts festivals.

See Travel Tips pages 353–4 for contact details of theatre and performing arts venues.

THE CONTEMPORARY MUSIC SCENE

Thankfully, New Zealand's once-thriving pub rock scene hasn't been entirely decimated by the onslaught of dance music. If anything, the international success of such rock bands as The Datsuns (once seen as something of an embarrassment for ploughing the musical furrow of retro hard rock when it was far from fashionable) and The D4 have created a pro-rock backlash at home.

The "alternative" tradition of the country's legendary Flying Nun Records – which during the 1980s produced such locally popular cult groups as The Clean, The Chills and Straitjacket Fits – is also maintained in pubs and bars in the major cities and radio stations countrywide. Other names to look out for are the Polynesian hip-hop success

stories Nesian Mystik and Che Fu, and the singer-songwriter Bic Runga.

If jazz is more your style, be sure to catch the annual Waiheke Island Jazz Festival over the Easter weekend in Auckland, with international names on the bill, or Wellington's smaller jazz festival every October/November.

The popular world-music festival Womad has appeared sporadically in New Zealand, but is now tentatively pinned down to every second year as part of New Plymouth's Taranaki Arts Festival. Along with an international line-up, Womad usually includes the very best of Maori and Polynesian groups and it's a big, friendly event attended by New Zealanders from all over the nation.

Film

New Zealand directors produced the occasional film prior to the 1970s, the most notable being by John O'Shea who specialised in bicultural themes, for example his interracial melodrama *Broken Barrier*, and *Don't Let It Get You*, a kitsch musical masterpiece featuring a young Kiri Te Kanawa. However, it wasn't until Roger Donaldson's 1977 thriller *Sleeping Dogs* that a wave of commercial filmmaking was launched – which continues to this day. Donaldson moved on to Hollywood, where his biggest commercial hit was the 1988 Tom Cruise movie, *Cocktail*. Others to emerge around this time were the

MAORI MUSIC AND DANCE

Music has always played a major role in Maori life, and as far back as the Classic (pre-European) era, instruments were fashioned from wood, whalebone and even stone. Traditional chants and songs *(waiata)* are an important feature of ceremonies such as funerals *(tangi)* and weddings. So too is Maori dance, which is both rhythmic and physical, with the beat added by the slapping of chest and thighs with the hand, foot-stamping or sometimes the hitting of sticks. Drums were unknown. *Kapa Haka* (Concert Parties) now take part in competitions each year to find the best performers, and some groups travel the world to share their impressive and entertaining cultural arts.

art-house favourite Vincent Ward (*Vigil* and *The Navigator*), Geoff Murphy, whose "Maori western", *Utu*, was vastly underrated, and Gaylene Preston, whose *Mr Wrong* was a slyly subversive feminist thriller.

One of the most successful exports was Jane Campion, who followed the distinctively New Zealand, but globally successful, *The Piano* (1993) with the equally accomplished *The Portrait of a Lady* (1996). Nominated in 1993 for the Academy Awards filmmaker award, Campion didn't win the title, but did take home the Oscar for best screenplay. She was also recognised at the Cannes Film Festival, and was the first woman to receive the prestigious Palme d'Or for directing. *The Piano* launched the talent of the new generation: 11-year-old actress Anna Paquin, Academy Award-winner for her outstanding performance, and New Zealander and Hollywood star, Sam Neill.

Niki Caro followed her dazzling debut *Memory and Desire* with the international hit *Whale Rider*, based on a Maori legend as told by one of the country's foremost Maori writers, Witi Ihimaera. Peter Jackson did the impossible by making a *Lord of the Rings* trilogy *(see pages 80–81)* that won 11 Oscars and pleased critics, Tolkien fans and audiences who had never even heard of the book. Earlier Jackson had made his mark with the 1994 movie, *Heavenly Creatures*. Although his remake of *King Kong* (2005) lacked the same magic, it still had its following.

Another New Zealander director, Andrew Adamson, has made his mark with worldwide blockbuster films including *Shrek I* (2001), *Shrek II* (2004) and *The Chronicles of Narnia, the Lion, the Witch and the Wardrobe* (2005). The last, filmed in New Zealand, featured superb graphics produced by Weta Workshop, which also animated Jackson's *Rings* trilogy. Adamson dazzled the world once more with *Prince Caspian*, the second in the Narnia series, in 2008.

For its size, New Zealand seems to have given the world a disproportionate number of international film stars, notably Sam Neill (who started out in the aforementioned *Sleeping Dogs*), and the Oscar winners Anna Paquin and Russell Crowe. Among the contemporary generation of film actors, Danielle Cormack and Joel Tobbeck are two stand-out performers. ❏

LEFT: a scene from *The Piano*. *RIGHT:* an orc in *The Lord of the Rings.*

BONANZA OF THE RINGS

New Zealand's sumptuous landscapes provided local director Peter Jackson with the perfect fantasy backdrop for one the most ambitious projects in cinematic history

The landscapes of Middle Earth, the fantasy creation of JRR Tolkien, are filled with dramatic mountains, wild forests, verdant pastures and grasslands. When the decision was made to create a definitive film version of the famous book, New Zealand was quickly chosen as the real life equivalent.

New Zealanders, who have something of a weakness for praise from other parts of the world, are immensely proud of the success of *The Lord of the Rings* trilogy. Forgive them, though, if they appear to be just a little blasé about the movie's locations. For them, this is simply home, and it has always looked like this.

For a detailed guide to the locations used in the film, see www. movie-locations.com.

ABOVE: Frodo is tormented by the power of the Ring.

LEFT: Peter Jackson directs a battle scene during the filming of part II, *The Two Towers*.

ABOVE: Tongariro National Park provided the location for Mordor; the vast bleakness and volcanic devastation of much of this barren area makes it clear why it was a suitable site for Sauron's realm. And in the form of Mount Ngauruhoe, one of the three peaks that dominate the park, you have Mount Doom itself.

BELOW: the Dead Marshes, where Frodo and Sam were stalked by Gollum *(pictured)* were filmed at a swamp called Kepler Mire on the Kepler Track near Te Anau. Also filmed near Te Anau (on Takaro Road) is Fangorn Forest, home of the Ents, where Merry and Pippin haggled with Treebeard to persuade him to join the battle for Helms Deep.

THE TOLKIEN TOURIST BOOM

The *Lord of the Rings* trilogy of movies were shot at locations that ranged almost the entire length of New Zealand, and, while some computer enhancements were inevitably employed, many of the sites are natural, unique and almost unbelievably spectacular. The movies have sparked enormous outside interest in the country and its pristine landscapes, and also ignited a boom in commercial tours taking fans – quite literally millions of them since the first movie was screened – to many of the sites.

While some of the places featured in the movie trilogy are relatively inaccessible or on private land, and can only be visited under the aegis of a tour operator, others are easy to reach by individuals. Anyone can get a glimpse, for instance, of large tracts of "Mordor" or the "Misty Mountains". But don't expect to find actual movie sets – due to the environmental considerations so dear to New Zealanders' hearts, all but one of them has since been demolished.

ABOVE: from almost any point in the South Island you can enjoy views of the Misty Mountains, along which the Fellowship trudged before being broken. Of course, hereabouts (and on all the maps) they are known as the Southern Alps.

RIGHT: Arwen, played by Liv Tyler. Most of the cast spent many months filming in New Zealand.

ABOVE: Saruman's citadel, Isengard, was filmed – with the help of computer wizadry – at Harcourt Park, Akatarawa Road, Upper Hutt, 30 km (20 miles) north of Wellington.

LEFT: the only movie set that has been left in place is Hobbiton, the home of Bag End itself, or at least the front door – the interior was a set in Wellington. It stands on private land at Matamata but can be visited for a fee. Much of this verdant, intensely farmed area will suggest the peaceful Shire to visitors.

CUISINE

Kiwi cooking is distinguished by ingredients that are fresh and flavourful, and a style that fuses a medley of influences, reflecting the country's cultural diversity

At the heart of New Zealand's exuberant cuisine is the pristine freshness of its fruit and vegetables, meat, seafood and dairy products. Most often, the principal ingredients on your plate will have been grown within a two-hour drive of your table. But what New Zealand cooks do with those ingredients has none of the simplicity of a traditional peasant cuisine. Indeed, there are very few indigenous foods eaten at all. Except for the wealth of seafood, the raw materials are descended from those brought here from many parts of the world, each one finding a suitable environment, whether in the year-round warmth of the north or the less benign climate of the south.

Cosmopolitan cuisine

When it comes to culinary styles, New Zealand cooks have a lot in common with their counterparts in Australia and California. Although all are located on the rim of the Pacific Ocean, they are less influenced by their place on the map than by a common mood of buoyant confidence, a love of vibrant flavours and a willingness to sample whatever food they come across. Mediterranean influences are encouraged by the fact that peppers, aubergines, olives, asparagus and garlic are easily grown. Pesto and hummus are as popular here as anywhere in the world. Not far behind are the foods of Asia. Curries, stir-fries, sushi and miso soup are commonplace.

New Zealanders also bring ideas from their travels abroad and keep up with international

PRECEDING PAGES: kiwi fruits. **LEFT:** freshly caught crayfish, also known as rock lobster. **RIGHT:** exotic foods from the Pacific Islands add colour.

trends through books, magazines and television. In addition, each smaller cultural group living in the country – Pacific, Indian, Chinese, Japanese, Greek, Cambodian, Croatian, Dutch, Thai, German and many others – has added its own colour and flavourful ingredients to the culinary melting pot, through importing speciality foods, opening restaurants and continuing to cook its traditional food at home.

Colonial roots

The culinary styles of England, Scotland and Ireland, the homelands of the largest number of immigrants since colonial times, remain a powerful element, particularly in home cooking. A typical family meal will consist of a roast leg of lamb, with crisp golden potatoes, pumpkin, parsnip and *kumara* (sweet potato) baked in the same pan and served with gravy, mint sauce, peas and silver beet (Swiss chard) or broccoli. In summer, the traditionally high status (and exceptional standard) of local meat is reflected in barbecues with a variety of steaks, lamb chops and sausages, or an array of seafood served with freshly baked bread, corn on the cob and salads.

Despite the influence of other cuisines, many main courses in restaurants still take the traditional form of a fine piece of meat or fish accompanied by vegetables. Many locals are dab hands

mously from the arrival of pigs and other farm animals, vegetables, fruit and grains from Europe and America.

Seafood has always been a vital part of the cuisine, and its continuing importance is recognised in the customary rights extended to Maori to allow the gathering of controlled species, such as the rare *toheroa*, a type of clam. The traditional Maori meal most likely to be offered to visitors is the *hangi* (earth oven), a tender and flavourful feast in which meat and vegetables are packed into baskets and steamed over hot rocks in a covered pit. A hearty broth ("boil-up") includes pork or beef, potatoes, onions, carrots

when it comes to home-baked scones, pikelets and muffins, as well as cakes and biscuits plus jams, marmalade, chutney and pickles.

Maori cooking

Many of the country's indigenous foods – birds, berries and fern root – were laborious to gather, prepare and preserve. Such traditional Maori delicacies include mutton birds (the distinctly fishy-flavoured young of the sooty petrel), freshwater eels, and seafood such as *paua* (abalone), *pipi* and *tuatua* (surf clam) and *kina* (prickly sea urchin). While the *kumara*, a sweet potato brought from Polynesia, enhanced the range of nourishing foods that could be grown in warmer regions, Maori cuisine benefited enor-

and watercress, *rauraki* or *puha* (sow thistle) and sometimes dumplings ("doughboys"). *Paraoa rewana* ("Maori bread") is a large wheaten loaf made with flour and potato.

Fresh fruit

Each season brings with it an amazing range of fresh fruit, none of which is native to New Zealand. However, over the past two centuries each has become a much-loved part of the local cuisine, and several are now important exports. Fruit and vegetable shops and supermarkets stock a good range, although some fruit is barely ripe when sold and needs to be kept for a few days. Delicious tree-ripened fruit can be bought direct from roadside stalls right where it is grown, throughout the country. Weekend farmers' markets nationwide are an increasing phenomenon, and a significant number of supermarkets, stalls and speciality shops offer organic produce.

Autumn is perhaps the most exciting season of all, when subtropical fruit, grown in the warmer parts of the country, is widely available. First in the season is the *tamarillo* or tree tomato, an intensely tart ruby-red fruit with a smooth skin and bright orange interior laced with black seeds. Then comes the *feijoa*, a scented, oval green fruit with a smooth skin and flavour reminiscent of pineapple and strawberries. The

should be eaten while they still feel hard in the hand. Varietal honey and locally grown chestnuts, walnuts, hazelnuts and macadamia nuts are other treats to look out for on your travels.

Some citrus fruit also ripen in the winter – easy-to-peel mandarins, navel oranges and the New Zealand grapefruit, an unusual variety with golden peel and sweet-sour golden-hued flesh. Strawberries start to ripen in spring, and by December they will be joined by raspberries, blackberries, loganberries, boysenberries, black and red currants. By Christmas, cherries, the first of the stone fruits, will also be ripe; small boxes of top-quality fruit are a popular gift.

wrinkled purple passionfruit holds a spoonful of black seeds in an aromatic golden juice. Kiwi fruit, with tart green flesh or the more mellow, golden-fleshed types, marketed under the Zespri label, have been joined by a cherry-sized, smooth-skinned variety.

Autumn also brings apples, including the flavoursome Braeburn, pears, notably the luscious Doyenne du Comice, *nashi* – an apple-shaped type of pear with crisp, juicy white flesh – and glossy orange non-astringent persimmons, which

As summer progresses, other stone fruits appear – plums, peaches (locally bred Golden Queens, white-fleshed early in the season and with deep golden flesh later), nectarines, peaches

> New Zealand's abundant produce is widely available at the ubiquitous roadside stalls dotted around the country roads. Larger stalls sometimes have a cashier; at others, customers simply leave payment in the honesty box.

LEFT: the purple-skinned *kumara* is almost a staple. **ABOVE:** the kiwi fruit is native to southern China; it was introduced to New Zealand in the early 20th century. **RIGHT:** high-quality produce.

and apricots – and in their primary growing regions of Hawke's Bay and Central Otago can often be bought from roadside stalls.

From the seas

In every season of the year commercial fishing boats bring in a wonderful variety of species, from the delicate hoki, gurnard and flounder, to the local favourites, the flavoursome tarakihi and snapper, flaky blue cod and firm John Dory, as well as the meaty hapuka and bluenose. All year round, excellent farmed Pacific salmon is available. Salmon and other species are often enjoyed skilfully smoked.

While winter is the season for highly regarded Bluff oysters, the closely related Nelson variety is a delectable alternative. Farmed Pacific oysters are also often available. Large and succulent Green-

Meat and dairy produce

Wide grassy pastures are the year-round home of millions of lambs and sheep, raised for wool as well as meat, cattle for beef and milk, and also smaller numbers of deer. The pastures, known locally as paddocks, are licked by salty sea breezes, which give the meat a delicious and distinctive flavour. All local meats are available throughout the year. A rack of lamb, seared on the outside and still pink inside, is always delicious, or for old-fashioned comfort, look for braised lamb shanks. Lamb's liver, known as lamb's fry, is also good. For steak-lovers, fillet is the most tender, while sirloin, porterhouse, rump or Scotch fillet

shell mussels, which are farmed in the Marlborough Sounds, can be bought live from most supermarkets. Smaller shellfish collected from sandy beaches include *pipi, tuatua* and little neck clams, known locally as cockles. Abalone *(paua)* cling to the rocks along many shores and can be collected in controlled numbers. Another springtime treat is dredged scallops, while eels are particularly delicious when smoked.

Salted mutton birds are also sometimes available from seafood providers. These are the chicks of *titi* (sooty shearwaters), which are collected from a few tiny islands near Stewart Island. Their rich meaty flavour is relished by aficionados. Crayfish, also known as rock lobster, is found along the Kaikoura coast.

have a richer flavour. Tender farm-raised venison, often marketed as Cervena, is best when cooked quickly and served medium rare.

Milk, butter and cheese have long been an important part of local cuisine. Thick cream and tangy yoghurt are of excellent quality. More than 60 varieties of cheese are produced in New Zealand – look out for Aorangi, kirima, blue supreme and Dutch-style cheeses made by several small producers – although cheddar remains the most popular and is widely available, from creamy mild to richly aged. Sheep and goat cheeses are a relatively new and growing part of the scene.

There are plenty of feral deer, pigs and goats in the bush for hunters (*see Travel Tips page 366*), although you don't often find wild meat on a restaurant menu. If you do, you can rest assured that it has been processed in a licensed abattoir and will be safe to eat. Trout, abundant in many rivers and streams, are reserved for licensed anglers and never sold. Big-game fishing – and eating the catch – is another attraction.

Picnic supplies

One takeaway meal that has a long local history is the meat pie. These are sold in convenience stores, bakeries and petrol stations, where they are heated to order. The single-serve pies are oval, round or square and most contain ground or diced beef in gravy. A layer of cheese is a popular addition, and some pies are topped with mashed potato instead of pastry.

Also at the bakeries and some cafés you will find sweet goodies that will often be the same distinctively New Zealand specialities that are traditionally baked in the home – Anzac biscuits, afghans with chocolate icing and walnut on top, peanut brownies, ginger crunch, bran or cheese muffins, and banana cake. The coffee is almost always espresso and often made with beans roasted by small speciality businesses. A range of teas and herbal teas is always available as well as local mineral water and fruit juices.

Despite the presence of the usual international franchises, owner-operated fish-and-chip shops still provide the most popular takeaway meal, comprising thick golden chips (french fries) and fish deep-fried in batter or crumbs, as well as seasonal oysters, scallops, sausages and other items. Wait while your meal is cooked to order, wrapped in absorbent paper or piled on a cardboard tray. Then take it to eat at a pretty spot by the sea. The seagulls will help out with the leftovers.

Fine dining

New Zealand has a large number of world-class restaurants, even in more remote locations where they flourish in the guise of luxury lodges and vineyards. The variety of food is dazzling. It can range from a reinvention of that controversial classic, tripe, to the finest of freshly caught game and seafood. Inspiration is eclectic – drawing from the world's great cuisines – and creativity seemingly boundless as chefs strive to find a balance between respect for their ingredients and the true artist's desire to improve on nature.

The relatively small size of the market means that competition is intense, which in turn helps keep standards high. But top-end restaurants in Auckland, Wellington and other cities are vulnerable to a domestic tendency to faddishness. It is not unusual for a new restaurant to be booked solid for its first three months, then find itself almost empty as the next shiny new establishment to open catches the locals' attention. However, plenty of fine restaurants have survived changing times and tastes to assure a memorable dining experience.

See Travel Tips pages 342–52 for a list of recommended restaurants across the country. ❑

PAVLOVA

If New Zealand has a national dessert, it is the pavlova, traditionally eaten at Christmas barbecues. And if Australia has a national dessert, it is also the pavlova. The two countries maintain a rivalry over where this giant egg-white meringue, smothered in whipped cream and topped with fresh fruit, was first concocted. An equally contested side issue is the best way of preparing the confection. Two things are incontestable, however: firstly, that the dessert was originally made in honour of Russian ballerina Anna Pavlova, who visited both countries more than a century ago; and secondly, that it is an unbeatable way to consume a large amount of sugar in one sitting.

LEFT: eating out in Auckland. **RIGHT:** mussels, a New Zealand favourite.

The Farming Life

Although New Zealand's prosperity was built on its farm produce, changing times have made life tough for farmers

It's early morning, high summer in the heart of the South Island. Daniel Jamieson, second-generation farmer, father of two and sometime recreational cricket player, has breakfast with his wife, then heads outdoors to start work on the land

where he was born and raised. More than 600 dairy cows await him and his staff in a high-tech milking parlour not far from where the woolshed once stood. Daniel remembers the heat, sweat and dust of summer shearing back when he used to be a sheep farmer. In the early 2000s he and his wife were among the first on the plains of North Canterbury to switch from sheep to dairy. Now theirs is one of many grazing cattle herds, in a region where sheep had been raised for nearly a century.

Fields of change

Such changes are sweeping the rural heartland of New Zealand. The rapid spread of dairy farming from traditional North Island regions like Waikato, Taranaki and Manawatu to former sheep-farming strongholds in Canterbury, Otago and Southland has been one of the biggest trends, but is certainly not the only shift to alter the look of the land.

Thousands of hectares of pine trees now cloak hills too steep to support profitable livestock farming, particularly in parts of the North Island. Horticulture, including an abundance of apples, stone fruit and kiwi fruit, remains a mainstay in the Bay of Plenty, Gisborne, Hawke's Bay, Nelson and Otago, but new crops, particularly in the form of large-scale vegetable production, have made inroads into other fertile coastal areas. Profitable new crops such as olives, avocados and lavender have emerged. Grapes now flourish on many hillsides. Deer, ostriches, emus, alpacas and goats are all in commercial production. The expansion of dairy farming and forestry is predicted to continue for some time.

The humble sheep, it seems, is under siege. For decades a cornerstone of New Zealand agriculture, and indeed of the nation's export-driven economy, pastoral sheep production and its supporting industries have arguably borne the brunt of radical political and market changes. The loss of secure markets in the UK when Britain joined the EEC was the first blow, and was followed after 1984 by the systematic dismantling of extensive farm subsidies. New Zealand's rural industries are now among the least subsidised in the world.

New growth

Farmers met these challenges head-on. They've scoured the world for fresh opportunities and continued as guardians of New Zealand's largest industry, responsible for producing more than half of the country's merchandise exports, with dairying currently the biggest single export earner of all.

Traditional commodity sales to Europe may have withered, but sophisticated new products have found buyers elsewhere, most notably throughout Asia and in Australia. The same spirit of innovation that allowed New Zealand to begin refrigerated shipment of frozen sheep carcasses way back in 1882 has led to rapid advances in food-processing technology and farm production systems, not to mention a whole new attitude down on the farm.

The sheer diversity of New Zealand's land-based exports, from powdered deer antler and fresh flowers to chilled gourmet meat cuts and handmade boutique cheeses, reflects only part of the transformation that has taken place. Equally important, though less apparent, has been the farmers' willingness to adapt to new market trends. For the thousands who remain committed to the nation's sheep industry, this has meant increasingly specialised production of specific types of meat and wool, many of which are now brand-marked. For others, it has meant branching out into different types of agriculture or horticulture altogether.

Pressures and possibilities

New Zealand's farmers have been quick to respond to the increasing worldwide consumer concern about chemical residues, animal welfare and food safety. Gifted with a sparse population, clean air and water, and a productive, temperate climate, the country's exports of organic products have shown tremendous growth, and strict animal welfare codes and quality

farms" owned by large corporations, and at the other end of the scale there has been a boom in lifestyle block (2–4-hectare/5–10-acre block) ownership.

Possession of the land itself remains a source of contention in several regions, as many Maori tribes seek redress for the grievances of the past (see pages 36–9, 46 and 54), including the confiscation of large tracts of land. The tortuous process of government compensation for these losses has largely centred on cash settlements, with some return of public land to Maori ownership. While today's farmers face little risk of being themselves dispossessed after 150 years of European settle-

assurance programmes have now been implemented in many of New Zealand's rural industries.

Contrary to the doomsayers of the mid-1980s, who predicted the industry would barely survive without subsidies, farms owned and operated by rural families have remained the backbone of New Zealand agriculture. Admittedly, these properties now tend to be bigger than they used to be and with fewer staff. One or other of the spouses is likely to have a job off-farm to help supplement income; and the tradition of passing land down to the children is by no means as secure as it used to be. In addition, there is a growing number of "mega-

LEFT: mainstay of the rural economy. ABOVE: a farm on the road to Hahei, Coromandel Peninsula.

ment, indigenous land claims have nonetheless heightened tensions in many small rural communities, especially in Taranaki and Northland.

Protecting the future

Beyond these domestic issues, and beyond its borders, insect pests and animal and plant diseases from other countries continue to pose serious potential threats to New Zealand. Border control is among the strictest in the world, implemented with more than a little obsession as the country strives to protect itself from tiny invaders which could scupper multimillion-dollar export markets.

Having survived these changes and challenges, it's hardly surprising that farmers like Daniel Jamieson have much on their minds these days.   ❏

WINES

New Zealand, a latecomer to the world of
winemaking, now produces outstanding vintages
that are sold worldwide

New Zealand was the last temperate place on earth inhabited by humans, so it is no surprise that it is also the last (suitable) place on earth to make wine. Still, it has made an impressive run, especially in the realm of small-scale, high-quality production.

It all began in the Bay of Islands in 1819 when Samuel Marsden introduced the grapevine, and James Busby, the official British Resident, planted the first vineyard on his property at Waitangi in 1833. A couple of years later the very first New Zealand wine was produced. It was sampled by French admiral Dumont d'Urville, who pronounced it to be light, sparkling and delicious.

From there on the history of winemaking in New Zealand becomes obscure (prepare to hear a different story depending on who you are talking to). It is undisputed fact, however, that early French settlers planted small vineyards at Akaroa in the South Island and, more importantly, that members of the Marist Catholic brotherhood established a winery at Mission Estate in Hawke's Bay in 1865. This is now a commercial venture and is known as New Zealand's oldest existing vineyard.

By the end of the 19th century, small commercial vineyards were established in other parts of Hawke's Bay and in the Auckland–Northland region. All suffered from the scourge of prohibition politics between 1900 and 1920. For decades the industry languished, until finally in the 1980s vineyards were again established and by the 1990s several distinct wine-growing regions were formed. Today, each has its own wine trails to follow, featuring vineyards of every size and description, many offering a cellar-door experience.

International standing

If New Zealand has a "signature wine", it is sauvignon blanc, produced here with as much – and often greater – success as anywhere in the world. But hot on its heels are the reds from the nation's superb pinot noir grapes, and more recently, white wines from the pinot gris. The Oyster Bay Marlborough Pinot Noir (www.oysterbaywines. com) won gold at the 2007 San Francisco International Wine Competition (America's largest and most prestigious) along with another medal-

LEFT: a winemaker samples pinot noir from a barrel.
RIGHT: luscious grapes at a Hawke's Bay vineyard.

winner, Stoneleigh's Rapaura Marlborough Pinot Gris (www.stoneleigh.co.nz). Experts have also predicted a shiraz revolution. Needless to say, New Zealand wines are the only complement to the local cuisine that visitors should consider during their stay.

With an eye on the export market, New Zealand winemakers are enthusiastic participants in international competitions, and many return home every year bearing medals. Enthusiasm has equally been applied to marketing, with a high proportion of the country's wine production is exported – around 72 million litres (16 million gallons), with further growth expected.

Wineries in this area have a strong sense of old-time hospitality. At Collards (tel: 09-838 8341), on Lincoln Road in Henderson, Auckland, you can sample some of the classiest white wines made anywhere in the nation, along with a little across-the-counter conversation. Kumeu Valley, northwest of the city, is home to the fabulous Kumeu River Vineyard (www.kumeuriver.co.nz), as sophisticated as anything in Burgundy, and with chardonnay to match. Down the road, Matua Valley (www.matua.co.nz) could be in California, with its restaurant and visitors centre, while both Westbrook (www.westbrook.co.nz) and Soljans (www.soljans.com) are more like

Over the past 10 years markets have diversified significantly, and whilst sauvignon blanc is still the dominant export, accounting for some 40 percent, pinot noir figures (at 18 percent) and chardonnay (at 17 percent) are closing the gap.

North Island wineries

Wines produced on Auckland's west coast are among the finest you will find anywhere in the country. It's a region dubbed "Dally Country" because the wine culture is based on the sterling efforts of immigrants from the Croatian province of Dalmatia. Many of the wineries, including Babich (www.babichwines.co.nz) at the original site in Henderson, are still run by descendants of the Dalmatian founders.

restaurants with wineries attached – but the wine is every bit as good as the food.

Also close to Auckland is exotic Waiheke Island, where the Goldwater Estate (www.goldwaterwine.com) provides the ultimate Pacific idyll. To the south of Auckland, Rongopai (www.rongopaiwines.co.nz) produces lavish sweet wines in the hills of Te Kauwhata. The Matakana wine trail, an hour's drive north of Auckland, is also worth exploring.

Hawke's Bay and Wairarapa

Down the lumpy eastern coast of the North Island is Hawke's Bay, where winemaking operates on a large scale. This lifestyle destination had at the last count more than 50 wineries, most of which offer a cellar-door experience. Drive or cycle the region to enjoy the Mediterranean microclimate and the delicious produce offered at roadside stalls along the way. Wine trail highlights include Craggy Range Vineyard (www.craggyrange.com), set beneath breathtaking Te Mata Peak; Mission Estate (www.missionestate.co.nz), established by Marist Brothers in 1851 and housed inside a former seminary building; Taradale's award-winning Church Road (www.churchroad.co.nz) wines; and the boutique vineyard of Clearview Estate (www.clearviewestate.co.nz), with its range of organic wines. Here you can enjoy lunch among the vines or relax at an informal dining table and chairs built around an 80-year-old olive tree.

Wairarapa is another exciting wine region, the centre of pinot noir excellence. And because the wineries are so close to each other, you can see a few of them on foot. Don't miss places like Ata Rangi (www.atarangi.co.nz), Martinborough Vineyard (www.martinborough-vineyard.co.nz) and Te Kairanga (www.tkwine.co.nz); the wines are very popular and sell fast, so don't expect everything to be available.

South Island wineries

Marlborough is the only place in New Zealand that actually feels like a totally dedicated wine community – not unlike Burgundy, with winery visitor centres crying out for your attention. Two A-list establishments are Montana (www.montanawines.co.nz) and Cloudy Bay (www.cloudybay.co.nz). Also well worth a visit is Villa Maria's (www.villa maria.co.nz) impressive modern winery, built confidently to allow for expansion.

The wine-growing region of Nelson is different altogether, ravishingly bucolic, sun-baked, both maritime and mountain-lined and full of potters and artists. Wineries here include Neudorf (www.neudorf.co.nz), which is one of the country's best producers, and Ruby Bay (www.rubybayvineyard.co.nz).

Wineries at Waipara in North Canterbury produce top pinot noir, but for the greatest wine-and-landscape spectacle, go south to central Otago, where mountains soar over clinging vineyards, the lakes are deep blue-green, rivers rush down craggy valleys with chilly enthusiasm, and you can sit outside, sip wine and gaze

at the mountains against a crisp sky. Pinot noir is king here, but there are some scintillating rieslings too. Almost every winery that is open to the public is worth a visit, notably Gibbston Valley (www.gvwines.co.nz) and Chard Farm (www.chardfarm.co.nz), which are both good for their food as well as their wine.

For that final memory of New Zealand wine, meander down to Black Ridge (www.blackridge.co.nz) in Alexandra to experience wine craft at its mythical best – challenging, fiercely individual and triumphantly satisfying. *See Travel Tips pages 375–6 for more wineries and contact details of vineyard tour operators.* ❑

WINES OF CHARACTER

New Zealand wine has a character, a crystalline purity of fruit flavour, that no one has yet been able to explain. It is certainly not the climate, mostly maritime, and like the landscape tremendously varied – and in the South Island classified in wine-growing terms as distinctly cool. It may be the soil, which is uniquely young by geological standards, or it may have something to do with how bright daylight is here, a similar phenomenon to that of Cognac in France, where locals say it contributes to the finesse and concentrated flavour of that region's famous brandy. The unusually clean air may also contribute. Most likely it is a combination of all these things.

LEFT: vineyards at Marlborough. **RIGHT:** New Zealand produces some of the world's best sauvignon blanc.

ENVIRONMENTAL ISSUES

Conservationists wage constant war against introduced
pests like possums, stoats and deer in a battle to save
unique species of flora and fauna

New Zealand is one of the most isolated places in the world. The vast expanse of ocean that has separated these islands from any other appreciable land mass for millions of years has meant that local flora and fauna have evolved in complete isolation from the rest of the world. Because of this lonely evolutionary history, around 80 percent of New Zealand's plant species and 25 percent of its birds are found nowhere else on earth, and the same applies to nearly all of the country's insects and marine molluscs.

When people first arrived here around AD 800, the only terrestrial mammals to be found were bats. The islands were, instead, a haven for over 120 species of birds, 70 of which were unique to New Zealand. Many were flightless, and, with a lack of mammals, the top predator in the ecosystem was the giant Haast eagle, preying on the flightless moa *(see page 100)*, up to 20 times heavier than itself. However, it was no match for humans or the four-legged predators they brought with them, and it is now extinct.

With human settlement came increased frequency of fire, resulting in the permanent removal of large areas of forest and the extinction of numerous bird species. Hunting brought the demise of the moa within a few hundred years, while introduced rats and dogs took their toll on other birdlife long before the first Europeans arrived. The arrival of Europeans from the late 18th century onwards sped up what the Maori had begun. Large areas of forest were

PRECEDING PAGES: autumn colours at Wanaka Lake.
LEFT: trekking through the temperate rainforest at Hollyford Valley. **RIGHT:** the introduction of European species, such as deer, decimated indigenous wildlife.

milled or burnt. The introduction of browsing mammals and farming dramatically altered the landscape. Introduced European species such as weasels, stoats, cats and various rodents wrought havoc on the native birdlife. Possums, rabbits, wild goats and deer browsed native plants so heavily that they killed them.

Conservation measures

While environmental strategies including the management of marine resources, sustainable use of water, the reduction of waste and improvement of energy efficiency have been implemented nationwide, New Zealand's most pervasive environmental issue remains the decline of its unique plants, animals and ecosystems. Over the past 25 years conservation efforts including extensive pest eradication programmes and afforestation projects have succeeded in rescuing many species from the brink of extinction. New Zealand's land and marine reserves – some of which have no public access to ensure they remain pristine – have also been extremely successful.

Many species, including the tuatara which have been around for 250 million years *(see opposite page)*, are bred in captivity before being moved to sanctuaries which prepare them for a safe return to the wild.

The kiwi

New Zealand's national icon, the kiwi is highly protected. It is the only bird known to have nostrils at the end of its bill and it also has one of the largest egg-to-body weight ratios of any bird, with the egg averaging about 15 percent of the female's body weight. Kiwis live in pairs and mate for life, sometimes as long as 30 years.

There are five recognised species, all unique to New Zealand: the Great spotted kiwi (roroa; the largest species and fairly numerous in parts of South Island); the Little spotted kiwi (some 1,300 live on Kapiti Island off the southwest coast of North Island *(see page 220)*, with smaller

THE MOA

This giant, flightless bird, once a mainstay of the Maori diet, weighed up to 250kg (550lbs) and could be 3 metres (10ft) tall. Its size, and lack of natural predators, made it easy prey for the early human settlers, and all 10 species of the bird were hunted to extinction by the early 16th century. Nevertheless, it became as big in myth as it was in stature, with stories of sightings including that of two gold prospectors in the 1860s (considered mad, they were locked up for their troubles), and an alleged sighting on the beach of Martins Bay in the early 20th century. Theories of their survival in the remote southwest of South Island persist, but are considered a near-impossibility by zoologists.

introduced populations on other offshore islands); the Brown kiwi (the most common of the five, still widespread in the central and northern North Island); the tokoeka (fairly common in the southern parts of South Island); and the Okarito brown kiwi (rowi; restricted to western parts of South Island). The total kiwi population is estimated to be around 75,000.

Introduced predators are the kiwis' biggest threat. Stoats and cats kill 95 percent of kiwi chicks before they are six months old – well short of the 20 percent survival needed for a population to increase. Eggs are also lost when possums disturb nests, and adult kiwis are often killed by ferrets and dogs. New Zealand's Department of Conservation (DOC) works to protect nests in the wild by trapping, shooting and poisoning predators, raising chicks in captivity and releasing them into the wild when they are able to defend themselves, and researching and working with landowners in areas where kiwis live on private land.

The largest project, Operation Nest Egg, collects wild kiwi eggs and young chicks in the summer breeding season and looks after them in captive-rearing facilities until they reach about 1.2kg (2.6lbs) in weight and can better fend for themselves, then releases them back into their wild home where they have a good chance of survival. The project relies on the knowledge, time and commitment of hundreds of different institutions and individuals involved in hatching the eggs and raising the chicks, as well as the ongoing financial support of the New Zealand public.

Operation Nest Egg has been particularly effective for rapidly recovering the populations of the rarest kiwi, the Okarito brown kiwi, or rowi, whose numbers have recovered by some 25 percent over six years, and re-establishing populations that had hitherto declined to just a few individuals. To preserve unique gene pools and adaptations of each population, chicks are always returned to the wild populations they came from and are never mixed up.

Tuatara

These medium-sized reptiles, the only survivors of the order *Sphenodontia* which comprised many species during the age of the dinosaurs, are of huge international interest to biologists and are under active conservation management.

Tuatara once roamed the mainland but were thought to survive in the wild only on 32 offshore islands which are free of rodents and other introduced mammals that prey on their eggs. However, in early 2009 scientists were astonished by the discovery of a wild tuatara at the Karori Wildlife Sanctuary in Wellington, the first sighted on the mainland for over 200 years. Rats are considered the most serious threat, and visitors to Kapiti Island have their bags thoroughly searched prior to their arrival on the island, while conservation initiatives focus on keeping existing habitats free of

rodents. Captive individuals play an important part in conservation, education and research, and can be seen at Southland Museum, Wellington Zoo and Auckland Zoo.

Bats

Bats are New Zealand's only native land mammals and in the past have been a challenge to move successfully to safer locations due to their finely honed homing instincts. However, in the past three years the DOC team at Pukaha Mount Bruce cracked the code when they transferred pregnant bat mothers to their facility where the pups were born, then transferred them to pest-

free Kapiti Island, and in doing so pulled off the world's first successful translocation of bats for conservation purposes.

Yellow-eyed penguin

New Zealand is also home to the world's rarest penguin (one of six species found on the islands; *see below*), the hoiho (noise shouter), or Yellow-eyed penguin, named for its call and distinctive yellow headband. These penguins are found along the southeast coast of the South Island, Stewart Island, the Auckland Islands and Campbell Island, and their total number is estimated to range between 6,000 and 7,000, with around 630 breeding pairs found on the South Island's southeast coast. Chicks are threatened

LEFT: kiwi in close-up at Rainbow Springs, Rotorua.
RIGHT: newly hatched tuatara.

by stoats, rats, cats and dogs. These last also worry adult penguins and they are banned from entering penguin breeding areas. In some readily accessible sites the popularity of ecotourism is also having an effect on nest survival rates. On beaches where there is extensive unsupervised human interaction (adult penguins need ready access to their nests and chicks), chick survival rates can be lower than 1 percent. A DOC species conservation plan was put into place in 1985 and has achieved considerable success. Another notable success story has been that of the Penguin Place project at Otago Peninsula in the South Island, where a private landowner converted his farm to a penguin sanctuary when penguins began to nest there some 20 years ago.

There are five other penguin species in New Zealand, but three of these (Rockhopper, Snares and Erect-crested) are restricted to the remote sub-Antarctic islands far to the south. The Blue penguin (korora) is the world's smallest penguin and its range extends across all of New Zealand's coasts – one of the best places to see it is on the Banks Peninsula near Christchurch, as well as the Otago coast. The Fiordland penguin (tawaki) is restricted to the fiords of South Island, parts of the southern coast and Stewart Island.

Kakapo

The kakapo is the world's only flightless parrot, which historically inhabited all three islands but is now confined to areas of Fiordland and Stewart Island – two of the most remote spots in the country. Kakapo have also been transferred to predator-free islands. In 1974 it was unclear whether any existed at all, then, incongruously, a population of males was found in Fiordland followed by a population of males and females on Stewart Island. The Department of Conservation has 10 people working full-time on kakapo-related projects (www.kakaporecovery.org.nz), but the bird remains at great risk.

Where to see wildlife

It is relatively easy to see whales, seals and dolphins as well as marine birds such as albatrosses and penguins on boat trips from Kaikoura *(see page 237)* on the upper east coast of the South Island. Sightings of half a dozen Sperm whales

---

MARINE MAMMALS

New Zealand's marine fauna is diverse, and all marine mammals in New Zealand waters are fully protected by law. Incredibly, sightings of almost half of the world's cetaceans (whales, porpoises and dolphins) have been reported here. Also seen are the endemic Hector's dolphins (found nowhere else), rare beaked whales, New Zealand sea lions (found only in New Zealand's southern waters), and the widely distributed New Zealand fur seals. Other seals that visit New Zealand's shores include the Southern elephant seal and the Leopard seal, both of which are found in larger numbers in Antarctic and sub-Antarctic waters. The most common threat to the nation's populations of large whales, including the Southern right whale and the Humpback whale, is habitat degradation, global climate change, fishing by-catch, entanglement and accumulation of pollutants in the oceans.

Didymo, a slimy organism otherwise known as rock snot, is found in some South Island rivers, and conservation controls to prevent its spread include disinfecting fishing gear at an approved cleaning station prior to departure on a fly-fishing trip.

New Zealand's Marine Exclusive Economic Zone covering some 4,053,049 sq km (1,564,882 sq miles) of ocean (more than 1 percent of the earth's surface), is the fourth-largest zone in the world, and is still being definitively mapped.

and pods of several hundred dolphins are common. Back on shore, Kaikoura has a seal colony located not far from the town centre.

A number of offshore islands have been cleared of predators and have become wildlife hotspots, home to a variety of endangered birds, reptiles and insects. Islands such as Tiritiri Matangi and Kapiti off the coast of North Island, Motuara off South Island and Ulva off Stewart Island are all easy to visit, and here, for example, you can see birds such as the takahe, the saddleback and the stitchbird, and get some idea of what New Zealand must have been like before Europeans arrived.

and although these trees can still be seen they are under conservation management by Project Crimson, which is assisting with pest and weed control, propagation and fencing to prevent stock and possums from dining on newly planted trees. Mysterious illnesses are also preying on the mighty kauri, and visitors should heed signs to protect these trees, whose roots are easily damaged, and scrape dirt off footwear before entering and leaving forested areas.

New Zealand boasts some of the most spectacular stands of forest in the world. There is not much that can beat the magnificent kauri forests of Northland, the splendid broadleaf-

Native flora

The trees and forests of New Zealand are also unique, evolving in isolation for millions of years. Eighty percent of the native fauna is found only here, and ranges from magnificent kauri forests, ferns and flaxes, dune plants, Alpine and sub-Alpine herb fields, to stands of rainforest dominated by rimu, beech, matai and rata. The last, along with its northern partner, the pohutukawa, which once completely painted the coastline red in the summer with its tiny crimson petals, has been ravaged by introduced possums,

podocarp forests of Pureora or Whirinaki in the central North Island, or the great, ancient beech forests that you pass through when crossing over the Main Divide in the South Island.

It is also worth taking a bit of time to seek out the Alpine vegetation, which includes some 600 species of plants, the vast majority of which are endemic. Although the best known is the Mount Cook lily, which is actually a type of buttercup, there is a host of other striking and unusual plants, such as the vegetable sheep – a strange, decidedly woolly-looking plant which grows together in "flocks" – and the spaniards, to mention just a couple. Many of these plants have evolved in a peculiar way in order to cope with the sometimes harsh environment. ❏

LEFT: Yellow-eyed penguin on the Otago Peninsula near Dunedin. **ABOVE:** the waters off Kaikoura are one of New Zealand's prime whale-watching areas.

OUTDOOR ACTIVITIES

With wide open spaces and a healthy lifestyle, New Zealanders are passionate about sport and adventure – and are keen to share it with others

New Zealanders embrace the great outdoors, and easy access to the oceans and wilderness areas is just one explanation for the great Kiwi sporting passion. In fact, it would be difficult to grow up in this country without spending a significant amount of time hiking in the mountains, fishing the rivers or riding the surf. Many of the country's most adored heroes are those who have achieved great things on the world's outdoor stages: Sir Edmund Hillary, the late Sir Peter Blake, the All Blacks rugby team.

From the moment children start school, sport and physical activity are a big part of the educational curriculum. More than 90 percent of the country's young people are actively engaged in sport through clubs or schools. This has helped make New Zealand a breeding ground for sportsmen and women, and a playground for adrenalin-seeking adventurers.

Team sports

Rugby union is the main national sport. More than 140,000 people play club rugby, and the national team, the All Blacks, is among the most successful in the world. February marks the start of the season with the regionally based Super 12 Competition, and it all ends in late October with the National Provincial Championships.

A good season for the All Blacks guarantees A-list celebrity status for players whose names and personal details will dominate nearly every tabloid and magazine in the country for months. The nation's obsession with the sport can be felt most strongly during international matches, when tens of thousands of fans decorate themselves in supporting colours. Failure to win results in collective mourning and a general post mortem of each player's performance.

Cricket is the main summer game, and New Zealand takes part in the Test Match series and other international competitions. Cricketing heroes include the legendary Sir Richard Hadlee, a Christchurch man who had a record-breaking career between the early 1970s and 1990 and was knighted for his services to the game. The excitement of one-day matches has raised the profile of what some people considered a rather dull and tedious pastime.

LEFT: mountain biking in the Southern Alps.
RIGHT: inside a zorb *(see page 113).*

The women's winter sport of netball also has a high profile, partly due to television coverage of all major international events and the feisty competitiveness between New Zealand and its greatest rival, Australia. Volleyball has moved outdoors onto New Zealand's most beautiful beaches. Beach volleyball for two- or four-person teams has become a popular spectator sport and is sufficiently casual for teams to be thrown together at the last minute.

Other team sports – hockey, soccer, touch rugby, rugby league and basketball – all have healthy numbers of followers, with the games' codes taught in schools throughout the country.

bag deer, chamois, wild pigs, goats and tahr (a Himalayan goat species). In an effort to diversify, farmers in more remote areas actively encourage hunters onto their properties. The Southern Alps hold some of the world's finest wild game species for trophy hunting. The main hunting period is from March to September during the "rut", when the big males are looking for mates. Hunting here can be challenging and conditions harsh; a high level of fitness is therefore necessary.

Trout fishing became popular after its introduction by British settlers, and the seasons vary between the two main islands. Both start in

On any winter Saturday, nearly every sports field in the country will be busy with children participating in one or more sporting events. Large numbers of parents gather along the sidelines, cheering, calling and offering unnecessary instructions to their protégés.

Hunting, fishing and skiing

Many sports considered elite in other parts of the world are readily accessible in New Zealand. Very few towns are without a carefully manicured golf course and fast-growing club memberships. No longer the domain of the retired population, golf has a growing popularity among younger people.

There are ample opportunities for hunters to

October, but in the North it finishes at the end of June, while in South Island the season closes at the end of April. Licences can be obtained from any sports shop in any one of the 22 fishing districts.

Game fishing is equally popular in New Zealand. Ever since writer Zane Grey alerted the world to the game-fishing opportunities in the Bay of Islands, fishermen have dreamed of reeling in a giant marlin or swordfish. Although many like to take their catch home, others prefer to tag and release the giant specimens caught off the east coast of Northland and Bay of Plenty. Game fishing is possible throughout the year, but the period from mid-January until the end of May is considered the prime time.

Clear blue skies, lofty mountains and dazzling snow slopes guarantee the popularity of skiing and snowboarding here, with commercial ski fields, Nordic cross-country and heli-ski areas. The North Island has three fields, two on Mount Ruapehu and another on Mount Taranaki. The South Island fields are spread throughout the Southern Alps, with Queenstown's Remarkables Ski Field and Coronet Peak being the southernmost and among the best. These fields are a favourite training venue for Northern Hemisphere ski teams. Heli-ski and glacier-skiing operators offer an extensive range of off-piste skiing from July to October.

regardless of duration or recommended fitness level, are available from information centres and Department of Conservation (DOC) offices. New Zealand walks are safe. There is no dangerous wildlife and tracks are well signposted and maintained. However, be aware that the weather is extremely changeable, and walkers of every level must always go well prepared.

Bookings with the doc are required for some of the most popular and world-renowned tracks, such as the Milford, Heaphy and Routeburn. The number of visitors is closely monitored to ensure preservation of the special nature and wildlife of these pristine areas.

Take a hike
New Zealand has some of the greatest walks in the world. From remote Fiordland forests to the vast wilderness areas of Te Urewera National Park, the volcanic plains of Tongariro National Park or heli-hiking on the Franz Josef Glacier, there is no disputing the diversity and beauty of the walks available.

If you are particularly energetic, you can walk the length of the country on marked trails (see Travel Tips pages 364–6). Details of most walks,

On the water
On any fine weekend the waters which embrace Auckland ripple with the wakes of thousands of watercraft. From Westhaven to Buckland's Beach, from the East Coast Bays to Whangaparaoa, they fly in the prevailing southwesterly breeze, skim-

> On the last Monday of January, the Auckland Anniversary Regatta takes place. With more than 1,000 entries it is the world's biggest one-day yachting event.

LEFT: fisherman snagging a Brown trout at Nelson Lakes National Park. **ABOVE:** Treble Cone, high above the shores of Lake Wanaka in the Southern Alps, is one of New Zealand's premier skiing areas.

ming like tiny white butterflies over the water with barely a gap between them. Then, as the shore is left behind, they spread out, revealing themselves as a mix of yachts, launches, fizz boats, windsurfers and jet skiers. The scenario is repeated all around the country's coastline.

Winning the America's Cup, the world's oldest sporting trophy, in 1995 highlighted the sport, which reached a climax in 2000 when Team New Zealand defended, and won the America's Cup for a second time.

Adrenalin action

Early in the 19th century, "adventure" meant people pushed to the edge of human endurance. There were things to be discovered, unex-

rap, the adventure is the world's first flight offering full pilot control of a high-speed, tethered plane. Based at Queenstown, the planes are suspended from an overhead suspension point 55 metres (180ft) high. Speeds of up to 125kph (77mph) have been recorded.

Parasailing, paragliding and parachuting are other ways to obtain an adrenalin fix while also getting an aerial sightseeing tour. During the summer months, commercial parasailers operate on most of the major lakes. Small airfields near main tourist destinations will generally have gliding or skydiving centres on site or nearby. For many, completing a tandem skydive

plored territories to be conquered, land to chart. Those were the days before double-edged harnesses, poly-prop garments and satellite navigation. Adventure, real adventure, meant facing hardships, discomfort and often death. Today's adventurers need only the spirit of adventure, some cash and a slight dose of insanity.

New Zealand's capacity for inventing and commercialising adventures is legendary (see pages 112–13). Leaping from aeroplanes, mountains and bridges, pounding down untamed rivers and over terrifying waterfalls, sinking beneath surging seas in search of wrecks or swimming with sharks are all readily available.

Fly by Wire is indicative of Kiwi ingenuity. Invented and patented worldwide by Neil Har-

is high on their list of "must-do" adventure activities. Taupo, Christchurch, Wanaka and Queenstown are notably popular areas for skydiving. After leaving the plane, jumpers will spend the first 30 seconds in freefall, plummeting to the ground at 200kph (124mph) before enjoying the leisurely drift down to earth. Others might prefer a hot-air balloon ride over the Canterbury Plains or aerobatics in a biplane near Rotorua. For those wanting a more sedate aerial adventure, Wairarapa, Matamata and Omarama are renowned for their superb gliding conditions.

Surfing and diving

For many thrill-seekers, the waters of New Zealand are the biggest, wildest and most exciting playgrounds of them all. Big-wave surfing, windsurfing, traction kiting and scuba diving pit the participant's human-sized strength and courage against one of nature's most powerful and untameable elements.

Kite surfing is one of the country's fastest-growing new watersports. Surfers use the power of both the waves and the wind to propel themselves as high as 30 metres (100ft) into the air and can cover some long distances across the water. Riders are strapped by their feet to "surfboards" and connected to a billowing kite by a harness similar to that used by windsurfers. Kite surfing has been described as a combination of aerobatics, windsurfing and skysurfing.

New Zealand's coastline and offshore islands have some of the best temperate-water diving in the world. From the rocky headlands of the far north to the fiords of the deep south, you can explore wrecks, swim under ice, enter dark caves, meander through forests of black coral trees, frolic with fish and confront camera-shy sharks. The coastal waters reflect the diversity of the land, providing a huge range of diving experiences within a very small area.

The Poor Knights Islands, off the coast from Tutukaka, are undoubtedly the jewel of New Zealand diving. Affectionately referred to as "The Diver's Knights", the labyrinth of caves, archways, air-bubble caves, and drop offs, combined with the prolific fish life which thrives due to the island's Marine Reserve status, ensure the diving is nothing less than spectacular. Experienced divers could never be disappointed with dive sites like Taravana Cave, Kamakazi Drop Off, Northern Arch and Wild Beast Point. For the less experienced and meandering photographers, Maomao Arch, Middle Arch and the Cream Garden offer colour and action at shallower depths. Close by lie two scuttled frigates, the *Tui* and the *Waikato*. Both make great wreck dives, as does the *Rainbow Warrior*, which lies further north at Matauri Bay. Dive operators at Tutukaka offer a variety of trips and cater for divers at all levels. Gear and guides are provided for those who require it.

South Island diving is colder but no less exciting. The Russian cruise liner *Mikhail Lermontov*, lying in 36 metres (120ft) of water near

Port Gore in the Marlborough Sounds, excites wreck divers, the cave system of the Riwaka Source in the Takaka Valley challenges cave divers, and Fiordland intrigues budding marine biologists. The heavy rainfall in Fiordland makes it one of the wettest places on earth and is also responsible for creating unique diving conditions. A permanent layer of tannin-rich fresh water up to 10 metres (32ft) deep sits above the sea water. The result is a great sun-blocking filter, which tricks deep-dwelling creatures into the shallow depths. The 14 fiords support the world's biggest population of black coral trees, about 7 million colonies, some up

to 200 years old and in depths only accessible to sport divers.

> *Inexperienced rafters need to listen to all the instructions handed out before setting off: take note of how to front paddle and back paddle, how to swap sides and how to hold on tight!*

White-water thrills

Every year thousands of adrenalin-hungry thrill-seekers climb into kayaks or bouncy orange inflatable rafts and attempt to navigate some of the most scenic, dramatic and dangerous rivers imaginable. Undaunted by nature's obstacles,

---

LEFT: a parachutist is happy with her successful descent. **RIGHT:** surfer riding a wave at a Christchurch beach.

they plummet over waterfalls and career through sharp-rocked rapids in a frenzy of foam and madness. Then, when the waters are quiet, they let their crafts and their minds drift in aimless contentment. There are more than 80 commercial white-water rafting operations in New Zealand, carrying a total of 130,000 clients annually on 57 rivers. Between Christmas and the end of February each year about 13,000 people will pour down the Shotover River alone. The rapids encountered range from grades one to five, so you can choose your level of excitement. Participants are provided with wetsuits, life jackets and helmets.

Kayaking is a more sedate pursuit, and trips on fresh or coastal waters are available everywhere. Fiordland is high on the list of most spectacular kayaking sites, with towering mountains rising sheer from the mostly navigable fiords. Abel Tasman National Park is also memorable for day, overnight or longer adventures. The pretty coastline is speckled with safe overnight campsites, and the chance of being accompanied by dolphins or an inquisitive seal is high.

Deep down and dirty

Cavers Dave Ash and Peter Chandler took the underground experience into the commercial

realm when they established The Legendary Black Water Rafting Company at Waitomo in 1987. Cavers float on inner tubes through underground flooded caves lit with glow-worms and decorated with stalactites and stalagmites, before surfacing to warm up with hot soup and crumpets. Be prepared to get wet, cold and scared. The same company can also introduce you to wilder adventures, including abseiling. Another reliable operator, Waitomo Adventures (which measures its adventure danger level at "Rambo Rating"), will have you abseiling down waterfalls or dropping 100 metres (330ft) down into a gaping hole in the earth known as The Lost World. The South Island's answer to Waitomo is found on the west coast, where The Wild West Adventure Company provides a similar range of heart-stopping activities.

Canyoning is the exploration and descent of steep-sided, confined river gorges using specialised ropes, abseiling skills, and sometimes the less specialised arts of jumping and swimming. The Deep Canyoning Company introduced it to New Zealand when it began exploring the spectacular gorges carved out of the schist rock around Wanaka. The thrill comes from abseiling down, in and behind huge cascades and witnessing the grandeur of the rock sculptures.

edge of a platform where, after summoning together their last reserves of courage, they leap off the building towards the city below.

There are various bungee-jumping sites throughout New Zealand, with one of the most notable being on the Auckland Harbour Bridge. The Bridge Walk to the jump site is equally exciting for spectators. Jumpers who opt for the South Island have a choice of Queenstown jumps. They can leap 43 metres (141ft) off the original bungee site at Kawarau Bridge, drop 47 metres (154ft) off the Ledge bungee in central Queenstown, or brave the Nevis Highwire bungee, the ultimate high-wire jump of 134

Off the edge

New Zealanders seem to have this obsession with throwing themselves off things, and the higher the better. None is higher than Auckland's Sky Tower, the tallest tower in the Southern Hemisphere. It protrudes 192 metres (630ft) above the Sky City casino in central Auckland. This is the site of Skyjump, best described as base-jumping without the parachute. Jumpers are escorted to a lift, which takes them to the 53rd floor. After donning a harness and having equipment checked, they make their way to the

LEFT: white-water action on the Rangitata River in Canterbury. **ABOVE:** plunging off Kawarau Bridge, Queenstown.

metres (440ft) from a gondola that overlooks the meeting of the Nevis and Kawarau rivers.

A similar thrill is on offer at the Shotover Canyon Swing where you jump in a harness from 109 metres (358ft) and freefall 60 metres (197ft) into the canyon before a twin rope system pendulums you in a smooth 200-metre (656ft) arc at 150kph (90mph).

A more recent attraction is the Skywire, located just 10 minutes from Nelson town. You are strapped into a four-seat carriage, after which you are launched 1.6km (1 mile) on an endless cable across a valley at a speed of 100kph (62mph). ❏

See also pages 362–75 of Travel Tips and its regional listings for contact details of operators.

THRILLSEEKERS' PARADISE

There's no end to the variety of adventure sports in New Zealand. Just as your heartbeat slows to normal, a new crazy activity comes along

New Zealanders have become famous for their willingness to jump off bridges, speed down shallow rivers, or roll down hills inside inflatable balls. They're happy to help others do the same, too, and have introduced new heart-pumping sports to the world – but they do it safely. Every week thousands of visitors experience the heady euphoric feeling of an adrenaline rush.

New Zealanders seem to be addicted to adrenaline. It's the best legal drug you can get, but like any drug you have to get more of it in different forms. So adventure addicts now consider bungee-jumping "boring" – rap jumping and kite-surfing is currently their way to get a high. Another favourite thrill is jet-boat rides down river gorges, travelling at breakneck speeds perilously close to the rocky banks.

The industry is strongly regulated and the operators highly trained. They've all been to the same charm school and so delight in making any activity seem more dangerous than it really is. They reason that the higher you think the risk is, the higher the adrenaline rush when you "miraculously" survive the experience.

Should you ask your parachute jump partner how long he's been doing tandem jumps, he'll tell you that today is his first time with a paying customer. Stand on a bridge and ask how many jumps a bungee rope is used for before it's retired, and you'll be told "100, and yours is the 99th". Such tricks are simple but extremely effective. In fact, the adventure sports industry in New Zealand has a remarkably good safety record.

Nobody has ever satisfactorily explained why New Zealanders are so successful at dreaming up new adventure activities. It must be a combination of the beautiful outdoors and their isolation from the rest of the world. They have to get their kicks at home and they will try anything once. If it works, they will develop it for their visitors' fun and enjoyment.

LEFT: river sledging on the Dart River, one of many unusual ways to experience New Zealand's waterways.

ABOVE: aerobatics. The plane looks tiny and the pilot looks crazy. They don't even give you a sick bag, although you can tell the pilot to stop. Loops and rolls, upside-down flying, inverted turns and more all conspire to twist your stomach into unbelievable shapes.

BELOW: face-forward abseiling was invented by the SAS. It allows you to safely see the city from a new angle.

ZORBING YOUR WAY DOWN THE HILL

Zorbing is the epitome of New Zealanders' love of the bizarre. An NZ Air Force pilot described zorbing as "the same sensation as spinning loops and barrel rolls and then crashing to the ground in a jet. Only in a Zorb it doesn't hurt." Lesser mortals say it's like "being inside a tumble drier".

The Zorb is actually two spheres, one suspended inside the inflated outer one. The view from inside is a tumbling blur of blue sky and green grass which eventually seems to blend into one as you bounce and fall and roll down a hillside. Aficionados throw a bucket of water in first just to remove any chance that they can cling to the sides. There are also plans to take it onto the country's fast-flowing rivers and over waterfalls.

Like many adventure sports, it's almost as much fun to watch as to participate. It starts with mirth as a vacuum cleaner working in reverse is used to pump up the Zorb, and finishes with hilarity as the dizzy participant tries to climb out of the sphere.

Zorbing is probably the safest of all the adventure sports. Like all of them, there is no logical reason to do it. The late Sir Edmund Hillary, New Zealander's most loved adventure sportsman probably climbed Everest in 1953 for the same reason as today's adrenaline seekers: because it's there.

ABOVE: glacier walking on what appears to be a living, moving, creaking, mountain of ice is awe-inspiring. You may be roped up to your guide in case you slip and fall down a crevasse.

RIGHT: tandem skydiving is a 30-second, 200 kph (120 mph) freefall with a professional attached to your back. The 4-minute final descent by parachute is the perfect way to calm down.

PLACES

A detailed guide to the entire country,
with principal sites clearly cross-referenced
by number to the maps

People aside – albeit friendly, heart-warming people – it's the places in New Zealand that arouse your sense of wonder and make you catch your breath. The pristine beauty of Milford Sound, the silver dazzle of the Southern Lakes, the bush-wrapped solitude of Lake Waikaremoana, the boiling surprises of the thermal regions… these have inspired even the most travelled of visitors to wax lyrical.

The Maori story of creation explains that land and human beings are all one – flesh and clay from the same source material. The indigenous Maori's emotional attachment to place is profound and has influenced Pakeha culture, contributing to the national belief that "clean and green" is a philosophy, not just a tourism marketing tool.

Initially the first European settlers tried to make New Zealand's countryside look British. They cut and burnt the forest and sowed grass, but when they had spare time to look around, they soon realised how special their new home was. The North Island's spas and hot pools earned an early reputation for their curative powers. As early as 1901, the government hired an official balneologist and formed a tourist department, the first government-sponsored tourism promotion organisation in the world.

The thermal regions still draw enormous attention from travellers, but nowadays it's mainly the unsullied, uncluttered landscape, and the sense of space and timelessness that bring thousands of visitors to its shores. Some come just to soak in the scenery, while an ever-increasing number want to walk in the wilderness; for them a tramp through this scenic wonderland is a sort of purification rite.

New Zealand's remoteness from the rest of the world has served both to limit the number of visitors and preserve the land from over-exploitation. Those who did come were delighted by what they found packed into a country whose length can be driven in a couple of days, and whose width can mostly be crossed in a few hours. ❑

PRECEDING PAGES: hiking at the head of the Hollyford River, Fiordland; scenery near Whangara, North Island east coast; sheep on the road, Banks Peninsula. **LEFT:** Lake Rotoiti, Nelson Lakes National Park. **TOP:** Wellington Harbour. **ABOVE LEFT:** scenery on the Routeburn Track. **ABOVE RIGHT:** Champagne Pool, Rotorua.

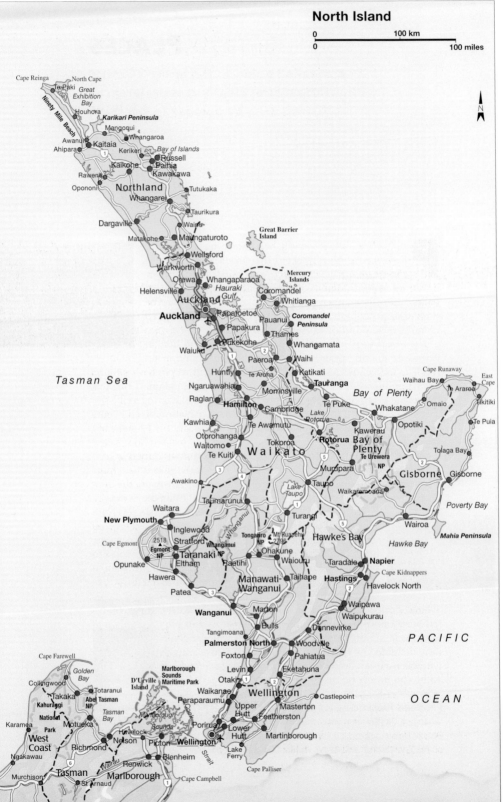

North Island

0   100 km

0   100 miles

N

Cape Reinga
Te Paki
North Cape
Great
Exhibition
Bay
Houhora
Karikari Peninsula
Mangonui
Awanui
Whangaroa
Kaitaia
Ahipara
Kerikeri
Bay of Islands
Russell
Kaikohe
Paihia
Kawakawa
Rawene
Opononi
Northland
Tutukaka
Whangarei
Taurikura
Dargaville
Waipu
Matakohe
Maungaturoto
Wellsford
Warkworth
Great Barrier
Island
Otewa
Whangaparaoa
Mercury
Islands
Helensville
Hauraki
Gulf
Coromandel
Auckland
Whitianga
Auckland
Papatoetoe
Pauanui
Coromandel
Peninsula
Papakura
Thames
Pukekohe
Whangamata
Waiuku
Paeroa
Waihi
Huntly
Te Aroha
Katikati
Ngaruawahia
Morrinsville
Tauranga
Raglan
Hamilton
Cambridge
Te Puke
Bay of Plenty
Whakatane
Waihau Bay
Cape Runaway
East
Cape
Te Araroa
Kawhia
Te Awamutu
Lake
Rotorua
Kawerau
Opotiki
Omaio
Tikitiki
Te Puia
Otorohanga
Tokoroa
Rotorua
Bay of
Plenty
Waitomo
Te Kuiti
Waikato
Te Urewera
NP
Tolaga Bay
Awakino
Murupara
Gisborne
Gisborne
Taupo
Waikaremoana
Taumarunui
Lake
Taupo
Poverty Bay
Waitara
Turangi
Wairoa
New Plymouth
Whanganui
Mahia Peninsula
Inglewood
Tongariro
NP
Mt Ruapehu
2796
Hawke's Bay
Cape Egmont
2518
Stratford
Whanganui
NP
Hawke Bay
Egmont
NP
Taranaki
Ohakune
Opunake
Eltham
Raetihi
Waiouru
Taradale
Napier
Hawera
Taihape
Hastings
Cape Kidnappers
Patea
Manawati-
Wanganui
Havelock North
Wanganui
Marton
Waipawa
Tangimoana
Bulls
Waipukurau
Dannevirke
PACIFIC
Palmerston North
Woodville
Foxton
Pahiatua
Levin
Eketahuna
Otaki
Castlepoint
OCEAN
Waikanae
Wellington
Paraparaumu
Masterton
Upper
Hutt
Featherston
Porirua
Lower
Hutt
Martinborough
Wellington
Lake
Ferry
Cape Palliser

Tasman Sea

Cape Farewell
Golden
Bay
Collingwood
Totaranui
Takaka
Abel Tasman
NP
Kahurangi
Karamea
Tasman
Bay
National
Park
Motueka
West
Coast
Havelock
Ngakawau
Richmond
Nelson
Picton
Murchison
Renwick
Tasman
Marlborough
St Arnaud
Cape Campbell
Marlborough
Sounds
Maritime Park
D'Urville
Island
Marlborough
Sounds
Blenheim
Wairau
Cook
Strait

NORTH ISLAND

North Island is New Zealand's hub, where
frenetic activity is a feature of business,
leisure and even the earth itself

The North Island, according to Maori legend, is the fish pulled from the sea by Maui. And what a catch it is, with a superb range of sights to see and things to do. New Zealand's largest and (by far) most worldly cities – Auckland and Wellington – are located here. Auckland, home to more than a quarter of New Zealand's population, is the largest Polynesian city in the world, and its wide range of shops, restaurants and activities make it truly cosmopolitan.

Laid-back Northland, in the subtropical far north beyond Auckland, has a strong Maori heritage and was one of the first areas settled by Europeans. Visit the Bay of Islands townships of Paihia and Russell and it's easy to understand why. Activities here centre on the sea: sailing, big-game fishing, pleasure cruising. There are also numerous sites of historical interest, from the place where the Treaty of Waitangi was signed to the nation's oldest stone building.

Like most of New Zealand, a change of scenery is never far away. An hour's drive south through fertile dairy country is Waikato – its name borrowed from New Zealand's longest waterway, the Waikato River, which winds its way through the region. On the east coast the Coroman-

del Peninsula's beautiful beaches and secluded bays urge travellers to slow down, while the East Cape and its remoteness offers a special charm of its own.

Inland things heat up considerably. Hot mineral springs, boiling mud, geysers and volcanoes have led to Rotorua's title: "thermal wonderland". Fly-fishing is popular further south at Lake Taupo, New Zealand's largest lake. The fertile grounds of Taranaki and the Manawatu are among the most intensely farmed regions in New Zealand, and their small service towns provide friendly stopover points for travellers. Though situated at the bottom of the North Island, Wellington, the nation's capital, is at the centre of New Zealand both geographically and culturally. Within its harbour-fringed confines are the head offices of many of the country's major companies. ❏

TOP: Waitangi Treaty House, Northland. **ABOVE LEFT:** New Zealand's northernmost point, Cape Reinga. **ABOVE RIGHT:** Maori dance performance.

AUCKLAND

Auckland is one of the world's most sprawling
cities, yet you can easily walk across it in
less than 20 minutes. Volcanoes and the sea
define its landscape, but its people are still
defining themselves

Auckland is built on an isthmus located between two stunning harbours and has, from the beginning, been defined by the water that surrounds it. The harbour that laps at the foot of what would become the city's main street was called Waitemata – sparkling water – by the pre-European Maori, and from every vantage point, man-made and natural, the aptness of the name can still be seen today.

Even when the sun is not shining – and Aucklanders like to think of their city as a sun-kissed gem of the South Pacific – the water glistens, silver under overcast skies, and becomes positively diamantine when the clouds part.

So insistent is the sea – nosing up creeks and estuaries and lapping on the shores of a hundred bays – that less than a mile of *terra firma* stops it from cutting Auckland completely adrift. The 19th-century townships that have linked up to make the 21st-century city were sprinkled along an S-shaped isthmus which at its narrowest point is barely 1.3km (¾ mile) wide. Across this corridor of land runs Portage Road, original crossing point between two harbours. Here, Maori would beach and haul their canoes across the only break in an aquatic highway leading from the sheltered eastern bays of the far north and joining up with the Waikato, the country's longest river, which leads to Lake Taupo, the liquid heart of the North Island.

The City of Sails

Waitemata Harbour is the gateway to the island-studded boating paradise of the Hauraki Gulf. Ownership of recreational boats – from ostentatious gin palaces and deep-sea fishing craft to aluminium "tinnies", battered rowboats and kayaks – is reputedly the world's highest per capita. Not for nothing has Auckland branded itself "The City of Sails".

The city's Anniversary Day, the last Monday in January, is marked by a regatta – first staged in 1840, it's as old

Main attractions
NATIONAL MARITIME MUSEUM
QUEEN STREET
SKY TOWER
CIVIC THEATRE
AUCKLAND ART GALLERY
ALBERT PARK
VICTORIA PARK MARKET
ANTARCTIC ENCOUNTER AND
UNDERWATER WORLD
MOUNT EDEN

**PRECEDING PAGES
& BELOW:** sailing in
Auckland Harbour.
LEFT: the Old
Customhouse.

Auckland

0 ——————— 500 m
0 ——————— 500 yds

Birkenhead

Stanley Bay

Waitemata Harbour

Devonport, Rangitoto

Bledisloe Wharf

Hamer Street

Brigham Street

Wynard Wharf

Jellicoe St

AMERICA'S CUP VILLAGE

Madden Street

Auckland Hilton

Passenger Terminal

Prince's Wharf

Pakenham Street

Beaumont Street

Gaunt Street

Daldy Street

New Zealand National Maritime Museum

Hobson Wharf

Queens Wharf

Cpt. Cook Wharf

Marsden Wharf

Powerhouse Lane

Tooley Street

Viaduct Basin

Ferry Building

VIADUCT HARBOUR

Ponsonby

Halsey Street

Customs St West

Market Place

Pakenham St

Sturdee St

Lwr Hobson St

Lower Albert Street

Quay Street

Tyler Street

Galway Street

Britomart

Timley St

Quay Street

Harbour Bridge, Whangarei and North Shore

Northern Motorway

VICTORIA PARK

Fanshawe Street

St Patrick's Cathedral

Wolfe St

Waite St

Swanson Street

Customs Street

Old Customhouse

Queen Elizabeth Square

Queen Street

Fort Street

Shortland Street

Britomart

Emily Road

Eden Crescent

Beach Road

Vector Arena

Auckland Station

Victoria Park Market

Victoria Street

Nelson Street

Hobson Street

Wyndham Street

Kingston St

Queen Street

High Street

Vulcan Lane

Chancery Street

Anzac Avenue

Waterloo Quadrant

Parliament St

Ronayne St

The Strand

Sky Tower

SKYCITY

Federal St

Albert Street

Wellesley Street West

Elliott St

Strand Arcade

AAG New Gallery

Bowen Avenue

Old Government House

ALBERT PARK

High Court

Rougan St

Parnell Rise

Parnell

Wellesley Street

Sale Street

Wellesley Street

St Matthew

Civic Theatre

Central City Library

Auckland Art Gallery Main Gallery

Old Arts Building

St Andrew's Church

University of Auckland

Stanley Street

Churchill St

The Strand

Cook Street

Union Street

Aotea Centre

Aotea Square

Town Hall

Rutland St

Auckland Institute of Technology

Alfred Street

Princes St

Grafton Road

WESTERN PARK

Howe Street

Pitt Street

Vincent Street

Mayoral Drive

White St

Airedale St

Wakefield St

Paul Street

Mount St

Symonds Street

St Pauls

CARLAW PARK

Hopetoun Street

Greys Avenue

Turner St

City Road

Liverpool Street

Whitaker Pl

AUCKLAND

Valkrie Fountain

MYERS PARK

Payton

Upper Queen's St

Rotunda

Teahouse

Karangahape Road

St James's St

East St

France St N

NEWTON

Grafton Bridge

GRAFTON

Auckland City Hospital

Winter Gardens

Auckland War Memorial Museum

DOMAIN

Cricket Pavilion

Grafton Road

Park Road

Seafield View Road

Park Avenue

Glasgow

Boyle

George Street

NEWMARKET

Carlton Gore Road

Huntley Avenue

Southern Motorway

Mountain Road

Maunganahui Road

Khyber Pass

Crowhurst Street

Kingdon St

Morgan St

Boston Road

Lauder Road

Hamilton

Beach Haven

Warkworth

Shoal Bay

Bayswater

Rangitoto Island

Northcote

Mt Victoria

Browns Island

Auckland Harbour Bridge

Devonport

Rangitoto Channel

Waitemata Harbour

Auckland

Ponsonby

Parnell

Kelly Tarlton's Antarctic Encounter & Underwater World

Melanesian Mission

St Heliers

MOTAT

Western Springs

Zoo

Mt Eden

Remuera

Orakei

Mission Bay

Glen Innes

Tamaki River

Mt Albert

Mt Eden

Epsom

Ellerslie

Pakuranga Heights

Royal Oak

One Tree Hill

Mt Roskill

Cornwall Park

Onehunga

Lynfield

Mangere Bridge

Manukau Harbour

Otara

0 ——————— 5 km
0 ——————— 5 miles

Puketutu Island

as the city itself – which crowds the harbour with as many as 1,000 sailing craft of all sizes in an organised mayhem of spectacle and competition.

A nation of boat owners produced a team of world-beating sailors. Team New Zealand was operating on a budget a fraction the size of its competitors' when it snatched the coveted yachting trophy the America's Cup in 1995 and successfully defended it in 2000. The pain of losing the cup to the affluent Swiss-based Alinghi syndicate in 2003 was somewhat eased by the knowledge that the victor boat's key crew members were all New Zealanders. With the America's Cup on hold due to court battles, the team gained their revenge in February 2009 when, skippered by Dean Barker, they won the Louis Vuitton Cup Pacific Series against Alinghi.

Technically, the Auckland region is made up of four cities. Auckland City itself is bordered by Manukau (the country's most populous municipal area) to the south, Waitakere to the west and North Shore City across the Waitemata. But Auckland City – which

has 30 percent of the region's and 10 percent of the nation's population – is undeniably the country's economic powerhouse. Auckland's population increased by almost 25 percent in the 1990s, but the growth has slowed somewhat since, with numbers rising only 12 percent between 2001 and 2009. Aucklanders produce and consume a disproportionate share of the national wealth, and this fact engenders a fair degree of hostility and resentment from the less well-off who choose to live in smaller cities and provincial centres.

Turbulent history

A geological newborn, Auckland came to life with a bang. Some 53 volcanoes were created by eruptions which started between 60,000 and 140,000 years ago. The youngest – the bush-clad Rangitoto Island *(see panel, below)*, whose blue-green hulk dominates the downtown waterfront view – last erupted only six centuries ago, burying a Maori settlement on adjoining Motutapu Island.

The city's human history is no less turbulent than its geological past. The

On Anniversary Day, Auckland's yachts come out to race in New Zealand's largest regatta. The city has the highest boat ownership per capita in the world, and it's easy to see why, with the myriad islands of the Hauraki Gulf lying beyond the beaches and bays of the Waitemata Harbour.

BELOW: Rangitoto at sunset.

Land of Lava

Auckland sits on top of a large volcanic field that has produced around 53 cones in the last 140,000 years, and from wherever you stand, a grassy volcanic slope is never far from view. Three of the more prominent examples include Mount Eden, One Tree Hill and Rangitoto; all offer a range of walks and, like many of Auckland's larger cones, offer panoramic city and harbour views. Rangitoto, a dormant marine volcano, can be easily reached by ferry (from Quay Street in downtown Auckland, departing every 1½ hours. The journey takes 25 minutes and costs NZ$25.) New Zealand's largest pohutukawa forest covers the island from top to toe and provides splendid viewing in summer, when its delicate red blossoms fall to the ground – which, being composed of black lava, creates a striking effect.

ancestors of the Maori are believed to have arrived from eastern Polynesia around AD 800 (although the debate continues). Traditional lore tells of incessant bloody inter-tribal warfare which gave Auckland its early Maori name, Tamaki Makaurau, meaning "battle of a hundred lovers": the poetic description alluded not to a love story but to the conflict, which was as fierce as a suitors' rivalry.

Contact between Maori and the white people they would come to call *Pakeha* had been occurred haphazardly in this part of New Zealand from the 1770s as traders and whale-hunters sought shelter along the coast. The British settlement of Auckland officially began with the visit of Samuel Marsden in 1820 *(see panel opposite)*, and the developing town became the national capital for a time following the signing of the Treaty of Waitangi in 1840.

Auckland's recent growth has been fuelled by the immigration boom of the 1990s, with an influx of Asians – wealthy immigrants in the southeastern areas of Howick and legions of students seeking a Western education. The change has caused palpable unease among long-established Kiwis who feel the ethnic composition of the city is changing too fast, but no one can deny that it has breathed new life into the place, making it reinvent itself as a vibrant Pacific-Asian metropolis.

An early arrival described Auckland as "a few tents and huts and a sea of fern stretching as far as the eye could see". Today, the gaze of the modern visitor ranges over a sea of suburbs. All four cities of sprawling Auckland cover 1,016 sq km (392 sq miles), an area considerably larger than London; in proportion to its population of 1.3 million, Greater Auckland is one of the world's largest metropolitan areas; today, however, land is running out and residential construction goes up, not out.

Generally, Aucklanders live, work and shop in the suburban hinterland, which is dotted with busy shopping malls, and venture into the city only on special occasions. From the mid-1980s the inner city area developed rapidly, with the building of office towers and (often shoddily constructed) apartment blocks. In aesthetic and heritage terms it has been something of a disaster; to some extent Auckland has butchered its past and replaced elegant Victorian buildings with cheap, characterless high-density apartments. Noteworthy modern architecture is lamentably rare in the city, although some exciting new developments have taken place in the Viaduct Harbour *(see opposite)*, the site of the America's Cup Village.

Auckland Harbour

Urban sprawl can make getting around the Greater Auckland area something of a challenge. Taxis are expensive by world standards, although there is a fairly efficient system of buses and ferries. The city centre's main historic highlights are, however, easily reached on foot.

The sturdy red-brick **Ferry Building** Ⓐ on Quay Street at the foot of Queen Street is a good place to start an exploratory ramble. The 1912 build-

ing, which once housed the offices of harbour officials, now contains two of downtown's better restaurants, and behind it you can board the ferries to the North Shore and the islands of the Hauraki Gulf (*for details see margin, page 146*).

If you stand in the street with your back to the building, the Viaduct Harbour precinct, including the excellent **New Zealand National Maritime Museum** Ⓑ (daily 9am–6pm; entrance fee; tel: 09-3730 8003; www.nzmaritime.org), is barely three minutes' walk to your right. Its collection covers maritime history all the way back to the earliest Polynesian explorers. Vessels on display include the *Rapaki* floating steam crane and *KZ1*, the yacht that launched New Zealand's America's Cup obsession when it sailed and lost in San Diego in 1988.

New Zealand's defence of the America's Cup prompted the redevelopment of the **Viaduct Harbour**. Site of the Southern Hemisphere's largest superyacht marina, the Viaduct is also a fashionable, if overpriced, restaurant and bar precinct offering that conjunction of fine food and water views which so many find irresistible. When the ostentatious super-luxury yachts are in port, particularly at the height of summer, they are a major attraction in themselves. At the northeast end of Viaduct Harbour is the **Auckland Hilton**, on the water's edge at Prince's Wharf, cleverly designed to suggest a cruise liner and one of Auckland's better examples of postmodern architecture.

Just across **Quay Street** is **Queen Elizabeth Square**, dominated by the city's main transport hub, **Britomart**. Housed in the former Chief Post Office, the neoclassical building dates back to 1910. As you leave the square to cross **Customs Street**, look again to your right (west). A block away, on the corner of **Albert Street** is the **Old Customhouse** Ⓒ, which was the financial heart of Auckland for more than 80 years. Designed in French Renaissance style, the building was completed in 1889 and is one of the last remaining examples of monumental Victorian architecture to be found in a central business district where the wrecker's ball has been far too busy.

*For a bird's-eye view of the city, try a half-hour guided climb over the **Auckland Harbour Bridge**. A maze of catwalks and surprising twists and turns add to the thrill of this outdoor adventure. Contact **Auckland Bridge Climb**, Curran Street, Westhaven Reserve, tel: 09-361 2000; www.bungy.co.nz.*

BELOW: the Ferry Building.

A Bargain Buy

British Auckland officially began with the visit of the enterprising Reverend Samuel Marsden in 1820. The Sydney-based missionary named the fledgling settlement (the town of Russell, further north, was already established as the main settlement on the North Island – *see page 153*) after the Earl of Auckland, George Eden, the Viceroy of India. This intrepid preacher crossed the Auckland isthmus on board the sailing ship *Coromandel* in November, the first European to do so, and his arrival heralded a process of land purchase which remains deeply problematic to this day.

It is more than likely that the Maori – whose traditional relationship with the land rendered the concept of ownership as meaningless – did not believe they were selling their real estate but rather accepting gifts in return for letting the new settlers live on their land.

Certainly the newcomers got a bargain: they purchased the area that now comprises the heart of Auckland for 50 blankets, 20 pairs of trousers, 20 shirts and other assorted sundries plus £50 cash, with another £6 paid the following year. The 1,200 hectares (3,000 acres) that the British settlers purchased covered the area from today's Freemans Bay to Parnell and inland as far as Mount Eden. Today, just 0.4 hectare (1 acre) of downtown land in the city is worth at least NZ$20 million.

At 328 metres (1,076ft), the Sky Tower is the tallest building in the Southern Hemisphere. This being New Zealand, it has attracted the bungee-jumpers: in 1998, a 192-metre (629ft) jump took place here, which remains the world's highest.

BELOW: Queen Street, in the heart of downtown Auckland.

Queen Street central

Downtown Auckland keeps long hours, and shops seeking the tourist dollar stay open until late in the evening on weekdays and through the weekends. Yet **Queen Street** ❶ – the city's main drag, traditionally known as the "Golden Mile" – does not glitter as it once did. Cheap noodle houses and Internet cafés cater to the huge number of Asian students, and convenience stores serve inner-city apartment dwellers, although there is also a sprinkling of upmarket boutiques and fashion brand stores. Much of corporate New Zealand headquarters itself in the Queen Street valley, which can be gloomy and sparsely peopled outside business hours.

Some excellent restaurants do good business in the streets that radiate out from Freyberg Place, but it's the inner suburbs – particularly Parnell to the east and Ponsonby to the southwest – where some of the city's best eateries are to be found. If you're so inclined, check out the touristy souvenir stores in the lower part of Queen Street: the prices, while not cheap, will not be extortionate, though half of the merchandise will be made in China – check the label.

As you walk south up the main street, pause at the intersection of Queen and Fort streets. Waves lapped the shore at this spot less than 150 years ago when Shortland Street, a block further up, was the main street; back then Queen Street was a bush-covered gully along which ran a canal serving as an open sewer.

You will have hardly failed to notice, some 500 metres (550 yards) to the southwest, the cloud-piercing **Sky Tower** ❷ (daily 8.30am–10.30pm, until 11pm on Fri and Sat; entrance fee; tel: 09-363 6000; www.skycity. co.nz) on Hobson Street, the western ridge of the valley. The tallest structure in the Southern Hemisphere at 328 metres (1,076ft), it was the butt of many jokes when it was built in the mid-1990s: critics saw its giant syringe shape as an apt symbol of the gambling addiction being generated by the casino at its foot. But it has rapidly become a familiar and dramatic feature of the city skyline – best seen from the

harbour or from Devonport's North Head. Visitors are whisked in high-speed lifts to the top for a view, which, on a clear day, can stretch more than 80km (50 miles). Those less prone to vertigo might like to consider the 192-metre (630ft) high base-jump off the tower (contact Skyjump, tel: 09-368 1835; www.skyjump.co.nz) – New Zealand's adventure-sport fixation is not restricted to the countryside.

Civic pride

Back down to earth on Queen Street, and some 400 metres (1,300ft) to the south is **Aotea Square** **F**, dominated by the monolithic **Auckland City Council** administration building, and, on the western side of the square, the city's main cultural complex, the **Aotea Centre**. Built over the howls of derision from those who could not understand why the city's pre-eminent public building was not being sited on the waterfront, the Aotea Centre is an impersonal and unwelcoming space. Its 2,300-seat multi-purpose theatre is acoustically problematic, to say the least – most classical music performances take place in the beautifully restored and acoustically warm **Town Hall** on the square's southeastern boundary – but it is popular as a convention centre. The Aotea Centre, The Civic, Auckland Town Hall and Aotea Square all come under the collective administrative umbrella, **The Edge** (tel: 09-309 2677). For programme details, check www.the-edge.co.nz.

Just down the road to the north at the corner with Wellesley Street is the opulent **Civic Theatre** **G**. Built in 1929, this was one of the world's finest atmospheric picture palaces, though now is mostly used for touring musicals and shows. Its ornate construction was a sign of the times – it employed many hundreds of tradesmen during the Great Depression – and the labyrinthine stairways are watched over by hundreds of glittering elephants. From 1997 to 1999 it underwent a multi-million-dollar refurbishment for the millennium, its mock sky, complete with twinkling stars, making it one of the city's finest sights.

Aotea Square and the Civic Theatre are separated by the city's major cinema centre. A block to the east in **Lorne Street** is the **Central City Library** (Mon–Fri 9am–8pm, Sat–Sun 10am–4pm; tel: 09-377 0209). Even in the internet age, its reading room remains popular with homesick travellers and immigrants devouring the foreign press.

A further block east on the corner of Kitchener and Wellesley streets is one half of the **Auckland Art Gallery** **H** (daily 10am–5pm; free, except for special exhibitions; free daily tour of collections at 2pm; tel: 09-307 7700; www.aucklandartgallery.govt.nz), called the **Main Gallery** since it was joined by the equally unimaginatively christened **New Gallery** in 1995 across the street. The former holds historical collections while the latter has fine exhibitions of contemporary art from New Zealand and overseas. Visitors are likely to be intrigued by the idealised 19th-century portraits of

Auckland's pre-eminent private art gallery is the Gow Langsford Gallery opposite the Auckland Art Gallery in Kitchener Street. Many of New Zealand's leading contemporary artists and a selection of international artists are represented here. Mon–Fri 10am–6pm, Sat 10am–4pm; tel: 09-303 4290; www.gowlangsford gallery.com.

BELOW: Auckland Art Gallery.

Albert Park combines Edwardian design features with some mildly incongruous contemporary sculpture.

Maori by Gottfried Lindauer and Charles Goldie in the Main Gallery.

The floral clock at 33–43 Princes Street, constructed in 1953 to commemorate Queen Elizabeth II's first visit to New Zealand, marks the main CBD pedestrian access to **Albert Park**, set on a ridge of thick ash formed by early volcanic eruptions. Once the site of a Maori village and then a defence post, it became a park administered by Auckland City Council from 1879 onwards. Paths, gardens and trees were established, and an elaborate Victorian fountain was built as a centrepiece. Albert Park House, formerly the gardener's cottage (now housing an aggregation of clocks and ceramics), was added along with a statue of Queen Victoria, unveiled in 1899 to mark her 60th jubilee.

From the park you can enter the leafy grounds of the **University of Auckland**. At the corner of Princes Street and Waterloo Quadrant, in part of the university grounds is the **Old Government House ❶**, built in 1856 as the home of the Governor. The building appears to be made of stone,

though in fact its exterior cladding is all kauri, the wood of the magnificent species of tree which once dominated the New Zealand bush and was the building material of choice until well into the 19th century.

The university's central attraction, however, a few metres south on Princes Street, is the **Old Arts Building ❶** with its intricate clock tower. It was completed in 1926 in Gothic style and immediately dubbed The Wedding Cake by locals because of its decorative pinnacled white-stone construction.

Note the refurbished **High Court**, some 250 metres (270 yards) to the northeast, where a series of grinning griffins and gargoyles adorn the exterior walls. It stands near the corner of Anzac Avenue and Parliament Street, whose name is another vestige of Auckland's former status as New Zealand's capital. It was only pressure from the gold-rich South Island and new settlements further south in the North Island that resulted in the movement of the capital from Auckland to Wellington in 1865.

East of the city centre

Continue east through the park known as **Constitution Hill**, named after the fact that businessmen took a "constitutional" walk up its steep slope from their Parnell homes to their city offices. Follow Parnell Rise, turning into Parnell Road for 2km (1¼ miles) and walk up through **Parnell ⓚ**. It's an oddity of the city's history – some say it's because the upper classes didn't like the sun in their eyes on the way to and from work in the city – that the suburbs east of Queen Street have always been the city's more affluent. So it's no accident that Parnell oozes a refined style. It's also the gateway to **Newmarket**, a busy shopping strip which is home to some of fashion's big-name outlets, and **Remuera**, where the serious, old money lives. Parnell largely overcame the unfortunate faux heritage refurbishment of the 1970s, which hideously attempted to re-imagine it as a pioneer village in low-maintenance materials.

At the end of Parnell Road, past the Anglican Cathedral, enter the **Auckland Domain** by turning right on Maunsell Road. This 75-hectare (185-acre) park is the city's oldest, with duck ponds, playing fields, traditional statuary and the Wintergardens – two large glasshouses displaying temperate and tropical plants.

This route provides easy access to the **Auckland War Memorial Museum ⓛ** (daily 10am–5pm; entrance fee, children free; tel: 09-306 7067; www.auckland museum.com), which presides over the rambling grounds of the Domain. Despite the name, the museum is not devoted to war artefacts but deals with subjects as diverse as natural history, ethnology and archaeology. The building was erected in 1929 as a memorial to soldiers who died in World War I. It houses one of the world's finest displays of Maori and Polynesian culture, with some artefacts dating as far back as AD 1200. A highlight is the 35-metre (115ft) war canoe *Te-Toki-A-Tapiri* (The Axe of Tapiri), carved in 1836 from a single giant *totara* tree and designed to seat up to 100 warriors.

Southwest of the centre

Auckland is the world's biggest Polynesian city. Almost 250,000 New Zealand-

WHERE

The impressive Manaia Maori cultural performance takes place at the Auckland War Memorial Museum (3 times daily, Apr–Dec 11am, noon and 1.30pm; 4 times daily Jan–Mar 11am, 12am, 1.30pm and 2.30pm). Admission to the 30-minute show is by ticket only (NZ$25 adult and NZ$12.50 child). Tel: 09-306 7924, 0800-256 873, or book direct at 09-306 7924.

BELOW: the Auckland War Memorial Museum.

WHERE

Auckland i-SITE Visitors Centres are found at the following locations: 137 Quay Street, Princes Wharf, Viaduct Harbour (daily 8am–8pm) and Atrium Sky City, corner Victoria and Federal streets (daily 8am–8pm). Enquiries at tel: 09-979 2333; www.aucklandnz.com.

ers – about one in 16 – are of Pacific Island ethnicity, with more than 60 percent of them residing in the Auckland region. In some cases, Auckland's Polynesian population outnumbers those back at home (for instance, nine out of 10 Niueans live here) and in most cases, more than half are New Zealand-born. Most of the Pacific peoples settled in the central part of the city in the mid-20th century, particularly in Ponsonby and adjoining Grey Lynn, until soaring property prices and the accompanying gentrification of those suburbs saw the islanders migrate again, to Manukau City *(see page 143)*.

Heading west from the Domain for some 1.25km (¾ mile) brings you to **Karangahape Road ⓜ** – known to locals as K Road – which runs west from Grafton Bridge, and where traces of the city's Pacific connections linger in shops displaying brilliantly coloured floral cloth, and where the occasional taro, yam, papaya and other tropical foods can be found. These days the vibe in this part of town is distinctly Indian, and for most visitors this is the

raffish but undeniably charming side of the city (even if the western end is home to some of the city's sex industry – the rest of which lurks downtown in Fort Street). Renewal and development have given the area a facelift, which is not an unalloyed improvement for those who enjoy urban diversity; it will take some years yet for the blandness to become completely entrenched.

About 1km (⅔ mile) north of K Road is the **Victoria Park Market ⓝ** (daily 9am–6pm; free; www.victoria-park-market.co.nz), built on the site (and under the tall brick chimney) of what was the city's rubbish destructor until the 1970s. The market is a seven-day tourist lure and the quality of most merchandise is high, although the prices can be too. Retail fruit and vegetable stalls operate here, though this is no atmospheric farmers' market.

Further west still – a 10-minute walk up Franklin Road or a short bus ride up the hill – is **Ponsonby ⓞ**. This ribbon of road, festooned with the best selection of restaurants in town, is the sister of Parnell, about the same distance from Queen Street. Once home to hirsute stu-

BELOW: an evening view of the sprawling city.

dents and whole streets of Pacific Island immigrant families, Ponsonby today is filled with refurbished turn-of-the-19th-century villas on pocket-handkerchief sections which fetch ludicrous prices at auctions, and the streets are full of the elegant and the self-regarding. It's not exactly Rodeo Drive – many of the city's more creative types live on its narrow streets – but it's definitely Auckland's Golden Mile.

Along Tamaki Drive

A return to the Ferry Building is as good a place as any to start Auckland's waterfront drive – the ribbon of tarmac that runs east from the port around the harbourside makes for a scenic tour of the city's waterfront. Quay Street becomes **Tamaki Drive**, which winds some 8km (5 miles) along the seafront. The safe beaches are good for swimming at high tide and excellent for picnics. Rangitoto Island looms ahead, seemingly close enough to touch. The footpath is busy with cyclists and walkers on sunny weekends, and bicycle-, boat- and windsurfer-hire businesses ply a roaring trade.

En route, **Kelly Tarlton's Antarctic Encounter and Underwater World P** (daily 9am–6pm; entrance fee; tel: 09-528 0603, 0800-805 050; www.kellytarltons.co.nz) can be considered a virtually compulsory stop. This world-class facility is constructed in what used to be a sewage pumping station before Auckland stopped pouring its effluent into the harbour in the 1960s. Today dozens of varieties of fish, including sharks, can be viewed from a moving walkway passing through a huge transparent tunnel. A 41-year-old 250kg (550lb) stingray with a metre-wide wingspan, named Phoebe, is the star attraction at Stingray Bay. The Antarctic section features a Snow Cat ride to view the colony of King and Gentoo penguins.

Mount Eden and Cornwall Park

Towering just 3km (2 miles) south of the city centre is the 196-metre (643ft) volcanic cone of **Mount Eden Q**,

The 19th-century town hall at Ponsonby, one of the city's most exclusive neigbourhoods.

BELOW: the Antarctic Encounter and Underwater World.

Taking the plunge at the Waitemata Harbour.

BELOW: the view from One Tree Hill.

Auckland's highest point. Long extinct in volcanic terms, it offers a dramatic 360-degree panorama of the region almost as good as the view from the Sky Tower. In an old lava pit on the eastern side, at 24 Omana Avenue, is **Eden Garden** (daily 9am–4.30pm; entrance fee; tel: 09-638 8395; www.edengarden.co.nz), which provides a heady floral display, including the largest collection of camellias in the Southern Hemisphere. It was created in 1964 on the site of an abandoned quarry and is entirely manned by volunteers. A café operates on site from 10am–4pm daily.

Another 3km (2 miles) southeast, in **Cornwall Park** ❼ (daily 7am–9pm; free; tel: 09-630 8485; www.cornwallpark.co.nz), is the landmark cone of **One Tree Hill** and the obelisk which crowns the tomb of the "Father of Auckland", Sir John Logan Campbell, the entrepreneur who set up Auckland's first commercial store at the bottom of Shortland Street on 21 December 1840. Campbell was the city's most prominent businessman until his death in 1912 at the age of 95.

The 135-hectare (334-acre) estate encompassing One Tree Hill, which he donated to the people of Auckland after becoming the city mayor, was given its name in 1901 when Campbell hosted Britain's Duke and Duchess of Cornwall. He also built **Acacia Cottage** in 1841: now Auckland's oldest building, the restored cottage is preserved in Cornwall Park at the base of One Tree Hill.

The Maori name for One Tree Hill is Te Totara-i-ahua, in deference to the sacred *totara* tree that stood here until 1852, when the early settlers replaced it with a pine. Today, the "One Tree" sobriquet is in fact something of a misnomer: the lone pine tree that used to stand on the summit was cut down in 2002, after failing to recover from an attack by a chainsaw-wielding Maori activist who was seeking to draw attention to political grievances.

Transport Museum and Zoo

At Western Springs, just off the northwestern motorway, the **Museum of Transport and Technology** ❾ (MOTAT; daily 10am–5pm; entrance fee; tel: 09-815 5800; www.motat.org.nz) has over 300,000 items in its collection, including working vintage vehicles, aircraft and machinery and excellent hands-on applied science displays. The museum also has an aircraft built by New Zealander Richard Pearse, who, some devotees claim, flew it in March 1903, several months before the Wright Brothers. Volunteer enthusiasts operate many exhibits at the weekends.

A brief ride from MOTAT in an old tram (or, alternatively, a pleasant walk eastwards around the lake at Western Springs Park) leads to **Auckland Zoo** ❼ (daily 9.30am–5.30pm, last admission 4.15pm; entrance fee; tel: 09-360 3800; www.aucklandzoo.co.nz), where you can see the kiwi, New Zealand's unique flightless bird, and the tuatara, a "living fossil" which has not changed since the age of the dinosaurs (*for more on these and other local wildlife see pages 100–103*). ❑

Trendsetting Kiwi Fashion

Something of a late starter in the global sartorial stakes, New Zealand's fashion industry has now come of age

New Zealand fashion may not have fully come of age just yet, but somewhere around the turn of the new millennium it developed the ability to walk. At that time, New Zealand designers – like others in an industry where, if imitation is the sincerest form of flattery, everyone is constantly paying compliments to everyone else – began developing a distinctive style of their own.

In 1997, four homegrown labels – Moontide, World, Wallace Rose and Zambesi – took part in Australian Fashion Week. Two years later, Kiwi designers took part in London Fashion Week. "There seems to be a remarkable difference between Australia and New Zealand. New Zealanders have a darker outlook. Less show-offy. More intellectual," observed French *Vogue*. In 2005, the labels Sabatini, NOM*D, WORLD and NG were showcased at the prestigious Tranoi show during Paris Fashion Week for the first time. All, plus Zambesi, made a return visit in 2006, launching New Zealand fashion further into new global markets.

Overseas fashion writers and opinion shapers are no longer the novelty at major New Zealand fashion events that they once were. Whatever the truth of *Vogue*'s pronouncement, the New Zealand style is less individualistic than it is a brilliant assimilation of a variety of influences. As in so many other areas, the country's isolation has forced the locals to come up with their own solutions – in fashion no less than in agriculture. While still heavily influenced by Northern Hemisphere designs, many designers draw on Polynesian styles, while others amass a globally eclectic mix and turn it into a coherent whole. (Much contemporary young Polynesian fashion, in turn, is strongly influenced by US hip-hop culture.)

Often those who do best in the fashion industry are those who market themselves as their brand – Karen Walker, Trelise Cooper and Sharon Ng are notable examples. Many of the prominent designers (and labels) who are matching local popularity with some overseas success – Walker, Cooper,

Kate Sylvester, Scotties, Zambesi and WORLD – are based in Auckland. But New Zealand's biggest city doesn't have the field entirely to itself.

While Wellington has stores representing the better-known local labels, local names to look out for include Andrea Moore, Madcat, Ricochet and Voon. Leading labels NOM*D, Carlson, Mild Red and Dot Com all call Dunedin home, and the student influence gives a lot of the city's fashion a slightly funkier air than the fashion favoured in other centres. Well supported, Dunedin is a hub for up-and-coming designers.

Other invigorating fashion is occurring on the fringes, produced by names that may well be big one day, or, fashion being fashion, disappear altogether. Away from Auckland's High Street, Lorne Street and Chancery you'll find the odd gem on Karangahape Road, but to find what bubbles beneath Auckland's polished veneer, head to the small studios of Ponsonby Road. Here, more often than not, as you make a purchase you will come face to face with the designers themselves in their role as cashier, fabric cutter and seamstress all rolled into one. Elsewhere, cutting-edge design is likely to be found in various small studios dotted around Dunedin.

As for men's fashion, for a Kiwi male to care about his appearance is still, except in certain circumstances, regarded as anomalous. ❑

RIGHT: local fashion designers are gaining status.

AUCKLAND'S SURROUNDINGS

Map on page 143

Auckland's hinterland exhibits different flavours depending on whether you travel west, north, south – or east, to the 47 islands of the Hauraki Gulf

Auckland is a sprawling city, the urban area extending for miles along the shores of the Hauraki Gulf, far to the south around Manukau Harbour and west to the fringes of the Waitakere vineyards. Beyond the suburbs, the countryside quickly becomes attractive, particularly to the north and west, where the kauri forests of the Waitakere Ranges are a major attraction. To the east, the blue waters of the Hauraki Gulf are dotted with islands, making this one of the world's most rewarding sailing destinations. Many of the islands are stunningly beautiful, notably Great Barrier Island, which can be reached from downtown Auckland in a couple of hours by ferry. The coasts on both sides of the northern peninsula extending towards Northland are blessed with wonderful sandy beaches, rather more windswept on the western shore.

Aucklanders are passionately, obsessively, blindly devoted to the motor car, as the rush-hour snarl on the motorways quickly reveals. Decades of political prevarication have prevented the development of an effective, useful rail system, and the buses all too often become gridlocked in traffic at busy times of day. Any visitor who wishes to avoid an eye-watering taxi bill will want to rent a car to make the most of a short stay by exploring beyond the city limits. Alternatively, there is no shortage of organised tours which take in the most important sights in the city's environs.

To the west

Travelling from downtown Auckland, the visitor's first taste of the western suburb of **Waitakere City** and its environs will be at **Henderson ❶**, west of SH16 at the Lincoln Road turnoff. The valley here was settled early by Dalmatian and Croatian wine-growers. Today, their dynasties are commemorated in many of the street names, and the roads of modern Waitakere are studded with vineyards, some world-class, others old family operations whose rough reds are still sold in half-gallon flagons.

Main attractions
WAITAKERE WINERIES
KAURI FORESTS,
WAITAKERE RANGES
MURIWAI BEACH
DEVONPORT
HAURAKI GULF ISLANDS
GREAT BARRIER ISLAND

LEFT: abseiling in the Waitakere Ranges west of Auckland.
BELOW: budding Kumeu farmer.

The Waitakere Ranges are known for their magnificent kauri trees.

BELOW: red-and-yellow flags mark safe places for swimming.

Beyond the city limits, stay on SH16 and you'll come to **Kumeu** ❷, 20km (12 miles) past the Henderson turnoff, where weekend farmers run horses on their farms. Here are to be found some of the more substantial vineyards, like **Kumeu River** (www.kumeuriver.co.nz), **Nobilo** (www.nobilo.co.nz) and **Matua Valley** (www.matua.co.nz).

In common with most of the developed world, the suburban areas of west Auckland are lined with shopping malls, bland commercial and light industrial developments. However, just beyond this, a mere 20km (12 miles) from downtown Auckland, lie the thickly forested **Waitakere Ranges**. Here tall kauri trees, giant ferns and nikau palms create a beautiful environment for bushwalkers – known locally as trampers – and for filmmakers. The popular TV series *Xena* and *Hercules* were filmed here in the **Waitakere Ranges Regional Park**. The ranges are easily explored by following the aptly named **Scenic Drive** (SH24) which runs for 28km (17 miles) along their spine from

Titirangi to Swanson. Some 5km (3 miles) from the **Titirangi** ❸ end of the drive, the **Arataki Visitors Centre** (daily 9am–5pm in summer, 10am–4pm in winter; tel: 09-817 4941) is the place to plan detailed explorations, with a series of walks of varying degrees of difficulty and suggestions for camping out overnight.

West coast beaches

Beyond the ranges, the west gets truly wild: the edge of the land is stitched by a line of black-sand surf beaches, windswept and pounded by the waves of the Tasman Sea. The northernmost beach, 32km (20-mile) long **Muriwai** ❹, is actually designated a public road (4WD only), leading north to Kaipara Harbour. Close to the township (also called Muriwai) is a gannet colony which, seen up close from viewing platforms, is one of the region's great sights. The breeding season, from September to May, is the best time to visit. Muriwai was one of the most important visual inspirations for the late Colin McCahon (*see page 62*), New Zealand's preeminent artist.

Waitakere City

Auckland's frontier, like the New World's, is out west. Waitakere City, 15km (9 miles) west of downtown Auckland on State Highway (SH) 16, burst into life in the mid-1950s when a causeway road was laid across part of the upper harbour, bringing the west much closer to the city. For all that, it still maintains a distinctive wildness. Residents are collectively nicknamed Westies, but any generalisation masks the city's variety. Artists, craftspeople, back-to-nature bush-lovers and substantial Maori and Polynesian populations are all part of Waitakere's mix. Well known internationally as an eco-city, even the council is in on the act, its new buildings winning several architectural and environmental awards for their green roof, covered in tussock, sustainable design and clean lines.

At the southernmost limit of Waitakere City and the Waitakere Ranges is Whatipu, where the sea seems to boil as it pours into the tidal Manukau Harbour. In between, the line of beaches raked by the sea includes **Piha**, the surfers' paradise and a favourite of holidaymakers, and **Karekare ❺**, where the spectacular opening sequence of Jane Campion's *The Piano* was filmed.

Be aware that these west coast beaches are very dangerous for swimming and their death tolls include many unwary tourists. Beaches are patrolled during the summer months, and for your own safety it is wise to swim between the flags. Also be wary of rogue waves that have been known to overwhelm people sitting on the rocks.

South Auckland

The words "South Auckland" are loaded for Aucklanders. The suburbs strung out on each side of the southern motorway beyond Otahuhu unquestionably include some the region's most economically depressed neighbourhoods – although there are parts of **Manukau City**, the region's southern city, that are extremely affluent. Here is to be found the social and physical landscape depicted in the 1994 movie *Once Were Warriors*, which showed the cost of drinking, domestic violence and gang warfare on Maori families.

Otahuhu ❻, 14km (9 miles) south of Auckland on SH1, gives a good glimpse of Manukau's cultural diversity: wander down the main street, where Asian and Pacific traders jostle cheek-by-jowl.

Some 3km (2 miles) further south is the colourful and noisy **Otara Market** (Sat only 6am–noon) on Newbury Street in the Otara Shopping Centre (take the East Tamaki Road/Otara turn-off on SH1). It's a great place to shop for souvenirs, not just because they are better value for money than the shops in the tourist traps, but because of the obvious authenticity. Standing in the midst of this multicultural community is **Mangere Mount**, which rises to 100 metres (330ft) and overlooks Manukau Harbour.

Travel another 5km (3 miles) south to **Rainbow's End** (daily 10am–5pm; entrance fee; tel: 09-262 2030; www.

The landmark Kiwi film Once Were Warriors, *based on a novel by Alan Duff and directed by Lee Tamahori, was released in 1994 to rave reviews. Set in south Auckland, it takes a painful look at the problems that plague working-class Maori families.*

BELOW: surfer on Piha beach.

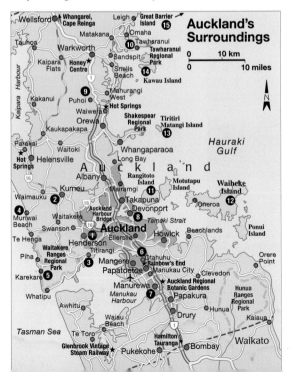

WHERE

The Riverhead Ferry's riverway and inner harbour chartered cruises provide a unique view of Auckland's sights and suburbs. They depart from Hobson West Marina, Viaduct Basin (tel: 09-376 0819; www. riverheadferry.co.nz).

rainbowsend.co.nz), the country's premier theme park, with crazy rides you won't find anywhere else in New Zealand. If you like that kind of thing, the park's "Power Surge" ride is comparable to a spin and tumble in a washing machine.

Elsewhere in Manukau, about 5km (3 miles) south of Rainbow's End, are the **Auckland Regional Botanic Gardens** (daily 8am–6pm; free; tel: 09-267 1457; www.aucklandbotanicgardens. co.nz) near **Manurewa** ❼, with a dazzling variety of species.

Manukau Harbour, which marks the city's western border, lacks the scenic charm of the east coast's Waitemata Harbour. At low tide its mudflats stretch for miles, and are home to numerous species of wader and other birds. It's uncrowded, too: many Aucklanders ignore it, partly because it used to be polluted with industrial and domestic run-off. The clean-up has been a triumph of conservation planning.

North Auckland

The opening of the **Auckland Harbour Bridge** in 1959 transformed the region immediately north of Auckland from countryside into city almost overnight. At a stroke, what had been a string of sleepy seaside settlements backed by rolling pastureland became part of the city.

Today the bridge, a 1km (2/3-mile) long "coathanger" stretching from the north end of the city centre at Fanshawe Street to Northcote Point across the harbour, carries an average of 141,000 vehicles a day. City and harbour views can be enjoyed with the help of an enterprising operator, **Auckland Bridge Climb** (tel: 09-361 2000; www.aucklandbridge-climb.co.nz) which offers a 1½-hour guided climb. This being New Zealand, there's a chance to take a bungee-jump off the bridge at the end of the tour. Two things you can't do on the bridge, strangely enough, are walk and ride a bicycle.

On the far side is North Shore City, a sprawling area of suburbia and industrial development fringed by beautiful white-sand beaches commanding tremendous views of Takapuna Beach, Milford Beach, Mairangi Bay and Browns Bay.

BELOW: Devonport basks in the sunshine.

Divine Devonport

A 10-minute ferry ride (30 times daily) across the harbour from downtown Auckland, Devonport is a waterside haven full of character and charm. Its streets are lined with preserved colonial villas and bungalows, many of them accommodating cafés and small boutiques selling local crafts, antiques and collectables. There are sandy beaches to relax on, and an enormous public playground for children is located right on the waterfront. Looming overhead are the volcanic cones of Mount Victoria and North Head, affording fine views of downtown Auckland and the eastern bays. At North Head there are old gun emplacements and connecting tunnels to explore, or linger in town following the Old Devonport Walk, a mapped route linking historical sites and museums of note such as the Devonport Historical Museum.

The best way to reach nearby **Devonport ❽** is to hop aboard one of the regular ferries departing from the Quay Street Ferry Building *(see margin, page 146)* in downtown Auckland. This is a decidedly affluent area with many grand Victorian houses, arts and craft galleries and a plethora of bars and cafés *(see panel, below left)*.

To the north of Devonport the coastline becomes an attractive procession of sheltered coves and white-sand beaches. One of these, Takapuna, has good shopping and a popular beach overlooking Rangitoto Island. Long Bay is a large regional park offering several good hikes.

Rodney District

But it's still further north, beyond North Shore City, that the day-tripper really begins to reap rewards. The newly completed **Northern Motorway Tollway** has opened up access to the region as never before.

The road bypasses the suburbs of Orewa and Whangaparaoa (the name means "bay of whales"), a region that was semi-rural pastureland and beach cottages barely a generation ago, but is now Auckland's northernmost dormitory suburb, and as a result has lost much of its former charm. There are some pleasant spots, though: the suburban neighbourhoods run down to safe swimming beaches and the well-manicured **Shakespear Regional Park** at the tip of Whangaparaoa Peninsula is still a nice picnic spot.

Some 6km (4 miles) north of Orewa is **Waiwera Thermal Resort** (daily 9am–10pm; entrance fee; tel: 09-427 8800; www.waiwera.co.nz). Tucked under the brow of the hill, the pools (whose Maori name means "hot water") are one of only two thermal areas in the Auckland region (the other is at **Parakai**, near Helensville, 55km (34 miles) northwest of the city on SH16).

If you continue to the end of the Northern Motorway Tollway, just after passing through the Johnson Hill Tunnels, watch out on the left for the sign to **Puhoi ❾**, the country's earliest Catholic Bohemian settlement. If you're passing by, be sure to stop for a drink at the **Puhoi Tavern**, full of old-world charm and pictures of the early Bohemian migrants and farming paraphernalia on display, or drop by the **Puhoi Bohemian Museum** (daily 1–4pm summer, weekends only 1–4pm during the rest of the year; www.puhoihistoricalsociety.org. nz) on Puhoi Road.

Beyond the Puhoi Junction, the countryside begins to open up. Interesting places to stop and stretch your legs include the **Honey Centre** (daily 8.30am–5pm; free; tel: 09-425 8003; www.honeycentre.co.nz), 4km (2½ miles) south of Warkworth, where you can buy varieties of New Zealand's excellent honey and watch the bees making it behind the glass walls of working hives. Its café serves a wide range of honey-inspired ice cream flavours. **Warkworth** itself is a pretty

A short ferry ride from downtown Auckland can transport you to the beauty of the Hauraki Gulf. Each island has a different character, ranging from dramatic lava landscapes to forested wildlife sanctuaries. (See margin tip page 146 for details.)

BELOW: Waiheke Island vineyards.

TIP

Ferries from the Quay Street terminal in Auckland travel to the following Hauraki Gulf Islands: **Rangitoto**, 3 daily, journey time 30 minutes; **Waiheke**, 20 daily, 40 minutes; **Tiritiri Matangi**, 1 daily, 1 hour 30 minutes; **Great Barrier Island**, 1 daily except Thursday, 2 hours 30 minutes. **Kawau** is only reached from Auckland by charter boat.

riverside country town which marks the northern boundary of the Auckland region. It's also the access point for some of the region's real gems. Turn east on the Matakana–Leigh Road for a drive through the wine-growing area of **Matakana** and take in **Tawharanui** ⑩, 25km (16 miles) from Warkworth, the northernmost of the regional parks, where – on a weekday at least – you stand a pretty good chance of having an endless white-sand beach entirely to yourself.

Hauraki Gulf islands

No visitor should leave without venturing onto the waters of the beautiful island-dotted **Hauraki Gulf**, or at least the inner harbour. All the islands described here are easily accessible by fast ferry from Auckland's Ferry Building along Quay Street *(see page 130)*.

In many ways the most striking island to visit is **Rangitoto Island** ⑪ – just 8km (5 miles) northeast of Auckland – the 600-year-old dormant volcano which dominates the city's skyline. The summit is a bracing, though not hugely demanding, walk, and there is a

tractor-trailer trip for those who don't fancy the exertion. Take stout shoes; the volcanic lava pathway butchers fancy leather. From the 260-metre (850ft) summit there are unforgettable 360-degree views of the city, the northern bays and the Hauraki Gulf. A causeway joins Rangitoto with **Motutapu Island**, which, by way of contrast, is mostly covered in farmland.

Barely 19km (12 miles) from downtown Auckland is **Waiheke Island** ⑫, the most populated of the Gulf islands. A generation ago it was a retreat for the impecunious and the artistic who had to brave the bouncy, hour-long ferry ride into town. These days a high-speed catamaran makes the commute shorter, and as a result the island's population and profile have changed beyond recognition. Much of the work of local craftspeople is now world-class rather than hippie-cottage. The steep slopes overlooking the many beautiful bays are now sprinkled with architect-designed houses where once only simple cottages stood. Chic cafés line the streets of the main settlement, **Oneroa**. The island's bus service is infrequent

BELOW: Kawau Island, popular with yachties.

– it's tied to the ferry timetable – but the taxis and rental cars are cheap and the walking is pleasant.

Waiheke has a burgeoning wine industry, too. And while it can be comfortably sampled in a day trip, if you decide to stay a while, you'll find accommodation to suit even the most extravagant of tastes.

Tiritiri Matangi Island ⓭, which must rank as one of New Zealand's greatest conservation success stories, makes for a lovely day trip from Auckland (guided tours are an option). Reclaimed from weeds and feral predators resulting from several centuries of settlement, it has been restored to a superb open wildlife sanctuary populated by many species of endangered New Zealand birdlife, including the Little spotted kiwi, *takahe* and Red-crowned parakeet *(kakariki)*.

Further to the north again, **Kawau Island ⓮**, 46km (29 miles) from Auckland, is a sleepy retreat ranged around a sheltered harbour popular with yachties. The stately **Mansion House** (daily 10am–3.30pm; entrance fee; tel: 09-422 8882), in the bay of the same name, was the country home of one of the early governors, Sir George Grey. It was he who introduced the wallaby, more commonly associated with Australia.

Those with more time to spend might set aside a couple of days to explore **Great Barrier Island ⓯**, the gulf's most remote at 90km (56 miles) northeast of Auckland. This is truly another country, where the small permanent population lives without mains power; electricity is supplied by private generators or alternative sources. The 700 or so islanders, who refer to their home as "the Barrier", are renowned as among the country's most reclusive; most live in Port Fitzroy on the southwest coast, the port of arrival for ferries from Auckland. There are some superb walks and beautiful beaches along the island's 30km (20-mile) length, and it is also a popular destination for diving, fishing, surfing and camping, as well as being home to several unique plant and bird species. In addition to the regular ferries there are also sightseeing cruises and flights, although to drop in for an hour is rather to miss the point. ❑

TIP

For more information on what to do on Great Barrier Island, phone the Great Barrier Information Line (daily 9am–4pm; tel: 09-429 0033) or visit www.greatbarrier.co.nz.

BELOW: Great Barrier Island is known for its beautiful beaches.

NORTHLAND

Northland's picturesque charm makes it an ideal holiday and retirement spot, while concealing a dramatic past of debauchery, excess, war, rebellion, conquest and settlement

Tribal warfare, bloody clashes between Maori and Pakeha, debauchery, insurrection, missionary zeal, a treaty of peace and promises – all are part of Northland's turbulent historical backdrop. But this subtropical side of New Zealand has more to offer than the past. It is a friendly, welcoming place where you can relax and enjoy the sun, food, sights and distinctive way of life. The irregular peninsula juts upwards some 450km (280 miles) from the farmlands north of Auckland to the rocky headlands of Cape Reinga, and is famed for its scenery, fine game fishing, unspoilt beaches, thermal pools and magnificent kauri forests.

The region is often labelled the winterless north because of its mild, damp winters and warm, humid summers. A distinctive feature are its pohutukawa trees, which in early summer rim the coast and decorate the hinterland with their bright red blossoms.

Bay of Islands

For those wanting to explore the region freely, **Paihia ❶**, a Bay of Islands township on the far northeast coast, is a good base to work from. It's a smooth and scenic 3½-hour (240km/150-mile) drive up State Highway (SH) 1 from Auckland via the Northern Motorway and its new extension, the Northern Motorway Tollway. Further on, the route becomes a single-lane road, travelling north through the small farming towns of Warkworth and Wellsford to

Waipu, an excellent lunch stop. Take time to visit the **House of Memories Museum** highlighting the extraordinary journey of the town's original Scottish settlers. From here it's a further 40km (25 miles) up to Northland's largest city, Whangarei *(see page 159)*.

Leave the main highway at **Kawakawa** – home to New Zealand's most interesting public toilets, a bizarre baroque confection designed by Austrian artist emigrant Frederick Hundertwasser – and snake down into the harbourside resort of Paihia.

Main attractions
THE BAY OF ISLANDS
WAITANGI NATIONAL TRUST
 TREATY GROUNDS
RUSSELL
NINETY MILE BEACH
CAPE REINGA
WAIPOUA FOREST
POOR KNIGHTS ISLANDS

PRECEDING PAGES: Cape Reinga. **LEFT:** sand dunes at Ninety Mile Beach. **BELOW:** Kawakawa's famous toilets.

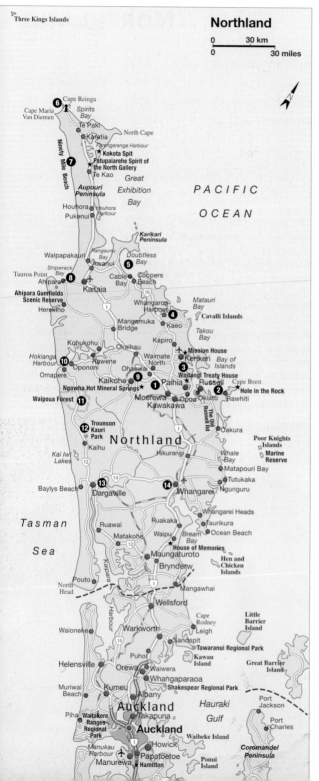

Northland

0 — 30 km

0 — 30 miles

Three Kings Islands

Cape Reinga
Cape Maria Van Diemen
Spirits Bay
Te Paki
North Cape
Karatia
Parengarenga Harbour
Kokota Spit
Patupaiarehe Spirit of the North Gallery
Te Kao
Aupouri Peninsula
Great Exhibition Bay
Houhora
Houhora Harbour
Pukenui
Ninety Mile Beach
Karikari Peninsula
Waipapakauri
Rangaunu Bay
Awanui
Doubtless Bay
Tauroa Point
Shipwreck Bay
Cable Bay
Coopers Beach
Ahipara
Kaitaia
Ahipara Gumfields Scenic Reserve
Herekino
Whangaroa Harbour
Matauri Bay
Cavalli Islands
Mangamuka Bridge
Kaeo
Takou Bay
Kohukohu
Okaihau
Kapiro
Mission House
Waimate North
Kerikeri
Bay of Islands
Hokianga Harbour
Rawene
Opononi
Ohaeawai
Omapere
Kaikohe
Waitangi Treaty House
Paihia
Russall
Cape Brett
Ngawha Hot Mineral Springs
Opua
Okiato
Rawhiti
Hole in the Rock
Waipoua Forest
Moerewa
Kawakawa
Trounson Kauri Park
Oakura
Kaihu
Hikurangi
Whale Bay
Poor Knights Islands
Marine Reserve
Kai Iwi Lakes
Matapouri Bay
Baylys Beach
Dargaville
Whangarei
Tutukaka
Ngunguru
Ruawai
Ruakaka
Whangarei Heads
Matakohe
Waipu
Taurikura
Ocean Beach
Bream Bay
House of Memories
Maungaturoto
Hen and Chicken Islands
Pouto
Brynderwn
North Head
Mangawhai
Wellsford
Cape Rodney
Little Barrier Island
Waioneke
Warkworth
Leigh
Sandspit
Tawaranui Regional Park
Puhoi
Kawau Island
Great Barrier Island
Helensville
Orewa
Waiwera
Whangaparaoa
Shakespear Regional Park
Muriwai Beach
Kumeu
Albany
Hauraki Gulf
Port Jackson
Piha
Waitakere Ranges Regional Park
Takapuna
Port Charles
Auckland
Waiheke Island
Manukau Harbour
Howick
Coromandel Peninsula
Manurewa
Papatoetoe
Hamilton
Ponui Island

PACIFIC OCEAN

Tasman Sea

Northland

This is the **Bay of Islands**, the cradle of New Zealand. Its irregular 800km (500-mile) coastline, embracing 144 islands, is steeped in historical association as the site of the country's earliest European settlement.

Polynesian explorer Kupe is said to have visited the bay in the 10th century, followed by another canoe voyager, Toi, some 200 years later. Captain James Cook discovered the harbour for Europeans in 1769. Impressed, he gave the sheltered waters of the bay their current name. In the scattered group are eight larger islands and numerous islets; the largest measures 22 hectares (54 acres). Many are uninhabited; some are privately owned; others are reserves. The region's small permanent population is multiplied during the traditional New Zealand summer holiday period, from Christmas to late January, when thousands of Kiwis head north to camp, boat, swim, fish and relax. As most Northland visitors head for the bay, a visit during this period requires accommodation reservations well in advance.

Since the 1950s, Paihia has been revamped to meet the challenge of tourism. Modern hotels surround a neat, expanded shopping centre, with a good variety of eating places and modest nightlife. The wharf, its focal point, caters for island cruises and fishing trips around the bay. Places of historical note are marked with bronze plaques along the sandy seafront. It is also a town of many firsts: New Zealand's oldest Norfolk pine stands here; a mission station was created on the town site in 1823, and missionaries built and launched the country's first ship, the *Herald*, here in 1826; from the first printing press, brought from England in 1834, was published the first Bible in Maori. Its colonial history is very obviously etched in Paihia's graveyard.

Waitangi Treaty House

The most significant act in New Zealand's early history took place on the lawn of the **Waitangi Treaty House**, set in the Waitangi Reserve about 2km

(1¼ miles) north of Paihia across a one-way bridge that also leads to the Wait-angi golf course. The house is now part of the **Waitangi National Trust Treaty Grounds** (daily 9am–5pm; entrance fee; tel: 09-402 7437; www.waitangi.net.nz; nightly cultural show www.culturenorth.co.nz).

On 6 February 1840, with Governor William Hobson signing on behalf of Queen Victoria, Maori chiefs and Eng-lish gentlemen agreed to end Maori–Pakeha conflict, guarantee the Maori land rights, give them and the colonists Crown protection and admit New Zea-land to the British Empire. At the time of the signing, the house was the home of James Busby, British Resident in New Zealand from 1832 to 1840.

The gracious colonial dwelling, with its commanding views of the bay, later fell into disrepair. It has since been restored, and today the Treaty House is a national museum. Also worth visit-ing is the adjacent Maori meeting house, or *whare runanga*, where one of the world's largest war canoes, the impressive 35-metre (115ft) *Ngatoki Matawhaorua*, is proudly displayed.

Russell – former Sin City

Runaway sailors, escaped convicts, lusty whalers, promiscuous women, brawlers and drunks: **Russell ❷**, 15km (9 miles) northeast of Paihia, formerly known as Kororareka and dubbed "hell-hole of the Pacific", has seen them all. Russell is easy to get to as it's linked by a regular passenger ferry service from Paihia and Waitangi. A vehicular ferry also travels between the deep-sea port of **Opua**, 9km (6 miles) south of Paihia, and **Okiato** near Russell.

Colonists first arrived in 1809, mak-ing Russell New Zealand's first white settlement. Today it's small, quiet and peaceful, though things liven up at Christmas and New Year with the influx of boaties and other visitors.

The town was briefly New Zealand's capital, and in the early 1830s lust and lawlessness prevailed, with up to 30 grog shops operating on the tiny waterfront.

Shocked early settlers responded by building **Christ Church**, at the corner of Robertson and Beresford streets, two blocks east of the harbour, in 1835. It is New Zealand's oldest surviving church; its bullet-holed walls are grim remind-ers of the siege that took place in 1845.

Maori chief Hone Heke, who signed the Treaty of Waitangi in 1840, later became discontented over government land dealings when the promised financial rewards did not materialise. In 1845, he defiantly chopped down the British flagstaff, symbol of the new regime, on Maiki Hill at the northern end of the beach. Meanwhile, Chief Kawiti, an ally of Heke, burnt and sacked Church property. A showdown duly took place in 1846 near Kawakawa, at Kawiti's *pa*, Ruapekapeka. A strong Redcoat force captured this formidable fortress, somewhat unfairly on a Sun-day when the converted Maori were busy worshipping their new Christian god. Heke was eventually pardoned and his men freed.

Pompallier (daily 10am–5pm; May–Nov five guided tours daily; entrance fee; tel: 09-403 9015; www.pompallier.

TIP

Russell is something of an epicurean hotspot and a haven for chefs of renown, who create culinary masterpieces with the pick of the Bay of Islands' legendary produce.

BELOW: the Waitangi Treaty House.

Prior to the arrival of the Europeans, the Maori used carvings instead of a written language. Each carved item tells a story (kaupapa); it is possible to interpret the precise shape and position of various features and patterns to reveal the messages within.

BELOW: fishing off Russell wharf.

co.nz) is housed in the sole surviving building of the French Catholic missionaries, who erected it in 1842 to serve as their printing press. Today, extensively restored as a working museum, its original printing press, bookbindery and tanning pits reproduce the Roman Catholic books in the Maori language, which were printed here in the 1840s. **Russell Museum** (daily 10am–5pm, until 5pm January; entrance fee; tel: 09-403 7701), one block east on York Street, has a seagoing model of Cook's *Endeavour*, and numerous colonial curios. The **Duke of Marlborough Hotel** (tel: 09-403 7829), one of the country's oldest, is a pub of great character dishing up steaming plates of seafood chowder and freshly caught fish and chips.

The Old Russell Road

There is an alternative route to Russell, turning off to the coast 17km (11 miles) north of Whangarei. Known as the Old Russell Road, the days of bumping along its dusty gravel length are long gone; the smooth sealed road now runs all the way through to the Bay of Islands. Along the way there is a lot to

linger over, including **Mimiwhangata**, an 800-hectare (2,000-acre)Coastal Farm Park under marine conservation offering excellent snorkelling and diving. Birdwatchers will be enthralled by the local populations of NZ dotterel, Pied stilt and oystercatcher, and 30 or so kiwis also make their home here.

Oakura was once the site of 10 Maori *pa*, and the pretty horseshoe of Bland Bay is anything but insipid, with deep-blue waters and a myriad of scattered islands. **Rawhiti** is the starting point for the **Cape Brett Walkway**, a hilly, seven-hour one-way hike, with a DOC hut at the end where hikers can camp overnight, or the option to catch a water taxi to Paihia. A less strenuous option is the three-hour return hike to the ruins of an old whaling station in the **Whangamumu Scenic Reserve**.

The Old Russell Road continues through Oke Bay and scenic Parekura Bay, past rows of oysters at Orongo Bay to Russell.

Trips on the bay

The true beauty of the islands in the bay can best be appreciated on one of

Fishing in the Bay of Islands

Deep-sea fishing for some of the world's biggest game fish is a major lure in the Bay of Islands. The main fishing season is from December to June, when the huge marlin are running. Many world records for marlin, shark and tuna have been set here. Yellowtail kingfish, running on until September, provide good sport on light rods. Snapper, one of New Zealand's favourite table fish, is also plentiful.

Fighting fish up to 400kg (880lbs) are caught in the bay, and weigh-ins attract appreciative crowds. At the end of the day listen out for the low tolling of a bell; this signals that a large fish has been caught and is being weighed on the wharf. Competitions for line-fishing and surf-casting are frequently held, and, despite the "seasons", fishing is a year-round sport here. Charter boats are available at Paihia or Russell for half- or full-day hire, and on a share basis. But a more laid-back fishing experience is also possible. The towns' numerous small wharves are seldom without at least one small-scale angler hopefully dangling a line in the water.

The bay is also popular as a sea-kayaking destination with its numerous sandy coves within short reach of each other. In the summer months the waters become crowded with yachts, many sailed by their owners up from Auckland for a holiday on the water.

the daily "Cream Trips" operated by **Fullers** (www.fboi.co.nz) from both Paihia (Marsden Road; tel: 09-402 7422) and Russell (Cass Street; tel: 09-403 7866). These six-hour boat trips retrace the voyages of bygone days when cream was regularly collected from island farms. Mail and provisions are still handled this way today. The Fullers cruise covers about 96km (60 miles), and passengers can see the island where Captain Cook first anchored on his 1769 voyage; the cove where French explorer Marion du Fresne, along with his 25 crew members, was slain by Maori in 1772; and the bays where the earliest missionaries landed.

Fullers also offers a shorter four-hour cruise to the Cape Brett lighthouse and Piercy Island, and, weather permitting, the boat passes right through the famous **Hole in the Rock** at the end of Cape Brett. For a bit more of a thrill, try the Mack Attack, operated by Kings Tours on Marsden Road (tel: 09-402 8180; www.kings-tours.co.nz), a 90-minute blast to the Hole in the Rock and back in a powerful catamaran with a top speed of 90kph (56mph).

With its remarkably clear waters, the Bay of Islands is also a diving paradise. By world standards, top-quality diving is cheap and accessible, with numerous reliable commercial operators (see Travel Tips pages 367–8).

Kerikeri and surroundings

The next major stop in Northland is **Kerikeri ❸**. Located 23km (14 miles) north of Paihia, beside a pretty inlet, it is a township of unusual interest and character, which has a rich backdrop of early Maori and European colonial history. Here, missionary Samuel Marsden planted the country's first vineyard in 1819. Today, much of New Zealand's finest citrus and subtropical fruits, including avocados, are grown on Kerikeri's fertile volcanic soils.

The township and its immediate environs, with a population of 5,000, are a thriving centre for handicrafts and cottage industries. The climate and relaxed lifestyle have attracted many creative residents, along with wealthy retirees from other New Zealand centres. Two vineyards and a plethora of quality restaurants do nothing to discourage new residents.

The oldest surviving European building in the country, **Mission House**, formerly **Kemp House** (daily 10am–5pm; entrance fee; tel: 09-407 9236), is on Kerikeri Road, 1km (2/3 mile) to the east of the township. It was built in 1822 of pit-sawn kauri and *totara*. The **Stone Store** (daily 10am–5pm; free; tel: 09-407 9236) next door, built in 1836 to house New Zealand mission supplies, is the country's oldest standing European stone building. It still serves as a shop and has a museum upstairs.

Just to the northeast, the site of **Kororipa Pa** should not be overlooked. This was celebrated warrior chief Hongi Hika's forward army base between 1780 and 1826. Maori warriors were assembled here before launching raids on tribes throughout North Island. It can be reached via a short walkway. For a

The tui is a large indigenous bird known for its raucous call and ability to mimic a variety of sounds. The Pakeha name "Parson Bird" is rarely used.

BELOW: the Hole in the Rock at Cape Brett.

A tall ship takes shelter in Russell Harbour.

Below: craft shop, Hokianga Harbour. The region is home to numerous artists and designers.

longer hike, take the path upriver to the impressive cascade of Rainbow Falls.

Across the river from the Stone Store is **Rewa's Village** (daily 9.30am–4.30pm; donation; tel: 09-407 6454), a replica 18th-century Maori fishing village built by traditional methods and using only materials that would have been available at the time.

Some 15km (9 miles) southwest of Kerikeri is **Waimate North**, New Zealand's first inland settlement for white people. Built in 1831–2, the **Te Waimate Mission** (Nov–Apr 10am–5pm daily, May–Oct Mon–Wed and Sat–Sun 10am–5pm; entrance fee; tel: 09-405 9734) in Waimate North was the home of Bishop George Augustus Selwyn, New Zealand's first Anglican bishop.

North to Cape Reinga

In Maori mythology, Cape Reinga is where the spirits of the dead depart on their homeward journey to the ancestral land of Hawaiki. Coach tours now make their way up this legendary flight path, along the Aupouri Peninsula to its northernmost point, and return via Ninety Mile Beach. As tourist hire cars

frequently get trapped on the sands of Ninety Mile Beach (mainly due to the drivers' lack of experience at driving on sand), coaches and four-wheel drive vehicles which leave Paihia, Kerikeri, Kaitaia and other Northland towns daily are the best option if you wish to travel via the beach. The east-coast route traverses the worked-out gum fields of the far north, a relic of the huge kauri forests that once covered this region. The dead trees left pockets of gum in the soil, which early settlers found to be a valuable export, used to make fine varnish. So valuable, in fact, that it triggered a "gum rush" – by the 1880s, more than 2,000 men were digging up a fortune.

In **Whangaroa Harbour** ❹, a deep-sea fishing base 25km (16 miles) north of Kerikeri, lies the wreck of the *Boyd*. The ship called in for kauri spars in 1809 and sent a party of 11 ashore. However, the group was murdered by the local Maori inhabitants, who donned the victims' clothes, rowed back to the vessel and massacred the rest of the crew, then set fire to the ship. Reliably serene now, Whangaroa

is another popular destination for cruising yachts and sea kayaking.

About 24km (15 miles) further is **Doubtless Bay ❺**, named by Cook, with its string of gently sloping sandy beaches, including **Coopers Beach**, lined with pohutukawa trees, and **Cable Bay**, with its peach-coloured sands and an array of pretty shells. There is a limited choice of accommodation and places to eat at both beaches.

At **Awanui**, the road forks north, passing through **Pukenui, Houhora** and **Te Kao**, to Cape Reinga with its lighthouse. The whole district is rich in Maori folklore. At **Cape Reinga ❻** itself, 130km (80 miles) north of Doubtless Bay at the tip of the **Aupouri Peninsula**, a gnarled pohutukawa, at least 800 years old, grows out of the rocks at the foot of the cape. Spirits are said to slide down its roots into the sea to begin their journey in the underworld. Views from the cape, where the lone lighthouse stands guard, are impressive. You can see the turbulent merging line of the Pacific Ocean and Tasman Sea, the **Three Kings Islands**, 57km (35 miles) offshore, neighbouring capes, including Cape Maria Van Diemen, and numerous secluded beaches. Steep trails lead down to several of these, including Te Werahi and Twilight Beach. Alternatively, take the road to Tauputaputa Beach, perfect for picnicking. For the complete sea-and-sand experience, join a kayaking tour at Karatia and paddle across the **Parengarenga Harbour** to the striking headland and sun-bleached dunes of **Kokota Spit** at the harbour mouth. This is the last landfall for migratory godwits flying across the planet to the Arctic.

Ninety Mile Beach

Ninety Mile Beach ❼, south of Cape Reinga and running along the western side of the Aupouri Peninsula, is actually 60 miles (96km) long (there are numerous explanations for this quirk, the most plausible being an early mapping error), lined with tall dunes and hillocks of shell and flanked by the

Aupouri Forest, populated by bands of wild horses of thoroughbred stature.

The route back to Paihia is via **Kaitaia**, New Zealand's northernmost town, and a place of little interest. Turn off for **Ahipara ❽**, a seaside village at the southernmost end of Ninety Mile Beach. Surfers come from all over the world to ply the waves here and at adjacent **Shipwreck Bay**.

Behind Shipwreck Bay is the **Ahipara Gumfields Scenic Reserve**, a ghostly and fascinating wilderness area where prospectors once excavated kauri gum from the sand. Hike or join a Tuatua Tours quad-bike adventure to explore the reserve and **Tauroa Point**, where there is an intriguing cluster of shanties with no running water and no power, used by transient seaweed-gatherers.

The west coast

From Ahipara, a more interesting west-coast route leads back to Auckland either via **Herekino** and **Kohukohu**, crossing the Hokianga Harbour by vehicular ferry, or via **Kaikohe ❾**, 150km (93 miles) south of Cape Reinga, where a hilltop monument to Chief

Ancient kauri is the oldest timber on earth, retrieved from swamps and dating back 30,000–50,000 years. At the Ancient Kauri Kingdom (tel: 09-406 7172; www.ancientkauri.co.nz) on Far North Road at Awanui, 8km (5 miles) north of Kaitaia, it is turned into beautiful craft pieces.

BELOW: sand-surfing on Ninety Mile Beach.

WHERE

After the desolate intensity of Cape Reinga, Ninety Mile Beach's sand highway offers the chance to let rip, entering or exiting on Te Paki Stream. Here where the road meets the stream, old boogie-boards are hired out by the hour or the day and become slick toboggans on Te Paki's giant golden dunes.

Hone Heke offers tremendous views of both coasts. Nearby are **Ngawha Hot Mineral Springs** (daily 9am–9.30pm; entrance fee), with tempting mineral-rich mercury and sulphur waters for a refreshing soak. From here it is a 40km (25-mile) drive west to **Hokianga Harbour** , a long sheltered harbour with a score of ragged inlets that keep the place quiet, serene and rural.

Across the harbour is Kohukohu, stamped with the architecture of the early 1900s, when it was a thriving timber town. Take time to wander its streets, visit the country's oldest stone bridge and peer through abandoned cannon from the *Boyd*. Stop for coffee at The Waterline, a picturesque café overhanging the harbour, before catching the vehicular ferry to **Rawene**, the gateway to northern Hokianga.

Rawene perches at the tip of the peninsula with many of its buildings hanging over the waterline, their foundation posts buried firmly in the sand. The village is home to some noteworthy buildings: the old courthouse and gaol, the Masonic Hotel, Clendon House, The Ferry House and

several old churches. The police station is also of note, for it was here in 1898 that the Mahurehure *hapu* of the Ngapuhi refused to pay the small fee required for licensing the ownership of a dog, marking New Zealand's last armed conflict.

Further towards the harbour mouth, the tiny seaside resort of **Opononi** briefly became world-famous in the summer of 1955–6, when a young dolphin began frolicking with swimmers at the beach. When "Opo" the dolphin died in somewhat mysterious circumstances, the nation mourned. She is remembered in a song and a monument.

The road then heads south through the **Waipoua Forest** with its 2,500 hectares (6,200 acres) of mature kauri trees, the largest stand of kauri left in the country. New Zealand's largest living kauri tree, Tane Mahuta (Lord of the Forest) is around 2,000 years old and is located a five-minute walk away from the car park. Its mighty girth spans 13.8 metres (45ft), yet this colossal kauri has fragile and easily bruised roots, and a well-formed wheelchair-friendly boardwalk has been constructed to protect them.

Waipoua Forest offers several other walks. The road to the DOC Visitors Centre follows a pretty stream with picturesque picnic spots and gas BBQs on its banks.

Further south at **Trounson Kauri Park** are more fine kauri, including one with four trunks. This park provides near-perfect growing conditions for large kauri, and a 40-minute loop track meanders among thick native bush dominated by the magnificent trees as well as kauri grass, taraire, kiekie, neinei and ferns.

Dargaville , 90km (56 miles) south of Hokianga Harbour, was founded on the timber and kauri gum trade. In Harding Park, **Dargaville Museum** (daily 9am–4.30pm; entrance fee; tel: 09-439 7555) is built of clay bricks brought in from China as ship's ballast and is full of memorabilia from

BELOW: Waipoua Forest.

this intriguing stretch of coast, including shipwreck artefacts and a pre-Maori carving unearthed from the dunes. There is also a display of the environmental vessel *Rainbow Warrior*, which was bombed by French agents in Auckland Harbour in 1985. It was scuttled near Kerikeri in 1987 and is now an artificial reef, teeming with marine life and popular with divers.

Whangarei and the Poor Knight Islands

The highway then turns east to **Whangarei** ⑭, a deep-sea port with a picturesque harbour and an industrial presence – the town is home to a glassworks, cement plant and an oil refinery. The Town Basin area on the waterfront, where international yachties moor their vessels, draws visitors from far and wide to dine at its wharfside cafés. Also a hub for talented Northland artisans, its galleries and studios offer something for every taste. Watch as molten glass is transformed into delicately blown vases at Burning Issues, and take a step back in time at **Clapham's Clocks – The National Clock Museum** (daily 9am–5pm; entrance fee; tel: 09-438 3993; www.claphamsclocks.co.nz), the largest collection of clocks and music boxes in the Southern Hemisphere, with 1,500 clocks and clockwork items dating back to the 17th century.

For panoramic views of the city and harbour visit Mount Parahaki or take the scenic drive to **Whangarei Heads** and hike up Mount Manaia for excellent views of **Bream Bay** and the **Hen and Chicken Islands**. Visit the Whangarei Falls, plunging 25 metres (82ft) into a deep, bush-fringed pool, or take kids to befriend Snoopy, the country's only tame kiwi, at the Native Bird Recovery Centre. There are plenty of hotels and restaurants in the city as well as safe swimming beaches.

The road out to the **Tutukaka** coast offers some real gems, including the quaint village of Ngunguru, once a busy port and now devoted to recrea-tional watersports, with great fishing, a boat ramp, ski lane, and picnic tables for enjoying takeaways alfresco overlooking the water.

The bustling nautical township of Tutukaka is the gateway to the **Poor Knights Islands** and some of the best diving, snorkelling and game fishing in the world. The islands stand alongside a spectacular marine reserve, and are also home to the world's largest sea cave, **Riko Riko**, a mammoth watery cavern covered from top to toe with lichen and moss. It's worth taking a speedboat tour across the water to experience its amazing acoustics and colourful parades of fish.

Further up the coast a horseshoe of holiday homes encircle **Matapouri Bay**, while Woolley's Bay and Sandy Bay are popular for swimming and surfing. A 20-minute hike through groves of ancient puriri trees and kowhai brings you to the isolated cove of **Whale Bay**, where pohutukawa trees overhang the sands. ❑

Clapham's Clocks, the national horological museum at Whangarei.

BELOW: picnic at Whangarei Falls.

THE WAIKATO

Dairy production and agriculture flourish in these rich, fertile lands south of Auckland, lands which also have a wealth of historical artefacts and cultural traditions

The central and western region of the North Island is one of New Zealand's great agricultural areas. Grass grows quickly here, and the free-grazing dairy herds that crop these fertile plains daily have brought prosperity to generations. The grass is fed by a mild, wet climate. On the flats – the area has more flat arable land than anywhere else in the North Island – farm diversification has expanded the production of fruit and vegetables. The Waikato is also thoroughbred horse-breeding country, and dairy cattle studs abound.

Much of the now-green pastures were the spoils of land wars between Maori and Pakeha in the 1860s. The Waikato was once relatively well populated by Maori tribes and its land communally owned, according to ancestry. This was a landscape of dense bush on the hills, with peat swamp and *kahikatea* (white pine) forests covering the extensive areas of flat land and the low hills of the Waikato and Waipa river systems.

The New Zealand Wars changed everything; it took nearly 20 years for the British and colonial forces to subdue Maori tribes who were intent on keeping what was left of their land. What land was not confiscated by the government was effectively taken through the 1862 legislation which forced the traditional Maori group ownership to be individualised. Single owners were easy prey for land agents, and the way was opened for the gradual taming, during the early 20th cen-

tury, of the natural wilderness into the intensively farmed land it is today.

Capital of the Waikato

Hamilton ❶, New Zealand's fourth-largest city, lies 136km (85 miles) south of Auckland on the banks of the **Waikato River**, New Zealand's longest waterway. Known to the Maori as Kirikiriroa, the city was renamed by Europeans after Captain Fane Charles Hamilton of the HMS *Esk*, who was killed at the Battle of Gate Pa, near Tauranga, in 1864.

Main attractions
WAIKATO MUSEUM,
HAMILTON
CAMBRIDGE
HOT SPRINGS DOMAIN,
TE AROHA
WAITOMO CAVES

LEFT: the magical Waitomo Caves.
BELOW: the Waikato is one of New Zealand's most productive agricultural areas.

Maori carvings at Turangawaewae Marae. The complex is open to the public on special occasions.

BELOW: a kaleidoscope of colourful balloons at Hamilton.

It was the Waikato River, long a vital Maori transport and trading link to the coast, that first brought the Europeans to the area and led to the establishment of Hamilton in the 1860s. The first businesses grew on the riverbank, and today the commercial hub of the city runs parallel to it on the west bank.

The city centre's most notable riverbank attraction is the **Waikato Museum** (daily 10am–4.30pm; free; tel: 07-838 6606; www.waikatomuseum.org.nz), situated at the southern end of the main thoroughfare, on the corner of Victoria and Grantham streets. Of particular note in its collection of fine arts, ethnography and Waikato history are 15,000 Tainui (Waikato's Maori tribe) artefacts, including wood and stone carvings, woven flax garments and tribal items. National and international touring exhibitions are a regular feature, but permanent displays worth noting are a magnificent war canoe and a contemporary Tainui carving and weaving commissioned for the museum's opening in 1987. Located within the complex is **Exscite Centre** (entrance fee; tel: 07-838 6606; www.exscite.org.nz), an interactive science and technology centre which boasts among its delights an earthquake simulator.

Another local favourite, the paddle steamer **MV *Waipa Delta*** (tel: 0800-472 335; www.waipadelta.co.nz), is found on the banks of the Waikato River by Memorial Park. Its lunch, dinner and afternoon-coffee cruises up the river are something of an institution.

Just south of the city centre on State Highway (SH) 1 are the 58-hectare (143-acre) **Hamilton Gardens** (daily 7.30am–5.30pm, until 8pm in summer; free; tel: 07-856 3200; www.hamiltongardens.co.nz). Organised by various themes including a tranquil Japanese garden and an Indian Char garden, these grounds are the city's most popular attraction.

The Waikato River is now a recreational asset for the region but it is also of primary importance for the power stations, which harness the waters to provide one-third of the nation's hydro-electric power. Behind each dam there are artificial lakes, popular spots for fishing, boating and rowing.

Maori stronghold

On the Waikato River north of Hamilton is **Ngaruawahia** ②, the hub of the Maori King Movement (*see page 39*) and an important Maori cultural centre. On the east riverbank is the **Turangawaewae Marae**, its name meaning "a place to put one's feet". It contains traditionally carved meeting houses and a modern concert hall, and is open to the public on special occasions. The **Waingaro Hot Springs** (daily 9am–9.30pm; entrance fee; tel: 07-825 4761; www.waingarohotsprings. co.nz) are 24km (15 miles) west of Ngaruawahia en route to **Raglan**.

Mount Taupiri, 6km (4 miles) downstream from Ngaruawahia, is the sacred burial ground of the Waikato tribes, with graves sprawling over the hill alongside the motorway. Nearby, the Waikato's waters are used to cool a massive coal-and-gas-fired power station at **Huntly**. Its two 150-metre (500ft) chimneys tower over the town.

Cambridge

The bucolic town of **Cambridge** ③ also sits on the Waikato River, 24km (15 miles) southeast of Hamilton. The charming **St Andrew's Anglican Church**, tree-lined streets and village green give it a very English atmosphere.

Cambridge is the renowned heart of the local equine industry. This is celebrated in mosaic tiles in the town centre, where local legends such as Zabeel, Sir Tristram and Empire Rose are commemorated, along with famous locally raised Olympians, including cyclist Sarah Ulmer and rowers Georgina and Caroline Evers-Swindell. It is also the location of **New Zealand Horse Magic** (daily; entrance fee; tel: 07-827 8118; www.cambridgethoroughbredlodge. co.nz), 6km (4 miles) south of Cambridge on SH1. Performances here showcase a variety of horse breeds, from a Lippizaner stallion (the only one in New Zealand) to the New Zealand wild horse, the Kaimaniwa, plus Arabian and Hackney specimens. Visitors can ride a horse at the conclusion of a show.

Provincial towns

To the east of the river are the Waikato towns of Morrinsville, Te Aroha and Matamata. **Matamata** ④ is well known

TIP

Visit the southern Waikato township of Tirau to see its signature art: wavy corrugated roofing iron which has become something of fashion statement adorning almost every high-street building in some shape or form, including a sheep and a dog.

BELOW: kayaking on the Waikato River.

Mangapu Cave in the amazing Waitomo subterranean complex is also known as the "Lost World".

for its thoroughbred racehorse stables. A three-storey blockhouse built by an early landowner, Josiah Clifton Firth, in 1881, stands as a reminder of the settlers' insecurity after the Land Wars with the Maori. It's now part of the **Firth Tower Historical Museum** (Thur–Mon 10am–4pm; entrance fee; tel: 07-888 8369), an entertaining interactive experience for families, sited on the Firth family homestead built in 1902.

Nearby, several walking tracks lead into and over the nearby **Kaimai-Mamaku Forest Park**, including one to the picturesque **Wairere Falls**. *Lord of the Rings* fans will enjoy a visit to **Hobbiton** (daily tours at 9.30am, 10.45am, noon, 1.15pm, 2.30pm, 3.45pm; entrance fee; tel: 07-888 9913; www. hobbitontour.com), further out of town. *For more on The Lord of the Rings film locations, see pages 80–81.*

Morrinsville is a centre for the surrounding dairy land, with its own large processing factory, while **Te Aroha ❺**, on the Waihou River, was once a gold town and fashionable Victorian spa sitting at the foot of 952-metre (3,123ft) bush-clad **Mount Te Aroha**. The

world's only known hot soda-water fountain, the **Mokena Geyser**, is here in the **Hot Springs Domain**, the 18--hectare (44-acre) thermal reserve that is the heart of the town's spa fame. The geyser erupts at 30–40-minute intervals, gushing at its highest to a modest 4 metres (13ft), while an elaborate piece of plumbing allows visitors to sample its allegedly health-giving waters at the source. The **Te Aroha Mineral Pools** (daily 9am–10pm; entrance fee; tel: 07-884 8717; www.tearohapools.co.nz) feature public and private pools – some in original 19th-century bathhouses – whose mineral waters are reputed to be good for aches and pains.

Southwest of Hamilton, heading towards Waitomo, is **Te Awamutu ❻**, which has been dubbed "the rose town" for its gardens and rose shows. One of the country's oldest and finest churches, **St John's Anglican Church**, built in 1854, stands in the main street. Another, St Paul's, built in 1856, lies to the east in Hairini.

The **Te Awamutu Museum** (Mon–Fri 10am–4pm, Sat 10am–1pm, Sun 1–4pm; entrance fee; tel: 07-872 0085;

www.tamuseum.org.nz) houses, alongside numerous important Maori treasures, a permanent exhibition, "True Colours", dedicated to the history of local boys made good, the Finn brothers of the rock band Split Enz.

Waitomo Caves

In the northern part of King Country, so named for its connections with the Maori King Movement (see page 39), is the little village of **Waitomo**, famous for its caves and glow-worm grottoes. The **Waitomo Caves** ❼ (daily 9am–5pm winter, daily 9am–5.30pm summer, tours depart at 10am, 11am, 1pm, 2pm and 3pm; entrance fee; tel: 07-878 8227; www.waitomocaves.co.nz) are sublime (see panel, below).

Waitomo is also a hotbed for black-water rafting, which duplicates the thrills of the white-water variety except underground and in the dark. One of the most reliable operators is **Waitomo Adventures** (tel: 07-878 7788; www.waitomo.co.nz), which offers a two-hour black-water journey as well as various permutations of abseiling down underground holes and waterfalls, and

a seven-hour Lost World adventure where participants abseil in and walk, swim and climb out. The same company also leads tours through the spectacular St Benedicts Caverns, only discovered in 1962 and long inaccessible to all but speleological specialists.

Before embarking on a visit to the caves, however, be sure to stop by the **Waitomo Museum of Caves** (daily, Dec–Feb 8.15am–7pm, Feb–May 8.30am–5.30pm, June–Nov 9am–5pm; entrance fee; tel: 07-878 7640; www.waitomodiscovery.co.nz), just beside Waitomo Village's visitors centre. It has informative displays on the fascinating geography and history of these underground labyrinths.

At **Te Kuiti**, 19km (12 miles) to the south, charismatic Maori leader Te Kooti Rikirangi took refuge from the British in 1864 and built a carved meeting house, later given to the local Maniapoto people as a gesture of thanks for their protection. Some 32km (20 miles) to the west of Waitomo are the thundering **Marokopa Falls**, located a 10-minute walk from the main Te Anga Road.   ❑

A glow-worm is actually the larva of the fungus gnat (related to the mosquito) which attaches itself to the Waitomo cave roof. The blueish-green glow the larva emits comes from the sticky silk threads on its body, which it uses to trap flying insects for food.

BELOW: glow-worms illuminate the Waitomo Caves to spellbinding effect.

Waitomo Wonderland

The glow-worms of Waitomo Caves are a truly stellar sight. Stairs lead down to the 14-metre (46ft) high Cathedral, adorned with stalactites and stalagmites on every conceivable surface, formed by the action of water on limestone over hundreds of thousands of years. It's incredible, but the highlight comes at the end: an awe-inspiring boat ride through enormous caverns, by the radiant light of millions of tiny glow-worms.

These caves were long known to Maori; the first Pakeha to visit them was surveyor Fred Mace in 1887. Today three caves are open to the public – the Glow-worm Cave, Ruakuri and Aranui – plus the self-guided Piripiri Cave located a 30-minute drive away, and best explored with a torch and solid footwear, as the ground is both slippery and steep.

COROMANDEL AND THE BAY OF PLENTY

This northeastern area is a place where the great outdoors comes to life in the form of camping, tramping and boating. The less energetic can laze at any number of glorious beaches

Main attractions
COROMANDEL
DRIVING CREEK RAILWAY
HAHEI AND CATHEDRAL COVE
WAIHI ARTS CENTRE
  AND MUSEUM
TAURANGA
WHITE ISLAND

The popular phrase "Coromandel: Mine Today, Gone Tomorrow!" reflects the strong feelings of its inhabitants that the region's greatest asset is not its abundant mineral wealth but its natural attractions. The region once yielded abundant treasures, and early European settlers who flocked here were gold-seekers and bushmen. Reminders of these earlier bonanzas abound, with colonial buildings, old gold-mine shafts and the like. Today, people flock to the area for a less material and much more accessible treasure: activities in the great outdoors including diving, fishing, boating, swimming, camping, tramping, and fossicking for gemstones.

Thames and environs

At the base of the Coromandel Peninsula, **Thames ❽** was officially declared a goldfield in August 1867. The ensuing gold rush swelled the town's population to 18,000 at its peak, with a total of more than 100 hotels. Today there are just four, the oldest (1868) being the atmospheric **Brian Boru Hotel** on the corner of Pollen and Richmond streets, at the southern end of town.

To appreciate Thames's past, one should head further north to the **Mineralogical Museum** and adjacent **School of Mines** (Sat–Sun 11am–3pm; entrance fee; tel: 07-868 6227) on Cochrane Street. This was one of 30 schools of mines around the country that used to provide practical instruc-

tion to a burgeoning population of miners. Nearby, around 500 metres (1,640ft) to the northeast on Tararu Road, is **Goldmine Experience** (daily 10am–3pm; entrance fee; tel: 07-868 8514; www.goldmine-experience.co.nz), an old gold mine now turned into a tourist attraction, where members of the Hauraki Prospectors' Association demonstrate the technology used to retrieve gold.

Kauaeranga Valley is the site of the **Department of Conservation Visitors Centre** (tel: 07-867 9080), 10km (6

LEFT: a giant kauri.
BELOW: garden art at Tauranga.

Scenery close to the tip of the Coromandel Peninsula, accessed by a narrow gravel road that hugs the shore most of the way.

miles) northeast of Thames. The first kauri spars were logged here in 1795, mainly for the use of the Royal Navy. By 1830, kauri trees were being cut in greater numbers, and the decimation of the forests was to continue for a century. Late in the 1800s, huge kauri timber dams were built across creeks on the peninsula to bank up water and then float the logs to sea. About 300 such dams were constructed, more than 60 of them in the Kauaeranga Valley. Many are still there, slowly disintegrating. Today the valley is a favourite spot for camping and tramping, and visitors have plenty of access to the wilderness along more than 50km (30 miles) of tracks.

Coromandel and surroundings

From Thames, follow the winding route north along the **Firth of Thames** up the west coast of the Coromandel Peninsula. The views across the water to Auckland in the far distance are spectacular. **Tapu**, 19km (12 miles) north of Thames, is the junction for the **Tapu–Coroglen Road**, a scenic route climbing to 448 metres (1,470ft) above sea level. The **Rapaura Watergardens** (daily 9am–5pm; entrance fee; tel: 07-868 4821; www.rapaurawatergardens.co.nz), 7km (4 miles) along this road, feature gentle walks, abundant native flora, lily ponds, bridges, streams, a waterfall and sculptures of *punga* (a native fern), as well as the delightful **Café Koru** (tel: 07-868 4821). The road continues over the peninsula to the east coast but it is rough and, in winter, somewhat dangerous. Most travellers to the east coast prefer to make the journey across at **Kopu**, just south of Thames.

Coromandel ➒ township, 55km (35 miles) north of Thames, near the northern end of the peninsula, offers a quiet, alternative life for creative types. The town and peninsula were named after the Royal Navy ship HMS *Coromandel*, which called into the harbour in 1820 seeking kauri spars. The township was less peaceful when it became the site of New Zealand's first gold

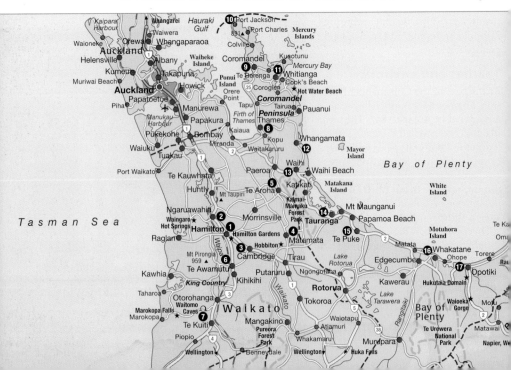

find, by Charles Ring in 1852. More than 2,000 people dashed across the gulf from Auckland at the news, but on arrival they found that the gold was deeply embedded in quartz rock and expensive to extract. It wasn't until 15 years later that a gold-bearing reef rich enough to warrant expensive extraction machinery was discovered. You can see the machine extraction process in action at the **Coromandel Battery Stamper** (tel: 07-866 7933), 3km (2 miles) north of the township at 410 Buffalo Road. Over 100 years old and fully operational, this huge machine, used for processing gold from rock, is powered by New Zealand's largest working waterwheel.

Coromandel has an air of the past about it and even at the peak of the summer holiday season the pace is slow and the lifestyle relaxed. Its sleepy history is recorded in the **Coromandel Historical Museum** (Mon–Fri 10am–1pm, Sat–Sun 1.30–4pm; entrance fee) at 841 Rings Road, which offers a glimpse of life in the gold-rush days. There is even a jailhouse at the back.

One of New Zealand's most idiosyncratic attractions is located some 3km (2 miles) north of town on Driving Creek Road. The **Driving Creek Railway and Potteries** (daily 10am–5pm; entrance fee; tel: 07-866 8703; www. drivingcreekrailway.co.nz), the creation of potter, conservationist and engineer Barry Brickell, is noted as much for its quirky train service as for the quality of its crafts. Brickell himself designed the train, built originally for carting clay from the hills for his pottery work. The miniature train takes passengers on a one-hour return trip into the hills, and up to the mountain-top terminus, "Eyefull Tower" for great views.

Beyond Coromandel, 28km (17 miles) north, is **Colville**, with the last store before Cape Colville and the northernmost tip of the peninsula. Enthusiasts insist that visitors cannot experience the full spirit of the peninsula unless they travel to the end of this road. En route, the road skirts the **Moehau Range**, whose 891-metre (2,923ft) peak is the highest point in the area. Keep an eye open for a rare native frog (*Leiopeima archeyi*) which lives only on the Coromandel Peninsula.

Driving Creek's narrow-gauge mountain railway runs on tracks only 388mm (15 inches) wide. Trains depart at 10.15am and 2pm daily, with more frequent departures in summer (bookings recommended).

BELOW: rural idyll in the Coromandel backwoods.

Central North Island

0   50 km
0   50 miles

N

PACIFIC

OCEAN

way
Whan-
gaparaoa
Hicks Bay 20
Te Araroa
East Cape 21
aukumara
orest Park
Hikurangi
1752
Tikitiki 22
Waiomatatini
Ruatoria
Te Puia
Tokomaru Bay
35
Anaura Bay
•orne
Tolaga Bay
Waihau Bay
aka Gisborne
Whangara 23

White sands and striking rock formations make Cathedral Cove one of the most attractive beaches on the east coast.

BELOW: rugged coastline near Whitianga.

The unspoilt beauty and isolation of **Port Jackson ⑩** and Fletcher Bay are worth sampling. **Fletcher Bay**, at the end of the road, is also the starting point for the **Coromandel Walkway**, a three-hour walk to **Stony Bay**. If you prefer less energetic pursuits, visit Stony Bay by taking the road just north of Colville, crossing the peninsula to Port Charles and returning via Kennedy Bay on the east coast to Coromandel township.

Whitianga and nearby beaches

Two roads lead from Coromandel Town to Whitianga, situated on the opposite coast of the peninsula. The first, the SH25, runs via the holiday resort of Matarangi and Kuaotunu Beach. The second route, some 15km (9 miles) shorter, is the 309 Road, which climbs to 300 metres (1,000ft) before descending to approach the town from the south along the Whitianga Harbour edge.

Whitianga ⑪ is said to have been occupied for more than 1,000 years by the descendants of the Polynesian explorer Kupe. Kauri gum was shipped

from Whitianga from 1844, peaking in 1899 with the shipment of 1,100 tonnes. Today's visitors enjoy fishing, swimming and rock-hunting, with the last drawing those in search of the area's semi-precious gemstones: jasper, amethyst, quartz, chalcedony, agate and carnelian.

Whitianga township is located on the shores of **Mercury Bay**, with the mouth of **Whitianga Harbour** situated at its southern end. If you follow the road south skirting the harbour to **Coroglen** (formerly Gumtown) and travel for a further 8km (5 miles), you will reach a junction which provides access to two of Coromandel's most important highlights. The first of these is **Cook's Beach**, where Captain Cook first hoisted the British flag in New Zealand in November 1769 to claim the territory in the name of King George III. While here, he also observed the transit of Mercury; a cairn and plaque at the summit of the dramatic Shakespeare Cliffs mark the occasion.

Nearby is **Hahei**, a wonderfully beguiling stretch of white sand, and a popular location for any number of

water activities thanks to its crystal clear waters. A track at the northern end of Hahei leads to **Cathedral Cove**, which is notable for its majestic rock formations. Also accessible by sea, it is a popular kayaking location.

The second essential site on the peninsula is **Hot Water Beach**, 9km (6 miles) south of Hahei, where thermal activity causes steam to rise from the sand and visitors can dig a thermal hot pool on the beach, using "sandcastle" walls to keep the sea out or let it in to regulate the temperature. It is a great way to relax travel-weary bodies from the bumps and bends of the roads.

The next centre southwards is **Tairua**, on the harbour of the same name. The area is dominated by 178-metre (584ft) **Mount Paku**, whose summit offers views of nearby Shoe and Slipper islands. Across the harbour is the affluent resort town of **Pauanui**, billed as a "Park by the Sea" but described by some as almost too tidy to be true. **Whangamata ⑫**, 40km (25 miles) further south, is a popular family holiday spot and one of the prime surfing beaches of the peninsula.

Inland from Whangamata

From Whangamata the road winds inland; 30km (19 miles) south is **Waihi ⑬**, where a rich gold- and silver-bearing lode was discovered in 1878. **Martha Hill Mine** was the greatest source of these minerals. Shafts were sunk to a depth of more than 500 metres (1,640ft) and in a period of over 60 years, more than NZ$50 million worth of gold and silver was retrieved. Fascinating mining relics are on display at **Waihi Arts Centre and Museum** (tel: 07-863 8386; www.waihimuseum.co. nz). Today, gold is still being mined from a venture which has laid bare the original mine shafts on Martha Hill.

The bullion trail led through the Karangahake Gorge to **Paeroa**, 20km (12 miles) from Waihi, from where the ore was shipped to Auckland. The Karangahake Gorge Walkway offers river views and old mining relics along the way.

A road through the Athenree Gorge south of Waihi leads to **Katikati** on State Highway (SH) 2, promoted as "The Gateway to the Bay of Plenty". In 1991, the town, concerned that its small

TIP

Swimmers beware: Hot Water Beach is notorious for rips and sudden changes in tides.

BELOW: kayakers at Cathedral Cove.

Lemon and Paeroa

The pride and joy of the small country township of Paeroa is a large concrete representation of a soft-drink bottle. The mineral waters of Paeroa were used to make Lemon and Paeroa, an indigenous soft drink and national icon. L&P, as it is now known, has long been mass-produced commercially, and the bottle, which used to stand beside the main road, was moved back several metres in 2002 because photographers angling for a good view were creating a traffic hazard. Bottles of L&P can be purchased at most supermarkets or at a dairy, the Kiwi lingo used to describe a convenience store. Today L&P comes packaged in either a can or a bottle which bears a distinctive yellow-and-brown label; the drink itself is said to taste somewhat like fizzy homemade lemonade.

Cricket on the beach at Mount Maunganui.

size and nondescript status was seeing it bypassed by travellers, decided to draw attention to itself by commissioning a series of public artworks. Within five years more than 20 outdoor murals adorned its buildings. Since then, as the number of murals depicting a variety of subjects connected to town life has increased, other art forms have also lent their weight to the "outdoor art gallery", including a number of sculptures and other installations.

Tauranga and the Bay of Plenty

Some 30km (19 miles) to the southeast of Katikati is the coastal city of **Tauranga ⑭**, which is both a tourist focal point and an important commercial centre served by the country's busiest export port. Located at the western end of the **Bay of Plenty**, Tauranga (meaning "safe anchorage") has a relaxed feel despite the obviously high level of commercial activity connected with the port. Its chief attractions are a benevolent climate and access to numerous beaches not far from the centre of town.

Tauranga has an interesting history. Flax trading became established here after the missionaries had arrived in 1838. In 1864, during the New Zealand Wars, Tauranga was the site of fierce fighting during the Battle of Gate Pa. That battlefield was the scene of heroic compassion when Maori warrior Hene Te Kirikamu heard fatally wounded British officers calling for water, and risked death in taking it to them.

The site of the original military camp, the **Monmouth Redoubt** and the mission cemetery, holds not only the remains of the British troops killed at Gate Pa but also the body of the defender of the fort, Rawhiri Puhirake, killed during the subsequent Battle of Te Ranga. **The Elms Mission House** (Wed, Sat, Sun and public holidays 2–4pm; entrance fee; tel: 07-577 9772; www.theelms.org.nz) in Mission Street, was built in 1847 by Reverend A.N. Brown (who treated the wounded from both sides at the Battle of Gate Pa) and occupied by members of the Brown family until 1991. Its library, finished in 1839, is the oldest in the country.

BELOW: lifesavers training at Mount Maunganui's popular beach.

For more down-to-earth thrills, try blokarting at Tauranga's **Blokart Heaven** (summer daily 10am–6pm, winter daily noon–5pm; tel: 07-572 4256; www.blokart.com) on Parton Road. A wind-powered Kiwi invention of 2002 vintage, the blokart is a cross between a go-kart and a land-sailer, with a top recorded speed of 90kph (56mph).

Across the harbour from Tauranga is the township of **Mount Maunganui**. Built around the 231-metre (758ft) dormant volcano, it affords views of Tauranga and the surrounding area. Near its foot are fine beaches and heated saltwater pools.

The Bay of Plenty was named by Cook, and his description proved prophetic. Perhaps the greatest evidence of plenitude was the phenomenal growth of the furry kiwi fruit, which has made the township of **Te Puke** ⓯, 28km (17 miles) southeast of Tauranga, the "Kiwi Fruit Capital of the World". Just beyond Te Puke is **Kiwi 360** (daily 9am–5pm; entrance fee; tel 07-573 6340; www. kiwi360.com), an orchard park, information centre and restaurant, with "kiwi karts" to take visitors for trips around the park.

Along the coastal road to Whakatane

About 100km (60 miles) southeast of Tauranga and 85km (53 miles) east of Rotorua is **Whakatane** ⓰, at the mouth of the Whakatane River and the edge of the fertile Rangitaiki Plains. Until it was drained 70 years ago, the area was a 40,000-hectare (100,000-acre) tract of swampland.

Whakatane takes its name from the arrival of the Mataatua canoe from Hawaiki at the local river mouth. Legend records that the men went ashore, leaving the women in the canoe, which began to drift away. Though it was *tapu* (forbidden) for women to touch paddles, the captain's daughter, Wairaka, seized one and shouted: *Kia whakatane au i ahau!* ("I will act as a man!"). Others followed suit and the canoe was saved. And thus the settlement was named Whakatane – to be manly. A bronze statue of Wairaka now stands on a rock at the river mouth. Above the area known as The Heads is

WHERE

There are several companies at Whakatane that organise tours of White Island. An excellent boat trip is offered by White Island Tours (tel: 07-308 9588; www.whiteisland.co.nz). More expensive are helicopter trips by Vulcan (tel: 07-308 4188; www.vulcanheli.co.nz).

BELOW: birdwatching at Mercury Bay.

TIP

Be sure to stop at Te Kaha Pub (tel: 07-325 2830) along the town's main road on a cliff. The pub was the setting for Taiki Waititi's Oscar-nominated short film *Two Cars, One Night*. It's a great place to meet the locals, especially if there is a rugby game on to kick-start the conversation.

Kapu-te Rangi ("Ridge of the Heavens"), claimed to be the oldest Maori *pa* (fortified village) site in New Zealand, established by the Polynesian explorer Toi.

Whakatane is known as an ecotourism centre, and one of its major attractions is **White Island**, in the midst of the Bay of Plenty 50km (30 miles) from the shore. Clearly visible from the town, the island is an active volcano. Daily boat trips include guided tours on the sulphuric moonscape, while scenic flights pass over the steaming cone, which was mined for sulphur ore between 1885 and the mid-1930s. In 1914, 12 men lost their lives here during a violent eruption. The island is also known for its thriving colonies of seabirds. Whakatane is also a good base for excursions that take you to swim with the dolphins that thrive in the bay.

Just over the hill, 7km (4 miles) from Whakatane, is the popular **Ohope Beach**, described with some justification by former New Zealand Governor-General Lord Cobbam as "the most beautiful beach in New Zealand".

The last centre of note between Whakatane and the eastern boundary of the Bay of Plenty at Cape Runaway is the rural centre of **Opotiki** ⓱. Here in 1865 missionary Reverend Carl Volkner was murdered by a Maori rebel leader, Kereopa of the Hau Hau sect, in a gruesome episode which saw Volkner's head cut off and placed on the church pulpit, with the communion chalice used to catch his blood.

Eight km (5 miles) to the southwest of Opotiki is the **Hukutaia Domain**, with some beautiful walks through the lush landscape. Many of the plants here are rare, and one of them is in a class of its own – a puriri burial tree, Taketakerau, estimated to be more than 2,000 years old. It was discovered in 1913 when a storm broke off one of its branches to reveal numerous human bones that had been interred by Maori. The bones were later re-interred and the *tapu* (sacred or taboo) status lifted from the tree.

Towards East Cape

From Opotiki there are two routes to the east coast: across or around. The route across is the more straightforward and follows SH2, which runs

BELOW: discover all you ever wanted to know about kiwi fruit at Kiwi 360, near Te Puke.

kiwi360™

Furry Fruits

Te Puke's horticulture has brought much prosperity to the region. The kiwi fruit, originally known as the Chinese gooseberry, was introduced to New Zealand from China in 1906, and thrived best in the Bay of Plenty. In the 1970s and early 1980s, fuelled by strong demand and high prices, many of Te Puke's farmers became rich from a harvest of only a few hectares. Over the years, cultivation expanded swiftly throughout other New Zealand regions, as well as to other countries including Chile, New Zealand's main kiwi fruit competitor. As iconic as it may be, these days the humble green kiwi fruit is just another orchard crop, and all eyes are now upon a contemporary yellow-fleshed cultivar dubbed 'Hort16A', a novelty hybrid which is attracting a lot of attention for its sweet-tasting flesh and smooth skin.

through the spectacular Waioeka Gorge. The gorge narrows and becomes steeper before crossing into the deep rolling hills that line the descent into Gisborne. The alternative route, which follows SH35 around East Cape, provides some of the most beautiful coastal driving the country can offer. The road winds along the coast for 115km (71 miles) to Cape Runaway. En route it crosses the Motu River and passes through the small settlement of **Te Kaha** ⑱, with its pretty crescent-shaped beach. As you drive around the coast from Te Kaha you will notice the distinctive **Raukokore Church**, an Anglican place of worship built in 1894, jutting out from the road almost into the sea. Nearby is **Waihau Bay** ⑲, a popular camping area and spot for divers to hire a boat and explore the rich seabed just metres from the shore. Several more beautiful bays are passed on the way to **Whangaparaoa**.

Rounding the cape, the next stop is **Hicks Bay** ⑳, which offers glow-worm caves for the adventurous night-time hill climber, and horse rides by day. **Te Araroa** is 10km (6 miles) further along. In the school yard by the road is a 600-year-old pohutukawa tree, Te Waha o Rerekohu, believed to be New Zealand's largest, with a total of 22 trunks, a girth of 19.9 metres (65ft) and an overall spread of 37.2 metres (122ft). The manuka tree also holds a special place in this community: harvested from much of the East Cape region, the leaves are brought to Te Araroa's manuka oil plant for extraction.

There's a turnoff here that leads 21km (13 miles) to **East Cape** ㉑ and its lighthouse. It is New Zealand's most easterly point and one of the first places in the world to see the new day.

Heading south from Te Araroa, SH35 runs inland through largely barren scenery. It passes through **Tikitiki** ㉒, with its **St Mary's Church**, built in 1924 to honour Maori servicemen killed in World War I. The building's Maori design is one of the most ornate in the country.

Just off the highway is **Ruatoria**, centre of the Ngati Porou tribe. Don't be surprised to see locals riding into town on horseback, or horses tied up outside the store. The hotel at **Te Puia**, 25km (16 miles) further south, has hot springs on site, and a short drive further on is **Tokomaru Bay**, where it is a delight to see the coast again. This entire stretch of coast, down to **Gisborne** (see page 194), is popular with surfers and holidaymakers for its unhurried pace and wide expanses of beach. The small roads leading off the main highway are rewarding to explore. Notable is **Anaura Bay**, where there is a campsite, and **Tolaga Bay**, the site of New Zealand's longest wharf.

Closer to Gisborne is **Whangara** ㉓, another beautiful white-sand beach and the location for the 2002 New Zealand film *Whale Rider*. As you approach Gisborne from Whangara, stop at **Wainui Beach**, where there are several motels. It is close to the town and provides a convenient beach location while you visit the city. ❑

Lush coastal scenery at Mount Maunganui.

BELOW: kayaking at Cathedral Cove.

ROTORUA AND THE VOLCANIC PLATEAU

On the surface it's quiet and even genteel, but Rotorua's tranquillity is punctuated by the hot and steamy thermal activity that has attracted tourists and health-seekers since Victorian times

Of his visit to Rotorua in 1934, playwright George Bernard Shaw declared: "I was pleased to get so close to Hades and be able to return." Shaw was not the first to draw an analogy between Rotorua and the fire and brimstone of the underworld. To pious Anglican pioneers the region must have had all the hallmarks of Dante's Inferno – a barren wasteland of stunted vegetation, cratered with scalding cauldrons, bubbling mud pools and roaring geysers hurling super-heated water into a sulphur-laden atmosphere.

Today, this part of central North Island represents pleasure and not torment – a place of thermal wonders, lush forests, green pastures and crystal-clear lakes teeming with trout. Anglers, campers, swimmers, water-skiers, yachtsmen, pleasure boaters, trampers and hunters are all drawn to the region. This is one of the major holiday areas in New Zealand, and the principal focus for adventure-sport activities on the North Island.

Rotorua is situated on a volcanic rift which stretches in a 200km (120-mile) line from White Island off the coast of the Bay of Plenty to Lake Taupo and the volcanoes of the Tongariro National Park in the Central Plateau of the North Island.

Cultural hotspot

Rotorua was settled by descendants of voyagers from the legendary Maori homeland of Hawaiki. Among the arrivals in the Te Arawa canoe around AD 1350 was the discoverer of Lake Rotorua, named in Maori tradition as Ihenga, who travelled inland from the settlement of Maketu and came across a lake he called Rotoiti, "little lake". He journeyed on to see a much larger lake which he appropriately called Rotorua, the "second lake".

About 68,000 people, around 35 percent of whom are Maori, reside in the Rotorua urban area and nearby smaller towns. This is the greatest concentration

Main attractions
ROTORUA MUSEUM
TE PUIA MAORI INSTITUTE
WHAKAREWAREWA
HELL'S GATE
WAIMANGU CAULDRON
WAI-O-TAPU
LAKE TAUPO
TONGARIRO NATIONAL PARK

PRECEDING PAGES: Orakei Korako thermal park. **LEFT:** visit a local *marae* for a taste of Maori culture. **BELOW:** Wai-O-Tapu.

WHERE

Rotorua's **i-site Visitors Centre** (tel: 07-348 5179; www.rotoruanz. com) in Fenton Street will provide assistance with hire cars, coach excursions and sightseeing. The majority of Rotorua's accommodation is located on Fenton Street, running north–south across the city. It is only a short drive to the popular tourist attractions of the surrounding region, but having your own transport is ideal.

of Maori residents of any New Zealand centre, and makes the town a national focus of Maori culture. Visitors will not fail to notice the strong smell of sulphur, all part of the geothermal activity, which pervades the entire area. Most people, fortunately, become accustomed to it in a matter of minutes.

City-centre attractions

Rotorua ❶ is 234km (145 miles) south of Auckland, following State Highway (SH) 1 through Hamilton to Tirau and turning southeast on SH5. Set beside the clear trout-filled waters of Lake Rotorua, the town is fairly compact. The downtown area is centred between two main thoroughfares, Fenton Street and Randolf Street.

At least some of a visitor's time here will be spent soaking in hot mineral water, an activity which can be enjoyed in an apparently infinite variety of ways. In 1874, former New Zealand premier Sir William Fox urged the government to "secure the whole of the Lake Country as a sanatorium owing to the ascertained healing properties of the water".

This immediately sparked off the development of Rotorua into a spa town. The building of its first sanatorium began in 1880 and, although the sulphurous waters of the baths are still regarded by some as useful in the treatment of arthritis and rheumatism, most people enjoy them simply as a pleasant form of relaxation.

East of the northern end of Fenton Street in the lovely grounds of the **Government Gardens** is the magnificent Tudor-style bathhouse, built in 1908 as a spa centre. Housing the **Rotorua Museum** Ⓐ (daily 9am–8pm; entrance fee; tel: 07-349 4350; www. rotoruamuseum.co.nz), it contains, alongside art exhibitions, fascinating displays of slightly sinister-looking apparatus used for various forms of hydrotherapy more than a century ago. Permanent exhibitions tell the story of the local Te Arawa people and the devastating eruption of Mount Tarawera (see page 186) in 1886.

A one-minute walk from the museum are the historic **Blue Baths** (daily 10am–7pm; entrance fee; tel: 07-350 2119; www.bluebaths.co.nz),

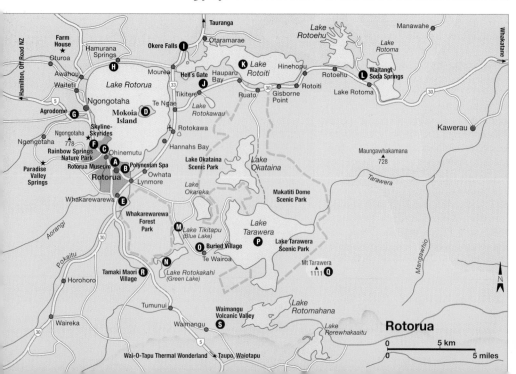

which occupy a Spanish mission building, first opened in 1933. They were beautifully restored in 1999.

A short stroll south of the museum is the **Polynesian Spa** Ⓑ (daily 8am–11pm; entrance fee; tel: 07-348 1328; www.polynesianspa.co.nz). Choose from the 26 thermal pools, each having its own special mineral content and varying temperatures. The Priest Pool was named after a Father Mahoney, who pitched his tent alongside a hot spring on the site in 1878 and bathed in the warm water until he reportedly obtained complete relief for his arthritis. Four years later the spa was established. Some pools are off-limits to children, and private pools and spa treatments are also available.

Legends of the pools

Further along the lakefront is the historic Maori village of **Ohinemutu** Ⓒ, once the main settlement on the lake. Its Tudor-style Maori **St Faith's Church**, built in 1910, is notable for its rich carvings, a window depicting a Maori Christ figure who looks as though he is walking on the waters of

Lake Rotorua, and a bust of Queen Victoria. The church was presented to the Maori people of Rotorua in appreciation of their loyalty to the Crown and is a noteworthy expression of how some of the Maori adopted Christianity into their traditional culture.

The adjacent 19th-century **Tamatekapua Meeting House** took 12 years to carve and is named after the captain of the Arawa canoe, Tama Te Kapua. It is said that Hine-te-Kakara, the daughter of Ihenga, Rotorua's discoverer, was murdered and her body thrown into a boiling mud pool. Ihenga subsequently set up a memorial stone, calling it Ohinemutu, or "the place where the young woman was killed".

Sightseeing cruises on the *Lakeland Queen* (tel: 07-348 0265; www.lakelandqueen.com), a 32-metre (105ft) paddle steamer, depart from the lakeside jetty four times daily. On its early morning cruise, you can view the sunrise over **Lake Rotorua** while enjoying a hearty breakfast. If you're not an early riser, opt for a lunch or dinner cruise.

The waters at the Polynesian Spa in Rotorua emanate from two deep thermal springs.

BELOW: the Rotorua Museum, housed in a Tudor-style former spa building.

Due to Rotorua's thermal activity, any construction or digging has to be carefully controlled. Houses do not have basements, and graves have built-in vaults that sit above the ground.

BELOW: bathing in a thermal pool.

If you wish to explore **Mokoia Island ** in the middle of Lake Rotorua, home to the rare saddleback, stitchbird and North Island robin, contact Mokoia Island Cruises (tel: 07-345 7456, 0800-665 642; www.mokoia island.com).

Mud and geysers

At the southern end of Fenton Street is the **Whakarewarewa** thermal area at **Te Puia** (www.tepuia.com), home to two major attractions. First is the impressive **Te Puia New Zealand Maori Arts and Crafts Institute** (daily 8am–6pm, until 5pm in winter; entrance fee; tel: 07-348 9047), where skilled Maori carvers and flax weavers can be observed at work. The intricately carved archway to the area depicts Hinemoa and Tutanekai embracing (see panel, opposite).

Bordering the institute is **Whakarewarewa Thermal Village** (daily 8.30am–5pm; entrance fee; tel: 07-349 3463, 0800-924 426; www.whakare warewa.com), whose residents inhabit an other-worldly terrain of bubbling mud pools and hot thermal springs.

Tribal people have, for generations, used thermal waters for cooking, washing and heating. Opposite the entrance to the village, colonial-style shops sell sheepskins, furs and handicrafts, including pounamu (greenstone).

The other attraction at Te Puia is **Pohutu** ("Big Splash"), the greatest geyser in New Zealand, thundering to a height of more than 30 metres (100ft) up to 20 times a day. In the evening concert performances and a hangi (traditional Maori earth-oven meal) are held here.

Rainbow country

About 4km (2½ miles) northwest of Rotorua off SH5 on Fairy Springs Road is the delightful **Rainbow Springs Nature Park** (daily 8am until late; entrance fee; tel: 07-350 0440; www.rainbowsprings.co.nz). Its natural pools, set amid 12 hectares (30 acres) of lush landscaped gardens, teem with thousands of Brown and Rainbow trout. These fish, which swim here from Lake Rotorua to spawn, can be hand-fed and viewed through an underwater window.

Adjacent to the nature park is **Kiwi Encounter** (daily 10am–4pm; entrance fee; tel: 07-350 0440; www.kiwiencounter.co.nz), a unique incubation facility, hatchery and nursery, the only one of its kind open to the public in the world. On your 45-minute guided tour, you can view kiwis, native geckos and skinks, plus adult and juvenile tuataras, New Zealand's living "dinosaurs", in a nocturnal house. There are also New Zealand native and exotic birds, and "Captain Cooker" wild pigs, introduced by the famous explorer himself.

Close to the springs is the terminus for **Skyline Skyrides** (daily 9am–late, tel: 07-347 0027, 0800-865 843; www.skylineskyrides.co.nz), one of Rotorua's main adventure attractions, but with plenty on offer for the less cavalier as well. Ride a gondola midway up **Mount Ngongotaha** for a breathtaking view of the city, lake and surrounding countryside. The more adventurous can plunge downhill again in a high-speed luge cart. The speed of the carts can be controlled, and there are three tracks totalling 5km (3 miles), including a relatively leisurely "scenic" option

with bays where riders can stop to take photographs. The Sky Swing takes the children's playground favourite a few notches higher, reaching a height of 50 metres (165ft) and speeds of 120kph (75mph).

About 10km (6 miles) northwest of Rotorua, on Western Road near **Ngongotaha**, is the spacious **Agrodome**  (daily 8.30am–5pm; entrance fee; tel: 07-357 1050; www.agrodome.co.nz), located on 160 hectares (395 acres) of pasture. Three times a day (9.30am, 11am and 2.30pm), 19 trained rams (showcasing New Zealand's 19 major breeds) are put through their paces by extremely well-trained sheepdogs. It's an educational and entertaining performance, and visitors receive handfuls of freshly shorn wool. Children love the chance to bottle-feed a lamb, though they're often less enthusiastic about the genuinely rural accompanying odours. There are a huge number of other activities, including farm tractor tours to feed sheep, deer, alpacas and emus by hand.

At the adjacent **Agrodome Adventure Park**, many thrilling rides are on

The lush environment of Rainbow Springs Nature Park.

BELOW: sheep-shearing performance at the Agrodome.

Hinemoa and Tutanekai

Rich with Maori folklore and legend, one of Lake Rotorua's greatest Maori love stories is set on the island of Mokoia: the romance of Hinemoa and Tutanekai. Hinemoa lived on the mainland and, against her family's wishes, fell in love with Tutanekai, a young island chieftain. Their marriage was forbidden, so the couple secretly planned for Hinemoa to paddle across the lake following the sound of Tutanekai's flute at night. When Hinemoa's family beached the canoes she was forced instead to swim across the lake, warming herself in the hot pool that bears her name, before reuniting with Tutanekai. Today visitors can join a boat cruise and bathe in Hinemoa's Pool, while spotting rare birds including the saddleback, stitchbird and North Island robin.

Trout pool at Rainbow Springs Nature Park.

BELOW: geyser at Wai-O-Tapu.

offer, perhaps the most unusual of which is Freefall Xtreme, which recreates the sensation of skydiving with a column of wind that holds the adventurer 5 metres (16ft) in the air. Also available are bungee-jumping, jet-boat racing, zorbing *(see page 113)*, and the Swoop, which is an exhilarating combination of bungee-jumping and flying that sees visitors being whisked 100 metres (330ft) through the air at 130kph (80mph).

There are more trout at **Paradise Valley Springs** (daily 8am–5pm; entrance fee; tel: 07-348 9667; www. paradisev.co.nz), 11km (7 miles) northwest of Rotorua, and at **Hamurana Springs** 17km (11 miles) away on the northern shore of Lake Rotorua.

To protect sports fisheries, it has been made illegal to buy or sell trout in New Zealand, but many visitors can still enjoy a fresh trout dinner, as the fish is an easy catch, with guides claiming a 97 percent daily "strike" rate. In fact, no trip to Rotorua or Taupo is complete without a fishing expedition on the lakes. Guides supply all tackle and will meet clients outside hotels,

with trailer boats ready for action, or at the boat harbour. **Clearwater Cruises** (tel: 07-362 8590; www.clearwater. co.nz) and **Mana Adventures** (tel: 07-348 4186; www.manaadventures. co.nz) both provide a variety of trout-fishing excursions.

Rainbow trout on most lakes around Rotorua and on Lake Taupo average 1.4kg (3lbs) and on Lake Tarawera *(see page 186)*, where they are tougher to catch, fish of 3.5–5.5kg (8–12lbs) are not uncommon. The icing on the cake after a day of fishing is having a hotel or restaurant chef prepare the catch – a service speciality which most are well used to providing.

Some 8km (5 miles) north of the Agrodome on SH5 is **Off Road NZ** (daily 9am–5pm; entrance fee; tel: 07-332 5748; www.offroadnz.co.nz). This is for those who like to go very fast and make a lot of noise, especially in self-drive four-wheel-drive vehicles or Off Road's monster truck, over rough and challenging terrain. Adjacent is the **Mamaku Blue Winery** (daily 9.30am–5pm; free; tel: 07-332 5840; www.mamakublue.co.nz), New Zealand's largest blueberry winery, where orchard tours are available.

Along Central Road, past Ngongotaha township at Sunnex Road, the **Farm House** (daily 10am–3pm; tel: 07-332 3771) hires out ponies and horses for riding over 245 hectares (605 acres) of bush-edged farmland. Carrying on clockwise around Lake Rotorua, the scenic road continues to **Okere Falls** ❶ where, after a short walk through native forest and down a cliff-side, the **Kaituna River** can be viewed thundering through a narrow chasm into the swirling pool below. This is the place to tackle the highest commercially rafted waterfall in the world (daily 9am, 12pm, 3pm; tel: 07-343 9500; www.raftabout.co.nz).

Knocking on Hell's Gate

Crossing the Ohau Channel outlet, which leads from northeastern Lake Rotorua into Lake Rotoiti, an east-

bound turn onto SH30 towards Whakatane takes you to the very door of **Hell's Gate** **❶** (daily 8.30am–8.30pm; entrance fee; tel: 07-345 3151; www.hellsgate.co.nz), reputedly the most active thermal reserve in Rotorua. The Maori name, Tikitere, recalls the legend of Hurutini, who threw herself into a boiling pool because her husband treated her with contempt. Tikitere is a contraction of *Taku tiki i tere nei* ("My daughter has floated away"), bestowed by George Bernard Shaw. The volcanic activity here covers 4 hectares (10 acres), highlighted by the hot-water **Kakahi Falls**, the largest of their kind in the Southern Hemisphere. Hell's Gate is home to the **Wai Ora Spa**, the only place in New Zealand where you can experience the singular cosmetic benefits of a mud bath. Follow this with a bath in the sulphur waters of the **Hurutini Pool** for surprisingly silky smooth skin.

On the shores of **Lake Rotoiti** **❻** is the family-run **Rotoiti Tours World of Maori** (nightly in summer, winter by arrangement; entrance fee; tel: 07-348 8969; www.worldofmaori.co.nz). Visitors are transported to the Rakeiao *marae* (meeting area) for a very traditional experience, which includes a concert performance and *hangi* meal, plus the opportunity for larger groups to sleep over communally in the *wharenui* (meeting house).

Further down SH30 along the shores of **Lake Rotoehu** and **Lake Rotoma**, a side road between the lakes heads off to **Waitangi Soda Springs** **❶**, located in front of the campground. Here hot water percolates in the Waitangi Stream, where you can take a dip. Heading south of Lake Rotoiti is unspoilt **Lake Okataina**, starting point of a walking track to Lake Tarawera (*see page 186*).

The eruption of Tarawera

Southeast of Rotorua, heading in the direction of the airport, is the turnoff to the forest-clad **Lake Tikitapu** **Ⓜ** (Blue Lake) and **Lake Rotokakahi** **Ⓝ** (Green Lake), a favourite stomping ground for joggers and a retreat for those who enjoy walking or riding

Hiring a camper van is a great way to see New Zealand.

BELOW: boiling mud pool at Hell's Gate. There is a total of around 1,200 geothermal features in the Rotorua region.

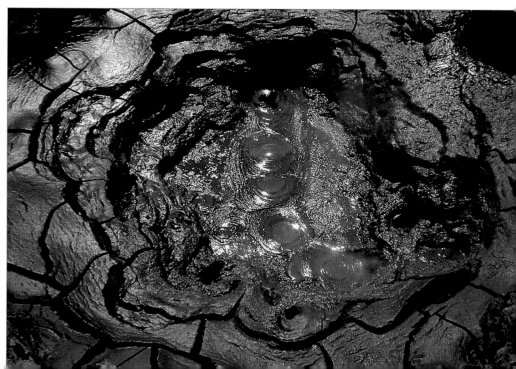

Te Wairoa's breath-taking waterfall is well worth the 20-minute hike from the Buried Village.

BELOW: the 1,111-metre (3,645ft) summit of Mount Tarawera.

along the well-marked and graded trails. Horses, ponies and kayaks are available for hire. The trails lead through pine forest and native bush. On a fine day, follow the signs to the lookout points between the lakes to observe that, although they are side by side, one is blue and the other green.

The road continues to the larger Lake Tarawera via the **Buried Village** Ⓞ (daily, 9am–5pm in summer, 9am–4.30pm in winter; entrance fee; tel: 07-362 8287; www.buriedvillage.co.nz), destroyed on 10 June 1886 when a devastating eruption of Mount Tarawera blasted rock, lava and ash into the air over a 15,500-sq-km (6,000-sq-mile) area and buried the villages of Te Wairoa, Te Ariki and Moura, killing 147 Maori and six Europeans. The Buried Village contains items excavated from Te Wairoa, including the *whare* (hut) of a *tohunga* (priest) who foretold the disaster *(see panel, below)* and was unearthed alive four days after the eruption. There is an inescapably eerie feeling here as

you walk past the remnants of Maori and European buildings frozen in time at the moment a community was extinguished.

Well worth the extra 20 minutes it takes at the end of your circuit of the village is the charming, if steep, **Te Wairoa Waterfalls Track**, a stroll through native bush to a 30-metre (100ft) waterfall.

From the Buried Village, it's a short drive further east to **Lake Tarawera** Ⓟ, with **Mount Tarawera** Ⓠ ("burnt spear") looming in the distance. From Te Wairoa, before the eruption, many Victorian tourists were rowed across Lake Tarawera to the fabulous Pink and White Terraces, two huge silica formations which rose 250 metres (820ft) from the shores of **Lake Rotomahana** and were billed as one of "the eight wonders of the world" *(see panel, below)*. Today, you can retrace the route to the former site with **Lake Tarawera Launch Cruises** (tel: 07-362 8595; www.thelandinglaketarawera.co.nz), when you take the Eruption Trail Cruise aboard the classic, kauri-hulled MV *Reremoana*. The return journey

Tarawera's Ghostly Sightings

Adding to the area's mysterious aura is the tale of a ghostly war canoe full of mourning, flax-robed Maori seen by two separate boatloads of visitors on Lake Tarawera on the misty morning of 31 May 1886. Earlier that morning, the visitors had ventured out by boat from Te Wairoa, the launch point for trips on Lake Tarawera, to view the famous Pink and White Terraces rising from the shores of nearby Lake Rotomahana.

When this sighting was reported back at Te Wairoa it filled the local Maori villagers with terror, for the ceremonial war canoe that had been described to them had ceased to exist in the region for over 50 years. Tuhuto, the *tohunga* (priest) of Te Wairoa, prophesied that the apparition was "an omen that all this region will be overwhelmed". Some Maori even left the area, but many stayed.

On a chilly moonlit night 11 days later, Mount Tarawera fulfilled his prophecy to the letter, blasting the Pink and White Terraces off the tourist map for ever, though not from Rotorua's memory. The eruption lasted some five hours, and an area measuring some 15,540 sq km (6,000 sq miles) – including the village of Te Wairoa – was covered with ash, lava and mud. Rotorua never seems to have come to terms with the loss of the terraces, and you may be surprised how often you are reminded of them during your stay.

cruises past the thermal activity at **Hot Water Beach** and across Lake Tarawera to Kariki Point. **The Landing Café** (tel: 07-362 8595), located within the cruise centre, is famous for its mussel chowder and should not be missed.

If you fancy a bird's-eye view, flights over the crater and thermal lakes depart from Te Puia, Agrodome Park as well as Skyline Skyrides. The flights are operated by **helipro** (tel: 07-357 2512; www. helipro.co.nz), which has exclusive landing concessions on both Mount Tarawera and Mokoia Island. A thrilling landing on the mountain's slopes allows close inspection of the 6km (4-mile) long, 250-metre (820ft) deep chasm caused by the volcanic explosion.

Waimangu Valley

On SH5, some 14km (9 miles) south of Rotorua, is the **Tamaki Maori Village** Ⓡ (evenings; entrance fee; tel: 07-349 2999; www.maoriculture.co.nz). The brainchild of two enterprising brothers, Doug and Mike Tamaki, the village features a recreated pre-European Maori village, bought alive by night by a tribal market where traditional crafts,

made on site, are sold and a stunning cultural performance is followed by a shared *hangi* (earth oven) meal.

Twenty km (12 miles) south of Rotorua, still on SH5 going towards Taupo, is the turnoff to **Waimangu Volcanic Valley** Ⓢ (daily 8.30am–3.30pm; entrance fee; tel: 07-366 6137; www.waimangu.com). This unspoilt thermal area contains the **Waimangu Cauldron**, the world's largest boiling lake. An easy walk downhill from a tea-room leads past bubbling crater lakes, hot creeks and algae-covered silica terraces to the shores of Lake Rotomahana, where a launch can be taken to the intensively active **Steaming Cliffs** and the former site of the lost Pink and White Terraces.

Waimangu is one of the more colourful thermal attractions, presenting a vivid palette of hues that only adds to the other-worldly impression it creates. The **Waimangu Geyser** was once the biggest in the world, reaching dizzy heights of 500 metres (1,640ft). Today it has less force and is dwarfed by Pohutu *(see page 182)*, New Zealand's biggest geyser.

(see page 182)

TIP

DON'T step off the designated path when visiting thermal attractions in the region. New Zealanders take a dim view of visitors desecrating their natural wonders, and besides which, what appears to be a firm surface may be the thin crust of a hot steaming pool. Accidents do happen.

BELOW: Waimangu Cauldron.

With trout abundant in the numerous lakes, no trip to Rotorua or Taupo is complete without a fishing expedition.

BELOW: white-knuckle jet-boat ride with thundering Huka Falls behind.

About 10km (6 miles) further along SH5, a loop road leads to another thermal area, **Wai-O-Tapu Thermal Wonderland** ❷ (daily 8.30am–5pm; entrance fee; tel: 07-366 6333; www.geyserland. co.nz). *Wai-O-Tapu*, Maori for "Sacred Waters", is the home of **Lady Knox Geyser**, which erupts daily at 10.15am – with a little encouragement from a staff member who adds some eco-friendly soap powder into the vent to create tension and cause the spectacular spurt of super-heated water and steam. Other attractions include the bubbly **Champagne Pool**, tinted silica terraces and **Bridal Veil Falls**.

About 70km (43 miles) south of Rotorua and 37km (23 miles) north of Taupo is the "Hidden Valley" of **Orakei Korako** ❸ (daily 8am–4.30pm; entrance fee; tel: 07-378 3131; www. orakeikorako.co.nz), which is a cave and thermal park comprising geysers, hot springs, mud volcanoes, underground caves and some of the largest silica terraces in the world. The geothermal area is accessible only by a short boat cruise across **Lake Ohakuri**. Maori chiefs painted themselves in the mirror pools here, hence the name, Orakei Korako – "adorning place".

The route to Taupo

If you've somehow emerged from Rotorua without being exposed to its geothermal wonders, you can rectify the omission on the way to Taupo. Some 7km (4 miles) before Taupo, just below the junction of SH1 and SH5, visitors will encounter the **Wairakei** ❹ geothermal area. At **Wairakei Terraces** (daily 9am–5pm in summer, until 4.30pm in winter; entrance fee; tel: 07-378 0913; www.wairakeiterraces.co.nz), natural silica terraces wiped out for the construction of a power station in the area have been recreated artificially and left to develop their brilliant colours of blue, pink and white over time. Whether they will eventually provide an adequate substitute for the much-missed Pink and White Terraces, only time will tell.

Wairakei hosts the **Maori Cultural Experience** with evening performances, *hangi* meals and craft displays (bookings essential). Tours of the power station are also available. Superheated water is drawn from the ground through a series of bores, enabling dry steam to be piped to electricity turbines in a nearby powerhouse.

Also located between Wairakei and Taupo, on a gravel road, are the **Craters of the Moon** (daily 8.30am–5pm; free; tel: 0274-965 131), another wild thermal area worth stopping at. Visitors can gaze into a frightening abyss of furiously boiling mud and walk around a track to see steam rising from natural fumaroles in the hillside. From here, the resort town of Taupo is only about 5km (3 miles) away.

Before reaching Taupo at the **Wairakei Tourist Park** on the Waikato River, you will encounter a world first, the geothermally heated **Huka Prawn Farm** (daily 9am–5.30pm; entrance fee; tel: 07-374 8474; www.hukaprawnpark. co.nz). Visitors can observe, hand-feed, catch and eat prawns here. Another

stop is the **Volcanic Activity Centre** (Mon–Fri 9am–5pm, Sat–Sun 10am–4pm; entrance fee; tel: 07-374 8375; www.volcanoes.co.nz), which explains all you need to know about geothermal and volcanic activity in the region – one of the most active areas on earth.

A further 200 metres (650ft) down the road is the **Honey Hive** (daily 9am–5pm; free; tel: 07-374 8553), where you can learn all about bees and honey production, and purchase a bottle of New Zealand's famous manuka honey to take home.

A nearby loop road leads to the spectacular **Huka Falls**, where the full force of the Waikato River hurtles from a narrow gorge over an 11-metre (36ft) ledge. Enough water goes over the falls every second to fill two Olympic-sized pools. When lit by sunshine, the water takes on a brilliant ice-blue colour before crashing into a foaming basin below. A footbridge passes over the river, offering spectacular views, and on the other side there are a number of pleasant hikes, including the walk downstream to **Aratiatia Rapids**. For water-level views, book a white-knuckle ride on the **Huka Falls Jet** boats (daily 10am–5pm; tel: 07-374 8572; www.hukafallsjet.com), which depart every 30 minutes and skim across the water near the base of the falls. A short distance along the loop road on the banks of the Waikato River is the renowned **Huka Lodge** (tel: 07-378 5791; www.hukalodge.co.nz), an exclusive retreat for the well-heeled.

Lake Taupo

Taupo is an abbreviation of Taupo-nui-Tia ("the great shoulder cloak of Tia"), which takes its name from the Arawa canoe explorer who discovered **Lake Taupo ❺**, New Zealand's largest. The lake covers some 619 sq km (240 sq miles) and was formed by volcanic explosions over thousands of years. It is now the most famous trout-fishing lake in the world, yielding in excess of 500 tonnes of rainbow trout annually. The rivers flowing into the lake are equally well stocked, so that fishermen frequently stand shoulder-to-shoulder at the mouth of the Waitahanui River, forming what has come to be known as the picket fence.

TIP

The magnificent Huka Falls are best experienced on the Huka Jet, which roars along Huka River and brings you in close proximity of the Huka Falls. The 30-minute trip runs all day (tel: 07-374 8572; www.hukafallsjet.com).

BELOW: Lake Taupo is a hot-spot for some mind-blowing adventure sports.

TIP

There are several useful websites on skiing in New Zealand, but skiers heading to Mount Ruapehu should check out www.mtruapehu. com. It has information on skiing at both Whakapapa and Turoa.

Apart from its trout-fishing fame, Taupo offers a full range of activities, from sedate boat and kayak trips on its lake to skydiving, bungee-jumping and other adrenalin-pumping sports. A major New Zealand events destination, both accommodation and restaurants are easy to find at this family-oriented township. For more information, drop by the **Taupo i-site Visitor Centre** at 30 Tongariro Street (tel: 07-376 0027; www.laketauponz.com).

Mount Ruapehu

At the southern head of Lake Taupo is the breathtaking 7,600-sq-km (2,930-sq-mile) **Tongariro National Park ❻**, containing the three active volcanic peaks of **Mount Tongariro** (1,968 metres/6,457ft), **Mount Ruapehu** (2,796 metres/9,173ft), as well as **Mount Ngauruhoe** (2,290 metres/7,513ft), which starred as Mount Doom in the film trilogy *The Lord of the Rings (see page 80)*.

The most scenic route from Taupo leaves SH1 at **Turangi** heading for **Tokaanu**, not far from the Tongariro Power Station, and winds up steeply up through native bush and around

the shore of Lake Rotoaira. The alternative route is to turn off the main highway at Rangipo on to SH47.

According to Maori legend, when the priest and explorer Ngatoro-i-rangi was in danger of freezing to death on the mountains his fervent prayers for assistance were answered by the fire demons of Hawaiki, who sent fire via White Island and Rotorua to burst out through the mountain tops. To appease the gods, Ngatoro cast his female slave into the Ngauruhoe volcano – called Auruhoe, by the local Maori. Mount Ngauruhoe, with its typical volcanic cone, is the youngest and most active of the three volcanoes and still bubbles and spits lava and ash occasionally. A major eruption in 1954 continued intermittently for nine months.

Mount Ruapehu is a perpetually snow-capped volcano with a flattened summit stretching 3km (2 miles) and incorporating an acidic, bubbling crater lake and six small glaciers. Ruapehu has blown out clouds of steam and ash a number of times in the past 100 years, raining dust over a

BELOW: trampers descending into a crater at Mount Tongariro.

90km (56-mile) radius in 1945, and closing the nearby Whakapapa and Turoa ski fields in 1996. On 24 December 1953, 151 people died in a tragic train disaster when a *lahar*, or violent discharge of water and mud, roared down the Whangaehu River from the Crater Lake. Fortunately, when the lake burst its banks again in March 2007, an alarm system provided warning before a torrent of mud and debris again poured through the river gorge.

Top-class skiing

Mount Ruapehu is the major ski area of the North Island, with the action taking place at two locations, comprising in total 1,800 hectares (4,450 acres) of slopes. **Whakapapa** on the mountain's northwestern face has excellent beginner slopes as well as more challenging areas. **Turoa** is on the southwestern slopes, with magnificent views of Mount Taranaki. Accommodation abounds in the area, with Turoa skiers tending to base themselves at **Ohakune**, while those skiing at Whakapapa stay at **Whakapapa Village**,

where the historic **Bayview Chateau Tongariro** (tel: 07-892 3809; www.chateau. co.nz) built in 1929 is found, or at **National Park**, a village located about 15km (9 miles) away. Apart from skiing, adventure tour operators also offer white-water rafting down the Tongariro and Rangitikei rivers.

Outside of the July–October ski season, Tongariro National Park has many fine walks, including the famous 16km (10-mile) **Tongariro Crossing**, which covers spectacular scenery in a matter of seven or eight hours. Rangers at the **Whakapapa Visitors Centre** (tel: 07-892 3729) have details on walking tracks and huts. The walk can easily be achieved in a day, but two days allows time for more diversions, including the summits of Mount Ngauruhoe and Mount Tongariro. Although the hike begins and ends at different locations, inexpensive transportation can be booked through your accommodation. ❑

Whakapapa, on the slopes of Mount Ruapehu, is the leading ski resort on the North Island.

BELOW: on the piste in Whakapapa.

HEALING WATERS OF ROTORUA

This strange, steamy landscape of bubbling springs and mud pools, saturated in Maori lore and history, has been attracting tourists for more than a century

Rotorua has been a top tourist resort for decades. A century ago genteel folk came to the spa from all over the world to promenade and take the waters. So it's a little surprising to learn that New Zealanders call the town "Stinkville" and "Rotten Egg Town". All becomes clear when you take your first breath of the sulphur-laden mist, but you'll soon forget the odour as you explore the surreal steamy surroundings. Every geyser, every spring, it seems, has a curious name with a story attached, like the Lobster Pool in Kuirau Park, so named because of the shade its acidic waters tinted fair European skins. And a concentrically ringed mud pool, charmingly named "Gramophone Record Pool".

LUNAR REBIRTH

One of these stories relates to the moon. Rotorua's healing waters have been described as "Wai-ora-a-Tane" (Living Water of Tane), where according to Maori legend the dying moon bathes each month in the great mythical lake of Aewa. Here, she receives the gift of life to sustain her on her journey through the heavens.

It's important to obey the signposts and keep to the paths in this region, where the earth is a bit less stable than most of us are used to. The thermal pools may look tempting, but some of them are boiling hot or highly acidic. If your vision gets blocked by steam, stand still until it clears – don't stagger on blindly.

ABOVE: Champagne Pool. Dinner parties and concerts are sometimes held in the misty, ethereal atmosphere of the Champagne Pool at Wai-O-Tapu Thermal Wonderland, just south of Rotorua. The pool is actually quite green and steamy, and doesn't really look like champagne at all, but it fizzes enthusiastically near the shoreline, just like a large glass of bubbly.

RIGHT: it's not a good idea to peer into the throat of an unpredictable geyser. Lady Knox Geyser's efficient timekeeping is kept to the minute with a daily dose of eco-friendly soap.

LEFT: some areas are dangerous, so pay heed to the signs.

DANGER
DO NOT ENTER

CROQUET AT THE BATH HOUSE

How very English! Splendid buildings like this one, the town's most frequently photographed edifice and superb backdrop to a croquet match, gives Rotorua its genteel charm. Now known as Tudor Towers, the elegant building which graces Government Gardens was originally constructed as a bathhouse in 1908, complete with ancient sculptures in the foyer. To the left and right of the entrance foyer, double doors led to men's and women's bathhouses, where treatment could be obtained for rheumatism. The baths had facilities for Aix massage, steam baths and mud baths.

The building is no longer a bathhouse – if you want a dip in a thermal pool, the nearby Polynesian Pools, built in 1886 and the site of Rotorua's first building and bathhouse, is open daily.

Today, Tudor Towers houses the Rotorua Museum *(see page 180)*, with a number of collections tracing the development of painting and printmaking in New Zealand, as well as contemporary paintings. There is also a kauri gum collection and a wildlife display, plus exhibitions about the local Te Arawa people who first settled the area. A video on the 1886 Mount Tarawera eruption shows how the magnificent Pink and White Terraces, formed of silica deposits, were annihilated.

ABOVE: Whakarewarewa. This famous thermal area's full name is Whakarewarewatanga-o-te-a-Wahiao, which means, "the uprising of a war party of Wahiao". New Zealand's highest geyser, Pohutu, bursts forth several times a day for up to 40 minutes at a time, reaching heights of 20–30 metres (65–100ft). The nearby Prince of Wales Feathers geyser generally goes off just before Pohutu.

ABOVE: Tudor Towers, the genteel side of Rotorua.

RIGHT: soaking up the therapeutic volcanic mud.

POVERTY BAY AND HAWKE'S BAY

Hawke's Bay and its neighbour, inappropriately
named Poverty Bay, are home to a wealth of
bountiful vineyards, colourful history,
interesting architecture – and New Zealand's
most easterly city

BELOW: the good
life in Gisborne,
one of the sunniest
places in New
Zealand.

There are several reasons why Gisborne and the area around it are special to New Zealanders. Situated on 178 degrees longitude, Gisborne is noted for being the first city in the world to greet the rising sun each day, a fortunate accident of geography made much of at midnight on 31 December 1999, when it led worldwide television coverage of the turn of the new millennium.

It is also a historic coast: Young Nick's Head, a promontory across the bay from the city of Gisborne, was the first piece of land that British explorer Captain James Cook and the crew of his ship Endeavour sighted in 1769. Cook's landing site is at the foot of Kaiti Hill, a great viewing platform for Gisborne and the surrounding areas. Over the Turanganui River stands an impressive statue of Captain Cook, and further around the beachfront is a statue of Nicholas Young, the cabin boy on the *Endeavour* credited with being the first on board to sight land.

Gisborne

Cook, who got most things right, erred badly, however, in calling the region **Poverty Bay** because "it did not afford a single article we wanted, except a little firewood". Poverty Bay retains the name grudgingly. It is now sheep and cattle country, rich in citrus, apple and kiwi fruit orchards, vineyards, vegetable gardens and a variety of food crops which all support a large processing industry. With 15 wineries in the area (www.gisborne.co.nz/wine) it's no surprise that its wines – particularly chardonnay and gewürztraminer – are among the best in the country and should be sampled at one of the many vineyards open to the public.

Poverty Bay offers spellbinding coastal vistas of white sands and sparkling blue waters, accompanied by the scarlet blossom of the pohutukawa, often known as the New Zealand Christmas tree because it is at its best and brightest in late December. Some of

this vibrancy rubs off on **Gisborne** ❼, a city of sun and water, parks, bridges and beaches. Watersports are a recreational way of life and the city is a magnet for surfers, with reliable conditions at the nearby beaches of Wainui, Okitu and Makorori.

The "City of Bridges", Gisborne is situated on the banks of the Taruheru and Waimata rivers and Waikanae Creek, all joining to form the Turanganui River. On Stout Street, adjacent to the city centre, **Tairawhiti Museum** (Mon–Fri 10am–4pm, Sat 11am–4pm, Sun 1.30–4pm; free; tel: 06-867 3832; www.tairawhitimuseum.org.nz) recounts the region's history. A section of the main building is a maritime museum, made up from parts of the steamship *Star of Canada*, which was wrecked on Kaiti Beach in 1912.

Gisborne lingers over its association with Cook, but the area's historic wealth pre-dates his visit. Maori landholdings – some of them leased to Europeans – are extensive. Meeting houses are numerous and can be seen at many Maori settlements along the coast. Most feature carved lintels,

panels and beams in traditional style, embellished with the unorthodox painting of patterned foliage, birds and mythical human figures. One of the largest meeting houses in the country is **Te Poho-o-Rawiri** (visits by arrangement only; tel: 06-867 2103), at the base of **Kaiti Hill** on Queens Drive. Built in 1925, it did not use the traditional ridge-pole structure because of its size. However, it still contains some impressive *tukutuku* (woven reed) panels and magnificent carvings. Almost every Maori settlement on the coast has its treasured meeting house.

As a major forestry centre, it's quite appropriate that Gisborne is the location of New Zealand's largest tree collection, at **Eastwoodhill Arboretum** (daily 9am–5pm; entrance fee; tel: 06-863 9003; www.eastwoodhill.org. nz). Located just 30 minutes west of town via Patutahi, it was founded by Gallipoli veteran soldier W. Douglas Cook. His lifetime's work sprawls over some 70 hectares (173 acres).

Children's artwork at the Tairawhiti Museum in Gisborne.

BELOW:
Eastwoodhill
Arboretum.

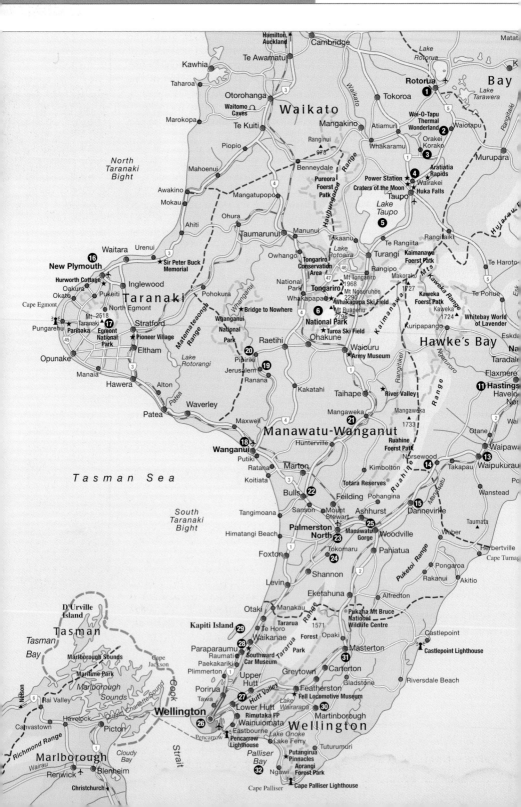

Legendary Te Kooti

While Poverty Bay is tranquil today, it has been the site of many tribal battles in the past. One of the most interesting stories concerns the Maori prophet Te Kooti, who in the 19th century led a rebellion against settlers. He was exiled to the distant Chatham Islands, hundreds of kilometres off the east coast of the North Island, along with dozens of other Maori arrested in the 1860s – but that wasn't to be the end of him. He masterminded a daring escape back to the mainland and, believing God had appeared to him and promised he would save the Maori as he had saved the Jews, founded a religious movement which still exists, called Ringatu ("The Upraised Hand"). The government sent an army in pursuit, but Te Kooti proved a formidable enemy in the wild bush of the **Urewera Range**, striking back with guerrilla attacks that kept him free and the government harassed. He was eventually pardoned in old age and allowed to live with his followers in the King Country (*see pages 163, 165*).

Many of Te Kooti's old haunts have been preserved in **Te Urewera National Park** ⑧, 212,000 hectares (524,000 acres) of rugged mountains, forests and lakes, much of it still inaccessible to all but the toughest trampers. Located some 164km (102 miles) northwest of Gisborne via Wairoa, the park's highlight is **Lake Waikaremoana** ("Lake of the Rippling Waters"), rich in trout and with bush thick to the water's edge on all but the eastern side, where it is hemmed in by steep cliffs. Chalet, motel and motor camp accommodation is available at Waikaremoana (tel: 06-837 3826; www.lake.co.nz), and there are tramping huts throughout the park.

Into Hawke's Bay

Poverty Bay runs southwards to the **Mahia Peninsula**, where it merges into the **Hawke's Bay** region. Sitting near the neck of the peninsula separating the two bays is **Morere**, 60km (37 miles) south of Gisborne, worth visiting if only to soak in a pool at the **Morere Hot**

Admiring the views on the Lake Waikaremoana Track, one of New Zealand's Great Walks.

A unique feature of Te Urewera National Park is Lake Waikare-iti, home of a lake within a lake. It contains tiny Ranui Island, which itself contains a lake called Te Tamaiti o Waikaremoana ("The Child of Waikaremoana").

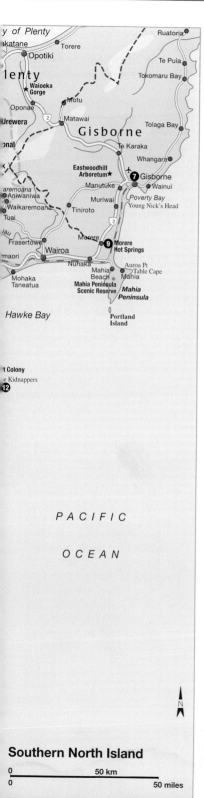

Southern North Island

0   50 km

0   50 miles

Hawke's Bay is New Zealand's oldest wine region.

BELOW: the Mahia Peninsula is one of New Zealand's best whale-watching areas.

Springs ❾ (daily 10am–5pm, until 9pm in summer; entrance fee; tel: 06-837 8856; www.morerehotsprings.co.nz). The Nikau Pool is the best; reached via a short track, it is set among a beautiful forest of ferns, and there are several rewarding hikes through the surrounding native forest.

Further on in **Nuhaka**, a road provides access to the dramatic, high white cliffs of the **Mahia Peninsula**. On the south side of the peninsula is **Mahia Beach**, a popular place with a large camping ground, friendly store and links-style golf course. Follow the road across the peninsula to Maungawhio Lagoon, a paradise for birdwatchers, and on to the small settlement of **Mahia** itself, located on a rocky coastline with a series of small sandy beaches punctuated by rocky outcrops boasting numerous rock pools. Café Mahia is a great place to sample paua fritters, a New Zealand delicacy, and is renowned, in the North Island at least, for its stunning chilli, lime and mango sauce.

Auroa Point provides great views of dramatic Table Cape, and whales are often seen passing through here.

Back on State Highway (SH) 2 some 40km (25 miles) past the town of **Wairoa**, a turnoff leads northwest to Te Urewera National Park (*see previous page*). Continue west for another 104km (65 miles), stopping to stretch your legs at Lake Tutira en route, until you meet the junction of SH2 and SH5. Turn off onto SH5 and travel 5km (3 miles) through the fruit-laden trees and vines of the Esk Valley.

In the heart of it all is the small community of **Eskdale** and **Whitebay World of Lavender** (daily 10am–4pm; free; tel: 06-836 6081; www.whitebay. co.nz). Apparently, wherever grapes grow well, conditions are right for lavender, so Hawke's Bay is ideal. Although the centre is open all year, harvesting at Whitebay is in January, so the time prior to that affords the best chance to soak up the spectacular sight of a sea of vivid purple lavender blooms. There are tours of the distillery, and plentiful opportunities to buy all things lavender-related: a shop sells lavender products and a café serves lavender-infused muffins, lavender ice cream and lavender tea.

Whale Strandings

The Mahia Peninsula has a long whaling history. Extensive commercial operations began in the 1830s, and it soon became the principal whaling point on the mid-eastern section of the North Island, with 11 stations located from Waikokopua to Mahanga. Whaling has long since ceased, and Sperm and Beaked whales are often spotted cruising past the peninsula. Unfortunately strandings (around 30 per year) are common, as the whales get confused by the unusual topography of the peninsula, and after following the land's curvature, find themselves wallowing in shallow waters. The largest recorded stranding was in April 1943, when 300 False killer whales came ashore; these days locals are better equipped to give those stranded a helping hand.

Art Deco Napier

Another 21km (13 miles) south is **Napier ⑩**, one of the two cities which, together with **Hastings**, further south, make up Hawke's Bay. Napier and Hastings may be twin cities but both are strongly independent and even competitive. Napier is a seafront city with a population of 55,000, while Hastings is an agricultural marketing centre of some 67,000. To their west plains sweep away to the Kaweka and Ruahine ranges, rugged areas for hunters and trampers. Both are thriving cities today, and there is little indication of the massive destruction they suffered in the tragic earthquake that rocked Hawke's Bay in 1931 *(see page 200)*.

The large-scale destruction wrought by the 1931 earthquake gave Napier a chance to reinvent itself, and a new city arose from the ashes with a distinctive Art Deco facade. Napier's collection of Art Deco buildings in the inner city, with their bold lines, elaborate motifs and pretty pastel colours, is recognised internationally. Widespread appreciation, however, has come only in the past few years. Napier's people are fiercely proud of the city's heritage. Building owners are encouraged to restore and preserve the facades, and civic leaders have done their bit too, developing the main street in a sympathetic fashion.

While New Zealand is well known for the effort it puts into preserving its many natural assets, it does not have a good record for preserving its architectural heritage. To this end, Napier's **Art Deco Trust** (www.artdeconapier.com) was formed in 1985 by a visionary group. Without their efforts it is entirely possible the construction-crazy 1980s would have seen "progress" do as much damage to the buildings of the 1930s as the earthquake did to their predecessors. The trust organises a number of activities, including informative daily walks for visitors, as well as spearheading the annual Art Deco Weekend held in February, when the whole town seems to step back in time to the 1930s. The Trust also runs the **Art Deco Shop** at the Deco Centre, 163 Tennyson Street (tel: 06-835 0022), which stocks a wide range of gifts and souvenirs relating to Napier's Art Deco heritage.

TIP

Napier's Art Deco Trust organises daily guided walks by volunteer guides. The 90-minute morning walk departs at 10am from the Napier Visitor Centre on Marine Parade. It costs NZ$14; bookings are not essential. The 150-minute afternoon tour departs at 2pm from the Art Deco Shop at 163 Tennyson Street. For further information contact the Art Deco Trust on tel: 06-835 0022; www.artdeconapier.com.

BELOW: The Daily Telegraph building – a fine example of Napier's Art Deco architecture.

TIP

Hastings has a scenic driving route, a signposted tour of its parks and attractions. Among these is Oak Avenue, a magnificent 1.5km (1-mile) stretch of road planted with oaks and other huge deciduous trees by a 19th-century landowner and lovingly tended by his successors ever since.

One exception to Art Deco's stranglehold on Napier's claims to architectural merit is the magnificent **County Hotel** (tel: 06-835 7800, 0800-843 468; www.countyhotel.co.nz) on Browning Street. Previously the County Council Chambers, it is a resplendent example of the Victorian-Edwardian Classical Revival style. And it is not just the design that harks back to those times. Quaintly, if not rashly, a complimentary decanter of port is always available in its library.

Another highlight of Napier is the city's 2km (1¼-mile) long **Marine Parade**. A large recreational collection of gardens, sculptures, fountains, earthquake memorials and varied visitor attractions, the seaside promenade is dominated by towering rows of Norfolk pines. Look out for the **Statue of Pania**, a maiden of local Maori legend who fell in love with a young chief but later lost her life and that of their child to the sea.

At No. 65 is **Hawke's Bay Museum** (daily 10am–4.40pm, until 6pm in summer; entrance fee; tel: 06-835 7781; www.hbmag.co.nz), which details

events surrounding the earthquake and the city's subsequent rebuilding, in addition to exhibits on Maori art and culture.

Also on Marine Parade is the **National Aquarium of New Zealand** (daily 9am–5pm, until 7pm in summer; entrance fee; tel: 06-834 1404; www.nationalaquarium.co.nz), which opened in 2002. Housed in a distinctive stingray-shaped building are more species than in any similar establishment in New Zealand. A moving footpath carries viewers under the "oceanarium", while sharks, stingrays and many other varieties of fish glide by. Land-based species are also featured: kiwis, tuatara and glow-worms among them. It's a hands-on, interactive experience centre in the manner that is now de rigueur for museums around the world.

The strip is also home to **Marineland** (daily 10am–4.30pm; entrance fee; tel: 06-834 4027; www.marineland.co.nz). Here, you can see dolphins, fur seals, otters, sea lions and other marine life.

Residential **Napier Hill** overlooks the city centre. This was one of the earli-

BELOW: Napier after it was devastated by the 1931 earthquake.

Rising from the Ashes

Hawke's Bay was where New Zealand's worst earthquake tragedy took place on 3 February 1931. Buildings crumpled under the impact of a 7.9 Richter Scale earthquake. What the shock did not destroy in Napier and Hastings, fire finished off. The resulting death toll of 258 included a number of people killed by falling parapets. The city of Napier was closest to the epicentre, and heroic deeds were performed by rescuers and by naval personnel from the HMS *Veronica*, which happened to be in harbour (along Napier's seafront today there is a colonnade named after the naval sloop).

As elsewhere in the world, the early 1930s was a time of economic depression, but a passionate government and a sympathetic world came to Hawke's Bay's post-quake aid with funds for a massive relief and rebuilding campaign. The opportunity was taken to widen streets, install new underground telephone lines, and a strict earthquake-proof building code was enforced, giving rise to a brand new city with architecture inspired by the Art Deco movement of the time.

It could be said that Napier today is a kind of memorial to the earthquake. Much of its suburban area, stretching out to the once-independent borough of Taradale in the southwest, is built on the 4,000 hectares (10,000 acres) of former marshland the earthquake pushed up.

est parts of the city to be developed by Europeans, as is evident in some of the fine Victorian and Edwardian homes and the maze of twisting, narrow streets, designed before motor cars were anticipated. On the north side of the hill, next to the busy port, is another historic locale, **Ahuriri**, the cradle of Napier and the site of the first European settlement in the area. A scenic road winds up **Bluff Hill** to a lookout for views over the city, harbour and bay.

Fruitful Hastings

Some 21km (13 miles) south from Napier, architectural treasures from the post-earthquake period are also a feature of **Hastings ⓫**, with a good number of them in the Art Deco and Spanish mission style. Despite this and despite their physical proximity, though, Hastings is rather a different city from Napier – laid out in a flat and formal fashion, and surrounded by rich alluvial plains which host a huge range of horticultural crops. Hastings's main role is, as it is proudly called by locals, "The Fruit Bowl of New Zealand". A Mediterranean-type climate, pure water from an underground aquifer, and innovative growers have made this one of the most important apple-growing regions in the world. Apricots, grapes, peaches, nectarines, plums, kiwi fruit, pears, berries and cherries also grow profusely and are on offer from roadside stalls during the harvesting season, along with tomatoes, sweetcorn, asparagus and peas.

Despite the horticultural bounty, the twin cities rely heavily on farming, which has generated the region's historic wealth. Only pine forests are challenging the supremacy of sheep and cattle in the rolling hinterland. The pastoral farms are the legacy of Victorian settlers who laid claim to huge tracts of Hawke's Bay, and made their fortunes from wool and, later, sheepmeat, beef and hides.

All this may be lost on younger visitors more likely to be awed by Hastings's **Splash Planet** (daily 10am–5.30pm; entrance fee; tel: 06-873 8033, 0508-775 274; www.splashplanet.co.nz), a family-friendly water theme park with more than 15 attractions and motorised rides, and a hit with toddlers, teens and the young at heart.

Marine Parade at Napier. The city's Art Deco buildings are among the finest in the world.

BELOW: Hastings fruit vendor.

The east coast resorts offer superb beaches and the most reliable weather in the country.

BELOW: Captain Cook and his crew were familar with this part of the east coast. Cook is commemorated by this statue on the Gisborne seafront, the first place he set foot on New Zealand soil.

A 3km (2 miles) across the plain from Hastings is "The Village", as the pretty, genteel town of **Havelock North** is known locally. It sits in the shadow of **Te Mata Peak**, a limestone mountain with a summit accessible by car. From the top you can enjoy the sweeping views or, if you are daring enough, you may go hang-gliding or paragliding from the steep cliff on one side. Havelock North is the also the home of **Arataki Honey** (daily 9am–5pm; entrance fee; tel: 06-877 7300, 0800-272 825; www. aratakihoneyhb.co.nz), with a total of more than 17,000 hives, and a major honey producer. At the "Bee Wall" you can see an entire colony at work, from the queen to the drones.

Gannets and wineries

Hastings and Napier may enjoy distinctive identities but they share some significant attractions – the Cape Kidnappers gannet colony, for example, and the local wine industry.
Cape Kidnappers ⑫ is 18km (11 miles) from Hastings and a 20- to 30-minute drive from either city, fol-

lowed by a ride along the beach aboard a tractor-towed trailer to what is thought to be the largest mainland gannet colony in the world. During the breeding season from June to October the cape is closed to visitors for scientific study. The Cape's name harks back to an incident in which local Maori attempted to abduct a Tahitian youth from the serving staff of Captain Cook's *Endeavour* while it lay at anchor nearby.

Hawke's Bay is the oldest of the country's wine-growing regions and sees itself as the finest. There are over 40 wineries established around Napier and Hastings. Certainly it enjoys ever-increasing recognition for the quality of its chardonnay, sauvignon blanc and cabernet sauvignon. Wine enthusiasts often wax lyrical over wineries like **Trinity Hill** (www.trinityhill.co.nz), **Te Mata Estate** (www.temata.co.nz) and **Church Road** (www.churchroad. co.nz). Church Road is one of New Zealand's leading producers and one of its oldest, having been founded in 1897. This was where pioneer wine-maker Tom McDonald earned the title

of father of quality red winemaking in New Zealand. Church Road has the country's only **wine museum**, which can be viewed on a winery tour departing from the cellar door at 2pm and 3pm daily. The museum has antiquities from the Mediterranean dating back to 1000 BC, including amphorae and other vessels. A wine tasting is held at the end of the tour.

There are numerous wineries in the region, all open to visitors. Many offer free wine tastings and have a restaurant on site. If you cannot find a willing designated driver, book a winery tour with one of the many operators in Napier or Hastings.

South of Hastings

Fifty km (31 miles) south of Hastings, pastoral farming is the reason for the existence of another set of Hawke's Bay twin towns, Waipukurau and Waipawa. Near **Waipukurau** ⓭ is a hill with one of the longest names of any place in the world: Taumatawhakatangihanga-koauauotamateapokaiwhenuakitana-tahu. The 57 letters translate into "The hill where the great husband of heaven,

Tamatea, caused plaintive music from his nose flute to ascend to his beloved".

Further south again, another culture has left its mark. In the 19th century, hardy Norwegian and Danish settlers cleared the rainforest in southern Hawke's Bay, which was so dense it had discouraged all others. They established such towns as Norsewood, 85km (53 miles) south of Hastings, and Dannevirke ("Dane's Work"), another 20km (12 miles) further south. The Scandinavian flavour is still evident at **Norsewood** ⓮. Although a tiny town, it has a well-known woollen mill producing a range of knitted goods bearing the settlement's name. **Dannevirke** ⓯ actively promotes its historic links with Scandinavia, though it once, probably wisely, rejected a plan to erect a giant statue of a Viking. It is a farm service town and a convenient staging post on the busy highway between Manawatu to the south and Hawke's Bay to the north. ❏

Typical east coast scenery.

BELOW: enjoying a picnic in Hawke's Bay wine country.

TARANAKI, WANGANUI AND MANAWATU

These predominantly rural regions encompass scenic splendour peppered with quiet, pleasant townships and crowned by Mount Taranaki's majestic peak

The 169km (105-mile) Te Kuiti to New Plymouth road leads southwards through a varied landscape. There is rugged farmed hill country, the Awakino River Gorge, and a beautiful stretch of coast with cliffs and placid sandy bays offering glimpses of **Mount Taranaki** in full view on a clear day. The road passes by a striking memorial to the famous Polynesian anthropologist Sir Peter Buck just north of Urenui, his birthplace. Approaching New Plymouth, Taranaki's main centre, the land flattens to fertile dairy plains which encircle the dormant volcano of Mount Taranaki, a near-perfect, permanently snow-capped cone soaring to a height of 2,518 metres (8,261ft).

New Plymouth

With Mount Taranaki as its backdrop, the town of **New Plymouth** ⓰, home to 48,000 people, spreads along the coast. Its location, fertile soil and climate were immediately attractive to European arrivals in the 1840s. Early missionaries and settlers found a Maori population depleted by inter-tribal wars, yet land disputes between the Maori and newcomers still beset the settlement. War broke out in 1860 and eventually placed New Plymouth under virtual siege.

Visitors should start at **Puke Ariki** (Mon–Tue and Thur–Fri 9am–6pm, Wed 9am–9pm, Sat–Sun 9am–5pm; free; tel: 06-759 6060; www.pukeariki.com),

a museum, public library and visitor centre rolled into one. Located on Ariki Street in the town centre, its exhibits and interactive displays will help you get acquainted with the history and culture of the Taranaki region. The museum also includes the historic **Richmond Cottage**, home of three of the first settler families.

To the east on Queen Street is the **Govett-Brewster Art Gallery** (daily 10am–5pm; free; tel: 06-759 6715; www.govettbrewster.com), home to a notable collection of contemporary art,

Main attractions
GOVETT-BREWSTER ART
  GALLERY, NEW PLYMOUTH
EGMONT NATIONAL PARK
WHANGANUI REGIONAL
  MUSEUM
MANAWATU GORGE

LEFT: cricket practice with Mount Taranaki in the background.
BELOW: Govett-Brewster Art Gallery, New Plymouth.

Blo-karting at Himatangi Beach.

including works by Len Lye, a New Zealand artist and filmmaker (*see page 63*). **St Mary's Church** (tel: 06-758 3111; www.stmarys.org.nz) on Vivian Street, completed in 1846, is the oldest stone church in New Zealand.

New Plymouth is best known for its beautiful parks. At **Pukekura Park** (daily 7.30am–7pm, until 8pm in summer), a few blocks southeast of Govett-Brewster Gallery, lovely lakes, gardens, a fernery, fountains and a waterfall are all lit in rainbow colours by night. The park is also home to the **Brooklands Zoo** (daily 8.30am–5pm; free; tel: 06-759 6060).

A pleasant **Coastal Walkway** runs the length of New Plymouth – fully 7km (4 miles) from the Waiwakaiho River Mouth to Point Taranaki. At roughly the mid-point, opposite Puke Ariki, is Len Lye's soaring 45-metre (148ft) kinetic sculpture *Wind Wand*, at first reviled, then embraced by the locals.

Around the town

BELOW: blooms at Pukeiti Rhododendron Trust.

Heading south 8km (5 miles) from New Plymouth, via Carrington Road, is **Hurworth Cottage** (Sat–Sun 11am–

3pm; charge; tel: 06-756 8606). One of the region's earliest homesteads, it was built in 1855 by Harry Atkinson, a young immigrant from England, who later became premier of New Zealand.

Some 12km (7 miles) out of town on Pukeiti Road is the **Pukeiti Rhododendron Trust** (daily 9am–5pm; charge; tel: 06-752 4141; www.pukeiti.org.nz), a 320-hectare (791-acre) park established in 1951, which showcases one of the world's best displays of rhododendrons and azaleas in a native bush setting.

Winter skiers and summer hikers will enjoy **Egmont National Park** ⑰, encircling the peak and slopes of **Mount Taranaki**, with its more than 300km (180 miles) of bush walks. Climbing the summit is not supremely difficult, but weather conditions change extremely quickly here, so it's important to have all the right gear, or for safety take a guided hike (*see margin note, opposite*). The easiest access to the park is via **Egmont Village**, 20km (12 miles) southeast of New Plymouth. The **North Egmont Visitor Centre** (daily 8am–5pm; tel: 06-756 0990) here can help with more information on what to do in the area.

Surf Highway

The Surf Highway, State Highway (SH) 45, which horseshoes around the bulbous Taranaki coastline from New Plymouth to Hawera, connects with SH3 up to New Plymouth for a complete circumnavigation of Mount Taranaki. There are plenty of reasons to tarry along the way on this beautiful coastal road.

Oakura, 15km (9 miles) southwest of New Plymouth, is a trendy beach outpost with a number of excellent cafés lining the main thoroughfare. Lucy's Gully nudges the edge of the Egmont National Park, while at **Okato** the Stony River Walk provides crystal-clear waterholes for a refreshing dip.

At **Pungarehu**, turn right at the school to Cape Egmont lighthouse (built in 1881), for beautiful views on

a clear day. Back on SH45 turn right to Parihaka to see the gravesite of the great Maori chief Te Whiti-O-Rongomai, who died here in 1907, aged 90.

In the 1870s, when Europeans settled on land confiscated from the Maori by the British following the Taranaki Wars, Te Whiti encouraged peaceful protest among his people. His campaign of passive resistance and civil disobedience ended at Parihaka in November 1881, when he was arrested. Earlier that day hundreds of British soldiers and militia marched to the *pa* (Maori fort) ready for battle, but to their surprise they were met by rows of children singing and dancing. As Te Whiti was led away he remained strong, telling his assembled followers, some 2,000 Maori, "Be you steadfast in all that is peaceful." Nevertheless, his words had no impact on the British troops and, in one of New Zealand's darkest moments, non-resistant Maori were raped and assaulted, crops destroyed and homes ransacked.

From Pungarehu the road continues on to **Opunake**, 65km (40 miles) from New Plymouth, where colourful murals decorate the town from top to toe. Opunake's landmark building, the eye-catching **Everybody's Theatre**, with Marilyn Monroe and Charlie Chaplin still gracing its billboards, is charming inside, with traditional movie chairs and posters. A tiny Art Deco building houses a boutique **Soap Factory** (daily 9am–5pm; free; tel: 06-761 8707), where everything is made from scratch, and across the road the eclectic **Sugar Juice Café** dishes out home-made fare.

In **Manaia**, an air of prosperity radiates from the freshly painted band rotunda and granite war memorial obelisks, surrounded by historic buildings. Wide streets lead inland to **Dawson Falls** and out to the coast to windswept **Kaupokonui Beach**.

In spring **Hawera** is blooming, and good views of the countryside can be enjoyed from its historic **Water Tower** on High Street. The town has some offbeat attractions, including Kevin Wasley's **Elvis Presley Museum** (daily; charge; tel: 06-278 7624; www.digitalus.co.nz/elvis), a shrine literally packed from floor to ceiling with memora-

TIP

The best time to explore Egmont National Park is during the flower season from Dec–Mar, or July–Aug (for snow). For guided walks, contact MacAlpine Guides, tel: 06-765 6234; 02-7441 7042; www.macalpine guides.com, or Top Guides, tel: 021-838 513, 0800-448 433; www.topguides.co.nz.

BELOW LEFT: bungee jumpers at Mokai Canyon. **BELOW:** Mount Taranaki.

Tales of Taranaki

Maori legend tells a sorrowful tale of how Mount Taranaki split from the mountains of the Central Plateau and came to reside in the Taranaki region. Pihanga, a small mountain and the beauty of the Central Plateau, set her heart on Mount Tongariro, spurning the advances of gentle, Zen-like Mount Taranaki, breaking his heart. While Mount Ruapehu and Mount Ngauruhoe looked on in wonder, mighty Mount Taranaki fled west, his sheer bulk carving the Whanganui River and his tears filling it into a raging torrent. Mount Taranaki found his way to the coast and finally stopped, in a region which embraces him still and has since been known as Taranaki.

Solace for any visitor can be found here, and it's not hard to imagine the rhythmic pounding of the ocean soothing his shattered ego, the strong westerly wind clearing his mind, and clouds providing a thick blanket of cover when he's feeling morose. But on a good day, when it dawns bright and clear, Mount Taranaki tosses aside his woes and holds his head high, parading his magnificent torso and icy crown for all to see.

New Zealand's
national rugby team,
the All Blacks, is
accorded almost god-
like status in a country
where the sport is
played with religious
fervour. For more
information, check
www.allblacks.co.nz.

BELOW: rugby shirts
drying in a field: the
sport has been part
of New Zealand's
culture for 150
years.

bilia, and the **Tawhiti Museum** (Mon–
Fri 10am–4pm; charge; tel: 06-278
6837; www.tawhitimuseum.co.nz), an
intricately detailed labour of love by
artist Nigel Ogle, in which the history
of the immediate area is recreated in
handcrafted life-size displays and scale
models. From Hawera SH3 leads southeast to Wanganui, or north to New Plymouth to complete a loop of Mount
Taranaki and passing through **Eltham**,
Stratford and **Inglewood**.

Stop in Eltham to explore its wealth
of Edwardian and Victorian buildings
on a self-guided walking tour, and Stratford to experience its **Clock Tower**
glockenspiel playing Romeo and Juliet
at 10am, 1pm and 3pm. The **Taranaki
Pioneer Village** (daily 10am–4pm;
charge; tel: 06-765 5399; www.pioneer
village.co.nz), is also well worth a visit.

Inglewood is home to the **Fun Ho!
National Toy Museum** (daily 10am–
4pm; entrance fee; tel: 06-756 7030;
www.funhotoys.co.nz), and from here
it's a short drive back to New Plymouth
via Lake Mangamahoe, where the mirror image of Mount Taranaki reflects
perfectly on a clear day.

Wanganui

Heading southeast along the coast
from Hawera, SH3 passes through lush
farming countryside to **Patea**, and on
to **Wanganui** ⓲, a city most famous
for its river – the Whanganui (note the
extra "h"), which is New Zealand's
longest navigable waterway and much
loved by canoeists and jet-boaters.

The main attraction in town is the
superb **Whanganui Regional Museum**
(daily 10am–4.30pm; charge; tel: 06-349
1110; www.wanganui-museum.org.nz)
on Watt Street, a treasure trove of Maori
artefacts, including the Te Mata-O-Ho-
turoa war canoe, and also featuring a
remarkable collection of paintings by
well-known New Zealand artist Gottfried Lindauer. Built in the form of a
Greek cross, the elegant **Sarjeant Gallery** (daily 10.30am–4.30pm; free; tel:
06-349 0506; www.sarjeant.org.nz)
graces the hill above the museum.

Before exploring Wanganui further,
take a trip up to the **Memorial Tower**
on **Durie Hill**. An elevator (daily 8am–
6pm), built in 1918, climbs 66 metres
(216ft) inside the hill, although the 176
tower steps are worth the trouble on a

fine day. You'll be rewarded with a magnificent view of the city and river.

About 2km (1¼ miles) south along Putiki Drive is **Putiki Church** (St Paul's Memorial Church). The exterior is plain white, but its interior is adorned with magnificent Maori carvings and *tukutuku* (weaving) wall panels.

Bason Botanical Reserve and **Bushy Park** scenic reserve, on the western outskirts of the city, are both within easy reach on SH3. With duck ponds and a range of short walks the parks are popular with families.

Heading upriver

The sooty departure of the lovingly restored coal-fired PS *Waimarie* from the **Whanganui Riverboat Centre** (Mon–Sat 9am–4pm, Sun 10am–4pm; charge; tel: 06-347 1863; www.riverboat.co.nz), provides a satisfying window into the days when paddle steamers plied the river. There is also an excellent museum on-site. Alternatively, follow the river up the 79km (49-mile) **Whanganui River Road** to Pipiriki, a journey of about two hours, 30km (19 miles) of which is unsealed.

As you approach the village of **Jerusalem** ⑲, you will understand why French Catholic missionaries established themselves along this bend in the river in 1854, and why New Zealand poet James K. Baxter chose the serenity of this site for a commune in the late 1960s. The mission remains today, but the commune disintegrated after Baxter's death in 1972. Prior to the establishment of the mission, Jerusalem was a larger Maori village known as Patiarero. In 1883 Mother Mary Aubert arrived and opened a school for Maori children. Her keen interest in native herbs led to the preparation of healing remedies and the subsequent establishment of a home for incurables.

Pipiriki ⑳ is the gateway to **Whanganui National Park**. From Pipiriki you can get to the **Bridge to Nowhere**, more accurately a bridge in the middle of nowhere, built to service a new settlement for soldiers after

World War I, but subsequently abandoned when they were forced out by the 1930s depression and farming difficulties. It can be accessed by a 40-minute walk from the Mangapurua landing, a two-day tramp from the Whakahoro Hut via the Kaiwhakauka and Mangapurua valleys, or by canoe or jet boat (contact Bridge to Nowhere Lodge, tel: 0800-480 308; www.bridgetonowhere-lodge.co.nz).

Another route into the interior north of Wanganui, the SH4 travels through the scenic Parapara Ranges.

White-water thrills

To the east of Wanganui and north of Palmerston North *(see page 210)* on SH1, **Taihape** and **Mangaweka** ㉑ provide access to the swift-flowing, canyon-carving **Rangitikei River**, famed for its excellent white water. At **River Valley** (daily; charge; tel: 06-388 1444; www.rivervalley.co.nz) near Taihape, gorges of violent white water, Grade 5 rapids and deep pools make for one of the top white-water-rafting destinations in the world. Or you can take a hair-raising 80-metre (260ft) bungee-

Putatara *conch shells, traditionally used by Maori to announce the arrival of visitors.*

BELOW: power-boating at Manawatu Gorge.

The lighthouse at Cape Egmont dates back to 1881.

BELOW: the fertile plains east of Mount Taranaki are ideal for dairy farming.

jump into the river at **Mokai Gravity Canyon** (daily 9am–5pm; charge; tel: 06-388 9109; www.gravitycanyon.co.nz) and catch a water-powered chairlift ride back to the top – where a 172-metre (560ft) high flying fox awaits. Onlookers can take in all the action from the safety of the viewing deck.

In Mangaweka itself, the **Up-the-Creek River Centre** (daily 8.30am–5.30pm; charge; tel: 06-382 5744; www.rra.co.nz) offers great family fun with a one-hour splash-about on stable sit-top kayaks, a scenic introduction to the river's gentler side.

South of Wanganui

The SH3 proceeds southeast from Wanganui to Palmerston North, 74km (46 miles) away. The largest township en route is **Bulls ㉒**, where there are 100 or so intriguing signs ranging from the medical centre "Cure-a-bull" through to the police station "Consta-bull", all niftily tucked in amid colourful murals and a pervasive aura of civic pride. Here you can add to your agricultural education with a visit to **Flock House,** an agricultural training institute. Built in 1895, it was purchased in 1923 by the New Zealand Sheepgrowers, who ran a scheme to train the sons of British seamen's widows as farmers.

The **Maize Maze**, on SH1 near Bulls, where the Watson family cuts a clever pattern in their maize plantings every year, is a great place to stop and stretch your legs – and get lost – on over 2km (1 mile) of pathways. For further information tel: 06-327 7615 or visit www.maizemaze.co.nz.

Palmerston North

On the approach to Palmerston North is **Mount Stewart**, with fine views of the rich pastures of Manawatu, the region surrounding the city of Palmerston North. A memorial near the road commemorates early settlers. It's a short hop from here to the historic homestead and gardens at **Mount Lees Reserve. Palmerston North ㉓** itself is the flourishing centre of agricultural Manawatu, with **The Square** as the city's focal point. Named in Maori as Te Marae-O-Hine or "Courtyard of the Daughter of Peace", it commemorates a female chieftain named Te Rongorito who sought an end to inter-tribal warfare during the early days of European settlement.

West of The Square, at 396 Main Street, is **Te Manawa** (daily 10am–5pm; charge; tel: 06-355 5000; www.temanawa.co.nz), an institution combining history, art and science in its museum, art gallery and interactive science centre. To the northwest, at 87 Cuba Street, is the **New Zealand Rugby Museum** (Mon–Sat 10am–4pm, Sun 1.30–4pm; charge; tel: 06-358 6947; www.rugbymuseum.co.nz). This shrine to the national sport displays items from blazers to whistles, with a section devoted to the country's famous All Blacks team. Palmerston North is a major national sporting venue with first-rate facilities.

Roads radiate outwards from the centre of "Palmy". **Fitzherbert Avenue** leads to the city's other major focal

point, the **Manawatu River**. The river is crossed by only one bridge, used by thousands of cars and bicycles each day en route to **Massey University** and a number of science research stations. Also over the bridge is the **International Pacific College**, and New Zealand's largest army base, at Linton. Given the number of educational institutions in Palmerston North, it's not surprising it calls itself the Knowledge Centre of New Zealand.

On the city side of the Manawatu River is the city's much-loved **Victoria Esplanade** (daily; free; www.pncc.govt. nz), an enchanting reserve featuring botanical gardens, a miniature train (www.esplanaderail.org.nz), a children's playground, an aviary and an education centre and conservatory. Don't miss the **Dugald Mackenzie Rose Garden** at the Esplanade, which has an international record for developing new varieties of the flower.

A stone's throw away, also on Park Road, is the **Lido Aquatic Centre** (Mon–Thur 6am–8pm, Fri 6am–9pm, Sat–Sun 8am–8pm; charge; tel: 06-357 2684; www.lidoaquaticcentre.co.nz), a water park replete with slides and chutes. Native bush reserves are close by.

Exploring Manawatu

A short drive south of Palmerston North on SH57 is **Tokomaru** ⧆, and its creative **Tokomaru Steam Engine Museum** (Mon–Sat 9am–3.30pm, Sun 10.30am–3.30pm; charge; tel: 06-329 8867; www.tokomarusteam.com). A railway track circles the grounds, and there are various contraptions on display, from steam rollers to sewing machines.

SH56 heads west to beaches at Tangimoana, Himatangi and Foxton, well patronised by locals and linked by bracing coastal walks. **Feilding**, 20 minutes north of Palmerston North on SH54, is a large town which boasts two squares, a motor-racing track and racecourse, and a stock sale on Friday mornings. Take a NZ$5 insider tour of the yards and auctions on a **Feilding**

Stock Saleyard Tour (tel: 06-323 3318; www.feilding.co.nz/saleyardtours. htm). The Feilding Stock Saleyard has the capacity to hold 35,000 sheep, and with a total turnover of around 1.2 to 1.3 million animals per week, these yards do more business than any other in the Southern Hemisphere.

Perhaps the most dramatic route in or out of Palmerston North and the Manawatu region is via the rugged **Manawatu Gorge** ㉕, to the east. SH3 first passes through the country town of Ashhurst. From here you'll get a good view of the **Tararua Wind Farm** (www.windenergy.org.nz), an impressive array of 40-metre (130ft) high 660kw turbines.

The route travels past **Pohangina** and **Totara** reserves, an area of virgin native bush favoured for picnics, then narrows, clinging to the southern side of the Manawatu Gorge and linking the region to Hawke's Bay. On the opposite bank of the river is the Hastings and Napier railway line, opened in 1891. Drive with care: this winding, and at times narrow, road demands your constant attention. ❑

The Feilding Farmers' Market held every Friday morning in the town square is a must-see, a showcase of local produce, from handmade pate, to bread, preserves, chocolates; from meat, through to fresh seasonal fruits and vegetables.

BELOW: Tararua Wind Farm in Manawatu.

WELLINGTON

Vibrant Wellington, the seat of government as well as the unofficial cultural centre of the country, has a cosmopolitan buzz that is readily discernible

awhiri-ma-tea, the Maori god of wind and storm, fought many fierce battles with his earthbound brother gods in Wellington and the Wairarapa. No wonder, then, that the Cook Strait, the stretch of water separating this end of the North Island from the South Island, has long been known as one of the most treacherous short stretches of open water in the world. The early Maori saw the North Island as a great fish, rich with food for their families. Today the mouth of the fish is as pretty a capital city as any in the world. Wellington's great blue bowl of harbour is only mildly scarred by its port reclamations and the high-rise offices set below green hills dotted with white wooden houses.

San Francisco's twin

Named after Arthur Wellesley, the first Duke of Wellington and victor of the Battle of Waterloo, **Wellington** ㉖ has long been compared to San Francisco, and accurately so. In addition to a susceptibility to earthquakes and a punishingly hilly topography, both cities have a superb coastal location with ocean vistas, an abundance of cool, sunny weather, and a shared penchant for old wooden houses done up in rainbow colours: the city's dwellers have made their homes the most architecturally attractive in New Zealand.

Like San Francisco, Wellington has a cable car, zooming out of its city belly on Lambton Quay to a fine view of the harbour, beside the ivy-clad, red-brick Victoria University. That it is also the seat of government has not seen it go short when it comes to funding public buildings.

Wellington is, however, rendered less than perfect not just by its earthquake risk but also with the near-constant presence of a nagging, often chilly wind. A cartoon image of residents bent double as they struggle to make their way against a chilly southerly bringing icy blasts borne down from the Southern Alps is not too far from the truth.

Main attractions
Te Papa Tongarewa
   Museum of New Zealand
Civic Square
Museum of Wellington
   City and Sea
Wellington Cable Car
Karori Wildlife Sanctuary
Kapiti Island
Hutt Valley
Martinborough
Ngawi

LEFT: old and new in central Wellington.
BELOW: a desirable seaside suburb.

Wellington

0	500 m
0	500 yds

Porirua

THORNDON

Katherine Mansfield's Birthplace

Hutt Valley, Silver Stream Railway, Petone Settlers' Museum

National Library

New St Paul's Cathedral

I

Old St Paul's Cathedral

J

Backbencher Pub

Thistle Inn

Archives New Zealand

New Zealand Portrait Gallery

H Parliament Buildings

Beehive

G Cenotaph

Old Government Buildings

F

Railway Station

Thorndon Container Terminal

PIPITEA

Karori Wildlife Sanctuary

L

ANDERSON PARK

EARLY SETTLERS MEMORIAL PARK

Lady Norwood Rose Garden

Botanic Gardens Cafe

WELLINGTON

LAMBTON

K BOTANIC

Education and Environment Centre

Carter National Observatory

GARDENS

Wellington Cable Car Museum

Cable Car

KELBURN

Centennial Fountain

KELBURN PARK

Cable Car

E

Wellington Harbour (Port Nicholson)

Queen's Wharf

Events Centre

D

Museum of Wellington City and Sea

Plimmer Steps

BNZ Building

FRANK KITTS PARK

WELLINGTON CENTRAL

Wellington City Library

City Gallery

C

Civic Square

Lambton Harbour

Clyde Quay Wharf

i Old Town Hall

Michael Fowler Centre

Film Centre

B Circa Theatre

A Te Papa Tongarewa Museum of New Zealand

Clyde Quay Marina

Freyberg Pool

Royal Port Nicholson Yacht Club

ORIENTAL BAY

Oriental Parade

Mt Victoria

Victoria University

State Opera House

TE ARO

GLOVER PARK

Bats Theatre

St James Theatre

Courtenay Place

Downstage Theatre

Embassy Theatre

MT VICTORIA

CHARLES PLIMMER PARK

Colonial Cottage Museum

M

National War Memorial & Carillon

CENTRAL PARK

BASIN RESERVE

BASIN RESERVE

Massey University

Tennis Centre

NAIRN STREET PARK

Wellington Polytechnic

St Marks

ALEXANDRA PARK

Mt Victoria Tunnel

Wellington College

MT COOK

Wellington Zoo **N**

In the second half of the 1970s the city was shaken by a man-made storm, as a downtown area of quaint Victorian wedding-cake two- and three-storey premises was demolished on the grounds of it being an earthquake risk. The skyscrapers of steel and glass that replaced them, however, look every bit as vulnerable.

After the decade of demolition, Wellington tarted up the few old buildings left, such as Victoria University, downtown relics like the baroque St James Theatre on Courtenay Place and the government buildings centred around The Terrace, which are built of native woods in the masonry style of European architecture.

Despite moving its port operations a mile or so north to a new container complex around this time, Wellington continues to rate as the busiest of the country's 13 large ports. This is mainly due to the all-weather sailing of the Cook Strait rail ferries and foreign fishing vessels that call here for registration and provisioning.

The buildings left behind when port operations moved north are a major part of Wellington's reinvention of itself after the public service, a major employer, was decimated in the 1980s. Physically confined by the sea on one side and the Rimutaka Ranges on the other, the capital went about the job with gusto.

The heart of the city

Any exploration of the city should start on Cable Street at **Te Papa Tongarewa – Museum of New Zealand** Ⓐ (daily 10am–6pm, until 9pm Thur; free; tel: 04-381 7000; www.tepapa. govt.nz), which is regarded as one of the finest in the country and houses some of the most important *taonga* (treasures) of New Zealand. There is no better introduction to the country to be found under one roof, and its aggressively postmodernist approach guarantees mental stimulation of a kind not always found in New Zealand museums.

Within its well-designed interior are a wide range of exhibits and experiences. Examples include Te Marae, a contemporary Maori gathering place, and Awesome Forces, where you get to experience the powerful geological forces that shape New Zealand's landscape. Don't miss the earthquake house. There are also discovery and state-of-the-art time travel and virtual reality centres, cafés, a souvenir shop and a bar. Visitors should set aside one full day to make the most of this landmark museum.

Leaving the museum and turning right out on the old wharf area, you will see a building with a wedding-cake facade, which was rescued from the demolished Westport Chambers to make a home for one of the city's liveliest and most innovative professional theatres, **Circa Theatre** Ⓑ (tel: 04-801 7992; www.circa.co.nz). The building is a perfect example of the born-again look that has transformed the original port area.

If you turn left after leaving the museum you'll find the city's two other major theatres. **Bats Theatre** (tel:

A downtown Wellington café.

BELOW: Te Papa Tongarewa, one of New Zealand's finest museums.

Wooden sculpture at Civic Square Bridge, a wide walkway connecting the square with Lambton Harbour.

04-802 4175; www.bats.co.nz), found by turning right from Cable Street onto Kent Terrace, is an intimate venue, home of the fringe, that presents diverse and challenging theatre. Turn right again on Marjoribanks Street to encounter the skew-whiff concrete, iron and wood pyramid of **Downstage Theatre** (tel: 04-801 6946; www.downstage.co.nz) offering great shows, a licensed bar and accommodation. The country's first professional theatre, established in 1964, Downstage marks the southern tip of **Courtenay Place**, the city's hip bar and restaurant centre.

To discover the commercial, retail and historic centre of Wellington, follow the wharf north from Circa Theatre to a place where a lagoon has been carved out beside two traditional city rowing clubs. Here, intricately carved arches lead across the main road to **Civic Square ◉**. In between the remnants of Wellington's Victoriana, colourful and architecturally impressive buildings and malls, and a slew of cafés, brighten the scene. Nowhere is this

more apparent than in the generous pink-and-beige piazza of Civic Square.

On one side of the square is the **Michael Fowler Centre** – the unmistakable steel colander housing the city's municipal chambers – and the rectangular **Old Town Hall**, saved after testimonials from visiting conductors, such as the late Leonard Bernstein, rated it one of the best symphonic halls in the world, a fitting venue for the home-base of the New Zealand Symphony Orchestra. The Michael Fowler Centre and Old Town Hall are the focus of the annual New Zealand Fringe Festival, reinforcing Wellington's status as the capital of the performing arts in New Zealand.

On the other side of Civic Square is the **Wellington City Library** (Mon–Thur 9.30am–8.30pm, until 9pm Fri and 5pm Sat, 1–4pm Sun; tel: 04-801 4040; www.wcl.govt.nz). The library's interior is like an industrial plant of exposed metal and awash with natural light; outside, its gorgeous plaster curve is decorated with metal palms. All was designed by the city's leading architect, Ian Athfield.

BELOW: Edward Gibbon Wakefield.

Wellington's Founding Father

The citizens of Wellington have shown scant respect for their Pakeha founding father, the English politician and advocate of emigration Edward Gibbon Wakefield. There is no memorial to Wakefield in the city other than his gravesite, perhaps partly due to lingering disapproval over a prison term he served for allegedly abducting an heiress; she was willing, but her father was not, and he brought a successful court case against the young Wakefield. It was in London's Newgate Prison that the unfortunate Wakefield witnessed at first hand the miserable lot of England's poor, and was moved to devise a scheme to that offered a chance to those with nothing by encouraging them to emigrate to Australia and New Zealand.

In practice, though, his ideas of orderly settlement proved to be something of a mess *(see pages 36–7)*. Idealists were thin on the ground in the new lands, and speculators as thick as shovels in a gold rush. Wakefield's brother, William, was in charge of acquiring land for the new emigrants, but he had only four months to do so. His quick deals with the Maori included buying Wellington for 100 muskets, 100 blankets, 60 red nightcaps, a dozen umbrellas and such goods as nails and axes. Wakefield claimed to have bought for £9,000 the "head of the fish and much of its body", a total of about 8 million hectares (20 million acres).

In between is the **City Gallery** (daily 10am–5pm; free; tel: 04-801 3021; www.citygallery.org.nz), which hosts a collection of contemporary local and international artworks in its 1930s Art Deco-style building.

Wellington's wharves

The streets between Wellington's skyscrapers are narrow and windswept with few parks or open spaces, but the city's office workers are never more than a stone's throw from the wharves with views of wide open skies and invigorating sea breezes. Turn right from the Civic Square towards the water and follow the **wharves** north again. These are open to the public; lunchtime joggers zip past the Russian and Korean fishing crews, and restaurants in converted stores offer haute cuisine. If you're not hungry, you can still see what the sea has to offer at the **Museum of Wellington City and Sea** ◐ (daily 10am–5pm; free; tel: 04-472 8904; www.museum ofwellington.co.nz) at Queens Wharf. The museum houses a captivating collection of maritime memorabilia.

Part of the museum is **Plimmer's Ark Gallery**, which contains the excavated remains of the 150-year-old sailing ship *Inconstant*, later known as Plimmer's Ark. Edward Gibbon Wakefield's *(see page 37)* controversial role in the struggles of the early settlers may explain why the title "Father of Wellington" was conferred on John Plimmer instead. A merchant settler who displayed less idealism, Plimmer complained that a place represented to him as "a veritable Eden" had proved "a wild and stern reality". In fact, he had little cause for complaint – he had converted the wreck of the *Inconstant*, the fallout from a bad day, into a flourishing trading enterprise on the beach. Like many of his fellow entrepreneurs, Plimmer added his own wharf, eventually becoming one of the solid citizens of the emerging town, and his wreck ended up as the boardroom chair in the country's Bank of New Zealand.

Lambton Quay and the Parliamentary District

Follow Grey Street, heading inland from the City and Sea Museum, until

The heritage building housing the Museum of Wellington City and Sea was first constructed in 1892 as the Bond Store (customs house), a warehouse where everything from coffee to corsets was stored until duty was paid. In fact, it is safe to say that from 1892 until after World War I, much of what Wellington ate, drank and wore had spent time here.

BELOW: Wellington harbour scene.

you reach Lambton Quay, turn right and you'll find **Wellington Cable Car** (Mon–Fri 7am–10pm, Sat–Sun 8.30am–10pm; tel: 04-472 2199). Given the city's precipitous downtown topography, the cable car, which terminates at the Botanic Gardens (see page 219), is a popular route between the shopping precinct and the numerous offices uphill.

Now a major shopping strip, **Lambton Quay** was once the beachfront where Plimmer and his fellow traders set up shop, its narrowness prompting reclamations ever since. The result today is that Lambton Quay is now situated several blocks from the harbour.

If you make a return trip on the cable car, you can continue north on Lambton Quay for 600 metres (660 yds) to the **Old Government Buildings** , the second largest wooden building in the world. Constructed in 1876, it comprises 9,300 sq metres (100,000 sq ft) of timber. The tides lapped at this site before land was reclaimed in 1840. Directly opposite, politicians, top public officials and business folk buzz around the capital's unique circular Cabinet offices, known as **The Beehive** . A large amount of the administrative and financial clout of the country is centred here.

Built in the late 1970s, the copper-domed Beehive is a soft contrast with the square marble angles of the adjacent **Parliament Buildings** (Mon–Fri 10am–4pm, Sat 10am–3pm, Sun 11am–4pm; free; tel: 04-471 9503; www.parliament.nz), completed in 1922, and the Gothic turrets of the **General Assembly Library**, dating back to 1897. To one side of the Beehive is the historic, red-brick **Turnbull House**, tucked below the skyscraper "Number One The Terrace", office for the Treasury, with the Reserve Bank across the road. North of the Beehive and Parliament are the **New St Paul's Cathedral**, larger than its predecessor (see following page) and with a pink concrete facade, as well as the **National Library** (Mon–Fri 9am–5pm, Sat 9am–1pm; free; tel: 04-474 3000; www.natlib.govt.nz). Within this is the **Alexander Turnbull Library**, housing a remarkable collection of New Zealand and Pacific history.

BELOW: city views on the Wellington Cable Car.

Leave the National Library via Aitken Street, turn left on Mulgrave Street and, surrounded by pohutukawa trees, you'll see **Old St Paul's**  (daily 10am–5pm; free; tel: 04-473 6722), a small but impressive Gothic Revival-style cathedral made entirely of native timbers, even down to the nails. Consecrated in 1866, this is the most noteworthy of the city's 30 churches; many of these were built in the wooden adaptation of the soaring stone Gothic style that was a unique colonial feature.

About 10 minutes' walk further north is the district of **Thorndon**, location of **Katherine Mansfield's Birthplace** (Tue–Sun 10am–4pm; charge; tel: 04-473 7268) at 25 Tinakori Road. The two-storey family home where the writer was born in 1888 has been beautifully restored and features an authentic Victorian town garden.

Wellington's suburbs

On the fringes of the city centre lie some of Wellington's premier attractions. Just over 1km (2/3 mile) southwest of Old St Paul's are the luxuriant grounds of the **Botanic Gardens**  (daily sunrise–sunset; free; tel: 04-499 1400; www.wellington.govt.nz/services/gardens), notable for the formal glory of the **Lady Norwood Rose Garden**. The gardens are perfect for a stroll, and in the summer months the colourful blooms are truly spectacular. There is also a good children's adventure playground here.

The **Carter National Observatory** in the Botanic Gardens (Mon–Fri 10am–5pm, Sat–Sun noon–5pm; tel: 04-472 8167; www.carterobs.ac.nz) gives enlightening talks and demonstrations about the southern night sky. There are also planetarium shows.

Another 1km (2/3 mile) southwest of the Botanic Gardens is the remarkable **Karori Wildlife Sanctuary**  (daily 10am–5pm, last entry 4pm; charge; tel: 04-920 9200; www.sanctuary.org.nz) on Waiapu Road. This oasis has 35km (22 miles) of tracks covering 252 hectares (623 acres) of regenerating forest. This

is a chance to see – or at least hear – birds such as kiwi, weka and morepork in their natural environment. Night guided tours are also available (booking is essential; tel: 04-920 9200). The sanctuary hit the headlines in 2009 when a baby tuatara was discovered here, the first sighting on the mainland for over 200 years.

Wellingtonians are seasoned campaigners when it comes to environmental battles. From the late 1960s, citizens of the gentrified Thorndon neighbourhood cut their conservation teeth when opposing the construction of an urban motorway; the campaign managed partly to achieve its aims. A more successful protest took place on the other side of the city in the raffish community of the Aro Valley below the Victoria University, when students and residents repelled council plans to demolish their wooden cottages in favour of concrete.

A high-profile example of the latter campaign can be seen in the presence of the **Colonial Cottage Museum**  (daily 10am–4pm; charge; tel: 04-384 9122; www.colonialcottagemuseum.

Tulips soaking up the sun at the Botanic Gardens.

BELOW: an antique telescope at the Carter National Observatory.

TIP

If time does not permit a day trip to Kapiti Island, visit Nga Manu (tel: 04-293 4131; www. ngamanu.co.nz), a 15-hectare (38-acre) park in Waikanae dedicated to the preservation of NZ flora and fauna. Breed and release recovery programmes for kiwi, brown teal, blue duck and tuatara operate here, and its wetland areas teem with native waterfowl, including scaup (NZ diving ducks).

co.nz). The building, at 68 Nairn Street close to the corner of Willis Street (which runs south from the city centre). The museum is located in Central Wellington's oldest building, a four-bedroom house dating from 1858. The house was to be demolished in the 1970s, but the tenacity of its occupant, a granddaughter of the original builders, inspired local support and it was saved.

From Te Aro, head southeast to the **Basin Reserve** cricket ground, which was a lake before an earthquake drained it. To the southeast of the basin is the suburb of **Newtown**, its narrow streets teeming with new migrants from the Pacific, Asia and Europe. At the local school, you can hear 20 different languages spoken, while shops that look like the clapboard facades of a Hollywood Wild West set sell exotic foods from a dozen lands. Newtown is also the site of **Wellington Zoo** (daily 9.30am–5pm; charge; tel: 04-381 6755; www.wellingtonzoo.com). This is New Zealand's oldest zoo, built in 1906 and now run on the natural-habitat conservation model favoured by zoos worldwide.

Wellington's environs: the Kapiti Coast

At weekends many Wellingtonians head northwest to the **Kapiti Coast**. One of the many good beaches in the area is at **Paraparaumu** ㉘, 57km (35 miles) from the capital and an hour away by train, where there are water slides and watersport facilities, and a range of accommodation options. It can be reached by commuter train in 45 minutes, or one hour by car (because of constant traffic).

It is possible to join tours from Paraparaumu to the unspoilt native bird sanctuary of **Kapiti Island** ㉙, the capital of the warrior chief Te Rauparaha, who ruled the Wellington region when the Pakeha arrived. Cats, goats and dogs blighted the native fauna of the island until the Department of Conservation embarked on an eradication programme, and Kapiti is now a valuable sanctuary for several species of native birds such as the kakariki, takahe, kea and kiwi. **Kapiti Tours Ltd** (tel: 04-237 7965; www.kapititours. co.nz), which is based at Paraparaumu, can take you there.

BELOW: Karori Wildlife Sanctuary.

A few kilometres further along the Gold Coast, as it is known, you can enjoy locally made gourmet cheeses, watch sheep-shearing and the milking of cows at the **Lindale Centre** (daily 9am–5pm; free; tel: 04-297 0916), or, alternatively, visit the vintage car collection in the **Southward Car Museum** (daily 9am–4.30pm; charge; tel: 04-297 1221; www.southward.org. nz), the largest and most diverse in the Southern Hemisphere.

The Hutt Valley

To enjoy the rest of what Wellington has to offer, head north again, leaving the city via the Hutt Road (NH2) and heading for the topographically blander environment of the **Hutt Valley**, the cities of **Lower Hutt** and **Upper Hutt** and their satellite suburbs. The first settlers had little to thank Edward Gibbon Wakefield for when they were dumped on a beach at the swampy bottom of the Lower Hutt Valley. After their tents flooded, the settlement moved to the narrow, but dry, site of the present city. The abandoned Lower Hutt area, today's

Petone, meaning the End of the Sand, evolved into a working-class industrial town. Times have changed, and the flat shoreline is now a recreational area and the workers' cottages have been gentrified. The **Petone Settlers' Museum** (Tue–Fri noon–4pm, Sat–Sun 1–5pm; tel: 04-568 8373; www. petonesettlers.org.nz) commemorates the early struggles. The museum is notable for its close involvement with the local community and is as much about the present as the past.

Further up the valley at Silver Stream, home to the exclusive red-brick Catholic St Patrick's College, is a chance to ride on a hillside steam train at the **Silver Stream Railway Museum** (Sun only 11am–4pm; charge; tel: 04-971 5747; www.silverstreamrailway. org.nz). It is operated by a group of volunteers and has one of the largest collections of working vintage steam trains in New Zealand.

Also in the Lower Hutt Valley, at Guthrie Street, is one of Wellington's essential attractions, **Maori Treasures** (Tue–Sat 10am–4pm; charge; tel: 04-939

A weka chick at a Wellington sanctuary. Fully grown, these are large, flightless birds, easy prey for the Maori and early Pakeha settlers. Unlike the ill-fated moa, however, they have survived.

BELOW: bikers take in views of the Hutt Valley.

The Toast Martinborough wine, food and music festival celebrates the produce of the bountiful Wairarapa region.

BELOW: Pencarrow Lighthouse.

9630). These are the private studios of the Hetet family, Maori artists of great distinction who work in ancient traditions of craft. Maori Treasures also houses temporary exhibitions of Maori artwork and gives visitors the opportunity to practise some of the traditional techniques themselves. One of the guiding principles of the enterprise is the importance of sharing knowledge in traditional Maori society.

Head back south towards Wellington and take the eastern turnoff to explore some of the small communities tucked into the steep eastern bays. **Wainuiomata**, famous for its rugby league club, is the gateway to the **Rimutaka Forest Park**, which provides a natural barrier between Wellington and the Wairarapa. The park features several good wilderness hikes, including the Whakanui Track, the McKerrow Track and the Mount Matthews track, leading to the summit of Mount Matthews.

Another hilly route leads to **Eastbourne**, across the bay from Wellington. It can also be reached by ferry or a drive around the bays from the city

centre, and is worth a visit for its craft shops and simply as a quiet contrast to the city. It is an easy 8km (5-mile) hike around this coast to view the **Pencarrow Lighthouse**, the country's first permanent lighthouse. This 1859 cast-iron structure was "manned" at the time by one Mary Jane Bennett, New Zealand's only woman lighthouse keeper.

Wairarapa region

Beyond the Hutt Valley are the farming lands of the **Wairarapa**. Wellington developed as a port partly for the shipping of the products from these fertile plains.

It takes an hour to drive northeast over the 300-metre (1,000ft) Rimutaka Range on NH2; cars sometimes need chains to negotiate the road during winter. In the old days, a Fell locomotive hauled people and goods up the mountain's almost vertical incline to the other side: a land of wide open spaces fringed by a handsome coastline, where it's warmer, sunnier and less windy than the capital. These same broad plains attracted some of New

Zealand's earliest European settlers – the ones responsible for its legacy of dollhouse-cute villas and homesteads.

Rolling down the hill into **Featherston**, the **Fell Locomotive Museum** (daily 10am–4pm; tel: 06-308 9379) houses the only Fell locomotive left in the world. Fells, of which only six were made, were designed to cope with steep gradients, such as on the Rimutaka Ranges where the track passed over a gradient of 1 in 13. The local **Heritage and World War Museum** outlines the grim role the town played as a POW camp for Japanese.

Greytown was New Zealand's first inland town and is arguably the prettiest and most Victorian of them all. City folk flock here to indulge in wine trails, antiques, arts, crafts, speciality shops and local produce. At the **Toy Soldier Museum** (daily 8am–5pm; tel: 06-304 8446; www.regaltoysoliders. co.nz) at 92 Main Street, an artwork unfolds under the magnifying glasses of brothers Allan and Ian Farley, who painstakingly mould, cast and hand-paint armies of tin-alloy soldiers. Also on Main Street, **Cobblestones**

Museum (Mon–Sat 9am–4pm, Sun 10am–4.30pm; tel: 06-304 9687; www. cobblestonesmuseum.org.nz) evokes the echoes of clattering stagecoaches and the heavy breathing of tired horses, pulling in with cargoes of new pioneers. Next door at number 177, **Schoc Chocolates** (daily; tel: 06-304 8960; www.chocolatetherapy.com) crafts divine organic and preservative-free chocolates and truffles on site.

Martinborough ③⓪, 18km (11 miles) southeast of Featherston, burst onto the world stage in the 1990s as a wine producer, particularly for its pinot noir. Take a vineyard tour from Wellington or visit the **Martinborough Wine Centre** at 6 Kitchener Street (tel: 06-306 9040; www.martinboroughwinecentre.co.nz), a fine place to learn all about the wineries in the region. The **Old Winery Café** (tel: 06-306 8333; www.theoldwinerycafe.co.nz) on **Margrain Vineyard** (tel: 06-306 9292; www.margrainvineyard.co.nz) makes a good lunch stop.

The Toast Martinborough festival takes place each November.

BELOW: sampling Wairarapa's vintage.

Wairarapa Wine

The Wairarapa region produces about 3,000 cases of wine per year and its success with pinot noir is well known. The potential to grow vines in the region was first recognised by William Beetham over a century ago when he planted vines in Masterton in 1883 and successfully managed to produce a quality vintage. A decade later, Beetham added another vineyard at Lansdowne (also in Masterton), which he planted with *vinifera* varietals including pinot noir. In 1905, prohibition brought an end to the Lansdowne vineyards, but in more recent years, riding the wave of Martinborough's success and wider global awareness of New Zealand wines, a flurry of boutique vineyards owned and run by passionate, quality-driven winemakers.

Further north on SH2, the eye-catching daffodil capital of **Carterton** has more historical buildings to explore, plus attractions including **Paua World** (daily; free; tel: 06-379 6777; www.pauaworld.com) at 54 Kent Street, with displays and information relating to the shellfish and its uses and the place to come for paua shell souvenirs of every description. Also in town is **Awaiti Gardens**, 2.4 hectares (6 acres) of rhododendrons, roses and hydrangeas, a gallery and a cottage serving Devonshire teas.

To the west, in the **Tararua Forest Park**, is the beautiful Waiohine Gorge, whose waters flow from the flanks of Arete Peak and Tarn Ridge. There are a number of good hikes here, beginning with a rather precarious-looking swing bridge suspended high above the river, just minutes from the car park.

North of Carterton, the town of **Masterton** ③ hosts the annual **Golden Shears** sheep-shearing competition (www.goldenshears.co.nz). Although New Zealand has long shed its image as one giant farm, the Golden Shears is still one of the few regular agricultural events in which the whole country takes an interest. Masterton's hills and rivers are popular with those who wish to get away from it all, and in the duck-shooting season its population rises dramatically.

For locals, life centres around **Queen Elizabeth Park** with its historic cemetery, super-sized duck pond, "Kids' Own" playground, steam train, mini golf and bowls. Across the road at 12 Dixon Street is **Shear Discovery New Zealand** (daily 9am–5pm; charge; tel: 06-378 8008; www.sheardiscovery.co. nz), with its Golden Shears Hall of Champions, sheep-shearing display, and information about all facets of wool production.

Other points of interest include peaceful **Henley Lake** and **The Pointon Collection** (daily; charge; tel: 06-378 6710; www.pointoncollection. co.nz), with its vast aggregation of vintage cars and motorcycles, plus a collection of clothes spanning 100 years from the 1860s through to the 1960s.

The bridge across Waiohine Gorge marks the entrance to Tararua Forest Park.

BELOW: the rolling countryside of Wairarapa.

Worthy excursions from Masterton include the drive north to **Pukaha Mount Bruce National Wildlife Centre** (daily 9am–4.30pm; charge; tel: 06-375 8004; www.mtbruce.org.nz), where threatened species such as the North Island kiwi, the kokako, and North Island kaka can be viewed in natural bush aviaries. A highlight here is the daily feeding at 3pm. The vineyards of Gladstone are nearby.

The southeast coast and Palliser Bay

Castlepoint is one of the few settlements on the ruggedly beautiful southeastern coast, accessed via a long road from Masterton. The Castlepoint lighthouse is perched among embedded fossils on a craggy wind-blown bluff, buffeted by the giant rollers of the Pacific Ocean and reached via a rickety causeway – an adventure in itself.

Another lighthouse and scenic drive of note is the route 60km (37 miles) southwest of Martinborough to the rough windswept coast of **Palliser Bay** ❸. From Lake Ferry take the Cape Palliser Road southeastwards to the strange **Putangirua Pinnacles**. Here a 30-minute walk leads to giant rock spires, some reaching up to 50 metres (165ft) in height, formed by the weathering away of silt deposits over the past 120,000 years.

In **Ngawi**, a picturesque fishing village nestled snugly into the base of the towering Aorangi Range, rows of rusty bulldozers, used for pulling fishing boats ashore, line the beach.

Seals are commonly sighted along this stretch of coast at the southern tip of North Island, and at the end of the road 258 steep steps lead to Cape Palliser Lighthouse, constructed in 1896 from materials brought by boat, as the road to the cape was not built until 1941. The windswept shores of Palliser Bay were once the principal points of access for early European settlers to the region. The settlers arrived in the mid- to late 1800s to set up sheep stations, build homes and farm the fertile plains.

From the lighthouse one can gain spectacular views across Palliser Bay to the South Island, and see Kaikoura's snow-capped mountains rising sharply from the sea. ❑

A tui feeds on nectar at Karori Wildlife Sanctuary.

BELOW: Castlepoint Beach and Lighthouse.

South Island

0   100 km

0   100 miles

Cape Farewell

D'Urville
Island

Marlborough
Sounds
Maritime Park

Golden
Bay

Totaranui

Cape
Jackson

Collingwood

Takaka

Abel Tasman
NP

Marlborough
Sounds

Kahurangi

Motueka

Tasman
Bay

Havelock

Picton

Wellington

National

Richmond

Nelson

Blenheim

Cook
Strait

Karamea

Park

Tasman

Renwick

Wairau

Marlborough

Cape
Campbell

St Arnaud

Lake Rotoiti

Inland Kaikoura Range

Murchison

Lake Rotoroa

Westport

Nelson
Lakes
NP

Cape Foulwind

Paparoa
NP

Reefton

Mauria
Springs

Kaikoura

Clarence

Punakaiki

Springs
Junction

Hammer
Springs

Lewis
Pass

Tasman Sea

Greymouth

Hurunui

Cheviot

Hokitika

Arthur's
Pass NP

Waipara

Ross

9243

Arthur's
Pass

Rangiora

Kaiapoi

West

ALPS

Lake
Coleridge

Darfield

Christchurch

Coast

Lyttelton

Okarito Lagoon

Methven

Akaroa

Franz Josef Glacier

Aoraki
Mt Cook
NP

Canterbury

Banks
Peninsula

Fox Glacier

3754 Mt Cook

Canterbury
Plains

Lake
Ellesmere
(Te Waihora)

Westland
NP

Mt
Cook

Canterbury

Ashburton

SOUTHERN

Lake
Tekapo

Geraldine

Canterbury
Bight

Haast

Lake
Pukaki

Fairlie

Temuka

Jackson Head

Mount
Aspiring
NP

Twizel

Timaru

Lake
Ohau

Lake
Benmore

Mt
Aspiring

Waimate

3030

Omarama

Milford
Sound

Treble Cone
2088

Lake
Hawea

Lake
Wanaka

971

Kurow

Waitaki

Oamaru

Milford
Sound

Wanaka

Lindis Pass

Glenorchy

Arrowtown

Ranfurly

Homer
Tunnel

Cromwell

Omakau

Fiordland

Queenstown

Alexandra

Otago

Palmerston

National

Lake
Wakatipu

Roxburgh

Port Chalmers

PACIFIC

Te Anau
Downs

Clutha

Otago
Peninsula

Lake
Te Anau

Mosgiel

Dunedin

Doubtful
Sound

Park

Te Anau

Mossburn

Lawrence

OCEAN

Manapouri

Riversdale

Milton

Lumsden

Dusky
Sound

Lake
Manapouri

Southland

Winton

Gore

Balclutha

Clifden

Catlins

Cape
Providence

Tuatapere

Owaka

Riverton

Invercargill

Forest
Park

Bluff

Waipapa Point

Foveaux

Strait

Oban

Stewart
Island

Paterson Inlet

Rakiura
National
Park

Southwest Cape

SOUTH ISLAND

An island of unparalleled scenic beauty and variety,
with magnificent snow-capped mountains, fabulous
empty beaches and dramatic fiords backed by
primeval rainforests

Variety is the essence of the South Island, a visual feast of towering snow-capped peaks, broad sun-parched plains, impenetrable rainforests, rich farmlands, spectacular waterfalls, giant glaciers, serene lakes and deep fiords. The boat from which Maui fished the North Island out of the sea, according to the ancient Polynesian legend, seems to have captured much of nature's bounty.

The South Island is remarkably uncrowded. Its two main points of entry are Christchurch, the very English "garden city" with its plethora of parks, and Picton in the picturesque Marlborough Sounds. Here at the top of the island, a region of sunken valleys and secluded bays, sun-drenched plains record New Zealand's highest sunshine hours, much to the pleasure of grape growers.

Hit the West Coast and things start to get wild; beaches pounded by the turbulent Tasman Sea meet with the immensity of the Southern Alps. Through the winding mountain passes the landscape opens up to one of wide braided rivers and high-country sheep farms. Hot mineral springs seep from the ground where the giant moa once roamed.

In the southern lakes region, Queenstown and Wanaka offer a magnificent setting with lakes, forests and mountains combining to create a scene of extraordinary beauty, with a range of adventure activities guaranteed to get the adrenalin pumping. To the east and on the coast is Dunedin, a university city where the influence of the early Scottish settlers is plain to see.

The rich farmland of Southland forms the base of the island. And then there is Fiordland, comprising 10 percent of New Zealand's land area but less than one-thousandth of its population. Found here are the renowned Milford Track, Milford Sound, Mitre Peak and Doubtful Sound.

Maui's anchor comes in the form of Stewart Island. Little-known to many New Zealanders themselves, those in the know say its friendly inhabitants and untouched landscapes make it the most phenomenal place of all. ❑

PRECEDING PAGES: scenic flight over Milford Sound; photo-op in the Southern Alps. **TOP**: St Kilda beach on the Otago Peninsula. **ABOVE LEFT**: MacKinnon Memorial on the Milford Track. **ABOVE RIGHT**: white-water rafting.

NELSON AND MARLBOROUGH

The South Island's northern tip is a haven for
wildlife and offers rest, relaxation and a slow
pace, which many travellers will welcome
after a bumpy journey across the Cook Strait

Across Cook Strait from Wellington, the provinces of Nelson and Marlborough are the gateway to the South Island for those arriving on the ferry (the three-hour trip from the capital terminates at Picton in the Marlborough Sounds). This is a picturesque region with marked differences in scenery – the dry scrubland of the east contrasting with the dripping rainforest further west. Collectively, the provinces enjoy the highest number of sunshine hours in the country (2,000–2,400 a year).

New Zealanders holiday here in droves. Nelson's population of 52,000 is said to double at Christmas and New Year. Its Tahunanui Motor Camp, empty much of the year, becomes a small city in its own right. At beach resorts like Kaiteriteri, numbers jump from several hundred to several thousand. Visitors pour into hotels, motels and motor camps in cars full of children, towing caravans or boats, with tents strapped to roof-racks.

Across Cook Strait to Picton

Cook Strait is a natural funnel for the strong westerly wind known as the Roaring Forties. On a bad day, this can be one of the most unpleasant short stretches of water on earth. But squeezing through the narrows to enter Tory Channel in the **Marlborough Sounds** ❶ is like entering another world, its sheltered coves and bays beckoning

with blissful hues of greens and blues. This complex configuration of sunken valleys has more than 1,000km (620 miles) of shoreline. Nonetheless, the journey down **Tory Channel** and **Queen Charlotte Sound** aboard the ferries gives only a glimpse of the glorious scenery. The shores invite exploration and are dotted with isolated houses, many offering holiday accommodation. Even today, few Sounds residents enjoy the luxury of road access to their homes, with launches still the main mode of transport; even mail and the

LEFT: the Kaikoura coast.
BELOW: idyllic Queen Charlotte Sound.

Northern South Island

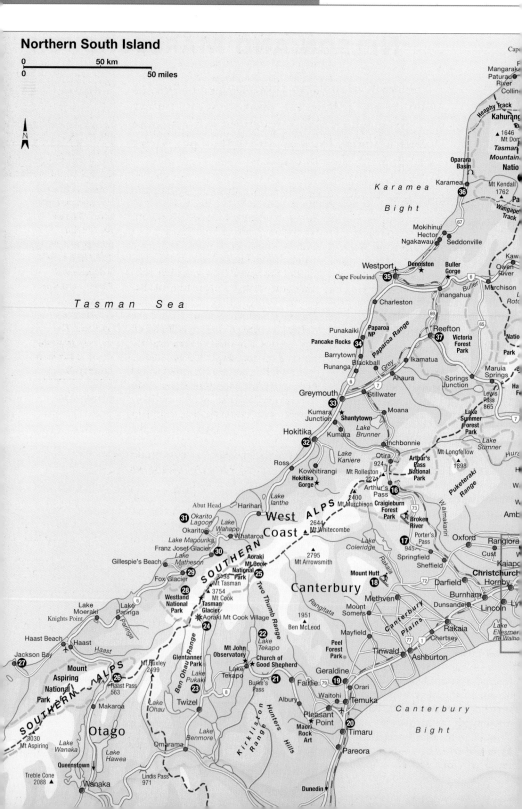

Arriving at Picton by ferry from the North Island. There are frequent daily crossings in both directions between Wellington and Picton: journey time is about three hours, depending on sea conditions. The crossing is frequently stormy, so take travel-sickness pills.

doctor come by boat. The area is encompassed by the Marlborough Sounds Maritime Park.

Derelict buildings from the last whaling station in the country can be seen just inside the entrance to Tory Channel. It closed in 1964, ending more than 50 years of pursuit of the migratory Humpback whale by the Perano family.

The most famous of all Pacific explorers, Captain James Cook, spent more than 100 days in and around Ship Cove during his travels. It was on the highest point of Moutara Island in Queen Charlotte Sound that Cook claimed New Zealand for King George III, and the Sound for his queen, an act commemorated by a monument erected near the entrance to Queen Charlotte Sound.

The commercial centre for almost all activity in the Sounds is the attractive town of **Picton ❷**, near the head of Queen Charlotte Sound. As well as being the terminal for the Cook Strait ferries to Wellington, Picton marks the start of the South Island section of both State Highway (SH) 1 and the main trunk railway. It is also the main base for the assorted launches, water taxis and charter boats on which locals and visitors rely for transport.

An old trading vessel, the *Echo*, usu-ally drawn up on the beach on one side of Picton's bay, was one of the last of New Zealand's old trading scows to remain in service, and is now a café bar (tel: 03-573 7498; closed in July). Its exploits during World War II, when the US Navy commandeered it, inspired the book and later film *The Wackiest Ship in the Navy*. A shipping relic of far greater antiquity, the teak hull of the *Edwin Fox*, lies in the purpose-built **Edwin Fox Maritime Centre** (daily 9am–3pm, until 5pm in summer; tel: 03-573 6868) at Dunbar Walk. Built in India in 1853, the *Edwin Fox*, in her long and colourful history, carried cargo worldwide, troops in the Crimean War, convicts to Australia and immigrants to New Zealand.

Picton has several museums, mostly devoted to its maritime heritage. Much of the activity here centres around scenic cruises, kayak trips and dolphin-watching expeditions to the labyrinthine waterways in the area.

Blenheim and the wineries

Some 30km (19 miles) south of Picton, **Blenheim ❸** is the administrative centre of sparsely populated Marlborough province. Sitting on the Wairau plain, this pleasant rural service town has truly blossomed since the establishment in 1973 of the original Montana vineyards, now owned by **Pernod Ricard New Zealand** (www.pernod-ricard-nz.com). They are New Zealand's largest winemaker, producing a bewildering array of wines. One of its wineries, **Montana Brancott Winery** (tel: 03-578 2099), is located just south of Blenheim. A guided tour of the vineyard, which departs from the visitors centre at 10am, 11am, 1pm and 3pm, is extremely informative and takes in some of the winery's special features, including rare, giant *cuves* made of French oak, New Zealand's first tradi-

tional Coquard champagne press, and 55-tonne tipping tanks.

Marlborough is one of the country's most important wine-producing regions, with wineries at every turn, including the renowned **Cloudy Bay** (www.cloudybay.co.nz), an abundance of fine restaurants and cafés, and a great variety of places to stay. The annual **Marlborough Wine and Food Festival** (www.wine-marlborough-festival.co.nz) in February celebrates the vital relationship between good food and wine and is now an important regional event. Other regional staples – grapes, apples, cherries, salmon, mussels and sheep – all take advantage of Marlborough's warmth to grow fat and juicy. The region's pleasant, sunny climate is down to the rainshadow (and *föhn*) effect produced by the mountains to the west and southwest. Nothing utilises the long, hot, dry days of summer more than the salt works at **Lake Grassmere**, 30km (19 miles) southeast of Blenheim, where sea water is ponded in shallow lagoons and then allowed to evaporate until nothing is left but blinding white salt crystals.

Whales are most likely to be spotted when they lift their flukes high into the air and slam them down on the water. This incredible manoeuvre can be witnessed regularly at Kaikoura.

BELOW: a Blenheim vineyard.

Kaikoura's whales and dolphins

The coastline along Marlborough's southern flank leading down to Canterbury is exposed and rocky. The province stretches all the way down to **Kaikoura ❹** (population 3,500), some 130km (80 miles) south of Blenheim, situated at the base of a small peninsula which provides shelter for the fishing boats that work out of here. The crayfish or rock lobster which they pursue on this rocky coast is sold freshly cooked from roadside stalls.

More important these days to Kaikoura's economy are the visitors who come to see the Sperm whales which congregate a few kilometres offshore. The sonar "clicks" from the submerged animals, chasing giant squid at depths of a kilometre or more, are tracked by a sensitive hydrophone so the boat can be positioned roughly where the whale will resurface to loll about for around 10 minutes. The highlight of the spectacle takes place when the leviathan throws up its big flukes and disappears. The 2½-hour-long tours, available throughout the year, are operated by **Whale Watch Kaikoura** (tel: 03-319 6767; www.whalewatch.co.nz).

It's ironic that this quaint seaside town, founded on the killing of whales over a century ago, should find new prosperity showing them off. Whale-watching trips can also be taken in a light plane (Wings Over Whales, tel: 03-319 6580; www.whales.co.nz; or Kaikoura Aero Club, tel: 03-319 6579), or helicopter (tel: 03-319 6609; www. worldofwhales.co.nz). The Maori-run whale-watching business has provided a big boost for the town, and it's now a worthy stopover activity on any journey in the area.

Another of Kaikoura's attractions is also found offshore. Dolphin-watching tours by **Dolphin Encounter** (tel: 03-319 6777; www.dolphin.co.nz) allow swimmers to frolic in the waters with these friendly creatures. The tours are hugely popular, so make sure you book in advance during summer.

Inland from Kaikoura, two parallel mountain ranges thrust skywards, with the highest peak, **Mount Tapuaenuku**, soaring to 2,885 metres (9,465ft). Beyond that is the **Awatere Valley** and **Molesworth Station**, New Zealand's largest sheep and cattle mountain ranch, which stretches over 182,000 hectares (450,000 acres).

Mussels and gold

State Highway (SH) 6, running northwest from Blenheim to Nelson, takes you 39km (24 miles) down the attractive Kaituna Valley to **Havelock ❺**. This fishing and holiday settlement at the head of Pelorus Sound, the furthest point that the Marlborough Sounds penetrate inland, is like a smaller version of Picton, without the bustle of the interisland ferries but with the same feeling that all the important businesses are waterborne. Pelorus and Kenepuru sounds are key to New Zealand's aquaculture industry, their uncrowded and sheltered waters being used for growing salmon in sea cages and green-lipped mussels on buoyed rope lines. Scallops and Pacific oysters are harvested here.

The Kaikoura coast yields a bountiful harvest, including crayfish – freshly cooked at roadside stalls.

BELOW: Kaikoura's Dolphin Encounter.

BELOW: the World of Wearable Art and Classic Cars Museum in Nelson.

Just beyond Havelock is **Canvastown**, named after the tent village which popped up when gold was discovered on the **Wakamarina River** in the 1860s. It was a short-lived rush, with most of the diggers going south to Otago. Canvastown remembers its brief heyday with a memorial of old mining tools and equipment set in concrete. Visitors can hire pans and still get a "show" of gold on the Wakamarina.

Rai Valley further north provides a rest stop for buses travelling the 115km (71 miles) between Blenheim and Nelson. A smaller road heads off northwards to **French Pass** ❻ at the outermost western edge of the sounds. A narrow, reef-strewn waterway separates the mainland and **D'Urville Island**, resembling a raging river as it tries to equalise the waters of Admiralty and Tasman Bays. New Zealand's fifth-largest island, it was named after 19th-century French explorer Dumont d'Urville, who sailed through the pass in 1827, narrowly avoiding the wrecking of his corvette, the *Astrolabe*, when it was dragged over the reef.

Nelson and environs

Marlborough and **Nelson** ❼ were once a single province, but the conservative sheep farmers of Marlborough ceded away Nelson in 1859, colonised as it was by progressive artisans and craftspersons perceived as troublemakers. It set the tone for a city unlike any other in New Zealand, a hotbed of creative flair.

In part, the city owes its arty identity to Andrew Suter, Bishop of Nelson from 1867 to 1891. Suter bequeathed what is considered to be the country's finest collection of early colonial watercolours to the people of Nelson. They are housed in the **Suter Gallery** (daily 10.30am–4.30pm; charge; tel: 03-548 4699; www.thesuter.org.nz) on Bridge Street, one of the centres of cultural life in the city, along with the **School of Music** (tel: 03-548 9477) two blocks south on Nile Street and the **Theatre Royal** (tel: 03-548 3840) to the west on Rutherford Street, the oldest theatre building in the country. One block to the east is Trafalgar Street, with **Christ Church Cathedral** set imperiously at the head of a flight of steps at its southern end.

A few hundred metres north on Trafalgar Street, at Montgomery Square, is **Nelson Markets** (Sat 8am–1pm; tel: 03-546 6454), a good opportunity to see and buy some of the region's best produce as well as a cross-section of local crafts.

On Atawhai Drive at Nelson's northern end is **Founder's Historic Park** (daily 10am–4.30pm; charge; tel: 03-548 2649), a collection of historical buildings, including a windmill, a 3-D maze, an organic brewery and nautical exhibits in a garden setting. Further north are the **Miyazu Gardens** (daily 8am–sunset; free), a traditional Japanese garden, and a better bet for garden-lovers than **Botanical Hill** on Milton Street at the town's eastern border.

Art that you can wear

Until 2004, Nelson hosted the world-famous **World of Wearable Art Awards** (WOW), an annual theatrical extravaganza that attracted local and overseas competitors. Designers competed to create the most outlandish garment that encompassed it all – fashion, sculpture and art.

In 2005 the WOW awards show moved to the Queens Wharf Events Centre in Wellington, but the creations from previous competitions have a permanent home in Nelson at the **World of Wearable Art and Classic Cars Museum** (daily 10am–5pm; charge; tel: 03-547 4573; www.wowcars.co.nz) at 95 Quarantine Road. Allow at least an hour to take in the wearable art and classic car galleries, audio-visual theatre and illumination room.

Some of the prettiest churches in the area are found in **Richmond**, 12km (7 miles) southwest of Nelson and **Wakefield**, 15km (9 miles) southwest of Richmond, where the parish church of **St John's** was built in 1846, making it New Zealand's second-oldest church and the oldest in the South Island. Halfway between Nelson and Richmond, at **Stoke**, is the pioneer homestead **Broadgreen Historic House** (daily 10.30am–4.30pm; tel: 03-547 0403; www.geocities.com/broadgreen_house) at 276 Nayland Road. Built circa 1855, this 11-room stately cob house provides a glimpse of an earlier and more genteel era.

The Marlborough area is New Zealand's premier wine-producing region, most famous for its sauvignon blanc. Harvest time is from late Febraury into April.

BELOW: Broadgreen Historic House, a glimpse of 19th-century life.

Motueka and Abel Tasman National Park

Nelson contributes a large part of the nation's production of nashi pears, kiwi fruit, berryfruit and apples. It also produces the entire national crop of hops. Flavouring the country's beer, these are grown near **Motueka** ❽, 35km (22 miles) northwest of Richmond on SH60, where large fields of tobacco once filled every paddock. Vineyards in Nelson are increasing in number, particularly in Waimea and the Moutere Hills. Forestry, fishing and ship servicing are other big local industries.

The handicraft revival of the 1960s saw the Nelson region develop as an important pottery centre, largely due to the good local clay, and nowhere more so than in Motueka – a thriving artistic community (with excellent trout fishing on the Motueka River). Potteries still abound, but weaving, silver working, glass blowing and other crafts are also well represented.

Some 20km (12 miles) north of Motueka is the **Abel Tasman National Park** ❾, with its emerald bays and granite-fringed coastline. This is best savoured by walking the **Coastal Track** (*see page 243*) connecting **Marahau** at its southern end to **Totaranui** in the north. The full walk takes three or four days, but the less energetic can take coastal launch or yacht services from Kaiteriteri or Marahau to a selection of bays along the way. Kayak trips around the bays, both guided and unguided, have grown in popularity in recent years. A memorial to Abel Tasman, the 17th-century Dutch navigator who first sighted New Zealand, stands at **Tarakohe** on the road to the park which bears his name.

Golden Bay

Ascending to an altitude of 791 metres (2,595ft), **Takaka Hill Road**, a section of SH60 which runs west of the park to **Golden Bay**, is not the country's highest mountain pass, but its 25km (16 miles), featuring a total of 365 bends, makes it the longest single hill drivers in New Zealand will tackle. Rainwater has etched this marble mountain into a bizarre landscape of rifts, rills, run-

The Interislander ferry makes its way through the Marlborough Sounds.

BELOW: Abel Tasman National Park is fringed with superb beaches.

nels and flutings. A walk of 400 metres (440 yds) from the end of a road up the Riwaka Valley, on the Nelson side of Takaka Hill, will take you to the first visible part of the Riwaka River, where it emerges in full flow from its invisible source inside the hill.

Down a side road to Canaan, **Harwoods Hole** plunges an awesome 183 metres (600ft), giving abseilers the ultimate test of plunging into the void. The first descent, taking place in 1957, was marked by tragedy when one member of the party was killed by a falling rock while being winched back up. After the summit is the hill's hairpin bend lookout, with wonderful views down to Golden Bay.

Just 5km (3 miles) west of **Takaka ⓾**, the town which serves as the gateway to Golden Bay, **Pupu Springs** (also known as Waikoropupu Springs) made world news in 1993 when scientists recorded that New Zealand's largest freshwater springs discharge the world's clearest water – giving near perfect underwater visibility for a stunning 62 metres (203ft). The effect is spectacular. Aquatic plants grow profusely, providing the glorious freshwater equivalent of a coral reef. Further up, at the head of the mist-clad valley, a car park marks the start of the **Pupu Walkway**. This 2km (1¼-mile) section of curving, cliff-hugging water channels and aqueducts remains a tribute to the eight men who built it with picks and shovels in 1901 in order to provide water for the gold sluicers below.

The **Wholemeal Café** (tel: 03-525 9471), established 1977 in Takaka as the Wholemeal Trading Company, was once the only eatery around. Now it competes with nearly a dozen cafés and restaurants around the bay. The **Mussel Inn** (tel: 03-525 9241), about midway on the 30km (19-mile) road north from Takaka to **Collingwood** (the last town near the end of the highway), is something of an institution. The owners believe small is beautiful when it comes to brewing beer, and this microbrewery is one of the smallest in the country.

Golden Bay takes its name from the precious metal that inspired the Aorere gold rush in 1857. Today it is synonymous with the long, lazy curve of sandy beaches that arch northwest up to **Farewell Spit ⓫**. Covered in huge sandhills and scrub, this unique 35km (22-mile) long sandspit, declared a nature reserve in 1938, is the longest in the world and curves out across Golden Bay like a scimitar, with turbulent waves on one side and vast tidal flats on the other. Built from schist sands washed north along the west coast, the spit is slowly growing, spreading, lengthening and widening as the action of the strong winds and currents bring their forces to bear on the constantly shifting sands of this dynamic environment. The Department of Conservation (DOC) manages the spit, with strict limits on access. Walking is permitted from **Puponga**, 26km (16 miles) from Collingwood. Four-wheel-drive sightseeing trips also regularly leave from Collingwood for the lighthouse and the gannet colony near the spit's end.

Farewell Spit also makes Golden Bay the world's deadliest whale trap. Pilot

BELOW: Pupu Springs' pristine waters.

Planning a kayak trip at Picton. Local companies offer guided kayaking trips and kayak hire: see pages 368–9 for details.

BELOW: Farewell Spit, the northern tip of South Island.

whales migrating past in summer become stranded in shallows, often hundreds at a time, when armies of residents and holidaymakers can be relied upon to refloat them.

Kahurangi and Nelson Lakes

South of Golden Bay, even four-wheel-drive vehicles are of no use. This is the area set aside for **Kahurangi National Park** ⑫, at 452,000 hectares (1 million acres), the country's second-largest national park and home to more than half of New Zealand's 2,400 plant species, including 67 found nowhere else. Many people come here to hike over 550km (342 miles) of trails, the most popular being the 85km (53-mile) **Heaphy Track** *(see opposite)*. This is a tramp of four to five days which starts 30km (19 miles) south of Collingwood and heads up through the mountains, then down the west coast to Karamea. Overnight accommodation along the way is available, for a small charge, in DOC huts.

There are other oases, too, for people of softer feet and softer muscles. A restored 1920s fishing lodge on the shores of **Lake Rotoroa**, 90km (56 miles) southwest of Nelson in the scenic **Nelson Lakes National Park** ⑬ area, boasts "blue-chip" fishing waters within a short walk of the front door, and 26 top-class fishing rivers teeming with trout are within an hour's drive. **St Arnaud** village on the shores of nearby **Lake Rotoiti** also offers comfortable accommodation and (for winter visitors) two ski fields nearby.

If you don't want to head on to Christchurch or the west coast, another route from St Arnaud follows the Wairau Valley back to Blenheim.

Wild west

Facing the raging Tasman Sea, Nelson's wild western flank can be an inhospitable, even dangerous, coastline, but is always inspiring. From Puponga, the 30-minute walk to **Wharariki Beach** is second to none, with bold cliff lines, arches, caves, rock pools galore and row upon row of massive dunes. The road over Pakawau Saddle gets you to Westhaven Inlet. When it was gazetted as a marine reserve in 1994, disgruntled locals put up a sign: "Westhaven Human Reserve. No birds, DOC or bird brains".

The narrow, dusty road around the inlet affords excellent views. The best reflections are at high tide if it's not windy. Echo Point is worth a stop and a good scream for an eightfold reverberation sound effect. Remnants of the once-thriving town of **Mangarakau** give little hint of an industrious past based on coal, timber, flax and gold. Spare a thought as you drive on past the old school house, another closure. Just off to the right is the overgrown entrance to the town's coal mine, where an explosion of built-up gas killed four miners on 17 January 1958, their first day back after summer vacation. The town's fifth miner, who rushed in to help the others, was seriously gassed. ❑

South Island Tracks

The very best way to experience the superior landscapes of South Island is to take an extended hike along the numerous tracks

Seeking the great New Zealand outdoor experience can be as simple as a walk in the park. The **Department of Conservation** (www.doc.govt.nz) administers walking tracks, including its 10 best Great Walks, through national parks scattered throughout the length of the country. Behold New Zealand's very best scenery. Bookings for the Milford, Kepler and Routeburn tracks must be made with the Department of Conservation – see page 365 and visit www.doc.govt.nz for more information.

Perhaps the most famous is the **Milford Track** in Fiordland, extending through glorious South Island landscapes for some 53 km (33 miles). It leads from an inland lake through a deep river valley and over an Alpine pass to finish four days later at a fiord. The track follows the Clinton River from the head of Lake Te Anau up to the Mintaro Hut. From there it crosses the scenic MacKinnon Pass and descends to the Quintin Hut. Packs can be left here while walkers make a worthwhile return journey to Sutherland Falls, the highest waterfall in New Zealand. From the Quintin Hut the track leads out through rainforest to Milford Sound.

Due to its immense popularity, you must book well in advance (ie before you leave home) if you want to walk the Milford Track. It can be completed either as part of a guided walk or independently as a "freedom walker". The track attracts people of all ages, but a reasonable standard of fitness is required and all-weather clothing is essential.

Only slightly less well known, but equally spectacular, is the three-day **Routeburn Track** that links the Fiordland National Park with the Mount Aspiring National Park. This track was part of an early Maori route to find greenstone (jade). It leads from the main divide on the Te Anau–Milford Road over Key Summit to Lake Howden before dropping into the Mackenzie Basin. From there it crosses the Harris Saddle into the Routeburn Valley. The highlight is the view from Key Summit. Permits are available from the DOC office in Te Anau.

A very different experience is offered by the **Coastal Track** at Abel Tasman National Park. This three- to four-day track idles through bush and dips down into golden sand beaches. The exceptional beauty of the track has made it immensely popular in recent years and it can be difficult getting hut accommodation, so bring a tent. If the tide is in, you occasionally have to divert around the inlets: check tide times in the local paper before you leave or at huts along the way.

The **Heaphy Track**, from Collingwood to Karamea, takes between four and six days. Most of the track lies within the boundary of Kahurangi National Park. From Brown Hut the track rises through beech forest to Perry Saddle. One highlight is the view from the summit of Mount Perry (a two-hour return walk from Perry Saddle Hut). The track then winds through the open spaces of the Gouland Downs and on to the Mackay Hut. Nikau palms are a feature of the section from Heaphy Hut along the spectacular coastal section, where the route drops down along the beach. This is the most beautiful part of the walk, but as for all the above hikes, bring plenty of insect repellent to ward off sandflies.

Detailed information on these and other tracks can be obtained from offices of the Department of Conservation. There is no charge for using the tracks, and reasonable rates apply to accommodation. ❑

RIGHT: a hiker on the Heaphy Track takes in views of Kahurangi National Park.

CHRISTCHURCH

The South Island's largest city has always prided itself on its Englishness – and, true to fine old British tradition, among the pleasantly cultivated gardens and elegant edifices you can generally find the odd eccentric

Christchurch enjoys its traditional pleasure – punting on the Avon River, riding a tram through the inner-city streets, having coffee alfresco in the old university precinct. Such pastimes say much about the way Christchurch sees itself – as a peculiarly English city.

Yet of all New Zealand's main centres, Christchurch was the first to adopt some rather more aggressive tactics to entice tourists. As a result, it's possible to take an aerial gondola up the Port Hills, the city's volcanic backdrop, shop in one of the many multilingual souvenir shops that dot the inner city, gamble in a casino, ride a hot-air balloon over the city and plains at dawn or fly in a helicopter to sample the French charms of Akaroa, out on Banks Peninsula.

Orientation in the Garden City

But first, the city itself. Start at Cathedral Square, where a lofty neo-Gothic Church of England cathedral, whose spire once made it the city's tallest building, presides *(see page 246)*. From its base, a grid of streets spreads across the plains. The central streets assume the names of English bishoprics – minor ones, because by the time the city was planned in the early 1850s, the best names had already been taken for other communities in the province.

At the limits of the city centre run four broad avenues. They enclose a square mile that mirrors the City of London. Within their bounds are extensive parklands and tidy, tree-lined squares with names such as Cranmer, Latimer and Victoria. Winding through the parklands and the city is the Avon River. On one 1849 Canterbury map, the Avon River appears as the "Shakespeare", and Christchurch as "Stratford". Indeed, many locals mistakenly believe that the Avon is named after the river in Shakespeare's Stratford but, in fact, the name is taken from that of a stream, a little larger than the Avon, which burbled past the home of the city's

Main attractions
CATHEDRAL SQUARE
CHRISTCHURCH ART GALLERY
CANTERBURY MUSEUM
BOTANIC GARDENS
CHRISTCHURCH GONDOLA
AKAROA (BANKS PENINSULA)

LEFT: town crier at Victoria Square.
BELOW: the Botanic Gardens, a highlight in a city of gardens.

pioneering Deans family. The Avon borders the **Riccarton House & Deans Bush** (tel: 03-341 1018; www.riccarton house.co.nz), the Deans' beautiful home at 16 Kahu Road. Guided tours are available (Sun–Fri, 2pm; charge), and the 1-hectare (3-acre) property includes the sole remnant of native kahi-katea forest in the Canterbury Plains.

Christchurch holds its traditions dear. It has also recognised that its charms have more tangible values: Japanese newlyweds come to Christ-church to have their marriage vows blessed in the Gothic charm of churches such as **St Barnabas**, on Tui Street in the leafy suburb of Fendalton, to the west of Hagley Park.

And there are gardens – acres and acres of them – both public and private. On Fendalton Road, the 6-hectare (13-acre) **Mona Vale** (daily, Oct–Apr 9.30am–5pm, May–Sept until 4pm; free; tel: 03-348 9660; www.monavale. co.nz) with beautiful gardens is a real delight, even more so if you have time for a leisurely punt on the Avon, which flows through the grounds. The "Garden City" label became official in 1997,

when Christchurch was named Garden City of the World. Visit in late summer and you will see this aspect of the city at its finest.

Cathedral Square and environs

Christchurch is an enjoyable city in which to walk, and where better to start than in the heart of the city at **Cathedral Square Ⓐ**. The square is officially countenanced, London's Hyde Park-style, as a public-speaking area. Lunch-time on a sunny weekday is best, while during summer the square is alive with festivals of fun and food, and stalls selling art, crafts and ethnic foods. The annual World Buskers Festival (www. worldbuskersfestival.com) held in late January is a popular event, with more than 450 live shows. Lunchtime concerts also run through December and January. Sadly, the square takes on a more unpleasant tone after dark, when it is not advisable to walk there alone.

Christchurch Cathedral (daily 9am–5pm; free; tel: 03-366 0046; www. christchurchcathedral.co.nz), on the east side of the square, is worth a visit.

TIP

The Christchurch and Canterbury i-site Visitor Centre is located at Cathedral Square in the former Post Office (tel: 03-379 9629; www.christchurchnz.net). It is open daily from 8.30am–5pm.

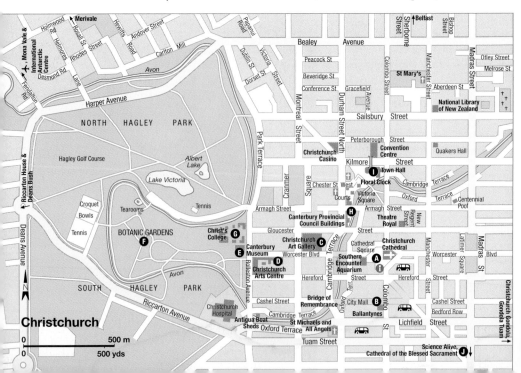

Dating back to the mid-19th century, it is one of the Southern Hemisphere's finest neo-Gothic churches. Building began in 1864 but was halted soon after due to a lack of funds. Some argued that the Church had better things to spend its money on – a recurring theme in New Zealand ecclesiastical history – and construction only resumed after the bishop of the time promised to contribute some of his own salary. The cathedral was finally completed in 1904. A visitors centre was added 90 years later. For a small admission fee, climb the 134 steps up the tower past the belfry for a view across the city.

West across the Square is the **Southern Encounter Aquarium** (daily 9am–5pm, last entry 4.30pm; entrance fee; tel: 03-359 0581; www.southernencounter. co.nz), a walk-through, hands-on-style aquarium and kiwi display. South down Colombo Street is **Ballantynes**, on the corner of the **City Mall ⓑ** pedestrian precinct. It is the establishment department store, Christchurch's Harrods if you like. The assistants dress in black and are known for being unfailingly helpful.

A walk down City Mall – prime Christchurch shopping territory – takes you to the **Bridge of Remembrance**, under which much water has flowed since it was opened on 11 November 1924. From here, just a short stroll along the river south of the bridge, on the corner of Oxford Terrace and Durham Street, stands the Anglican **St Michael and All Angels Church**. Completed in 1872, this historic church is built entirely of native wood and ranks among the largest timber Victorian Gothic churches in the world. The belfry, which stands apart from the church, houses the bell brought out from England with the first four ships.

The heart of Christchurch

North along the Avon up Cambridge Terrace, the city's old library, a small, architectural gem, is on the left. Like many others in the city, the building has been carefully restored – but now houses offices. A little further on is **Worcester Boulevard**, route of the restored trams. At the corner of Montreal Street stands the **Christchurch Art Gallery ⓒ** (daily 10am–5pm, Wed

Performance art by the Wizard of Christchurch, a long-running and well-known local eccentric, on Cathedral Square.

BELOW: punting along the Avon River.

For Ever England

A city does not become more English than England without putting its mind to it. Named after an Oxford college, Christchurch was a planned Anglican settlement, masterminded by one John Robert Godley. Repelled by the egalitarianism and industrialisation of the 19th century, Godley aspired to a medieval notion of a harmoniously blended Church and state, presided over by a benevolent gentry. He founded the Canterbury Association, with no fewer than two archbishops, seven bishops, 14 peers, four baronets and 16 Members of Parliament as backers. The idea was to raise money and find settlers – and only the best sort of migrant needed apply. To qualify for an assisted passage, a migrant had to furnish a certificate from his vicar vouching that "the applicant is sober, industrious and honest", and that "he and all his family are amongst the most respectable in the parish". From such ideals came the first Canterbury pilgrims in 1850. By 1855, 3,549 migrants had made the journey.

Inevitably, things went wrong. Dreams of an ecclesiastical utopia crumbled under the harsh realities of colonial life. It was as difficult to revitalise Anglicanism in New Zealand as it was anywhere else. Yet dreams endure. To be of First Four Ships stock still brings some cachet, even today. The names of those first official migrants are engraved on plaques in Cathedral Square.

Street buskers, part of the city's lively performing arts scene. The World Buskers Festival takes place every year in late January.

BELOW: the glass-and-steel frontage of Christchurch Art Gallery.

until 9pm; free; tel: 03-941 7300; www. christchurchartgallery.org.nz), a glass-and-steel building housing an impressive collection of New Zealand art.

Continue down Worcester Boulevard and you will come to the **Christchurch Arts Centre** (daily 9.30am–5pm; free; tel: 03-366 0989; www. artscentre.org.nz). A mass of dreaming spires, turrets and cloisters, this was once the site of the University of Canterbury. When the university moved to more spacious grounds in the suburbs, the site was dedicated to arts and crafts studios, theatres, restaurants and apartments, all nestled within the granite Gothic shells. The centre is home to the **Court Theatre** (tel: 03-963 0870; www.courttheatre.org.nz), a professional company long established as one of New Zealand's best.

This is the heart of old Christchurch. Directly across Rolleston Avenue is another Gothic structure, designed by the country's most distinguished Victorian architect, Benjamin W. Mountfort (1825–98). Opened in 1878, this significant landmark was designed to house the **Canterbury Museum**

(daily 9am–5.30pm in summer, until 5pm in winter; free; tel: 03-366 5000; www.canterburymuseum.com). Besides displays exploring Canterbury's pre-European and pioneer history and showcasing a fine collection of European decorative art and costume, the museum also devotes space to the discovery and exploration of Antarctica, and to **Discovery** (entrance fee), the museum's natural history centre for children.

Beyond, moving further into Hagley Park, the 30-hectare (74-acre) **Botanic Gardens** (daily 7am–sunset; free; tel: 03-941 6840; www.ccc.govt.nz/parks) are a truly splendid celebration of the city's gardening heritage, from English herbaceous borders to native sections and glasshouses of subtropical and desert specimens. Considered one of the top botanic gardens in the world, the area is enclosed within a loop of the Avon River as it winds through the 160-hectare (500-acre) **Hagley Park**. The park also includes a golf course, playing fields, tennis courts and a duck pond.

Immediately north along Rolleston Avenue is **Christ's College** , a very Anglican, English public school for boys. The buildings, old and new, are marvellous. Guided tours are available from October to mid-April (Mon, Wed and Fri 10am; charge; book at the college office). Head back to town down Armagh Street and you'll pass **Cranmer Square**. On the far side is the former **Christchurch Normal School**, built in 1878 to provide trainee teachers with a "normal" school environment in which to observe experienced teachers in a classroom situation. Long since deserted by educationalists, the building is now known as **Cranmer Courts**, and houses luxury apartments.

Further along Armagh Street, on the Durham Street corner, stand the old **Canterbury Provincial Council Buildings** (Mon–Sat 10.30am–3pm; donation requested), occupied in part by an establishment worthy of patronage, the pleasant **Belgian Beer Café Torenhof** (tel: 03-377 1007). Con-

structed between 1858 and 1865, these Gothic Revival-style buildings are the work of Benjamin Mountfort.

Architectural triumphs

Continue east along Armagh Street to **Victoria Square**. Once the city's market place, it is now a restful expanse of green anchored by the **Town Hall ❶**. Opened in 1972, after the city had dithered for 122 years over a civic centre, it remains the pride of modern Christchurch. Designed by local architects Warren and Mahoney, the building is restrained and elegant, with an auditorium, concert chamber, conference rooms and a restaurant overlooking the Avon River and square.

The Town Hall has been linked to one of the city's newer architectural features, the **Crowne Plaza Hotel**, and via an overhead walkway to a new convention centre for the city. Just another block away on Victoria Street stands **Christchurch Casino** (tel: 03-365 9999; www.christchurchcasino.co.nz; dress code applies), New Zealand's first, with its distinctive, stylised roulette-wheel facade.

Further down Armagh Street on the right is **New Regent Street**, with its charming Spanish mission-style facades in pastel blues and yellows. The street is closed to traffic (except the tram) and has cafés, restaurants and boutiques.

The "other" cathedral

If you're interested in ecclesiastical architecture, the city's other cathedral is worth seeking out. Two km (1 mile) south of Cathedral Square, on Barbadoes Street, is the Roman Catholic **Cathedral of the Blessed Sacrament ❷** (daily 9am–4pm; tel: 03-377 5610). This high Renaissance Romanesque basilica, opened in 1905, replaced a wooden church that was moved to a new site on Ferry Road. George Bernard Shaw visited the city soon after the building opened and praised Christchurch's "splendid cathedral". The pride of local Anglicans turned to chagrin when they realised that he was not referring to the main cathedral, but to the Catholic basilica. The building's architect, Francis W. Petre, though born in New Zealand, was descended from one of England's foremost Catholic families.

TIP

Hire a canoe or paddle boat from Antigua Boat Sheds (Cambridge Terrace at the end of Rolleston Avenue; tel: 03-366 5885; www.boatsheds.co.nz) beside the Avon and explore the river as it winds through the Botanic Gardens and Hagley Park. Or simply relax and enjoy the "Punting in the Park" option, courtesy of a boatman on a classic Cambridge punt.

BELOW: Polynesian cultural performance at the Christchurch Art Gallery.

Turn right from Barbadoes Street onto Moorhouse Avenue, where the old railway station has been converted into a hands-on science centre, **Science Alive** (daily 10am–5pm; entrance fee; tel: 03-365 5199; www.sciencealive.co.nz), an interactive temple to technology. Visitors can experience New Zealand's highest vertical slide, sample astronaut training on a human gyroscope and look into a Black Hole – all for the best scientific motives, of course.

Port Hills and the Banks Peninsula

Further from the city centre in the suburbs you can tour countless streets of fine homes. Christchurch's real estate is fiercely class-conscious, along lines that are somewhat inexplicable. **Fendalton** and **Merivale**, northwest of the city, are easily recognised, with their fine trees and secluded gardens, as havens of the wealthy. Yet cross the wrong street and values plummet.

To the south, the **Port Hills** enjoy a clear geographical advantage over the rest of the city. Their elevation lifts them above the winter smog, which can be severe. The **Summit Road** ❶, along the tops of the hills, gives tremendous views across the city, the plains and the Southern Alps and, on the other side, the port of Lyttelton and the hills of Banks Peninsula. There are extensive walking tracks over the Port Hills and peninsula beyond. They range from one- or two-hour strolls to ambitious hikes, with shelters to rest in. Ask at an information centre for details.

The hills can also be tackled by the **Christchurch Gondola** (daily 10am–10pm, last gondola leaves at 9pm; tel: 03-384 0700; www.gondola.co.nz), which has become one of the city's big attractions. A restaurant, bar and souvenir shops have been installed for diversions after the ride. The hardier can hire mountain bikes at the summit for an alternative route down, or an exploration of the hills.

There are many gardens in the hills. One of the most notable is **Gethsemane Gardens** (daily 9am–5pm; entrance fee; tel: 03-326 5848; www.gethsemanegardens.co.nz) on Revelation Drive, a private garden that nurtures many unusual plant species. Its

BELOW: the Christchurch tramway.

little avenues and tiny trellised chapel are worth a visit, but the highlight – the Noah's Ark, a chapel set inside a large wooden boat, is a new addition and a must-see.

It's also worth taking a drive or bus to **Lyttelton ②**, 12km (7 miles) to the southeast, the sleepy-looking port over the hill from Christchurch, with its charming cottages that cling to the slopes. You can return through the Lyttleton road tunnel or drive over the hill to the beachside suburbs of Ferrymead, Redcliffs and **Sumner ③**. The last has the air of an artists' retreat. It's also slightly bohemian and gets extra busy at weekends, when families come to enjoy its golden sand beach.

Back towards the city, **Ferrymead Heritage Park ④** (daily 10am–4.30pm; entrance fee; tel: 03-384 1970; www.ferry mead.org.nz) is a working re-creation of a pioneer village. Members of no fewer than 18 volunteer societies keep the village alive, and tram and train rides are available. A steam train runs the first Sunday of every month.

On the other side of the city, a short distance from the airport, is the fascinat-ing **International Antarctic Centre ⑤** (daily 9am–5.30pm, until 7pm in sum-mer; entrance fee; tel: 03-353 7798; www.iceberg.co.nz), which celebrates Christchurch's history as the embarka-tion point for ice-bound expeditions *(see page 316)*. As part of the "Snow and Ice Experience" visitors are exposed to Antarctic temperatures, as well as get-ting the chance to explore a snow cave. Generally considered the next best thing to being in Antarctica – if not slightly better because it omits the pri-vations that accompany the real thing – it's well worth a visit. The centre's newest attraction is the **New Zealand Little Blue Penguin Encounter**, fea-turing the world's smallest penguins.

Nearby is **Orana Wildlife Park ⑥** (daily 10am–5pm; entrance fee; tel: 03-359 7109; www.oranawildlifepark. co.nz), New Zealand's largest wildlife and conservation centre and open-range, safari-style zoo. Visitors can enjoy a hands-on experience with domestic animals in a farm enclosure, but the most attention is given to the rhinoceroses, cheetahs, giraffes, zebras and other exotic species. The park also

The Cathedral of the Blessed Sacrament at Barbadoes Street.

BELOW: modern art flanks Christchurch Cathedral.

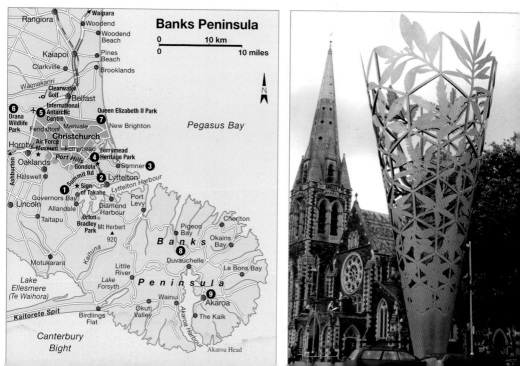

Get an overview of Christchurch's countryside on a balloon flight. Contact Up Up and Away, tel: 03-381 4600; www. ballooning.co.nz.

BELOW: Clearwater Golf Course.

has excellent displays of New Zealand wildlife, including the rare tuatara, and endangered birds such as the kiwi, kereru and kaka.

There are more refined pleasures to be had at the many wineries that have dotted the rural outskirts of Christchurch since Canterbury became one of New Zealand's boutique wine-growing regions in the late 1980s.

To the northeast, on Travis Road, is **Queen Elizabeth II Park ❼** (Mon–Fri 6am–9pm, Sat–Sun 7am–8pm; entrance fee; tel: 03-941 8999; www. qeiipark.org.nz). The stadium and swimming sports complex was built for the 1974 Commonwealth Games. City taxpayers didn't want to be landed with a white elephant, so it's been turned into an all-round family attraction, with wave machine, fountains and a pirate ship among other diversions.

French-influenced Akaroa

If you have time before you head south to the mountains and lakes, you might want a change from the city lights. **Banks Peninsula ❽**, over the Port Hills to the east, is the best destination for a short trip. It is the scene of one of two blunders made by Captain James Cook when he circumnavigated New Zealand in the 18th century. He mapped the peninsula as an island – which would have been correct if he had come several millennia earlier, as the extinct volcanoes which formed the peninsula were once separated from the mainland. (Cook's other gaffe was Stewart Island, at the southern tip of the South Island, which he linked to the mainland.)

The once bush-covered hills of Banks Peninsula were long ago logged for timber, but there are still some small remnants of bush and plenty of delightful valleys and bays. Sheltered microclimates support many horticultural products and plants that cannot be cultivated anywhere else this far south, including kiwi fruit. There are also some exotic nuts and herbs grown in the area.

To experience the real charm of the region, seek out **Diamond Harbour**, Okains Bay, Okuti Valley and **Port Levy**. These places are fertile, inviting and unspoilt – in many other parts of the world they would be bristling with condominiums.

But the real gem of the peninsula is **Akaroa ⑨**, about 80km (50 miles) from Christchurch. This little settlement began its European life in 1838 when a French whaler, Captain Jean-François Langlois, landed on its shores and bought – or so he thought – the entire peninsula from the Maori. Sixty-three settlers set out from France on the *Comte de Paris* to create a South Seas outpost. But they arrived in 1840 to find the Union flag flying. Pipped at the colonial post, the French settlers nevertheless stayed. They planted poplars from Normandy, named streets after places in their home country and grew grapes. By 1843, however, they were outnumbered by the English.

Nonetheless this French outpost lingers on, and has been spruced up for visitors. Little streets, with names such as Rue Lavaud and Rue Jolie, wind up the hill from the harbourfront. A charming colonial style predominates, and has been protected by town planning rules. Of most note is the **Langlois-Eteveneaux House**, now fitted out as a display and part of the **Akaroa Museum** (daily 10.30am–4.30pm; tel: 03-304 7614; entrance fee) at the corner of Rue Lavaud and Rue Balguerie.

Churches are also among Akaroa's notable sights. The Roman Catholic **St Patrick's Church** on Rue Lavaud is the oldest in anything like original form. It was built in 1864 and was in fact the third in town to serve Akaroa's French and Irish (hence the name) Catholics. It is a charming and cluttered little building with a noteworthy Bavarian window on the east wall.

The nearby Anglican **St Peter's Church** at Rue Balguerie was built in 1863, and generously enlarged about 15 years later. Compared to St Patrick's, this is a more austere building in the Protestant style. Most distinctive of all is the tiny **Kaik**, a Maori church some 6km (4 miles) south of the township along the foreshore. It is a remnant of a once strong Maori presence around Akaroa Harbour, in a haunting and evocative setting.

In the town of Akaroa, a climb through the domain, called the **Garden of Tane**, is worthwhile on its own count, and will take you to the spectacularly sited graveyard. Its graves must have the best views in the country, and they make up a rich record of the region's history. The **Old French Cemetery**, however, on the other side of town, is a disappointment. It was the resting place of Akaroa's earliest Europeans; the long slog up the hill affords a good view of the harbour, but a benevolent government tidied the place up in 1925, in the process destroying most of the headstones for a mediocre memorial.

Akaroa Harbour, on the south coast of Banks Peninsula, is on the doorstep of the habitat of the rare Hector's dolphin. There are regular sea cruises to catch glimpses of the dolphin and other features of the region.

Many Christchurch people own holiday houses in Akaroa or nearby, and the town can become crowded in January and February. There are numerous bars, restaurants and cafés – but due to the isolation, restaurants tend to be pricey. ❑

EAT

If driving to Akaroa from Christchurch, take the south fork off the SH75 at Barry's Bay for the French Farm Winery and Restaurant (tel: 03-304 5784). It makes its own range of wines (the chardonnay is excellent) and runs a highly recommended restaurant.

BELOW: otters at Orana Wildlife Park.

CANTERBURY

Canterbury's flat coastal and inland plains are bordered by mountain ranges of breathtaking beauty. There can be no finer place to be – when the wind's in the right direction

Canterbury is a mariage of mountain and sea, linked by snow-fed rivers that cut braided courses across the plain. The Southern Alps, Pacific Ocean and two rivers (the Conway in the north and Waitaki in the south) form the boundaries of the province, which surrounds Christchurch on the eastern side of South Island.

The popular view of Canterbury as a patchwork plain where lambs frolic under a nor'west sky really does exist. The plain, 180km (112 miles) long and an average of 40km (25 miles) wide, is New Zealand's largest area of flat land. Canterbury lamb, bred for meat and wool, is regarded as the country's best. And the Canterbury nor'wester is a notorious wind, a true *föhn* that creates warm, dry and blustery conditions as it descends from the high peaks to the west. It whips up dust from the river beds and furrowed farmlands, and is blamed for the moodiness of the locals.

Further west, Canterbury province also encompasses New Zealand's highest mountains and its widest rivers, alongside pastoral and forested hills, some superb beaches, extinct volcanoes and the sheltered bays of Banks Peninsula *(see page 252)*. Settlement is diverse, from cities to high-country sheep stations where genteel English traditions are vigorously upheld.

North Canterbury

Heading north from Christchurch, the main State Highway (SH) 1 crosses the Canterbury Plain to reach **Waipara**, one of New Zealand's most rapidly expanding wine regions. Stop for a tasting at a cellar door, or sample the fare at one of its award-winning wineries, including **Pegasus Bay** (www.pegasusbay.com) and **Waipara Hills** (www.waiparahills.co.nz).

At the town of Waipara, NH7 peals off inland, climbing up the Waiau Valley and the rolling hills of north Canterbury to reach **Lewis Pass**, from where it winds its way down to the west coast. It's an all-weather route which opened

Main attractions
HANMER SPRINGS
ARTHUR'S PASS
    NATIONAL PARK
GERALDINE
TIMARU
LAKE TEKAPO
AORAKI MOUNT COOK
    NATIONAL PARK

LEFT: rock climbing at Aoraki Mount Cook.
BELOW: newborn lamb on the Canterbury plains.

Choose your poison at Thrillseeker's Canyon (tel: 03-315 7046; www.thrillseekers canyon.co.nz), a short drive from Hanmer – rafting, jet boating, go-karting or bungee-jumping.

BELOW: autumn colours along Hanmer's Mount Isobel Track.

in 1939, offering a comparatively gentle, picturesque crossing to the west coast.

North of Waipara the road passes through small rural settlements including **Hurunui**, where a famous limestone tavern was built in 1868 to accommodate weary drovers, and the limestone landscape of **Waikari**, with its ancient Maori rock art and naturally sculpted animal forms.

Further on, in the mountains, is a favourite retreat of Cantabrians. **Hanmer Springs** ⓮, a little Alpine village an easy 136km (85-mile) drive north of Christchurch, nestled in a sheltered, forested valley. The **Hanmer Springs Thermal Pools and Spa** (daily 10am–9pm; entrance fee; tel: 03-315 7511; www.hanmersprings.co.nz), on Amuri Avenue, has hot mineral pools set in a garden of giant conifers. Few experiences are more pleasurable than relaxing in these open-air pools on a winter's night, watching the snowflakes dissolve silently in the steam.

A European settler stumbled upon the springs in 1859 and they were har-

nessed by the government in 1883. Since then their recuperative powers have been used at various times to help rehabilitate wounded soldiers, the mentally ill and alcoholics. The landscaped rock gardens include numerous thermal pools and a separate family area where children can enjoy waterfalls and slides.

Several easy, well-defined paths meander through **Hanmer Forest Park**, the first exotic forest established by the government in the South Island. More demanding walks to the summits of **Conical Hill** and **Mount Isobel** provide magnificent panoramas. The **Mount Isobel Track**, which passes 200 different kinds of sub-Alpine flowering plants and ferns, is a naturalist's delight.

Hanmer's 18-hole golf course is one of the highest in New Zealand, while fishing, hunting, jet boating, river rafting, bungee-jumping, skiing and horse-trekking are also available. Although there is accommodation in the form of small hotels and guesthouses, the main street has retained the low-key atmosphere of a typical rural township.

To the west of Hamer, NH7 reaches an altitude of 865 metres (2,838ft) at **Lewis Pass**, passing through beautiful beech-covered mountains. The highway descends to **Maruia Springs**, where the **Maruia Springs Thermal Resort** (daily; entrance fee; tel: 03-523 8840; www.maruiasprings.co.nz) offers a chemical-free thermal soak in perfectly formed rock pools situated beside the burbling Maruia River. The route then continues on to the Rahu Saddle, Reefton and Greymouth on the west coast (see page 273).

In the far north of the province, the isolated **Clarence Valley** ⑮ is worth exploring for its rugged tussocked beauty, especially upstream. Note, however, that the road that runs along it is not accessible from Hanmer – there are locked gates at the Acheron River Bridge (downstream from Jack's Pass) and at the Rainbow Station over the Main Divide. The road, originally built to install and maintain the high-voltage transmission lines from the hydro schemes of Otago to Blenheim, Nelson and beyond, is an unsealed, often steep track, suitable only in good weather.

South Canterbury: a touch of Switzerland

Canterbury's finest scenery is inland, along the foothills and valleys of the **Southern Alps**. Three main roads provide easy access to passes to the mountains, beyond which lies Westland. Northernmost is the aforementioned Lewis Pass, central is spectacular Arthur's Pass and the surrounding national park of the same name; southernmost is Burke's Pass, which leads to the Mackenzie Country and the magnificent panorama of glacial lakes and Alps of the Aoraki Mount Cook region.

The quickest route between Christchurch and Westland is the West Coast Road (SH73) through Arthur's Pass, which boasts New Zealand's version of a Swiss village. Although **Arthur's Pass** ⑯ township, in the heart of the Southern Alps 154km (96 miles) west of Christchurch, lacks green pastures and tinkling cowbells, it does have chalet-style accommodation and a railway station. The **TranzAlpine** train stops here twice daily on its journey between Christchurch and Grey-

TIP

One way to get really stunning views of Canterbury is to drift over it sipping champagne in a hot-air balloon, gazing at the Southern Alps. Aoraki Balloon Safaris operate from Methven (tel: 03-302 8172; www.nzballooning.com).

BELOW: snowboarder in action.

Winter Wonderland

Winter transforms the vast windswept plains and pleated foothills of the Mackenzie Country into a sports wonderland. While local ski fields like Mount Dobson (www.dobson.co.nz), Fox Peak (www.foxpeak.co.nz) and Lake Ohau (www.ohau.co.nz) rely on naturally forming snow, Round Hill Ski Field (www.roundhill.co.nz) in the Two Thumb Range is always open during the winter thanks to its snow-making machines. The ski field offers magnificent views across Lake Tekapo, and its wide gentle slopes are ideal for beginners and those making the transition from skiing to snowboarding who need to put in concentrated effort on predictable terrain. Qualified instructors provide tuition for beginners, intermediate and advanced, and you can hire all the equipment you need.

mouth *(see page 321)*. For information on walks and climbs in the area, and on weather conditions, call the DOC information centre (tel: 03-318 9211; www.apinfo.co.nz).

Arthur's Pass marks the eastern portal of the **Otira Tunnel**, the only rail link through the mountains. The 8km (5-mile) tunnel, completed in 1923 after 15 years of construction, remains a vital rail link between the west coast and Canterbury.

Arthur's Pass is also the headquarters of **Arthur's Pass National Park**. Its proximity to Christchurch and access to numerous tracks of varying difficulty through inspiring scenery, mountain climbing and skiing make the 114,500-hectare (282,930-acre) park one of the most popular in the country. You can also enjoy night skiing on the floodlit slopes of Temple Basin (www.templebasin.co.nz) on the main divide of the Southern Alps. Within its borders are 16 peaks over 2,000 metres (6,500ft), the highest being **Mount Murchison** at 2,400 metres (7,870ft), while the most accessible is **Mount Rolleston** at 2,271 metres (7,451ft).

The 924-metre (3,032ft) pass, named after Arthur Dudley Dobson who rediscovered the former Maori route in 1864, marks the boundary between Canterbury and Westland. Storms are often as intense as they are sudden, dropping as much as 250mm (10 inches) of rain in 24 hours. Bad weather in winter often forces the closure of the highway, which in the Otira Gorge is very steep, with a series of tight bends requiring special care in wet weather and in winter.

The road is not suitable for vehicles towing caravans, and in bad weather it is advisable for camper vans to take the longer, but easier and safer, Lewis Pass route to Westland.

Porter's Pass and Mount Hutt

Arthur's Pass is not the highest point on the West Coast Road. That distinction belongs to **Porter's Pass** ⓱, just 88km (55 miles) west of Christchurch, which traverses the foothills at 945 metres (3,100ft). It's a popular winter destination for day-trippers from Christchurch who enjoy tobogganing

TIP

One of New Zealand's most spectacular train journeys is the Tranz-Alpine from Christchurch to Greymouth. It passes through farmland, mountains and valleys on a 233km (145-mile) journey which takes 4½ hours one-way. Contact Tranz Scenic at tel: 04-495 0775; www.tranzscenic.co.nz.

BELOW: Canterbury sheep jam.

and ice-skating at Lake Lyndon and skiing on the many ski fields in the vicinity, such as the commercial field at **Porter Heights** (www.porterheights. co.nz) and the club fields at **Craigie-burn** (www.craigieburn.co.nz), **Broken River** (www.brokenriver.co.nz) and **Mount Cheeseman** (www.mt cheeseman.com).

Canterbury's most popular and best-developed ski field is **Mount Hutt** ⑱, 100km (60 miles) west of Christchurch and serviced by the small town of **Methven**, 11km (7 miles) away, which provides accommodation to suit all budgets. Ski aficionados regard Mount Hutt as one of the best ski fields in New Zealand. It has a vertical rise of 672 metres (2,205ft) – the longest run stretches for about 2km (1¼ miles) – and is well suited to both skiing and snowboarding.

Nearby is the **Rakaia Gorge**, world-famous for its salmon and its landmark bridges. Experienced local guides lead backcountry fishing excursions, or to ride the rapids aboard the **Rakaia Gorge Alpine Jet** (daily; entrance fee; tel: 03-318 6574; www.rivertours.co.nz).

To Aoraki Mount Cook via Burke's Pass

Although New Zealand's highest peak, Aoraki Mount Cook, is almost directly due west from Christchurch, the journey by road is a circuitous 330km (205 miles), heading first south, then west, then north again. Getting there, however, is half the fun.

The main route from Christchurch follows SH1 south for 121km (75 miles), marching easily across plain and braided river alike, casually belying the mighty challenges this journey once posed for Maori and pioneer. The wide rivers proved major obstacles to travel and settlement in the 1850s, and difficult river crossings caused numerous drownings in Canterbury. Throughout New Zealand 1,115 people lost their lives in river accidents between 1840 and 1870, and it was even suggested in Parliament that drowning be classified a natural death. Nowadays motorists speed over the Rakaia, Ashburton and Rangitata rivers without a thought for the hazards that once confronted travellers.

The kea is a native parrot, a fairly common sight in the mountains.

BELOW: Geraldine's country-style cinema.

Jammy Geraldine

Set on the banks of the Waihi River, Geraldine is a friendly settlement, jam-packed with craftspeople who have moved here for the creative synergy and the relaxed lifestyle. A hive of edible creativity, there are gourmet treats on every corner of this town. Tempt your tastebuds at Talbot Forest Cheese, inhale the aromatic world of speciality jams at Barker Fruit Processors, and indulge yourself in the chocolatey confines of Chocolate Fellmann, where a legendary Kiwi favourite, the chocolate fish (a marshmallow sweet covered in rich creamy chocolate), can be sampled.

At Michael and Gillian Linton's Giant Jersey, gorgeously soft Perendale, mohair and merino wools are crafted into stylish made-to-measure garments, and at the Belanger-Taylor Glass Studio visitors can witness the fascinating birth of intriguing works of art. Vintage-car enthusiasts will be in their element at the Vintage Car and Machinery Museum, while an evening at Barry and Anthea McLauchlan's classic country-style cinema will never be forgotten. "Reverend Barry" (as he's known around town) greets guests at the door and will usher you to your seat – a cosy couch downstairs, or a regular seat up top. Art-house and mainstream films are screened on an old Ernemann 2 projector and, unless the movie is subtitled, an intermission is standard.

The Church of the Good Shepherd at Tekapo.

BELOW: winter sports on the slopes of Mount Hutt.

Immediately past the Rangitata River, the road to the Mackenzie Country (SH79) veers off westwards from the main highway. It leads to the foothills and the tiny inland country town of **Geraldine ⓳**, 138km (86 miles) southwest of Christchurch. The town nestles into the hills, a base for detours to a historic pioneer homestead in the Orari Gorge and excellent picnic and fishing spots in the nearby Waihi and Te Moana gorges and Peel Forest Park.

Thirty-one km (19 miles) further south is **Timaru ⓴**, the urban heart of the Central South Island, a vibrant town that has preserved much of its Edwardian heritage and buildings. Timaru's first colonists started building a breakwater in 1859, and its harbour was finally completed in 1906. The addition of many stately Edwardian buildings and a striking piazza overlooking Caroline Bay (site of the town's annual summer carnival) has created a respectable town centre with an air of quiet dignity.

The renowned artist Colin McCahon was born here, and many of his works can be seen at the **Aigantighe Art Gallery** (daily; free; tel: 03-688 4424; www.timaru.govt.nz). The city has an excellent network of walkways. You can visit **the South Canterbury Museum** (daily; free; tel: 03-684 2212; www.timaru.govt.nz) or inhale the heady scents of the 529 named old rose varieties planted in the **Trevor Griffiths Rose Garden** (daily; free; tel: 03-684 8199; www.timaru.govt.nz).

Head inland to **Pleasant Point**, where the surrounding countryside offers wine tasting at the café at **Opihi Vineyard** (Sept–May Wed–Sun 11am– 4pm; tel: 03-614 8308; www.opihi.co. nz), **Maori Rock Art** at Raincliff Reserve (free) and in **Upper Waitohi**, the memorial of unsung aviation pioneer Richard Pearse. At **Pleasant Point Museum and Railway** (daily; entrance fee; tel-03 614 8323; www.pleasantpoin-trail.org.nz) you can ride the world's only Ford Model T Railcar (departs 11am, 12pm, 1pm, 2pm and 3pm),

admire the restored railway relics, or wait in the Old Time Movie Theatre, with a bunch of cinema classics.

The small country town of **Fairlie**, reached by travelling through Geraldine or Pleasant Point, has a tiny historical museum. From here onwards the gentle countryside is left behind as the road, now SH8, rises with deceptive ease to **Burke's Pass ㉑**. At this gap through the foothills a different world stretches beyond – the great tussocked basin known as the **Mackenzie Country**, named after a Scottish shepherd who in 1855 tried to hide stolen sheep in this isolated high-country area.

Long, straight stretches of road take you for about 100km (62 miles) southwest, eventually to **Twizel** (www.twizel.com), a town built to provide accommodation for workers on the region's major dam projects, and thought likely to become a ghost town when the projects were completed. Twizel, however, has defied pundits, and is enjoying a mini boom as a budget-friendly base for exploring the area.

Winding across the stark, bronzed landscape, 58km (36 miles) from Twizel, the road reaches **Lake Tekapo ㉒**, a lovely turquoise glacial lake reflecting the surrounding mountains. At 710 metres (2,329ft) above sea level, the lake's gorgeous turquoise colour is caused by "rock flour", finely ground rock particles suspended in glacial meltwater. By the water's edge is the simple stone **Church of the Good Shepherd**. Nearby, the high-country sheepdog which has played an essential role in building New Zealand's prosperity is commemorated in a bronze statue erected by runholders from Mackenzie Country.

For stunning views and star-gazing tours take the road to **Mount John Observatory** (daily; entrance fee; tel: 03-680 6960; www.earthandsky.co.nz), where telescopes probe deep space searching for dark matter, Black Holes and distant planets. Below is Tekapo's all-new **Winter Park** (daily 10am–9pm; entrance fee; tel: 0800-235 382; www.

winterpark.co.nz), an ice-skating rink where skates are hired by the hour. The adjoining **Alpine Springs and Spa** (daily 10am–9pm; entrance fee; tel: 0800-235 382; www.alpinesprings.co.nz) promises to soothe away any aches and pains, or you can try your hand at fishing, hiking, mountain biking or horse riding. During the winter **Round Hill Ski Field** (www.roundhill.co.nz) offers a pleasant drive to gentle, open slopes and cosy clubrooms.

Beyond Tekapo there is a choice of two routes, either the main SH8 or the **Canal Road**, a scenic route which follows the course of the man-made canal that drains Tekapo's waters to the first of the Waitaki hydroelectric scheme's powerhouses on the southern shore of **Lake Pukaki ㉓**.

Pukaki today is twice the size it was in 1979, when its waters were allowed to flow unimpeded to Lake Benmore. Concrete dams now hold Pukaki in check, forcing it to rise to a new level for use in hydroelectric power generation. About 2km (1¼ miles) north of

The sheepdog monument at Lake Tekapo.

BELOW: the view across Lake Pukaki.

BELOW: the "Shoe Fence" just east of Burke's Pass has become known as a quirky sight. Over 1,000 items of footwear are strung along a length of wire fence.

the turnoff to **Aoraki Mount Cook** is a lookout with spectacular views of the area, including, on a clear day, the towering hulk of the mountain itself.

Aoraki Mount Cook National Park

Travellers on the highway that skirts the southern slopes of the Pukaki Valley and concludes at **Aoraki Mount Cook Village** ㉔, 99km (62 miles) west of Tekapo, might catch glimpses of the old road undulating above and disappearing into the surface of the lake far below. The new sealed highway, with an easy gradient, has halved the driving time to the lodge with the million-dollar views, **The Hermitage** (tel: 03-435 1809; www.hermitage.co.nz), with rooms nearly as pricey.

The village is the gateway to the monarch of New Zealand's parks, the **Aoraki Mount Cook National Park** ㉕, where the highest peaks in the land soar above the crest of the Southern Alps. Supreme is Aoraki Mount Cook itself, which until 1991 was 3,764 metres (12,349ft) high. However, the famous mountain lost about 10 metres

(33ft) from its summit in that year in a massive avalanche. The re-surveyed official height today is 3,754 metres (12,316ft), which allows it still to retain its standing as New Zealand's highest mountain.

The Aoraki Mount Cook Alpine region was the training ground for the late Sir Edmund Hillary, the first person to scale Mount Everest. The narrow park extends only 80km (50 miles) along the Alpine spine, yet it contains 140 peaks over 2,100 metres (7,000ft), as well as 72 glaciers, including five of New Zealand's largest – the Godley, Murchison, Tasman, Hooker and Mueller. Of these, the **Tasman Glacier** is the largest and longest in the Southern Hemisphere, extending 27km (17 miles) – it has retreated a couple of kilometres in recent times – and in places some 3km (2 miles) wide. The ice in this glacier can reach over 600 metres (2,000ft) in depth.

Due to its sacrosanct status within a national park, accommodation in the village has been limited. Nevertheless, in addition to The Hermitage hotel, there are also self-contained A-frame

chalets, a camping ground, a well-equipped youth hostel and a new lodge. Well-defined tracks lead from the village up to the surrounding valleys. These eventually become "climbs" that are definitely not for novices and should only be tackled with the right equipment, and then only after consultation with the park rangers. Easier mountain ascents are provided by ski-equipped scenic aircraft which land on the high snowfields.

Skiing is available from July to September, the most exciting run being the descent of the Tasman Glacier. As the spectacular upper reaches of the glacier slopes can only be accessed via fixed-wing skiplane, skiing the Tasman can be an expensive affair. The Aoraki Mount Cook-based **Alpine Guides** (tel: 03-435 1834; www.alpineguides.co.nz) operate ski trips to the Tasman during the season. The same company also organises guided climbs of Aoraki Mount Cook and mountaineering instruction courses in the summer.

On SH80 near Aoraki Mount Cook Village is a tiny airport from where

Aoraki Mount Cook Skiplanes (tel: 03-435 1026; www.mtcookskiplanes.com) offer magnificent scenic flights to view the glaciers up close and, on some routes, land on them. The Grand Circle Option lasts nearly an hour and flies first to the west side of the Alpine Divide to land on either Franz Josef or Fox Glacier (*see page 269*) before returning via Tasman Glacier. Flights incorporating a landing on the *neve* of Tasman Glacier are highly recommended.

The spectacular views of Aoraki Mount Cook, especially when the last rays of the midsummer sun strike its blushing peak in late twilight, form the highlight of many a traveller's exploration of Canterbury. The mountain, named Aoraki (Cloud Piercer) by the Maori, is frequently shrouded in cloud, depriving sightseers of its face. But come rain or shine, this Alpine region is ever masterful, ever dramatic, and a corner of Canterbury where people are dwarfed into comparative insignificance. ❏

Take a scenic flight over Mount Cook and the Southern Alps.

BELOW: sublime scenery at Lake Tekapo.

THE WEST COAST

Wild and rugged, this area's inhospitable terrain makes many of its scenic spots difficult to reach: those who persevere will be rewarded with untamed nature at its best

Main attractions
FOX AND FRANZ JOSEF GLACIERS
OKARITO LAGOON
GREYMOUTH
PUNAKAIKI

M ost New Zealanders refer to their South Island's western flank as simply "the Coast", a rugged and primeval region that plummets westwards from the South Island's Main Divide, through luxuriant rainforest hemmed in by a breathtaking coastline. Weeks can be spent exploring this region, which Rudyard Kipling referred to as "last, loneliest, loveliest, exquisite apart". No other area in the country is so stamped with identity or character.

In the gold-rush days of the 1860s men lit their cigars with £5 notes and dozens of towns sprang up in the middle of the bush around the promise of buried riches. Yet the hard-drinking, hard-fighting and hard-working men and women of those bygone days have left behind little more than a legend. After decades of decline, the population along the 500km (300-mile) coast is now almost back to what it was in 1867, when it peaked at 40,000 and comprised 13 percent of New Zealand's total population. Today, West Coasters number around 38,000 – a mere one percent of the country's 4 million people. Old buildings ramble into misty landscapes and rainforest relentlessly reclaims sites where towns such as Charleston (home to 12,000 souls and 80 grog shops) once boomed.

Living here is still for the hardy. There are more "settlements" than towns, and no cities. Along with the mist and mountains, a pioneering spirit still hangs in the air. The Coasters who remain have developed a strong identity, with a reputation for being down-to-earth, rugged, independent and hospitable. For years, they made a habit of flouting liquor licensing laws, in particular that which forbade the sale of alcohol after 6 o'clock, which was regarded as some kind of joke originating from the city. Many West Coasters still harbour a deep suspicion of "Greenies", conservationists who want to preserve intact the area's native forests and birdlife. Some locals,

PRECEDING PAGES: climbing at Fox Glacier. **LEFT:** the coast at Ship Creek. **BELOW:** polished *paua* (abalone) shells.

The Bushman's Centre at Lake Ianthe recreates the lives of the pioneering bushmen – mainly fur trappers – who lived in the west coast region in the 19th century.

BELOW: the TranzAlpine train en route to Greymouth.

struggling to scratch a living from coal-mining and timber-milling, angrily oppose the environmentalist concerns of these outsiders.

Early explorers

The west coast has never seduced its inhabitants with an easy life. It was settled late by the Maori, from about 1400, the main attraction being the much-coveted *pounamu* greenstone at Arahura, the hard and translucent jade traded up and down the country to make fine-quality tools and weapons. Because of the stormy sea conditions along this stretch of coast, the stone had to be arduously carried out on men's backs, first through a route north to Nelson and later across Alpine passes in the Main Divide to Canterbury.

Neither of the two great European discoverers, Abel Tasman and James Cook, was enamoured of what he saw when sailing past the west coast, in 1642 and 1769 respectively. "An inhospitable shore" was Cook's description. "One long solitude with a forbidding sky and impenetrable forest" was the view, about 50 years later, of an officer in a French expedition.

Travelling up the coast

The west coast is accessed from elsewhere in South Island via one of three spectacular mountain passes, or through the scenic Buller Gorge that winds back to Nelson in the north. The southernmost route, snaking up from the Southern Lakes and the dry, tussocked scenery of central Otago, is State Highway (SH) 6. Crossing the 563-metre (1,867ft) high **Haast Pass** ㉖, this was the last major arterial route to be pushed through in New Zealand, completed in 1965. Having descended to the coast, SH6 then follows the seaboard northwards from the town of Haast all the way up to Westport, enabling travellers to follow almost the entire length of the coast as part of a South Island round trip.

The **Haast Visitors Centre** DOC (daily Nov–Mar 9am–6pm, Apr–Oct 9am–4.30pm; tel: 03-750 0809; www.haastnz.com) near the Haast junction has useful information on attractions in the area. Turn south at Haast town-

ship and you enter an especially lonely corner of the country, traversed by a road which extends 36km (22 miles) to the fishing village of **Jackson Bay** ㉗. This small community swells in size during the spring, when whitebaiters descend en masse to the nearby river mouth, an annual occurrence which is repeated beside swift-flowing rivers all along the coast.

Fishing is a major preoccupation in this southern part of Westland. Haast is known for its river fishing, while 45km (28 miles) north at the quiet holiday spot of **Lake Paringa**, anglers are enticed by the prospect of Brown trout and Quinnat salmon. Meanwhile, eco-tourism is breathing new life into rural communities once entirely reliant on fishing or other local resources. Thirty km (19 miles) north of Haast, at **Wilderness Lodge Lake Moeraki** (tel: 03-750 0881; www.wildernesslodge. co.nz) in South Westland, guests are immersed in the nature experience while cosseted in luxury. For many, gazing up at the Southern Cross and hearing the screech of a kiwi are among the highlights of their stay. In the light of

day, there is the Fiordland penguin colony near **Knights Point** to visit, or dolphins to be seen cavorting in the surf off **Ship Creek**.

Fox and Franz Josef glaciers

Many of the country's finest mountains lie in the geographical region of the west coast, comprising that chain of spectacular cloud-piercing peaks called the **Southern Alps**. Aoraki Mount Cook *(see page 262)* is the highest and a serious challenge to the Alpine climber. Dozens of other peaks over 3,000 metres (9,850ft) are named after early navigators, including Tasman, Magellan, La Perouse, Dampier and Malaspina.

About 120km (75 miles) north of Haast, an astonishing total of 15 metres (49ft) of snow is dumped annually at high altitudes, giving rise to some 140 glaciers. Uniquely, two of these – **Fox Glacier**, and, further up the road, **Franz Josef Glacier** – penetrate the lower forest. Few sights equal the spectacle of these giant tongues of ice grinding down through the temperate

EAT

If you like seafood, and you're in the west coast in spring, make sure you sample that scrumptious New Zealand speciality, whitebait fritters. Small but nutritious worm-like fish, bound in a light batter or just with egg, they're irresistible.

BELOW: Jackson Bay is famous for its Brown trout.

A handcarved greenstone pendant. It is also known as jade or nephrite or, in Maori, pounamu.

rainforest to just 300 metres (1,000ft) above sea level. Explorer and geologist Julius von Haast made the first recorded visit to the glaciers in 1865. His unbridled enthusiasm soon made them known as far away as Europe. Within two decades, guided glacier trips had become fashionable. One old photo of the period shows a party of 90 picknickers high in the jumbled ice. Venturing onto the ice alone has never been recommended, and successions of mountain guides have made their living sharing their glacial passion.

Years of heavy snowfall high in the mountains caused both glaciers to begin a spectacular advance in 1982. Such was the progress of Franz Josef Glacier that its sparkling white ice could be seen again for the first time in 40 years from the altar window of St James Anglican Church, which sits hidden in a superb setting of native bush in Franz Josef township. Although the advance of both glaciers had ground to a halt at the end of the first decade of the 21st century, neither is showing any signs of retreating. Fox Glacier still extends 600 metres

(2,000ft) further down the valley now than it did in 1982.

Both glaciers are located, about 25km (16 miles) apart, in the **Westland National Park** ㉘, with its 88,000 hectares (217,000 acres) of Alpine peaks, snowfields, forests, lakes and rivers. The main highway which traverses the park's western edge passes close to both. As well as guided walks on the ice (*see below*), narrow bush-clad roads provide easy access to good vantage points for postcard views from reasonably close vantage points. But take note that the glacier terminals are very fragile, and towering blocks of ice have been crashing down with increasing frequency resulting in some fatal accidents: it is important to stay within the boundary ropes. Helicopter and skiplane flights over the glaciers provide remarkable views of the greenish-blue tints and the apparently infinite crevasses.

Two small but lively townships, **Fox Glacier** ㉙ and **Franz Josef** ㉚, each with a decent range of accommodation and restaurants on offer, cater to the

needs of visitors. **Department of Conservation** offices in Fox Glacier (Mon–Fri 9am–4.30pm; tel: 03-751 0807) and Franz Josef (daily 8.30am–6pm in summer, until 5pm in winter; tel: 03-752 0796) provide information about the activities available in the area.

There are some 110km (68 miles) of walking tracks accessible from these townships, passing through the varied native forest and dominated by the lofty peaks of Cook, Tasman and La Perouse. This trio of mountains is stunningly mirrored in **Lake Matheson**, one of the park's three calm lakes formed by the glacial dramas of 10,000 years ago. Just 10 minutes north of Franz Josef Village on SH6 is **Lake Mapourika**, the largest and arguably the most stunning of South Westland's glacial lakes.

Coastal highlights

A short detour 19km (12 miles) west of Fox Glacier township is **Gillespie's Beach**, noted for its miners' cemetery and seal colony. Some 60km (37 miles) further north on the main road, another detour leads to **Okarito**

Lagoon ③, New Zealand's largest natural wetland, which covers 3,240 hectares (8,000 acres). It is famous as the only breeding ground of the rare white heron. A survey taken just 12 years after the birds' discovery there in 1865 showed only six breeding pairs had escaped the plume hunters. Today, a sedate 20-minute jet-boat ride takes nature-lovers to a riverside hideaway within the sanctuary to view the colony, now numbering 250-strong. The Maori called them kotuku, the "bird of a single flight", to be seen perhaps once in a lifetime.

The town of **Okarito** once boasted 31 hotels, but now only a few holiday cottages remain. For the more adventurous, guided kayak trips organised by **Okarito Nature Tours** (tel: 03-573 4014; www.okarito.co.nz) are an excellent means of exploring the lagoon and the white heron colony.

Northwards, the main highway passes the idyllic, forest-enclosed and trout-filled **Lake Ianthe** before arriving in the town of **Ross**, at the heart of a once-flourishing goldfield which produced the largest nugget (2,970g/99oz)

New Zealand author Keri Hulme's Booker Prize-winning novel Bone People *is set in the township of Okarito. The novel examines the lives of three troubled individuals caught between Maori and European traditions.*

BELOW: an ice cave on Fox Glacier.

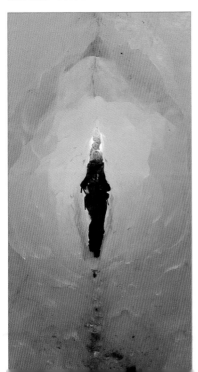

Walking on Ice

You can't come all the way to Westland National Park and not walk on the glaciers. Guided walks range from a half- to full day, while a more expensive option is a heli-hike, which takes you on a scenic helicopter flight and lands you on the glacier for a guided walk. More adventurous travellers can try their hand at ice climbing – scaling pinnacles and vertical crevasse walls. You will be outfitted with a helmet and harness, ice crampons (metal spikes to be fastened onto boots), an axe and a rope. Needless to say, a high degree of fitness is necessary.

Less fit mortals are better off on the half-day glacier walk, which itself is a strenuous affair if you've never walked on ice before. Dress warmly in layers, although you will be provided with boots, socks and gloves, crampons, a Gore-Tex raincoat and a trekking pole.

For walks on Fox Glacier, contact Fox Glacier Guiding (daily 8.30am, 9.10am, 1.30pm; tel: 03-751 0825; www.foxguides.co.nz). For Franz Josef, contact Franz Josef Glacier Guides (daily 9.15am, 11.45am, 2.15pm; tel: 03-752 0763; www.franzjosefglacier.com).

If the idea of walking on ice – even if it's not thin – doesn't appeal, hop onto a helicopter or light plane instead. There is a range of options, with the more expensive trips featuring a brief snow landing on either of the glaciers.

BELOW: huhu grubs served at Hokitika's Wild Food Festival – not for the squeamish.

– the "Honourable Roddy" – ever recorded in New Zealand. Relics of its once proud history and a replica of the aforementioned nugget can be seen at the **Ross Goldfields Information and Heritage Centre** at 4 Aylmer Street (daily 9am–4pm; tel: 03-755 4077; www.ross.org.nz).

About 30km (19 miles) north of Ross is **Hokitika** ㉜, formerly the "Wonder City of the Southern Hemisphere" with "streets of gold" and a thriving seaport. It is much quieter these days, but has regained something of its prosperous feel. It is served by the west coast's main airfield, and its many tourist attractions include a historical museum, greenstone factories, a gold mine, gold panning and a glowworm dell. One of the country's best kiwi-viewing facilities is here at the **National Kiwi Centre** (daily 9am–5pm; entrance fee; tel: 03-755 5251; www.thenationalkiwicentre.co.nz) at 64 Tancred Street. You can view kiwis in a recreated habitat, giant eels (best at feeding times 10am, noon and 3pm), tuatara and various aquatic species. A celebration of the coast's bush

tucker is held annually in mid-March at the **Hokitika Wild Foods Festival** (www.wildfoods.co.nz). The one-day gala event gives visitors the chance to sample wild boar, venison, huge roasted larvae called huhu grubs and gourmet "westcargot" snails, not to mention whitebait patties. At the other end of the culinary scale, the town's **Café de Paris** (tel: 03-755 8933) on Tancred Street serves authentic French cuisine and has won various awards for its fine fare.

Both **Lake Kaniere** and the **Hokitika Gorge**, 18km (11 miles) and 35km (22 miles) from Hokitika respectively, make worthwhile side trips. Otherwise continue 23km (14 miles) north of the town, to Kumara Junction and the turnoff to the dramatic **Arthur's Pass Highway** *(see page 257)*, the second of the three mountain passes linking the east and west coasts of South Island. A few kilometres along this road is the old gold-mining town of **Kumara**, from where a scenic detour to **Lake Brunner**, the largest lake on the west coast, winds its way through dense native forest.

From Shantytown to Greymouth

Towards Greymouth, about 10km (6 miles) north of Kumara Junction, is **Shantytown** (daily 8.30am–5pm; entrance fee; tel: 03-762 6634, 0800-742 689; www.shantytown.co.nz), a replica of a late 19th-century goldfield town offering gold panning and a bush steam locomotive ride to the gold-panning area. Thirty historic buildings include a local saloon, gift shop, bank, jail, church, hospital and school. You are welcome to try your hand at panning for gold, but if that does not appeal, down a Monteith's beer instead at the Golden Nugget Hotel.

At nearby **Wood's Creek**, take the 1km (2/3-mile) walking track around the New River diggings dating back to 1865. Diggers smeared their bodies with rotten mutton fat to ward off sandflies, risking their lives working in

the river and its tributaries, where water levels could rise in a matter of minutes after heavy rain (a frequent occurrence on this coast). Take a torch so you can investigate the tunnels, but leave immediately should the water begin to rise.

Greymouth ㉝, 41km (25 miles) north of Hokitika on SH6, is the terminus of the TranzAlpine train route from Christchurch *(see page 257)*. The largest town on the west coast (population 13,900), it owes its commanding position to its seaport and its proximity to timber mills and coal mines. Nowadays it is reinventing itself as the coast's adventure capital. The pioneering spirit still drives tourist ventures that cajole visitors to try their hand at gold mining, four-wheel-drive quad-bike safaris, dolphin-watching and cave rafting. Greymouth is a good base with enough diversions for a short stay. Inquire at the **i-site Visitors Centre** at 112 Mackay Street (tel: 03-768 5101; www.greydistrict.co.nz).

The **Jade Boulder Gallery** (daily 8am–6pm in summer, 9am–5pm in winter; free; tel: 03-768 0700) in Guin-

Carving pounamu *greenstone.*

ness Street showcases greenstone with innovative displays, while **History House** (daily 10am–4pm, closed winter weekends; entrance fee; tel: 03-768 4149; www.history-house.co.nz) features a collection of photographs and memorabilia of the district dating back to the 1850s.

Another of Greymouth's varied attractions are tours of **Monteith's Brewery Company** (booking essential; entrance fee; tel: 03-768 4149; www.monteiths.co.nz) at the corner of Turumaha and Herbert streets. You can see the beer being brewed in open fermenters by coal-fired boilers, learn about each beer's origin and taste profile, and, of course, down a couple at the end of the tour.

A 20-minute drive inland from Greymouth is **Blackball**, a former coal-mining town now enjoying something of a nostalgic renaissance. A room at the **Blackball Hilton Hotel** (tel: 03-732 4705; www.blackballhilton.co.nz) comes with a candlewick bedspread and hot water bottle. Spend the day

BELOW: the steam locomotive at Shantytown.

The Pancake Rocks at Punakaiki.

BELOW: gold was discovered in the region in the 1860s.

wandering around the old coal workings or explore the start of the **Croesus Track** to Barrytown. Evenings are best huddled around a fire, sipping Monteith's beer.

Pancakes at Punakaiki

Beyond Greymouth, the spectacular Coast Road to Westport hugs the coastline which, 43km (27 miles) north at **Punakaiki**, takes on the extraordinary appearance of a pile of petrified pancakes. The **Pancake Rocks** ❸❹ and their blowholes comprise layers of stratified limestone. Reached by a short, scenic walk from the main road, the rocks are best visited when there is an incoming tide, when the brisk westerly wind causes the tempestuous sea to surge explosively and dramatically into the chasms, spouting spray through skylight-type holes.

Take a stroll along the nearby coastal tracks and look out for native wood pigeons (kereru) and tui feeding on the abundant kowhai trees, or hike along the shoreline to see the nests of Westland petrels. Punakaiki is situated on the edge of the **Paparoa National Park**, where the peculiarities of the limestone landscape continue inland. Here, rainwater has created deep gorges, fluted rocks and cave networks, many still unexplored.

Thirty-two km (20 miles) north is **Charleston**, the once-booming centre of the Buller district, with old gold workings nearby. At a junction 21km (13 miles) further to the north, the coastal road becomes SH67, leading to nearby **Westport** ❸❺, a useful launching pad for side trips to attractions in the area.

At **Cape Foulwind**, west of the township, a walkway follows the coast for 4km (2 miles). The highlight is a view of a breeding colony of New Zealand fur seals. About 14km (9 miles) north of Westport, along the Karamea Highway, is the deserted coal-mining town of **Denniston**, once the largest producer of coal in New Zealand. The **Denniston Walkway**

Gleam of Gold

Back in the early days the west coast was so forbidding that European exploration inland did not begin in earnest until 1846. The opinion of one of the early first explorers, Thomas Brunner, who described it as "the very worst country I have seen in New Zealand", only served to discourage others. His distaste resulted from the great hardships suffered during his nightmarish 550-day journey, when he got so hungry he had to eat his dog. There must be something about this place and desperate eating; the last act of cannibalism reputedly took place here in the late 1800s.

It was only in 1860, after favourable reports of huge low-level glaciers in the south and possible routes through the Alps to Canterbury, that the central government purchased the west coast from the Maori for 300 gold sovereigns. Discovery of gold in 1864 at Greenstone Creek, a tributary of the Taramakau River, would change everything here. Hordes of gold-hungry miners converged on the area from all over the world. New strikes followed up and down the Coast, in the river gorges and gravels, the precious metal even being found in the black sand of the beaches. These "diggers" brought a cheerful camaraderie that gave a distinctive character to the new province. The boom did not last long, but the surviving town sites, workings and rusty relics provide glimpses of that golden past.

climbs the high plateau to the old coal town and provides views of the once breathtakingly steep tramway called the **Denniston Incline**.

The west coast's northernmost town, 97km (60 miles) north of Westport, is **Karamea 36**, gateway to the vast 4,520 sq. km (1,745 sq. mile) **Kahurangi National Park** (see page 242) with its famous Heaphy Track.

A visit to Karamea is not complete without a trip to the **Oparara Basin**, an area of majestic limestone arches and caves northeast of the town. Westport shop owner Phil Wood and three caving mates discovered the entrance to **Honeycomb Cave**, just 1km (2/3 mile) further up from the **Oparara Arch**, in 1980. So far, the bones of 27 extinct species of birds – giant moa and eagles, even a goose that no one knew existed – have been found in its 17km (11 miles) of passages. Honeycomb Cave, with its delicate straw stalactites, pedestal "elephant feet" and cascades of rougher flowstone, can be viewed with **Oparara Guided Tours** (daily 10am and 2pm; tel: 03-782 6652; www.oparara.co.nz).

Buller Gorge and Reefton

Five km (3 miles) south of Westport, SH6 turns inland (becoming the Buller Gorge Highway) to follow one of the South Island's most beautiful rivers, the Buller, through its lower and upper gorges for 84km (52 miles) to Murchison. At this point the west coast is left behind and the road continues to Nelson and Blenheim at the northern end of the island. Prior to Murchison, two branches extend southwards: SH69 and SH65, both of which connect with the Lewis Pass Highway at Springs Junction, the last major route across the South Island.

SH69, which turns off at the Inangahua Junction, traverses one of the most mineralised districts of New Zealand. About 34km (21 miles) south, it enters **Reefton 37**, named after its famous quartz reefs. This region was once abundant with gold and coal. The other route (SH65) winds its way up to the Lewis Pass from the outskirts of Murchison, joining up with the main Lewis Pass Highway at Springs Junction, 72km (45 miles) to the south. ❑

Heavy rainfall on the west coast – some 5 metres (200 inches) pours annually – accounts for its lush greenery and vibrant colours. In fact some Kiwis refer to it as the "wet coast". When the rain is exhausted and the cloud rolls back from the mountain tops, the air fills with birdsong and – the sole flaw in this Eden – sandflies with their craving for human blood. Be sure to slather yourself with plenty of insect repellent.

BELOW: display at a Punakaiki motel.

EXPLORING THE NATIONAL PARKS

Well-marked tracks with plenty of accommodation along the way make it easy to find your way around New Zealand's great outdoors

New Zealand's 14 national parks are some of the country's foremost attractions. Department of Conservation (DOC) offices, in all cities and in many towns, provide information on the flora and fauna found in each park, and on walking the trails. Visitor Centres generally provide useful DOC leaflets and information, too.

People come from all over the world to tramp the famous tracks within the National Parks, such as the three-day Coastal Track, along the north coast of the South Island; the Milford Track, which gets so crowded that booking well in advance is necessary; and the Routeburn, in the south of the South Island. Yet there are many other beautiful routes, including much shorter walks where you can hike for hours without seeing a soul. A bonus of hiking in New Zealand is that hot springs are often found en route, just in time to soothe those aching joints.

UNIQUE ECOLOGY

The country's many flightless birds reflect the absence of predators, yet many of its trees are not so fortunate. Possums, imported in 1837 from Australia to start a fur trade, are highly destructive to New Zealand's native forests. In Australia the trees have a built-in protection against being stripped bare by the creatures; New Zealand's trees do not: one reason why the country often seems to be engaged in a running battle to preserve the natural ecological balance. The life forms found in this country are so distinctive that scientists have likened studying New Zealand's native species to studying life on another planet.

ABOVE: Lake Matheson in Westland National Park, with Mount Tasman and Mount Cook beyond. The park also contains the Fox and Franz Josef glaciers, and has some great walks.

ABOVE LEFT: a giant kauri tree at Waipoua Kauri Forest, Northland, a protected nature reserve. Many of New Zealand's kauri forests were decimated in the 18th and 19th centuries.

SAFETY IN THE NATIONAL PARKS

A few simple precautions will help you enjoy some of the most beautiful scenery in the world. Always check with the local DOC office or Visitor Centre before you go tramping, as weather conditions can change very rapidly in New Zealand. Even in the height of summer it is essential to be prepared for very adverse weather conditions. DOC offices will also be able to advise you on the availability of accommodation, time and food supplies required, and even volcanic activity. You may get more out of some walks and climbs with the assistance of a guide who knows the area well – guided group walks are available in a lot of areas.

Do not set out on a tramp – long or short – without suitable thermal clothing and footwear. Bring a map, compass, torch, matches and a first-aid kit. Sunblock, sunglasses and a good raincoat are also essential. If required, there are plenty of shops where you can purchase or hire decent gear, and some hostels and hotels can supply clothes, gloves and hats.

Always inform someone else where you're going before you depart and on your return. For your own safety all movements should be logged at DOC offices and the huts en route. Once you step off the main road, if you set out in the wrong direction it's extremely easy to get lost and your hike could become a much longer walk than you'd planned.

ABOVE: Mount Taranaki. Despite being one of New Zealand's wettest places, Taranaki offers a plethora of fine walks, including the hike to its summit, and is a popular winter skiing venue.

LEFT: Mount Cook is the crowning glory of the magnificent Southern Alps range. The training ground for Everest conqueror, the late Sir Edmund Hillary, it's a terrain that is not to be taken lightly.

ABOVE: world heritage area of Tongariro National Park.

RIGHT: Lake Ohakuri in the Orakei Korako park south of Rotorua.

QUEENSTOWN AND OTAGO

Located in an area of spectacular natural beauty, it's easy to understand why Queenstown is unashamedly a tourist town, with its huge range of leisure activities and great shopping

The hub of central Otago is the jewel in New Zealand's tourism crown. It has become such a popular destination for overseas visitors that some New Zealanders complain that they can't get a look in. In less than 30 years, **Queenstown** has grown from a sleepy lakeside town into a sophisticated all-year tourist resort, a sort of Antipodean Saint Moritz. This is a place that has been nurtured on tourism, and while other rural towns have struggled to survive in a sluggish economy, it has flourished. Within a radius of just a few kilometres, the ingenuity and mechanical wizardry of New Zealanders have combined with the stunning landscape to provide an unrivalled range of adventure activities.

Central Otago possesses a personality quite distinct from other parts of the country. Some of the Southern Alps' most impressive peaks dominate its western flank, towering over deep glacier-gouged lakes. Yet the enduring impact is more subtle, encapsulated in the strange landscape chiselled and shaved from central Otago's plateau of mica schist rock. In the dry continental climate of the inland plateau, the pure atmosphere aids the play of light, evoking nuances few other landscapes permit. The overwhelming impression is of a stark, simple landscape burnished in glowing browns tinged with white, gold, ochre and sienna. The effect has attracted generations of landscape painters to the area.

Yet scenery alone is not enough to lure people into staking out a patch of earth in what in the past has been an arid and often inhospitable region. Over nine centuries of sketchy human habitation, central Otago's lure has been successively based on moa, jade, grazing land, gold, hydroelectric power and now tourism.

Gold in them hills

The first humans to set foot in the region were Maori moa-hunters who pushed inland around the 15th century.

Main attractions

BOB'S PEAK GONDOLA
LAKE WAKATIPU
QUEENSTOWN GARDENS
SHOTOVER JET
SKIPPERS CANYON
ARROWTOWN
CORONET PEAK
ROUTEBURN TRACK
BENDIGO

LEFT: Lake Wanaka.
BELOW: thrills on the Shotover River.

However, through over-hunting and the effects of fire, the moa and other birds disappeared for ever. Some of New Zealand's best moa remains have been found in the banks of the Clutha River as it winds through the plateau on its 320km (200-mile) journey to the Pacific.

Europeans first arrived in central Otago in 1847 when a surveyor blazed a trail for pioneers searching for land to establish large sheep runs. By 1861 the new settlers were squatting on most of the potential grazing land, battling against the harsh environment of winter snows, spring floods, summer droughts and bush fires, as well as wild dogs and other vermin.

These pioneers, predominantly of Scottish origin, were just settling in when, in 1861, the first major gold strike was made in a gully along the Tuapeka River. Central Otago's gold boom had begun. In just four months, 3,000 men were swarming over the 5km (3-mile) valley, probing and sifting each centimetre for glowing alluvial gold. A year on, the population of the Tuapeka goldfield was 11,500, double that of the fast-emptying provisional capital, Dunedin. Otago's income trebled in 12 months, while the number of ship arrivals quadrupled, many of the 200 vessels bringing miners from Australia's goldfields.

As prospectors moved inland to the then inhospitable hinterland of central Otago, new fields were discovered in quick succession in other valleys – the Clutha at the foot of the Dunstan Range, the Cardrona, Shotover, Arrow and Kawarau. In 1862 the Shotover, then yielding as much as 155g (5oz) of gold by the shovelful, was known as the richest river in the world. In one afternoon two Maori men going to the rescue of their near-drowned dog recovered no less than 11kg (388oz) of gold.

Queenstown

One of the best introductions to **Queenstown ❶** is to admire the magnificent views of the town and surroundings from **Bob's Peak** by taking an exciting gondola ride (daily 9am until late; entrance fee; tel: 03-441 0101; www.skyline.co.nz) at the end of Brecon Street.

Maori Succession

The moa-hunters, the first people to arrive and settle in this region at the end of the 15th century, were subsequently conquered by the Ngati-Mamoe tribe, who were defeated in turn by another invading Maori tribe, and fled into the forests of Fiordland. The victors, the Ngati-Tahu, controlled the supply of the Maori's precious stone – the New Zealand jade known variously as *pounamu*, nephrite or greenstone. Hard, durable and workable, it was in demand for adzes, chisels and weapons. So desirable was the jade, in fact, that the Maori made epic expeditions through central Otago and the Alpine Divide to bring it out from the west coast, via the head of Lake Wakatipu to the east coast. It was then "processed" and exported to northern tribes.

After the 790-metre (2,592ft) climb, take the chairlift higher up the peak and ride the thrilling luge downhill, back to the gondola's viewing deck.

Also on Brecon Street is the **Kiwi and Birdlife Park** (daily 9am–6pm; entrance fee; tel: 03-442 8059; www.kiwibird.co.nz). Easy walks through native bush lead to aviaries where you can see tui, bellbird, fantail and kiwi as well as endangered species such as the black stilt and banded rail.

As you would expect from a major tourist hub, Queenstown has a wide variety of accommodation, restaurants, entertainment and shops displaying handcrafted New Zealand products such as suede and leather goods, sheepskin and woollen products, and attractive greenstone jewellery. But for most people, these are mere distractions from the lure of great outdoors all around. The **i-site Visitors Centre** at the corner of Shotover and Camp streets (daily 7am–6pm, until 7pm in summer; tel: 03-442 4100, 0800-668 888; www.queenstown-vacation.com) has all the details you need on how to spend your time in Queenstown.

Commercial water adventures on Queenstown's lakes and rivers include canoeing, yachting, windsurfing, parasailing, water-skiing, canyoning, rafting and hobie-cat sailing. Queenstown is also synonymous with bungee-jumping, and you don't even have to leave town to get your first bungee under your belt. A short but spectacular jump called **The Ledge** bungee is found at the top of the Skyline Gondola; here too you'll find the **Ledge Sky Swing** (tel: 03-442 4007; www.bungee.co.nz).

Some of the world's finest scenic flights, on both helicopter and light plane, operate from Queenstown, providing access to spectacular lake, Alp and fiord scenery and locations which cannot easily be reached in any other way. For those with enough daring to dispense with machines, there is also paragliding, hang-gliding and sky-diving, strapped to your guide of course (the Visitors Centre has all the details).

Riding the luge down the twisting track on Bob's Peak is heaps of fun. But try the beginners' "scenic" route before progressing to the more winding advanced route.

BELOW: Bob's Peak with views over Lake Wakatipu.

TSS Earnslaw steams across Lake Wakatipu every two hours in summer.

Milder pastimes

Rather more sedate activities are available around the town, too – trout fishing in rivers and streams, or an excursion on the steamship TSS *Earnslaw* (daily 10am–8pm, summer departures every two hours; tel: 03-249 7416; www.realjourneys.co.nz), a grand old coal-fuelled vessel which has graced the waters of **Lake Wakatipu ②** since 1912, when it was first used to carry goods to remote settlements. What's inside is almost as fascinating as the views beyond, and passengers are encouraged to view the engine room and historic displays. An optional extra is a visit to a working farm in a magnificent location, the **Walter Peak High Country Farm**, where you can have lunch or tea and the chance to see New Zealand's all-important agriculture at first hand. In summer you can also opt for a wine heritage tour (daily 4pm) and sample a range of central Otago wine and cheese.

Passenger launches take visitors trout fishing on the lake. In season (1 Oct–31 July), jet-boat, helicopter and four-wheel-drive excursions are available to transport anglers to various pristine and remote stretches of water.

Lake Wakatipu is central Otago's most haunting body of water and has long captured people's imagination with its strange serpentine shape and rhythmic "heartbeat" *(see below)*, as well as its constant coldness (swimming is enjoyed during summer in other lakes in the South Island – but here, even during the height of summer, it is nothing short of a teeth-chattering experience). According to Maori legend, the lake is the "Hollow of the Giant" (Whakatipua), formed when an evil sleeping giant was set on fire by a brave youth, thus melting the snow and ice of the surrounding mountains to fill the 80km (50-mile) double-dog-legged hollow. In fact, the major lakes of Wakatipu, Wanaka and Hawea were all gouged by glaciers, and the peculiar rise and fall of Wakatipu every five minutes is not the effect of a giant's heartbeat, as legend dictates,

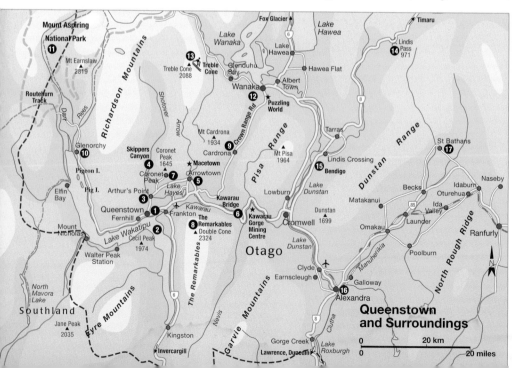

Queenstown and Surroundings

but of a natural oscillation caused by variations in atmospheric pressure.

Directly opposite the lake from the steamer wharf are the **Queenstown Gardens**, a tranquil, fir-surrounded expanse of broad lawns and rose gardens that also afford excellent views of Walter Peak, Ben Lomond and The Remarkables. If you prefer a more structured horticultural experience, **Queenstown Garden Tours** (tel: 03-442 3799; www.queenstowngarden tours.co.nz) depart from Queenstown's visitor centre, and take in three splendid local residential gardens in the spring and summer months. Devonshire tea is served.

Outside Queenstown

To enjoy most of the activities for which the area is renowned, you will have to venture a little further from Queenstown itself.

Following the **Gorge Road** north out of town will bring you to **Climbing Queenstown** (tel: 03-409 2508; www.climbingqueenstown.com). A first in the Southern Hemisphere, this series of iron rungs, ladders and wires attached to a mountainside enables the inexperienced to replicate the experience of rock climbing. Abseiling and rock-climbing options cater for both first-timers and experts.

The region's swift-flowing rivers set the scene for white-water rafting and jet-boating adventures. The latter is New Zealand's home-grown style of running rivers, upstream as well as down. Propellerless powerboats speed over rapid shallows barely ankle-deep. These nifty craft are thrust along by their jet-stream as water, drawn in through an intake in the bottom of the hull, is pumped out at high pressure through a nozzle at the rear. The typical jet boat can skim over shallows no more than 10cm (4 inches) deep, and can execute sudden 180-degree turns within a single boat length. The best-known of the dozen or so commercial options, **Shotover Jet** (daily dawn until dusk; tel: 03-442 8570; www.shotover jet.com) takes passengers from **Arthur's Point ❸**, 5km (3 miles) north of Queenstown, on a thrilling ride, swerving up and down the **Shotover River** just a hair's breadth away from jagged cliffs. It is without a doubt one of the more accessible adventure experiences in Queenstown. Free shuttle service from Queenstown is available.

White-water rafting on the 14km (9-mile) stretch of the Shotover River with its Grade 3–5 rapids *(see margin box)* is more challenging than the **Kawarau River** to the east, which has a 7km (4-mile) run more suitable for inexperienced rafters. Several companies – such as **Queenstown Rafting** (tel: 03-442 9792; www.rafting.co.nz) – offer trips with bus transfers to the launch point, wetsuits and a brief lesson before you take off.

North of Arthur's Point is **Skippers Canyon ❹**, the epicentre of the region's gold-mining activity from the 1860s until recently. Also known as Skippers Grand Canyon, this 8-hectare (20-acre) area encompasses a number of attractions. The dramatic **Skippers Road**, hand-hewn from solid rock, is

White-water rafting grades are weather-dependent. If a lot of rain falls the river will be higher and therefore fewer rocks are exposed, making it a lower-grade river, ie Grades 1, 2 or 3. When little rain has fallen there is less water and therefore more rocks and more challenge, hence a Grade 5 river. Rain can come at any time of the year, so the rivers fluctuate, but it does tend to rain a lot less in summer, so there is far more chance of a Grade 5 experience.

BELOW: Skippers Canyon.

an adventure in itself. Self-driving is not recommended; a sign advises that car insurance is invalid here. **Nomad Safaris** (tel: 03-442 6699; www.nomad safaris.co.nz) offers daily four-wheel-drive tours into the canyon to the old settlement with a restored school house, cemetery and the **Skippers Canyon Suspension Bridge**, which spans the swift waters of Shotover River 102 metres (335 feet) below.

Gold towns

Just past Arthur's Point is the steep road leading to Coronet Peak, but if you continue on straight ahead you will wind up in the tiny village of **Arrowtown** ❺. This is the most picturesque and best-preserved gold-mining settlement in central Otago and arguably the prettiest small town in New Zealand, never more so than in autumn, when the foliage colours are truly spectacular.

Arrowtown is home to what may well be New Zealand's quirkiest movie house – **Dorothy Brown's Cinema, Bar and Bookshop** (tel: 03-442 1964; www.dorothybrowns.com) on Buck-ingham Street, which shows art-house films in an opulent setting (red possum fur cushions, chandeliers, unusually comfortable seating), with an open fire and a bar.

At the end of Buckingham Street, heading towards the river, lie the evocative remains of the **Chinese Settlement**. At the peak of the gold rush in the 1880s, this sad collection of tiny stone buildings was home to some 60 Chinese miners. Their story is told in the **Lakes District Museum** (daily 8.30am–5pm; entrance fee; tel: 03-442 1824; www.museumqueenstown.com) further along Buckingham Street. There are gold and other mineral specimens, miners' tools, miners' personal effects (typically old photos and old domestic appliances), plus colonial-era memorabilia, a collection of horse-drawn vehicles, a recreated streetscape and a Victorian school room.

Ghost towns are scattered throughout the region, shadows of the calico, sod and corrugated-iron settlements that seemed ugly to visiting English novelist Anthony Trollope in 1872. One such place, **Macetown**, haunts the

> "
> *Lake Wakatipu is indisputably handsome. "I do not know that lake scenery can be finer than this,"* enthused English novelist Anthony Trollope in 1872.
> "

BELOW: autumn in Arrowtown.

hills 15km (9 miles) northwest of Arrowtown and is a worthwhile detour. To get there a 4WD vehicle is essential, so it is best visited with a reputable tour company such as **Nomad Safaris** *(see page 284)*. The town now consists of a handful of buildings in various states of ruin, yet has an almost park-like quality, in part thanks to remnants of old gardens which have gone their own way. Macetown began life last century as a collection of tents for miners who hunted first for gold and, later, quartz. When the resources were exhausted, the town declined. The last mine closed in 1914.

Leaving Arrowtown, take the Arrowtown/Lake Hayes Road back to Queenstown. For most of this section of the trip you will be driving alongside the much-photographed mirror-like **Lake Hayes** and bypassing the luxury **Millbrook Resort**, with its Bob Charles-designed golf course. New Zealand's own distinctive architectural styles are visible in the thoughtfully designed farm dwellings where craftspeople, artists and retired folk enjoy a gentle way of life.

At the junction of State Highway (SH) 6 turn left and you will soon be at the world's first commercial bungee-site, the historic **Kawarau Bridge ❻**, 6km (4 miles) south of Arrowtown, opened in 1988 by A.J. Hackett. For those who don't fancy the real deal, there is the behind-the-scenes **Secrets of Bungee Tour** (tel: 03-442 4007, 0800-286 498) at the adjacent **Kawarau Bungee Centre**. This includes a look at bungee-cord making and exclusive access to viewing decks. After taking the plunge or just watching the expressions of those who do, you may feel in need of a little something at the centre's **Freefall Wine Bar** or at the **Winehouse and Kitchen** (daily; tel: 03-442 7310; www.winehouse.co.nz), a farm-style restaurant specialising in wine tasting. From here return to Queenstown via SH6 or continue on through the Gibbston Valley. At **Gibbston Valley Wines** (www.gibbstonvalley.co.nz) tastings are held in the candlelit ambience of a deep schist cave-turned-wine-cellar, with the wine complemented by cheese produced on site.

The original bungee-jump, off the Kawarau Bridge into Kawarau River.

BELOW: paragliding over Bob's Peak.

Skippers Canyon

Skippers Canyon is an adventurous scenic drive snaking along a treacherously narrow trail along a schist bluff with sheer vertical drops to the vivid ice-blue of the Shotover River below. Hell's Gate, Castle Rock and Devil's Elbow flash past, before you're deposited in a vast tussock-draped landscape framed by the Richardson and Harris mountains. Steeped in history, the route is littered with old gold-mining settlements and ruins, with informative displays and numerous picnic spots.

Follow in the footsteps of miners at Skippers Bridge, or explore the ruins of the Long Gully Pub, Mount Aurum Recreation Reserve, and the pipeline that once brought water to the goldfield. To get safely there and back team up with Nomad Safaris (www.nomadsafaris.co.nz).

TIP

The highlight of the ski season in Queenstown is the week-long Queenstown Winter Carnival in the third week of July. One of the best websites for skiing in this region is www.nzski. com. Also worth checking out is www.cardrona. com and www.treble cone.co.nz.

A.J. Hackett also run one of the highest bungee-jumps in the world, the mind-blowing 134-metre (440ft) Nevis Highwire Bungee, on the Nevis River (a tributary of the Kawarau) 32km (20 miles) from Queenstown. The site can only be accessed by four-wheel drive.

Skiing and tramping

The largest ski fields in the South Island are Coronet Peak, The Remarkables, Treble Cone and Cardrona. **Coronet Peak** ❼ is Queenstown's backyard ski field, located just 18km (11 miles) by sealed road to the north. The ski season here extends from July to September (sometimes into October) and is noted for the variety of its terrain and innovations such as night skiing under floodlights. In the summer, sightseers can take chairlifts to the summit (1,645 metres/5,397ft) for a wonderful view, while thrill-seekers can enjoy a rapid descent in a Cresta Run toboggan.

The second major ski field is **The Remarkables** ❽, 20km (12 miles) east, the rugged range that forms the famous backdrop to Queenstown. Its ski runs are popular with beginner and inter-mediate skiers, although there are also more challenging runs for the more experienced. The third ski area is **Cardrona** ❾, 57km (35 miles) from Queenstown, on the way to Wanaka via the Crown Range Road. The highest road in New Zealand, it offers a series of stunning views.

Some 42km (26 miles) northwest of Queenstown at the head of Lake Wakatipu is **Glenorchy** ❿, an area of exceptional beauty in a region where exceptional beauty seems to be the norm. For much of the distance from Queenstown, the road follows the shores of the Wakatipu's western arm. Some 25km (16 miles) from town you will reach the top of a hill which provides a spectacular view across the lake with its three islands – Tree Island, Pig Island and Pigeon Island.

Glenorchy is a hotbed of activity. Kayaking, jet boating, horse riding, fishing, canoeing and canyoning are all popular pursuits here. **Dart River Safaris** (tel: 03-442 9992, 0800-327 853; www.dartriver.co.nz), leads groups on many of these activities, including a jet-boat excursion to Sandy Bluff at the

BELOW: dock at Lake Wakatipu.

edge of **Mount Aspiring National Park** ⓫; a wilderness safari incorporating jet boating and a nature trail; and full-day Funyak (inflatable canoe) trips. All explore the **Dart River**, which passes through a landscape of mountains and glaciers, and scenery from Tolkien's "Middle Earth" *(see pages 80–81)*.

The mountains of the Mount Aspiring National Park, a World Heritage Site, loom ahead, dominated by **Mount Aspiring** (3,030 metres/9,941ft). The park and the lonely valleys extending into Lake Wanaka *(see following page)* present unrivalled opportunities for hiking, tramping and fishing in unspoilt wilderness.

Of all the numerous hiking trails in the Wakatipu Basin, the most rewarding is the **Routeburn Track**, which commences at Glenorchy. Winding its way through splendidly isolated country at the head of Lake Wakatipu to the Upper Hollyford Valley, this four-day trek is one of New Zealand's best, but requires a greater degree of experience and fitness than the famed Milford Track in neighbouring Fiordland. High

points of the walk include a variety of flora – and some fauna – waterfalls and rapidly changing landscapes.

Wanaka and its environs

Wanaka ⓬, 34km (21 miles) north of Cardrona, is a sort of mini-Queenstown (though it dislikes being described so). It may be relatively devoid of the bigger centre's in-your-face commercialism and crowds, but with its own lake, ski fields and everything else that's required of a southern playground, it's still a popular resort – with a good range of accommodation and restaurants. Wanaka's **i-site Visitors Centre** (tel: 03-443 1233; www.lake wanaka.co.nz) has all the details you need to plan a stay here.

One of the more unusual attractions is Stuart Landsborough's **Puzzling World!** (daily 8.30am–6pm, until 5.30pm in winter; entrance fee; tel: 03-443 7489; www.puzzlingworld.co.nz), about 2km (1¼ miles) south from Wanaka. Its main features are the tilted

The area around Queenstown is a major tourist hub, and there is a commensurate number of "novelty" attractions. At Wanaka's Puzzling World!, your senses will be challenged in more ways than one.

BELOW: the road north from Wanaka to Haast Pass and the west coast.

The Queenstown area is well supplied with scenic hiking trails.

BELOW: Wanaka's pristine lake.

buildings that make up the complex and a challenging 1.5km (1-mile) maze. Inside are numerous fascinating "how-does-that-work?" optical illusions and holograms as well as the unique Hall of Following Faces, in which faces of famous people seem to float and follow you everywhere.

Treble Cone ⓭, (tel: 03-443 7443; www.treblecone.co.nz) is a ski resort 19km (12 miles) northwest of Wanaka. Proud of its powder and the number of international awards it has won, it styles itself as the ski field where the locals go, and boasts the longest vertical rise in the district. In the summer it's worth a visit to marvel at the stupendous views.

Follow SH6 east of Wanaka and head north on SH8 to the **Lindis Pass** ⓮, linking northern central Otago with Mount Cook and the Mackenzie Country. The road winds through some of the most beautiful hill country anywhere in New Zealand.

Former gold-rush towns

Bendigo ⓯, near the Clutha River 40km (25 miles) southeast of Wanaka (off SH8), is a near-perfect ghost town, especially when the wind whistles through the tumbledown stone cottages at the bleak crossroads. The southern extension of SH8 is the main artery to the heart of central Otago, running parallel with the Clutha River, past the former gold towns of Roxburgh, Alexandra, Clyde and Cromwell. These towns are still relatively prosperous today thanks to their connection with Otago's lifeblood: that same mighty Clutha. The river that once surrendered gold has since, through irrigation, transformed parched land into fertile country famous for its stone fruit. These days it is also a major generator of electricity.

The road south of Bendigo runs for 15km (9 miles) to **Cromwell**. This is wine- and fruit-growing country, although Cromwell's greatest asset is **Lake Dunstan**, the body of water on which the town sits. The lake is used extensively for watersports and has an abundance of birdlife. In 1993 a dam

was built close to where the Clutha River leaves the Cromwell Gorge near **Clyde**, 20km (12 miles) southeast of Cromwell. The water behind expanded through the gorge, drowning the old town of Cromwell and much of the lower Clutha Valley.

Alexandra , 31km (19 miles) southeast of Clyde, distinguishes itself yearly by its colourful, blossom-parade tribute to spring. In winter, ice-skating and curling take place on natural ice on the Manorburn Dam. Heading south there are tiny gold-rush towns that have refused to die. The original gold-rush settlement – which was then known as Tuapeka, now **Lawrence** – still survives with a strongly Victorian flavour. Pockets of old gold towns are stitched into the ranges, gullies, gorges and valleys elsewhere in central Otago. The town of Lawrence has earned a place in New Zealand history as the home of Thomas Bracken when he wrote the words to the national anthem, "God Defend New Zealand".

SH85 leads northeast of Alexandra before looping back southeastwards to the Otago coast. En route it passes through the Manuherikia Valley, offering a worthwhile side trip to historic **St Bathans** , one of the best-preserved sites in the Otago goldfields. Among its 19th-century wood, stone and mud-brick buildings is the celebrated **Vulcan Hotel**, built in 1882, and famous for its resident ghost. The town stands on the edge of disused goldfields, and contained therein is the **Blue Lake**, whose intense colour is caused by the presence of mica, which reflects the light to memorable effect on a sunny day. Ice-skating and curling are popular sports here in winter. Another worthwhile destination via SH85 is **Naseby**, a quaint hillside hamlet with period buildings, craft shops, a village green and the Cottage Garden Café.

Central Otago is an intense experience, whatever the time of year. The area enjoys greater variety between seasons than most other parts of New Zealand. In autumn, poplars planted by the settlers glow gold. In winter, nature transforms power lines into glistening lace-like threads of white across a frosty fairyland. ❏

DRINK

If visiting wineries is more your scene, book a tour with Queenstown Wine Trail, which takes you to premier wineries in central Otago – like Gibbston Valley, Peregrine, Waitiri Creek and Chard Farm. Tel: 03-442 3799; www.queenstownwinetrail.co.nz.

BELOW: view from The Remarkables.

DUNEDIN

Behind the solid, sombre facade of a city built by Scots and leavened in gold-rush wealth lies a lively university town, splendidly placed to take advantage of surroundings rich in natural treasures

Dunedin reclines, all-embracing, at the head of a bay, a green-belted city of slate and tin-roofed houses, of spires, chimneys and churches, of glorious Victorian and Edwardian buildings, of culture, of learning. In the opinion of its 125,000 friendly citizens, almost 20,000 of whom are students, this is as it should be, for here in the deep south is a way of life, a peace and a tranquillity that few cities can match.

The best first view is from the haven of Otago Harbour, the 20km (12-mile) long, shallow-bottomed fiord where container ships and coastal traders now ply in place of Maori war canoes, whaling ships and three-masters. Around the road-fringed harbourside sprout green hills, including the 314-metre (984ft) extinct volcano of Harbour Cone on the steep and skinny Otago Peninsula, and the perpetually cloud-carpeted cap of the 680-metre (2,230ft) Mount Cargill.

A proud history

While Dunedin is still a very proud city, it was once also the richest and most populous in all New Zealand. In the 1860s, with the discovery of gold in the Otago hinterland and a rush that rivalled California's, Dunedin rapidly became the financial centre of the country. Immigrants flocked from around the world, head offices of national companies sprang up, industry and civic enterprise flourished.

Here was the country's first university, medical school, finest educational institutions, its first daily newspaper, first electric trams, and the first cable-car system in the world outside United States.

Before the gold strikes, it was religious fervour on the other side of the world that led to Dunedin's European colonisation. Disruption in the Presbyterian Church of Scotland gave birth to the idea of a new settlement in the colony of New Zealand where "piety, rectitude and industry" could flourish.

Main attractions
DUNEDIN PUBLIC ART GALLERY
DUNEDIN RAILWAY STATION
OTAGO SETTLERS MUSEUM
GLENFALLOCH WOODLAND GARDEN
TAIAROA HEAD
LARNACH CASTLE
OAMARU

LEFT: conversation at Moeraki Boulders.
BELOW: Dunedin is New Zealand's Scottish city.

BELOW: Dunedin
Railway Station
dates from 1904.

Free Kirk advocates Captain William Cargill, a veteran of the Peninsular War, and the Rev. Thomas Burns, nephew of poet Robbie, were the leaders. The ships *John Wickliffe* and *Philip Laing* landed 300 Scots in March and April 1848 to a site already chosen by the London-based New Zealand Company and purchased – for £2,400 – from the local Maori. Its first name was New Edinburgh; soon it became Dunedin (Edin on the Hill).

Once gold was discovered inland, there was no holding Dunedin back. In two years, the population of Otago rocketed from 12,000 to 60,000 – 35,000 of them immigrant gold-seekers. Dunedin was the arrival point for the miners, the service centre for the goldfields and the bank for the gold. With all this new prosperity came saloons, gambling dens, brothels and dubious dance halls. Pubs there were aplenty, breweries too. Dunedin to this day has retained a high reputation for its well-patronised licensed premises.

For a quarter of a century, Dunedin boomed. And where Dunedin went, the rest of New Zealand followed, until the gold ran out. Gradually, commercial attractions and a kinder climate in the north led to the decline of the southern cities and provinces. For the past few decades, Dunedin has fought the inevitable drift north. The most significant means of stemming the flow is through its educational prowess: the greatly expanded university – now with more than 17,000 students – together with the College of Education for training schoolteachers and the Otago Polytechnic, pour over 20,000 youngsters into the Dunedin community, consolidating its status as a leading city of learning.

Around the Octagon

To explore Dunedin, start in the **Octagon Ⓐ**, which links Princes and George streets in the heart of the city. Tall, leafy trees bordered by historic buildings make this a popular lunch spot. Immediately west is the **Dunedin Public Art Gallery** (daily 10am–5pm; tel: 03-477 4000; www.dunedin.art.museum), the oldest in New Zealand. It houses one of the country's finest collections, with works by Van der Velden, Frances Hodg-

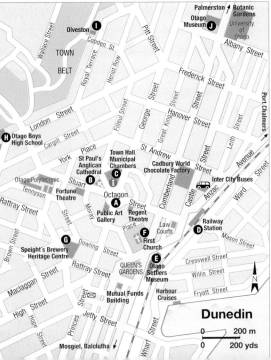

kins, Constable, Gainsborough, Monet, Pissarro and Reynolds.

Just north of the gallery is **St Paul's Anglican Cathedral** Ⓑ (tel: 03-477 4931), its Gothic Revival pillars rising 40 metres (130ft) to support the only stone-vaulted nave roof in New Zealand. Built between 1915 and 1919, it is constructed entirely of stone quarried from nearby Oamaru *(see page 298)*.

Next door are the century-old **Municipal Chambers** Ⓒ, which were designed by the noted colonial architect Robert Lawson, and behind it the 2,280-seat **Town Hall**, which was once the largest in the country. The Chambers, also built from Oamaru stone, have been replaced by the adjacent **Civic Centre** as local government offices, although the modern, stepped design of the latter has drawn criticism for the contrast with its Victorian-era antecedents. The city's **i-site Visitors Centre** (tel: 03-474 3300; www.dunedin.govt.nz), as well as conference facilities, are housed in the Municipal Chambers, whose imposing clock tower and spire were re-erected in 1989 amid an overall spring-cleaning of the city centre.

Moving east down Lower Stuart Street, look out for classic old buildings such as the Allied Press newspaper offices, the law courts and the police station, which are excellent examples of art in stone.

Near the junction of Castle Street and Anzac Avenue is the **Dunedin Railway Station** Ⓓ, perhaps the finest stone structure to be found anywhere in the country. It earned designer George Troup a knighthood and the nickname "Gingerbread George". Built between 1904 and 1906 in the Flemish Renaissance style, it has a 37-metre (121ft) high square tower, three huge clock faces and a covered carriageway projecting from the arched colonnade.

In the main foyer is a mosaic-tiled floor with nine central panels showing a small English "Puffing Billy". The original floor was comprised of a total of 725,760 half-inch Royal Doulton porcelain squares. Other ornamentation in the station is in original Doulton china and stained glass. From here, trains depart daily for the spectacular Taieri River Gorge *(see page 298)* and beyond.

Local Oamaru stone, as used in the construction of St Paul's Cathedral, is a feature of Dunedin.

BELOW: St Paul's Cathedral and the Municipal Chambers.

Dunedin is full of Victorian details, such as wrought-iron fences and latticework, which are part of the city's charm.

BELOW: the Robbie Burns statue.

On the first floor of the station is the **New Zealand Sports Hall of Fame** (daily 10am–4pm; entrance fee; tel: 03-477 7775; www.nzhalloffame.co.nz), the national sports museum that pays tribute to that great New Zealand obsession with a dizzying array of memorabilia and exhibits – such as the arm guard All Blacks rugby player Colin Meads wore when he played a test match with a broken arm.

Maybe it's not surprising that Dunedin has such a remarkable railway station, as the city has a fascination with trains. *Josephine*, one of the country's first steam engines (a double-boiler, double-facing Fairlie) is protected in a glass case on display beside the **Otago Settlers Museum E** (daily 10am–5pm; entrance fee; tel: 03-477 5052; www.dunedin.govt.nz/facilities/otago-settlers-museum) at 31 Queens Gardens, just south of Dunedin Railway Station. Established in 1898, it is one of New Zealand's finest social history museums, showcasing the ancestral journeys of the people who live here today, including southern Maori tribes, Scottish pioneers and Chinese gold miners.

Also among its displays is *JA1274*, the last Dunedin-made steam locomotive to haul the main trunk-line trains.

Other city highlights

The country's first skyscraper, the **Mutual Funds Building** (1910), stands near the station, close to the original centre of Dunedin, the Stock Exchange area. Land reclamation has forced many of the fine old office buildings that used to line the harbour into a new role as storage areas (others have been demolished). A gargoyled "bride's-cake" monument in here pays homage to founder Captain Cargill. It sat atop men's underground toilets until public opprobrium led to the conveniences being closed.

First Church F, in Moray Place, is another Robert Lawson design and arguably his best work. Actually the third church to be built on this site, it has a magnificent spire rising 54 metres (180ft) heavenwards. Inside, the wooden gabled ceiling and rose window above the pulpit are worthy of inspection.

Two blocks west at 200 Rattray Street lies **Speight's Brewery Heritage Cen-**

Tartan Town

Dunedin is known as New Zealand's Scottish city and its Victorian city. A giant statue of Scottish poet Robbie Burns sits in the town centre, fittingly with his back to the Anglican St Paul's Cathedral, and facing what was formerly a corner pub. Here too are the country's only kilt manufacturer, lots of highland pipe bands and regularly celebrated Burns Nights.

But Dunedin folk are a little weary of continual references to the "Edinburgh of the South" and "Victorian City"; there are equally fine examples of Edwardian and later-style buildings that qualify the city as the most architecturally interesting and diverse in the country. The range is delightful, from full-fashioned ornate Victoriana through Edwardian splendour to impressive Art Deco and modern concrete-and-glass structures that have won national awards.

tre **G** (guided tours Fri–Sun 10am, noon, 2pm, 6pm, 7pm; entrance fee; tel: 03-477 7697; www.speights.co.nz). You can tour the brewery where the beer in which southerners take so much pride is brewed, and there is, of course, a tasting session at the tour's conclusion.

Many of the banks and other churches in the central city area are of architectural merit, as is the Lawson-designed **Otago Boys High School** **H** tower block, dominant above the city. It is situated just below the **Town Belt**, a 200-hectare (490-acre) and 8km (5-mile) long green swathe that separates the city from its suburbs. A walk here offers some of the best views of the city and its harbour. Listen out for the call of the tui and the bellbird; this expansive green space is an area of wooded reserves and sports fields, golf courses, cotula-turfed bowling greens, huge heated swimming pools and fine swimming and surfing beaches.

Within the Town Belt area also lies "the jewel in Dunedin's crown", **Olveston** **I** (booking essential; guided tours only; entrance fee; tel: 03-477 3320; www.olveston.co.nz). Built between 1904 and 1906 to the design of celebrated English architect Sir Ernest George for a local businessman, David Theomin, it was bequeathed to the city in 1966. The 35-room house of double brick and oak is rated the best example of a grand Edwardian-style manor found in New Zealand.

North of the Octagon

In the north of the city are the (almost) combined campuses of the University of Otago, Otago Polytechnic and Dunedin College of Education. Dominating the Gothic rockpiles of the university, beside the grass-banked water of the Leith, is the main clock tower. Just west is the fascinating **Otago Museum** **J** (daily 10am–5pm; free; tel: 03-474 7474; www.otago museum.govt.nz) on Great King Street, with Pacific Island and Maori artefacts, maritime relics and colonial-era collections. If you have time for only one museum visit in Dunedin, this has to be it. **Discovery World** (entrance fee) on Level 1 will appeal to children.

Baldwin Street, north of the city centre, is believed to be the world's steepest residential street. With a 38-degree gradient, it's indisputably a remarkable sight. Motorists are advised not to try driving up it; however, this doesn't stop innovative thrill-seekers who attempt to devise ever more ingenious ways of propelling themselves down it.

BELOW: Speight's Brewery.

Also in the north, on the slopes of Signal Hill, are the **Botanic Gardens** (daily daylight hours; free). New Zealand's oldest, it covers 65 hectares (160 acres) and is world-renowned for its rhododendron dell and its great variety of gardens.

Otago Peninsula drive

To appreciate fully the **Otago Peninsula** and its views of the city, take the "low road" and return via the "high". The following 64km (40-mile) round trip can take anything from 90 minutes to a full day. The narrow, winding road calls for careful driving as part of it was built by convict labour for horse and buggy traffic. (The prisoners were housed in an old hulk that was dragged slowly along the seafront.)

The first sight you will see along the curving western coastline is **Glenfalloch Woodland Garden ⓚ** (daylight hours; free; tel: 03-476 1006; www. glenfalloch.co.nz), 12 hectares (30 acres) of lovely rambling gardens encircling a 1871 homestead. It has a café on-site which is open daily from 11am to 4pm.

The winding Portobello Road runs along the peninsula coast to **Portobello ⓛ**, 8km (5 miles) from Glenfalloch. In Portobello village, you can visit the **Otago Peninsula Museum Historical Society** (Sun 1.30–4.30pm, or by appointment; free; tel: 03-478 0255) and on Hatchery Road the **New Zealand Marine Studies Centre and Aquarium** (10am for a 60-minute guided tour and noon–4.30pm for self-guided tours; entrance fee; tel: 03-479 5826; www.marine.ac.nz). Operated by the University of Otago as a marine laboratory, the centre has a life-size model of a colossal squid, and its aquariums are filled with everything marine from seahorses to octopuses. The touch pool allows a tactile experience with smaller sea creatures.

At **Otakou ⓜ**, about 4km (2½ miles) further north, is a Maori church and meeting house which appear to be carved, but are actually cast in concrete. In the cemetery behind are buried three great Maori chiefs of the 19th century – the warlike Taiaroa, Ngatata (a northern chief said to have welcomed the Pakeha to Cook Strait) and Karetai,

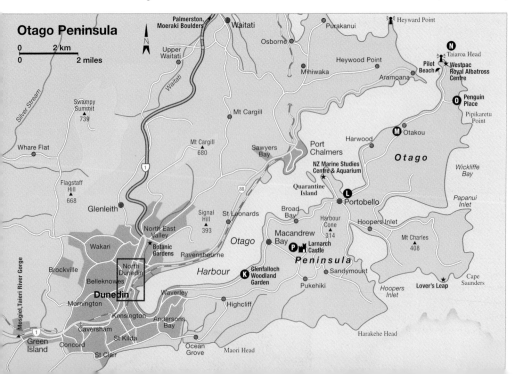

Otago Peninsula

induced by missionaries to abandon cannibalism and take up the Bible. The *marae* here is sacred to local Maori and is still the most historic Maori site in Otago. (The name "Otago", in fact, is a European corruption of "Otakou".)

Just north lie remains of the whaling industry founded in Otago Harbour in 1831, 17 years before European settlement took root. The old factory is clearly visible and marked by a plaque. Another plaque across the road commemorates the first Christian service held in Otago Harbour, by Bishop Pompalier, in 1840.

Wildlife and a castle

As you crest the hill past Otakou and look towards lofty **Taiaroa Head** , the tip of the peninsula, glance up. Those huge seabirds resting lazily on the wind are the world's largest birds of flight, rare Royal albatrosses. Incredibly graceful, they swoop, turn and soar with barely a flick of their 3-metre (10ft) wings. They mate for life, and up to 30 pairs from this tiny colony circle the globe before returning here to mate and produce a chick every two years.

The **Westpac Royal Albatross Centre** (daily 9am–5pm, until 8pm in summer; entrance fee; tel: 03-478 0499; www.albatross.org.nz) has viewing galleries and display areas. Escorted groups observe the breeding cycle and the pre-flight peregrinations of the fledglings. While here, take in (for free) the antics of a southern fur seal colony at nearby **Pilot Beach**, and visit also **Fort Taiaroa**, where the unusual **Armstrong Disappearing Gun**, transported here in 1886 on the perceived threat of an attack by Tsarist Russia, is found. The 15cm (6-inch) cannon is hidden in the bowels of the earth, rising to fire, then sinking again for reloading.

Two km (1¼ miles) to the east, along a farm road, is **Penguin Place** (daily tours from 10.15am, every hour at quarter past until 7pm; entrance fee; tel: 03-478 0286; www.penguinplace. co.nz). Here, rare Chaplinesque Yelloweyed penguins (*see page 101*) strut in the surf and can be observed at close proximity through a unique system of hides and tunnels.

The MV *Monarch* provides a regular service from Dunedin down Otago Harbour to Taiaroa Head, but for a very different view of the peninsula and its wildlife, contact **Wild Earth Adventures** (tel: 03-489 1951; www.wildearth. co.nz), which leads kayak tours, visiting the Royal albatross and fur seal colonies by sea and taking in a great variety of other wildlife on the way.

The return route follows the Taiaroa Head access road to Portobello in order to reach the "high road" leading back to the city. Along the way, visit **Larnach Castle** (daily 9am–5pm; entrance fee; tel: 03-476 1616; www.larnachcastle.co. nz), a century-old baronial manor that is New Zealand's only castle. It took 14 years to build (from 1871) as the home of the Hon. William J.M. Larnach, financier and later Minister of the Crown. An English workman, along with two Italian craftsmen, spent 12 years carving the ceilings. The castle fell into disrepair but has now been fully restored, and most of its 43 rooms, including accom-

Larnach Castle features a remarkable range of craftsmanship – a spectacular example being the detail in its Venetian stained-glass windows.

BELOW: Larnach Castle grounds.

TIP

If you're making a special effort to see the albatrosses at Taiaroa Head, do check to see if they're going to be at home. Sept: adults arrive; Oct: courting and mating; Nov: eggs are laid; Feb: chicks hatch; Sept: chicks fly the nest.

modation, are open to the public. The "high road" that leads back to suburbia has commanding views of the harbour.

Taieri Gorge and railway

Dunedin visitors should not restrict themselves to the city. Within easy reach both north and south there are areas of immense natural beauty, sparsely populated and as yet undiscovered by the tourist hordes.

Special excursion trains run north and sometimes south on the main trunk line from the Dunedin Railway Station *(see page 293)*. On the **Taieri Gorge Railway** (tel: 03-477 4449; www.taieri.co.nz), both vintage 1920s wooden carriages renovated by the Otago Excursion Train Trust and modern air-conditioned steel carriages enter Otago's hinterland through the rugged and spectacularly bridged **Taieri River Gorge ❶**, northwest of Dunedin. Here, jet-boat and whitewater raft tours tumble adventurous tourists between virgin bush-edged cliffs. You can make a return journey to **Pukerangi**, 58km (36 miles) away, or continue another 19km (12 miles) to the railway's terminus at

Middlemarch in central Otago, where coach connections can take tourists onward to Queenstown *(see page 280)*.

North to Oamaru

The Otago coast north from Dunedin is of interest, too. At **Kaitiki Beach** Common dolphins are often spotted, while further north are the bizarre **Moeraki Boulders ❷**, huge round stones that lie "like devil's marbles" on the seashore. The food baskets of a wrecked canoe according to legend, they were actually formed by the gradual erosion of the mudstone cliffs just behind the beach. Over a period of 60 million years, salts accumulated around the eroded pieces, forming the boulders. Some measure 4 metres (13ft) in circumference.

Oamaru ❸, 117km (72 miles) north of Dunedin, is the site of the largest collection of protected heritage buildings to be found in New Zealand. Crafted from a creamy textured local limestone known as Oamaru stone, these gorgeous Victorian buildings with their huge columns and extensive ornamentation are a rare sight to behold. Pick up a walking map from the informa-

BELOW: the Clutha River inland from Dunedin.

Nomadic Communities

For much of the period prior to the arrival of Europeans, the coast of Otago was more densely settled than any part of the North Island. The moa-hunters lived here, thriving on fish, waterfowl and the giant, flightless moa bird. But when Captain Cook sailed past in 1770, he missed the harbour entrance and the moa-hunters, noting only long white beaches now called St Kilda and St Clair. "A land green and woody but without any sign of inhabitants," he logged. Thirty years later, sealers and whalers gathered in the Otago region, but were not always popular with the locals. In 1813, four sailors were killed and eaten by Maori; then, in 1817, at Murdering Beach, just north of the harbour entrance, three sealers offended natives and were killed.

tion centre (daily 8.30am–5pm; tel: 03-434 1656; www.visitoamaru.co.nz) at 1 Thames Street, for insights into the features and history behind their exquisitely restored facades.

Also in town are **St Luke's Anglican Church** (1866), the **North Otago Museum** (1882) and the old **Courthouse** (1882–3), its well-proportioned classical design reflecting a Palladian architectural influence. The old **Bank of New South Wales** with its Corinthian columns is now home to the **Forrester Gallery** (tel: 03-434 1653; www.forrestergallery.co.nz) at 9 Thames Street.

Pop inside the impressive **St Patrick's Basilica** on Reed Street, built in 1893, to see its coffered Renaissance-style ceiling and great dome over the sanctuary. Nearby, at 56 Eden Street, is the house where New Zealand author **Janet Frame** lived for 14 years. A number of extracts from her earlier manuscripts can be seen in Oamaru. Follow Chelmer Street, Toby's route described in *The Edge of the Alphabet*: "Now up the damp road… the high bank on the right with the houses and gardens in the shadow of it not yet rid of the night dew; on the other side the Town Gardens…" Established in 1876, the latter boast some magnificent trees, shrubs and flower beds, and a burbling Italian marble fountain.

Just beyond the information centre is the **Harbour and Tyne Historical Precinct**, the old quarter of town. Here craftsmen sculpt wedges of Oamaru stone, and a local bookbinder practises his age-old craft. The district is full of arty types whose works are on display in the **Grainstore Gallery** (Mon–Fri noon–4pm, Sat–Sun 10am–2pm; tel: 027-261 3764). Stop for a drink in the olde-worlde bar of the **Criterion Hotel** (tel: 03-434 6247; www.criterion.net.nz) and learn of its resident ghost.

As evening falls, make your way along the waterfront to the **Oamaru Blue Penguin Colony** (daily, summer 9.30am–10pm, winter 9.30am–8pm; tel: 03-433 1195; www.penguins.co.nz) at Oamaru Harbour and take a seat in the open-air grandstand. As it gets dark, the Little Blue penguins come ashore and waddle past to the colony's nesting area. During the day the facility offers a 30-minute behind-the-scenes experience. Yellow-eyed penguins can be seen at the **Bushy Beach Penguin Colony** (free) at Bushy Point from DOC hides.

Waimate's wallabies

Some 49km (31 miles) north of Oamaru is **Waimate ④**, wallaby country where you can kiss, kill or eat a wallaby, all in a single day! To hunt, team up with the **Ngahere Game Ranch** (tel: 03-689 7809; www.tournz.com), but if a cuddle is more your scene, visit **EnkleDooVery Korna** (daily Sept–June 10am–5pm; tel: 03-689 7197) to befriend hand-reared orphaned joeys.

Waimate's other claim to fame is its strawberries, and the annual "Strawberry Fare" in December. Head to Waimate's main street for an architectural flashback to the Edwardian era, but don't leave without tasting the **Savoy Tearooms'** famous wallaby pies, a mix of steak, onion, salt and pepper and plum sauce. ❏

The view across to Dunedin from the Otago Peninsula.

BELOW: mural in Dunedin's Octagon.

SOUTHLAND

Stepping into Southland's staggeringly beautiful landscape, you could be excused for feeling that you were at the ends of the earth

I t's the expansiveness of the place that first takes ou – wide open spaces with a distinctive quality of bold light which so impressed the early European landscape painters. Signs of Maori settlement go back as far as the 12th century around the southern coast; the first white inhabitants were a determined breed of Scottish settlers who began to arrive in 1848 and within 13 years were demanding provincial government. The 1860s were a time of heady development – in towns, country, rail and roads – to such extent that the state coffers were emptied. As a result, the province was legally and administratively fixed to neighbouring Otago in 1870.

The 100,000 people who proudly call themselves Southlanders today have scant regard for the historical purist's arguments about their legitimacy. They live in New Zealand's southernmost land district – Murihiku, the last joint of the tail, as the Maori called it. This "province" takes in about 28,000 sq km (some 11,000 sq miles), its boundary starting just above the breathtaking hills and valleys of Milford Sound on the west coast, skirting the southern shores of Lake Wakatipu bordering central Otago, and meandering its way through some of the lushest, most productive farmland in New Zealand to join the southeast coast near an unspoilt area called the Catlins. The grittiness in the local character manifests itself in an agrarian excellence –

the region is responsible for a quarter of New Zealand's export receipts.

Contrasts abound in the land itself. On the spectacular west coast, deep fiords lap against towering mountains and snow-capped peaks reach skywards in an area that is called, not surprisingly, Fiordland. In the lee of the mountains are the two extensive plains on which the province's prosperity has grown to depend. These lowlands surround the city of Invercargill, extending across the South Island to reach the southeastern coastlands.

Main attractions
SOUTHLAND MUSEUM AND
    ART GALLERY, INVERCARGILL
SOUTHERN SCENIC ROUTE
CURIO BAY
FIORDLAND NATIONAL PARK
TE ANAU GLOW-WORM CAVES
MILFORD SOUND
MILFORD TRACK
ROUTEBURN TRACK

PRECEDING PAGES & LEFT: contrasting moods at Milford Sound. **BELOW:** mossy trees on the Routeburn Track.

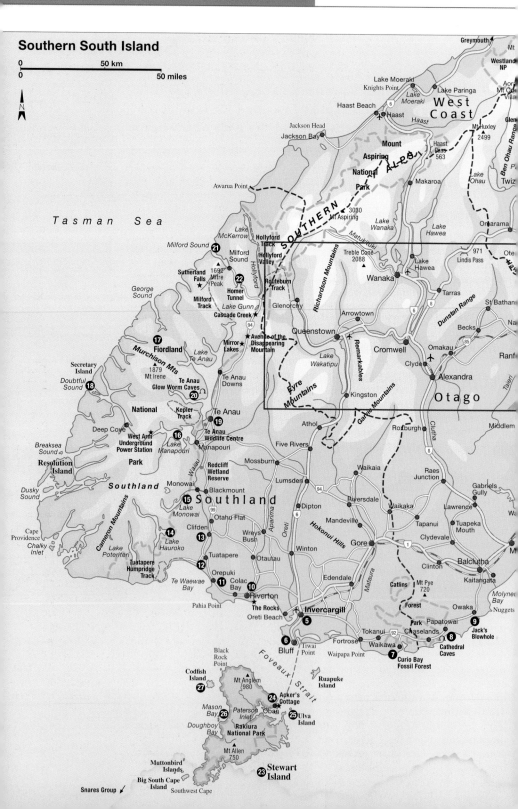

Southern South Island

0 ————————— 50 km
0 ————————— 50 miles

N

T a s m a n   S e a

Greymouth
Mt
Westland
NP

Lake Moeraki
Knights Point
Lake Moeraki
Lake Paringa
Aora
Mt Co
Villa

Haast Beach
Haast
Haast

**West
Coast**

Jackson Head
Jackson Bay

**Mount
Aspiring**
MtHuxley
2499
Glen

Haast
Pass
563

Makaroa
Lake
Ohau
Twiz

**National
Park**

Awarua Point

3030
Mt Aspiring
Lake
Wanaka
Lake
Hawea
Onarama

SOUTHERN ALPS

Matukituki

971
Lindis Pass
Ote

Lake
McKerrow
Hollyford
Track
Milford Sound **21**
Milford
Sound
Hollyford
Valley

Treble Cone
2088

Lake
Hawea

Wanaka

St Bathan

Na

Sutherland
Falls
1692
Mitre
Peak
22
Homer
Tunnel

Routeburn
Track

Richardson Mountains

Tarras

Dunstan Range

George
Sound

Milford
Track

Hollyford

Lake Gunn

Cascade Creek

94

Glenorchy

Arrowtown

Lake
Hawea

6

8

Becks

17 **Fiordland**
Murchison Mts

Avenue of the
Disappearing
Mountain

Queenstown

Omakau

85

Ranf

Secretary
Island

1879
Mt Irene

Mirror
Lakes

Lake
Te Anau

Cromwell

Clyde

Remarkables

Doubtful
Sound **18**

Te Anau
Glow Worm Caves
20

Te Anau
Downs

Lake
Wakatipu

Alexandra

O t a g o

Tatei

National

Kepler
Track

Te Anau **19**

Eyre
Mountains

Kingston

Deep Cove

16

Te Anau
Wildlife Centre

Athol

Garvin Mountains

Roxburgh

Middlem

Breaksea
Sound

West Arm
Underground
Power Station

Lake
Manapouri

Manapouri

Five Rivers

Clutha

Park

Mossburn

Waikaia

8

Resolution
Island

Park

Redcliff
Wetland
Reserve

Raes
Junction

Gabriels
Gully

Dusky
Sound

Monowai

Blackmount

Lumsden

94

Riversdale

Waikaka

Lawrence

Wa

Southland

15 **S o u t h l a n d**

Dipton

6

Riverdale

Tapanui

Tuapeka
Mouth

Cape
Providence
Chalky
Inlet

Lake
Monowai

99

Otahu Flat

Mandeville

Tapanui

Clydevale

Clifden

Wreys
Bush

Oreti

Hokonui Hills

Gore

1

Balclutha

M

14

Lake
Hauroko

13

Winton

Clinton

Lake
Poteriteri

Tuatapere
Humpridge
Track

Tuatapere

Otautau

Edendale

Mataura

Kaitangata

Cameron Mountains

12

Orepuki

11 Colac
Bay

10

Riverton

Catlins

Mt Pye
720

Owaka

Molyne
Bay
Nuggets

Te Waewae
Bay

Pahia Point

The Rocks
Oreti Beach

5

Invercargill

Forest

Papatowai

Jack's
Blowhole

9

6

Bluff

Tiwai
Point

Fortrose

92

Chaselands

8

**Cathedral
Caves**

Black
Rock
Point

Tokanui

Waikawa

7

Waipapa Point

Curio Bay
Fossil Forest

Foveaux Strait

Codfish
Island

27

Mt Anglem
980

Acker's
Cottage

Ruapuke
Island

Mason
Bay

26

Paterson
Inlet

Oban

24

25 Ulva
Island

Doughboy
Bay

**Rakiura
National Park**

Muttonbird
Islands

Mt Allen
750

23 **Stewart
Island**

Big South Cape
Island

Snares Group

Southwest Cape

Scottish Invercargill

The 50,000 people who live in **Invercargill ❺** – located some 217km (135 miles) southwest of Dunedin, or 283km (176 miles) south of Queenstown – reside close to an estuary once plied by steamers and sailing ships. The Scottish heritage of New Zealand's southernmost city is well reflected in its street names, many elegant buildings, neat gardens and tree-lined parks. The original town planners were generous in the amount of space devoted to main thoroughfares and public spaces. Today, **Queens Park**, the green heart of the city, provides a wide range of recreational pursuits, from sunken rose gardens and statuary created by Sir Charles Wheeler, to a golf course and swimming pool.

Downtown Invercargill on a stormy day.

Invercargill's biggest attraction is the **Southland Museum and Art Gallery** (Mon–Fri 9am–5pm, Sat–Sun 10am–5pm; donation fee; tel: 03-219 9069; www.southlandmuseum.com) at the Gala Street entrance of Queens Park. There are galleries devoted to the Maori, history and art, but the displays on the sub-Antarctic region – the cluster of islands between New Zealand and the Antarctic – alone make a visit worthwhile. The audio-visual film *Beyond the Roaring Forties* will add immeasurably to your understanding of this windswept and isolated region. Another highlight of the pyramid-shaped museum is a "tuatarium" where visitors can observe tuatara lizards, last survivors of the dinosaur era, roaming at leisure in a large, natural sanctuary.

At the ground level of the museum is Invercargill's **i-site Visitors Centre** (tel: 03-214 6243; www.invercargill.org.nz), where you can get more information on the rest of the attractions in the city.

Just 10km (6 miles) south of the city centre is **Oreti Beach**, a long stretch of sand popular among the hardy locals for swimming, yachting and water-skiing. The beach is also famous for the succulent toheroa, a rare and strictly protected shellfish that grows up to 15cm (6 inches) in length.

EAT

For an afternoon energy boost, follow your nose to The Seriously Good Chocolate Company, bordering Queens Park, for a glorious finger-licking feast: truffles of every conceivable description, southern rabbit "droppings", and "tuatara" chocolate eggs, to name but a few. Phone: 03-217 5107; www.seriouslygood chocolate.com.

Bluff's highlights

About 27km (17 miles) south of Invercargill is the land's-end port of **Bluff ❻**. The next stop after here is Stewart Island (*see page 312*) and the cold, stormy sub-Antarctic waters. _

Aside from its busy port area (*see panel below*), Bluff is famous, above all, for the plump oysters from the Foveaux Strait, the 35km (22-mile) stretch of water that separates Stewart Island from the mainland. In the early 1980s, the oyster beds were stricken with *Bonamia*, a protozoan disease, but careful management has ensured their recovery and a quota system prevents over-harvesting. Unique to New Zealand, this shellfish is not exported as the local market takes the full quota. The oyster season runs from March to August, with the highlight being the hugely popular annual **Bluff Oyster and Southland Seafood Festival** (www.bluffoysterfest.co.nz) in April.

If you're interested in local maritime history, the small **Bluff Maritime Museum** (Mon–Fri 10am–4.30pm, Sat–Sun 1–5pm; entrance fee; tel: 03-212 7534), at 241 Foreshore Road, is worth a visit. Here you can climb aboard and explore the workings of the oyster boat *Monica II*.

East to the Catlins coast

Head southeast of Invercargill for 80km (50 miles) towards the small fishing port of **Waikawa**, reached by a well-surfaced road that passes through rolling countryside which not long ago was covered in bush. This is part of the **Southern Scenic Route**, stretching from Balclutha in south Otago, along the southern coast, past Waikawa, and eventually terminating at Te Anau (*see page 309*). Heading northeast from Waikawa the scenic route (State Highway SH 92) takes in much of the **Catlins**, an area whose diverse natural beauty is supplemented by the many opportunities it affords to see such wildlife as fur seals, sea lions, the occasional, awe-inspiring elephant seal and rare Yellow-eyed penguins.

Turn off to Waikawa (the town lies just off the scenic route) and travel a further 6km (3¾ miles) to the remains of a petrified forest buried millions of years ago at a place called **Curio Bay ❼**.

A Bluff local, Jim Burke, is the world record-holder for opening the most oysters – 1,719 – in an hour. That equates to opening 28 oysters a minute, for a solid hour.

BELOW: hoisting a dredge full of oysters from the waters of Foveaux Strait.

Industrious Bluff

There is no mistaking Bluff's importance as a port. Large vessels tie up at the large man-made island within the inland harbour, workers toil around the clock as snake-like conveyor machines, their tails buried in a large building and their heads in ships' holds, load hundreds of thousands of frozen carcasses of lamb and mutton for export to markets across the globe.

Across the harbour, a series of imposing structures is dominated by a chimney stack 137 metres (450ft) high. This is the Tiwai Point aluminium smelter, which produces 334,000 tonnes of aluminium a year. Tucked away on the lonely Tiwai Peninsula where almost non-stop winds disperse smoke-laden effluent, the smelter is the major industrial employer in the south. Free tours can be arranged; call 03-218 5999 for details.

This freeze-frame of time has caught every grain of timber in the fossilised stumps; boulders which have been broken open by some unknown force show patterns of leaves and twigs. It's best viewed at low tide. Adjacent is **Porpoise Bay**, a pleasant swimming beach named after the rare, small Hector's dolpins, with their distinctive black-and-white markings, which frequent the bay.

Further east, 34km (21 miles) from Porpoise Bay, is the vast **Waipati Beach**, where a walkway leads to the spectacular 30-metre (98ft) **Cathedral Caves ❽**. The caves can only be entered two hours either side of low tide. A torch is essential lest you tread on a sleeping seal or sea lion. Travel another 10km (6 miles) north to **Papatowai**, which is home to a few essential stores and the starting point for numerous magnificent beach and forest walks.

Follow the Southern Scenic Route another 24km (15 miles) to **Owaka**, a thriving – albeit remote – township, stopping off at the stunning **Purakaunui Falls** along the way. Follow the road signs to reach this three-tiered waterfall, then hike for 10 minutes on a trail through the forest to the actual cascade. At Owaka, there are restaurants and accommodation; it makes a good base from which to explore bush walks and waterfalls, or indulge in some bird-watching. The **Catlins Visitors Centre** here (tel: 03-415 8371; www.catlins-nz.com) can supply you with all the details you need. Some 6km (4 miles) southeast of Owaka is **Jack's Blowhole ❾**, a 55-metre (180ft) deep hole of surging seas located some 200 metres (220yds) from the beach.

From here you can continue 30km (19 miles) north to **Balclutha**, and then either turn northeast to Dunedin or take the faster inland route back to Invercargill and head into isolated Fiordland.

West to the mountains

Invercargill may be flat, but its residents cannot help but raise their eyes west-

The view from Bluff Lookout. Stewart Island, 35km (22 miles) distant, can be seen on a clear day.

BELOW: petrified tree stumps at Curio Bay.

Macrocarpa trees near the shore at Orepuki, shaped by years of beating by fierce winds.

ward to the distant mountains that border Fiordland. For those in a hurry, this vast natural area can be reached in less than two hours, travelling northwest across the central Southland plains via Winton and Lumsden: this is prime farmland, carrying several million head of stock. At Lumsden, turn westwards on State Highway (SH) 99 towards Te Anau and the highlands: the scenery soon changes, with the rolling tussock country indicating that you are in land of an altogether tougher nature.

For those with more time, the coastal road to the mountains – the western section of the Southern Scenic Route – makes for a more interesting drive. Some 38km (24 miles) due west of Invercargill is the historic coastal township of **Riverton** ❿. Sealers and whalers made this their home in 1836, and Southland's first European settlement still bears signs of those times. Preservation is a way of life here. In 2002 the New Zealand Historic Places Trust offered a whaler's cottage for sale for

BELOW: Purakaunui Falls near Owaka.

the sum of just NZ$1, so long as the owner promised to preserve it according to the trust's specifications.

A further 10km (6 miles) west is **Colac Bay**. Once a Maori settlement, it grew into a town with a population of 6,000 during the gold-rush days of the 1890s, and now is a popular holiday spot for Southlanders. Further west is **Orepuki** ⓫ township, where history merges with the present: an old courthouse is now a sheep-shearing shed. Along the shore, look out for macrocarpa trees turned inwards by salt-laden southerly winds.

Travellers have a fine view of thundering surf between Orepuki and **Tuatapere** ⓬, 20km (12 miles) away. Across **Te Waewae Bay**, where Hector's dolphins and Southern right whales can sometimes be spied, bush-clad mountains loom, the first signs of what is to come. The **Tuatapere Hump Ridge Track** (www.humpridgetrack. co.nz), a 53km (33-mile), three-day circuit, starts and finishes at the western end of the bay.

From the timber town of Tuatapere, where fishing and deer-hunting stories are as common as logs from the town's mills, the road heads inland 12km (8 miles) to **Clifden** ⓭, notable for the nearby **Clifden Suspension Bridge** (built in 1899) and the spooky **Clifden Caves**. The caves can be explored without a guide, but make sure you have a good torch and follow the signposted instructions. From Clifden, a 30km (19-mile) unsealed road leads to New Zealand's deepest lake, **Lake Hauroko** ⓮, set among dense bush and steep slopes. Its name means "sounding wind" after the exposure it has to winds from both north and south.

Continuing north from Clifden, the road passes through Blackmount and then to the **Redcliff Wetland Reserve**, where birdwatchers might catch sight of a Bush falcon in action. The town of Monowai is 6km (4 miles) northwest of Blackmount, a base for the recreational Mecca of **Lake Monowai** ⓯, with its excellent fishing and hunting.

Fiordland National Park

Beyond the wetlands is **Lake Manapouri** , 28km (17 miles) north of Monowai. It has been described as a soft, feminine lake, with a scattering of wooded islands, banks dense with bush and a horizon bounded by the **Kepler Mountains**. It is indeed in a magnificent setting, with the high mountains of Fiordland rising majestically ahead.

With an area of 1.2 million hectares (3 million acres), **Fiordland National Park** is New Zealand's largest, and forms part of the South West New Zealand World Heritage Area. That first glimpse across Lake Manapouri, to sheer mountains and remote deep valleys on the other side of the lake, gives the observer some understanding of why ancient Maori legends never lose their romantic hold in this wild region.

To experience the scenery first-hand, you can take a launch across Lake Manapouri to its **West Arm**. There was a scheme to raise this lake by 27 metres (89ft) for hydroelectric purposes, but thankfully conservation interests prevailed, although the massive **Manapouri Underground Power Station** was built at West Arm to supply power to the Tiwai Point aluminium smelter (*see page 306*). Guided tours to the vast machine hall located 200 metres (660ft) underground are operated by **Real Journeys** (tel: 03-249 7416, 0800-656 501; www.realjourneys.co.nz) as part of their Doubtful Sound day excursion.

The construction of the power station involved the building of a road from West Arm, at the westernmost point of Lake Manapouri, across the wild Wilmot Pass, to the head of **Doubtful Sound**, the deepest of Fiordland's sounds, in an area known as **Deep Cove**. Bottlenose and Dusky dolphins frolic in the deep-blue waters of the fiord, and divers can view black coral, which grows at an unusually shallow depth due to the darker, fresh, tannin-infused water that pours into the cove from the power station and surrounding hills.

The hub of this magnificent wilderness is the town of **Te Anau**, 22km (14 miles) north of Manapouri, with its many hotels, motels and lodges. According to Maori legend, Lake Te

TIP

The road trip from Queenstown to Milford Sound is a tiring 4–5 hours each way, so book a coach and boat trip with Real Journeys (tel: 03-249 7416 or 0800-656 501; www.realjourneys.co.nz) instead. Better still at the end of the day, take the flight option back to Queenstown.

BELOW: bottlenose dolphins, one of the largest species in New Zealand waters.

The spellbinding scenery of Milford Sound.

Anau was created when local Maori chief Te Horo found a sacred spring. He asked his wife not to reveal its existence, but after he'd departed on a journey, she nonetheless showed it to her lover. As soon as his face reflected in its waters, a torrent drowned the village and formed the lake.

A highlight of this area is the **Te Anau Glow-worm Caves ㉔** on the western shores of **Lake Te Anau** at the base of the Murchison Mountains. The caves, believed to have been known to early Maori explorers, were only rediscovered in 1948. A trip to the caves takes 2½ hours and can be booked at **Real Journeys** *(see page 309)* in Te Anau. A walkway and a short punt ride take people to the heart of the cave system, which also features whirlpools, magical waterfalls and a glow-worm grotto. The Department of Conservation runs the **Te Anau Wildlife Centre** (daily 24 hours; tel: 03-249 7921; www.doc.govt.nz),

BELOW: a kaka, endemic species of parrot.

just outside the town on the road to Manapouri. It is one of the very few places where you can see the rare takahe, among other bird species.

Mighty Milford Sound

The second, still more spectacular way to the sea through Fiordland is the 120km (75-mile) long road to **Milford Sound ㉕** from Te Anau, world-renowned and described by Rudyard Kipling as "the eighth wonder of the world". Authors and artists have struggled to put into words the beauty that unfolds as the road, following Lake Te Anau for the first 30km (19 miles), enters dense forests, then passes serenely beautiful places such as the **Mirror Lakes**, 58km (36 miles) from Te Anau, and the **Avenue of the Disappearing Mountain**, where the eyes are not to be believed as the mountain appears to shrink while driving towards it. Forests, river flats and small lakes pass by, until the road drops towards the forested upper **Hollyford Valley** at Marian Camp.

The road then splits in two. One arm ventures into the no-exit **Hollyford**

Valley with its **Gunns Rest**, a well-established motor camp run by one of Fiordland's most interesting characters. At the end of this road is the start of the **Hollyford Track**. The other fork proceeds west, heading steeply up the mountain towards the eastern portal of the **Homer Tunnel** ㉒. Work on this 1,240-metre (4,118ft) unlined tunnel, hewn from solid rock, began in 1935 as an employment project for five men who lived in tents and used only picks, shovels and wheelbarrows. It was completed in 1954, but not before avalanches had claimed the lives of three men. Homer can be Fiordland at its roughest.

From the Milford side, the road drops 690 metres (2,264ft) in 10km (6 miles) between sheer mountain faces to emerge in the **Cleddau Valley**, with its awe-inspiring **Chasm Walk**, where you can stroll to a series of steep falls formed by the plunging Cleddau River. Back on the road, it's another 10km (6 miles) to the head of Milford Sound, where a small clutch of boats await. These carry visitors from the southernmost end of Milford Sound out to the open sea. The trips are extremely popular, and it is wise to book well in advance. **Red Boat Cruises** (tel: 03-441 1137, 0800-264 536; www.redboats.co.nz) operate short boat trips that take in most highlights, while **Real Journeys** *(see page 309)* offer short scenic cruises as well as overnight trips on the *Milford Wanderer* and *Milford Mariner*.

The Sound is dominated by the unforgettable **Mitre Peak** – a 1,692-metre (5,551ft) pinnacle of rock – and several landmarks, notably the 162-metre (532ft) **Lady Bowen Falls**. Milford tends to buzz with day-trippers, but remains remarkably empty at either end of the day. It also buzzes with sandflies, so insect repellent should be liberally applied.

From Milford Sound, it is possible to travel north towards Queenstown via Te Anau, **Mossburn** and **Kingston**, where a vintage steam train, the *Kingston Flyer* (www.kingstonflyer.co.nz) chugs to and fro between Fairlight and Kingston from October to May. Alternatively, motorists can proceed northeast toward Dunedin via the Mataura Valley. ❏

TIP

Bring your waterproof coats and wellingtons (gumboots to a Kiwi) if visiting Milford Sound or walking the Milford Track – in this area the rainfall is measured in metres. Insect repellent is also a must, to keep the voracious sandflies away.

BELOW: cruising Milford Sound.

Milford Marvels

Maori legends tell of Tu-te-raki-whanoa, the master carver who crafted the beautiful fiords of Fiordland with his adze, beginning in the south and working his way slowly up the coastline, fiord by fiord until he reached Milford Sound, his pièce de résistance.

One way to reach his masterpiece is to board a ferry from Te Anau Downs to the beginning of the **Milford Track** *(see page 243)* and hike a 54km (34-mile) route over four or five days, staying in huts along the way. Described as one of the finest walks in the world, this trail is so popular that it's fully booked for months in advance (it is necessary to arrange access to the track through the Department of Conservation, *see page 365*), but there is no better way fully to appreciate the Sound's beauty than to hike along its length.

Fiordland boasts other famous treks, including the Routeburn Track and the spectacular **Kepler Track** also reached from Te Anau. But don't rush away from Milford Sound just yet. If you have time and energy, consider a sea-kayaking trip or hop aboard a boat and visit Harrison Cove's underwater observatory. Here you can peek below the shallow top layer of tinted fresh water to spy on weird and wonderful deep-water species and corals that thrive in this place oblivious to the bright light above.

STEWART ISLAND

Little-known, even to New Zealanders, the country's "third island" is a wildlife paradise and ecotourist's dream come true

BELOW: sunset at Paterson Inlet.

The Maori called it Te-Punga-o-te-Waka-a-Maui – "Anchorstone of Maui's Canoe" – the weight that held the other islands of New Zealand together. The most commonly used and known Maori name is, however, Rakiura, meaning "glowing skies". One William Stewart, first officer on a sealing expedition in 1809, began charting the island's coasts and lent it the name by which it is now known. Today, **Stewart Island ㉓** metaphorically serves as one of the great foundation stones of the New Zealand environment, acting as a safe haven for many kinds of wildlife which otherwise would struggle to survive. It helps that it has just 28km (17 miles) of sealed roads and a grand total of 350 inhabitants.

Stewart Island can be reached by plane from Invercargill Airport, which takes just over 20 minutes, or by express catamaran ferry from Bluff to Oban, across Foveaux Strait, which takes an hour. If you take the ferry, particularly in the winter months, be prepared for a fairly rough trip, as the Strait has a well-earned reputation as one of the rough-

est stretches of water in New Zealand (the winds aren't called the "roaring forties" for nothing). On the bright side, the larger seabirds, such as albatrosses and mollymawks, need strong winds to remain aloft, so the rougher the weather, the more you are likely to see.

From the air, Stewart Island looks deceptively small. It is roughly triangular in shape, with the west coast stretching almost 60km (37 miles) from Black Rock Point in the north to the **Southwest Cape**. There are two large bays, Doughboy and Mason, with all-weather anchorage provided by Paterson Inlet on the east coast. On the western side, rollers constantly thunder onto the shore from the Tasman Sea. The southeast coast is also fairly exposed.

Oban and Ulva Island

Centred around Half Moon Bay and Horseshoe Bay, with its charming cottages almost hidden among the trees, **Oban** ㉔ is one of the most delightful settlements in New Zealand. Some of the houses date back to the days when the Norwegians had a whaling base at nearby **Paterson Inlet**, with others built by the descendants of whalers and sealers. There is a wide range of accommodation, from hostels for backpackers to some expensive homestays. (Prices on Stewart Island tend to be a bit steeper than those on the mainland, as just about everything, except fish, needs to be imported.) There is also accommodation available at the local watering hole, the **South Seas Hotel** (tel: 03-219 1059; www.stewart-island. co.nz) at the shore end of Main Road, which claims to be the most southern hotel in the world (conveniently ignoring those in southern Chile and Argentina – both of which extend several hundred miles further south than Stewart Island).

Rakiura Museum (Mon–Sat 10am–noon, Sun noon–2pm; entrance fee) in Ayr Street holds many items relating to the island's maritime history and pre-European days, and is a good place to learn about the local wildlife.

Not far east of town on the way to Acker's Point is **Acker's Cottage**, New Zealand's oldest surviving dwelling. Built of stone and clay-mortar, it was constructed by an American whaler, Lewis Acker, and his wife, Mary Pi, in 1835. Acker set up a coastal trading and boatbuilding business, which he operated until the late 1950s. Since then the cottage has been used as a smithy, storeroom, brewery and workshop. More recently the NZ Historic Places Trust and the Department of Conservation restored it to its current state. Some say it is unsympathetically restored; nonetheless, it is still worth a visit.

Around Oban are many delightful shore walks for a wide range of fitness levels. There are some fine stands of trees, and the native fuchsia is particularly prolific. Birdlife is abundant, and, as they are seldom harassed, they will allow you to approach quite near. Kakariki, bellbirds, fantails, tui and tomtits are among the species commonly encountered, and also the native pigeon, the kereru. The raucous cries of one of the native parrots, the kaka, flying overhead, can often be heard around Oban.

Blue penguins on Stewart Island, one of the best places to see birds in New Zealand.

BELOW: hiking the Rakiura Track.

Well worth a visit is **Ulva Island** 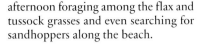, about 3km (2 miles) offshore in Paterson Inlet. It is accessed by water taxi, or, for the more adventurous, a kayak. The island is covered in primeval forest. Mature rimu, totara, miro and kamahi are all present in good numbers, as are smaller plants such as ferns and orchids. Ulva has been cleared of predators in recent years, and a number of bird species have been introduced. The most conspicuous of these is the South Island saddleback, but there are also Stewart Island robins, riflemen and yellowheads. Also on Ulva is a flourishing population of Stewart Island weka. Signs discourage you from feeding them, but weka are nothing if not optimists, and are certainly not above helping themselves to an unattended lunch. There is also a population of *tokoeka* kiwis; because they sometimes forage during the day due to the short nights of midsummer, there is a better chance of seeing them here than in any other part of New Zealand.

Mason Bay , on the west coast, is another kiwi stronghold. The birds here are often to be seen in the late afternoon foraging among the flax and tussock grasses and even searching for sandhoppers along the beach.

A haven for birdwatchers

Another good place for viewing birds is at the relatively exposed **Acker's Point**, 3km (2 miles) to the east of Oban. Larger seabirds such as albatrosses and mollymawks tend to stay out of the sheltered bays, as the winds there are generally not strong enough to keep them aloft. If you walk out to Acker's Point in the evening, you'll hear Blue penguins calling to each other as they float in rafts (or groups) just offshore, waiting until it is dark enough to venture safely ashore to their burrows. During the summer breeding season, you'll also hear the calls of the home-coming sooty shearwater, or *titi*, which nests in burrows under and around the beacon.

Sooty shearwaters generally go by the rather unflattering name of mutton birds – derived from the taste of their meat: either like fish-flavoured mutton or mutton-flavoured fish. In any event, it is a rather unhappy gastro-

Spectacular views across Stewart Island.

BELOW: green fern fronds at Ulva Island.

Giant Seabirds

One of the best places to spot seabirds lies to the south of Stewart Island towards the Snares Group. Although landing is not permitted, sailing or motoring just offshore is, and in the evenings the cacophony of home-coming shearwaters and penguins is impossible to miss.

For dedicated birdwatchers wanting to add magnificent albatrosses, sooty shearwaters and mollymawks to their lifelist, there is no other way of seeing them, and you had better see them while you can. With the craven attitude taken by the New Zealand government on enforcing the regulations on long-line fishing in the southern waters, the numbers of these birds are fast plummeting. Several thousand are drowned each year when they get hooked on the fishing lines of boats.

nomic combination. For the curious, the South Seas Hotel in Oban sometimes features them on its menu.

The waters around Stewart Island offer some of the best opportunities in the world for viewing seabirds. Over half the world's known albatrosses and mollymawks frequent the coastal waters here, along with a plethora of other seabirds, including petrels, shearwaters, skuas, prions, Blue penguins and Fiordland penguins. Also commonly encountered are Cape pigeons, known somewhat irreverently by the locals as "Jesus Christ birds", because of their habit of pattering across the water. There is also a plethora of seabirds found near the **Snares Group**, 125km (78 miles) from the southernmost tip of Stewart Island (*see opposite*).

Rakiura National Park

However, if you choose to keep your feet on dry land, there is plenty to keep you occupied on Stewart Island itself, as there are about 245km (152 miles) of walking tracks. A particularly good tramp is the 29km (18-mile) long **Rakiura Track**, which starts and ends at Oban and takes three days to complete. There are huts along the way for overnight stays. The tracks in the north take you through stands of totara, rimu and rata, while those in the south run up from beautiful forested bays out into shrublands and sub-Alpine vegetation. These southern areas, around the Tin Range, were until fairly recently home to New Zealand's rarest bird, the kakapo. In the 1970s they were moved to the safety of offshore islands like **Codfish Island** ㉗, which lies not far off Stewart Island's west coast.

With 85 percent of the island encompassed by the **Rakiura National Park**, there is a multitude of areas to visit and things to do. And even if you are not the tramping sort, there are few other places where it is as pleasant just to sit and take in nature at its finest. The fern groves, particularly those around **Dynamite Point**, are luxuriant, especially now that the introduced white-tail deer are being kept under control, and there is a particularly good collection of plants in the gardens at the **Motarau Moana Reserve**, on the road to Horseshoe Bay. ❑

TIP

The South Seas Hotel is a good place to meet up with the locals, mostly fishermen or workers from the local salmon farm. If the urge takes you, visits to the salmon farm (tel: 03-219 1282; www.seabuzzz.co.nz) can be arranged, and you can also visit the local mussel farms.

BELOW: Stewart Island's huge albatrosses are a sight to behold.

Antarctica: Last Bastion for Heroes

New Zealand has long had a stake in the planet's most extreme environment, one that represents the final frontier for tourism

Adventurous travellers, like the brave explorers who blazed their trail, are succumbing to the lure of Antarctica, a continent with an exceptional and utterly unique beauty. The coldest, windiest and most hostile place on earth, the frozen continent has teased our curiosity for centuries, and heroes populate its short human history. Those who have been there report awesome encounters with the raw forces of nature, but also times of ineffable, luminous peace and beauty.

The city of Christchurch has long been a base for Antarctic expeditions – Robert Falcon Scott spent three weeks there in 1901 preparing for his journey. Today, several commercial operators *(see page 375)* sail from Christchurch to Antarctica and the sub-Antarctic islands of New Zealand – far-flung islands teeming with wildlife which have been described as the Galapagos of the South.

Last wilderness

Antarctica is the last great wilderness, with close to 90 percent of the world's ice sprawling over an area larger than the United States. If all this ice were to melt, the continent would shrink to about three-quarters of its present size and rising sea levels would inundate most of the world's lowlands.

Antarctica's exploration has close associations with New Zealand. When Abel Tasman arrived off the west coast of New Zealand in 1642 he believed it might be the western edge of a continent that stretched across to South America. Accordingly, he called it Staten Landt, then the name for South America. A year later, when it was decided there was no huge landmass across the South Pacific, the name was changed to Zeelandia Nova.

The next European visitor to New Zealand, Captain James Cook, also showed an interest in a possible southern land mass, the *terra australis*. In one of the most daring voyages ever made, Cook sailed along 60 degrees latitude and then penetrated as far as 71 degrees south without sighting the legendary continent. He stayed south so long, his crew verged on mutiny. Fifty years later, the Russian navigator Fabian Gottlieb von Bellinghausen circumnavigated the world between 60 and 65 degrees south, dipping to 69 degrees on two occasions, and became the first man to see land inside the Antarctic Circle.

New Zealander Alexander von Tunzelmann, the 17-year-old nephew of a pioneer settler of central Otago, is believed to have been the first person to step ashore on Antarctica, at Cape Adare in January 1895. Exploration on the land began soon afterwards, and New Zealanders took part in the explo-

LEFT: snow-crusted Antarctica explorer.
ABOVE: Edmund Hillary at Scott Base, 1957.
RIGHT: Scott base, population 19.

rations by Englishman Robert Falcon Scott and the Anglo-Irish Ernest Shackleton between 1900 and 1917, and Australia's Sir Douglas Mawson during the years before World War I. As every schoolboy knows, Scott and his party reached the South Pole in January 1912, only to learn that the Norwegians under Roald Amundsen had beaten them to it. Scott and his team died on their return journey.

In 1923, the territory south of 60 degrees and between 160 degrees east and 150 degrees west was claimed by the British, and placed under the administration of the Governor-General of New Zealand. In 1933 the New Zealand Antarctic Society was formed, although it was another 15 years before the first New Zealand onshore base was established on the continent.

In 1957, Everest conqueror Sir Edmund Hillary led a group of five fellow countrymen on an overland dash to the South Pole. He was supposed to have acted solely as a support for Britain's transpolar expedition, laying down supply bases on the New Zealand side of Antarctica. But Hillary and his small group made such progress that they decided to push for the Pole themselves, becoming the first to make it overland since Scott 45 years before.

Since 1958, parties from New Zealand have explored and mapped huge areas of the frozen continent, and intensively researched the geology of the region. In 1964, New Zealand erected a new base of its own, named Scott Base after Captain Scott, at McMurdo Sound.

Care of resources

Five years earlier, the Antarctic Treaty designed to "ensure the use of Antarctica for peaceful purposes only and the continuance of international harmony" was signed by 12 nations, including New Zealand. This culminated in a Convention on the Regulation of Antarctic Mineral Resource Activities (CRAMRA) in Wellington in 1988. In 1991, the CRAMRA signatories signed a protocol that prohibits mining on the continent until 2041. It is probable that mineral-bearing rocks of the sort prevalent in Australia and South Africa are common on the Antarctic mainland. There are also known to be huge deposits of sub-bituminous coal and large deposits of low-grade iron ore.

Tourism interest in Antarctica remains strong, but access is still extremely difficult, and likely to stay that way for many years. The majority of tourists travel by ship from southern South America, although a few intrepid travellers make the trip from Christchurch (see page 375). If it becomes easier, protection of this special environment may have to include stringent controls on tourism. For now, visitors who can't get to Antarctica can get a taste of the continent at Christchurch's International Antarctic Centre and Auckland's Kelly Tarlton's Antarctic Encounter and Underwater World (see page 137). ❑

INSIGHT GUIDES TRAVEL TIPS
NEW ZEALAND

TRANSPORT

ACCOMMODATION

EATING OUT

ACTIVITIES

A – Z

TRANSPORT

GETTING THERE AND GETTING AROUND

By Air

More than 99 percent of the 2 million tourists who visit New Zealand each year arrive by air.

International Airports

The main gateway is the **Auckland International Airport** (www.auckland-airport.co.nz) at Mangere, 24km (15 miles) southwest of downtown **Auckland**. Bus, shuttle and taxi transfers into the city are available.

There is also an international airport in **Hamilton** (www.hamiltonairport.co.nz), 15km (9 miles) south of the city, although this tends to service only New Zealand and Australian flights.

The airport at **Wellington** (www.wellington-airport.co.nz), the capital city, has restricted access for most wide-bodied aircraft types because of the runway length.

There is a good international airport at Harewood, close to the main South Island city of **Christchurch** (www.christchurch-airport.co.nz). Many international airlines run scheduled flights there.

Direct flights to and from Australia land at and take off from the airport at **Queenstown** (www.queenstownairport.co.nz), 8km (5 miles) east of Frankton. The majority of scheduled flights are domestic.

New Zealand has direct air links with the Pacific Islands, all the major Australian cities, many Southeast Asian destinations, and cities in North America and Europe. Passengers arriving on long-haul flights should allow themselves a

DVT Caution

To prevent deep-vein thrombosis (DVT) on long-haul flights, take note of the following guidelines:
- Be comfortable in your seat.
- Bend and straighten your legs, feet and toes every half-hour or so while seated during the flight.
- Press the balls of your feet down hard against the floor or footrest to help increase the blood flow.
- Do some upper-body and breathing exercises to improve circulation.
- Take occasional short walks up and down the aisles.
- If the plane stops for refuelling, get off the plane and walk around, if this is permitted.
- Drink plenty of water.
- Don't drink too much alcohol.
- Avoid taking sleeping pills, which also cause immobility.

couple of rest days on arrival.

The no-frills subsidiary of Air New Zealand, **Freedom Air** (www.freedomair.com) flies between Australia and New Zealand.

By Sea

A few cruise ships visit New Zealand, but there are no regular passenger-ship services to the country. Most cruises in the South Pacific originate in Sydney, Australia, so cruise operators generally fly their passengers to and from New Zealand. However, some cruise lines, including P&O Line (www.pocruises.co.nz), regularly travel to New Zealand, mostly between November and April. Some cargo vessels also take small groups.

By Air

Air New Zealand, Qantas and Pacific Blue are the main domestic carriers.

Helicopters are readily available in main cities and in the main tourist resort areas.

Although domestic flights can be expensive, there are plenty of deals around for flying in off-peak times, for example Air New Zealand's Grabaseat website (www.grabaseat.co.nz), and other internet deals rewarding those who book well in advance. Flights can be booked online or with travel agents and accredited agents.

Air New Zealand, Sales and Reservations, tel: 0800-737 000 (reservations) or 0800-737 767 (travel centres); www.airnewzealand.co.nz

Qantas New Zealand, 191 Queen Street, Auckland, tel: 0800-808 767; for reservations, tel: 09-357 8900; www.qantas.co.nz

Pacific Blue, Auckland Domestic Terminal, Mangere, tel: 0800-670 000; www.pacificblue.co.nz

Departure Tax

A tax of NZ$25 must be paid when you leave New Zealand unless it has been prepaid when you purchased your ticket. Auckland International Airport introduced this streamlined prepaid system in mid-2008, and other New Zealand airports are expected to follow suit. Check your ticket with your travel agent if you are departing from any airport other than Auckland.

By Sea

Modern ferries operated by two competing companies, Interislander and Bluebridge, link the North and South Islands. The ferries sail between Wellington and Picton and carry passengers, vehicles and freight. There are frequent daily crossings in both directions, though it is important to book vehicle space in advance during summer. The journey time takes about 3 hours, depending on sea conditions.

There is a wide range of facilities and entertainment on board the *Interislander* including a bar, lounges and a café.

Ferry tickets can be purchased at NZ Post outlets, travel agents and visitor information centres.

The *Interislander*, tel: 04-498 3302 or 0800-802 802; www.interislander.co.nz

Bluebridge, tel: 0800-844 844; www.bluebridge.co.nz.

A passenger ferry operated by Real Journeys (tel: 0800-656 501; www.realjourneys.co.nz) from Bluff in Southland connects Stewart Island with the South Island.

Passenger ferries (departing from the terminal behind the Ferry Building on Quay Street, Auckland), service Great Barrier Island and Waiheke Island as well as vehicular ferries. For further information on transporting your vehicle across to either island, contact **SeaLink**, car, passenger and freight ferry services, tel: 0800-732 546; www.sealink.co.nz

By Rail

By international standards the New Zealand rail network is extremely limited. The infrastructure is there, although rail is mainly used for freight. To travel the country completely by rail is not an option.

The New Zealand government has set aside money to improve the rail network, so chances are that over the next 10 years things will change. In the meantime, the following limited services are available.

TranzScenic (tel: 04-495 0775, 0800-872 467; www.tranzscenic.co.nz) offers three routes, one in the North Island and two in the South Island, which travel through some of the most spectacular scenery in the world aboard trains comfortably outfitted with an onboard dining car serving light meals and beverages.

TranzAlpine: This scenic train journey is also offered as a return one-day trip, and travels between Christchurch in the east of the South Island and Greymouth in the west.

TranzCoastal: This train travels along the coast and connects Christchurch with the inter-island ferries at Picton. From here you can catch a ferry across the Cook Strait to Wellington in the North Island.

The Overlander: This service runs between Wellington and Auckland.

Tickets can be purchased online, from any TranzScenic accredited agency, travel agents and visitor information centres. Enquire about the **Scenic Rail Pass**, which allows you to hop on and off TranzScenic trains (*see box on page 323*).

By Bus and Coach

City transport: Major cities all have extensive local bus services for getting you out and about economically. Check with visitor information centres in each town for details of how they operate. Have coins ready, as you usually pay on boarding. Bus passes are available from visitors centres and local convenience stores.

Inter-city coaches: There is an excellent inter-city coach network throughout the country, using modern and comfortable coaches (some with toilets). It is wise to reserve seats in advance, especially during summer months.

The major bus operators are **InterCity Coachlines** and the **Naked Bus Company**. Travel and information centres throughout New Zealand can book bus tickets and multi-day passes for visitors aboard InterCity Coachlines. In addition, several smaller bus and shuttle companies operate regional and inter-city coach services. Check with local visitor information centres for contacts.

InterCity Coachlines

www.intercitycoach.co.nz
Auckland, tel: 09-623 1503
Wellington, tel: 04-385 0520
Christchurch, tel: 03-365 1113
Dunedin, tel: 03-471 7143

Naked Bus

www.nakedbus.co.nz
This low-cost and reliable coach transport company operates almost entirely online, enabling it to offer cut-price fares on its fleet of comfortable coaches which travel throughout New Zealand. A limited number of fares starting at NZ$1 can often be found. Should you wish to call, tel: 0900-62533, but note that calls are charged at premium rates.

Taxis

All cities and most towns have 24-hour taxicab services. Chauffeur-driven cars are also readily available.

By Car and Campervan

Driving offers one of the best ways to see New Zealand's extremely diverse landscape, and on any single journey you can expect to enjoy a wealth of spectacular scenery. It is worth noting, however, that some journeys involve winding roads through hill country, and therefore the time to travel from one place to another can take a lot longer than you may expect. To make the most of your time in New Zealand, allow adequate time to journey from one place to another.

Approximate Driving Times

North Island

Auckland–Whangarei	3 hours
Whangarei–Paihia	1 hour
Paihia–Cape Reinga	4½ hours
Auckland–Hamilton	2 hours
Hamilton–Rotorua	1½ hours

BELOW: Auckland's free City Circuit bus operates in the city centre.

Hamilton–Whakatane	3 hours
Hamilton–New Plymouth	4½ hours
Hamilton–Taupo	2 hours
Taupo–Napier	2½ hours
Whakatane–Napier	5 hours
Taupo–Palmerston North	3½ hours
Palmerston North– Wellington	2 hours

South Island

Picton–Christchurch	5 hours
Christchurch–Greymouth	4 hours
Christchurch–Kaikoura	3 hours
Christchurch–Mount Cook	5 hours
Christchurch–Dunedin	5 hours
Mount Cook–Queenstown	4 hours
Queenstown–Invercargill	3 hours
Invercargill–Dunedin	4½ hours
Queenstown–Fox Glacier	7 hours
Fox Glacier–Greymouth	3½ hours
Greymouth–Westport	2 hours
Greymouth–Nelson	4½ hours

Road Conditions

Multi-lane highways are few – they generally only provide immediate access to and through major cities – and single-lane roads are the norm. While traffic is generally light by European standards, the winding and narrow nature of some stretches of roads means you can only go as fast as the slowest truck, so do not underestimate driving times. Main road surfaces are good and conditions are usually comfortable; the main problem you might encounter is wet road surfaces after heavy rains. Signposting is generally good.

Petrol

Unleaded 91- and 96-octane petrol is sold, along with diesel, at all service stations. Compressed natural gas and liquid petroleum gas are also offered. Prices vary from place to place.

Rules of the Road

• In New Zealand, you drive on the left side of the road and overtake on the right.
• Give way to traffic on the right.
• If you are turning left, give way to right-turning oncoming traffic.
• The wearing of seat belts – by the driver and all passengers – is compulsory.
• The legal speed limits are 100kmh (60mph) on open roads and 50kmh (30mph) in built-up areas, but watch for signposts superseding these limits.
• New Zealand's road signs follow the internationally recognised symbols.
• For drink-driving, see page 379.

ABOVE: bike hire is available nationwide.

Motoring Associations

A comprehensive range of services for motorists is available from the Automobile Association, and reciprocal membership arrangements may be available for those holding membership of foreign motoring organisations.
Automobile Association, Head Office, 99 Albert Street, Auckland City, tel: 0800-500 543; www.aa.co.nz
Documentation: You can legally drive in New Zealand for up to 12 months if you have a current driver's licence from your home country or an International Driving Permit (IDP).

Vehicle Hire

To hire a vehicle, you must be 21 years of age or over and hold a current New Zealand or international driver's licence. Third-party insurance is compulsory, although most hire companies will insist on full insurance cover before hiring out their vehicles.
    It is wise to book in advance. Major international hire firms such as Avis, Hertz and Budget offer good deals for pre-booking. If you have not pre-booked, tourist information desks at most airports can direct you to other operators to fit your budget.
    The approximate cost per day for rental of a mid-sized car is NZ$80–110, with competitive rates negotiable for longer periods.
    Campervans/motorhomes are very popular in New Zealand and are both an economical and flexible means of exploring the country. The average daily charge for a two-berth/six-berth works out at approximately NZ$190–300 in the high season.

Vehicle Hire Companies
Ace Rental Cars
Nationwide, tel: 0800-502 277
Auckland, tel: 09-303 3112
Wellington, tel: 0800-535 500

Christchurch, tel: 0800-202 029
Queenstown, tel: 0800-002 203
www.acerentalcars.co.nz
Avis
Auckland, tel: 09-275 7239
Wellington, tel: 04-801 8108
Christchurch, tel: 03-379 6133
Queenstown, tel: 03-442 3808
Dunedin, tel: 03-486 2780
www.avis.com
Budget
Nationwide, tel: 0800-283 438
Auckland, tel: 09-976 2270
Wellington, tel: 04-802 4548
Christchurch, tel: 03-366 0072
www.budget.co.nz
Hertz
Auckland, tel: 09-367 6350
Wellington, tel: 04-384 3809
Christchurch, tel: 03-366 0549
Queenstown, tel: 03-442 4106
Dunedin, tel: 03-477 7385
www.hertz.com
KEA Campers
Nationwide, tel: 0800-520 052
Auckland, tel: 09-441 7833
Christchurch, tel: 03-359 2820
www.keacampers.co.nz
National Car Rentals
Nationwide, tel: 03-366 5574 or
0800-800 115; www.nationalcar.co.nz

Cycling

If you are fit, cycling is another good way to get around New Zealand. It is becoming increasingly popular, especially in the South Island. However, as the countryside is extremely hilly and mountainous and can be quite hard-going, you may wish to sit some sectors out, and travel aboard a coach. If doing so, advise the coach companies when you book to ensure there will be adequate space for your bicycle. Bikes are hired out all over the country, and are a fantastic way to get around New Zealand's smaller towns.

TRANSPORT BY REGION

North Island

Auckland

The main gateway to New Zealand is the **Auckland International Airport** at Mangere, 24km (15 miles) southwest of the city's downtown area. Bus, shuttle and taxi transfers are available into the city. You'll find them lined up outside the main terminal. Shuttles and buses cost about NZ$18 (Airbus) and take about an hour to reach the city. A taxi takes about half the time, but will cost NZ$50 plus.

As New Zealand's largest city, Auckland is well connected by a network of domestic flights and inter-city coaches, as well as rail services.

There is a great inner-city bus service (including the free City Circuit service around the immediate city centre every 10 minutes 8am–6pm) and plenty of taxi services to choose from. You'll find taxi stands throughout the central city. Contact **Auckland Co-operative Taxis**, tel: 09-300 3000; www.cooptaxi.co.nz. Flagfall is NZ$3 and trips are charged at NZ$2.50 per kilometre; waiting time is charged at NZ90 cents per minute.

A NZ$13 **Auckland Discovery Day Pass** (tel: 09-366 6400; www.maxx. co.nz) gives you unlimited rides on most buses, train and ferries for a day. This is also available as a monthly pass for NZ$220 per calendar month. You can buy the pass on any Link or Stagecoach bus, or at the ferry office. The Link bus is a convenient way to travel around the inner city. It travels both clockwise and anti-clockwise in a loop travelling through Ponsonby, K Road and the city. A ride costs only NZ$1.60.

Auckland also has a commuter train system, **Connex**, linking the city to the outer suburbs.

For all public transportation enquiries, call MAXX, tel: 09-366 6400; www.maxx.co.nz

Northland

The Bay of Islands is about 250km (155 miles) north of Auckland. **Air New Zealand** operates daily flights from Auckland to **Kerikeri** Airport, Northland's main airport. The flight time is around 45 minutes. There's a shuttle service from the airport.

The **Northliner** operates a daily luxury express coach service from Auckland to the Bay of Islands and to Kaitaia in the far north. Prices are NZ$49–72 one way. Contact:

Northliner Travel Centre, Sky City Terminal, Auckland, tel: 09-307 5873; www.intercitycoach.co.nz

The Bay of Islands is 3½ hours' drive from Auckland via the East Coast Highway, or 5 hours if you travel past the mighty Waipoua forest (the largest kauri forest in New Zealand).

Northland is well served by buses in and out of the region, as well as inner-city bus and taxi services in most towns.

The Waikato

Hamilton

Hamilton, is located about 2 hours south of Auckland, with bus links to most cities and towns. **Hamilton International Airport** is 15km (9 miles) or so south of the city, with daily links with major New Zealand cities. **Freedom Air** flies direct from Australia's Gold Coast.

Hamilton is also on the main trunk line, with rail services on TranzScenic Rail's **Overlander** between Auckland and Wellington. Journey time is just over 2 hours.

Hamilton is serviced by excellent inner-city bus and taxi services. There are also plenty of car-hire agencies in the city. **Hamilton City Buses**, tel: 07-846 1975; www.busit.co.nz **Hamilton Taxis**, tel: 07-847 7477; www.hamiltontaxis.co.nz

Coromandel and the Bay of Plenty

About 90 minutes from Auckland and Rotorua, the Coromandel is on the Pacific Coast Highway. There are flights to Whitianga from Auckland with Great Barrier Airlines (tel: 0800-900 600), but only on Friday. There are also door-to-door shuttle services between Whitianga, Tairua, Thames and Auckland, which cost from NZ$60 through to NZ$108, depending on how far you travel. Contact: **Go Kiwi Shuttles and Adventures**, tel: 07-866 0336; www.gokiwi.co.nz. Or drive the 2½-hour scenic, winding route following the Pacific Coast Highway from Auckland.

Tauranga/Mount Maunganui

From the Coromandel, you can take the Pacific Coast Highway to the Bay of Plenty. The trip into Tauranga takes 1 to 2 hours. Or catch an **InterCity** bus to Tauranga from most North Island destinations. Also try **Bayline Coaches**, tel: 07-578 3113.

Rotorua and the Volcanic Plateau

Rotorua

Air New Zealand has flights in and out of Rotorua. The airport is about 15 minutes from the centre of Rotorua. You can also catch one of a number of inter-city coaches such as the **Naked Bus** and **InterCity** in and out of all major New Zealand destinations.

Most thermal activities in Rotorua offer shuttle services that will take you from the city centre to their attraction, for a small charge or free of charge. There is a good public bus service; contact **Rotorua Super Shuttle**, tel: 07-345 7790, 0800-748 885. For taxis, contact **Rotorua Taxis**, tel: 07-348 1111.

Taupo

Taupo is about midway between Auckland (4 hours to the north) and Wellington (4 hours south), on the classic touring route – which runs through Taupo en route from Auckland to Rotorua and Hawke's Bay. There are direct **Air New Zealand** flights daily from Auckland and Wellington to Taupo Airport with connections to the South Island.

Whakapapa Village/National Park

To get to the Whakapapa Village– National Park area and Ohakune – from where the North Island's ski slopes are easily accessible – take the **Overlander** train from Auckland, or the **InterCity** bus that connects with Ohakune from Auckland and Wellington.

Poverty Bay and Hawke's Bay

Gisborne

Gisborne is an 8½-hour car ride south on the Pacific Coast Highway from Auckland. Regular flights connect major North and South Island centres to Gisborne Airport. Coaches

ABOVE: Wellington's cable car.

also operate regular schedules from around the country.

Hastings
Hastings is 3½ hours' drive from Gisborne. Regular flights connect major centres to Hawke's Bay airports. Coaches also operate regular schedules from around the country.

Napier
Napier is 3 hours' drive from Gisborne. Regular flights connect major North and South Island centres to Hawke's Bay airports. Coaches also operate regular schedules from around the country.

Taranaki, Wanganui and Manawatu
New Plymouth
Off the beaten track, this region has its own airport, which is serviced by **Air New Zealand**. Inter-city coaches also run services. **New Plymouth** can be reached on a 6½-hour drive from Auckland by following SH1 and SH3.

Palmerston North
Palmerston North, the heart of the Manawatu, is about 1 hour's drive south of Wanganui. It is serviced by **Air New Zealand**. Inter-city coaches also run to the region. The town is also on the main Auckland to Wellington trunk line with rail services on the **Overlander**.

Wanganui
Wanganui has its own airport serviced daily by **Air New Zealand**. Inter-city coaches run services to the region. It is a 3-hour drive from Wellington or Taupo, 2½ hours from New Plymouth, and 4 hours from Napier. You can also reach Wanganui from Auckland – an

8-hour drive – via New Plymouth or via Taumarunui on SH4.

Wellington and Surroundings
Wellington
Wellington International Airport has services from Australia and some South Pacific islands, as well as having good regional and national links. It's about half an hour's drive from the city centre – taxis cost about NZ$50 and a shuttle, which takes a little longer, costs about NZ$15. The **Stagecoach Flyer** runs from the airport to the city, Lower Hutt and Upper Hutt, taking 15 minutes to 1¼ hours.

Wellington is also well served by inter-city coaches and can be reached from Auckland by train aboard Tranz-Scenic Rail's Overlander.

Ferry services link Wellington with Picton on the South Island. *See "By Sea", page 321.*

The Wellington public transport system, **Metlink** (tel: 0800-801 700 or 04-801 7000; www.metlink.co.nz), runs regular bus, commuter train and ferry services throughout the city and outer regions, including the Daytripper Pass (NZ$5 day pass) that loops the inner city every 15 minutes. There are plenty of taxi stands around the inner city. However, Wellington is so compact that it's easy to walk from one end of Lambton Quay to Courtenay Place.

You can visit historic Somes Island or Eastbourne on the **Dominion Post Ferry** (tel: 04-499 1282; www. eastbywest.co.nz), or catch the unique **Cable Car** (tel: 04-472 2199) from Cable Car Lane off Lambton Quay, to the suburb of Kelburn and the top of the Botanic Gardens. Wellington also has a commuter train system, the **Tranzmetro** (contact Metlink on tel: 0800-801 700), linking the city to the outer suburbs as far as Upper Hutt.

South Island

Nelson and Marlborough
Blenheim
Air New Zealand flies to Blenheim, which is on SH1, 36km (22 miles) south of Picton.

Kaikoura
Kaikoura, the world's whale-watching capital, is midway between Blenheim and Christchurch. It can be reached by road or rail. The journey down the east coast to Kaikoura is picturesque and magnificent.

Nelson
Nelson Regional Airport has regular airlinks with Auckland, Wellington and

Christchurch, as well as a range of provincial centres.

Plenty of coach services link Nelson with Motueka and the southern entrance of the Abel Tasman Park. Contact: **Abel Tasman Coachlines**, tel: 03-548 0285; www.abeltasmantravel.co.nz. You can also hire a car or motorhome and drive to most surrounding towns in less than 2 hours. Contact the nearest visitors centre for more details.

Picton and the Sounds
Ferry services between Wellington and Picton are frequent. The Inter-islander and Bluebridge ferries take 3 hours to get you across Cook Strait.

Christchurch and Surroundings
Christchurch
Christchurch is served by a busy international airport, and has comprehensive road and rail links and a thriving deep-water port. There's a public bus service from the airport to the city, which will cost about NZ$5 per person and take 30–40 minutes; the shuttle will take around 20–30 minutes at a cost of NZ$18 per person. The more expensive option of a taxi will cost NZ$35, but it will get you there much faster – about 12–20 minutes.

If travelling from Greymouth, on the west coast, you should try to take the scenic **TranzAlpine** train (tel: 0800-277 482; www.tranzscenic.co.nz), which cuts through some spectacular scenery. Christchurch is also well served by inter-city coaches from other New Zealand destinations.

There are plenty of inner-city bus and taxi services, but to experience a taste of old-world charm, take one of Christchurch's historic trams. The trams do a circuit from Worcester Street, past the Arts Centre, museum and Christ's College, and you can hop off and on at any of the stops along the way, making this ideal for sightseeing (tel: 03-366 7830; www.tram.co.nz).

There is a dedicated shuttle service to Hanmer Springs, which leaves the Christchurch Information Service at 9am every day and arrives in Hanmer Springs 2 hours later. Contact: **Hanmer Connection**, tel: 0800-242 663.

Reliable taxi companies operating in the Christchurch region are **Blue Star Taxis**, tel: 03-3799 799, or **Gold Band Taxis**, tel: 03-379 5795.

The West Coast
If you drive, access is either through the Buller Gorge from Nelson, through

the Lewis Pass via historic Reefton, over the high Alpine Arthur's Pass from Christchurch or via Haast Pass from Queenstown. Driving time is about 3–5 hours.

There are airports at Hokitika and Westport, with regular scheduled services. A scenic alternative is to take the **TranzAlpine** train through the Southern Alps from Christchurch to Greymouth, or vice versa *(see page 321 for details)*. The west coast is also well served by **InterCity Coachlines**.

Queenstown and Otago

Queenstown

Air New Zealand has regular flights to Queenstown, and you can reach it direct from main centres such as Wellington, Christchurch and Auckland. Daily flights also operate to and from Sydney, Australia and Brisbane. There are daily coach and shuttle services to and from Christchurch, Mount Cook, Dunedin, Te Anau, Wanaka, Franz Josef and Milford Sound.

In Queenstown, you can reach most places by walking or taking a short taxi ride. You'll need to hire a car to get out and really see the countryside, and there are plenty of car-hire companies in Queenstown. Getting to and from Arrowtown is also easy, with a regular coach service.

Wanaka

Wanaka is about an hour's drive north of Queenstown. Alternatively, you can take a shuttle service or inter-city bus. There are also scenic flights – the one from Queenstown to Wanaka takes approximately 20 minutes.

Dunedin and Surroundings

Dunedin

Dunedin has an international airport with direct flights on **Freedom Air** (www.freedomair.com) from Australia's Gold Coast, Sydney, Melbourne and Brisbane, as well as Auckland, Wellington, Christchurch and Rotorua. Airport shuttles to the city cost from NZ$25–32 per person and taxis at NZ$60 are also available. The airport is about half an hour south of the city. You can also drive, catch a train or take a bus from anywhere around the country. Driving from Dunedin to Christchurch takes about 5 hours, while the journey from Queenstown is about 4½ hours.

Dunedin, like Queenstown, is easily covered on foot or by taxi: **Dunedin Taxis**, tel: 03-477 7777; www.dunedintaxis.co.nz. There are also regular city bus services. For all shuttle, rail, coach and domestic flight bookings, go to the **Dunedin Railway Station** in Lower Stuart Street, tel: 03-477 4449, extension 811.

Southland

Invercargill

Invercargill Airport is a 5-minute drive west of the city centre and is serviced by **Air New Zealand** flights. Coach services also connect Invercargill with other points in New Zealand.

Te Anau

Te Anau is about a 3-hour drive south of Queenstown, with shuttle services and inter-city buses between the two towns. **Top Line Tours** in Te Anau (tel: 03-249 8059) travel from Te Anau to Queenstown every day, and there's a 45-minute flight from Queenstown.

Stewart Island

Real Journeys' **Stewart Island Express Ferry Service** (tel: 0800-000 511; www.realjourneys.co.nz) operates daily between Bluff (departs from Bluff Visitor Terminal, Foreshore Road) and Stewart Island (departs from Stewart Island Visitor Terminal, Main Wharf).

The ferry company also runs a **Coach Connections** service to the ferry from Invercargill (pick-up and drop-off at the airport and **i-site** Visitors Centre), Queenstown and Te Anau (pick-up and drop-off at Real Journeys Visitors Centres in both cities).

Stewart Island Flights also fly directly from Invercargill Airport to Stewart Island, tel: 03-218 9129; www.stewartislandflights.com

Real Journeys' **Stewart Island Experience** (Stewart Island Visitor Terminal, Main Wharf, Halfmoon Bay, Oban, tel: 0800-000 511; www.realjourneys.co.nz) has cars, scooters and mountain bikes for hire. It also operates various tours and cruises, as do **Aurora Charters** (tel: 03-219 1126; www.auroracharters.co.nz), which have tours for fishing, sightseeing, bird-watching and nature walks. **Sails Ashore** (tel: 0800-783 9278; www.sailsashore.co.nz) offers an **SUV Scenic Road Tour** that explores virtually every road on the island, all 28km (17 miles), with an interesting commentary on the island's history.

Another good way to visit some of the major sites is by **water taxi**. Contact **Sails Ashore**, **Stewart Island Water Taxi & Eco-Guiding** (tel: 03-219 1394; www.sailsashore.co.nz) or **Sea Buzzz** (tel: 03-219 1282; www.seabuzzz.co.nz).

BELOW: Picton harbour.

A CCOMMODATION

HOTELS, YOUTH HOSTELS, BED AND BREAKFAST

Hotels and Motels

International-standard hotels are found in all large cities, in many provincial cities, and in all resort areas frequented by tourists. In smaller cities and towns, more modest hotels are the norm.

Motels are generally clean and comfortable, with facilities ideal for families. Many offer full kitchens and dining tables, and some provide breakfast.

The New Zealand tourism industry uses Qualmark as a classification and grading system to help you find the best accommodation, shopping and activities to suit your needs. There are five levels of grading from one star (minimum) to five stars (best available). Participation in the Qualmark system is voluntary, so if a motel or hotel doesn't have a grading, its location and tariffs will usually give a reliable indication of what to expect. Expect to pay surcharges for additional occupants and peak season.

Travel agents will be able to give details of concessions for children. (A guide is: children under two years of age, free; two to four, quarter of tariff; five to nine, half tariff. 10 years and over, full tariff.) Goods and Services Tax (GST) of 12.5 percent should be inclusive of the price you are quoted.

Farmstays, Homestays, Bed and Breakfasts (B&B)

More New Zealanders are opening their homes to visitors. There is a large number of B&B properties in cities, towns and rural locations, ranging from historic and heritage buildings to boutique inns.

ABOVE: The Langham Hotel Auckland.

Farmstays are an excellent way for visitors to see the real New Zealand, which has been dependent on farming since the colonial days. You may share the homestead with the farmer and his family, or, in many cases, have the use of a cottage on the farm. Depending on the farm, you may get the chance to share home-cooked meals with your hosts and join in activities like sheep shearing and fruit harvesting.

If you are on a limited budget, you can try working farmstays. Over 180 farms offer free accommodation, meals and friendly hospitality in exchange for 4 hours of light work a day, doing tasks such as gardening and feeding animals. It is also possible to work flexible hours so that you have time to explore the area. Contact visitor information centres, or check the websites listed below.

New Zealand Farmstays and Homestays: 10 Locarno Street, Opawa, Christchurch, tel: 03-960 4394; www.nzhomestay.co.nz.

Rural Holidays New Zealand, PO Box 2155, Christchurch 8140, tel: 03-355 6218; www.ruralholidays.co.nz.
Rural Tours NZ, PO Box 228, Cambridge, North Island, tel: 07-827 8055; www.ruraltourism.co.nz.

Hostels

The **Youth Hostel Association of New Zealand** offers an extensive chain of hostels to members throughout New Zealand. Details of membership and hostel locations can be obtained from its National Office at Level 1, 166 Moorhouse Avenue, PO Box 436, Christchurch, New Zealand, tel: 03-379 9970, 0800-278 299; www.yha.co.nz.

Motor Camps

Most motor camps (caravan parks with tent sites as well) offer communal washing, cooking and toilet facilities. Campers are required to supply their own trailer or tent, but camps in larger towns and cities have cabins available, ranging from tiny huts to Alpine-style cabins.

Motor camps are licensed under the Camping Ground Regulation (1936) and are all graded by the New Zealand Automobile Association. It is a good idea to check with the AA on current standards within the camps.

In summer, do book ahead, as New Zealanders are inveterate campers. For details, contact:

Automobile Association, Head Office, 99 Albert Street, Auckland, tel: 0800-500 543; www.aa.co.nz.

Top 10 Holiday Parks, 294 Montreal Street, Christchurch 8015, New Zealand, tel: 03-377 9900, 0800-867 836; www.topparks.co.nz.

NORTH ISLAND

AUCKLAND

Barrycourt Suites Hotel
10–20 Gladstone Road, Parnell
Tel: 09-303 3789
www.barrycourt.co.nz
Located 2km (1¼ mile) from the city, 1km (²/₃ mile) from the beach, this hotel offers rooms, motel units with kitchens and serviced apartments, many with grand harbour and sea views. Licensed restaurant, bar and café, and hot spa pools. 107 units and suites. **$–$$$$$**

The Great Ponsonby Bed and Breakfast
30 Ponsonby Terrace, Ponsonby
Tel: 09-376 5989, 0800-766 792
www.greatpons.co.nz
Located close to all the major attractions, this small hotel in a restored 1898 weatherboard villa offers a range of tastefully decorated rooms and studios, surrounded by New Zealand artworks. **$$$–$$$$$**

Heritage Auckland
35 Hobson Street
Tel: 09-379 8553
www.heritagehotels.co.nz
Located downtown near the America's Cup Village and transformed from a landmark building which used to house Auckland's most significant department store. Two distinctive wings

offer full services. The Tower Wing has an indoor lap pool, sauna, spa and gym, while the Hobson Street Wing (the old department store) has a rooftop pool, spa and gym. Other facilities include an all-weather tennis court, two restaurants and a bar. 467 rooms and suites. **$$$–$$$$$**

Hilton Auckland
147 Quay Street, Princes Wharf
Tel: 09-978 2000
www.hilton.com
One of Auckland's contemporary five-star properties, this boutique hotel occupies a prime position 300 metres/yds out to sea on Princes Wharf, commanding uninterrupted views of the harbour. 166 rooms and suites. **$$$$–$$$$$**

Hyatt Regency Auckland
Corner Waterloo Quadrant and Princes Street
Tel: 09-355 1234
www.auckland.regency.hyatt.com
The hotel has 385 rooms, many with stunning views of the harbour, city and parks. Guests have access to a luxury health and fitness spa. **$$$–$$$$$**

Langham Hotel Auckland
83 Symonds Street
Tel: 09-379 5132

www.langhamhotels.com
Situated in the heart of the city, the Langham offers five-star luxury in its 410 rooms. Featuring 24-hour service, butler service, an outdoor heated pool, rejuvenating spa, gym and business centre with high-speed broadband. **$$$–$$$$$**

New President Hotel
27–35 Victoria Street West
Tel: 09-303 1333
www.newpresidenthotel.co.nz
Comfortable air-conditioned rooms and standard studios, suites and apartments. Ideally situated between Sky City and Queen Street. **$$–$$$$**

Parnell Village Motor Lodge
2 St Stephens Avenue, Parnell
Tel: 09-377 1463
www.parnellmotorlodge.co.nz
Choose between elegant Edwardian rooms and modern apartments near Parnell shops. Five minutes from downtown Auckland. **$–$$$**

Ranfurly Evergreen Motel
285 Manukau Road, Epsom
Tel: 09-638 9059
www.ranfurlymotel.co.nz
Spacious self-contained units, sleeping up to five, located 500 metres/yds from restaurants and 1km (²/₃ mile) from the racecourse and showgrounds. On airport bus route. 12 units. **$$**

Rendezvous Hotel Auckland
Corner Vincent Street and Mayoral Drive
Tel: 09-366 3000
www.rendezvoushotels.com/auckland
Near the waterfront and within walking distance of the main commercial and entertainment area. The Rendezvous has 24-hour room service, shops, currency exchange and

some executive rooms. 452 rooms. **$$$$–$$$$$**

Sky City Grand Hotel
90 Federal Street
Tel: 09-363 7000, 0800-804 111
www.skycityauckland.co.nz
Located in the heart of the city adjacent to Sky City Hotel, this is one of Auckland's newest hotels, with 316 rooms, a spa, gym, indoor lap pool, club lounge and business centre. It also has two restaurants, most notably the highly acclaimed Dine by Peter Gordon (tel: 0800-759 2489), which serves superlative food with imagination and flair. **$$–$$$$$**

Sky City Hotel
Victoria Street
Tel: 09-363 6000, 0800-759 2489
www.skycityauckland.co.nz
Located in the Sky City complex, this hotel has luxury and premier suites, a heated rooftop pool and gym, restaurants and bars. Among its range of nightlife options are two on-site casinos. Free parking. 344 rooms. **$$$$$**

PRICE CATEGORIES

Price categories are for two people in a double room, including GST:
$ = below NZ$100
$$ = NZ$100–150
$$$ = NZ$150–200
$$$$ = NZ$200–250
$$$$$ = over NZ$250

BELOW: Auckland city view.

AUCKLAND'S SURROUNDINGS

Devonport

Devonport Motel
11 Buchanan Street
Tel: 09-445 1010
A historic building, close to all the main attractions, provides privacy, comfort and great value. 2 units. **$$**

Esplanade Hotel
1 Victoria Road
Tel: 09-445 1291
www.esplanadehotel.co.nz
Built in 1903, this lovingly restored luxury boutique hotel has it all – charm, ambience and friendly service. It's a 10-minute ferry ride from downtown Auckland. 17 suites.
$$$-$$$$$

Peace and Plenty Inn
6 Flagstaff Terrace
Tel: 09-445 2925
www.peaceandplenty.co.nz
Enjoy tranquillity and grandeur at this lovingly restored waterfront Victorian villa. Minutes by ferry from the CBD, its guest suites are spacious and ooze colonial charm, yet offer all modern conveniences including en suite bathrooms and wireless broadband. Highly recommended.
$$$-$$$$$

Great Barrier Island

Great Barrier Lodge
Whangaparapara, RD1
Tel: 09-429 0488
www.greatbarrierlodge.com
Modern studios and cottages in a waterfront setting. **$-$$**

Medlands Beach Backpackers
Masons Road
Tel: 09-429 0320
www.medlandsbeach.com
Comfortable family accommodation with great views. **$**

Tipi & Bob's Waterfront Lodge
38 Puriri Bay, Tryphena
Tel: 09-429 0550
www.waterfrontlodge.co.nz
Qualmark-rated lodge with spectacular sea views and right on the waterfront. Licensed restaurant and bar. **$$$-$$$$**

Kawau Island

The Beach House Resort
Vivienne Bay
Tel: 09-422 8850
www.kawauresort.co.nz
Email: beachhouse@paradise.co.nz
Comfortable accommodation located on a pristine beach ideal for swimming, kayaking, snorkelling and fishing.
$$$$$

Kawau Lodge
Tel: 09-422 8831
www.kawaulodge.co.nz
An island homestay set amid native bush, accessible only by water. Queen rooms with en suites, kayaks for guests' use, plus sailing and fishing options.
$$$-$$$$

Orewa

Anchor Lodge Motel
436 Hibiscus Coast Highway, Orewa
Tel: 09-427 0690
www.anchorlodge.co.nz
Next to the seafront and a safe swimming beach and close to shops and restaurants. **$-$$$**

Edgewater Motel
387 Main Road, Orewa Beach
Tel: 09-426 5260
www.edgewaterorewa.co.nz
One- and two-bedroom family units, plus a luxury beachfront honeymoon suite with spa bath.
$$-$$$

The Nautilus Apartments
9–13 Tamariki Avenue, Orewa
Tel: 09-427 0131
www.thenautilus.co.nz
Modern luxury apartments at Orewa Beach, North Auckland; all apartments have private balcony and spectacular elevated views. Shops and beach nearby.
$$$$$

South Auckland

Airport Goldstar Motel
255 Kirkbride Road, Mangere
Tel: 09-275 8199
www.airportgoldstar.co.nz
Airport-handy accommodation in a quiet setting. **$-$$$**

Cedar Park Motor Lodge
250 Great South Road, Manurewa
Tel: 09-266 3266
www.cedarparkmotorlodge.co.nz
Conveniently sited for the airport and other South Auckland attractions. **$-$$**

Jet Inn Airport Hotel
63 Westney Road, Mangere
Tel: 09-275 4100, 0800-538 466
www.jetinn.co.nz
Five minutes from the airport and 15km (9 miles) from downtown, this 131-room hotel has four room types to accommodate different needs. Courtesy shuttle. **$$-$$$$**

Waiheke Island

Beachside Lodge
48 Kiwi Street, Oneroa
Tel: 09-372 9884
www.beachsidelodge.co.nz
Self-contained apartments or bed and breakfast, situated near the beach with views of Blackpool Bay.
$$$-$$$$

Le Chalet Waiheke Apartments
14 Tawas Street, Little Oneroa
Tel/fax: 09-372 7510
www.waiheke.co.nz/lechalet
Self-contained luxury apartments with private decks and sea views. **$$$**

Waitakere City and West Coast Beaches

Auckland Waitakere Estate
573 Scenic Drive, Waiatarua
Tel: 09-814 9622
www.waitakereestate.co.nz
A private paradise surrounded by rainforest, perched at 244 metres (800ft) above sea level, yet within easy reach of the city centre. **$$$-$$$$**

Hobson Motor Inn
327 Hobsonville Road, Upper Harbour
Tel: 09-416 9068
www.hobson.co.nz
This inn has fully self-contained units, plus swimming pool, spa, sauna and mini-golf course. 29 units. **$$-$$$**

Karekare Beach Lodge
7 Karekare Road, Karekare Beach
Tel: 09-817 9987

www.karekarebeachlodge.co.nz
A secluded getaway opposite one of the coast's most beautiful beaches – the location for the movie *The Piano*, it makes ideal base for local walks.
$$$-$$$$$

Lincoln Court Motel
58 Lincoln Road, Henderson
Tel: 09-836 0326
www.lincolncourtmotel.co.nz
Ideally located for exploring the Waitakere Ranges and west-coast beaches. **$-$$**

Piha Lodge
117 Piha Road, Piha
Tel: 09-812 8595
www.pihalodge.co.nz
This small, award-winning facility has magnificent views of the sea and bush, plus pool, spa and games room. 2 units. **$$**

Vineyard Cottages
Old North Road, Waimauku
Tel: 0800-846 800
www.vineyardcottages.co.nz
Self-contained cottages set in an attractive vineyard and gardens. **$$$$$**

Warkworth Area

Bridgehouse Lodge
16 Elizabeth Street, Warkworth
Tel: 09-425 8351
www.bridgehouse.co.nz
Comfortable rooms, gaming room and the most stunningly appointed bar and restaurant. Overlooking the Mahurangi River. **$-$$**

Walton Park Motor Lodge
2 Walton Avenue, Warkworth
Tel: 09-425 8149
www.waltonpark.co.nz
Studio and family units, handy for the town centre and Kawau Island ferry.
$-$$

Bream Bay

Bream Bay Motel
67 Bream Bay Drive, Ruakaka
Tel: 09-432 7166
www.breambaymotel.co.nz
Located on a popular surf beach with friendly hosts. Walk straight out of your motel, across the grass and onto Ruakaka Beach. One-bedroom units or self contained studios.**$–$$**

Doubtless Bay

Acacia Lodge
Mill Bay Road, Mangonui
Tel: 09-406 0417
www.acacia.co.nz
A comfortable motel on the waterfront, with all rooms facing the sea. **$$**
Taipa Bay Resort
22 Taipa Point Road
Tel: 09-406 0656
www.taipabay.co.nz
A top-rated complex with its own beachfront café, pool and tennis court.
$$–$$$$$

Kerikeri

Kerikeri Homestead Motel
17 Homestead Road
Tel: 09-407 7063
www.kerikerihomesteadmotel.co.nz
In a tranquil area, with views of Kerikeri golf course, each boutique unit has cooking facilities and four have spa baths. Huge pool and outdoor spa. Close to a restaurant and bar. 12 units. **$$**
Ora Ora Resort
28 Landing Road
Tel: 09-407 3598
www.oraoraresort.co.nz
This upmarket resort promises a panoply of pampering options, and its Makai Restaurant serves fine organic food, wines and beer. **$$$$$**

Omapere/Opononi

Harbourside Bed and Breakfast – Omapere
Corner SH12 and Pioneers Walk, Omapere
Tel: 09-405 8246
Email: harboursidebnb@xtra.co.nz

This beachfront house, with great views of the sandhills, is an easy walk from restaurants and close to the Waipoua Forest and west-coast beaches. Two rooms, both with en suites and private decks. **$**
Copthorne Omapere
SH12, Omapere
Tel: 09-405 8737
www.omapere.co.nz
Restaurant, bar and wonderful rooms right on the harbour's edge. An extremely relaxing place to stay close to the Waipoua Forest, Opononi and all the delights of the peaceful Hokianga Harbour.
$$–$$$$

Paihia

Abel Tasman Lodge
Corner Marsden and Bayview roads
Tel: 09-402 7521
www.abeltasmanlodge.co.nz
Superior waterfront apartments plus family motel units. Just one minute's walk to Paihia wharf and town centre. 25 units. **$$–$$$**
Beachcomber Resort
1 Seaview Road
Tel: 09-402 7434, 0800-732 786
www.beachcomber-resort.co.nz
The Beachcomber is a splendid resort with a private beach for safe bathing, plus heated swimming pool, tennis courts and sauna. It also has an award-winning restaurant and bar, and is close to all town centre amenities and restaurants. 45 rooms. **$$–$$$$$**
Blue Pacific Quality Apartments
166 Marsden Road
Tel: 09-402 0011
www.bluepacific.co.nz
Just minutes from Paihia township, these high-quality one- to three-bedroom apartments have breathtaking views of the Bay of Islands. Each has a full kitchen plus a private balcony or courtyard. 11 units and 1 studio. **$$$–$$$$$**

Edgewater Apartments
8–10 Marsden Road
Tel: 09-402 0090
www.edgewaterapartments.co.nz
Pleasant beachfront location with saltwater lap pool. A range of apartments to choose from, all with a sea view. It's a short, flat walk to the shops, wharf and water activities.
$$–$$$$$
Paihia Beach Resort and Spa
116 Marsden Road
Tel: 09-402 0111
www.paihiabeach.co.nz
Panoramic sea views from its suites and studios, which have private patios, spa baths, and kitchen and dining facilities. Spa and heated seasonal swimming pool. **$$$$$**

Russell

Commodore's Lodge Motel
The Waterfront
Tel: 09-403 7899
www.commodoreslodgemotel.co.nz
These spacious and luxurious self-contained studio apartments open onto a subtropical garden on the waterfront. There's a solar-heated pool, a children's pool, spa and barbecue. 11 units.
$$–$$$$$
The Duke of Marlborough Hotel
Waterfront
Tel: 09-403 7829
www.theduke.co.nz
"The Duke" holds New Zealand's oldest liquor licence and has been a haven of hospitality for over 150 years. An elegant refurbished hotel, it offers superb dining and well-equipped en suite rooms of various types, including a self-contained bungalow. It is situated right on the waterfront, next to the ferry terminal. 25 rooms.
$$$–$$$$$
Eagles Nest
60 Topeka Road
Tel: 09-403 8333
www.eaglesnest.co.nz
Luxury retreat with

self-contained villas, a spa, sauna and 20-metre (65ft) horizon-edge heated lap pools. The restaurant serves Pacific Rim cuisine, and the extensive cellar stocks some of the best local and French wines. Beautiful native bush walks lead to private beaches. **$$$$$**
Orongo Bay Homestead
Aucks Road, Orongo Bay
Tel: 09-403 7527
www.thehomestead.co.nz
Built in the 1860s and known as New Zealand's first American Consulate, this wonderfully luxurious place is set on 7 private hectares (17 acres) on the coast. Organic wines from the cellar, a vintage grand piano, spacious grounds and tremendous sea views are all part of the package. Rooms are equipped with super-king beds. Gourmet meals by arrangement.
$$$$$

Waipoua Forest

Waipoua Lodge
SH12, Waipoua Forest
Tel: 09-439 0422
www.waipoualodge.co.nz
Perched on a ridge overlooking the Waipoua Forest, this villa was built as a private home over a century ago. Now restored,

PRICE CATEGORIES

Price categories are for two people in a double room, including GST:
$ = below NZ$100
$$ = NZ$100–150
$$$ = NZ$150–200
$$$$ = NZ$200–250
$$$$$ = over NZ$250

ABOVE: Northland coastal scenery.

Central Court Motel
54 Otaika Road
Tel/fax: 09-438 4574
www.centralcourtmotel.co.nz
Close to Whangarei and next door to a restaurant. Finnish sauna and spa room available. 21 units. **$**

Pacific Rendezvous
73 Motel Road, Tutukaka
Tel: 09-434 3847
www.pacificrendezvous.co.nz
This resort overlooks Tutukaka Harbour, with accommodation ranging from one-bedroom chalets to three-bedroom suites. Two private beaches, *pétanque* and swimming pool. 30 units. **$$$–$$$$**

Settlers Hotel
61–69 Hatea Drive

it includes three pioneer-style, self-contained cottages with super-king and queen bedrooms, en suite bathrooms, lounge and kitchenette. There is a restaurant and bar on site. **$$$$$**

Tel: 09-438 2699
www.settlershotel.co.nz
In the city centre, overlooking the river, this quaint hotel has en suite rooms, a restaurant, spa pool and swimming pool. 53 rooms. **$–$$**

Kingfish Lodge
Whangaroa Harbour
Tel: 09-405 0164
www.kingfishlodge.co.nz
A premier sport-fishing resort with a fine seafood restaurant, this exclusive family-owned retreat is on the water's edge at the headland of Whangaroa Harbour in Kingfish Cove. Access is by cruise up the harbour. 12 rooms. **$$$$$**

THE WAIKATO

Anglesea Motel
36 Liverpool Street
Tel: 07-834 0010, 0800-426 453
www.angleseamotel.co.nz
A five-star hotel close to the city centre. Studio and one-bedroom units have modern facilities. Outdoor swimming pool, spa bath units and gym. **$$$–$$$$**

Barclay Motel
280 Ulster Street
Tel: 07-838 2475, 0800-808 090
www.barclay.co.nz
Luxury spa suites and family units and studios, 21 in all, set around a spacious courtyard dotted with colourful geraniums and potted palms. Solar-heated swimming pool, spa pool and children's playground. **$$–$$$**

Kingsgate Hotel Hamilton
100 Garnett Avenue
Tel: 07-849 0860
www.kingsgatehotels.co.nz
Good value city-centre hotel with 24-hour room service. 147 rooms. **$$**

Novotel Tainui Hamilton
7 Alma Street
Tel: 07-838 1366
www.accorhotels.co.nz
A four-star hotel on the banks of the Waikato River

in the Central Business District. Luxurious rooms, restaurant and bar, plus gym, spa and sauna. 177 rooms. **$$$**

Ventura Inn and Suites Hamilton
23 Clarence Street
Tel: 07-838 0110, 0800-283 688
www.venturainns.co.nz
Some rooms have king-size beds and spa baths. Central location. 50 rooms. **$$**

Southern Belle
101 Firth Street
Tel: 07-888 5518
www.southernbelle.co.nz
Popular B&B located in a classic, two-storey house built in 1936. Three rooms located on self-contained upper-storey guest wing. **$–$$**

Brooklands Country Estate
RD1, Ngaruawahia
Tel: 07-825 4756
www.brooklands.net.nz
This country retreat has a reputation for being one of the finest five-star lodges in New Zealand. Originally the

gracious homestead of a pioneer farming family, it retains beautiful decor, fine paintings and large open fireplaces. The there is the award-winning food, a tennis court and swimming pool. Sumptuous rooms overlook the garden. 10 rooms. **$$$$$**

Aroha Mountain Lodge
5 Boundary Street
Tel: 07-884 8134
www.arohamountainlodge.co.nz
Cosy lodgings in a picturesque villa. **$–$$$**

Villa Dale
13 Terminus Street
Tel: 07-884 4248
Bed and breakfast in a lovely old villa set in a beautiful garden. Guided garden rambles in the district also available. **$**

Rose Lodge
4 Rose Street
Tel: 07-883 1162
Email: jennysayers@xtra.co.nz
Provincial setting with friendly hosts. Once a Masonic Lodge, this historic building in the heartland of

rural Waikato offers two rooms, each with its own entranceway and shady, private veranda. Breakfast available. **$–$$**

Abseil Inn
709 Waitomo Caves Road, Waitomo Village
Tel: 07-878 7815
www.absailinn.co.nz
Comfortable bed and breakfast with nice views of the countryside. **$$–$$$**

Waitomo Caves Hotel
Lemon Point Road
Tel: 07-878 8204
www.waitomocaveshotel.co.nz
Victorian-style hotel, 19km (12 miles) from Te Kuiti and near the limestone caves. 37 rooms. **$–$$$**

COROMANDEL AND THE BAY OF PLENTY

Hahei

The Church Accommodation and Restaurant
87 Hahei Beach Road
Tel: 07-866 3533
www.thechurchhahei.co.nz
Eleven cosy cottages set in beautiful gardens. **$$**

Hahei Holiday and Cathedral Cove Villas
Harsant Avenue, Hahei Beach
Tel: 07-866 3889
www.cathedralcove.co.nz
Beachfront accommodation a short walk from Cathedral Cove. Rooms have sea or garden views. 16 units. **$–$$$$$**

Hot Water Beach Bed and Breakfast
48 Pye Place
Tel: 07-866 3991
www.hotwaterbedandbreakfast.co.nz
Award-winning bed and breakfast on Hot Water Beach, 6km (4 miles) south of Hahei. It's a short walk to the beach. **$$$$**

Pauanui

Pauanui Pines Motor Lodge
174 Vista Paku, Pauanui Beach
Tel: 07-864 8086
www.pauanuipines.co.nz
Next to a golf course, this award-winning motor lodge has one- and two-bedroom units in nine colonial-style cottages. All include a TV and kitchen, and there's a tennis court and heated swimming pool. 18 units. **$$$$**

Tauranga/Mount Maunganui

Accommodation at Te Puna
Corner Minden Road and
SH2, RD6, Tauranga
Tel: 07-552 5621
www.tepunalodge.co.nz
A comfortable motel with family-size units, some with spa baths. **$–$$**

Bay Palm Motel
84 Girven Road, Mount Maunganui
Tel: 07-574 5971
www.baypalmmotel.co.nz
Comfortable units with spa baths, close to shops and beach. Heated swimming pool. 16 units. **$–$$$**

Best Western Summit Motor Lodge
213 Waihi Road, Tauranga
Tel: 07-578 1181
www.summitmotorlodge.co.nz
With quiet, private and spacious self-contained units, sleeping up to six. Close to the city, Mount Maunganui, the surf and shops. There's a spa pool, a games room and laundry facilities. 25 units. **$$**

Oceanside Twin Towers Resort
1 Maunganui Road, Mount Maunganui
Tel: 07-575 5371, 0800-466 868
www.oceanside.co.nz
A premier resort with motel and apartment accommodation. The motel rooms are spacious and feature en suite bathrooms and kitchenettes. The complex also has hot pools, gym and sauna and is close to shops, restaurants and the beach. The apartments, with en suite baths and full kitchens, have impressive views. Minimum two-night stay required in the apartments. **$$$–$$$$$**

The Terraces
346 Ocean Beach Road, Mount Maunganui
Tel: 07-575 6494
www.terraces-oceanbeach.co.nz
Spacious three-level apartments with full kitchen, laundry and balcony. **$$$**

Tairua

Pacific Harbour Lodge
223 Main Road, Tairua Beach
Tel: 07-864 8581
www.pacificharbour.co.nz
Thirty-one Island-style lodges, set amidst tropical vegetation with shell-covered pathways to the chalets, beach and award-winning restaurant. Spacious units. **$$–$$$$$**

Thames

Rapaura Watergardens
586 Tapu–Coroglen Road
Tel: 07-868 4821
www.rapaurawatergardens.co.nz
The accommodation here is located at a sightseeing attraction – water gardens with gentle walks, abundant native flora, lily ponds, bridges, streams, waterfall and sculptures of *ponga* (native fern). **$$–$$$$**

Tuscany on Thames
SH25, Jellicoe Crescent
Tel: 07-868 5099
www.tuscanyonthames.co.nz
Italian-style motel nestled between beautiful coast and bush-covered hills. It has modern facilities, including large en suite bathrooms. 14 units. **$$–$$$**

Whangamata

Breakers Motel
324 Hetherington Road
Tel: 07-865 8464
www.breakersmotel.co.nz
Tucked away in a reserve bordering the estuary, this attractive motel building resembles a wave. The units all overlook a swimming-pool complex with a water-fall and large barbecue area, and include a private deck with spa pool. 21 suites. **$$–$$$$**

Cabana Motel
101–103 Beach Road
Tel: 07-865 8772
The only motel on the water's edge, with fully self-contained units, close to excellent fishing, swimming and other outdoor activities. 9 units. **$–$$**

Whitianga

Kuaotunu Bay Lodge
SH25, Kuaotunu
Tel: 07-866 4396
www.kuaotunubay.co.nz
An elegant beach house, 18km (11 miles) north of Whitianga, with beach access and a private deck with panoramic views of the peninsula. It's a great winter getaway, with open-fire, underfloor heating and en suite bathrooms. 3 rooms. **$$$**

Mercury Bay Beachfront Resort
111–113 Buffalo Beach Road
Tel: 07-866 5637
www.beachfrontresort.co.nz
This has one to three bedrooms, and its full range of facilities includes a heated spa pool and barbecue site. 8 units. **$$$$**

Waterfront Motel
2 Buffalo Beach Road
Tel: 07-866 4498
www.waterfrontmotel.co.nz
Overlooking Buffalo Beach with magnificent sea views, the apartments and suites are all self-contained, with private balconies and spa baths. **$$$–$$$$$**

BELOW: Coromandel vista.

PRICE CATEGORIES

Price categories are for two people in a double room, including GST:
$ = below NZ$100
$$ = NZ$100–150
$$$ = NZ$150–200
$$$$ = NZ$200–250
$$$$$ = over NZ$250

TRANSPORT

ACCOMMODATION

EATING OUT

ACTIVITIES

A – Z

ROTORUA AND THE VOLCANIC PLATEAU

National Park

Adventure Lodge and Motel
Carroll Street, National Park Village
Tel: 07-892 2991
www.adventurenationalpark.co.nz
Studio motel units, standard lodge rooms and budget bunk beds. Transport to the ski slopes can be arranged. **$–$$**

Ski Haus
Carroll Street, National Park Village
Tel: 07-892 2854
www.skihaus.co.nz
Basic double, bunk and family rooms, and campervan sites. Bar and spa pool. **$**

Ohakune

Alpine Motel and Sassi's Bistro
7 Miro Street
Tel: 06-385 8758
www.alpinemotel.co.nz
In the town centre, this motel offers quality studios, family units and spacious chalets, most with cooking facilities. Casual dining at its Sassi's Bistro. **$–$$$$**

Hobbit Motor Lodge and Restaurant
Corner Goldfinch and Wye streets
Tel: 06-385 8248, 0800-843 462
www.the-hobbit.co.nz
Beds are normal size, despite the lodge's name, and accommodation includes family units and studio apartments. Also has a licensed restaurant and bar open every evening except Sun. **$–$$$**

Powderhorn Château
Bottom of Mountain Road
Tel: 06-385 8888
www.powderhorn.co.nz
The Château, 20 minutes' drive from Turoa ski area, combines the ambience of a traditional European ski chalet with the luxury of a hotel. Rooms include the Mansion, a luxury apartment which can sleep up to eight adults. Dine at the downstairs restaurant, soak in the hot pool, or enjoy a drink around the log fire in the main bar, the

Powderkeg. The Powderhorn ski and board shop is next door. 30 rooms. **$$$$**

Tussock Grove
3 Karo Street
Tel: 06-385 8771
www.tussockgrove.co.nz
Boutique hotel in park-like setting with a restaurant and a bar. Lounge with log fire, sauna, spa, drying room and adjacent tennis court. **$$–$$$$**

Rotorua

Acapulco Motel
Corner Malfroy Road and Eason Street
Tel: 07-347 9569, 0800-100 069
Email: acapulco@xtra.co.nz
Quiet location near city centre, just a short walk from restaurants and shops. 15 rooms. **$**

Birchwood Spa Motel
6 Sala Street
Tel: 07-347 1800, 0800-881 800
www.birchwoodspamotel.co.nz
Close to the thermal reserve and golf course, these luxury units all have a spa bath or spa pool. 17 units. **$$–$$$**

Duxton Hotel Okawa Bay
Mourea, Lake Rotoiti
Tel: 07-362 4599
www.duxtonhotels.com
Award-winning resort on the shores of Lake Rotoiti, with trout fishing and hot pools trips. 44 rooms. **$$$–$$$$$**

Kingsgate Hotel Rotorua
Fenton Street
Tel: 07-348 0199, 0800-808 228
www.kingsgatehotels.co.nz
This hotel is adjacent to the racecourse, sports ground and golf courses. 136 rooms. **$$**

Lake Plaza Rotorua Hotel
1000 Eruera Street
Tel: 07-348 1174
www.lakeplazahotel.co.nz
Opposite the Polynesian Pools, with superb views of the lake and thermal areas, this hotel is also close to the city centre. Golf packages available. 250 rooms. **$$**

Millennium Rotorua
Corner Eruera and Hinemaru streets
Tel: 07-347 1234, 0800-645 685

www.millenniumrotorua.co.nz
Ask for a room overlooking the Polynesian Pools and Lake Rotorua. You get a great view from the balcony. Friendly staff, and facilities include a gym and pool. **$$$**

The Princes Gate Hotel
1057 Arawa Street
Tel: 07-348 1179, 0800-500 705
www.princesgate.co.nz
Built in 1897 and recently refurbished, this boutique accommodation comes complete with spas, sauna, heated pool, gym and tennis court. **$$–$$$$$**

Silver Fern Motor Inn
326 Fenton Street
Tel: 07-346 3849, 0800-118 808
www.silverfernmotorinn.co.nz
A touch of California in this city-centre motor inn. Executive suites have spa pools and other modern facilities. 20 suites. **$$**

Solitaire Lodge
Lake Tarawera, RD5
Tel: 07-362 8208, 0800-765 482
www.solitairelodge.com
Luxury accommodation in a stunning lake-edge location with superb views. Suites have timber cathedral ceilings, large beds, private deck and spacious bathroom. Open fire in the main lounge. 10 suites. **$$$$$**

Westminster Lodge
58A Mountain Road
Tel: 07-348 4273, 0800-937 864
www.westminsterlodge.co.nz
Nestled on the slopes of Mount Ngongotaha but away from the sulphur smells, yet only five minutes from the city centre. Friendly hosts Barry and Gill Gillette offer superb hospitality and delicious Continental breakfasts. Five bedrooms, three en suite units, plus a two-bedroom self-catering cottage. **$**

Wylie Court Motor Lodge
345 Fenton Street
Tel: 07-347 7879, 0800-100 879
www.wyliecourt.co.nz
Resort-style complex, with private heated pools, in park-like grounds. Modern facilities include a large heated swimming pool. 36 rooms. **$$–$$$**

Taupo

Bayview Wairakei Resort
SH1
Tel: 07-374 8021, 0800-737 678
www.wairakei.co.nz
In the heart of the Wairakei Thermal Valley, this resort is located just 9km (6 miles) north of central Taupo. There is a sauna, gym, six large spa pools and two swimming pools. More than 180 rooms and villas. **$$–$$$$**

Baywater Motor Inn
126 Lake Terrace
Tel: 07-378 9933, 0800-926 822
www.baywater.co.nz
Magnificent lake and mountain views from this motel 1km (2/3 mile) from the town centre. Self-contained units have a large in-room spa bath and balcony or patio. 12 units. **$$**

Boulevard Waters Motor Lodge
215 Lake Terrace
Tel: 07-377 3395
www.boulevardwaters.co.nz
Lake-edge motel with luxury features, such as in-room spas, king-size beds, underfloor heating and thermal pool. 10 suites. **$$–$$$**

The Cove
213 Lake Terrace
Tel: 07-378 7599
Luxury boutique hotel

PRICE CATEGORIES

Price categories are for two people in a double room, including GST:
$ = below NZ$100
$$ = NZ$100–150
$$$ = NZ$150–200
$$$$ = NZ$200–250
$$$$$ = over NZ$250

TRANSPORT

situated on the lake shore, 3km (2 miles) from the edge of town. There are lake views, as well as a restaurant with an extensive menu and a comprehensive wine list. **$$–$$$$$**

Gables Motor Lodge
130 Lake Terrace
Tel: 07-378 8030
www.gablesmotorlodge.com

Opposite Taupo's main swimming pool, with lake and mountain views. 12 one-bedroom suites, each with a private spa pool. **$$**

Whakapapa Village

Château Tongariro
Whakapapa Village, Tongariro National Park

Tel: 07-892 3809
www.chateau.co.nz
Completed in 1929, this is one of New Zealand's few hotels located in the middle of a World Heritage park. Known as "the grand old lady of the mountain", it is renowned for its grandeur, and offers a range of rooms. **$$$–$$$$**

Skotel Alpine Resort
Whakapapa Village, Tongariro National Park
Tel: 07-892 3719
www.skotel.co.nz
Located at the edge of the village, this resort has accommodation ranging from deluxe rooms to straightforward cabins and chalets. **$–$$$**

POVERTY BAY AND HAWKE'S BAY

Gisborne

Alfresco Motor Lodge
784 Gladstone Road
Tel: 06-863 2464, 0800-222 550
www.alfrescolodge.co.nz
Located close to the airport and golf courses. Comfortable ground-floor units, some with spa baths, all with cooking facilities. 14 units. **$–$$$**

Champers Motor Lodge
811 Gladstone Road
Tel: 06-863 1515, 0800-702 000
www.champers.co.nz
Modern complex, close to the city centre and airport, with luxurious ground-floor units and studios, some with double spa baths. Heated outdoor pool in landscaped grounds. 14 units. **$–$$**

Ocean Beach Motor Lodge and Sandbar Restaurant
Wainui Beach
Tel: 06-868 6186, 0800-250 800
www.oceanbeach.co.nz
Mediterranean-style luxury motor lodge, located at Wainui Beach. One- and two-bedroom apartments with spacious private

courtyards and designer kitchens. **$$–$$$**

The Quarters
Te Au Farm, Nuhaka, Mahia
Tel: 06-837 5751
www.quarters.co.nz
Modern and stylish holiday cottage with ocean views. Complimentary home-made bread and cheese on arrival. The surroundings are great for scenic walks, bush tramping, swimming, hunting and surfing. **$$$–$$$$**

Hastings

Black Barn
Black Barn Road, RD2
Tel: 06-877 7985
www.blackbarn.co.nz
Beautiful rural vistas from cottages located on a vineyard. Range of accommodation available. **$$$–$$$$$**

Omahu Motor Lodge
357 Omahu Road
Tel: 06-870 7061, 0800-166 248
www.omahumotorlodge.co.nz
Quality air-conditioned units opposite Hawke's Bay Hospital. **$$–$$$**

Napier

Bella Tuscany On Kennedy
371–373 Kennedy Road
Tel: 06-843 9129
www.bellatuscany.co.nz
The Bella Tuscany offers architecturally stunning Mediterranean-style accommodation, with spa bath suites, private courtyards and tasteful furnishings. **$$–$$$$**

The County Hotel
12 Browning Street
Tel: 06-835 7800
www.countyhotel.co.nz
Luxurious Edwardian Art Deco building in a central location. Its restaurant, Chambers, serves award-winning international cuisine. **$$$$**

Deco City Motor Lodge
308 Kennedy Road
Tel: 06-843 4342
www.decocity.co.nz
Provides mid-range accommodation in lovely Art Deco-style buildings. **$$–$$$**

McHardy Lodge
11 Bracken Street

Tel: 06-835 0605
www.mchardylodge.com
With fabulous food, this is possibly the only former maternity home providing visitor accommodation in the country. **$$$$$**

Te Urewera National Park

As well as the motor camp beside Lake Waikaremoana, there are numerous Department of Conservation (DOC) huts dotted around the park. For bookings, contact the Aniwaniwa Visitors Centre.

ACCOMMODATION

EATING OUT

ACTIVITIES

TARANAKI, WANGANUI AND MANAWATU

Hawera

Tairoa Lodge
3 Puawai Street
Tel: 06-278 8603
www.tairoalodge.co.nz
Set on 4 hectares (10 acres) of established gardens with mature rhododendron, magnolia, copper beech and kauri trees, Tairoa Lodge is one of Hawera's oldest residences. Built in 1875

from Northland kauri, it has been restored to its former elegance. A relaxing place to stay. **$$–$$$$**

New Plymouth

93 By the Sea
93 Buller Street
Tel: 06-758 6555
www.93bythesea.co.nz
A cosy bed and breakfast on the coastal walkway, near

ocean and rivers. **$$–$$$**

Brougham Heights Motel
54 Brougham Street
Tel: 06-757 9954, 0800-107 008
www.broughamheights.co.nz
Executive and spa-bath units, plus business lounge and conference facilities. 34 suites. **$$–$$$**

Copthorne Hotel Grand Central New Plymouth
42 Powderham Street
Tel: 06-758 7495

A – Z

ABOVE: Mount Taranaki.

www.copthornenewplymouth.co.nz
Central hotel, with premier to executive rooms, most with spa bath, and a first-class café. 60 rooms and suites. **$$–$$$$**
Nice Hotel and Restaurant
71 Brougham Street
Tel: 06-758 6423
www.nicehotel.co.nz
Formerly a small hospital,

this hotel has individually styled bedrooms with contemporary art and designer bathrooms with double spa baths. Award-winning Table Restaurant. 7 luxury suites. **$$$**

Palmerston North

Ann Keith's Bed and Breakfast
123 Grey Street
Tel: 06-358 6928
www.grandmas-place.com
Comfortable accommodation in a 1920s villa, complete with period furniture and modern en suite facilities. Hearty breakfast inclusive. Children and pets welcome. Hosts Don and Liz also run the nearby motel units and Grandma's Place. **$–$$**
Chancellor Motor Lodge
131 Fitzherbert Avenue
Tel: 06-354 5903
www.chancellormotel.co.nz

Close to the city centre, this motel has comfortable units, with fully equipped kitchens and spa baths. 18 units. **$$**
Hotel Coachman
134–140 Fitzherbert Avenue
Tel: 06-356 5065
www.hotelcoachman.co.nz
Colonial-style boutique hotel with gym and pool, handy for all the town's amenities and attractions. **$$**
Rose City Motel
120–122 Fitzherbert Avenue
Tel: 06-356 5388
www.rosecitymotel.co.nz
Offers studio and mezzanine units, and one- to two-bedroom suites. Sauna, spa pool and squash court. Convenient location. **$$**

Wanganui

Kings Court Motel
60 Plymouth Street
Tel: 0800-221 222

www.kingscourtmotel.co.nz
Clean and tidy accommodation in a convenient central location. **$$**
Kingsgate Hotel The Avenue Wanganui
379 Victoria Avenue
Tel: 06-349 0044
www.theavenuewanganui.com
Offers an extensive range of accommodation, international cuisine at its award-winning 379 The Avenue Restaurant, and a swimming pool. Located a 10-minute walk from the central business area, arts and cultural centres and sports venues. **$$–$$$**
Rutland Arms Inn
48–52 Ridgway Street, Wanganui
Tel: 0800-788 526
www.rutland.arms.co.nz
Modern facilities are combined with sophisticated old-world surroundings, and a top-quality restaurant. **$$–$$$**

WELLINGTON AND SURROUNDINGS

Wellington

Apollo Lodge Motel
49 Majoribanks Street
Tel: 04-385 1849
www.apollo-lodge.co.nz
Motel units, executive suites and apartments for up to five people, close to the shopping centre and five minutes from Oriental Bay. 50 units. **$$**
Copthorne Hotel Oriental Bay
100 Oriental Parade
Tel: 04-385 0279
www.millenniumhotels.co.nz
Fine modern hotel overlooking the harbour and close to city centre. 117 rooms. **$$$–$$$$$**
Duxton Hotel Wellington
170 Wakefield Street
Tel: 04-473 3900
www.duxton.com
In a good mid-town location, near Michael Fowler Centre and the waterfront, business travellers favour this hotel. Burbury's restaurant on the top floor offers fine dining.
$$$–$$$$$

InterContinental Wellington
2 Grey Street
Tel: 04-472 2722
www.intercontinental.com/wellington
In an excellent waterfront location, this hotel is good for both business and leisure guests. It has a restaurant, bars and room service, fitness centre with a heated pool. 232 rooms and suites. **$$$$–$$$$$**
James Cook Hotel Grand Chancellor
147 The Terrace
Tel: 04-499 9500
www.grandhotelsinternational.com
Well-managed landmark hotel in a central location close to the shops. It was one of the first grand hotels in Wellington, but has kept up with the times.
$$$–$$$$$
Mercure Hotel Willis Street
355 Willis Street, Te Aro
Tel: 04-803 1000
www.accorhotels.co.nz
Modern hotel with indoor swimming pool, fitness suite, restaurant and bar. 84 rooms. **$$–$$$**

Novotel Capital Wellington
133–137 The Terrace
Tel: 04-918 1900
www.novotel.co.nz
Modern hotel in the centre of the CBD, near Lambton Quay, with swimming pool. **$$–$$$$$**
Tinakori Lodge Bed and Breakfast
182 Tinakori Road, Thorndon
Tel: 04-939 3478
www.tinakorilodge.co.nz
Hosts Neville and Linda see to your every need in the comfort of their historic guesthouse situated close to Wellington's inner city. Quality facilities and restful atmosphere with a conservatory lounge overlooking native bush-clad hills. Within easy walking distance of Wellington's main attractions. **$–$$$**
Victoria Court Motor Lodge
201 Victoria Street
Tel: 04-472 4297
www.victoriacourt.co.nz
Located near the city centre, the pleasant units and off-street parking make this a

good option. From here it is only a short stroll to the eateries of Cuba Street and the shopping facilities of Manners Mall. **$$–$$$**

Outside Wellington

Parehua Country Estate
New York Street, Martinborough
Tel: 06-306 8405
www.parehua.co.nz
Twenty-eight modern villas and cottages located at the edge of Martinborough's wine district in landscaped grounds overlooking farmland and distant mountains. **$$$$**

SOUTH ISLAND

NELSON AND MARLBOROUGH

Blenheim

Criterion Hotel
2 Market Street
Tel: 03-578 3299
Handy for the centre of
town, with a good restaurant
and comfortable bars. **$**

Marlborough Hotel
20 Nelson Street
Tel: 03-577 7333
www.marlboroughhotel.co.nz
Classy, contemporary hotel
with a very good restaurant.
$$–$$$$$

Swansdown Cottage
Riverina Riverlands, RD4
Tel: 03-578 9824
www.swansdown.co.nz
Experience New Zealand
farm life in the seclusion and
tranquillity of your own
private self-contained
bed-and-breakfast
accommodation. **$$$–$$$$**

Uno Piu
75 Murphys Rd
Tel: 03-578 2235
www.unopiu.co.nz
Boutique accommodation
set on 1.6 hectares (4 acres)
of established gardens. Two
modern guest suites with
en suite bathrooms and
self-contained cottage. Ten-
metre (33ft) pool, cobbled
patio. Charming hosts.
$$$–$$$$

Nelson

Beachside Villas Hotel
71 Golf Road
Tel: 03-548 5041
www.beachsidevillas.co.nz
A Mediterranean-style
boutique motel in a
beautiful garden setting,
offering luxurious self-
contained apartments. The
cast and crew of *The Lord of
the Rings* stayed here while
filming in the Nelson region.
6 units. **$$–$$$**

Bella Vista Motel
178 Tahunanui Drive
Tel: 03-548 6948
www.bellavistamotels.co.nz
A bit of a walk from the city
centre (30 minutes), but
close to a beautiful beach

and the harbour entrance.
Good cafés and shops
nearby. One unit has a spa
bath, while two rooms are
wheelchair-accessible.
18 units. **$$–$$$**

**DeLorenzo's Studio
Apartments**
43–55 Trafalgar Street
Tel: 03-548 9774
www.delorenzos.co.nz
These luxury apartments,
close to business and shop-
ping areas, are furnished in
a modern style and have
super-king beds, en suite
bathrooms, spa baths and
Sky TV. **$$–$$$$$**

Kimi Ora Spa Resort
Kaiteriteri
Tel: 0508-546 4672
www.kimiora.com
Swiss-style chalet
apartments with sea views.
The resort has a health
complex with an extensive
range of spa treatments,
heated indoor and outdoor
pools, sauna, steam room,
spa pool, tennis courts and
fully licensed vegetarian
restaurant with panoramic
ocean views. 20 units.
$$–$$$$$

**Tuscany Gardens
Motor Lodge**
80 Tahunanui Drive
Tel: 03-548 5522
www.tuscanygardens.co.nz
Studio one- and two-
bedroom family units have
full kitchens, but it's only a
five-minute walk to local
eateries (and the beach).
12 units. **$$–$$$**

Wairepo House
22 Weka Road, Mariri
Tel: 03-526 6865
www.wairepohouse.co.nz
A three-storey colonial
homestead with rich native
timbers, chapel ceilings and
sunny decks, set in an apple-
and-pear orchard. **$$$$$**

Picton and the Sounds

Bay of Many Coves Resort
Queen Charlotte Sound
Tel: 03-579 9771, 0800-579 9771

www.bayofmanycovesresort.co.nz
In the heart of the
Marlborough Sounds, this
is a quiet and attractive
holiday retreat with a
swimming pool, hot tub
and massage spa therapy.
Kayaks and dinghies are
available free of charge,
as are wilderness tours
within the bay to see
shag colonies, seals
and dolphins. 11 self-
contained apartments and
great food. **$$$$–$$$$$**

Furneaux Lodge
Endeavour Inlet
Tel: 03-579 8259
www.furneaux.co.nz
This exclusive bush retreat
and eco-resort in the heart
of the Marlborough Sounds
offers a range of luxury
suites, self-catering cabins
and backpacker hostels.
Facilities include a
restaurant-bar. All scuba-
diving requirements are
supplied. Good fishing off
the wharf. From here you
can embark on the Queen
Charlotte hike.
$$$–$$$$$

Harbour View Motel
30 Waikawa Road, Picton
Tel: 03-573 6259
www.harbourviewpicton.co.nz
Twelve tastefully furnished
studios with great harbour
views. **$$–$$$**

Portage Resort
Kenepuru Sound
Tel: 03-573 4309
www.portage.co.nz
A famous resort in the
beautiful Marlborough
Sounds. Facilities include
swimming pool, spa, leisure
activities and the superb
Portage Restaurant. Kayaks
can be rented. Hillside and
garden rooms, bunk rooms
and lodges available.
$$–$$$$$

Punga Cove Resort
Endeavour Inlet
Tel: 03-579 8561
www.pungacove.co.nz
Chalets are nestled in the
bush, with superb views of
the surrounding bay. Each

has an en suite bathroom,
modern facilities, a sun
deck and barbecue (on
request). The Punga Lodge
sleeps 10 people, while the
studio chalets can accom-
modate two to three. It has
a private beach, with good
swimming and excellent
fishing. **$$–$$$**

Raetihi Lodge
Kenepuru Sound
Tel: 03-573 4300
www.raetihi.co.nz
Luxury lodge with 14 theme
rooms, all with en suites and
elegant furnishings. Large
guest lounge, licensed bar,
restaurant, games room and
plenty of outdoor activities.
$$–$$$$

Sennen House
Oxford Street, Picton
Tel: 03-573 5216
www.sennenhouse.co.nz
Set on a quiet street away
from the wharf area but
within easy walking distance,
this historic B&B and self-
catering apartments is
housed inside a historic
colonial villa built in 1886.
Each apartment within the
home is beautifully restored
and offers a private lounge
and full kitchen facilities.
$$$$$

PRICE CATEGORIES

Price categories are for two
people in a double room,
including GST:
$ = below NZ$100
$$ = NZ$100–150
$$$ = NZ$150–200
$$$$ = NZ$200–250
$$$$$ = over NZ$250

TRANSPORT

ACCOMMODATION

EATING OUT

ACTIVITIES

A – Z

CHRISTCHURCH AND SURROUNDINGS

Akaroa

Akaroa Criterion Motel
75 Rue Jolie
Tel: 03-304 7775, 0800-252 762
www.holidayakaroa.co.nz
Twelve luxury studio units
and a penthouse apartment,
all with harbour views.
$$–$$$$$

Akaroa Waterfront Motel
56–64 Rue Jolie
Tel: 03-304 7292
www.akaroawaterfront.co.nz
Family-size accommodation
on the seafront; within
walking distance of shops
and restaurants. **$$–$$$**

Christchurch

Admiral Motel
168 Bealey Avenue
Tel: 03-379 3554
www.admiralmotel.co.nz
Near Cathedral Square and
the Town Hall, this motel
has units sleeping up to six
people. 9 units. **$–$$**

**Airport Gateway
Motor Lodge**
45 Roydvale Avenue, Burnside
Tel: 03-358 7093
www.airportgateway.co.nz
Free stretch-limo airport
transfers. Larger units sleep
up to six people per unit. 40
studios. **$$–$$$$$**

Ashleigh Court Motel
47 Matai Street West,
Lower Riccarton
Tel: 03-348 1888
www.ashleighcourtmotel.co.nz
A short walk from the
museum, shopping centre
and gardens, units have

kitchen facilities and en
suite bathrooms. **$–$$$**

Belmont Motor Inn
172 Bealey Avenue
Tel: 03-379 4037
www.belmontmotorinn.co.nz
This conveniently located
motor inn is only 10
minutes from the city centre
and has one- and two-
bedroom units. **$–$$$**

The Charlotte Jane
110 Papanui Road
Tel: 03-355 1028
www.charlotte-jane.co.nz
Located near Merivale
Village, this charming
boutique property is only a
20-minute walk to the city.
Converted from an old
Victorian school for girls and
named after one of the first
four ships that brought
Christchurch's founding
fathers to its shores, its 12
spacious en suite rooms are
tastefully furnished and
come with a gourmet
breakfast each morning and
a glass of sherry or wine in
the evenings. **$$$$$**

Christchurch YMCA
12 Hereford Street
Tel: 03-365 0502
www.ymcachch.org.nz
Quality accommodation for
all budgets, located next to
the Arts Centre and just
opposite the Botanic
Gardens and museum.
$–$$$

Country Glen Lodge
107 Bealey Avenue
Tel: 03-365 9980, 0800-229 980
www.glenlodge.com
Luxurious apartments close

to the city centre. Extensive
facilities including luxury
spa bath units. **$$–$$$**

**Crowne Plaza Hotel
Christchurch**
Corner Kilmore and Durham
streets
Tel: 03-365 7799
www.crowneplaza.com
Magnificent location on
Victoria Square in the city
centre, connected to town
hall and convention centre.
Immaculate rooms,
spacious corridors and top-
class amenities. 298 rooms.
$$$–$$$$

The George Hotel
50 Park Terrace
Tel: 03-379 4560
www.thegeorge.com
A low-rise luxury hotel on a
great site across the road
from the Avon River and
Hagley Park. Nice willow-
shaded rooms with
balconies. Ten-minute walk
to the city centre. Top-rated
fine-dining restaurant. **$$$$**

Gothic Heights Motel
430 Hagley Avenue
Tel: 03-366 0838
www.gothicheightsmotel.co.nz
Opposite Hagley Park, within
walking distance of the
museum, the Arts Centre,
restaurants and botanical
gardens. 15 studio and
family units. **$$**

Holiday Inn City Centre
Corner Cashel and High streets
Tel: 03-365 8888
www.holidayinn.co.nz
In a central location, close
to retail and business
districts, this hotel has its
own restaurant and bar. 146
rooms and 3 apartments.
$$–$$$$$

Hotel Grand Chancellor
161 Cashel Street
Tel: 03-379 2999
www.ghihotels.com
Excellent location in central
Christchurch, only a short
walk from Cathedral Square.
Comfortable rooms and
prompt service. **$$$**

**Latimer Hotel and
Apartments**
30 Latimer Square
Tel: 03-379 6760
www.latimerhotel.co.nz
Low-rise travellers' lodge
close to the city centre, with

good-value rooms and off-
street parking. Locally
owned and operated, it has
a distinct Kiwi flavour of
service. There is a popular
restaurant located on site
with a wide-ranging menu.
$$–$$$$$

**Millennium Hotel
Christchurch**
14 Cathedral Square
Tel: 03-365 1111, 0800-645 536
www.millenniumchristchurch.co.nz
Modern, city-centre hotel
with restaurant, bar,
gymnasium, sauna and
business centre. 179
rooms. **$$$–$$$$$**

**Scenic Circle
Cotswold Hotel**
88–96 Papanui Road
Tel: 03-355 3535
www.scenic-circle.co.nz
Modern comforts are
combined with old-world
charm and authentic period
furnishings at this hotel,
just five minutes from the
city. Nearby restaurant
offers Continental cuisine.
99 rooms and suites.
$$–$$$$

**Windsor Hotel Bed and
Breakfast**
52 Armagh Street
Tel: 03-366 1503
www.windsorhotel.co.nz
Family-run traditional bed
and breakfast in a centrally
located, attractive colonial-
style accommodation. **$$**

PRICE CATEGORIES

Price categories are for two
people in a double room,
including GST:
$ = below NZ$100
$$ = NZ$100–150
$$$ = NZ$150–200
$$$$ = NZ$200–250
$$$$$ = over NZ$250

BELOW: Hagley Park.

CANTERBURY

Aoraki Mount Cook National Park

Aoraki Mount Cook Alpine Lodge
Aoraki Mount Cook Village
Tel: 03-435 1860
www.aorakialpinelodge.co.nz
Located in the heart of Aoraki Mount Cook National Park. Quality, self-catering accommodation for the budget-conscious traveller, with superb panoramic views of Mount Cook and the Southern Alps. 16 en suite rooms. **$$–$$$**

The Hermitage Hotel
Terrace Road, Mount Cook
Tel: 03-435 1809
www.hermitage.co.nz
Luxurious accommodation and amazing scenery at the foot of New Zealand's tallest mountain in the Aoraki Mount Cook National Park. Sauna, clothing outlet, coffee shop, two restaurants and a bar. Sir Edmund Hillary Museum and Planetarium on site. 250 rooms. Well worth splashing out for a room in the Aoraki Wing. **$$$$–$$$$$**

The Hermitage Mount Cook Chalets and Motels
Terrace Road, Mount Cook
Tel: 03-435 1809
www.hermitage.co.nz
Nestled deep in the Aoraki Mount Cook National Park, this Alpine resort comprises the Hermitage Hotel and self-contained family-size motels and chalets. There is a range of restaurants and bars – and the views are tremendous. **$$$–$$$$$**

Mount Cook Youth Hostel
Corner Kitchener and Bowen drives, Mount Cook
Tel: 03-435-1820
www.yha.co.nz
A modern complex with a wide range of facilities. Single-sex and mixed dormitories, double and twin rooms. Shop, TV room, central-heating showers, toilets, free sauna, coin-operated laundry. Newmans and Great Sights buses arrive and depart from outside the hostel daily. **$**

Hanmer Springs

Albergo Lodge
88 Rippingdale Road
Tel: 03-315 7428
www.albergohanmer.com
The priority at Albergo is relaxation, restoration and recreation, with an emphasis on well-being. No matter how grumpy or travel-weary you arrive, you are guaranteed to leave refreshed. The buildings and grounds have been designed along the harmonious principles of *feng shui*, with whimsical details that create a delightful ambience. All your creature comforts are here, a highlight of which is the three-course gourmet breakfast, which arrives at a time to suit. **$$–$$$$$**

Alpine Lodge
Corner Amuri Drive and Harrogate Street
Tel: 03-315 7311, 0800-993 377
www.alpinelodgemotel.co.nz
Accommodation, close to shops and pool complex, ranges from traditional chalets to luxurious tower suites. Facilities vary in each unit. 23 units. **$$–$$$$$**

Greenacres Chalets and Apartments
84 Conical Hill Road
Tel: 03-315 7125, 0800-822 262
www.greenacresmotel.co.nz
Separate units in park-like setting overlooking the Hanmer Basin. Chalets and deluxe townhouse apartments have decks, balconies and full kitchen facilities. Close to Hanmer township and thermal pools. **$–$$**

Hanmer Resort Motel
7 Cheltenham Street
Tel: 03-315 7362, 0800-777 666
www.hanmerresortmotel.co.nz
Motel units here accommodate up to six people. It's located adjacent to hot mineral pools. 15 rooms. **$–$$$**

Hanmer Springs Larchwood Motel
18 Bath Street
Tel: 03-315 7281
www.larchwoodmotel.co.nz
Spacious rooms, which can sleep up to six, handy for squash courts, hot pools and forest walks. 16 rooms. **$–$$$**

Kaikoura

Admiral Court Motel
16 Avoca Street
Tel: 03-319 5525
www.kaikouramotel.co.nz
In a quiet location with mountain and sea views, this motel has units equipped with kitchens. There's off-road parking, courtesy car to bus or rail stations, and a spa pool. **$$–$$$**

Donegal House
School House Road
Tel: 03-319 5083, 0800-346 873
www.donegalhouse.co.nz
Located 3km (2 miles) north of Kaikoura, this award-winning Irish pub has 28 bed-and-breakfast en suite rooms furnished with an Irish theme. Outdoor spas, three huge open fires, tranquil gardens and lake. There's also an excellent restaurant and an Irish bar serving over 100 Irish and Scottish whiskies. **$$**

Hapuku Lodge and Tree Houses
Station Road, Kaikoura
Tel: 03-319 6559
www.hapukulodge.com
A luxury lodge with five distinctive designer Tree Houses a short drive from Kaikoura, in landscaped grounds of a deer farm with spectacular scenery. **$$$$–$$$$$**

Panorama Motel
266 Esplanade
Tel: 03-319 5053
www.panoramamotel.co.nz
Beachfront location, with sea and mountain views from all units. Plenty of off-street parking for boats and cars. 22 units. **$–$$**

Lake Tekapo

Lake Tekapo Grandview
32 Hamilton Drive
Tel: 03-680 6910
www.laketekapograndview.co.nz
Living up to its name, this luxury bed-and-breakfast accommodation has stunning views of the Alps and lake from every room. **$$$–$$$$$**

Lake Tekapo Scenic Resort
Main Highway
Tel: 03-680 6808
www.laketekapo.com
Centrally located accommodation with good views. Budget accommodation available. **$$–$$$$**

Methven

Canterbury Hotel (Brown Pub)
Mount Hutt Village
Tel: 03-302 8045
www.thebrownpub.co.nz
A historic hotel that has been a haven for travellers for more than 120 years. Basic but comfortable facilities. Good family restaurant. **$**

Mount Hutt Motels
205 Main Street
Tel: 03-302 8382
www.mounthuttmotels.com
This has the distinction of being the closest motel to Mount Hutt. Spacious, self-contained studio units and apartments set in park-like surroundings with spa and tennis courts. 10 units. **$**

Powderhouse Country Lodge
3 Cameron Street, Mount Hutt
Tel: 03-302 9105
www.powderhouse.co.nz
A beautifully restored Edwardian villa. Luxurious bedrooms have private en suites. Eight-person spa available, plus breakfast. 3 rooms. **$$$**

THE WEST COAST

Arthur's Pass

Trans Alpine Lodge
Main Road, Arthur's Pass
Tel: 03-318 9236
www.arthurspass.co.nz
Great Alpine scenery and
chalet-style accommodation
in the Southern Alps.
Restaurant specialises in
lamb, venison and beef. 14
rooms. **$–$$**

Fox Glacier

Fox Glacier Lodge
Sullivan Road, Fox Glacier
Tel/fax: 03-751 0888,
0800-369 800
www.foxglacierlodge.co.nz
This lodge is right is in the
heart of the scenic area by
Fox Glacier, and close to a
forest walk known for its
glow-worms. Modern units
with en suites, some with
double spa baths, cooking
facilities and mountain
views. Parking is available
for self-contained
motorhomes/campervans.
Mountain-bike hire
available. **$–$$$$**
Fox Glacier Resort Hotel
Corner Cook Flat Road and SH6
Tel: 03-751 0839
www.resorts.co.nz
Built in 1928, the hotel has
been refurbished to retain
its charm and atmosphere.
Restaurant, lounge bar,
guest lounge and Internet
services. 80 rooms. **$–$$**

Franz Josef Glacier

Alpine Glacier Motel
Condon Street
Tel: 03-752 0226, 0800-757 111
www.alpineglaciermotel.com
Warm, spacious studio and
family units close to
restaurants, 5km (3 miles)
to the glacier. **$–$$$$**
**Glacier Gateway
Motor Lodge**
Main Road
Tel: 03-752 0776
www.franzjosefhotels.co.nz
Among the closest
accommodation to any
glacier in New Zealand.
Basic facilities, but two
rooms have baths, and
there's a spa and sauna.
Close to shops and
restaurants. 23 units. **$–$$**
**Karamea Bridge
Farm Motels**
Bridge Street, RD3, Karamea,
Westport
Tel: 03-782 6955, 0800-527 263
www.karameamotels.co.nz
One- and two-bedroom
suites on a private farm, with
views across the wilderness
of Kahurangi National Park.
Suites have large private
lounges. Close to the centre
of Karamea. 8 units. **$–$$**
**Scenic Circle
Franz Josef Glacier Hotel**
SH6
Tel: 03-752 0729
www.scenic-circle.co.nz
Comprising two distinctive
properties 1km (²/₃ mile)

apart, the hotel has three
wings surrounded by lush
native bush and superb
Alpine views. 177 luxury
rooms. **$$–$$$$$**

Greymouth

Aachen Place Motel
50 High Street
Tel: 03-768 6901
www.aachenmotel.co.nz
Award-winning studio
apartments and units with
great views of the sea and
mountains.Centrally located
and self-contained. **$–$$**
Gables Motor Lodge
84 High Street
Tel: 03-768 9991
www.gablesmotorlodge.com
Luxury units with large beds
and fully equipped kitchens.
Some have spa baths, while
others have showers. Handy
for the shops. **$–$$$**

Haast

**Wilderness Lodge,
Lake Moeraki**
SH6
Tel: 03-750 0881
www.wildernesslodge.co.nz
The Wilderness Lodge has a
stunning and tranquil
setting, with fantastic bush
and coastal walks teeming
with wildlife. Guest-only
tours include hikes to
secluded penguin sites.
Breakfast and dinner are
included in the tariff. **$$$$$**

Hokitika

**Best Western Shining Star
Beachfront Chalets**
11 Richards Drive
Tel: 03-755 8921
www.shiningstar.co.nz
Centrally located, these fully
self-contained timber
chalets have their own decks
and direct beach access.
Near glow-worm cave. **$–$$**
Fitzherbert Court Motel
191 Fitzherbert Street
Tel: 03-755 5342
www.fitzherbertcourt.co.nz
Luxury units with self-
contained kitchens, some
with spa baths. Near town,
airport and beach. **$–$$**
Kapitea Ridge and Cottage
Chesterfield Road, SH6,
Kapitea Creek, RD2
Tel: 03-755 6805
www.kapitea.co.nz
Luxury lodge
accommodation with sea
views. **$$$$$**

QUEENSTOWN AND OTAGO

Arrowtown

Millbrook Resort
Malaghans Road
Tel: 03-441 7000
www.millbrook.co.nz
Luxury resort with a range of
accommodation from
cottages to two-bedroom
villas. There's a superb golf
course, restaurant and
health and fitness spa.
$$$$$
Settlers Cottage Motel
22 Hertford Street
Tel: 0800-803 801
www.settlerscottagemotel.co.nz

Pretty, cosy and quiet rooms
just off the main street. **$$**
Shades of Arrowtown
9 Merioneth Street
Tel: 03-442 1613/1824
www.shadesofarrowtown.co.nz
Tastefully furnished studios
and apartments in a garden
setting on Arrowtown's tree-
lined avenue. **$–$$**

Queenstown

Azur
23 McKinnon Terrace
Tel: 03-409 0588
www.azur.co.nz

This nine-villa luxury lodge
is in the Sunshine Bay area,
five minutes from
Queenstown. Each villa
boasts sensational
panoramic views, a lounge
area with a fireplace and an
outside deck. Rates include
breakfast, afternoon tea
and pre-dinner drinks, plus
all transfers. **$$$$$**
**Copthorne Lakefront
Resort and Hotel**
Corner Adelaide Street and
Frankton Road
Tel: 03-442 8123
www.millenniumhotels.co.nz

Four-star accommodation
with 241 cosy rooms, many
with views of the lake and

mountains. Within walking distance of the main shopping area. Shuttle service available. **$$$–$$$$$**

The Heritage Queenstown
91 Fernhill Road
Tel: 03-442 4988
www.heritagehotels.co.nz
A European-style lodge, with forest and waterfall rooms and lakeside suites, crafted from centuries-old schist and cedar. Facilities include a well-equipped day spa, sauna, gym and swimming pool. **$$$–$$$$$**

Kingsgate Hotel Terraces
88 Frankton Road
Tel: 03-442 7950
www.kingsgatehotels.co.nz
Ten minutes' walk from the town centre. The rooms all have magnificent views of the lake and mountains, and some have cooking facilities. Private spa pool. 85 rooms. **$$–$$$$**

Mercure Resort
Sainsbury Road
Tel: 03-442 6600
www.accorhotels.co.nz
Overlooking The Remarkables mountain range, with expansive lake views, just five minutes from the town. Facilities include a

spa, tennis courts, gym, saunas and an observation deck. **$$–$$$$$**

Millennium Queenstown
Corner Frankton Road and Stanley Street
Tel: 03-441 8888
www.millenniumhotels.com
A top-class hotel with tasteful rooms, a restaurant, bar, parking, gym and spa. 220 rooms. **$$$–$$$$$**

Novotel Gardens
Corner Marine Parade and Earl Street
Tel: 03-442 7750
www.accor.co.nz
A modern hotel on the lakefront. The spacious and welcoming foyer gives a hint of the quality of the rooms refurbished in 2008. Management and staff provide top-class and unobtrusive service. **$$–$$$$**

Nugget Point Boutique Hotel
Arthur's Point
Tel: 03-441 0288
www.nuggetpoint.co.nz
Award-winning boutique hotel with a fine restaurant, only 10 minutes' drive from Queenstown. The suites are impeccably furnished, and the more expensive ones

have stunning views of the Shotover River and Coronet Peak. Competent staff provide first-class service. **$$$$$**

Oak Shores
327–343 Frankton Road
Tel: 03-450 005
www.theoaksgroup.com.au
New, luxury apartments, all with stunning views of The Remarkables. Kitchens, en suites, laundry facilities. Comfortable and immaculately presented. **$$$$–$$$$$**

Wanaka

Alpine Motel Apartments
7 Ardmore Street, Lake Wanaka
Tel: 03-443 7950
www.alpinemotels.co.nz
Centrally located and within walking distance of the town centre, lake and golf course, these basic family and studio suites are self-contained and comfortable. **$$–$$$$**

Brook Vale Motels
35 Brownston Street
Tel: 0800-438 333
www.brookvale.co.nz
Close to the centre of town, but private, with views of the Southern Alps. All units have kitchens, and there's a

spa pool outdoor pool, bbq area and guest laundry. **$$**

Edgewater Resort
Sargood Drive, Lake Wanaka
Tel: 03-443 8311, 0800-108 311
www.edgewater.co.nz
Modern luxury apartments and rooms with large bathrooms – some can be configured to provide family suites. Set on the edge of Lake Wanaka, with great views. Award-winning restaurant. **$$$–$$$$$**

Mount Aspiring Hotel
109 Mount Aspiring Road, Lake Wanaka
Tel: 03-443 8216
www.wanakanz.com
Built in natural stone and wood, this picturesque family-owned hotel has 57 studio rooms with private bath and shower facilities; some have a spa bath. There is also a good restaurant. **$$$**

Oak Ridge Pool and Spa Resort
Corner Studholme and Cardrona roads
Tel: 03-443 7707
www.oakridge.co.nz
Comfortable accommodation located just a stone's throw from the town centre. **$$–$$$$**

DUNEDIN AND SURROUNDINGS

Dunedin

Cargill's Hotel
678 George Street
Tel: 03-477 7983, 0800-737 378
www.cargills.co.nz
Central hotel, with its own restaurant, that's perfect for business travellers. Basic, but comfortable rooms. **$$$**

Fletcher Lodge
276 High Street
Tel: 03-477 5552
www.fletcherlodge.co.nz
Luxurious accommodation a

PRICE CATEGORIES

Price categories are for two people in a double room, including GST:
$ = below NZ$100
$$ = NZ$100–150
$$$ = NZ$150–200
$$$$ = NZ$200–250
$$$$$ = over NZ$250

few minutes' walk from the centre of the city. Exclusive, with only six rooms. **$$$$–$$$$$**

Hulmes Court Bed and Breakfast
52 Tennyson Street
Tel: 0800-448 563
www.hulmes.co.nz
A beautiful 1860s Victorian mansion in the heart of Dunedin. A large marble fireplace is cosy during winter and there's a relaxing drawing room with authentic furnishings. **$–$$$**

Larnach Lodge
145 Camp Road, Otago Peninsula
Tel: 03-476 1616
www.larnachcastle.co.nz
Bedrooms with private bathrooms are individually decorated in period style, and each has an amazing view of the ocean 305

metres (1,000ft) below. Lodge guests may dine in the historic Larnach Castle dining room. 12 rooms. **$$$$$** There is also a much cheaper option with shared bathrooms. 6 rooms. **$$**

Mercure Leisure Lodge
Duke Street, Dunedin North
Tel: 03-477 5360, 0800-334 123
www.mercure.co.nz
Close to the shopping centre and adjacent to the Botanical Gardens, this lodge occupies the original location of McGavin's Brewery and still retains the original stonework and brewery theme. 76 rooms. **$$–$$$$**

Scenic Circle Southern Dunedin Cross Hotel
118 High Street
Tel: 03-477 0752, 0800-696 963
www.scenic-circle.co.nz

In a central location, with a spacious and welcoming lobby, this historic landmark hotel has plenty of superior and premium rooms from which to choose, but some rooms by the road can be a bit noisy. There's a great café attached to the hotel, and service is good. **$$–$$$$$**

SOUTHLAND

Catlins Coast

Catlins Farmstay B&B
174 Progress Valley Road, Catlins
Tel: 03-246 8843
www.catlinsfarmstay.co.nz
Roomy accommodation on a working farm, midway between Cathedral Caves and Curio Bay. Breakfast available, and you'll get an exceptionally warm Kiwi welcome here. **$$$–$$$$**

Nadir Outpost
Slope Point, The Catlins
Tel: 03-246 8544
www.catlins-slopepoint.co.nz
A range of basic accommodation, from tent sites to bed and breakfast, set amid forest with spectacular views. Facilities include small souvenir and supplies shop. **$**

Invercargill

Ascot Park Hotel/Motel
Corner Racecourse Road and Tay Street
Tel: 03-217 6195
www.ascotparkhotel.co.nz
A large complex in quiet surroundings, with indoor swimming pool, spa, sauna, gym and restaurant. **$–$$**

Beersheba
58 Milton Park Road
Tel: 03-216 3677
www.beersheba.co.nz
Michael and Anne Broad

offer warm and thoughtful Southern hospitality in their sprawling home. Set in 4.4 hectares (11 acres) of landscaped woodland gardens, featuring an enormous pond, provide a restful setting. There's a hideaway cottage offering private, self-contained accommodation, or guests can stay in the Tamarisk or Magnolia rooms within the main homestead. **$$–$$$$**

Birchwood Manor
189 Tay Street
Tel: 03-218 8881
www.birchwoodmanor.co.nz
Award-winning motel with good family and business accommodation in spacious and affordable units and rooms. Closest motel to supermarket, opposite city centre. **$$**

Victoria Railway Hotel
3 Leven Street
Tel: 03-218 1281, 0800-777 557
www.hotelinvercargill.com
Intimate family-owned hotel in a historic building, with a restaurant and bar. **$$**

Te Anau

Aden Motel
57–59 Quintin Drive
Tel: 03-249 7748
www.adenmotel.co.nz
Self-contained units with

kitchen, close to lake and shops. 12 units. **$–$$**

Dunluce B&B
Apirama Drive
Tel: 03-249 7715
www.dunluce-fiordland.co.nz
A great base from which to explore Te Anau and Milford. Mountain views from all rooms and friendly hosts. **$$$$–$$$$$**

Explorer Motor Lodge
6 Cleddau Street
Tel: 03-249 7156, 0800-477 877
www.explorerlodge.co.nz
Bright, spacious apartments (studio, one- and two-bedroom) with fully equipped kitchens in this accommodation set amid the glorious scenery of Fiordland National Park. Close to the town centre. 17 units. **$$**

Kingsgate Hotel Te Anau
20 Lakefront Drive
Tel: 03-249 7421
www.millenniumhotels.com
Set on the shores of Lake Te Anau, with manicured gardens and a restaurant and bar. 94 rooms. **$$–$$$$**

Lakeside Motel
36 Lakefront Drive
Tel: 03-249 7435
www.lakesideteanau.co.nz
Central motel in a garden, near restaurants and with unobstructed views of lake and mountains. Nineteen

units with full kitchens and en suite bathrooms. **$–$$**

Luxmore Hotel
Main Street
Tel: 03-249 7526, 0800-589 6673
www.distinctionluxmore.co.nz
Located close to Te Anau's services and attractions, and a mere 100 metres/yds from the lake front. The rooms are comfortable and well heated. 106 rooms. **$$$–$$$$$**

Te Anau Hotel and Villas
Lakefront Drive
Tel: 03-249 7947, 0800-223 687
www.distinctionhotels.co.nz
This hotel has 80 rooms, four deluxe suites and 28 garden villas, commanding lake and mountain views. Outdoor pool, spa and sauna, business centre, and a restaurant/bar overlooking Lake Te Anau. **$$$$–$$$$$**

STEWART ISLAND

Greenvale Bed & Breakfast
Kaka Ridge Road, Halfmoon Bay
Tel: 03-219 1357
www.greenvalestewartisland.co.nz
Close to the centre of Oban and the sea, with magnificent views of Foveaux Strait. Exclusive,

with just the two individually designed rooms with king-size beds and en suite bathrooms. **$$$$$**

Pania Lodge
Tel: 03-215 7733
Email: halstead@xtra.co.nz
Set in secluded bush, this is an ideal location from which to explore Oban Town and Paterson Inlet. **$$**

Sails Ashore Luxury B&B
Halfmoon Bay
Tel: 03-219 1151
www.sailsashore.co.nz
Luxury boutique bed and breakfast overlooking Halfmoon Bay and the islands of Foveaux Strait, a

short stroll from the village. Two-night stay minimum in summer. **$$$$$**

South Sea Hotel
Elgin Terrace, Halfmoon Bay
Tel: 03-219 1059
www.stewart-island.co.nz
A friendly country-style hotel, a 25-minute walk from town. The restaurant serves local seafood. Also has studio units adjacent to the hotel. Great views. **$–$$**

Stewart Island Lodge
14 Nichol Road, Halfmoon Bay
Tel: 03-219 1085
www.stewartislandlodge.co.nz
Secluded setting with fantastic views of the bay;

each suite has a super king-size bed, central heating and en suite bathroom. Gourmet meals feature fresh local seafood. **$$$**

E ATING OUT

RECOMMENDED RESTAURANTS, CAFES & BARS

WHERE TO EAT

General

An abundance and variety of quality fresh meat, fish and garden produce fill the New Zealand larder with riches on which a world-class cuisine has been built.

The variety of produce offered by New Zealand's market gardens is perhaps rivalled only by those of California. Vegetables such as asparagus, globe artichokes and silver beet (Swiss chard) – luxuries in some countries – are abundant here, as are pumpkins and kumara, the waxiest and most succulent of the world's sweet potatoes. Kiwi fruit, apples, tamarillos, strawberries, passion fruit, pears, blueberries and boysenberries are shipped all over the globe, but while you are here, it's also well worth trying less famous fruits, such as feigoa, pepinos, babacos and prince melons.

The waters surrounding New Zealand contain an abundant harvest and are the source of at least 50 commercially viable types of fish and shellfish – including crayfish, mussels, oysters, *paua* (abalone) and the tiny whitebait.

New Zealand lamb is superb and richly deserves its worldwide acclaim. Dishes that are particularly worthy of note are crown roast lamb and lamb spare ribs. The beef is excellent, too, and game – including venison – is plentiful.

If you want to savour a national dish, you won't go far wrong with a helping of pavlova – a delectable concoction of meringue, topped with fresh fruit and whipped cream.

Where to Eat

Good restaurants abound in the major cities and in major resort towns. Many of them specialise in international cuisines, most notably Japanese, Vietnamese, Indonesian, Chinese, Korean, Indian, Italian and Thai.

There are formal restaurants, of course, but New Zealanders tend to be more casual, and outdoor dining is popular in the summer months. If you are invited to a BBQ it is customary to ask what you can bring along to contribute. The answer may range from "just yourself" through to "bring a salad". If you are unsure, take a bottle of wine for your hosts. If the answer, however, is to "bring a plate", this actually means to fill a dish with food to share with everyone, similar to "pot luck".

What to Drink

Wine: New Zealand wines win awards all over the world and are well worth trying. The country's cool maritime climate and its summer rains produce light, elegant, fruity white wines – and, in recent years, some very fine red wines, in particular pinot noir. See *Cuisine, pages 85–9*, and *Wine, pages 93–5*, for more details.

Wine purchased with your meal at a licensed restaurant will be more expensive: add roughly NZ$10 extra per bottle. Look out for the restaurant's "house" wine as these can be extremely good, often local, and offer significantly better value.

Beer: New Zealanders, with Australians, are among the biggest beer-drinkers in the world: many of New Zealand's beers – Steinlager, Speights, Tui, DB Draught, Monteiths

– rank with the great beers of Denmark and Germany.

BYO mean "Bring Your Own" bottle, and indicates that a restaurant is licensed for the consumption of alcohol, but not for selling it. At BYO restaurants you are likely to be charged a small "corkage" fee for supplying glasses and opening your bottle.

Most nightspots, restaurants and cafés serve liquor, and you can buy alcohol from liquor outlets, wine shops and supermarkets (beer and wine only) – if you're 18 or over.

Fruit juice: In addition to alcoholic beverages, licensed restaurants also offer a range of fruit juices (New Zealand's feigoa juice is delicious), soft drinks and water.

Water: Drinking tap water in New Zealand is perfectly safe, and in most restaurants this will automatically be supplied to your table in a vessel such as a glass bottle or jug. At more casual eateries, for example cafés, it is up to the individual to help one self to tap water. This is most often located somewhere on the counter area, again served in a jug, sometimes with ice, mint, cucumber or lemon added. Again this attracts no charge.

Bottled water, either still or sparkling, can also be ordered. Well-known European brands are often available, but you are far better off to order a New Zealand brand – at the last count there were some 126 varieties available – of which most are classed as spring or artesian with variants including mineral, sparkling and still. Brands such as New Zealand Natural are widely available, but look out for other boutique brands, as each has its own regional flavour. Two you may like to try include Waiwera water and 420 Volcanic Spring Water.

NORTH ISLAND

AUCKLAND

Antoine's
333 Parnell Road
Tel: 09-379 8756
www.antoinesrestaurant.co.nz
Elegant, highly innovative gourmet restaurant, on a busy shopping street with many other good eateries located in the same area. The menu offers New Zealand cuisine with French undertones. **$$$**

Cibo
91 St Georges Bay Road, Parnell
Tel: 09-303 9660
www.cibo.co.nz
Mediterranean plus Asian-influenced cuisine and superb service have kept Cibo at the top of its game for more than a decade. **$$$**

De Post Belgian Beer Café
466 Mount Eden Road, Mount Eden
Tel: 09-630 9330
www.depost.co.nz
This very popular bar has a great range of Belgian beers and some of the best mussel dishes anywhere. **$$**

Dine by Peter Gordon
Sky City, 90 Federal Street
Tel: 09-363 7030
www.skycitygrand.co.nz
"Superstar chef returns home and takes the town by storm with his trademark fusion style." Ignore such silly labels and concentrate on the menu, which is always exciting and intelligent. Excellent service of a level seldom found in New Zealand. **$$$**

Euro Restaurant and Bar
22 Princes Wharf
Tel: 09-309 9866
Fashionable restaurant that was *the* place to be during the America's Cup. The high-quality food and service is still maintained, and the focus is on fresh New Zealand produce. **$$$**

The French Café
210 Symonds Street
Tel: 09-377 1911
www.thefrenchcafe.co.nz
Winner of many prestigious awards, The French Café serves contemporary European cuisine in a friendly and intimate environment. There's a relaxed bar for pre- and post-dinner drinks and a conservatory room that overlooks the courtyard, where one can enjoy dining alfresco. **$$$**

Harbourside Seafood Bar and Grill
1st Floor, Ferry Building, 99 Quay Street
Tel: 09-307 0556
www.harboursiderestaurant.co.nz
Like CinCin on the ground floor, this restaurant offers imaginative seafood cooking. Great views. **$$$**

Iguacu
269 Parnell Road
Tel: 09-358 4804
www.iguacu.co.nz
A large, busy bar and restaurant featuring Pacific Rim food. **$$**

Kermadec Ocean Fresh Restaurant
Viaduct Quay (opposite the Maritime Museum)
Tel: 09-309 0412
www.kermadec.co.nz
Very good fish dishes. **$$**

KK Malaysian Cuisine
463A Manukau Road, Epsom
Tel: 09-630 3555
Malaysian food doesn't come any fresher or tastier, and you're spoilt for choice in this unpretentious, inexpensive eatery set amongst Epsom's antique shops. **$**

The Observatory Restaurant
Level 52, Sky Tower
Tel: 09-363 6000
www.skycityauckland.co.nz
Venture nearly 200 metres (660ft) up Auckland's tallest structure to the highest restaurant in the tower for

ABOVE: the Ferry Building.

buffet-style New Zealand seafood specialities. **$$$**

Prego
226 Ponsonby Road, Ponsonby
Tel: 09-376 3095
Great food, Italian classics and more cooked with panache. A top restaurant. **$$$**

Rice
10–12 Federal Street, CBD
Tel: 09-359 9113
www.rice.co.nz
International cuisine, with mouth-watering recipes derived from 20 types or derivates of rice. Try the entrée platter, especially the barbecue pork and crispy vermicelli. Modern and chic, it has a stylish bar. **$$**

Rocco
23 Ponsonby Road, Ponsonby
Tel: 09-360 6262
www.rocco.co.nz
Modern and healthful cuisine is served in an intimate and cosy atmosphere, with an extensive range of wines. **$$$**

Soul Bar and Bistro
Viaduct Harbour
Tel: 09-356 7249
www.soulbar.co.nz
By far the best choice at the Viaduct Harbour, with fabulous fish dishes. Enjoy some of New Zealand's most popular soul food while appreciating the harbour views. Very popular with locals. **$$–$$$**

SPQR
150 Ponsonby Road, Ponsonby
Tel: 09-360 1710
www.spqrnz.co.nz
One of Auckland's most famous and best-loved restaurants, with great cuisine, notably the linguine and clams. It becomes a popular nightspot once the plates are cleared away. Dark interior; pavement tables. **$$$**

Vivace
Level 1, 50 High Street
Tel: 09-302 2303
www.vivacerestaurant.co.nz
Italian-style food served tapas fashion makes for a tasty quick meal or a pleasant evening out if you feel like lingering to savour a few of the delights on one of Auckland's better wine lists. **$$$**

Wildfire
Shed 22, Princes Wharf
Tel: 09-353 7595
www.wildfirerestaurant.co.nz
Meat and seafood abound in this Mediterranean eatery by the waterfront. Try the tapas menu, or something more substantial such as a gourmet pizza or items from the wood-fired grill. **$$–$$$**

PRICE CATEGORIES

Price categories are per person for dinner, including service and tax:
$ = NZ$10–15
$$ = NZ$15–25
$$$ = NZ$25 and over

Auckland's Surroundings

Devonport

Manuka Restaurant
49 Victoria Road
Tel: 09-445 7732
Superior dining with a relaxed and friendly atmosphere. **$$–$$$**
Monsoon Café Restaurant
71 Victoria Road
Tel: 09-445 4263
Specialises in Thai and Malay food, to eat in or take out. **$–$$**

Great Barrier Island

Claris Texas Café
Hector Sanderson Road
Tel: 09-429 0811
Standard café fare for breakfast and lunch. Daily from 8am. **$**
Currach Irish Pub
Pah Beach, Stonewall, Tryphena
Tel: 09-429 0211
Authentic Irish atmosphere, great pub food, with Guinness and Kilkenny on tap. **$$**

Helensville

Macnuts Farm Café and Shop
914 South Head Road
Tel: 09-420 2501
www.macnut.co.nz
Book to tour the macadamia orchard and enjoy lunch from a somewhat macadamia-dominated menu at the farm café. **$–$$**

Riverview Restaurant and Corridor Bar
88 Commercial Road
Tel: 09-420 6040
Enjoy good food and great views from the deck overlooking the Kaipara River.

Kawau Island

Mansion House Café
Mansion House
Tel: 09-422 8903
Open for light snacks and coffee from 10am–4pm. **$**

Orewa

Kaizen Café
350 Hibiscus Coast Highway, Orewa
Tel: 09-427 5633
www.kaizencafe.co.nz
Delicious Italian-style food made with organic and free-range produce. Try the organic Italian coffee and fruit gelato. The queue for the very addictive breakfast starts at 7am. **$$**
Sahara Café and Restaurant
336 Hibiscus Coast Highway
Tel: 09-246 8828
Mediterranean-style cuisine. **$$**

South Auckland

Broncos Steak House
712 Great South Road, Manukau
Tel: 09-262 2850
As reliable as restaurants with "steak house" as part

of the name the world over. **$–$$**
Volare
91 Charles Prevost Drive, Manurewa
Tel: 09-267 6688
Famous for its convivial atmosphere and one of the most popular restaurants in South Auckland. International cuisine. **$$**

Waiheke Island

Nourish Café
3 Belgium Street, Oneroa
Tel: 09-372 3557
Fresh, seasonal gourmet café fare with takeaways available. **$–$$**
Vino Vino Restaurant
3/153 Ocean View Road, Oneroa
Tel: 09-372 9888
www.vinovino.co.nz
Casual Mediterranean platters or à la carte dining, on a deck with stunning bay views. Reservations are essential. **$$$**

Waitakere City and West Coast Beaches

Beesonline Honey Centre and Café
791 SH16, Waimauku
Tel: 09-411 7953
www.beesonline.co.nz
It's not just for apiarists – this stylish licensed café serves first-class food with an emphasis on fresh organic produce, local ingredients and honey. Well worth the drive if only to

dine here. **$$–$$$**
The Elevation
473 Scenic Drive, Waiatarua
Tel: 09-814 1919
Good food, wine and music in a prime location high on top of the Waitakere Ranges, with fantastic panoramic views of Auckland city. A great stopover on a day trip to Piha, serving brunch at weekends. Dinner reservations are recommended. **$$$**
The Hunting Lodge
Waikoukou Valley Road, Waimauku
Tel: 09-411 8259
www.thehuntinglodge.co.nz
Fine dining; game is a speciality. **$$$**

Warkworth Area

"86"
1 Omaha Flats Road, Matakana
Tel: 09-422 7360
Hearty meals are the hallmark of this large, family-friendly country café. The complex includes a children's playground, Saturday craft market and horse-riding centre. Very popular, so reservations are recommended. **$$$**
Leigh Sawmill Café
142 Pakiri Road, Leigh
Tel: 09-422 6019
www.sawmillcafe.co.nz
One of the area's most esoteric cafés, specialising in fresh local fish (straight from the commercial fishery next door) and pizzas. **$$$**

Northland

Doubtless Bay

Mangonui Fish Shop
Beach Road
Tel: 09-406 0478
This place wins prizes for its traditional fish and chips, and its seafront location is unbeatable. When available, be sure to sample succulent blue nose. **$**
Waterfront Café and Bar
Waterfront Road
Tel: 09-406 0850
Reliable fare for breakfast,

lunch and dinner, right on the waterfront. **$$–$$$**

Kerikeri

Café Blue
582 Kerikeri Road
Tel: 09-407 5150
www.cafeblue.co.nz
Great family-friendly indoor and outdoor dining with a children's playground. Set in an orchard that provides oranges, figs, macadamias and culinary herbs. **$$$**

Fishbone Café
88 Kerikeri Road
Tel: 09-407 6065
Good, straightforward café fare and friendly atmosphere. **$–$$**

Paihia

Pure Tastes Restaurant
Paihia Beach Resort
116 Marsden Road
Tel: 09-402 0003
www.puretastes.co.nz
Award-winning chef Paul

Jobin serves superlative dishes using local produce. Reservations are recommended. **$$$**
Waikokopu Café
Treaty Grounds, Waitangi
Tel: 09-402 6275
This award-winning café is set in a shady tropical garden at the entrance to Waitangi Treaty Grounds. The food ranges from breakfast and light snacks to main meals of lamb, beef and seafood. **$–$$**

Russell

The Duke of Marlborough Hotel
Waterfront
Tel: 09-403 7829
The hotel has a fine restaurant, where you can't go wrong with the locally caught seafood – oysters and mussels are brought straight from the sea to the table. **$$–$$$**

The Gables
The Strand
Tel: 09-403 7618
Housed in one of New Zealand's oldest buildings, built in 1847, The Gables has retained many original features, including kauri panelling, open fires, original maps and old photographs. The menu is contemporary Mediterranean. Seating is available inside and out, with views across the bay. **$$$**

Gannets Restaurant
York Street
Tel: 09-403 7990
www.gannets.co.nz
Recommended by locals, Gannets offers a varied menu with plenty of seafood. Everything is home-made, including the ice cream. Dinner Tue–Sun. **$$$**

Kamakura
The Strand
Tel: 09-403 7771
www.kamakura.co.nz
The best waterfront location, with outdoor tables set beneath giant native *pohutukawa* trees. Superb fine dining and an excellent wine list. **$$$**

York Street Café
1 York Street
Tel: 09-403 7360
Fresh local food at reasonable prices. The chowder is widely praised. Several vegetarian options as well. Daily 8am–3pm.**$$**

Whangarei

A Deco Restaurant
70 Kamo Road, Kensington
Tel: 09-459 4957
www.a-deco.co.nz
Nationally acclaimed cuisine using Northland's best produce, in a stunning Art Deco setting. Open for lunch and Tue–Sat for dinner from 6pm. Reservations essential. **$$$**

Caffeine Espresso Café
4 Water Street
Tel: 09-438 6925
www.caffeinecafe.co.nz
Serves some of the best coffee in the country and provides mouth-watering meals in a cosy atmosphere. Open for breakfast and lunch. **$**

Killer Prawn
26–28 Bank Street
Tel: 09-430 3333
www.killerprawn.co.nz
New Zealand and Pacific Island cuisine at its best. Try the restaurant's signature Killer Prawn bowl and other tasty seafood. Enjoy a cocktail in the main bar or soak up the sun in the garden bar. **$$$**

Reva's on the Waterfront
31 Quay Side, Town Basin Marina
Tel: 09-438 8969
www.revas.co.nz
Located right on the harbour overlooking moored boats, Reva's has an extensive menu of traditional and contemporary cuisine, pizzas and seafood, plus "famous original" Mexican dishes. **$$–$$$**

THE WAIKATO

Cambridge

The Lily Pad Café
1242 Kaipaki Road
Tel: 07-823 9134
www.lilypadcafe.co.nz
It takes a little drive to reach this countryside café, but it is well worth the trip. Set in a delightful garden filled with sculptures, the café serves wholesome seasonal fare prepared with artistic flair. Has a hand-picked selection of wines. Open daily for breakfast and lunch, Thur–Sat for dinner (summer only). **$$–$$$**

BELOW: seafood platter.

Hamilton

Domaine Restaurant
575 Victoria Street
Tel: 07-839 2100
Teeming with locals, this eatery serves Mediterranean-style and Asian-inspired dishes. **$$**

The Narrows Landing
431 Airport Road
Tel: 07-858 4001
www.thenarrowslanding.co.nz
Gourmet cuisine with New Zealand and European influences. Huge wooden doors, lots of iron, a metal mesh staircase and candlelight enhance its medieval style. **$$$**

OneZB
20 Alma Street
Tel: 07-838 3718
www.onezb.co.nz
This spacious eatery beside the Waikato River occupies Hamilton's old broadcasting building. Extensive wine list and great service complement top ingredients and original fare. **$$$**

Thai Village Café
The Market Place, Hood Street
Tel: 07-834 9960
www.thaivillage.co.nz
Excellent Thai cuisine with a wide range of curry, rice and noodle dishes. Generous servings and cheap prices. **$$**

Te Aroha

Domain Cottage Café
Te Aroha Domain
Tel: 07-884 9222
Lovely setting inside historic building. Café fare daily; evening meals by arrangement. **$**

Mokena Restaurant
6 Church Street
Tel: 07-884 8038
Licensed restaurant serving home-style cooking. **$$$**

Other Locations

Bosco Café
57 Te Kumi Road, Te Kuiti
Tel: 07-878 3633
In the heart of King Country, a great stopover for some good hearty food, decent coffee and excellent home-made cake and muffins. **$**

Out in the Styx Guesthouse
2117 Arapuni Road, Te Awamutu
Tel: 0800-461 559
www.styx.co.nz
A bed-and-breakfast retreat with an adjacent restaurant focusing on New Zealand cuisine. It offers only a four-course set menu, plus coffee. Bookings only. **$$$**

Roselands
579 Fullerton Road, Waitomo Caves
Tel: 07-878 7611
An award-winning restaurant amid native bush in a rural landscape. The mouth-watering menu is prepared using fresh Kiwi produce. Try the barbecue-style lunch. Open for lunch only. **$$$**

COROMANDEL AND THE BAY OF PLENTY

Hahei

Café Luna
1 French Road
Tel: 07-866 3016
Good food and great coffee served by friendly staff.
$$–$$$

The Grange Road Café
7 Grange Road
Tel: 07-866 3502
Good home-cooked comfort food and the only place in Hahei where you'll find beer on tap. Laid-back courtyard and deck dining.
$–$$$

Tauranga/Mount Maunganui

Bravo Café and Restaurant
Red Square
Tel: 07-578 4700
www.cafebravo.co.nz
All-day dining, good service and sunny tables. The spicy mussels, gourmet pizzas and wood-fired bread are all excellent. Dinner Tue–Sat.
$$–$$$

Harbourside Brasserie and Bar
The Old Yacht Club, The Strand, Tauranga
Tel: 07-571 0520, 0800-721 714
Waterfront dining at its best – watch the boats come in as you dine on imaginative cuisine. A wide range of dishes, from lamb shanks Provençal to apple-roasted pork rack. Or try some of New Zealand's finest seafood here. **$$$**

The Lobster Club
Harbourside, Tauranga
Tel: 07-574 4147
Set on the water's edge in the Harbour Bridge Marina. Fine dining with a wide range of dishes, from light meals to fabulous platters and a huge variety of seafood. **$$$**

Tairua

Manaia Café and Bar
Corner Main and Manaia roads
Tel: 07-864 9050
Menus change regularly with the seasons and focus

on fresh flavours. Dine alfresco in the spacious courtyard or indoors. Happy hour on Friday from 5.30pm; great music and atmosphere. Open 10am until late for brunch, lunch and dinner. **$–$$**

Shells Restaurant and Bar
227 Main Road
Tel: 07-864 8811
One of the peninsula's most popular restaurants, situated next to Pacific Harbour Lodge. **$$$**

Thames

Sola Café
720 Pollen Street
Tel: 07-868 878
A vegetarian café/restaurant offering dining indoors, on the street or amongst its extensive herb gardens out back. **$–$$**

Whangamata

Nero's
Port Road
Tel: 07-865 6300

Gourmet-style pizzas with exotic toppings. **$$**

The Whanga Bar and Café
101 Winifred Avenue
Tel: 07-865 6472
Café fare; open daily for breakfast and lunch, plus dinner at weekends. **$–$$**

Whitianga

Eggsentric Café and Restaurant
1049 Purangi Road, Flaxmill Bay, Cooks Beach
Tel: 07-866 0307
Good food, live music nightly, art exhibitions. **$$**

The Fire Place
9 The Esplanade
Tel: 07-866 4828
www.thefireplace-restaurant.com
The seafood and wood-fired pizzas are particularly popular in this rustic eatery. With its lovely waterfront location, it's a treat to dine alfresco on the lovely big deck in summer. In winter, cosy up to the fireplace.
$$–$$$

ROTORUA AND THE VOLCANIC PLATEAU

Ohakune

Alpine Restaurant and Bar
Corner Clyde and Miro streets
Tel: 06-385 9183
European-style meals in a warm and welcoming fine-dining environment.
$$–$$$

Altitude 585
79 Clyde Street
Tel: 06-385 9292
www.altitude585.co.nz
A great place for hearty and reasonably priced pub fare.
$–$$

Powderkeg Restaurant and Bar
Mountain Road
Tel: 06-385 8888
Good-value meals served beside a roaring fire on huge, slab tables and benches. Open 7am until late. **$$–$$$v**

Sassi's Bistro
7 Miro Street
Tel: 06-385 8758

This is the place to go for a family meal. **$–$$**

Utopia Café
47 Clyde Street
Tel: 06-385 9120
Enjoy superb Santos coffee, all-day breakfasts and delicious café meals. **$–$$**

Rotorua

Abracadabra Café/Bar
1263 Amohia Street
Tel: 07-348 3883
A Moroccan-themed café/restaurant open for breakfast, lunch and dinner. Tapas and meze served from 5pm until closing provide excellent value. Recently gained a top score on New Zealand reality TV show *Target* for its cuisine, cleanliness and service.
$–$$

Bistro 1284
1284 Eruera Street
Tel: 07-346 1284

www.bistro1284.co.nz
An award-winning restaurant set in a historic 1930s building in Rotorua.
$$$

Cableway Restaurant
185 Fairy Springs Road
Tel: 07-347 0027
www.skylineskyrides.co.nz
Buffets normally aren't to be trusted, but the selection here is first-rate, from multitudinous seafood to perfectly roasted meats. A bonus is the ride in the gondola to the hilltop site.
$$

Capers Epicurean
1181 Eruera Street
Tel: 07-348 8818
Casual deli-style café serving freshly prepared fare including salads, hot dishes, cakes, slices, sandwiches and wraps, for breakfast, lunch and dinner – and everything inbetween. Highly recommended. **$–$$**

Cicco Italian Café
1262 Fenton Street, Rotorua
Tel: 07-481 828
Authentic Italian fare at an affordable price. Sit by the fire in the winter, or dine alfresco during the summer.
$–$$

Fat Dog Café and Bar
1161 Arawa Street
Tel: 07-348 8411
Reasonably priced breakfasts, lunches and coffees make this a good place to start the day, or to sit and enjoy a coffee. **$**

Freos Café
1103 Tutanekai Street
Tel: 07-346 0976
Contemporary New Zealand

PRICE CATEGORIES

Price categories are per person for dinner, including service and tax:
$ = NZ$10–15
$$ = NZ$15–25
$$$ = NZ$25 and over

ABOVE: kiwi fruits.

fare served with casual café-style service. Open daily for breakfast, lunch and dinner. **$$–$$$**

Katsubi Restaurant and Sushi Bar
1123 Eruera Street
Tel: 07-349 3494
Authentic Japanese and Korean cuisine is served at this restaurant specialising in sushi, teriyaki, tonkatsu and bento. **$**

The Landing Café
Lake Tarawera
Tel: 07-362 8595
www.thelandinglaketarawera.co.nz

Nestled on the shores of Lake Tarawera, this café features a mouth-watering menu of traditional winter fare like venison, bacon and mushroom pie and more delicate summer dishes like scallops in a boysenberry sauce. **$–$$$**

Lewishams Café and Restaurant
1099 Tutanekai Street
Tel: 07-348 1786
www.lewishamsrestaurant.co.nz
Established over 20 years ago, serves European cuisine with Pacific Rim accents. Daily 9am until late. **$–$$$**

Restaurant Nikau
Millennium Hotel Rotorua, corner Eruera and Hinemaru streets
Tel: 07-347 1234
New Zealand and Maori ingredients are used to create innovative and delicious fare. **$$$**

Zanelli's
1243 Amohia Street
Tel: 07-348 4908

A popular Italian restaurant famous for mussels topped with garlic and crumb gratin, home-made gelato and tiramisu. Reservations essential. **$$$**

Taupo

Huka Vineyard Restaurant
56 Huka Falls Road
Tel: 07-377 2326
This is Taupo's only winery restaurant, and serves up mouth-watering cuisine in an exquisite setting of landscaped gardens and pinot noir vines. Enjoy one of the chef's signature platters while seated on the expansive patio with panoramic views of Mount Tauhara and surrounds. Sample Huka Vineyard's fine wines at the cellar door adjacent to the restaurant. **$$$**

Huka Prawn Park
Wairakei Tourist Park
Tel: 07-374 8474
The Wairakei Geothermal

Field harnesses the power of about 30,000 tonnes of hot water, and Huka Prawn Farm makes the most of the warmth to raise succulent tropical prawns. Tour the farm, fish for your own lunch using bamboo rods, or enjoy a delicious prawn feast while surveying the Waikato River as it begins its 425km (265-mile) journey to the sea. **$$–$$$**

Pimentos
17 Tamamutu Street
Tel: 07-377 4549
A popular evening eatery with an eclectic menu. Wed–Mon from 5.30pm. **$$**

Zest Café
65 Rifle Range Road
Tel: 07-378 5397
Owner-chef Greg Heffernan of the acclaimed Huka Lodge fame applies his considerable skills to this small café serving great food. Takeout is also available. Tue–Fri 8.45am–4pm, Sat–Sun 8.45am–2pm. **$–$$**

POVERTY BAY AND HAWKE'S BAY

Gisborne

The Colosseum Café and Wine Bar
4 River Point Road, Matawhero
Tel: 06-867 4733
Country café cuisine in a vineyard setting. **$$**

Gordon Gecko Restaurant and Bar
1 Wharf Shed, 60 The Esplanade
Tel: 06-868 3257
www.gordongecko.co.nz
Quality food using fresh local produce, generous servings; great atmosphere, excellent wine list and a harbourfront location. Daily from 3.30pm. **$$–$$$**

Trudy's Restaurant
Gisborne Hotel, corner Huxley and Tyndall roads
Tel: 06-868 4109
Good, wholesome local produce is used for a menu that specialises in lamb, beef and seafood. **$$$**

Ussco Bar and Bistr
16 Childers Road
Tel: 06-868 3246
Located in the old Union

Steam Ship Company Building – hence the name. Its menu caters to all, from kids, to those who want to enjoy a platter with a glass of wine, to others who want substantial meals. The Szechuan squid is a must. Lunch Wed–Sun from 10am and dinner from 5pm. **$–$$$**

Wharf Café Bar and Restaurant
Waterfront
Tel: 06-868 4876
www.wharfbar.co.nz
Seafood and the use of lots of local produce is the speciality here. Features one of the best wine lists in the country. Bookings recommended. **$$$**

Hastings

Rush Munro's Ice Cream Gardens
704 Heretaunga Street
Tel: 06-878 9634
www.rushmunro.co.nz
This all-natural hand-

churned ice cream has to be tasted to be believed, a testament to the extraordinary quality of New Zealand dairy products. **$**

Terroir
253 Waimarama Road, Havelock North
Tel: 06-873-0143
www.craggyrange.com
The restaurant attached to Craggy Bay winery has an impeccable pedigree and sophisticated, original fare, including notable desserts. Lunch Mon–Sun from noon and dinner Mon–Sat from 6pm. **$$$**

Napier

Pacifica Restaurant
209 Marine Parade
Tel: 06-833 6335
A contemporary seafood/game restaurant with a strong Pacific ambience. Voted in the top 10 of New Zealand's fine dining by *Cuisine* magazine 2008. **$$$**

Ujazi
28 Tennyson Street
Tel: 06-835 1490
Cosy café that is particularly interesting for its exhibitions by local artists. **$$**

Westshore Fish Café
112A Charles Street, Westshore
Tel: 06-834 0227
Slightly outside the centre of town, but worth the journey for the excellent and inexpensive fish. Dinner Tue–Sun, lunch Thur–Sun. **$$**

Taradale

Church Road Winery Restaurant
150 Church Road
Tel: 06-845 9140
Fresh local produce is used to create dishes that complement the vineyard's range of wines. Dine indoors in the Tiffen Room or alfresco in the winery garden. Open for lunch from 11am. Bookings recommended. **$$–$$$**

TARANAKI, WANGANUI AND MANAWATU

New Plymouth

André L'Escargot Restaurant and Bar
37–41 Brougham Street
Tel: 06-758 4812
www.andres.co.nz
Run by Frenchman André Teissonnière, L'Escargot has a definite French feel, including the namesake dish – baked Burgundy snails – and the music playing in the bar. **$$$**

Arborio
Puke Ariki Museum,
St Aubyn Street
Tel: 07-759 1241
www.macfarlanes.co.nz
Lively café in the museum overlooking the foreshore walkway. Enjoy authentic Italian risottos, home-made pizzas and pasta dishes indoors or alfresco. Daily 9am until late. **$$–$$$**

Salt
1 Egmont Street
Tel: 06-769 5301
Right on the waterfront with superb views from every table, Salt offers contemporary New Zealand cuisine until 10pm daily.
$$–$$$

Table Restaurant
Nice Hotel, 71 Brougham Street
Tel: 06-758 6423
www.nicehotel.co.nz
This award-winning restaurant in the gorgeous Nice Hotel serves designer food using the best of locally sourced ingredients. A huge selection of wines plus superb service. Also has an outdoor deck surrounded by a lush tropical garden. **$$$**

Palmerston North

Aberdeen Steakhouse
161 Broadway Avenue
Tel: 06-952 5570
www.aberdeensteakhouse.co.nz
Marbled walls, an earthen fireplace and the menu provide a Mediterranean atmosphere, and there's an all-weather courtyard for year-round alfresco dining. Wide range of dishes; steak is obviously the speciality. **$$**

The Herb Farm Café
Grove Road, Ashhurst
Tel: 06-326 7479
www.herbfarm.co.nz
A short drive from Palmerston North, this is Manawatu's most popular destination café, situated in a tranquil rural setting. It serves beautifully presented, garden-fresh meals. Also offers a range of herbal tours and workshops, and a well-stocked studio with herbal products, many of which are manufactured on site. **$–$$**

Spostato
213A Cuba Street
Tel: 06-952 3400
A real wee gem, hidden up a narrow staircase. Offers fine evening dining in a cosy, old-fashioned set-up with eclectic decor. Daily from 6pm. **$$$**

Wanganui

Redeye Café
96 Guyton Street
Tel: 06-345 5646
Freshly prepared food available from the chilled cabinet of this popular café.
$

Victoria's Restaurant
13 Victoria Avenue
Tel: 06-347 7007
This award-winning restaurant offers an à la carte menu, comprising mostly traditional Kiwi fare, and a café menu that's more European with fettuccine, spaghetti and sandwiches. **$$**

WELLINGTON AND SURROUNDINGS

Wellington

Arbitrageur
125 Featherstone Street
Tel: 04-499 5530
Described by *Cuisine* magazine as "a serious temple of gustatory pleasure", serves exquisite food in an elegant 1930s European ambience. It has a wine list of 600 bottles, 60 of which are available by the glass. **$$$**

Boulcott Street Bistro
99 Boulcott Street
Tel: 04-499 4199
www.boulcottstreetbistro.co.nz
A pretty cottage just off Willis Street houses this fine restaurant, which has an air of relaxed formality. New Zealand's finest game and seafood imaginatively prepared and served with grace and style. Lunch Mon–Fri, dinner Mon–Sat. **$$$**

Café Bastille
16 Majorbanks Street,
Mount Victoria
Tel: 04-382 9559
www.bastille.co.nz
Traditional French bistro serving good old-fashioned French food and some very good French and New Zealand wines, served by the glass. Mon–Sat 5.30pm until late. Reservation recommended. **$$$**

Café L'Affare
27 College Street
Tel: 04-385 9748
www.laffare.co.nz
This place serves excellent breakfasts and roasts its own coffee. It's very popular, so you'll need to arrive early to avoid disappointment. **$**

Citron 270
Willis Street
Tel: 04-801 6263
Set in a tiny two-storey colonial house, Citron offers wonderful flavour combinations and impeccable presentation. Tue–Sat from 6.30pm. **$$$**

The Flying Burrito Brothers
Corner Cuba and Vivian streets
Tel: 04-385 8811
www.flyingburritobrothers.co.nz
Fun Mexican-styled eatery and bar in the Bohemian Cuba quarter. **$$**

Logan Brown Restaurant
192 Cuba Street
Tel: 04-801 5114
www.loganbrown.co.nz
Book in advance to secure a table at one of the city's top restaurants. **$$$**

Martin Bosley's Yacht Club Restaurant
Royal Port Nicholson Yacht Club,
103 Oriental Parade
Tel: 04-385 6963
www.martin-bosley.com
Location doesn't come any better, and with Bosley's flamboyant dishes to match, the combination is perfect.
$$$

Monsoon Poon
12 Blair Street, Courtney Place
Tel: 04-803 3555
www.monsoonpoon.co.nz
A melting-pot of the cuisines of the Far East, this richly decorated eatery resembles an Eastern trading house. Diners can feast their eyes directly on the large open kitchen where it all happens. Take-out is also available.
$$–$$$

One Red Dog
Steamship Building,
North Queens Wharf
Tel: 04-918 4723
Wellington's leading gourmet pizza restaurant, with a bubbly atmosphere, more than 50 wines by the glass and award-winning beers on tap. **$$**

Shed 5 Restaurant and Bar
Queens Wharf
Tel: 04-499 9069
www.shed5.co.nz
This restaurant occupies a well-converted 1800s wool shed opposite the Maritime Museum and serves smartly prepared seafood.

PRICE CATEGORIES

Price categories are per person for dinner, including service and tax:
$ = NZ$10–15
$$ = NZ$15–25
$$$ = NZ$25 and over

The menu includes a range of meats as well. **$$$**

Taste
2 Ganges Road, Khandallah
Tel: 04-479 8449
Taste is a good example of the type of relaxed restaurant that features dishes reflecting New Zealand's diverse cultural influences. Dinner Wed–Sat from 6pm; brunch Sat–Sun 10am–2pm. Dinner bookings are essential. **$$$**

The Tasting Room
2 Courtenay Place
Tel: 04-384 1159
www.thetastingroom.co.nz
In the heart of the entertainment district, a "gastro-pub" specialising in traditional pub fare with a

twist, matched to a wide range of beers. **$$$**

Wholly Bagels
Corner Willis and Bond streets
Tel: 04-472 2336
Bagels made fresh daily using locally sourced ingredients. Boiled and baked in traditional New York style using no preservatives or additives. **$**

Zibibbo
25–29 Taranaki Street
Tel: 04-385 6650
www.zibibbo.co.nz
Contemporary cuisine in a stylish restaurant upstairs. Cocktail and lounge bar downstairs. Resident DJ on Friday and Saturday nights. Lunch Mon–Fri, dinner Mon–Sat. **$$–$$$**

Outside Wellington

The Old Winery Café
Corner Ponatahi and Huangarua roads, Martinborough
Tel: 06-306 8333
Fresh local New Zealand cuisine matched with a superb range of Martinborough's famous wine. **$$–$$$**

Salute
83 Main Street, Greytown
Tel: 06-304 9828
Recognised as one of the country's best Middle Eastern restaurants, Salute offers deliciously robust flavours and fine wines that can be enjoyed next to a blazing log fire on chilly Wairarapa winter nights, or,

come balmy summer afternoons, served alfresco under shady oaks. **$$$**

Wendy Campbell's French Bistro
3 Kitchener Street, Martinborough
Tel: 06-306 8863
Owners and hosts Jim and Wendy Campbell fled Wellington to Martinborough, 80km (50 miles) away, to establish this small restaurant which specialises in regional produce and serves wonderful local wines. The handwritten menu is always well thought out. The bistro got some much-deserved publicity when Oscar-winner Adrien Brody dined there and raved about it. **$$$**

SOUTH ISLAND

NELSON AND MARLBOROUGH

Blenheim

Bellafico Restaurant and Wine Bar
17 Maxwell Road
Tel: 03-577 6072
www.bellafico.co.nz
Modern New Zealand cuisine, imaginatively prepared seafood with a wine list featuring a wide range of the area's great wines. **$$**

Hotel d'Urville Restaurant
52 Queen Street
Tel: 03-577 9945
www.durville.com
A world-acclaimed restaurant with accommodation, set in a historic building. It also includes an international cooking school. 11 rooms. **$$$**

Rocco's Italian Restaurant
5 Dobson Street
Tel/fax: 03-578 6940
Run by Italians, this place specialises in home-made fresh pasta and prosciutto, as well as New Zealand seafood, lamb and chicken cooked in the traditional Italian way. Extensive menu and wine list. **$$$**

Twelve Trees Vineyard Restaurant
Allan Scott Wines and Estate, Jacksons Road
Tel: 03-572 7123
www.allanscott.com
A winery restaurant with a menu which perfectly showcases Allan Scott's full-bodied wines. Gorgeous indoor/outdoor setting seven minutes out of town towards the airport. Daily year-round for lunch. **$$–$$$**

Kaikoura

The Craypot Café and Bar
70 West End Road
Tel: 03-319 6027
www.craypot.co.nz
Centrally located, this restaurant has an open fire, and the varied menu includes mulled wine, fresh crayfish and vegetarian options. All-day dining until late. **$$$**

Donegal House
School House Road
Tel: 03-319 5083, 0800-346 873
www.donegalhouse.co.nz
Located 3km (2 miles) north of Kaikoura, this acclaimed Irish pub has an excellent

restaurant serving fresh local seafood; Kaikoura crayfish and the local rib-eye steak are specialities. Good local wine selection, and, of course, Guinness on tap. **$$$**

Nelson

Boat Shed Café
350 Wakefield Quay
Tel: 03-546 9783
www.boatshedcafe.co.nz
A very pleasant and popular restaurant, with views across the water and imaginative seafood dishes. 10am until late. Bookings essential. **$$$**

The Honest Lawyer
1 Point Road, Monaco
Tel: 03-547 8850
www.honestlawyer.co.nz
An old-style country pub in a historic building just outside Nelson, with a large beer garden and accommodation. Delicious New Zealand and British cuisine plus a wide-ranging wine list and selection of beers on tap. **$$**

The Smokehouse Café
Shed Three, Mapua Wharf, Mapua
Tel: 03-540 2280

www.smokehouse.co.nz
A unique smokehouse and café using the freshest local seafood. The menu is based on fish, mussels and vegetables, delicately hot-smoked on site using a traditional brick kiln and manuka shavings. **$$$**

Picton and the Sounds

The Barn Café, Restaurant and Bar
High Street, Picton
Tel: 03-573 7440
The traditional steak, chicken and seafood dishes cater to mainstream tastes but are no less worthy for that. Daily for breakfast, lunch and dinner. **$$$**

Le Café
14–26 London Quay, Picton
Tel: 03-573 5588
www.lecafepicton.co.nz
Great location on the waterfront, with an excellent menu featuring seasonal local produce, and, wherever possible, organic fare. Over 50 wines, beers and a selection of cigars. **$$**

CHRISTCHURCH AND SURROUNDINGS

Akaroa

C'est La Vie Bistro/Café
33 Rue Lavaud, Akaroa
Tel: 03-304 7314
Specialising in French cuisine and seafood dishes. **$$$**

French Farm Winery and Restaurant
Winery Road
Tel: 03-304 5784
www.frenchfarm.co.nz
One of the highlights of dining here is the glorious scenery around the outdoor dining patio. The menu emphasises fresh local ingredients, including Akaroa salmon and vegetables. Lunch daily 10am–4pm, dinner by arrangement. Next to it is La Pizzeria, serving traditional European-style pizzas. Sat and Sun only. **$$**

Little River Café and Store
Main Road, Little River, Banks Peninsula
Tel: 03-325 1933
This unpretentious café and general store is a popular halfway stopover on the road to Akaroa. Enjoy scrumptious country food, made on the premises, and good coffee in a private sculpture garden. **$**

Ma Maison Restaurant and Bar
6 Rue Balguerie
Tel: 03-304 7668
Waterfront location with quality food and a good wine list. Open 10.30am until late. **$$**

Christchurch

Asian Food Court
266 High Street
Tel: 03-365 0168
The only truly Asian food court in the South Island. A veritable melting pot of Asian cuisines: India, Thai, Indonesian, Malay, Chinese and Vietnamese. **$**

Cook 'N' With Gas
23 Worcester Boulevard
Tel: 03-377 9166
www.cooknwithgas.co.nz
The atmosphere is casual but the food is seriously good in this converted villa

opposite the Arts Centre. Canterbury ingredients and New Zealand heritage foods feature on the menu. There's also a good selection of boutique beers. This was Canterbury's Restaurant of the Year in 2006. Mon–Sat from 6pm. **$$$**

Coyote Café
18 Marshhead Road
Tel: 03-386 0556
An eclectic blend of Tex-Mex, Mexican and New Zealand flavours. Well-priced fare catering to a mostly younger crowd. **$–$$**

Cup
Corner Hackthorne and Dyers Pass roads
Tel: 03-332 1270
The food is good and the view is probably the best in Christchurch, taking in the whole city. **$$**

Dux de Lux
The Arts Centre, corner Montreal and Hereford streets
Tel: 03-366 6919
www.thedux.co.nz
Laid-back dining in a buzzing restaurant-bar complex. The menu is extensive, and includes a large number of seafood and vegetarian options. Try the brewed-on-the-premises beer. There's a great outdoor garden bar which can be used in all seasons. **$$$**

Ginko
153–157 Hereford Street
Tel: 03-374 2523
This restaurant prides itself on serving the spicy specialities of Szechuan from original recipes without Western adaptations. Here, it's the real deal. Lunch 11.30am–2pm; dinner Mon–Sun 5pm until late. **$–$$**

Honeypot Café
114 Lichfield Street
Tel: 03-366 5853
Casual eatery serving full meals as well as sandwiches. The pizzas include innovative toppings such as tandoori chicken, and Cajun with sour cream. Great desserts and coffee too. **$$**

ABOVE: dining alfresco.

Indochine
209 Cambridge Terrace
Tel: 03-365 7323
www.indochine.co.nz
The food is an eclectic mix of Asian-inspired fare. The atmosphere, cocktails and desserts are a blend of the exotic and seductive. **$$$**

Pedro's
143 Worcester Street
Tel: 03-379 7668
www.pedrosrestaurant.co.nz
Pedro comes from the Basque country, and is a popular local figure. The restaurant features superb Basque cuisine served in a relaxed atmosphere. **$$$**

Raj Mahal
Corner Worcester and Manchester streets
Tel: 03-366 0521
www.rajmahal.co.nz
The wide-ranging menu features Punjabi, northern and southern Indian, Mughlai, Goan and Gujarati dishes. There's also a good array of vegetarian dishes and breads. Takeaway service available. Tue–Sun 4.30–10pm. **$–$$**

Retour
Corner Cambridge Terrace and Manchester Street
Tel: 03-365 2888
www.retour.co.nz
Formerly a band rotunda, now a glass-sided restaurant overlooking the Avon River. Perfect for a romantic dinner, it specialises in premium New Zealand cuisine. Tue–Sun for dinner. **$$$**

Saggio di' Vino
Corner Victoria Street and Bealey Avenue
Tel: 03-379 4006
A "vinotheque" where the food is designed to complement the 80 or so wines that are offered by the glass. Daily for dinner. **$$$**

Sign of the Takahe
200 Hackthorne Road, Cashmere Hills
Tel: 03-332 4052
www.signofthetakahe.com
Silver service and fine dining in a baronial hilltop castle. This unique restaurant offers modern and traditional New Zealand cuisine. Reserve well in advance. **$$$**

Tiffany's Restaurant
Corner of Oxford Terrace and Lichfield Street
Tel: 03-379 1350
www.tiffanys.co.nz
Fine wines, first-rate regional cuisine and top-class service are on offer here. Tiffany's has a picturesque riverside location, but is still close to the centre of town. Their alfresco lunches are recommended. **$$$**

PRICE CATEGORIES

Price categories are per person for dinner, including service and tax:
$ = NZ$10–15
$$ = NZ$15–25
$$$ = NZ$25 and over

TRANSPORT

ACCOMMODATION

EATING OUT

ACTIVITIES

A – Z

CANTERBURY

The Old Mountaineers Café Bar and Restaurant
Aoraki Mount Cook Village, next to the DOC Visitor Centre
Tel: 03-435 1890
Sir Edmund Hillary is one of the mountaineers this café is named after. The extensive menu covers just about everything, from towering mountain burgers and steaks to chicken and apple crumble. Of note are the house speciality pork sausages named after the late Sir Ed. **$–$$$**
Panorama Restaurant
Inside the Hermitage Hotel
Tel: 0800-686 800
Outstanding views, particularly at sunset, the Panorama is where Chef Franz Blum creates world-class cuisine including seared venison

Denver leg, Mount Cook Salmon, Pithivier of Pheasant, medallions of South Island beef and deceptively simple, sublime desserts such as chocolate pots and vanilla rice pudding soufflé. Well worth splashing out. Bookings absolutely essential; ask for a window seat. **$$$**

Hot Springs Hotel
2 Fraser Close
Tel: 03-315 7799
www.hotsprings.co.nz
This is a friendly pub with a bistro menu. **$$**
Malabar Restaurant and Cocktail Bar
5 Conical Hill Road
Tel: 03-315 7745
The finest Asian and Indian cuisine with an excellent selection of local wines.

Reservations are essential. **$$$**

Pepe's Pizza
SH8
Tel: 03-680 6677
In a niche of its own among the many fine-dining establishments along Tekapo's ridge, Pepe's Pizza has a great atmosphere with fireside dining and a cosy bar, and incredibly good pizza. The Smoked Salmon Siesta – thin-crust pizza topped with smoked Mount Cook salmon, onion, zucchini and wasabi sauce – as well as Vinnie's Venison, topped with roast venison, roast kumara and pumpkin served with lashings of spiced plum sauce, are especially recommended. **$$**

Reflections Restaurant
At the Lake Tekapo Scenic Resort, Main Highway
Tel: 03-680 6234
Fresh local produce including salmon and venison are on the menu here, accompanied by spectacular mountain and lake views. **$$$**

Abisko Lodge
74 Main Street, Mount Hutt Village, Main Road
Tel: 03-302 8875
www.abisko.co.nz
Specialists in feeding hungry skiers. Open for breakfast, lunch and dinner. **$–$$**
Café 131
131 Main Street
Tel: 03-302 9131
Hearty breakfasts, lunches and snacks, all reasonably priced. Closes at 5pm daily. **$–$$**

THE WEST COAST

Café Neve
Main Road
Tel: 03-751 0110
Award-winning café in the heart of Fox Glacier township offering indoor and alfresco (summer only) dining. The menu features fresh seafood, lamb, beef, vegetarian meals and a selection of pasta dishes and salads. **$$–$$$**
High Peaks Bar and Restaurant
163 Cook Flat Road
Tel: 03-751 0131
The place to sample authentic west-coast cuisine: the venison hotpot is one of its most popular dishes. The restaurant has an extensive wine list; the café has a good selection of bistro meals. Great views from every table. **$$**

Beeches Restaurant
SH6, Franz Josef Glacier

Tel: 03-752 0721
Specialising in authentic west-coast cuisine, including venison and beef, it also offers light meals and has an extensive wine list. Open from 9am daily. **$$**
Blue Ice Café
SH6
Tel: 03-752 0707
The eclectic menu ranges from Italian and Indian dishes to New Zealand cuisine, but pizzas are the speciality. Extensive wine list. Upstairs bar with pool table. **$$**
The Glasshouse Restaurant
Scenic Circle Hotel, SH6
Tel: 03-752 0729
Stunning rainforest views and a superb showcase of classic west-coast cuisine, including tempting entrées such as whitebait fritters served with fresh Lake Mapourika watercress, Fox Glacier duck breast served on udon noodles, and mains like South Westland lamb rump, venison medallions,

and Aoraki salmon. **$$$**

The Bay House Café
Tauranga Bay (near Westport)
Tel: 03-789 7133
www.thebayhouse.co.nz
Good food in an oceanside location, tucked away under the shelter of Cape Foulwind, well worth going out of your way for. The seasonal menu features west-coast specialities, fish in particular. Don't miss the chowder. Wash it down with a glass or two of Good Bastards, Green Fern or Monteith's local beer. **$$$**
Café 124 On Mackay
124 Mackay Street
Tel: 03-768 7503
Situated in newly built premises. Great food and coffee. Indoor and outdoor dining. **$$–$$$**
The Smelting House Café
102 MacKay Street
Tel: 03-768 0012
Set in a converted historic west-coast bank building

and run by a registered dietician. Specialising in home-style food. Mon–Sat 8am–5pm. **$–$$**

Fantail Café
Corner Mark Road and SH6
Tel: 03-750 0055, 0800-681 682
Dine in or get takeaway at this conveniently located café. Serves standard café fare such as fish and chips, pies, vegetarian food and sandwiches. Menu features blue cod when available. Whitebait is a favourite here. Daily 7.30am–5pm. **$–$$$**
Haast World Heritage Hotel
SH6
Tel: 03-750 0828, 0800-502 444

Price categories are per person for dinner, including service and tax:
$ = NZ$10–15
$$ = NZ$15–25
$$$ = NZ$25 and over

www.world-heritage-hotel.com
Wild west-coast food, such as lamb, monkfish, venison, salmon and whitebait, are on the menu here. **$–$$$**
McGuires Lodge Restaurant and Bar
SH6
Tel: 03-750 0020, 0800-624 847
www.mcguireslodge.co.nz
One of the best eateries

around. Its menu draws on local ingredients from whitebait to Hereford steak to blue cod. Part of the McGuires Lodge with 19 rooms. **$$–$$$**

Hokitika

Café de Paris
19–21 Tancred Street

Tel: 03-755 8933
Featuring genuine French cooking, with a fabulous range of mouth-watering desserts in a place that's about as far from Paris as you can possibly get. **$$–$$$**
Stumpers Bar And Café
2 Weld Street
Tel: 03-755 6154

www.stumpers.co.nz
This warm and cosy café offers a wide-ranging menu featuring lamb shanks, fresh pasta, locally caught whitebait (in season) and venison, to name a few. Check out the copper artwork by local artists that adorns the walls. **$$–$$$**

QUEENSTOWN AND OTAGO

Arrowtown

The Postmasters House Restaurant
54 Buckingham Street
Tel: 03-442 0991
www.postmastershouse.com
Award-winning restaurant in a meticulously restored historic house. Superb food, fine wine list and excellent service. Tue–Sun. **$$$**
Saffron
18 Buckingham Street
Tel: 03-442 0131
www.saffronrestaurant.co.nz
With its classy Asian-influenced menu, Saffron has been included in *Condé Nast Traveller's* list of the most exciting restaurants in the world. **$$$**

Queenstown

The Bathhouse
28 Marine Parade
Tel: 03-442 5625
www.bathhouse.co.nz
An old bathhouse, built in 1911, right on the beach with amazing lake and mountain views. It offers nostalgic indoor and awe-inspiring outdoor dining from an award-winning menu. **$$$**
Boardwalk Seafood Restaurant and Bar
Steamer Wharf Village
Tel: 03-442 5630
www.boardwalk.net.nz
Popular with tourists – and Bill Clinton once dined here – this restaurant serves both meat and seafood dishes with a modicum of flair. **$$$**
The Bunker
Cow Lane
Tel: 03-441 8030

www.thebunker.co.nz
Small, stylish restaurant serving simple, fresh, modern cuisine. Reservations advised. Daily for dinner. **$$$**
Glenorchy Hotel & Bar
Mull Street, Glenorchy
Tel: 03-442 9902
Rustic fully licensed restaurant open for country-style breakfasts, and lunch and dinner. Sit beside the large stone fireplace during the winter or on the sun-drenched decks during the summer. **$–$$**
Lone Star Café and Bar
14 Brecon Street
Tel: 03-442 9995
www.lonestar.co.nz
As the name implies, a Western-style restaurant where the portions are huge and the food is good. **$$**
Minami Jujisei
45 Beach Street
Tel: 03-442 9854
Award-winning traditional Japanese cuisine, mixed

with modern influences; particularly good for those who have never tried Japanese food before. **$$$**
Roaring Megs Restaurant
53 Shotover Street
Tel: 03-442 9676
www.roaringmegs.co.nz
Set in a gold miner's cottage dating back to the late 1800s, this restaurant has won awards for its European/Pacific Rim style of cuisine. Candlelit dining in a relaxed, cosy atmosphere. **$$$**
Solera Vino
25 Beach Street
Tel: 03-442 6082
An attractive place serving French Mediterranean cuisine and a good range of wines. **$$–$$$**
Tatler Restaurant
5 The Mall
Tel: 03-442 8372
www.tatler.co.nz
Evocatively sited in a gold-rush-era building. Akaroa salmon fillet served with

basmati rice is typical of the lunch menu. **$$$**

Wanaka

Finchy's Restaurant and Bar
2 Dunmore Street
Tel: 03-443 6262
Built in rustic stone, wood and iron on the old 1880 Wanaka jail site, this spacious, upmarket but casual restaurant has an inviting ambience. The open fireplace is a draw, as is the long menu and wine list. **$$$**
Kai Whakapai Café and Bar
Lakefront
Tel: 03-443 7795
www.kaiwanaka.co.nz
Easy to find on the edge of Lake Wanaka, this café has panoramic views and prides itself on its freshly baked breads, pies, pasta and vegetarian selections. Daily 8am–4pm. **$–$$**

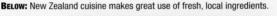

BELOW: New Zealand cuisine makes great use of fresh, local ingredients.

DUNEDIN

Dunedin

Bell Pepper Blues
474 Princes Street
Tel: 03-474 0973
www.bellpepperblues.co.nz
Pleasant, high-quality
restaurant with fireside
atmosphere and
outstanding food. Always
very full. **$$$**

Bennu Café and Bar
12 Moray Place
Tel: 03-474 5055
Brasserie with imaginative
Pacific Rim flavours,
Mediterranean
gourmet pizzas and great

desserts, served amid the
stylish decor of the old
Savoy building. It's also
renowned for great coffee.
Late-night lounge bar
upstairs. **$$**

A Cow Called Bertha
199 Upper Stuart Street
Tel: 03-477 2993
Swiss-style country cuisine.
A variety of meat dishes
with the emphasis on big
flavours and sauces. Mon–
Sat for dinner. **$$$**

Etrusco at the Savoy
8A Moray Place
Tel: 03-477 3737
www.etrusco.co.nz

Located on the first floor of
the historic Savoy Building,
offering an extensive menu
of Tuscan favourites – pasta
dishes, thin-crust pizzas,
Italian breads and antipasti.
Strong Italian coffee,
desserts and extensive wine
list. **$$–$$$**

Ombrellos
10 Clarendon Street
Tel: 03-477 8773
www.ombrellos.com
This restaurant features
highly imaginative cuisine
in an attractive, wood-
panelled interior.
Excellent wine list. Lunch

Tue–Sun 10am–2.30pm,
dinner Tue–Sat 6pm until
late. **$$$**

The Palms Restaurant
18 Queens Gardens
Tel: 03-477 6534
Popular with the locals,
this elegant, relaxed
restaurant serves up
generous portions from a
varied menu. Enjoy lovely
views over the Queens
Gardens (on summer
evenings) from the huge
windows of this spacious
turn-of-the-century building.
Lunch and dinner Mon–Sat.
$$$

SOUTHLAND

Colac Bay

The Pavilion
188 Colac Foreshore Road,
Tel: 03-234 8445
Sample fresh local fare
including Colac Bay *paua*
and beefburgers, fresh
Stewart Island salmon,
seafood chowder, and that
good old Southland stable,
blue cod and chips. It
comes cooked to your liking,
battered or egg-washed,
with potatoes or chips,
salad and home-made
tartare. Highly
recommended. **$–$$$**

Invercargill

The Cabbage Tree
379 Dunns Road, Otatara, RD9
Tel: 03-213 1443
www.thecabbagetree.com
A European-inspired

restaurant and wine bar
with a warm atmosphere
(four fireplaces) and
delicious local seafood and
produce. There is a choice
of à la carte or set menus.
$$–$$$

El Tigre Café Bar
16 Kelvin Street
Tel: 03-214 6914
El Tigre is an upbeat café
serving stylish fare ranging
from tiger prawns and
yellowfin tuna to ostrich
steaks. **$–$$**

**Flannagans Seafood
Restaurant**
Bainfield Road, Queens Drive
roundabout, Waikiwi
Tel: 03-215 8156
Housed in a rambling old
villa, this restaurant
specialises in seafood but
also caters amply to meat
eaters. Open Tue–Sat.
$$

HMS Kings Restaurant
80 Tay Street
Tel: 03-218 3443
Classic New Zealand
seafood, prepared simply to
do it justice: crayfish,
oysters, whitebait, prawns,
fish. **$$**

Te Anau

Kepler's Restaurant
23 Town Centre
Tel: 03-249 7909
The menu consists of 50
percent seafood. Sautéed
garlic prawns and orange
roughy feature alongside
traditional favourites
(pavlova, lamb, venison, fish
and chips) on the menu
here. Kepler's has excellent
food and good service.
$$–$$$

La Toscana
108 Town Centre

Tel: 03-249 7756
www.latoscana.co.nz
A true taste of Tuscany in Te
Anau with excellent service.
Word from the locals is that
the *al nonno* pasta and
cheesecake are divine.
Open daily 7am–10pm.
$–$$

Olive Tree Café
52 Town Centre
Tel: 03-249 8496
A pleasant café open
7am–10pm for breakfast,
lunch and dinner with good
coffee. **$**

Redcliff Café and Bar
12 Mokonui Street
Tel: 03-249 7431
Big-city-style fusion fare
served in a delightful old
cottage, with live
entertainment. Evenings
only. Friendly true-blue Kiwi
service; highly
recommended. **$$**

STEWART ISLAND

Charliez Pizzeria
10 Main Road, Oban
Tel: 03-219 1419
In the middle of Oban,
adjoining the Rakiura
Theatre where NZ heritage
movies are shown by day
and feature and arthouse
movies play at night,
Charliez Pizzeria dishes up
steaming coffee, cake and a

wide range of pizzas which
can be eaten in house or
while watching a movie.
$–$$

Church Hill Café
36 Kamahi Road, Oban
Tel: 03-219 1323
Offers a la carte and stone-
grill dining with panoramic
sea views. Local dishes
blue cod and mutton bird

are specialities here.
$$–$$$

South Sea Hotel
Foreshore, Oban
Tel: 03-219 1059
No visit to Stewart Island is
complete without dining at
the South Seas Hotel, a
local watering hole and the
best place to sample freshly
caught blue cod served with

chunky fries and thick
wedges of lemon.
$–$$

PRICE CATEGORIES

Price categories are per
person for dinner, including
service and tax:
$ = NZ$10–15
$$ = NZ$15–25
$$$ = NZ$25 and over

A CTIVITIES

THE ARTS, NIGHTLIFE, FESTIVALS, SHOPPING, OUTDOOR ACTIVITIES AND CHILDREN'S ACTIVITIES

THE ARTS

General

New Zealand's culture comprises a blend of influences, including Maori and Pacific Island, European, US and Asian. New Zealand performers, film-makers, writers, designers and musicians have made their mark with their own unique style and talent.
Art Galleries: New Zealand has a vibrant contemporary art scene, and most towns have art galleries. Keep an eye out for works by some of the country's leading artists, including Ralph Hotere, Colin McCahon, Michael Parekowhai and Robyn Kahukiwa. The Dunedin Public Art Gallery (www.dunedin.art.museum) is the country's oldest viewing room.
Classical Music and Ballet: The country has three professional symphony orchestras, including the New Zealand Symphony Orchestra, and its own professional ballet company, the Royal New Zealand Ballet. A number of contemporary dance companies are operating throughout the country, including Black Grace Dance Company (Auckland) and Footnote Dance Company (Wellington).
Contemporary Music: The music scene varies from rappers and DJs to jazz musicians and opera singers. It has produced some world-class performers, from Kiri Te Kanawa to Neil Finn (Crowded House) and Pauly Fuemana (OMC). Other Kiwi performers making a name for themselves include Pacifier, Bic Runga, Stellar, The Datsuns, D4 and Hayley Westenra.

Theatre: Theatre is a thriving industry and New Zealand boasts a number of theatre companies, including Taki Rua in Wellington and the Auckland Theatre Company. There are venues for live theatre in most towns and cities, and many fine repertory theatre companies throughout the country.
Festivals: Festivals are plentiful, and there are arts festivals in most major New Zealand towns – from Bluff in the South to the Bay of Islands in the North. *(See pages 357–60 for listings.)*
Film: Movies such as Peter Jackson's *The Lord of the Rings*, Lee Tamahori's *Once Were Warriors* and the hit cult television series *Xena, Warrior Princess* have established the country's filmmakers as some of the best in the world.
Listings: To find local cultural events, check the entertainment pages of the local newspaper or go to: www.artscalendar.co.nz. Other useful sources of information are: the monthly magazine *Theatre News*; *NZ Musician* (modern music); *Music in New Zealand* (classical); *Rip it Up; Real Groove* (pop/rock) and *Pulp*, all available at major newsagents or in libraries.

North Island

Auckland

New Zealand's biggest city is home to several dance and theatre companies, its own arts festival and three theatres: the **Civic**, **Aotea Centre** and **Sky City Theatre**. The entertainment section of the *New Zealand Herald* is the best source of performance listings. Book for major events through **Ticketek** (Aotea Centre, Aotea Square, Queen Street, tel: 09-307 5000; www.ticketek.co.nz).

Concert Venues

The main concert and opera venues are the modern **Aotea Centre** and the **Town Hall** (Aotea Square, Queen Street, tel: 09-309 2677; www.the-edge.co.nz). There's also the **Bruce Mason Theatre** on the North Shore, which is mostly used for larger productions. For bookings, tel: 09-488 2940; www.bmcentre.co.nz. Smaller, part-time venues include the old theatre complexes in the city centre, which host concerts and shows by international DJs and musicians.
Authentic Maori ceremonies and dances are performed daily at 11am, noon and 1.30pm in the **Auckland War Memorial Museum** (Domain, tel: 09-309 0443). Performances last approximately 45 minutes.

Theatre/Dance
The 700-seat **Sky City Theatre**, which opened in 1997 in the Casino Complex (entrance at the corner of Hobson and Wellesley streets), tel: 09-912 6000; www.skycity.co.nz; **Maidment Theatre** (in the university, corner of Princes and Alfred streets, tel: 09-308 2383; www.maidment. auckland.ac.nz), the **Herald Theatre** and **ASB Auditorium** (Aotea Centre complex, tel: 09-309 2677; www.the-edge.co.nz) are three of the most popular venues for drama. The opulent **Civic** (tel: 09-309 2677; www. civictheatre.co.nz) is usually used for touring musicals and shows.
Details of performances at various venues by Auckland's main theatre group, **Auckland Theatre Company**, are available at tel: 09-309 3395;

Ticketek Tickets

Most major events can be booked through the national ticketing agency, **Ticketek**. There are more than 200 Ticketek outlets in New Zealand. Contact: **Auckland**, tel: 09-307 5000; **Wellington**, tel: 04-384 3840; **Christchurch**, tel: 03-377 8899; www.ticketek.co.nz.

www.atc.co.nz. For the **Auckland Music Theatre Company**, contact tel: 09-846 7693.

Smaller venues producing more innovative work include **Silo**, Lower Greys Avenue in central Auckland, tel: 09-366 0339; www.silotheatre.co.nz, and **Depot Arts Space**, 28 Clarence Street, Devonport, over the Harbour Bridge on the North Shore, tel: 09-963 2331; www.depotartspace.co.nz.

Auckland is also home to the all-male dance company **Black Grace**, featuring some of New Zealand's finest and most respected contemporary dancers, tel: 09-358 0552; www.blackgrace.co.nz.

Hamilton

Hamilton has a variety of entertainment on offer – from arts and film festivals to live theatre, music and dance. National and international touring groups visit Hamilton and play at one of three venues – **Founders Theatre**, the **Clarence Street Theatre** and **The Meteor**, tel: 07-838 6600.

Check out **The Fuel Festival**, held in Hamilton in June every other year (next held in 2010). The city has an abundance of nightclubs and bars, and some of the top DJs from Auckland often perform here.

Rotorua

The **Civic Theatre** is a popular venue for *kapa haka* and Maori performing arts, and there are Maori concerts and shows throughout Rotorua. The famous **Opera In The Pa** concerts are held in January at Rotowhio Marae. For more information, contact the **Rotorua i-site Visitors Centre**, tel: 07-348 5179; www.rotoruanz.com. With **Rotoiti Tours** (daily in summer, winter by arrangement; charge; tel: 07-348 8969, 0800-476 864; www.worldmaori.co.nz), visitors enjoy a very traditional experience, including a concert and *hangi*, at the Rakeiao *marae* (meeting area), plus the opportunity to sleep over communally in the *wharenui* (meeting house), although this is usually only available for large groups.

Tauranga/Mount Maunganui

Tauranga hosts a vast range of events, including jazz festivals, arts festivals and sports marathons. It also has a vibrant nightlife scene, and most bars around the Tauranga and Mount Maunganui region are packed during the weekends. The **Baycourt Theatre** stages a number of exhibitions, festivals and events, tel: 07-577 7198.

Wellington

Wellington has three repertory theatres, a wide range of musical events and numerous music, art and theatre festivals. It's also home to the Royal New Zealand Ballet, New Zealand Symphony Orchestra, New Zealand String Quartet, Chamber Music New Zealand, Wellington Sinfonia and NBR New Zealand Opera. At the end of the year, there are performances by the New Zealand School of Dance and the New Zealand Drama School, Toi Whakaari.

For ticketing details, contact Wellington's **Ticketek** office at tel: 04-384 3840; www.ticketek.co.nz.

Theatre/Ballet

Bats Theatre, 1 Kent Terrace, tel: 04-802 4175; www.bats.co.nz. This small and cosy venue has the courage to experiment with lesser-known works, which means you can often book tickets at short notice.
Circa Theatre, 1 Taranaki Street, tel: 04-801 7992; www.circa.co.nz. This theatre, managed by the actors themselves, offers stimulating drama in a waterside location, by Te Papa Museum. You can get cheap stand-by tickets an hour before the show.
Downstage Theatre, 2 Courtenay Place, tel: 04-801 6946; www. downstage.co.nz. Located in the restaurant and café district, this professional theatre stages a variety of plays – from modern authors to Shakespeare – plus performances by the leading Maori theatre company, Taki Rua.
Royal New Zealand Ballet, 77–87 Courtenay Place, tel: 04-381 9000; www.nzballet.org.nz. The country's principal ballet company was formed in 1953, and is based at the St James Theatre. Tickets from Ticketek, tel: 04-384 3840.
St James Theatre, 77–87 Courtenay Place, tel: 04-802 4060; www.stjames. co.nz. The finest lyric theatre in New Zealand. This restored heritage building is the Wellington venue for opera, ballet and major musical shows. Also the site of the Ticketek box-office agency.

South Island

Christchurch

Christchurch is a fairly laid-back city with many artists and craftspeople. The theatre and concert scene is varied, and events are listed in the *Christchurch and Canterbury Visitors' Guide*. The *Press* newspaper also has details of current arts events. Christchurch is also home to the yearly Arts Festival, the Festival of Romance and the Winter Carnival.

Theatre

Court Theatre, 20 Worcester Boulevard, tel: 0800-333 100; www. courttheatre.org.nz. This is regarded as New Zealand's leading theatre, with a small, high-quality ensemble and guest actors from Britain playing middle-of-the-road modern drama. It's also home to the Southern Ballet and Dance Theatre.
Isaac Theatre Royal, 145 Gloucester Street, tel: 03-366 6326; www. isaactheatreroyal.co.nz. Built in 1908, this Edwardian-style lyric theatre seats about 1,300 people and hosts concerts, comedy and a range of other events and arts performances.

Concerts

Convention Centre, **Town Hall**, and **Westpac Centre**, 95 Kilmore Street, tel: 03-366 8899; www.convention.co.nz. This modern building near the casino plays host to major musical events. It is also the headquarters of a leading nationwide theatre and concert-ticket agency – and New Zealand's largest indoor sports stadium.

Dunedin

Behind the facades of its once elegant buildings, Dunedin is still a very youthful town. It is the home of New Zealand's oldest university, and the large numbers of students give it a relaxed atmosphere, with plenty of pub music and theatre on offer. Dunedin has a vibrant live-music scene, and a number of excellent New Zealand bands have originated here. The **Fortune Theatre**, 231 Stewart Street, tel: 03-477 8323; www. fortunetheatre.co.nz, has a particularly good reputation and hosts both local and touring performances. Also the **Globe Theatre**, 104 London Street, tel: 03-477 3274, a Dunedin institution dedicated to bringing the best in classical and modern plays, although no further productions are currently scheduled until 2010. The **Dunedin Casino**, 118 High Street, tel: 03-477 4545; www.dunedincasino.co.nz is also worth a visit. Minimum age is 20.

NIGHTLIFE

New Zealand's nightlife options can vary considerably, depending on the size of the place you are visiting. In small towns, you will find little more than a humble pub. Pubs are a great New Zealand social institution, and you will seldom find yourself short of conversation or an opinion. In recent years, many city pubs have become more sophisticated, with "boutique" beer brewed on the premises and brasserie-style food.

The main cities have a variety of cosmopolitan dance clubs with a predominantly young clientele, as well as late-night bars. In Auckland and Wellington, and to a growing extent Christchurch, activity in the bars doesn't peak until after midnight. Auckland and Wellington are busy most nights of the week, while it is a little quieter in Christchurch until Thursday, Friday and Saturday nights. Queenstown reaches a critical mass at times, such as during the winter festival, when the parties don't seem to stop.

North Island

Auckland

It's hard to escape the buzz of Auckland's nightlife. Walk along Ponsonby Road, turn left into K Road, then down Queen Street and through to the viaduct and you'll hear music pulsating from every doorway.

Most clubs have dress codes and you won't get in wearing shorts or gym shoes. Some clubs are discreetly hidden away up staircases or down alleyways, and only the locals know they exist, but follow the music and you're bound to find them. Some of the popular bars include:

Caluzzi, 461–463 Karangahape Road, CBD, tel: 09-357 0778; www.caluzzi.co.nz. For a unique, unforgettable night out with great food, this is the place. Plus a disco, DJs and an interactive show by award-winning drag artistes. NZ$60 for dinner and show.

Chapel Bar, 147 Ponsonby Road, Ponsonby, tel: 09-360 4528. Recently voted best bar in New Zealand, this popular venue on the corner of Ponsonby Road and Anglesea also has a full menu from 6–10pm, and thereafter serves pizza and finger food until it closes.

Clooney, 33 Sales Street, CBD, tel: 09-358 1702. Tucked in behind Victoria Park Market, this bar is set inside a converted warehouse and has an extensive cocktail list.

Danny Doolans, Viaduct Harbour, 204 Quay Street, CBD, tel: 09-358 2554. Popular Irish bar in a good location with lots of old-world charm. Decor even includes a confessional box.

The Dog's Bollix, corner Newton and K roads, tel:09-376 4600; www.dogsbollix.co.nz. Great live-music pub.

The Drake, 2 Drake Street, Freemans Bay, tel: 09-307 3220. Serves Monteith's beer and tasty pub grub.

Fu/Zen Bar, 166 Queen Street, tel: 09-309 3079. Fu Bar is a relaxed hideaway with friendly staff, attracting drum-and-bass fans.

Hush Lounge Bar, corner of Paul Matthews Road and Omega Street, Albany, North Shore, tel: 09-414 5679. A swish watering hole in the heart of Albany. Boasts a comprehensive cocktail list, small dinner menu and has a sunny outdoor courtyard.

Khuja Lounge, 3rd Floor, 536 Queen Street, tel: 09-377 3711. An intimate Moroccan-themed bar hidden away up three flights of stairs. Great DJs, soulful jazz and excellent chocolate Martinis.

Rakinos, Level 1, 35 High Street, CBD, tel: 09-358 3535. Trendy lounge bar playing a blend of hip-hop, soul and funk. DJ on Thursday evenings, jazz on Sundays.

Ruby, 484 New North Road, Kingsland, tel: 09-845 6990. Upmarket bar that is always open and filled with an interesting and offbeat crowd. A great place to people-watch. Well worth the short taxi ride.

The Wine Cellar, St Kevin's Arcade, K Road, tel: 09-377 8293. Cosy bunker-like space beneath arcade and the hang-out for creative types who come here to enjoy wines from the Coromandel in an unpretentious environment. Live acoustic entertainment Sat–Sun.

Northland

Nightlife is pretty relaxed in Northland, but there are plenty of bars and restaurants to choose from. The town of Paihia or the trendy area of the Town Basin in Whangarei are the best places to head for live music and bars.

Rotorua

Pubs/Bars

Barbarella, 1263 Pukuatua Street, tel: 07-347 0409. Rotorua's main live-music venue, where you are just as likely to find the latest punk band from Auckland as a DJ keeping things happening.

Fuze Bar, 1122 Tutanekai Street, tel: 07-349 6306; www.fuzebar.co.nz. This upmarket café and bar is bright and airy and offers light gourmet meals and great coffee. In the evenings, it's one of the most popular dance clubs in town.

Henneseys Irish Bar, 1210 Tutanekai Street, tel: 07-343 7901; Mon–Sat 11am until late, Sun noon–1am. Live entertainment on Thursday. Outside seating available. Full bar menu and snacks.

O'Malleys Irish Bar, 1287 Eruera Street, tel: 07-347 6410. Daily 2pm until late. Nice atmosphere, friendly people and good music. Comedy night once a month, quiz night Wednesday, happy hour daily from 4–6pm with full bar menu.

The Pheasant Plucker, Arawa Street, tel: 07-343 7071. Live music Thur–Sat nights, bar snacks and meals. Mon–Fri 4pm until late, Sat 3pm until late, Sun 11.30am until late.

Pig and Whistle, corner Haupapa and Tutanekai streets, tel: 07-347

BELOW: Auckland and Wellington are the main nightlife centres.

3025; www.pigandwhistle.co.nz. Naturally brewed beers, a garden bar with two big screens, hearty pub meals and live entertainment on Thur, Fri and Sat.

Taupo

For a town of its size, Taupo has quite a number of bars to while away the evening hours. **Holy Cow!** (tel: 07-378 0040) at 11 Tongariro Street is one of the most popular nightspots. **Finn MacCuhal's** (tel: 07-378 6165; www. finns.co.nz), an Irish bar at the corner of Tuwharetoa and Tongariro streets, is another lively place to down a pint of Guinness. It has live entertainment Thur–Sat.

Wellington

Beaujolais Wine Bar, 11 Woodward Street, tel: 04-472 1471. A great destination for wine-lovers as it serves an excellent range of quality wines from New Zealand and around the world, sold by the glass or the bottle.
Bodega, 101 Ghuznee Street, tel: 04-384 8212; www.bodega.co.nz. Bodega specialises in New Zealand ale, including the local Tuatara beer, and serves the city's only hand-drawn ales plus 17 different tap beers. Also famous as a venue for live, original New Zealand music.
Boogie Wonderland, 25–29 Courtney Place, tel: 04-385 2242. Those who love to dance are guaranteed a good night. Featuring a *Saturday Night Fever* dance floor.
Boulot, 15 Blair Street, tel: 04-801 6615. European-style restaurant and bar with an excellent wine list.
Concrete Bar, Level 1, Cable Car Lane, tel: 04-473 7427. Light evening meals and a superb range of cocktails are served in a distinct New York-style atmosphere.
Courtney Arms, 26 Allen Street, tel: 04-801 6026. Reminiscent of an English pub, with decor to match. English beers available on tap. Large open fireplace and a dance floor with a DJ playing most nights, and a jukebox when not.

Films

Wellington has more screens per capita than anywhere else in the country, which show mainstream and arthouse, international and local films. There is a highly regarded film festival every year. The **Embassy Theatre** (tel: 04-384 7657), at the end of Courtenay Place, is Wellington's grandest cinema.

Hummingbird, 22 Courtenay Place, tel: 04-801 6336. This is a stylish café and bar in a great location, and it attracts a more mature crowd than some of the other establishments along Courtenay Place.
Welsh Dragon Bar, Middle of the Road, Cambridge Terrace, tel: 04-385 6566. This has been compared to the best pubs in Ireland for atmosphere, yet it is Welsh – complete with Welsh beer and owners. Live music three nights a week; there's a piano for impromptu performances. Closed Mondays.

South Island

Christchurch

On Fridays and Saturdays, nearly all pubs have live bands performing. The **Christchurch Casino** (tel: 03-365 9999) in Victoria Street is also a hive of activity.
Work your way through the various establishments such as **Viaduct** (tel: 03-377 9968) on **The Strip** along **Oxford Terrace**. Cafés by day, they become bars by night.
The Dux de Lux, 299 Montreal Street, tel: 03-366 6919; www.thedux.co.nz. This has a trendy but laid-back crowd. Brews its own beers, and you can drink in one of three bars inside or outside. Food is vegetarian and seafood. Live music, often folk and blues.
The Loaded Hog, corner of Cashel and Manchester streets, tel: 03-366 6674; www.loadedhog.co.nz. The premier bar on a busy corner. Like its Auckland counterpart, it is big, bold and a popular place to be seen.
Lone Star, 76 Manchester Street, tel: 03-365 7086. The Jack Ruby Bar within this complex is a comfortable place to meet for a casual beer. Meals are also served.
The Ministry, 90 Lichfield Street, tel: 03-379 2910; www.ministry.co.nz. Plays the latest sounds from around the world to a frequently gay crowd. Big dance floor and great sound system add to the frenetic atmosphere late at night.
Speights Ale House, 263 Bealey Avenue, tel: 03-379 8660; www. speights-alehouse.co.nz. Owned by an ex-All Black, this is a good place to rub shoulders with locals.
Torenhof Belgian Café, 88 Armagh Street, tel: 03-377 1007. Housed in the historic Canterbury Provincial Chambers, this bar serves a range of Belgian and New Zealand beers.
The Twisted Hop, 6 Popular Street, tel: 03-962 3688. The only brewery in New Zealand to produce traditional

English-style cask-conditioned ales. If you need a proper pint head here. An extensive range of draught beers from New Zealand and around the globe is also served here. Family-friendly during the day.

Queenstown

Queenstown has plenty of superb bars and nightclubs that are often packed with international travellers and backpackers as well as local skiers and adventurers.
Altitude, 49 Shotover Street, tel: 03-441 0846. A new bar with lots of entertainment most suited to a younger crowd.
Bardeaux, Eureka Arcade, off The Mall, tel: 03-442 8284. Sumptuous surroundings with comfy leather armchairs, extensive wine and cocktails list, plus a huge open fireplace make this a very popular spot for locals and tourists alike. Best to dress smart.
Barup, Searle Lane, tel: 03-442 7067. Cocktail bar with comfy couches, a large fireplace and good cocktails. A DJ plays on Friday nights.
The Boiler Room, Steamer Wharf, tel: 03-441 8066. A groovy cocktail bar with friendly bar staff. Leather loungers and music from the 70s, 80s and 90s. Frequented by locals and visiting New Zealanders, this is the place to see and be seen.
Pog Mahone's, 14 Rees Street, tel: 03-442 5328. As Irish as they come in Queenstown. The Guinness flows smoothly, and it packs out when live bands are playing (usually Wed and Sun). Food available.
Surreal, 7 Rees Street, tel: 03-441 8492. It's a restaurant in the early evening, but as the night comes on, techno music takes hold and this venue transforms into one of the cooler nightspots in town. Great food and service.
Tardis, Cow Lane, tel: 03-441 8397. Hip-hop every night of the week played by leading DJs. A small venue that fills quickly, so it pays to go early.
The World Bar, Restaurants and Nightclub, 27 Shotover Street, tel: 03-4426 757. Often filled with backpackers and young adventurers, this is a lively and often very noisy venue renowned for happy hours that go on until late.

Wanaka

Like Queenstown, the nightlife and entertainment in Wanaka tend to centre around the après-ski crowd in winter and adventure bunnies in summer. There are plenty of bars and a few nightclubs. Check out the

Slainte Irish Bar, tel: 03-443 6755, in Lower Helwick Street, open daily from noon. It serves Irish and Kiwi fare, plus a huge variety of New Zealand and Irish beers.

Dunedin

A true university town, Dunedin's nightlife is lively and incorporates a mix of live music and poetry evenings, and is a hothouse for contemporary up-and-coming bands.
Di Lusso, 12 The Octagon, tel: 03-477 3776. A live – and loud – music venue, that stays open until late.
Iris Lounge, 68 Princes Street, tel: 03-477 8001. Friendly atmosphere with live music; a good place to relax over a cocktail.
Mornington Tavern, 36 Mailer Street, tel: 03-453 6099. A popular sports bar perfect for catching live sports coverage on huge screens.
Ra Bar, 21 The Octagon, tel: 03-477 6080. DJs on Friday and Saturday nights, and live local bands play here in the heart of the city. Happy hour 5–8pm on Fridays.
Scotia Whisky Bar, 20 Anzac Avenue, tel: 03-477 7704. New Zealand's only true whisky bar, with over 300 whiskies and Emersons award-winning beer and Bellhaven Scottish ale on tap.

FESTIVALS

January

Auckland

Anniversary Regatta – Annual sailing regatta that celebrates Auckland's birthday (one-day event).
ASB Bank Classic – Leading international and national women tennis players battle it out in this annual one-week tournament.
Auckland Festival – The region's biennial arts festival, presenting performance and arts events from New Zealand and the Pacific.
Heineken Tennis Open – International men's ATP tennis tour that precedes the Australian Open (week-long event).
New Zealand Golf Open – New Zealand's official golf championship. An open event that features players from throughout Australasia (three-day event).

Christchurch

World Buskers Festival – The world's best street acts converge on Christchurch (10-day event). www.worldbuskersfestival.com.

ABOVE: sailing in the Hauraki Gulf.

Rotorua

Opera in the Pa – International performers thrill capacity audiences in the ancestral grounds of Ohinemutu Geothermal Village on the shores of Lake Rotorua.

Wellington

Summercity – A series of small festivals around the city supported by the local council (two-month event).

February

Auckland

Devonport Wine and Food Festival – A two-day food and wine festival that is one of the highlights of the Auckland summer calendar.
Waiheke Island Wine Festival – An event for wine-lovers showcasing the island's vineyards. Located on Waiheke Island in the Hauraki Gulf (two-day event).

Blenheim

Marlborough Wine Festival – Gourmet cuisine, local wine, workshops and music make up this extremely popular festival (one-day event). www.wine-marlborough-festival.co.nz.

Canterbury

Coast to Coast – Longest-running multi-sport event in the world. National and international participants run, kayak and cycle 238km (148 miles) from the west coast to Sumner Bay (two-day event). www.coasttocoast.co.nz.

Christchurch

Garden City Festival of Flowers – Helps Christchurch live up to its billing as New Zealand's garden city with abundant floral displays centred on Christchurch Cathedral. www.festivalofflowers.co.nz.

Hamilton

Hamilton Gardens Summer Festival A celebration of opera, theatre, concerts and performing arts in a garden setting. www.hamiltongardens.co.nz.

Napier

Art Deco Weekend – This Deco jewel of a town steps back in time en masse. Many Deco landmarks are open to the public on this weekend. www.artdeconapier.com.

Waitangi

Waitangi Day – The signing of the nation's founding document is celebrated in the Treaty House grounds with much pageantry, including a spectacular display of waka (canoes).

Wanganui

Masters Games – The largest multi-sport event in New Zealand (one-week event). Held in Wanganui odd-numbered years and Dunedin even-numbered years; www.nzmastersgames.com

Various Locations

Aotearoa Maori Traditional Performing Arts Festival – Teams of Maori performers compete in traditional Maori performing arts (kapa haka) in even-numbered years. For locations, check its website at www.maoriperformingarts.co.nz.

March

Auckland

Auckland Cup – One of the biggest days in New Zealand for thoroughbred horse racing.
Pasifika Festival – The biggest one-day Pacific Island Festival, celebrating Pacific Island cultures with food, crafts, music, theatre, comedy and art.

Round the Bays – Its moderate distance of 8.6km (5 miles) makes for a high level of participation in this fun-run. www.roundthebays.co.nz.

Hokitika Wild Foods Festival – This festival celebrates such gourmet delights as possum pie, huhu grub sushi, scorpions and the ever-popular euphemism – mountain (or prairie, depending where you come from) oysters. www.wildfoods.co.nz.

Ngaruawahia

Ngaruawahia Regatta – The town's location at the meeting point of two rivers makes it the natural site for highly competitive Maori *waka* (canoe) races. This is an exciting event held annually for more than 100 years. It is also the only time the Turangawaewae Marae is open to the public.

Taupo

Ironman New Zealand – This is the longest endurance triathlon in New Zealand. It is one of the six qualifying races for the Ironman Triathlon World Championships (one-day event). www.ironman.co.nz.

Tauranga

National Jazz Festival – Tauranga's bars and nightclubs come alive with the sounds of jazz during this weekend festival. www.jazz.org.nz.

Waipara

Waipara Wine and Food Festival – Described as the "biggest little best wine-and-food celebration", this festival features leading winemakers and purveyors of fine food.

Wairarapa

Golden Shears – The world's premier shearing and wool-handling championships (four-day event) celebrate one of New Zealand's foremost rural industries. www.goldenshears.co.nz.

Wellington

New Zealand Arts Festival – Taking place on even-numbered years only, this is unquestionably New Zealand's premier arts festival, featuring national and international acts (four-week event).

April

Arrowtown

Arrowtown Autumn Festival – There's no prettier town in autumn, and local heritage is celebrated with numerous performances, parades and markets. www.arrowtownautumnfestival.org.nz.

Auckland

Auckland Wine and Food Festival – Food event of the year. A unique opportunity for Aucklanders to treat their taste buds to a feast laid on by New Zealand's premier suppliers of cheeses, antipasto, continental meats, wine and premium beer. www.aucklandwineandfoodfestival.com.

Royal Easter Show – Livestock competitions, arts and crafts awards, wine awards and one of the largest equestrian shows in the Southern Hemisphere (one-week event). www.royaleastershow.co.nz.

Waiheke Jazz Festival – First-rate acts in a magnificent setting, and an opportunity to hear quality New Zealand (and overseas) musicians. www.waihekejazz.co.nz.

Bluff

Bluff Oyster and Southland Seafood Festival – The annual celebration of Southland's most precious gourmet delight, with numerous oyster-themed events. www.bluffoysterfest.co.nz.

Christchurch

Montana Christchurch International Jazz Festival – New Zealand's biggest jazz festival, an annual event featuring local and international jazz luminaries. www.jazzfestivalnz.com.

Hamilton

Balloons Over Waikato – A five-day event during which up to 40 hot air balloons grace the skies over the Waikato landscape. Includes a mass ascension of balloons at sunrise and sunset. The Night Glow event is unforgettable. www.balloonsoverwaikato.co.nz.

Taihape

Gumboot Day – Find out why Taihape is the gumboot capital of the world, as rural New Zealand puts on a light-hearted celebration of itself.

Wanaka

Southern Lakes Festival of Colour – Wanaka hosts some of the country's most respected names in art, music, theatre and dance during this biennial celebration. www.festivalofcolour.co.nz.

May

Auckland

Great Barrier Island Seafood Celebration – a lively celebration of the island's bountiful seafood. www.seafoodgreatbarrier.com.

New Zealand International Comedy Festival – Comedy festival showcasing the best local, national and international comedians (two-week event). www.laugh.co.nz.

Christchurch

Savour New Zealand – Every two years (next on in 2010), a mouth-watering weekend of food, wine, cooking demonstrations and wine workshops takes place. www.savournewzealand.co.nz.

Manawatu

Manawatu International Jazz Festival – Live jazz at various venues throughout Palmerston North (one-week event).

Rotorua

International Rally of Rotorua – FIA Pacific Rally championships takes place on Rotorua's winding forest roads (two-day event). www.rallyrotorua.co.nz.

Rotorua Tagged Trout Competition – Rotorua's premier fishing competition, with a NZ$50,000 trout waiting to be hooked (two-day event). www.taggedtrout.co.nz.

BELOW: mural in Katikati, Bay of Plenty.

June

Queenstown

Queenstown Winter Festival – One of the Southern Hemisphere's biggest and brightest winter parties, in downtown Queenstown. The events range from the zany and hilarious to serious winter sports competitions (two-week event). www.winterfestival.co.nz.

The Waikato

Fuel Festival of New Zealand Theatre – A biennial, three-week national festival of theatre held in Hamilton. www.fuelfest.co.nz.
National Agricultural Field Days – One of the largest agricultural shows in the world, held at Mystery Creek (three-day event). www.feildays.co.nz.

July

Auckland and Wellington

International Film Festival – Three weeks of movie madness and the year's best cinematic offerings.

Volcanic Plateau

The Ruapehu Mountain Mardi Gras The Ruapehu and Turangi skiing areas of the North Island host a more sedate version of the Queenstown event *(see above)*. www.ohakune-mardigras.co.nz.

Wanaka

World Heli-Challenge – The annual gathering of the world's leading snowboarders and skiers in the premier helicopter-accessed free ski and free-ride competition. The two-week event ends with the Wanaka Big Air (free-style ski and snowboard championships).

August

Christchurch

Bay of Islands Jazz and Blues Festival – Jazz and blues on the streets and in selected venues in Paihia and Russell during this three-day event that draws both international and national talent.
Christchurch Winter Carnival – The week-long winter carnival celebrates the great features of Christchurch and Canterbury with skiing and snowboarding championships, "extreme" winter games, and a celebrity charity ball and dinner.

September

Alexandra

Alexandra Blossom Festival – Central Otago celebrates the coming

of spring with a parade, sheep-shearing competitions, entertainment and garden tours.

Auckland

New Zealand Fashion Week – A showcase of some of New Zealand's best fashion designers, with catwalk shows and a trade exhibition (one-week event).

Hastings

Hastings Blossom Festival – Hawke's Bay is one of the country's leading apple exporters and Hastings is known as the fruit bowl of New Zealand, so the blossoms are outstanding this time of the year. Highlights of this celebration of spring include a huge parade, performances by celebrity artists, concerts and a big fireworks finale. www.blossomfestival.co.nz.

Rotorua

Rotorua Trout Festival – Marks the annual opening of the Rotorua Lakes. Anglers, who have been kept at bay since June, are out in full force (one-day event).

Te Puke

Kiwi Fruit Festival – The national fruit is celebrated in style, with a festival covering all aspects of kiwi fruit, in the "home town" of the furry delicacy.

Wellington

Montana World of Wearable Art Awards – A fashion extravaganza of weird and wonderful designs by national and international designers and artists (three-day event).
Wellington Fashion Festival – The capital kicks off spring in style with fashion shows and in-store promotions (one-week event).

October

Gisborne

Gisborne Wine and Food Festival and International Chardonnay Challenge – The festival brings together a range of Gisborne wines and the culinary expertise of top New Zealand chefs using quality Gisborne produce (one-day event). www.internationalchardonnaychallenge.com.

Hawke's Bay

Hawke's Bay Show – One of Hawke's Bay's biggest events, attracting 60,000 spectators each year. Plenty of attractions, competitions and entertainment, with and without an agricultural bias (two-day event). www.hawkesbayshow.co.nz.

Nelson

Nelson Arts Festival – An annual two-week showcase of artists from all over New Zealand, with cabaret, music, theatre, comedy and visual art. www.nelsoncitycouncil.co.nz/artsfestival.

Taranaki

Taranaki Rhododendron Festival – This regional garden festival encompasses over 60 private gardens that are open to the public during the 10-day blooming period for rhododendrons (one-week event). www.rhodo.co.nz.

Tauranga

Tauranga Arts Festival – Street theatre, dance, literature and other performing arts are brought to the fore in this biennial event, which is staged throughout the region (10-day event).

Wellington

Kaikoura Seafest – A celebration of the abundance of the ocean and fine wines and foods predominantly from the Kaikoura, Marlborough and North Canterbury regions, with continuous live entertainment. Bookings essential. www.kaikoura.co.nz/seafest.
Wellington International Jazz Festival – One of the country's largest jazz festivals, representing many different kinds of music from New Orleans, swing and fusion to experimental jazz (three-week event). Features legendary musicians.

Various Locations

Fiji Day celebrates the anniversary of Fiji's independence, and involves communities throughout the country. A different theme is chosen every year. Call the Fiji High Commission, tel: 04-473 5401, for details.

November

Auckland

Waitakere Pacifica Living Arts Festival – Enjoy fashion shows and try creative activities in traditional craft workshops during this cultural celebration of Pacific art, music, crafts and fashion.

Christchurch

Cup Carnival – The strongly contested New Zealand Trotting and Galloping Cups are just a part of the celebrations that form the Christchurch A&P Show *(see below)*.
Royal New Zealand Show – The country's biggest A&P (agriculture and pastoral) show, with a programme of events for all ages (two-day event).

TRANSPORT
ACCOMMODATION
EATING OUT
ACTIVITIES
A – Z

Martinborough

Toast Martinborough – A wine, food and music festival that promotes the top-quality wine region of Martinborough. This is a hugely popular festival, so get tickets early (one-day event). www.toastmartinborough.co.nz

December

Nelson

Nelson Jazz Festival – A variety of local and national jazz bands saturate Nelson with music in a week-long festival.

Taranaki

Festival of Lights – New Plymouth's Pukekura Park is beautifully illuminated by lights each December; fluorescent pebble-paths and waterfalls come alight. The festival that is held when the lights are switched on is a one-day event, but the lights stay on for several weeks.

Wellington

Summercity – Not a big bash, but a series of small festivals that take place all around the city over two months.

SHOPPING

New Zealand offers a wide range of shopping opportunities, from exclusive high-street designer stores in its larger cities through to boutique shops, and arts and crafts stores in its smaller towns and villages. If you are seeking quality and/or goods with a creative twist, look out for New Zealand-made products, which usually bear a black and gold, or blue, white and red sticker with a kiwi in the centre. These goods are guaranteed to be designed and manufactured in New Zealand; quality workmanship is a given.

What to Buy

Sheepskin

With more than 45 million sheep in New Zealand, it comes as no surprise that among the country's major shopping attractions are its sheepskin and woollen products. You are unlikely to find cheaper sheepskin clothing anywhere in the world, and the colour and variety of items make them ideal gifts or souvenirs. Many shops stock a huge range of coats and jackets made from sheepskin, possum, deerskin, leather and suede.

Woollens

New Zealand is one of the world's major wool producers, and experienced manufacturers take the raw material right through to quality finished products such as the beautiful possum-merino garments, light, soft and so warm. Hand-knitted, chunky sweaters from naturally dyed wool or mohair are ideal if you are heading back to a northern winter. Innovative wall hangings created from home-spun yarns make another worthwhile purchase.

Woodcarvings

The time-honoured skills involved in Maori carvings have been passed down from one generation to the next. Carvings usually tell stories from mythology and often represent a special relationship with the spirits of the land. Maori carvings of wood and bone can command high prices.

Greenstone

New Zealand jade, more commonly referred to as greenstone, is a distinctive Kiwi product. The jade, found only on the west coast of the South Island, is worked into jewellery, figurines, ornaments and Maori *tiki*. Factories in the west-coast towns of Greymouth and Hokitika allow visitors to see the jade being worked.

Jewellery

Jewellery made from greenstone and the iridescent *paua* (abalone) shell and bone have been treasured by Maori for centuries. You can buy such ornaments and unique contemporary jewellery from specialised stores.

Jewellery Workshop

Bonz and Stonz, 16 Hamilton Street, tel: 03-755 6504, 0800-214 949; www.bonz-n-stonz.co.nz. Offers a full-day workshop where you can design and carve your own pendants in jade, bone, *paua* and mother-of-pearl shells. Advance bookings essential, especially in the summmer months. No previous carving experience is necessary.

Handicrafts

There has been an explosion of handicrafts in recent years – sold by local craftsmen and craftswomen and by local shops catering specifically to tourists. Pottery is perhaps the most widely available craft product, though patchwork, quilting, canework, kauri woodware, wooden toys, glassware and leather goods are among the enormous range of crafts available at the major tourist centres.

Sportswear and Outdoor Equipment

New Zealanders love the great outdoors, so it should come as little surprise that they have developed a wide range of hard-wearing clothing and equipment to match tough environmental demands. Warm and rugged farm-wear like Swanndri bush shirts and jackets are popular purchases, while mountaineering equipment, camping gear and backpacks set world standards. Some items have even become fashion success stories, such as the Canterbury range of rugby and yachting jerseys.

Contemporary Art

Quality contemporary art, from the conservative to the ground-breaking, is surprisingly affordable in New Zealand. Artist's prints in particular are well priced and easy to transport. The larger cities have private galleries that usually keep a wide range of artwork in stock.

Designer Clothing

New Zealand designers, such as World, Karen Walker, Trelise Cooper, Sharon Ng, Sabatini, Nom*D and Zambesi, are making their mark on the international catwalks. Boutiques in the principal cities stock these award-winning New Zealand labels, as well as a range of international designers.

Food and Wine

Processed items like local jams, chutney, pates, smoked beef and honey do not need documentation, and make excellent gifts as they are attractively packaged.

Wines are a real New Zealand success story. The country's young wines, with their fresh and exciting flavours, are jumping up and demanding attention in the international market. Red and white varietal wines such as sauvignon blanc, chardonnay and pinot noir are consistent winners in New Zealand and have received numerous international awards.

Bookstores

Bearing in mind that New Zealand boasts the highest per capita readership of books and periodicals anywhere in the world, it is well worth paying a visit to some of New Zealand's fine bookshops. Whitcoull's (www.whitcoulls.co.nz) is the country's major bookstore (and stationer) and offers a good selection of quality titles. There is a wealth of reading related to New Zealand. *See page 387.*

Where to Shop

North Island

Auckland

Auckland's **Queen Street** is a good place to start, as it has a range of souvenir shops, and from here other interesting shopping streets can be easily reached on foot. Modish **Vulcan Lane**, fashionable **High Street** and the **Chancery** shopping area are home to many chic boutiques and stores of New Zealand designers such as Karen Walker, World, Zambesi and Ricochet. Pauanesia in High Street stocks designer jewellery and ornaments from throughout the Pacific, while The Old Customhouse, corner of **Customs and Albert streets** (near the downtown Ferry Building) is the place to go for luxury labels and duty-free shopping.

Make sure you pay a visit to **Victoria Park Market** (www.victoria-park-market.co.nz), with its distinctive chimney stack on Victoria Street. It's filled with stalls, shops and cafés. On Friday and Saturday the stallholders in the **Aotea Square Markets** outside the Aotea Centre, Queen Street, offer a variety of Pacific Rim arts and crafts, souvenirs and clothing – some collectable, some forgettable.

At the top of Queen Street is **Karangahape Road**. "Karangahape" translates as "winding ridge of human activity", an apt description of one of Auckland's busiest and oldest commercial streets (not to mention red-light district), where small second-hand clothing and furniture shops compete for business with spacious department stores.

Further afield, the inner-city suburbs of Parnell, Ponsonby and Newmarket also offer a wide choice. Check out the backstreets in **Newmarket**, where there are many interesting shops, and Elephant House at 237 Parnell Road, where over 300 Kiwi craftspeople exhibit their handcrafted wares.

Across the harbour, **Devonport** has a range of boutique stores, including: **Art of this World**, Shop 1, 1 Queens Parade, tel: 09-446 0926; www.artofthisworld.co.nz, with art and sculpture by New Zealand-based artists; **Flagstaff Gallery**, 30 Victoria Road, tel: 09-445 1142; www.flagstaff.co.nz, offering contemporary New Zealand art; and **Green Planet Enterprises Ltd**, 87 Victoria Road, tel: 09-445 7404; www.greenplanet.co.nz, with its high-quality, New Zealand-made eco-friendly merchandise.

For mainstream international brands, head to St Lukes in Mount

ABOVE: a gift shop selling Maori designs.

Albert, or Westfield in Albany, or 277 in Newmarket.

Not to be missed is New Zealand's largest street market, the **Otara Market** (Sat 6am–noon; tel: 09-274 0830), located behind Otara Shopping Centre in the car park between Watford and Newbury streets in South Auckland. It's where sensible tourists shop for souvenirs – not just because they are better value for money than the shops in the tourist traps, but also because of the obvious authenticity.

Bay of Plenty

There are several major shopping centres in the Bay, from Tauranga to Mount Maunganui's Phoenix Centre, Bayfair and Palm Beach Plaza. Walk the streets of an earlier age at the Village on 17th (www.villageon17.co.nz), on 17th Avenue West in Tauranga, and discover colonial buildings and craft shops, then rest your feet at the village café (tel: 07-571 3700).

Paihia

Bring home New Zealand-made gifts from The Cabbage Tree shops (tel: 09-402 7318; www.thecabbagetree.co.nz) in Paihia. Choose from merino wool garments, hand-blown glassware, greenstone jewellery and more from either of its two shops, one in Williams Road and the other at the Maritime Building on the wharf.

Rotorua

With attractive wide streets, Rotorua provides an abundance of shops from clothing and fashion to souvenirs, food and pharmacies. Tutanekai and Hinemoa are the streets to visit, while City Focus Square is within walking distance. There are souvenir shops galore in the city, including **The Jade Factory** in Fenton Street, tel: 07-349 3968, which showcases quality jade from throughout New Zealand and

elsewhere. **The Souvenir Centre**, tel: 07-348 9515, also in Fenton Street, stocks a wide range of New Zealand arts and crafts.

Russell

The Strand is Russell's premier all-weather retail therapy centre, with everything from fine food to high fashion and gifts.

Warkworth

Craft Co-Op @ Sheepworld, 324 SH1, Warkworth, tel: 0800-227 433, www.sheepworld.co.nz. This is New Zealand's largest arts and crafts co-op, with a dazzling variety of locally produced goods made from both traditional and more innovative materials. It has a good café, open daily 9am–5pm.
Honey Centre, corner SH1 and Perry Road, Warkworth, tel: 09-425 8003; www.honeycentre.co.nz. Sells all varieties of New Zealand's excellent honey.
Morris and James Pottery and Café, 48 Tongue Farm Road, Matakana, tel: 09-422 7116; www.morrisandjames.co.nz. This establishment has a devoted following among locals and tourists alike for its brightly coloured pottery.

Wellington

Wellington City is divided into several distinct shopping precincts – **Cuba Quarter** is where you'll find the more alternative, funky stores and second-hand shops. **Lambton Quarter** is home to five shopping centres, including the famous Kirkcaldie & Stains – the oldest classic department store in New Zealand – while **Willis Quarter** has local designer stores, sports shops and cafés. For antiques shops, head to the character-filled streets of Wellington's historical district, **Thorndon**. Otherwise, nip over to the **Wairarapa**, where you'll discover amazing wineries and antiques and craft shops located inside beautiful historic houses.

South Island
Arrowtown
The Gold Shop on Buckingham Street makes reasonably priced contemporary jewellery, including lockets, from local natural gold nuggets; www.goldshop.co.nz.

Christchurch
Christchurch offers excellent prospects for shopping, and you will find a selection of designer stores, nationwide chain stores, souvenir shops and shopping malls.

The **Arts Centre** in Worcester Boulevard has more than 40 craft studios, galleries and shops, all offering unique New Zealand-made souvenirs.

Canterbury Museum specialises in *paua* shell jewellery and souvenirs, New Zealand-designed pottery, glass, stone and wood pieces. It also features a selection of Maori carvings. For New Zealand-made products with a wintry theme, check out the **Antarctic Shop** at the International Antarctic Centre and Christchurch International Airport.

On the corner of Colombo Street and the City Mall, you will find **Ballantynes**, the city's foremost department store, considered as Christchurch's Harrods or Marshall Field's. The assistants dress in black and are notoriously helpful.

Dunedin
Shopping in Dunedin is relaxed and unhurried. The main shopping centre is located around the Octagon, and radiates out onto Lower Stuart Street, Princes Street, George Street and St Andrews. There are also a number of suburban centres with good shops at Mornington, The Gardens, Andersons Bay Road and Mosgiel.

Nelson/Marlborough
There are more than 350 full-time artists and craftspeople in the Nelson region, so expect to see plenty of craft shops in the centre of town. The Saturday morning market in Montgomery Square is popular, and there are stalls with everything from arts and crafts to regional produce and gourmet foods. There are also weekend markets in Motueka and Golden Bay. At the Nelson or Motueka information centres you can get a copy of *Creative Pathways*, a guide to the studios of more than 30 local artists and craftspeople.

Queenstown
Visitors to Queenstown will find streets bristling with souvenir shops. Prices are usually fixed, but bargaining is becoming increasingly common here. To meet demand, Queenstown does not follow normal retail hours – most shops are open seven days a week for extended hours.

Wanaka
Everything you need is within walking distance in Wanaka. You'll find shops selling local arts and crafts, plenty of souvenir shops and such basic amenities as pharmacies, hardware and stationery shops.

West Coast Crafts
For genuine handcrafted South Island *pounamu* (greenstone), check out **Te Waipounamu Jade**, 27 Sewell Street, Hokitika. **Possum People**, at 20 Sewell Street, specialise in making items from possum fur and sheep skins, tel: 03-756 8090; www.possum-nz.com.

OUTDOOR ACTIVITIES

General
New Zealanders love the outdoors, and there are plenty of places to cycle, walk, swim, ski, climb, bungee-jump, fish, play golf or go rafting. Because the country has a low population density and spectacular scenery, you are never very far from an outdoor activity, whether it's an organised adventure or a peaceful walk in the bush. The opportunity to participate in so many activities at low cost in some of the world's most beautiful locations is a major tourist draw, and local tourism operators have risen to the challenge by meeting this demand with a high level of professionalism and, equally important, safety.

Watching sport of all descriptions is easily accessible. Attending an **All Blacks** match is often high on visitors' agendas, although it is worth noting that during the summer season the team is often touring overseas, during the Northern Hemisphere's winter. Chances of catching a game are a lot higher during New Zealand's winter, and each of New Zealand's stadiums, mostly located in major cities, has its own methods of ticketing. Local i-sites will be able to assist (free of charge) to secure tickets and advise of matches that are being played. Alternatively, visit www.allblacks.co.nz and follow the tickets link

on the left of the screen. Information on games and ticketing is posted here, as it becomes available.

In 2011 New Zealand will host the Rugby World Cup. For information regarding match times and ticketing visit www.nzrugbyworldcupinfo.co.nz. Tickets should be booked as far in advance as possible.

Watching regional and local rugby matches is also popular; again local i-sites will be able to assist, although on a local level many games and practice matches can be attended free of charge. Join the spectators: New Zealanders will love any interest you show for their national game. Summer spectator sports that can be attended include cricket, sailing, motor racing, horse racing, tennis and softball. For further information ask at the local i-site.

Land Sports
Abseiling
New Zealand provides numerous opportunities to abseil down cliffs, waterfalls, canyons and some spectacularly deep holes in the ground. In some cities, it is possible to perform the urban equivalent and rappel down the outside of skyscrapers.

Ballooning
Ballooning is a wonderful way to see New Zealand's unique landscape. Balloons depart in the early morning, so be prepared to be up at the crack of dawn. On some tours you will get to assist in preparing the balloon for take-off; all will offer a safety briefing before your departure.

Hastings
Early Morning Balloons, 71 Rosser Road, tel: 06-879 4229; www.hotair.co.nz. You'll spend an hour drifting peacefully above Hawke's Bay, with a traditional balloon picnic at the end of the flight.

Methven
Aoraki Balloon Safaris, 20 Barkers Road, tel: 03-302 8172, 0800-256 837; www.nzballooning.com. Soar aloft for views of Mount Cook and the National Park Mountains, plus a full panorama of the entire Canterbury Plains.

Bungee-Jumping
Developed in the 1980s by New Zealand adventurers A.J. Hackett and Henry Van Asch, this exhilarating experience of throwing oneself off a high platform with a large rubber-band attached to the ankles has become world-famous.

Today, there are four official **A.J. Hackett** (www.ajhackett.com) bungee-jump sites in **Queenstown**, including the world's first 43-metre (141ft) site at Kawarau Bridge, and a site at **Auckland Bridge**.

Bungee-jumps are also offered by other operators.

Auckland

A.J. Hackett Bungy, Curran Street, Westhaven Reserve, tel: 09-360 7748; www.ajhackett.com. This was the world's first harbour-bridge bungee-jump, run by the outfit that originally developed the sport. The latest in adventure technology is used – with a purpose-built jump pod and retrieval system for maximum safety and comfort for the jumpers.

Skyjump, Sky Tower, corner Victoria and Federal streets, tel: 09-368 1835, 0800-759 586; www.skyjump.co.nz. Touting itself as a world-first adventure experience, the 192-metre (630ft) Skyjump is a cable-controlled base jump with great views. Jumpers drop at up to 80kmh (51mph).

Queenstown

Queenstown is the home of bungee-jumping, the place where it all began in 1988. The world's first bungee site, the Kawarau Bridge, has evolved into the **Kawarau Bungy Centre**, a busy hub from where A.J. Hackett (tel: 03-442 4007, 0800-286 495; www.ajhackett.com) operates the Bungy Shop, a café, the **Freefall Wine Bar** and the newest addition, the **Secrets of Bungy Tour**, a behind-the-scenes insight into the bungee phenomenon for those who don't fancy the real deal. This tour leaves hourly and includes the Bungy Theatre and Interactive Zone where you can get a first-hand look at bungee-cord making as well as exclusive access to viewing

decks where you observe alongside the jump crews. At the end of the car park is another new addition, **The Winehouse & Kitchen** (tel: 03-442 7310; www.winehouse.co.nz), a farm-style restaurant with a special wine-tasting experience.

In addition to the Kawarau Bridge Bungy (adults NZ$165 child 10–15 years NZ$110), A.J. Hackett operates two other bungee sites around Queenstown, **The Ledge Bungy** (adults NZ$125, child 10–15 years NZ$80), and the **Nevis Highwire Bungy** (NZ$240 for adults and children), billed as the wildest. Their Thrillogy package gives the option of all three for NZ$425, or try the new Nevis Arc, a 120-metre (787ft) rope swing. The world's highest, this can be also be done in tandem (adults NZ$170, tandem NZ$300, child 10–15 years NZ$110).

Taupo

Taupo Bungy, Spa Road, tel: 07-377 1135, 0800-888 408; www.taupobungy.co.nz. Solo and tandem jumps from above the Waikato River.

Caving

New Zealand offers some of the most challenging and spectacular caving in the world, although you do not need to be a professional caver to make the most of the underworld. Guided tours range from easy to as daring as you like, but for the best range of activities head to the Waitomo region.

Waitomo

Waitomo Adventures, Waitomo Caves Road, tel: 07-878 7788, 0800-924 866; www.waitomo.co.nz. Offers a two-hour black-water journey, as well as various permutations of abseiling into underground holes and down waterfalls.

Te Anau

Real Journeys, Real Journeys Visitors Centre, Lakefront Drive, Te Anau, tel: 03-249 7416, 0800-656 501; www.realjourneys.co.nz. Enjoy a scenic cruise across Lake Te Anau, then venture underground on foot and on a small boat into the glow-worm grotto for a magical sight. This tour takes just over two hours.

Climbing

Rock climbing has experienced a phenomenal growth in New Zealand. There are now lots of indoor climbing walls in towns and cities, rock-climbing clubs and excellent terrain to discover throughout the country. New Zealand has adopted the Australian "Ewbank" numerical grading system which uses a single numerical value to indicate route difficulty. Some of the best rock-climbing areas include **Wharepapa**, south of the Waikato, which has more than 700 climbs, and the **Canterbury** area, which has more than 800 climbs.

For more information, contact: **Climb New Zealand**; www.climb.co.nz.

Queenstown

Climbing Queenstown, Via Ferrata, tel: 03-409 2508; www.climbingqueenstown.com. The Southern Hemisphere's first "Iron Way" is simply a series of iron rungs, ladders and wires, attached to a mountainside, which enables the inexperienced to duplicate the experience of rock climbing. Rock-climbing and abseiling tours also depart daily at 9am and 1.30pm.

Wharepapa

Wharepapa is one of the best rock-climbing areas in New Zealand, with over 800 routes, short, easy walks to the climb, and an equipment store nearby. Wharepapa is located between Te Awamutu and Mangakino. For accommodation, equipment and information, contact the **Wharepapa Outdoor Centre**, tel: 07-872 2533; www.rockclimb.co.nz.

Cycling

New Zealand's windy, rainy weather can sometimes take the pleasure out of cycling, as can the hilly terrain and narrow winding roads crowded with badly driven recreational vehicles. Cycle touring nevertheless offers huge rewards, and some organised tours include a bus to carry your luggage. Mountain bikes are widely available for hire throughout the country. Some of the best places for cycling are in the South Island, in areas such as

BELOW: bungee-jump, Bob's Peak.

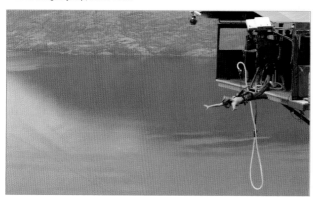

Wanaka, **Glenorchy**, and **Queenstown**. Highlights include abandoned gold-diggers' villages such as Macetown, breathtaking ravines in the Nevis Valley, and the roads leading up to the ski resorts, which offer superb lakeland views. One book providing detailed route descriptions is *Classic New Zealand Mountain-Bike Rides*, which has over 400 rides researched from Cape Reinga to Scott Base. You can order the book online: www.kennett.co.nz.

New Plymouth
Cycle Inn, 133 Devon Street East, tel: 06-758 7418. Bicycle hire.

Rotorua
Planet Bike, tel: 07-346 1717; www. planetbike.co.nz. Rotorua has world-class mountain biking in **Whakarewarewa Forest** close to the city centre. Choose from flat, easy rides for first-timers or fast, technical single-track action for the more experienced. There are half-day or two-day adventures, and combination packages incorporate other activities such as kayaking. A half-day single track exploration costs NZ$65, or you can take a 2-hour night ride for NZ$79. Equipment, bikes, guides and refreshments are included.

Te Aroha
Te Aroha Mountain Bike Track. This 1-hour round trip through native bush and hilly terrain is one of the best cycle tracks in the country.

Wanganui
Some of the region's best biking trails are within minutes of Wanganui. Contact 06-347 2770 for information about precise sites.

Wellington
There are scores of exhilarating mountain-bike tracks around the city, meaning that you don't have to travel far to enjoy the outdoors. Classic rides include the town belt on **Mount Victoria**, the **Rollercoaster** from the Wellington wind turbine to Highbury, the **Te Kopahau Reserve** and the **Makara Peak Mountain Track**.

Golf
There are around 400 golf courses in New Zealand, with an average green charge of around NZ$15 at smaller clubs, and equipment for hire at low cost. The finest courses are in the Bay of Islands (Waitangi), near Taupo (Wairakei International Golf Resort), in Auckland (Titirangi) and in Arrowtown (Millbrook Golf and Country Club). Just

turn up: you will be sure of a warm welcome.

Auckland
Akarana Golf Club, 1388 Dominion Road, Mount Roskill; tel: 09-620 5461; www.akaranagolf.co.nz. This course has tree-lined fairways, with bunkers protecting most greens and panoramic views from the clubhouse. **Aviation Country Club of NZ**, Tom Pearce Drive, Auckland International Airport, tel: 09-275 6265. Part of this 18-hole course at the airport runs beside the Manukau Harbour. **Muriwai Golf Club**, Muriwai Beach, tel: 09-411 8454; www.muriwaigolfclub. co.nz, is a links course with fantastic views over the west coast and undulating fairways over the natural landscape. **Titirangi Golf Club**, Links Road, New Lynn, tel: 09-827 5749; www. titirangigolf.co.nz. One of New Zealand's top courses, with tight fairways, deep gullies and subtle bunkers set amid exotic trees, native bush and streams.

Hanmer Springs
Hanmer Springs Golf Club, 133 Argelins Road, tel: 03-315 7110; www. hanmersprings.nzgolf.net. A challenging 18-hole course, amid breathtaking mountain scenery.
Thrillseekers Canyon Adventure Centre, Hanmer Springs, tel: 03-315 7046; www.thrillseekerscanyon.co.nz. Located 8 minutes from Hanmer, this one-stop action adventure land has it all – bungee, jet boating, quad biking, claypigeon shooting, river rafting and paintball.

Paihia
Waitangi Golf Club, Paihia, tel: 09-402 8207; www.waitangigolf.co.nz. One of New Zealand's finest golf courses with impressive scenery.

Queenstown
Millbrook Resort, Malaghans Road, Arrowtown, tel: 03-441 7010; www. millbrook.co.nz. Play a round of golf at the Millbrook Resort's spectacular par-72 championship golf course, which was designed by New Zealand's renowned master golfer, Sir Bob Charles.

Taupo
Wairakei International Golf Course, SH1, PO Box 377, Taupo, tel: 07-374 8152; www.wairakeigolfcourse.co.nz. Voted one of the top 20 golf courses outside the USA by *Golf Digest*, the Wairakei International Golf Course has magnificent fairways and large greens with 101 bunkers.

Whitianga
Mercury Bay Golf and Country Club, Golf Road, tel: 07-866 5479. An 18-hole course north of Thames. Idyllic surroundings with level walking.

Hiking
New Zealand has 14 national parks, and more than 5 million hectares (12½ million acres)– a stunning one-third of New Zealand – are protected in parks and reserves. There are hundreds of walking opportunities in conservation areas and other places throughout New Zealand, as well as heritage walks which explore the country's cultural and natural history.

There are nine routes, known as the **Great Walks**, for which you need a pass if you plan to stay overnight. These are obtainable from offices of the Department of Conservation (DOC), and cost NZ$7–35 per night if you sleep in a hut during high season (Oct–Apr), or NZ$5–10 for a serviced campsite (which has flush toilets, tap water, kitchen, laundry, hot showers, rubbish collection, picnic tables and some powered pitches).

If you like hot showers and other home comforts, it is best to book a guided walk. But if you don't mind "roughing it", then try independent walking, staying in basic huts and tents. For detailed maps and information on hikes and hiking passes nationwide, contact the **Department of Conservation** (DOC), Ferry Building, Quay Street, Auckland, tel: 09-379 6476. There are DOC offices in all the main cities, or check out the department's national website, www.doc.govt.nz.

Guided walking tours amid some of the country's most impressive scenery are available. Contact: **Active Earth** (tel: 0800-201 040; www. activeearthnewzealand.com), which takes small groups on hiking and trekking trips off the North Island's beaten track. **Hiking New Zealand** (tel: 0800-697 232; www.nzhike.com) is another company that conducts small-group hiking tours throughout the South, with knowledgeable guides.

Auckland
The west coast of Auckland, near Helensville, has a range of forest and beach walks. From SH16 take the Rimmers Road turnoff for some bracing walking along lesser-known beaches of the west coast.
The Arataki Park Visitor Centre, Scenic Drive, Titirangi, tel: 09-817 0077. Provides guided walks of varying degrees of difficulty through some of West Auckland's most

Hiking Hints

With the increase in the number of visitors to New Zealand, the impact on the country's natural environment has increased. There are several things you can do to protect the environment.
• Do not damage or remove plants in the forests.
• Remove rubbish. Do not burn or bury it.
• Keep streams and lakes clean.
• Take care when building fires.
• Keep on the track when walking.
• Respect New Zealand's cultural heritage and *tapu* (sacred) sites.
To find out more information about how you can protect New Zealand's environment, visit the nearest Department of Conservation office or check out the Department's website, www.doc.govt.nz, and the Biosecurity New Zealand website, www.biosecurity.govt.nz.

impressive stands of forest. Alternatively, contact Friends of Arataki at 09-827 3803.

Blenheim
Southern Wilderness and Wilderness Guides, tel: 03-546 734 or 0800-666 044; www.southernwilderness.com. Guided walks and sea kayaking. Gourmet food and wine on the way.

Catlins Coast
Catlins Wildlife Trackers Ecotours, Papatowai, RD2 Owaka, tel: 03-415 8613; www.catlins-ecotours.co.nz. Award-winning multi-day tours that get you to see penguins, sea lions and rare birds, with a fascinating commentary on history, from 180 million years ago to the present. Catlins Traverse is a two-day fully catered walk through the inland beech forest to Papatowai Beach, with self-catering accommodation in special cottages.

Central Plateau
The primary activity in the Tongariro National Park in the Central Plateau is skiing during the winter and tramping – the one-day Tongariro Crossing or multi-day Tongariro Northern Circuit or Round the Mountain Track – in summer.
For information on the Tongariro Crossing, contact Taupo-based Alpine Scenic Tours, tel: 07 378 7412; www.alpinescenictours.co.nz. Whakapapa's Bayview Grand Château (www.chateau.co.nz) also has packages which include the Tongariro Crossing.

Gisborne
The east coast has a selection of excellent walking tracks to explore, including beach walks, privately owned walkways and old piers. You can also enjoy a leisurely historic walk through Gisborne city or take an early-morning Alpine climb to the top of Mount Hikurangi, which, at 1,752 metres (5,748ft), is the first point on mainland New Zealand to see the sunrise. For details, contact the local DOC office or visitor information centre.

New Plymouth
There are fabulous walks both in the **Egmont** and **Whanganui** National Parks. It's best to check the weather before you embark on any walk or hike, but especially if you intend to climb **Mount Taranaki**. The nearest Department of Conservation office will be able to advise about weather and hiking conditions. Professional guiding services are available in Taranaki. There are also many fabulous river and coastal walks to be found throughout both regions. For details, contact **North Egmont Visitor Centre** at Egmont Village, Egmont Road, tel: 06-756 0991. Alternatively, call Mount Taranaki Guided Tours, tel: 06-765 6234; www.macalpineguides.com.

Southland
Southland is blessed with rainforest retreats, coastal tracks and unspoilt beaches, plus vast tracts of stunning national park land. The 53.5km (33-mile) **Milford Track** is one of the most popular. Bookings for the **Milford**, **Kepler** and **Routeburn tracks** must be made with the Department of Conservation at **Great Walks Booking Desk**, Lakefront Drive, PO Box 29, Te Anau, tel: 03-249 8514; www.doc.govt.nz. For maps, further information on the walks and area, contact: **Fiordland National Park Visitor Centre** in Te Anau, tel: 03-249 7924. No booking is required for the **Hollyford Valley Track**.
Try the relatively new **Tutapere Humpridge Track** at the southeastern end of Fiordland National Park. This track is a 3-day, 2-night, 43km (27-mile) walk that starts and finishes at the western end of Te Wae Wae Bay. It is owned by a charitable trust and can be booked at tel: 03-226 6739, 0800-486 774; www.humpridgetrack.co.nz.
Near Bluff, the **Foveaux Walkway**, a 7km (4½-mile) walk along rugged coastline, offers great views of the

coast and bush. For all walks in Southland, contact the nearest Department of Conservation office or Visitor Information Centre or check out the Department of Conservation at www.doc.govt.nz.

Stewart Island
There are many tracks to explore – some walks take as little as 15 minutes, others as long as three days. The three-day **Rakiura Track**, the most popular, crosses forest and is suitable for anyone with moderate fitness. It provides a good introduction to the island and its bird life, including Stewart Island kiwi and the Blue penguin.
Kiwi Wilderness Walks, 31 Orawia Road, Tuatapere, tel: 0800-733 549; www.nzwalk.com, conducts multi-day guided walks with a chance of spotting kiwi in their natural environment.
Ulva's Guided Walks, tel: 03-219 1216; www.ulva.co.nz. Ulva Amos is a direct descendant of the indigenous people of Stewart Island, an authority on the area's flora and fauna, and leads gentle half-day walks which showcase the island's natural heritage.

Te Aroha
Waiorongomai Valley Walk. This hike takes you through old gold-mining ruins. Another popular walk is the **Whakapipi Lookout Track**. A Department of Conservation brochure and map with full details of all walks is available from the Information Centre.

Te Urewera National Park
Some of the finest and least-known walks in the country are here. The DOC Visitor Information Centres at Rotorua or within the park at Aniwaniwa can advise and provide full mapping for exploration into this area.

Thames
Kauaeranga Valley DOC **Visitors Centre**, Kauaeranga Valley Road, tel: 07-867 9080, can provide information on more than 20 bush walks in the area.

Wellington
There are plenty of parks, reserves, rivers and forests to walk on the outskirts of Wellington. You can head to **Makara Beach**, 35 minutes west of Wellington city, for a 3- or 4-hour stroll along the coast, or take a 2-hour coastal walk to **Red Rocks** and visit its colony of New Zealand fur seals (May–Oct). There are also plenty of

city heritage walks that trace
Wellington's history.

West Coast
Experience the beauty and history of
the west coast on the numerous great
walks and hiking trails within the
region. These include the Heaphy
Track, the Wangapeka Track and the
Charming Creek Walkway. Check with
the local information office or
Department of Conservation for track
conditions.

Whangamata
Kiwi Dundee Adventures, Pauanui,
Tairua and Whangamata, tel: 07-865
8809; www.kiwidundee.co.nz. Two of New
Zealand's foremost guides offer
personalised walks, hikes and tours.

Horse Riding
Seeing New Zealand on horseback is
one of the best ways of experiencing
the country and its people at close
quarters. Operators throughout the
country organise treks which range
from half-day to full-day and overnight
trips.
New Zealand Horse Magic, SH1,
south of Cambridge, tel: 07-827
8118; www.cambridgethoroughbredlodge.
co.nz; daily 10am–3pm; charge. Daily
performances showcase a variety of
breeds, from a Lippizaner stallion (the
only one in New Zealand) to the New
Zealand wild horse, the Kaimaniwa,
plus Arabian, Clydesdale and Hackney
specimens. Bookings essential for
shows.

Hanmer Springs
Hurunui Horse Treks, Ribbonwood,
Hawarden (between Hammer Springs
and Christchurch), tel/fax: 03-314
4500; www.hurunui.co.nz. This company
conducts horseback tours through the
farmland of North Canterbury.

Lake Tekapo
**MacKenzie Alpine Trekking
Company**, Godley Peaks Road, tel:
0800-628 269; www.maht.co.nz.
Horseback treks through the tussock
grasslands, glacial lakes and forests
of the Mackenzie High Country at
Lake Tekapo, with the option for the
"Lake Stroll", a 6–7 day adventure
hike over three famous sheep
stations to enjoy stunning views of
Aoraki Mount Cook. All levels catered
for with treks from 1 hour to overnight.

New Plymouth
Gumboot Gully, Piko Road, Okoki.
Rides and overnight excursions with
this company range from half-day to
week-long treks, including river

crossings, old stock routes, native
bush tracks, pine forests and high
ridge tops with spectacular views and
quiet, misty gullies. Overnight treks
between November and May, and
year-round for day rides.

Palmerston North
Timeless Horse Treks, Gorge Road,
Ballance, Pahiatua, tel: 06-376 6157;
www.timelesshorsetreks.co.nz. Rides
include gentle river trails and
challenging hill country.

Rotorua
The Farm House, Sunnex Road,
tel: 07-332 3771. Hire ponies and
horses and ride over 245 hectares
(600 acres) of bush-edged farmland.
Daily 10am–3pm.

Te Anau
**High Ride Horse Treks and Quad
Bike Adventures**, Wilderness Road,
RD2, tel: 03-249 8591; www.highride.
co.nz. Scenic treks with wonderful
views, animal encounters and ancient
forests. A variety of horses is available
to suit all levels of experience, and
trained guides provide tuition. It also
offers quad-bike tours that take you
through Te Anau's backcountry, across
rolling paddocks and to the summit of
Danby Hill for attractive views of the
lakes, farmland and mountains.

Te Awamutu
Pirongia Clydesdales, RD6, Te
Awamutu, tel: 07-871 9711; www.
clydesdales.co.nz, is home to several
equine stars of *The Lord of the Rings*
and *Xena: Warrior Princess*. Wagon
rides are also available.

Warkworth Area
Pakiri Beach Horse Rides, Rahuikiri
Road, Pakiri Beach, Wellsford, tel:
09-422 6275; www.horseride-nz.co.nz.

Ninety minutes' drive north of
Auckland, Sharley and Laly Haddon
cater for all riding abilities, beginners
included. Daily 1- and 2-hour rides,
half- and full-day rides and also multi-
day safaris, including a 7-day Great
Northern coast-to-coast ride.

Wanaka
Backcountry Saddle Expeditions,
Cardrona Valley, tel: 03-443 8151.
Organised horseback tours of the
Cardrona Valley. Appaloosa horses
with Western saddles.

Hunting
In New Zealand's earlier colonial days,
Europeans introduced many unwanted
species, some of which have become
pests. Populations of these pests are
now controlled through hunting, a
popular rural pastime. Game includes
possum, deer, chamois, Himalayan
tahr, rabbits, pigs, goats, and near
Waimate in the South Island, wallabies.

Gisborne
New Zealand Safari Adventures,
Tangihau Station, Rere, tel: 06-867
0872; www.nzsafari.co.nz. Experienced
guides take you hunting for trophy red
stags. Bush hut and homestay
cottages available.

Waimate
Ngahere Game Ranch, tel: 03-689
7809; www.tournz.com. Hunting
wallabies in Waimate is something of
a local sport, and visitors can take
part by teaming up with locals, like
Bruce and Mieke Fiett at the Ngahere
Game Ranch. Trophy hunts for red
stags, elk, fallow buck, goats and
boars are also available.

Mountaineering
Before New Zealander Sir Edmund
Hillary conquered Everest, he

BELOW: horse riding on the beach at East Cape, easternmost point of North Island.

practised in the Southern Alps, an area stretching more than 700km (435 miles) and larger than the French, Austrian and Swiss Alps combined. But even if your ambitions are less lofty, you'll find plenty of climbing opportunities in New Zealand. There are numerous mountaineering and climbing clubs, including the New Zealand Alpine Club, which has a strong nationwide membership. Contact: **New Zealand Alpine Club**, Unit 6, 6 Raycroft Street, Opawa, Christchurch, tel: 03-377 7595; www.alpineclub.org.nz.

Aoraki Mount Cook

Alpine Guides Aoraki, the only resident guide company in Aoraki/ Mount Cook National Park, offers Alpine touring, mountaineering courses, private instruction, mountain expeditions and guiding programmes through the Southern Alps. The cost for a 7-day expedition up Mount Cook (3,754 metres/12,348ft) is NZ$4,850. Aircraft access is included in the price. Contact: **Alpine Guides** Aoraki, Bowen Drive, Mount Cook, tel: 03-435 1834; www.alpineguides.co.nz.

Lake Tekapo

Alpine Recreation Canterbury, Murray Place, tel: 03-680 6736; www. alpinerecreation.com. Climbing courses and guided ascents of major peaks and glaciers.

Wanaka

New Zealand Wild Walks, 10A Tenby Street, tel: 03-443 4476; www. wildwalks.co.nz. Specialists in tramping and climbing in Mount Aspiring National Park and guiding small groups on single-day as well as overnight climbing trips up the mountain and on treks over glaciers.

Orienteering

This is something of a specialist activity, but for those who like having to find their way across unknown terrain with just a map and a compass, New Zealand is the perfect spot. Its varied, often rugged terrain provides plenty of challenges, with the bonus, usually, of some splendid scenery along the way. Courses cater to a variety of competence levels. There are a lot of clubs located throughout the country; to join a group, check with local information centres for details.

Geocaching has also caught on in New Zealand in a big way. Basically it is a high-tech game of hide and seek and can be combined with hiking, mountain biking and orienteering. For

further information visit www.geocaching. com, which has the largest directory of New Zealand geocache sites.

Parapenting/Hang-Gliding

Parapenting involves unfurling a canopy that lifts you from the ground as you take off down a hill. Once airborne you gain height and drift lazily around the sky. It can be done in tandem with an experienced operator. In hang-gliding, you are strapped to a giant kite (together with the pilot of course!) and literally run off a mountain.

Queenstown

Coronet Peak Tandem Paragliding and Hang Gliding, tel: 0800-467 325; www.tandemparagliding.com. Take off from 700 metres (1,100ft) above the Wakatipu Basin while harnessed to an instructor. In winter you take off from Coronet Peak, a great way to descend after a day's skiing. **Queenstown Hang Gliding**, tel: 03-442 5747, 0800-878 4373; www. hangglide.co.nz. Fly in tandem with the world's most experienced pilot-instructors. You literally launch off the side of Coronet Peak, the highest take-off in town at 1,160 metres (3,800ft). Prices from NZ$185. Allow 2–2½ hours for the activity. Departs 9am, noon, 3pm, 6pm or on demand.

Wanaka

Wanaka Paragliding, Wanaka, tel: 0800-359 754; www.wanakaparagliding. co.nz. Wanaka offers New Zealand's highest tandem paragliding (NZ$180). Also has door-to-door Flying Bus Transport service to Treble Cone (NZ$28).

Skydiving

If launching yourself into the air from a mountainside is too passé for you, try jumping from a plane. Tandem skydiving has made this thrill accessible to all. Attached to an experienced skydiver by a special harness, there is little you need to do except follow the instructions and keep control of your fear. The bonus with this thrill is the stunning views offered by the plane ride as you circle above the drop zone. Operators are found throughout the country, but especially in Queenstown and Taupo.

Christchurch

Skydiving NZ.Com, Wigram Aerodrome, tel: 03-343 5542, 0800-697 593; www.skydivingnz.com. Experience the adrenalin rush from freefalling at speeds of up to 200kmh (124mph).

Queenstown

NZONE The Ultimate Jump, tel: 03-442 5867; www.nzone.biz. The tandem jumps are priced variably, depending on whether you jump at 2,743 metres (9,000ft), 3,658 metres (12,000ft) or the ultimate 4,572 metres (15,000ft).

Taupo

Skydive Taupo, tel: 0800-586 766 ; www.skydivetaupo.co.nz. Choose your jump height for stunning scenery of the Central Plateau. The higher you go, the longer it lasts! Prices start at NZ$250.

Watersports

Diving

Diving in New Zealand's clear waters is an absolute delight, and not surprisingly the country has more divers per head of population than anywhere else in the world. There are many shipwrecks to explore in the **Marlborough Sounds** and **Bay of Islands**, where you'll find the remains of the anti-nuclear Greenpeace ship, the *Rainbow Warrior*, which was bombed by French agents in 1985.

New Plymouth

Team Tasman Charters, tel: 06-758 6348 or 027-471 2012. Operates dive charters and a shop.

Paihia

Dive North, Main Wharf, tel: 09-402 5369; www.divenorth.co.nz. Takes divers to many dive locations in the Bay of Islands, including the wreck of the *Rainbow Warrior*, the Cavalli Islands and Cape Brett.
Paihia Dive, 12 Mako Lane, Paihia, tel: 09-402 7551, 0800-107 551; www. divenz.com. Trips to the *Rainbow Warrior*, as well as the Three Kings diving area.

Warkworth Area

Goat Island Dive, 142A Pakiri Road, Leigh, tel: 09-422 6925, 0800-348 369; www.goatislanddive.co.nz. Diving operation and boat charter based at the magnificent Goat Island Marine Reserve.

Whangarei

Poor Knights Dive Centre, Marina Road, Tutukaka RD3, tel: 09-434 3867; www.diving.co.nz. Centred on the Poor Knights Islands some 22km (14 miles) off the east coast at Tutukaka near Whangarei, this is rated among the 10 best dive spots in the world.

Fishing

From October to April, New Zealand's

tranquil waters attract anglers from all over the world. One in four New Zealanders enjoys fishing, but there are plenty of fish to go around. One of the best places for trout fishing is Lake Rotorua in the Nelson Lake District, where guides will help you find brown trout up to 50cm (20ins) in length. **Lake Tarawera**, in the Rotorua region, and **Gore** in Southland are other renowned spots to angle for trout.

Gisborne
Charter a fishing cruise on Poverty Bay with an experienced skipper for one day or several. Contact Glistening Waters Fishing Adventures, Harbour Marina, Gisborne, tel: 06-377 1281; www.nzfish.com.

Great Barrier Island
Tryphena Charters, tel: 09-429 0596; www.greatbarrierisland.co.nz/fishing.htm. Coastal charters of up to four people. Craig McInman is a fount of local knowledge and can tailor a charter to suit, be it fishing, diving or sightseeing, or a combination of all three.

Hastings
Jack Trout Fishing Guides, 27 Tainui Drive, Havelock North, tel: 06-877 7642; www.jacktrout.co.nz. Professional guides provide one-on-one fishing at Hawke's Bay, opportunities for all levels, reaching the best spots by helicopter and raft.

Invercargill
Riverside Guides in Gore, tel: 03-208 4922. Guided fishing tours of quality rivers and streams with an extremely experienced guide. The Mataura River in Gore is one of the best Brown trout rivers in the world – according to the locals.

New Plymouth
Whanganui, Manawatu and Taranaki offer great fishing and boating. Both regions have lakes with excellent trout and perch fishing. Licences must be purchased for sport fishing, contact: **Taranaki Fish and Game Council**, 1H Taupo Quay, Wanganui, tel: 06-345 4908.

Rotorua
There are plenty of trout-fishing guides and companies for hire in Rotorua. **Clearwater Cruises** (537 Spencer Road, Tarawera, tel: 07-362 8590; www.clearwater.co.nz) and **Hamill Adventures** (tel: 07-348 4186; www.hamillcharters.co.nz) both offer a variety of trout-fishing excursions.

ABOVE: power-boating, Rotorua.

Russell
Major Tom Charters, tel: 09-403 8553, 027-437 7844; www.majortom.co.nz. A serious fishing boat whose fun-loving crew hold numerous New Zealand and world records for marlin, broadbill, swordfish, tuna, kingfish, snapper and sea bass. For game fishing, plan for mid-December to mid-May; fishing for grouper, kingfish, sea bass, snapper and saltfly is available year-round.

Taupo
Central Plateau Fishing Guides, tel: 07-378 8192; www.cpf.net.nz. Famous for trout fishing, Taupo has numerous rivers and streams that are superb for fly-fishing. Rainbow trout in Lake Taupo average 2kg (4lb) while brown trout average 3kg (6lb).
Bryce Curle Fly Fishing Guide, 59 Kahotea Drive, Motuoapa, tel: 07-386 6813; email: bcurle@xtra.co.nz. Fly-fishing tuition and professional angling in all of Taupo's lakes, rivers and Central North Island backcountry streams and rivers. Quality tackle, waders, food and refreshments provided.

Tauranga/Mount Maunganui
Mission Charters, Tauranga Bridge Marina, Tauranga, tel: 0274-842 700; www.missioncharters.co.nz. This company organises a range of fishing trips, from single-day excursions to an extended cruise, anchoring in some idyllic bay for the evening. The crew are experienced and these trips are ideal for everyone, from novices to experts.

Whitianga
Waters Edge Charters, Whitianga, tel: 07-866 5760; www.watersedgecharters.co.nz. Experienced skipper Craig Donovan will take you out for a spot of bottom fishing, game fishing, diving or scenic tours, tailored to suit your needs.

Kayaking/Canoeing
With so much water around, both along the coast and on the lakes, this sport is enjoying a veritable boom in New Zealand, particularly in **Malborough Sounds** and the **Bay of Islands**. You can hire kayaks for guided or independent tours lasting one or more days.

Coastal Kayaking
Abel Tasman National Park, located some 60km (37 miles) from Nelson, has emerald bays and a granite-fringed coastline, and is best savoured by walking the Coastal Track *(see page 243)*. The full walk takes 3–4 days. If you prefer to take to the water, kayak trips around the bays, both guided and unguided, have exploded in popularity in recent years. The following operators are recommended:
Abel Tasman Kayaks, RD2 Marahau, Motueka, tel: 03-527 8022; www.abeltasmankayaks.co.nz. Half-day, single-day or multi-day guided sea-kayaking trips with camping and boat-stay options.
Ocean River Sea Kayaking, Marahau Beach, Marahau, tel: 03-527 8266; www.oceanriver.co.nz. Freedom rentals at the entrance to the park. Ocean River offers a fully equipped base, parking and luggage storage.
Abel Tasman Wilson's Experiences, 265 High Street, Motueka, tel: 03-528 2027. Choose from a wide range of one- or multi-day trips, including boat-cruise, walking and sea-kayaking options.

Akaroa
Akaroa Boat Hire and Akaroa Sea Kayaks, Foreshore, Beach Road, Akaroa, tel: 03-304 7866. Paddle boats, kayaks, sea kayaks, motor boats, double canoes and rowing boats available.

Dunedin
Wild Earth Adventures, daily by arrangement; tel: 03-489 1951; www.wildearth.co.nz. This company offers sea-kayak tours ranging in duration from a few hours to several days, visiting the royal albatross and fur seal colonies by sea, and taking in a great variety of other wildlife on the way.

Great Barrier Island
Aotea Kayaks, 6 Mulberry Grove, Tryphena, tel: 09-429 0664. Provides fully equipped rentals, guided kayaking and snorkelling trips.

Hahei
Cathedral Cove Sea Kayaking, Hahei, tel: 07-866 3877; www. seakayaktours.co.nz, organises both half- and full-day tours to Hot Water Beach and Cathedral Cove.

New Plymouth
Canoe and Kayak, 631 Devon Road, Ball Block, tel: 06-769 5506; www. canoeandkayak.co.nz. This company runs guided tours and courses, and has kayaks for hire, plus a large range of kayaks and accessories for sale.

Paihia
Coastal Kayakers, Te Karuwha Parade, Ti Bay, Waitangi, tel: 09-402 8105; www.coastalkayakers.co.nz. There are more than 150 scenic islands to explore by sea kayak. Coastal Kayakers conduct guided tours, from a half-day to three days. NZ$60 to NZ$480 per person.

Picton and the Sounds
Marlborough Sounds Adventure Company, The Waterfront, Picton, tel: 03-573 6078 or 0800-283 283; www. marlboroughsounds.co.nz. This company organises kayaking, and also conducts walks and bike trials around the 1,500km (930 miles) of bays in the area.

Stewart Island
Kayaking is another great way to explore this region. Call **Stewart Island Sea Kayaks**, tel: 03-219 1080, **Rakiura Kayaks**, tel: 03-219 1160; www.rakiura.co.nz, or **Ruggedy Range**, tel: 03-219 1066; www. ruggedyrange.com.

Tauranga/Mount Maunganui
Oceanix Sea Kayaking, Mount Maunganui, tel: 0800-335 800; www. oceanix.co.nz. This outfit leads kayaking trips that will take you island-hopping on an inner-harbour expedition visiting Maori *pa* sites along the foreshore.

Wanganui
Blazing Paddles, Piriaka (10km/6 miles south of Taumarunui on SH4), tel: 0800-252 946; www.blazingpaddles. co.nz/pricing.html. Self-guided canoe trips on the river from 1 hour to 5 days, with various canoe options to choose from.

Rafting/Jet Boating
Wild, untamed rivers and spectacular scenery provide the perfect backdrop for New Zealand's numerous wild-water rafting expeditions.
Jet boats, which are fast, manoeuvrable and skim the surface of the water, were invented by a New Zealand farmer. One of the best places for this activity is Queenstown's **Shotover River** and Rotorua's Kaituna River. Alternatively, many of New Zealand's rivers are ideally suited to white-water rafting, and you can enjoy the thrills and spills in an inflatable with up to seven other people.
Other intrepid souls can go black-water rafting through the caves of **Waitomo** in the Waikato. You'll discover a labyrinth of dark caves with waterfalls, lit by glow-worms and providing endless fun.

Greymouth
Wild West Adventure Company, 8 Whall Street, tel: 03-768 6649; www. fun-nz.com. Various activities including black-water and white-water rafting (eight rivers to choose from for the latter) as well as glow-worm-cave rafting. Rainforest cruises, gold and gemstone prospecting, guided walks and multi-day adventure tours.

Haast
Waiatoto River Jet Boat Safaris, The Red Barn, SH6, Haast Junction, tel: 03-750 0780. The world's only sea-to-mountain river eco-jet-boat safari explores a remote part of the Southwest World Heritage Area.

Palmerston North
River Valley, Mangahoata Road, Pukeokahu, tel: 06-388 1444; www. rivervalley.co.nz. This location in the Rangitikei River canyon offers New Zealand's premier Grade 5 rafting trip through great rapids such as Fulcrum and Max's Drop. Daily trips year-round. Family and scenic trips are available on gentler sections. Hill-country horse treks are another option. Accommodation in upmarket, self-contained riverside rooms, cabins or camping.

Queenstown
Shotover Jet, Shotover Jet Beach,

Arthurs Point, Queenstown, tel: 03-442 8570; www.shotoverjet.co.nz. One of the best places for jet boating in Queenstown – and all of New Zealand – is the Shotover River. Courtesy shuttle from Queenstown. Half-hour trips through the Shotover Canyons.
Dart River Safaris, Mull Street, Glenorchy and also 27 Shotover Street, tel: 03-442 9992; www.dartriver. co.nz. This company takes you on a 80km (50 miles) safari by jet boat between mountains and glaciers through the landscape of "Middle Earth" into Mount Aspiring National Park, a World Heritage Area.
Challenge Rafting, The Station, corner of Shotover and Camp streets, tel: 03-442 7318; www.totallytourism.co. nz. Enjoy the thrills and spills of white-water rafting in an inflatable; some of the most exciting rivers are the Shotover and Kawarau.

Rotorua
Agrojet, Western Road, tel: 07-357 2929; www.agroventures.co.nz. A 450hp 4-metre (13ft) raceboat offers a thrilling ride, accelerating up to 100kmh (62mph) in just four seconds, with no slowing down for corners on a man-made watercourse.
Kaituna Cascades Raft and Kayak Expeditions, Trout Pool Road, Okere Falls, tel: 07-345 4199, 0800-524 8862; www.kaitunacascades.co.nz. Offers single-day and multi-day adventures down the Kaituna, Wairoa, Rangitaiki and Motu rivers. The company has award-winning guides, custom-built rafts and first-class equipment.

Waitomo
Blackwater Rafting Company, 585 Waitomo Caves Road, tel: 07-878 6219; www.blackwaterrafting.co.nz. Well-known operator of cave-tubing trips; organises underground adventures of varying difficulty. Some trips involve abseiling (rappelling) and flying fox (zip line) rides.

Wanganui
Bridge to Nowhere Jet Boat Tours, tel: 0800-480 308; www. bridgetonowheretours. Escorted jet-boat tours of the magnificent Whanganui River, with an option to stay overnight at the Bridge to Nowhere Lodge.

Sailing/Cruises
The best conditions for sea sailing occur between October and April. You will find the widest range of sailing boats for one-day and longer trips, with or without a skipper, in the **Bay of Islands**, **Auckland** and the **Marlborough Sounds**.

TRANSPORT ACCOMMODATION EATING OUT ACTIVITIES A – Z

Chartering a fully equipped 12-metre (40ft) yacht costs between NZ$2,000 and NZ$3,000 a week, depending on the season. One of the most scenic trips you can make is the "coastal cruise" along the coast of Auckland into the Bay of Islands; a 10-day minimum charter charge applies. A day's sailing in a group costs around NZ$80–195 per person.

Aoraki Mount Cook National Park
Glacier Explorers, The Hermitage, Mount Cook, tel: 03-435 1077; 0800-686 800; www.glacierexplorers.com; Oct–May. Cruise the glacial lake formed by the melting face of New Zealand's' largest glacier; touch and taste 500-year-old ice. Guides give an informative commentary.

Auckland
Auckland isn't called the City of Sails for nothing. The best conditions for sailing occur between October and April. You will find a wide range of sailing boats for 1-day and longer trips. You can also take a daily cruise on the former America's Cup New Zealand yachts *NZL 40* and *NZL 41* (NZ$135 adult, NZ$110 child for 2 hours). Match racing in the yachts is also available from October to April (NZ$195 adult, NZ$175 child). Contact **Sail NZ**, tel: 0800-397 567; www.explorenz.co.nz. They also offer an Auckland Dolphin and Whale Safari, trips aboard the *Pride of Auckland*, and a 2½-hour dinner cruise on a 15-metre (49-ft) yacht around Auckland's magnificent harbour (NZ$95 adult, NZ$63 child).

Hahei
Hahei Explorer, Hahei Beach Road, tel: 07-866 3910; www.glassbottomboatwhitianga.co.nz. Daily adventure boat trips in a glass-bottomed boat to see Hahei Marine Reserve's Cathedral Cove, islands, reefs and sea caves (adults NZ$75, children 3–15 years NZ$40). Snorkel gear also available for hire.

Hokitika
Paddle Boat Cruises, Main South Road, 5km (3 miles) south of Hokitika, tel: 03-755 7239; www.paddleboatcruises.com. This 90-minute return trip takes you through magnificent scenery, including virgin rainforest, sighting rare birds. With an informative commentary. Seats up to 20, children under 5 free.

Kerikeri
Woodwind Yacht Charters, Wharau Road, RD3, tel: 09-407 5532; www.

woodwindyachtcharters.co.nz, offers fast, safe and comfortable sailing in a 15-metre (48ft) ocean-going kauri-built cutter.

Paihia
Fullers Bay of Islands, Maritime Building, Paihia Waterfront, tel: 09-402 7421; www.fboi.co.nz. The Bay of Islands is renowned for sailing, and Fullers has luxury cruises, the 90-minute high-speed Excitor Tour to Cape Brett and through the famous Hole in the Rock, plus "swimming with dolphins" adventures.

Picton and the Sounds
Compass Charters, Unit 1, Commercial Building, Waikawa Marina, tel: 03-573 8332; www.compass-charters.co.nz. Explore the magical Marlborough Sounds on a yacht, runabout or launch.

Queenstown
TSS *Earnslaw*, Lake Wakatipu, tel: 03-442 7500, 0800-656 503; www.realjourneys.co.nz; daily every 2 hours (summer 10am–8pm, winter noon–4pm). This grand, coal-fuelled old lady has graced the waters of Lake Wakatipu since 1912 when she was first used to carry goods to remote settlements. You may opt to visit Walter Peak High Country farm, a working farm, for lunch and a guided horse trek.

Russell
Fullers Russell, The Strand, tel: 09-403 7866; www.fboi.co.nz. The Cape Brett Hole in the Rock cruise includes the eponymous gap, Cape Brett Lighthouse and Grand Cathedral Cave, and includes a stop ashore on Urupukapuka Island.

Te Anau
Adventure Manapouri, 50 View Street, Manapouri, tel: 03-249 8070; www.adventuremanapouri.co.nz. This company will take you by water taxi to the beginning of the Manapouri Track, only accessible by boat.
Milford Sound Red Boat Cruises, Milford Wharf, Milford Sound, tel: 03-441 1137; www.redboats.co.nz. The highlight of a New Zealand holiday for many is a visit to the majestic scenery of Milford Sound, including Mitre Peak, waterfalls and abundant flora and fauna.

Te Urewera National Park
The Department of Conservation hires dinghies for the strong of shoulder to explore the glories of the lake. Tel: 06-837 3900.

Whitianga
Cave Cruzer Adventures, Whitianga Wharf, tel: 07-866 2574; www.cavecruzer.co.nz. You can explore the Coromandel's scenic coastline in an ex-Navy inflatable rescue boat, and head into a sea cave to hear the amazing sound of dolphins and whales calling, plus Maori instrument demonstrations.

Surfing
New Zealand's surrounding coastline ranges from gentle sloping beaches to rocky cliffs. There are excellent surfing conditions throughout the country, from **Raglan** in the North Island to **Dunedin** in the South. Water temperatures vary, and the best waves are usually found in the winter months. A wetsuit is required most of the year, although surfers can get by with a rash shirt in the North during the summer months (Dec–Feb). You'll find clean, barrelling waves on the **east coast** and heavier sets, sometimes as big as 3 metres (10ft), on the **west coast**.

For daily weather and surf conditions, up-to-date access to satellite images, surf cams and photographs of some of New Zealand's top surfing spots, plus information about contests, surf travel and surf stores around the country, check out: www.surf.co.nz, or call **Wavetrack Surf Report**, tel: 0900-99 777 (New Zealand only, calls are at premium rates).

Auckland
The best surf beaches in Auckland are on the west coast, and include Piha, Maori Bay, Muriwai and Bethells. Keep an eye on serious rips and tidal changes, as this coast is renowned for its danger spots. If unsure, check at the Surf Lifesaving Clubs before entering the water.

Dunedin
For anyone who is brave enough to

Swimming Baths

Most towns in New Zealand have community pools, and entrance to these is generally very reasonably priced. There is also bathing in many local lakes, most of which are crystal-clear, and swimming in the sea. Generally the east coast provides the safest sea swimming, but be sure to look for signs which may indicate rips, and if the beach has a Surf Lifesaving Club, be sure to swim between the flags.

ABOVE: surfers paddle out from Main Beach, Mount Maunganui, Bay of Plenty.

venture into the freezing cold ocean, Dunedin offers some of the best waves in the country – and there are 47km (29 miles) of beach within the city boundaries. The popular surf spots include **St Clair**, **St Kilda** and **Brighton**. If you plan to surf in winter, make sure you have a thick wetsuit, hat and booties.

Northland
At the top of the North Island above Auckland, sitting 12 degrees below the Tropic of Capricorn, this region's waters are mild throughout the year, and wetsuits are not required during the summer. Popular east-coast surf beaches include Mangawhai Heads, Waipu Cove and Ruakaka, while the west is famous for Shipwreck Bay, near Ahipara, and Bayleys Beach.

Waikato
Raglan Beach is a popular resort on Waikato's rugged west coast. The point breaks of Indicators and Manu are the fastest and best surfing spots in Raglan; Whale Bay tends to provide a slower ride.

Swimming/Pools
Christchurch
Queen Elizabeth II Park, 171 Travis Road, tel: 03-941 6849; www.qeiipark. org.nz; Mon–Fri 6am–9pm, Sat–Sun and public holidays 7am–8pm; charge. Stadium and sports complex built for the 1974 Commonwealth Games, but substantially upgraded with many special aquatic features.

Franz Josef
Glacier Hot Pools, Cron Street, Franz Josef, tel: 0800-044 044; www. glacierhotpools.co.nz. Daily noon–10pm. Located within easy walking distance

of town, these invitingly warm pools are set amid dripping rainforest.

Hanmer Springs
Hanmer Springs Thermal Pools and Spa, Amuri Avenue, daily 10am–9pm; charge; tel: 03-315 7511, 0800-442 663; www.hanmersprings.co.nz. These hot mineral pools are set in a garden of giant conifers. Few experiences are more pleasurable than relaxing in the warmth of these open-air pools on a winter's night, watching the snowflakes dissolve silently in the steam.

Hastings
Splash Planet, Grove Road, Hastings, summer Sat–Sun only, 10am–5.30pm; charge; tel: 06-873 8033; www.splashplanet.co.nz. This is a fun, family-oriented park, with such amusements as a full-size pirate ship, a castle, thrilling water slides and many more escapes from reality.

Helensville
Aquatic Park Parakai Springs, Parkhurst Road, Parakai, tel: 09-420 8998; www.parakaisprings.com. Enjoy a relaxing soak in the mineral pools, hire a private pool or have fun on the giant water slide. Daily 10am–10pm.

Rotorua
Polynesian Spa, Lake end of Hinemoa Street, daily 8am–11pm; charge; tel: 07-348 1328; www. polynesianspa.co.nz. There are 31 thermal pools of varying temperatures, each with its own special mineral content.

Tekapo
Alpine Springs and Spa, Tekapo Winter Park, tel: 03-680 6550. Fed by

underground spring water, there are three pools to choose from, each differently shaped to reflect the local glacier lakes of the region. Heated pathways lead between the pools and the sauna, steam room and plunge pool.

Te Aroha
Te Aroha Mineral Pools, tel: 07-884 8717; www.tearohapools.co.nz; daily 9am–10pm; charge. Public and private pools, some in original 19th-century bathhouses. Lovely small-town atmosphere.

Whale/Dolphin/Penguin/Seal Watch
You can get close to whales at **Kaikoura**, on the east coast of the South Island. Here, huge Sperm whales swim barely 1km (^{2}/$_3$ mile) off the coast between April and June; orcas can also be seen during the summer, and humpbacks put in an appearance during June and July.

In the **Bay of Islands**, you'll encounter Bottlenose dolphins, orcas and Sperm whales. Some trips also allow you to get into the water to cavort with the dolphins.

Akaroa
Black Cat, 61 Beach Road, tel: 03-304 7726; www.blackcat.co.nz. Two-hour cruises observing fur seals, Blue penguins and the rare Hector's dolphin. On the swimming tour, you can dive in and swim with the dolphins.

Dunedin
Penguin Place, Harrington Point, tel: 03-478 0286; www.penguinplace.co. nz; daily 10.15am to 90 minutes before sunset in summer, 3.15–4.45pm winter; charge. Here, rare Chaplinesque Yellow-eyed penguins strut in the surf and can be observed at close proximity utilising a unique system of hides and tunnels.
Monarch Wildlife Cruises Ltd, tel: 03-477 4276, 0800-666 272; www.wildlife.co.nz. Unrivalled viewing of albatross, seals and penguins in their natural environment. Explore Taiaroa Head, Otago Harbour and the Peninsula. One-hour cruises, half and full-day tours.

Kaikoura
Kaikoura is world famous for its whale and dolphin population. Huge Sperm whales swim barely a kilometre off the coast between April and June; orcas can also be seen during the summer, and humpbacks put in an appearance during June and July.

The following companies organise

trips to see both whales and dolphins; you should book a few days in advance:

Dolphin Encounter, 96 The Esplanade, tel: 03-319 6777, 0800-733 365; www.dolphin.co.nz.

Topspot Sealswims, 22 Deal Street, Kaikoura, tel: 03-319 5540. Slip into a wetsuit and get up close to New Zealand fur seals.

Whale Watch Kaikoura, Railway Station Road, tel: 03-319 6767, 0800-655 121; www.whalewatch.co.nz.

Wings Over Whales, Kaikoura Airfield, tel: 03-319 6580, 0800-226 629; www.whales.co.nz. Spectacular 30-minute whale-watching flights.

Paihia

Explore NZ, New Zealand Post Building, corner Marsden and Williams roads, tel: 09-402 8234; www.explorenz.co.nz. Runs regular dolphin discovery trips from Paihia and Russell to see Bottlenose dolphins, orcas and Sperm whales.

Wellington

Seal Coast Safari, departing i-site Visitors Centre, corner Victoria and Wakefield streets, tel: 0800-732 5277; www.sealcoast.com. These boat trips get you up close to Wellington's resident seal colony.

Windsurfing

New Zealand is an ideal place for windsurfing because windless days are few and far between and there are miles of coastline, harbours and lakes in which to enjoy the sport. Windsurfing conditions similar to those of Hawaii can be found in the North Island province of Taranaki. Other good windsurfing destinations include Auckland's Orewa Beach, Mission Bay and Piha Beach (professionals only), **New Plymouth and Makatana Island** near Tauranga, and **Gisborne**. In the South Island, the wind and waves are particularly good at **Kaikoura**, **Whites Bay** (Blenheim), **Pegasus** and **Sumner** bays near Christchurch, and the bays around **Dunedin** and **Cape Foulwind** (Westport).

Those who prefer lakes will find plenty of room at Lake Taupo, the largest in the country, Lake Rotorua or on the Alpine lakes of the South Island. For more information check out www.winzurf.co.nz, or call into local surf shops.

Auckland

There are plenty of great windsurfing spots in Auckland, including the popular **Point Chevalier** near the city centre, Orewa Beach and Piha Beach. Winds are consistent, but seldom very strong. You can hire from **New Zealand Board Store**, 5 Raymond Street, Point Chevalier, tel: 09-815 0683; www.nzboardstore.co.nz. This company offers lessons including kite surfing, and also rents out boards and gear from its branch at 532 Ellerslie/Panmure Highway.

Christchurch

Pegasus and Sumner bays near Christchurch offer the best windsurfing and surfing conditions, but the water is freezing, so it is advisable to wear a wetsuit.

Winter Sports

Skiing, Snowboarding and Heli-Skiing

With the spectacular triple peaks of the North Island and the magnificent Alps which run most of the length of the South Island, New Zealand is one of the world's great skiing destinations.

In winter, Kiwis are magically transformed into "Skiwis". Between July and October, as soon as sufficient new snow has accumulated, snow-loving New Zealanders migrate from the water to the mountains. There are 27 peaks higher than 3,000 metres (9,843ft), and another 140 exceeding 2,000 metres (6,562ft), and many of the ski resorts have spectacular views of green valleys and deep blue lakes far below. The snowline is usually at around 1,000 metres (3,300ft), and all the skiing areas are above the tree-line. This means there is plenty of space for everyone, and conditions are particularly ideal for the popular sport of snowboarding. Most ski fields have impressive, long runs and a range of slopes from beginner to professional-only. Fields pride themselves on having long vertical drops.

The main ski season runs from July to September, though this is extended at the larger fields by using artificial snow. Typically a day pass costs around NZ$74–79 for adults. Multi-day passes and season passes are also available. Ski gear including boots, skis and poles can be hired for around NZ$40–60 a day and snowboards and boots for around NZ$40–54.

Heli-skiing is an affordable luxury in New Zealand: three to five runs a day cost between NZ$645 and NZ$945. There are also week-long private heli-skiing charters, as well as daily heli-skiing packages tailored to your ability.

Ski Centres

The major **ski centres** in the **South Island** are at:
Cardrona: www.cardrona.com
Coronet Peak: www.nzski.com/coronet
Craigieburn: www.craigieburn.co.nz
Mount Hutt: www.nzski.com/mthutt
Ohau: www.ohau.co.nz
Porter Heights: www.skiporters.co.nz
The Remarkables: www.nzski.com/remarkables
Temple Basin: www.templebasin.co.nz
Treble Cone: www.treblecone.co.nz

The major **North Island** ski centres are located at Tongariro National Park and around Mount Ruapehu, specifically Whakapapa (National Park or Whakapapa Village) and Turoa (Ohakune): www.MtRuapehu.com.

For more information, look up www.nzski.com and www.snow.co.nz.

Aoraki Mount Cook National Park

Alpine Guides Aoraki, Bowen Drive, Mount Cook, tel: 03-435 1834; www.skithetasman.co.nz or www.alpineguides.co.nz. Tasman Glacier is open for skiing from July to September, but access to its magnificent slopes is only via fixed-winged skiplanes. Be warned that

Snow Safety

Be aware that even the most glorious mountain weather can deteriorate very rapidly, so be prepared for the worst conditions.

The NZ MetService provides weather forecasts for mountain areas, daily reports on ski conditions and the latest AA highway reports. Visit www.metservice.co.nz or phone (note premium rates apply).

Central North Island: tel: 0900-999 09
Nelson Lakes, Canterbury and Southern Lakes: tel: 0900-999 03

For up-to-date information from ski areas on snow conditions, snow-cams and operating facilities, check out www.snow.co.nz.

When you're up on a mountain, you need to protect yourself from the elements. If you become cold, don't wait until you are shivering, move to shelter and warm up; if possible, have a hot drink. Remember that children tire more easily than adults. Carry snacks and eat regularly, as skiing and snowboarding are high-energy sports, and drink plenty of fluids. Don't forget lip balm, sunblock and sunglasses or goggles to prevent snow blindness.

skiing the Tasman can be an expensive affair, although heli-skiing in New Zealand is cheap compared to the US and Europe.

Christchurch

Mount Hutt, **Methven** and **Porter Heights** are a 90-minute drive away from Christchurch. Contact: **Mount Hutt Ski Area**, tel: 03-308 5074; www.nzski.com/mthutt or **Porters Ski Area**, tel: 03-318 4002; www.skiporters.co.nz.

Methven

Methven Heliskiing, Main Street, tel: 03-302 8108; www.heliskiing.co.nz. This company flies skiers by helicopter, deep into the heartland where there are long ski runs through unbeatable scenery.

Queenstown/Wanaka

The best-organised ski centres in the South Island are Cardrona (www.cardrona.co.nz), Treble Cone (www.treblecone.co.nz), Coronet Peak (www.nzski.com/coronet) and The Remarkables (www.nzski.com/remarkables), all close to Queenstown and Wanaka. Visit their websites for more info or contact the visitors centres at Queenstown and Wanaka.

Harris Mountains Heli-Ski offers a range of packages, including private heli-ski charters as well as week-long and daily heli-skiing packages tailored to your skiing ability. Skiers get to explore the vast terrains of the Southern Alps, with its untracked powder, massive peaks, stunning valleys and challenging chutes. The best time for heli-skiing is July to September. Contact: Harris Mountains Heli-Ski, The Station, corner Shotover and Camp streets, Queenstown, tel: 03-442 6722 or 99 Ardmore Street, Wanaka, tel: 03-443 7930 (winter only); www.heliski.co.nz.

Whakapapa Village/National Park

Whakapapa ski area is located on the northwestern slopes of Mount Ruapehu and, on a clear day, has spectacular views across central North Island. Skiers either base themselves at Whakapapa Village, a 6km (4-mile) drive via Bruce Road to the foot of the slopes, or at the National Park area, 15km (9 miles) to the west.

Turoa ski area is located on the southwestern slopes of Ruapehu and has spectacular views out towards Mount Taranaki. A 17km (11-mile) drive up the Mountain Road above Ohakune Village (which has a wide range of accommodations, cafés and restaurants) will take you to the base of the slopes.

Check www.MtRuapehu.com for more information on skiing in these areas.

Ice Hiking/Glacier Walking

Ice hiking (also known as glacier walking) is the art of trying to stay upright while negotiating your way along an icy expanse full of stunning blue crevasses. This activity should certainly not be attempted alone: team up with a professional company which, as well as providing a knowledgeable and safety-conscious guide, will provide all the gear you will require, including crampons to attach to your hiking boots. Trips are either half- or full-day, with the full day being better to suited to those who are in good shape physically. Heli-hikes transport you quickly to the heart of the action and are suitable for people of all levels of fitness.

Fox Glacier Guiding, Main Road, SH6, Franz Josef Glacier, tel: 03-751 0825, 0800-111 6000; www.foxguides.co.nz. This company operates glacier walks, ice climbing and heli-hikes on Fox Glacier. Short hike to reach start point at the glacier's base.

Franz Josef Glacier

Franz Josef Glacier Guides, Main Road, SH6, tel: 03-752 0763, 0800-484 337; www.franzjosefglacier.com. Glacier walks, ice climbing and heli-hikes on Franz Josef Glacier; it is worth noting that a longer hike is required to reach the Franz Josef Glacier face.

Other Outdoor Activities

Four-Wheel-Drive Tours

Four-wheel-drive tours allow visitors to reach the seldom-seen scenery of New Zealand's backcountry with experienced and informative local guides.

Rotorua

Off Road NZ, SH5, daily 9am–5pm; charge; tel: 07-332 5748; www.offroadnz.co.nz. This is for those thrill-seekers who like to go very fast and make a lot of noise, especially in self-drive four-wheel-drive vehicles.

Queenstown

Nomad Safaris, Lord of the Rings Shop, 19 Shotover Street, tel: 03-442 6699, 0800-688 222; www.nomadsafaris.co.nz. Tours depart 8.30am and 1.30pm and last 4 hours. Various tour options include the spectacular off-road scenery of Middle Earth, Skippers Canyon and Macetown.

Star Gazing

Tekapo Tours Star Watching, Main Road, tel: 03-680 6960; www.earthandsky.co.nz. Take advantage of the unusually clear skies in this region to go on one of these spectacular, if chilly, night-time adventures. Tours depart at 10pm during the summer and 7–8pm during the winter months.

Scenic Flights

Scenic flights provide a great way to see New Zealand's landscapes and an overview of the area you are exploring. Flights range from relatively cheap to expensive, mostly depending on the size of the aircraft. You can choose to charter your own scenic flight (expensive) or join others with prices starting at around NZ$60 and increasing depending on the length of flight.

Aoraki Mount Cook National Park

Aoraki Mount Cook Skiplanes, Mount Cook Airport, SH80, near Aoraki Mount Cook Village, tel: 03-430 8034, 0800-800 702; www.skiplanes.co.nz. Offers scenic flights to view the glaciers up close and the only fixed-wing snow landing in the Southern Alps.

Helicopter Line, tel: 0800-650 651. Flights depart from Glentanner and fly directly up to Mount Dark or to any point you choose. Heli-flights can be tailor-made to suit any time frame.

Central Plateau

Mountain Air, SH4, tel: 07-892 2812; www.mountainair.co.nz. Breathtaking scenic views of the mountains of the Tongariro National Park, its many iridescent lakes and the broad sweep of Lake Taupo.

Franz Josef/Fox Glacier

Fox and Franz Josef Heliservices, SH6, Franz Josef; tel: 03-751 0866; www.scenic-flights.co.nz. There's no better way to gain a bird's-eye view of glacier country than aboard a helicopter with a glacier landing. A range of flights is on offer, including the Grand Tour, which explores both Fox and Franz Josef Glaciers, then flies around Mount Cook and Mount Tasman to the Tasman Glacier before returning to base.

Paihia

Salt Air, Paihia Waterfront, tel: 09-402 8338, 0800-472 582; www.saltair.co.nz. Operates light plane and helicopter flights to scenic spots in the Bay of Islands and to Cape

Reinga. The latter combines with a four-wheel drive tour of the sand dunes at Ninety Mile Beach.

Rotorua

Volcanic Air Safaris, Rotorua City lakefront, tel: 07-348 9984, 0800-800 848; www.volcanicair.co.nz. Floatplane and helicopter tours of the Rotorua region and central volcanic plateau, including Mount Tarawera and White Island. Costs range from NZ$60 for an 8-minute flight (minimum 4 persons) over the town area to NZ$665 for a 3-hour helicopter flight to White Island.

Marine Volcano Tours

Scrambling inside a volcano is not everybody's cup of tea, but there is nowhere else in the world where a live marine volcano is as easily accessible as at Whakatane, where regular tours depart to explore the fiery – and still active – crater of White Island.

Whakatane

White Island Tours with PeeJay, 15 The Strand East, Whakatane, tel: 07-308 9588; www.whiteisland.co.nz. Experience the awesome might of a live volcanic island. To get there, a boat ferries you across to the island, where you disembark to see the rusty ruins of a former sulphur mine, before hiking across a steaming, hissing crater floor, to the island's crater lake.

Wildlife and Garden Tours

Wildlife and garden tours provide the opportunity to view some of New Zealand's most important wildlife sites with an experienced guide who provides informative and in-depth information on native flora and fauna. Garden tours provide an insight into this art form, and here you will see native plants growing happily beside exotic species.

Franz Josef Glacier

Okarito Nature Tours, Franz Josef, Whataroa, tel: 03-753 4014; www.okarito.co.nz. Kayak deep into the heart of the forest for awesome Alpine views or to spot some of the 70 bird species in the area, notably the *kotuku* (White heron).

White Heron Sanctuary Tours, SH6, Whataroa, tel: 03-753 4120, 0800-523 456; www.whiteherontours.co.nz. Visit New Zealand's only White heron nesting colony from late September to March. Jet boating and sightseeing tours available all year round.

Hastings

Gannet Safaris Overland, Summerlee Station, 396 Clifton Road, Te Awanga, Hastings, tel: 06-875 0888, 0800-427 232; www.gannetsafaris.com. On these excursions, you ride in style and comfort in four-wheel-drive vehicles, for the unique experience of visiting the largest mainland colony of gannets in the world on the rugged Cape Kidnappers Coast. Tours depart daily at 9.30am and 1.30pm from Sept–Apr.

Whitebay World of Lavender, 527 SH5 Esk Valley, tel: 06-836 6081; www.whitebay.co.nz. Stunning lavender gardens; you can purchase lavender health-care products here.

Queenstown

Queenstown Garden Tours, tel: 03-442 3799; www.queenstowngardentours.co.nz; Oct–Mar daily 8.30am–noon. Tours include at least three splendid local residential gardens, chosen according to season, providing a delightful opportunity to see New Zealand domestic gardening at its best. Devonshire tea included. The Garden Tour can be combined with a Wine Tour – check details on www.queenstownwinetrail.co.nz.

Kiwi and Birdlife Park, Brecon Street, tel: 03-442 8059; www.kiwibird.co.nz; daily 9am–6pm; charge. Easy walking through native bush to aviaries where you will see not just *tui*, bellbirds, fantails and kiwis, but also rare and endangered birds and the rare tuatara. Conservation shows daily at 11am and 3pm. Kiwi feeding is held at 10am, noon, 1.30pm and 4.30pm.

Te Anau

The Te Anau Wildlife Centre, Lakefront Drive, Te Anau, tel: 03-249 7924. Focuses on native birds, including the rare takahe.

Wellington

Karori Wildlife Sanctuary, Waiapu Road, tel: 04-920 9213; www.sanctuary.org.nz. Daily 10am–5pm, last entry 4pm; charge. This wildlife oasis has 35km (21 miles) of tracks within the 252 hectares (622 acres) of regenerating forest. There's also a 19th-century gold mine on the site.

Skywire/Cable Car/Luge

Skywire is somewhat similar to a flying fox except you are seated inside a carriage – it is best not attempted immediately after lunch! A more sedate way to enjoy scenery in a moving carriage is aboard a cable car or gondola. Attached to a cable, these travel sedately uphill to a landing platform, most often with a café/restaurant or other optional activities available at the summit, including the luge, a three-wheeled cart that travels on a purpose-built track.

Nelson

Happy Valley Adventures, 194 Cable Bay Road, tel: 03-545 0304; www.happyvalleyadventures.co.nz. Fifteen minutes north of Nelson, this offers the world's first Skywire ride that is also New Zealand's longest flying fox. Strapped in a four-seat carriage suspended by a cable high over native

BELOW: riding the gondala from Queenstown to Bob's Peak.

Pan for Gold

Goldmine Experience, Main Road, SH25, Thames, tel: 07-868 8514; www.goldmine-experience.co.nz; daily 10am–4pm. In the heart of the gold-mining district, this unique attraction offers gold panning, guided tours underground and through the stamper battery, and a photographic museum.

forest, you are flown over 3km (2 miles) at speeds of up to 100kmh (62mph). Also popular are the four-wheel bike rides and horse treks through farmland and native forest.

Queenstown
Queenstown Paraflights, Queenstown Main Pier, tel: 03-441 2242, 0800-225 520; www.paraflights. co.nz. Take off from a boat on Lake Wakatipu and feel yourself lift gently into the air, to rise up to 200 metres (656ft). Land back on the boat. Minimum age is 3.
Shotover Canyon Swing, tel: 03-442 6990, 0800-279 464; www.canyonswing. co.nz. At 109 metres (358ft), this is the world's highest rope swing. You'll freefall 60 metres (197ft) into the canyon until the ropes pendulum you in a giant arc (200 metres/656ft) at 150kph (93mph). Minimum age is 10.
Skyline Gondolas, Brecon Street, tel: 03-441 0101; www.skyline.co.nz; daily 9am until late; charge. After the 790-metre (2,600ft) climb by cable car, take a ride on the thrilling downhill luge. Minimum age is 3 for luge rides.

Island Excursions
The main islands of the Hauraki Gulf – Rangitoto, Waiheke, Tiritiri Matangi and Great Barrier – are accessible by the fast ferries operated by **Fullers Cruise Centre** (Ferry Building, 99 Quay Street, Auckland, tel: 09-367 9111; www.fullers.co.nz). Don't miss the return ferry, as there is no accommodation on some islands, and alternative transport to the mainland is expensive.
If you wish to bring your car to Great Barrier Island, book with **Sea Link**, 45 Jellicoe Street, Auckland Viaduct, tel: 09-300 5900; www.sealink.co.nz.
Great Barrier Island is also serviced by flights scheduled three times daily. Contact **Great Barrier Airlines**, Auckland Domestic Airport Terminal, tel: 09-2759 120, 0800-900 600; www.greatbarrierairlines.co.nz.
Kawau Island and all the islands in the Hauraki Gulf are served by **Reuben's Water Taxis and Kawau**

Cruises, Sandspit Wharf, Warkworth, tel: 09-425 8006, 0800-111 616; www.reubens.co.nz.

Stewart Island
There are numerous local charter outfits, including adventure cruises, diving and fishing excursions.

Exploring Antarctica
Not a journey to be undertaken lightly, a visit to one of the world's most remarkable places can be booked and depart from Christchurch.
Heritage Expeditions, 53B Montreal Street, Christchurch, tel: 03-365 3500; www.heritage-expeditions.com. Cruises to Antarctica and the sub-Antarctic Islands – the "Galapagos of Antarctica" and among the last remaining unspoilt environments in the world. Groups number less than 50, and the emphasis is on getting you on shore as often and for as long as possible.

WINERIES AND TOURS

Scattered throughout the country are New Zealand's vineyards. Call in to sample local wines or join a vineyard tour. For more in-depth information regarding this booming industry (see pages 93–5).

North Island
Auckland
Fine Wine Tours, 33 Truro Road, Sandringham, tel: 09-849 4519, 021-626 529, 0800-023 111; www. insidertouring.co.nz. Conducts personalised wine-tasting tours for one to nine people.
Matua Valley Wines, Waikoukou Road, Waimauku, tel: 09-411 8301; www.matua.co.nz. Daily 10am–5pm. In a delightful garden setting, this winery offers cellar-door sales.
Soljans Estate Winery, 366 SH16, Kumeu, tel: 09-412 5858; www.soljans. co.nz. Offers complimentary tastings and a café. Daily 9am–5.30pm.
Villa Maria Estate, 118 Montgomerie Road, Mangere, tel: 09-255 0660; www.villamaria.co.nz. One of New Zealand's leading, and longest-established, wineries. Cellar-shop tastings, sales and winery tours, Mon–Fri 9am–6pm, Sat–Sun 10am–5pm.

Hastings
Vidal Estate, 913 St Aubyn Street East, tel: 06-872 7441; www.vidal.co.nz. Vidal Estates have many of their

award-winning bottles on the wine list at their restaurant, which was the first winery restaurant in the country.
On Yer Bike Wine Tours, 129 Rosser Road, Hastings, tel: 06-879 8735. Tour seven wineries on a bicycle, along reasonably level roads through the vineyards, orchards, ostrich farms and olive groves of Hawkes Bay. A unique one-day cycling experience.

Kerikeri
Marsden Estate Winery and Restaurant, Wiroa Road, tel: 09-407 9398; www.marsdenestate.co.nz. Original cuisine and wines can be enjoyed in a relaxed courtyard overlooking the lake and vines. Also wine sales, tastings and tours.
Cottle Hill, SH10, tel: 09-407 5203. This small family-owned winery offers tastings and platters in a casual and relaxed atmosphere.

Martinborough
Margrain Vineyard, corner Ponatahi and Huangarua roads, Martinborough, tel: 06-306 8333. A full selection of wines by Margrain Vineyard can be sampled at The Old Winery Café, where fresh local New Zealand cuisine is superbly matched to this region's famous wine.
Wairarapa Gourmet Wine Escape, run by Tranzit Coachlines, 316–318 Queen Street, Masterton, tel: 06-377 1227; www.tranzit.co.nz. Takes visitors on a lip-smacking tour of four Martinborough wineries, and finishes at the Martinborough Wine Centre.

Napier
Church Road Winery, 151 Church Road, Taradale, tel: 06-845 9137; www.churchroad.co.nz. This winery is one of New Zealand's leading producers and among its oldest, having been founded in 1897.
Mission Estate, 198 Church Road, Taradale, tel: 06-845 9350; www. missionestate.co.nz. New Zealand's oldest winery, established in 1851 and housed in a graceful building that is in itself worth a visit.
Royalty Wine Tours, 12 Browning Street, tel: 06-835 7800; www. countyhotel.co.nz. Named because both Queen Elizabeth II and Princess Diana enjoyed this jaunt. Operated by The County Hotel.

New Plymouth
Cottage Wines, 81 Branch Road, tel: 06-758 6910; www.cottagewines.co.nz. Visitors are welcome for complimentary tastings of the delicious range of fruit wines

TRANSPORT

ACCOMMODATION

EATING OUT

ACTIVITIES

A – Z

produced here. Winery tours are by prior arrangement. Daily 9am–6pm.

Whitecliffs Brewing Company Ltd, SH3, tel: 06-752 3676; www.organicbeer.co.nz. You can visit this fully organic working brewery to buy and sample Mike's Mild Ale, an award-winning handcrafted, English-style mild ale, and Mountain Lager, a full-strength German-style lager, both produced from only natural ingredients. Daily 10am–6pm.

Rotorua

Mamaku Blue Winery, SH5, tel: 07-332 5840; free; www.mamakublue.co.nz. Daily 10am–5pm. This is the only place in New Zealand making blueberry wine. Tours of the winery and orchard are available.

Russell

Omata Estate, Aucks Road, tel: 09-403 8007; www.omata.co.nz. Open daily for wine tasting.

Tauranga/Mount Maunganui

Tasting Tours and Charters, 31 Albero Drive, Tauranga, tel 07-544 1383; www.tastingtours.co.nz. Tours to local wineries, breweries and producers of gourmet foods.

Waiheke Island

Mudbrick Vineyard and Restaurant, Church Bay Road, tel: 09-372 9050; www.mudbrick.co.nz. A popular wine-and-dine location, featuring international cuisine.

Te Whau Vineyard Restaurant, 218 Te Whau Drive, Rocky Bay, tel: 09-372 7191; www.tewhau.com. With New Zealand's longest wine list, including its own, the restaurant has an absolutely stunning sea view and serves excellent New Zealand/Pacific cuisine.

Warkworth Area

Ascension Vineyards and Café, 480 Matakana Road, Matakana, tel: 09-422 9601; www.ascensionvineyard.co.nz. Open for tastings and sales daily from 10am–5pm, and excellent food is available in the café.

Heron's Flight Vineyards and Café, 49 Sharp Road, Matakana, tel: 09-422 7915; www.heronsflight.co.nz. Daily 11am–5pm, its courtyard café has a great view – and herons to spot.

Hyperion Wines, 188 Tongue Farm Road, Matakana, tel: 09-422 9375; www.hyperion-wines.co.nz. This winery produces mostly cabernet sauvignon and merlot, also pinot gris and chardonnay.

Whangarei

Longview Estate Vineyard and Winery, SH1, Otaika, tel: 09-438 7227; www.longviewwines.co.nz. Uses traditional techniques with modern technology to produce individual, handcrafted wines with intense fruit flavours.

South Island

Blenheim

Cloudy Bay, Jacksons Road, tel: 03-520 9140; www.cloudybay.co.nz. One of the best-known wineries, Cloudy Bay produces some of New Zealand's best wines. Offers tastings and sales of the vineyard's current releases, including limited-release wines.

Montana Brancott Winery, SH1, Riverlands, tel: 03-578 2099; www.montana.co.nz. One of New Zealand's largest wineries and host to the Wine Marlborough Festival in the second week of February. Wine tours and tastings, children's playground and restaurant.

Villa Maria Estate, corner Paynters and New Renwick roads, Fairhall, tel: 03-577 9530; www.villamaria.co.nz. Award-winning modern winery in an impressive location, specialising in pinot noir and sauvignon blanc.

Wairau River Winery, 264 Rapaura Road, tel: 03-572 9800; www.wairauriverwines.co.nz. Good food crafted from Marlborough's local produce at the Wairau River Restaurant, and award-winning wines at cellar-door prices.

Queenstown

Chard Farm, RD1, Queenstown, tel: 03-442 6110; www.chardfarm.co.nz. On a backcountry byway which used to be part of the main coach link between Queenstown and Cromwell.

Gibbston Valley Wines, SH6, Gibbston, tel: 03-442 6910; www.gvwines.co.nz. Award-winning winery in stunning location. The wine tour is not to be missed. Very impressive wine cave.

Lake Hayes Amisfield Cellars, 10 Lake Hayes Road, Lake Hayes, tel: 03-442 0556; www.amisfield.co.nz. A wine-tasting experience in a stunning lakeside location 10 minutes from Queenstown. Amisfield Bistro was voted best winery restaurant in *Cuisine* magazine's Restaurant of the Year Awards 2006.

Peregrine Wines, Kawarau Gorge Road, Queenstown, tel: 03-442 4000; www.peregrinewines.co.nz. Pinot noir specialists with a vineyard in rugged mountain country. Located in the Gibbston region of central Otago.

CHILDREN'S ACTIVITIES

Not all tourist attractions are suitable for children, and if you are travelling with children you will need to factor this into your travel plans. Fortunately, from restaurants to parklands, New Zealand is well equipped to cope with the wide-ranging needs of kids and provides a magnitude of entertainment – particularly outdoors – for all ages, just about everywhere you travel.

While all restaurants will be able to provide a high chair, many others also come with toy boxes, outdoor areas, and even separate play areas.

Children's parks are found in every small town and at a minimum offer swings and slides. **Outdoor playgrounds** of note include Masterton's Kids Own Playground, Whangarei's Town Basin Playground, and Rotorua's Lakefront Playground. In the larger cities there are large indoor playgrounds (look out for the franchised branches of Chipmunks and Lollipops), where, for a small charge, children have access to bouncy castles, huge slides and adventure play.

Rainbows End in Auckland is the country's largest **theme park**, and Auckland, Hamilton, Wellington and Christchurch all have their own **zoos**.

Other family activities available in most of New Zealand's larger townships include mini golf, mazes and nature parks. Throughout the country there is a variety of bush and beach walks on offer which range from 10–30 minutes – perfect for younger legs, as well as longer hikes for the teens.

New Zealand's wealth of **educational activities** – thermal-pool walks, dolphin watching, glow-worm caves, farm tours and birdlife tours – are ideal for keeping young minds stimulated. Other novel activities such as **Taupiri's Candyland** (Mon–Fri 10am–5pm, tel: 07-824 6818; www.candyland.co.nz, where you can make your own lollipops, and Wanaka's famous **Puzzling World** mazes (www.puzzlingworld.co.nz) can be found along the way.

What's more, in New Zealand age seems to be no barrier to many activities: you can go rafting at age 3, bungee-jumping at 10, tackle rapids at 13, and any age is considered suitable to swim with dolphins! Older kids can enjoy horse riding, hot-air ballooning and even paragliding.

A – Z

A HANDY SUMMARY OF PRACTICAL INFORMATION, ARRANGED ALPHABETICALLY

A dmission Charges

Unless visiting a beach, national park, scenic reserve or botanic gardens, the vast majority of attractions in New Zealand have an admission charge, as indicated in the Places chapters. Generally these average around NZ$15 for an adult NZ$5–10 for children, although there are many attractions such as museums located in small towns or small community-run enterprises that request only a NZ$1 or NZ$2 donation (you may come across the term *koha* – Maori for donation). Honesty boxes abound in New Zealand; respect the locals' trusting nature by paying your dues.

Adventure activities tend to attract higher costs. These range roughly between NZ$45–120 depending on the activity, its duration and what is included in the price (ie the cost of lunch or dinner, or entry into several attractions). Special multi-attraction deals are on offer in larger cities and key tourist destinations including Rotorua and Queenstown. For information, check at the local i-site information office. Major discounts (sometimes up to half-price) are often

available for children, students and senior citizens. Children under 5 often go free, while children under 3 years almost always do.

Age Restrictions

The minimum driving age in New Zealand is 15, so don't be surprised when you encounter very young-looking drivers on the road. The age of consent in New Zealand is 16, for both hetero- and homosexual persons. The legal drinking age is 18.

B udgeting for Your Trip

Ordering a standard beer and a glass of house wine at an average bar or pub will cost you around NZ$12–15. The main course meal for one person at a budget restaurant will set you back NZ$10–15, at a moderately priced establishment NZ$20–22, and anywhere between NZ$35–40 at a restaurant of high renown.

The price of accommodation varies from around NZ$80 to NZ$250 per night for two people. Motel rooms (self-contained units) tend to cost NZ$80–150, bed & breakfast NZ$100–150,

hotel rooms NZ$120–200 and boutique-style rooms NZ$250 and up.

Car hire ranges from around NZ$35 for a small vehicle hired for a hire period of seven days or more, and increase up to around NZ$120 for a large vehicle. Short hire periods cost more, starting at around NZ$70 per day for a small vehicle, or NZ$120+ for a larger vehicle.

Taxi fares are relatively expensive. Typical city-centre to airport fees are anywhere from NZ$35 (in Christchurch) to NZ$50 (in Auckland) one-way. Airport shuttle buses cost around NZ$15–25. Other bus tickets start at around NZ$2 (depending on the city) and a one-day travel pass costs between NZ$9–13.

C hildren

New Zealand is a great place to visit with children, with a range of activities for the whole family to enjoy. Most hotels offer a reliable babysitting service, and some have kids' clubs and activities. Motels and other accommodation usually have a contract with a local babysitting service and can organise fully police-vetted sitters on your behalf. Expect to pay around NZ$15 to NZ$20 per hour; many of the babysitters employed will be qualified nannies, so your children will be in good hands.

As a general rule children under 3 years of age gain free entry to attractions, and this sometimes applies to under 5s. Most attractions offer cut-rate prices for older children, sometimes half-price or less. There are special offers during off-peak holiday periods (mid-April, the first half of July and early October).

For more information about family holidays in New Zealand, contact: Familystophere.com, PO Box 12087, Wellington 6144, tel: 04-971 0646; www.familystophere.com. *See also children section, page 376.*

Climate

New Zealand's climate is the reverse of that of the Northern Hemisphere. This means New Zealanders enjoy a warm Christmas in the sun, while June and July are the coldest months.

The north of New Zealand, particularly Northland, enjoys an almost subtropical climate, with very mild winters. The climate in the south is generally temperate, with rainfall spread fairly evenly throughout the year, although the weather is very changeable – not too disimilar from that of the UK, albeit sunnier.

Winds can be strong at any time on the Cook Strait, which separates the two main islands, but summer days are generally warm and pleasant in most of the regions. Winters can be cold in the central and southern North Island and coastal districts of the South Island, and can be severe in the central regions of the South Island. The New Zealand weather service's website, www.metservice.co.nz, has details on weather conditions.

Temperature Ranges

Winter (June–August) and summer (December–February/March) temperature ranges are as follows:
Auckland: 8–15°C (48–59°F) in winter; 14–23°C (57–74°F) in summer.
Wellington: 6–13°C (43–55°F) in winter; 12–20°C (53–69°F) in summer.
Christchurch: 2–11°C (33–52°F) in winter; 10–22°C (50–73°F) in summer.
Queenstown: -1–10°C (30–50°F) in winter; 19–22°C (66–73°F) in summer.
Dunedin: 4–12°C (39–53°F) in winter; 9–19°C (48–66°F) in summer.

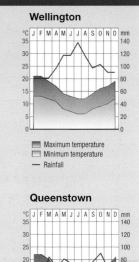

CLIMATE CHARTS

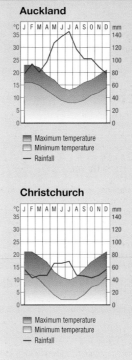

When to Visit

The summer and autumn seasons from December to May are the most settled and sunniest, and the best time for a visit. New Zealanders traditionally take their main family holiday break at Christmas and into January, so visitors are advised to make advance bookings for accommodation and domestic transport over this period.

Remember to stock up on plenty of sunscreen and insect repellent during summer; this is readily available throughout the country.

What to Wear

(See also Etiquette, page 379)
For summer visits, you are advised to bring sweaters or wind-breakers for the cooler evenings or brisk days, especially if you are planning to travel to regions in the South Island.

Medium-thick clothing, plus a raincoat or umbrella, is adequate for most regions most of the year, but in midwinter in Rotorua, Taupo and most of the South Island including Queenstown, sturdy winter clothing and footwear are essential. The South Island is considerably colder during

the winter than the North.

Note: New Zealand is noted for its high level of ultraviolet radiation and the brilliance of its light. This means you may get sunburnt even on days when the air temperature is quite low. It is important to wear sunscreen lotions, a hat, sunglasses and protective clothing. Stay out of the summer sun around the middle of the day (especially in the North) and follow the advice to "Slip, slop, slap-wrap and re-apply sunscreen regularly" – as the weather service says on its website.

Crime and Safety

New Zealand is considered to be one of the safer countries in the world for travellers and suffers only isolated incidences of serious crime. However, petty crime is a problem. Take precautions to secure and conceal your valuables at all times, and never leave them in a car.

To report a crime, contact your nearest police station, where you will find police who are approachable and helpful. New Zealand police carry tazer stun guns, and the special force within the police known as the armed defenders squad, only called upon in emergencies, are heavily armed.

In an emergency dial 111 for ambulance, police or fire service. Emergency calls are free from public call boxes. For further information regarding safety and other general information regarding travelling in New Zealand, visit www.nz-immigration. co.nz/newzealand/index.html.

Drink-Driving

Drink-driving penalties are tough, regardless of where you are from. Random breath tests by police are often conducted and care should be taken not to exceed the limit of 0.8g of alcohol for each litre of blood. Loosely this equates to four standard drinks for a male, and three standard drinks for a female in the first hour, followed by one standard drink every hour thereafter. The New Zealand government will be reviewing the law in late 2009, with a view to bringing it in line with the Australian standard of 0.5g per litre of blood.

Customs Regulations

New Zealand has three levels of control at all points of entry into the country: immigration, customs and The Ministry of Agriculture and Fisheries, otherwise known as MAF. On arrival, you must complete an arrival card. Present this to an immigration official with your passport, and, if required, a valid visa. *For more on visas and entry requirements, see page 386.*

A visitor over the age of 17 may import 200 cigarettes or 200g of tobacco; 50 cigars or a mixture of all three not exceeding 250g; 4.5 litres of wine or beer and one 1,125ml bottle of spirits. Excess quantities are subject to customs charges.

Strict laws prevent the entry of drugs, weapons, illicit material, wildlife products, firearms and quarantine items.

Farm Regulations

Because New Zealand relies heavily on agricultural and horticultural trade with the rest of the world, it has stringent regulations governing the import of animals, as well as vegetable and animal matter. Visitors planning to bring in any material of this sort should make enquiries at the New Zealand Government offices overseas before proceeding. Live animals legally brought into the country must undergo strict quarantine periods.

It is worth noting that if you complete your arrival card stating you are not carrying food of any kind, and food is in fact discovered, this attracts hefty fines of up to NZ$200,000. All baggage entering the country is X-rayed prior to entry, so if you are carrying food of any description with you, declare it.

D isabled Travellers

New Zealand law requires every new building or major reconstruction to provide "reasonable and adequate" access for people with disabilities. Most facilities have wheelchair access, but it pays to check when booking.

Parking concessions are available for people with disabilities, and temporary display cards can be issued for the length of the visitor's stay. For more information, check the **Weka** website, www.weka.net.nz, New Zealand's disability information website, which also provides brochures, or call tel: 0800-171 981. Weka can direct you to any of the 23 Local Disability Resource Centres around the country.

Most transport operators can cater for people with special needs, although most urban transport buses are not equipped to accommodate the disabled. A few tour operators provide custom holiday packages for individual and group travellers with disabilities. Contact:
Accessible Kiwi Tours, 1610 State Highway 30, RD4, Rotorua, New Zealand, tel: 07-362 7622; www.toursnz.com.
Ucan Tours New Zealand Ltd, 8 Campbell Street, Sumner, Christchurch, tel: 03-326 7881; www.ucantours.com.

E lectricity

New Zealand's AC electricity supply operates at 230/240 volts, 50 hertz, which is the same as Australia's. Most hotels and motels provide 110-volt, 20-watt AC sockets for electric razors only. A transformer is necessary to operate all other electrical equipment.

Emergency Numbers

If you are involved in an emergency in New Zealand you need to dial **111** (for ambulance, fire or police). This number is free regardless of whether you are using a mobile phone, landline, or public telephone.

Power outlets only accept flat three- or two-pin plugs, depending on whether an earth connection is fitted.

Embassies and Consulates

Overseas

There is a New Zealand Diplomatic Post finder at www.nzembassy.com, which details all New Zealand embassies and consulates around the world. Here are a few of them:
Australia: New Zealand High Commission, Commonwealth Avenue, Canberra, ACT 2600, Australia, tel: 02-6270 4211; email: nzhccba@bigpond.net.au.
Canada: New High Commission, 99 Bank Street, Suite 727, Ottawa, Ontario K1P 6GE, Canada, tel: 613-238 5991; email: info@nzhcottawa.org.
France: New Zealand Embassy, 7ter, rue Léonard de Vinci, 75116 Paris, France, tel: 01-4501 4343; email: nzembassy.paris@fr.oleane.com.
Germany: New Zealand Embassy, Friedrichstrasse 60, 10117 Berlin, Germany, tel: 030-206 210; email: nzembassy.berlin@t-online.de.
Singapore: New Zealand High Commission, 391A Orchard Road, #15-06/10, Ngee Ann City, Tower A, Singapore 238873, tel: 65-6235 9966; email: enquiries@nz-high-com.org.sg.
South Africa: New Zealand High Commission, 1110 Arcadia Street, Block C, 2nd floor, Hatfield Gardens, Hatfield, Pretoria 0028, tel: 012-342 8656; email: enquiries@nzhc.co.nz.
United Kingdom: New Zealand High Commission, New Zealand House, 80 Haymarket, London SW1Y 4TQ, United Kingdom, tel: 020-7930 8422; email: aboutnz@newzealandhc.org.uk.

BELOW: high-quality cuisine.

Above: Maori dance performance.

United States of America: New Zealand Embassy, 37 Observatory Circle, Washington DC 20008, USA, tel: 202-328 4800; email: info@nzemb.org.

In New Zealand

For information on foreign embassies in New Zealand, check the Ministry of Foreign Affairs and Trade website: www.mfat.govt.nz. Most foreign embassies are located in Wellington.
Australia: 72–76 Hobson Street, Thorndon, Wellington 6011, tel: 04-473 6411.
Canada: Level 11, 125 The Terrace, Wellington 6011, tel: 04-473 9577.
France: 34–42 Manners Street, Wellington 6011, tel: 04-384 2555.
United Kingdom: 44 Hill Street, Thorndon, Wellington 6011, tel: 04-924 2888.
United States: 29 Fitzherbert Terrace, Thorndon, Wellington, tel: 04-462 6000.
Note that Ireland and South Africa do not have an embassy or high commission in New Zealand.

Etiquette

New Zealanders are regarded as fairly casual dressers, although you will need to bring something dressy if you plan to go to any arts events and fancy restaurants. For clubbing, you should wear something smart. Some nightclubs and bars do not allow shorts, singlets, trainers or flip-flops (called jandells in New Zealand).

If you are invited to someone's home, casual dress is fine. If you are invited to attend church or a Maori *marae*, dress neatly but don't go over the top, as New Zealanders in general have a very laid-back approach to dressing up.

If you are invited to attend a barbeque, or meal at someone's home it is appropriate to bring something for your host; a bottle of wine, small box of chocolates or other small token will be graciously accepted.

If you happen to attend a community event that states everyone should "bring a plate" – this means a plate filled with something to share with others, most usually finger-food. For visitors it is perfectly acceptable, should this arise, simply to bring a packet of shop-bought biscuits. On arrival, place them on the table.

Gay and Lesbian Travellers

New Zealand is a gay-tolerant country, although some prejudice persists, particularly in small towns. Homosexuality ceased being categorised as a criminal offence in 1986, and the age of consent was set at 16 (same as heterosexuals).

There are plenty of facilities in New Zealand catering for the gay, lesbian and bisexual traveller, and festivals include Gay Ski Week in Queenstown and the Great Party weekend in Wellington.

The best organisations to contact for further information include:
Gay Tourism New Zealand: PO Box 11–462, Wellington 6015, tel: 04-917 9176; www.gaytourismnewzealand.com.
New Zealand Gay and Lesbian Tourist Association, QNZ Marketing Ltd: PO Box 638, Camp Street, Queenstown, tel: 21-762 796; www.gaypages.co.nz.
Other useful websites are www.gaytravel.co.nz and www.gaynz.net.nz.

Health and Medical Care

Visitors are charged for taxpayer-funded health care in New Zealand, so health insurance is highly recommended. To be eligible for the same health-care benefits as New Zealand residents, you must be able to prove your eligibility with a work permit for two years or more, refugee status, or proof that you are a Cook Islands, Niue or Tokelau New Zealand citizen. In the case of visiting children under 18 years, the child's legal guardian must prove their resident status.

Any ineligible patient who seeks general specialist treatment at a hospital – whether it is a public or a private hospital – or any medical centre will be prioritised alongside eligible patients if there is spare capacity. The estimated cost must be paid in advance and any additional costs paid at the end of the treatment.

All visitors, however, are entitled to initial, free acute (emergency) care following an accident, regardless of who is to blame, and this is covered by the government-run Accident Compensation Scheme (ACC). However, they must apply to the ACC for approval to undergo any further ongoing treatment.

Free care is also provided by the New Zealand government for any visitor who has been admitted to hospital under a compulsory treatment order issued under the Tuberculosis Act the Mental Health Act, or the Alcoholism and Drug Addiction Act.

Other Considerations

Tap water in New Zealand is safe to drink and is of a high quality thanks to its pristine environment. However, it is not wise to drink untreated water from lakes and streams, or to fill up a drink bottle in a public toilet, as it may be plumbed from a stream. In national parks, Department of Conversation (DOC) signs will state whether water sources are safe to drink.

Law prohibits smoking in all public buildings, restaurants and pubs. There are no snakes or dangerous wild animals in New Zealand, although a bite from the native Red-backed katipo spider and introduced White-tail spider may require medical attention. Sandflies and mosquitoes are prevalent in some areas, although insect repellents are widely available.

Medical Services

For non-emergencies, full instructions for obtaining assistance are printed in the front of telephone directories. Hotels and motels normally have individual arrangements with duty doctors for guests' attention, and they can also assist you in finding a dentist.

New Zealand's medical and hospital facilities, both public and private, provide a high standard of treatment and care. It is important to note that medical services are not free to visitors, except as outlined above, for the treatment of injuries sustained in an accident.

Pharmacies

Pharmacies, or chemists, are generally open 8.30am–5.30pm weekdays and until noon on Saturdays. Some are also open for one late night a week.

In New Zealand there is no single pharmacy that remains open 24/7: this task is a shared responsibility, although public hospitals, listed below, will be able to advise the address and phone number of pharmacies which are on duty on any given night.

As well as dispensing pharmaceuticals and medicines, chemists also sell cosmetics and insect and sun protections. Some drugs sold over the counter in other countries may not be available without a prescription – this will involve a visit to a medical centre to obtain one.

Major North Island Hospitals

Auckland Hospital, tel: 09-367 0000
Hawke's Bay Hospital, tel: 06-878 8109
Rotorua Hospital, tel: 07-348 1199
Taranaki Hospital, tel: 06-753 6139
Taupo Hospital, tel: 07-376 1000
Waikato Hospital, tel: 07-839 8899
Wellington Hospital, tel: 04-385 5999
Whangarei Hospital, tel: 09-430 4100

Major South Island Hospitals

Christchurch Hospital, tel: 03-364 0640
Clyde Hospital, tel: 03-418 0500 (closest to Queenstown)
Dunedin Hospital, tel: 03-474 0999
Greymouth Hospital, tel: 03-768 0499
Nelson Hospital, tel: 03-546 1800
Southland Hospital, tel: 03-218 1949
Timaru Hospital, tel: 03-684 4000

Health and Beauty

Health Spas

Since the 1800s, New Zealanders have been soaking in the country's natural mineral waters, and the Maori have been doing so for a great deal longer. But it wasn't until the latter part of the 19th century that the spa industry in New Zealand really began in earnest.

Today, there are numerous natural spas and thermal resorts in New Zealand. These include the **Polynesian Spa** in Rotorua, the **Taupo Hot Springs Health Spa** in the North Island, and **Hanmer Springs Thermal Pools and Spa** in the South Island, to name a few.

Beauty Therapy and Day Spas

Beauty-therapy clinics offering services such as sunbeds, day spas, manicures, pedicures, massages, body wraps, waxing, skin care and make-up can be found throughout New Zealand. Prices range from NZNZ$50 for a 40-minute massage to around NZNZ$500 for a full-day, complete beauty spa experience. Check the Yellow Pages (www.yellowpages.co.nz) for the nearest beauty salon or day spa.

Internet

There are numerous Internet cafés in every city and small town in New Zealand that provide access to Internet and email. All hotels provide Internet access, as do the majority of motels and other accommodations. Most often this is for an additional charge, although at some lodges and boutique accommodations it is complimentary. You will need an RJ45-type plug to be able to connect your laptop into a computer socket in New Zealand, and an adaptor with a flat two- or three-point power plug to connect to the power supply.

Wireless is widely available, but to access you will need to obtain correct passwords, etc. Your accommodation will be able to provide you with information on local hotspots, and how to access and pay for these.

Websites

www.newzealand.com Tourism New Zealand's award-winning website is loaded with useful information.

www.holiday.co.nz A travel guide and vacation planner with holiday options from motorcycle tours to accommodation.
www.aotearoa.co.nz New Zealand and Pacific arts and crafts. You can order bone carvings, glass art, woodcarvings and designer jewellery online.
www.nzedge.com A comprehensive and eclectic site that explores the lives and achievements of New Zealanders living overseas and connects them on a global scale. The site contains a unique online shopping guide, news stories, a section dedicated to New Zealand "heroes", image galleries,

Language

English is the common language of New Zealand. However, as this is a multicultural society, you may hear other languages spoken, including Te Reo Maori, the other official language. The vast majority of New Zealand place names are of Maori origin. There are also television and radio programmes which are broadcast entirely in the Maori language.

Useful Maori Phrases

Kia ora – your good health (hello)
Kia ora tatou – hello everyone
Tena koe – greetings to you (said to one person)
Tena koutou – greetings to you all
Haere mai – welcome
Haere ra – farewell
Ka kite ano – until I see you again (goodbye)
moana – sea
puke – hill
roto – lake
tomo – cave
wai – water
whanga – bay
waitomo – water cave

speeches, web links and a global register.

www.nzmusic.com The diversity of the Pacific sound is at your fingertips here. It has a catalogue of Kiwi artists, biographies, music, news, an extensive gig guide and a section dedicated to forums.

www.allblacks.com Official site of the New Zealand Rugby Football Union and the All Blacks.

www.aa.co.nz New Zealand's leading motoring organisation. Driver, accommodation and travel info.
www.nzmuseums.co.nz An exhaustive listing of museums great and small, throughout the country.

Left Luggage

Key-operated luggage-storage facilities are available at all major train stations and bus stations. Most are coin-operated; others you will need to pay for at a desk. Many hotels will also happily store extra luggage if you plan to return to the hotel after taking a tour.

Lost Property

There is no central lost-property service in New Zealand, so if you lose

ABOVE: old and new in Auckland.

something of value, advise your accommodation and contact the nearest police station. Chances are someone will hand the item in. If you lose your passport you will need to advise your embassy as soon as possible, and should your credit card go astray, phone your credit card provider immediately.

M aps

Tourist information offices (i-sites) and car-hire companies distribute free maps. The New Zealand Automobile Association also produces regional maps and excellent district maps; a nominal sum is charged for North and South Island maps. *Hema Maps, Wises Maps* and the *Shell Road Atlas* are also well produced and widely available. The laminated *Insight Fleximap New Zealand* is durable and detailed.

Media

Print

English is the most widely used language, followed by Maori, the indigenous language. There is a high level of literacy in New Zealand: most communities have a decent library, and sales of books, magazines and newspapers on a per capita basis are among the highest in the world. One in four people in Auckland buys *The New Zealand Herald*, the morning daily. Most large towns have their own newspaper, and community newspapers abound.

International newspapers can be found in the larger bookshops and outlets at New Zealand's international airports as well as in public libraries.

Cuisine magazine is an excellent guide to New Zealand food and wine, with regular new restaurant reviews from around the country; *RV &*

Motorhome Lifestyle magazine has in-depth features and reviews of New Zealand travel destinations, food and wine; and *The Listener* comments on contemporary New Zealand issues.

TV and Radio

New Zealand has several public broadcasting channels. Two television channels are administered by a nominally independent government corporation: Television One and TV2. Two more channels, TV3 and Prime, are run by a Canadian-owned company. National and international news and current affairs programmes are usually carried on Television One, TV3 and Prime.

Free-view (digital) has seen the start-up of several new regional television stations – some of which broadcast nationwide. In addition, many New Zealanders, and most hotels and motels, have long subscribed to the Sky satellite TV service for international sports and news, movie and music channels and a variety of other programming.

New Zealand has a selection of AM- and FM-band radio stations, satisfying a wide variety of tastes.

Money

The New Zealand dollar (NZ$), divided into 100 cents, is the unit of currency. Currency exchange facilities are available at Auckland, Wellington and Christchurch international airports, as well as most banks and bureaux de change in the larger cities and resorts.

There is no restriction on the amount of domestic or foreign currency (or traveller's cheques in New Zealand dollars) a visitor may bring into or take out of New Zealand. The New Zealand dollar is frequently called "the kiwi" because the dollar coin features a kiwi, the national bird, on one side.

At time of going to press (May 2009), NZ$1 was equivalent to US$0.57 while US$1 bought NZ$1.75. NZ$1 was equivalent to £0.38 while £1 was worth NZ$2.61.

Credit Cards

Credit cards, including Visa, American Express, Diners Club and MasterCard, are widely accepted throughout New Zealand, and you will be able to use them to withdraw cash from automatic teller machines (ATMs), situated at banks and shopping centres throughout the country.
Amex, tel: 0800-656 660
Diners Club, tel: 0800-346 377
Mastercard, tel: 0800-449 140
Visa, tel: 0508-600 300

Goods and Services Tax

A goods and services tax (GST) of 12.5 percent is applied to the cost of all goods and services and is generally included in all prices. GST is not charged on duty-free goods, or where the items are posted by a retailer to an international visitor's home address. Neither is GST included in international air fares purchased in New Zealand.

GST is added to accommodation, however, by law, and this is now included in the quoted price. There are no further hotel taxes.

Tipping

Tipping is becoming more widespread in New Zealand, although it is still regarded as a foreign custom. In the major centres, tipping is encouraged but not expected. You should tip 5–10 percent of your restaurant bill if you feel the service was worthy. Service charges are not added to hotel or restaurant bills.

O pening Hours

As a general rule, shops are open for business 8.30am–5.30pm (Mon–Fri), and usually stay open until 9pm one night of the week. Hours on Saturday are usually from 9am until the late afternoon. Main cities and the larger tourist areas have extended opening hours, with many shops open seven days a week.

Banks are open 9.30am–4.30pm (Mon–Fri), and ATMs are plentiful. Bars, pubs and taverns are open 11am–late (Mon–Sun). Nightclubs usually open their doors 7.30–8pm and close around 3am.

Banks, post offices, government offices and some shops close on public holidays. Most nightclubs and bars also close at midnight the night before each public holiday.

P hotography

Most New Zealanders don't mind being photographed, but it's best to ask before you click. There are professional photographic labs and camera centres throughout the country. They have the most up-to-date digital and film-processing technology, and the latest camera and video gear. At some stores you can even hire equipment. You can also drop your film off at local pharmacies to be processed and download your digital camera's memory card onto disk. There are also plenty of camera-repair services throughout New Zealand. Check the widely available

Public Holidays

January New Year's Day (1st) and next working day; provincial anniversaries: Southland (18th), Wellington (25th).
February Waitangi Day (6th); provincial anniversaries: Northland and Auckland (1st), Nelson/Buller Day (1st).
March Provincial anniversaries: Otago (22nd), Taranaki (8th). Good Friday and Easter Monday.
April Anzac Day (25th).
June Queen's Birthday (usually the first Monday).
September Provincial anniversaries: South Canterbury (27th).
October Labour Day (usually the last Monday), Provincial anniversaries: Hawke's Bay (22nd).
November Provincial anniversaries: Marlborough (1st), Canterbury (12th).
December Christmas (25th, 26th and next working day).
Note: Provincial anniversaries are usually observed on the Monday closest to the actual date. All banks, post offices, government and private office and some shops close on public holidays.

Yellow Pages directory or the Internet for camera store locations.

Postal Services

Post offices are generally open 9am–5pm (Mon–Fri). Some are also open Saturday mornings until midday. In smaller rural areas, postal services and stamps are also available in stationery shops and corner stores. In larger towns, in addition to stamps, post offices also sell magazines and a range of stationery. NZ Post also offers a courier service within New Zealand.

Post boxes are widely available and easily identified by their distinctive red-and-white design. If you are posting within New Zealand there is the choice of standard post or fast post. An average letter costs NZ50c to send by standard post, or NZ$1 by fast post.

Airmail is fairly swift, but because it is based on weight, it becomes expensive if you are sending a letter of more than one page. A one-page letter to in a standard airmail-sized envelope to Australia costs NZ$1.50, as does a postcard or aerogramme; to anywhere else in the world a standard letter costs NZ$2 and a postcard or aerogramme costs NZ$1.50.

Mail to Australia takes 3–6 days to reach its destination; the rest of the world takes 6–10 days.

Public Toilets

Public toilets can be found at most beaches, parks and town centres. In wilderness areas and national parks, environmentally friendly composting and long-drop toilets are found in or near most car parks and at huts. During the summer it is wise to travel with your own supply of toilet paper, as smaller places sometimes struggle to cope with the demands placed upon their facilities, which are free of charge.

Religious Services

More than half of New Zealanders affiliate themselves with a Christian religion, with Anglican, Catholic and Presbyterian being the largest denominations. The largest non-Christian religions include Buddhist, Hindu, Islam/Muslim, Spiritualism and New Age religions.

Churches and other places of worship are located throughout New Zealand. To find out about local services, ask at your accommodation or at the nearest i-site.

Smoking

Although statistics report that one in four New Zealanders smokes, these days smoking has a social stigma attached to it and is banned in all public places, including bars. Endeavour not to light up within close proximity of other people and never inside a public space. Some hotels/motels still provide smoking rooms, but there is a trend towards providing smokers with comfortable outdoor places to indulge their habit.

Student Travellers

Discounts are offered to travelling students, although in many cases you will need to ask. Identification will be required in the form of an International Student Identity Card, although International Youth Travel Cards (www.isiccard.com) will sometimes be accepted.

The Youth Hostel Association (www.yha.co.nz) is widely recognised in New Zealand. Its members are eligible for discounts of 10 to 25 percent on coach travel, adventure activities, and shopping. Visit the website www.yha.co.nz, click on membership, then on member discounts to see a sample list of savings.

Tax

A goods and services tax (GST) of 12.5 percent is applied to the cost of all goods and services. Goods are priced inclusive of GST.

GST is charged on accommodation, but again it is inclusive and will not be added when you settle your bill. There are no further hotel taxes or sales taxes, but when you leave the country there is a NZ$25 departure tax. In the case of some tickets, especially those departing Auckland, this will have been prepaid.

Telephones

To call New Zealand from overseas, dial its country code (64), but omit the 0 prefix on all area codes. Dial the 0 prefix of the area code only when calling within New Zealand. To phone overseas from New Zealand, dial 00 followed by the national code of the country you are calling.

Note: Some businesses have free 0800 or 0508 numbers which can only be dialled within New Zealand. 0900 numbers are charged to the caller by the minute, and are at premium rates.

Phone numbers appear in the White Pages (alphabetical listings) and the Yellow Pages (business category listings).
Public phones: Most public telephones accept cards that can be purchased from bookstalls and newsagents with a minimum value of NZ$5. Some public telephones also accept credit cards, and a few accept coins. Calls made from public telephones within the local area cost 50 cents.
Mobile phones: Check with your phone company before leaving home about international mobile roam facilities in New Zealand. Mobile phones can also be hired on arrival in New Zealand (outlets are available at international airports). To save on mobile phone bills, consider buying a prepaid phone card. Check with **NZ Telecom** (www.telecom.co.nz) and **Vodafone** (www.vodafone.com) shops in major towns and cities.

New Zealand Area Codes

Northland: 09
Auckland: 09
Waikato: 07
Bay of Plenty: 07
Gisborne: 06
Hawke's Bay: 06
Taranaki: 06
Wairarapa: 06
Wellington: 04

ABOVE: sheep outnumber people by around twenty to one.

Nelson: 03
West coast and Buller: 03
Christchurch: 03
Timaru/Oamaru: 03
Otago: 03
Southland: 03

International Codes from New Zealand

Australia: 0061
Canada: 001
Ireland: 00353
New Zealand: 0064
South Africa: 0027
United Kingdom: 0044
United States: 001

Time Zone

There is only one time zone throughout most of the country: 12 hours ahead of Greenwich Mean Time (GMT), and 17 hours ahead of Eastern Standard Time in the USA. However, from early October until late March, time is advanced by one hour to give extended daylight throughout summer. Therefore, and taking British Summer Time and the US Daylight Saving Time into account, New Zealand time is in fact GMT +13/EST + 18 for much of the October–March period, and GMT + 11/EST + 16 from late March to October.

Time in the remote Chatham Islands, 800km (500 miles) east of Christchurch, is 45 minutes ahead of that in the rest of the country.

Early Start to the Day

Travellers from the Northern Hemisphere moving west into New Zealand lose a full day crossing the International Dateline, and regain a full day returning eastwards. Because the country is so advanced in time, given its proximity to the International Date Line, it is one of the very first nations to welcome each day, preceded only by Fiji, Kiribati and some of the other small Pacific Islands.

Tour Operators

New Zealand tour operators employ highly trained, professional and friendly staff who will often go out of their way to make sure your experience is the very best they can provide. A huge range of activities is on offer: *for a comprehensive listing refer to the activities guide on page 353.*

Tourist Information: General

New Zealand is well served in terms of visitor information. Desks offering information and booking services at most airports and information can also be found at over 100 prime locations including i-sites (visitor information centres) around the country. A good start point is **Tourism New Zealand**'s website, www.newzealand.com.

The official **Tourism New Zealand** website, **www.newzealand.com**, has comprehensive information in several languages. Alternatively, contact one of the following Tourism New Zealand offices:

London: New Zealand House, Level 7, 80 Haymarket, London SW1Y 4TQ, tel: 020 7930 1662.
Los Angeles: 501 Santa Monica Boulevard, Suite 300, Santa Monica, CA 90401, tel: 310-395 7480.
Singapore: 391A Orchard Road, 15–01 Ngee Ann City, Tower A, Singapore 238873, tel: 65-6738 5844.

Sydney: Suite 3, Level 24, 1 Alfred Street, Sydney NSW 2000, tel: 02-8220 9000.

Tourist Information Offices: North Island

Auckland
Auckland i-site Visitors Centre, Atrium, Sky City, corner of Victoria and Federal streets; daily 8am–8pm; tel: 09-363 71825; www.aucklandnz.com.
New Zealand Visitors Centre, AMEX Princes Wharf, corner Quay and Hobson streets; daily 8.30am–6pm; tel: 09-979 2333; www.aucklandnz.com.

Cambridge
Cambridge Information Centre, corner of Victoria and Queen streets, tel: 07-823 3456; www.cambridge.co.nz.

Devonport
Devonport i-site Visitors Centre, 3 Victoria Road, tel: 09-446 0677.

Doubtless Bay
Doubtless Bay Information Centre, Waterfront Drive, tel: 09-406 2046; www.doubtlessbay.co.nz.

Great Barrier Island
Great Barrier Island Visitor Information Centre, Claris Postal Centre, tel: 09-367 6009; www.greatbarrier.co.nz. Note: there are no banks on the island so do bring cash, although credit card facilities are available at most commercial outlets.

Gisborne
Gisborne i-site Visitors Centre, 209 Grey Street, tel: 06-868 6139; www.gisbornenz.com.

Hamilton
Hamilton i-site Visitors Centre, Transport Centre, 373 Anglesea Street, tel: 07-839 3580; www.visithamilton.co.nz.

Hastings
Hastings i-site Visitors Centre, corner Russell and Heretaunga streets, tel: 06-873 5526; www.hastings.co.nz.

Kaitaia / Northland
Far North i-site Visitors Centre, Jaycee Park, South Road, Kaitaia, tel: 09-408 0879; www.visitnorthland.co.nz.

Napier
Napier i-site Visitors Centre, 100 Marine Parade, tel: 06-834 1911; www.napiervic.co.nz.

New Plymouth
New Plymouth i-site Visitors Centre
Puke Ariki, 1 Ariki Street, tel: 06-759
6060; www.pukeariki.com; daily 9am–
6pm, until 9pm Wed and 5pm
weekends; free. Town-centre
museum, public library and visitor
centre in one.

Ohakune
Ruapehu Visitors Centre, 54 Clyde
Street, tel: 06-385 8427; www.
visitruapehu.com.

Orewa
The Hibiscus Coast Visitor
Information Centre, 214A Hibiscus
Coast Highway, Orewa, tel: 09-426
0076.

Paihia
Bay of Islands i-site Visitors Centre,
The Wharf, Marsden Road,
tel: 09-402 7345; www.paihia.co.nz.

Palmerston North
Palmerston North i-site Visitors
Centre, 52 The Square, tel: 06-350
1922; www.manawatunz.co.nz.

Rotorua
Rotorua i-site Visitors Centre, 1167
Fenton Street, tel: 07-348 5179; www.
rotoruanz.com.

Russell
Russell Information Centre and
Wahoo Fishing Charters, end of the
Wharf, tel: 09-403 8020.

South Auckland
Franklin i-site Visitors Centre, SH1,
Mill Road, Bombay, tel: 09-236 0670;
www.franklincountry.com.
Auckland Airport i-site Visitors
Centre, International Terminal,
Mangere, tel: 09-275 6467; www.
aucklandnz.com.

Taupo
Taupo i-site Visitors Centre, 30
Tongariro Street, tel: 07-376 0027;
www.laketauponz.com.

Tauranga/Mount Maunganui
Tauranga i-site Visitors Centre, 95
Willow Street, tel: 07-578 8103; www.
tauranga.govt.nz; www.bayofplentynz.com.

Te Aroha
Te Aroha i-site Visitors Centre, 102
Whitaker Street, tel: 07-884 8052;
www.tearoha-info.co.nz.

Te Urewera National Park
Aniwaniwa Visitors Centre, SH38,
Aniwaniwa, Wairoa, tel: 06-837 3900;
www.doc.govt.nz. Daily 8am–5pm.

Thames
Tourism Coromandel, 1st Floor,
Goldfields Shopping Centre, 100 May
Street, tel: 07-868 0017; www.
thecoromandel.com.

Waiheke Island
Waiheke Island i-site Visitors
Centre, 2 Korora Road, Artworks,
Oneroa, tel: 09-372 1234; www.
waihekenz.com.

**Waitakere City and
West Coast Beaches**
Destination Waitakere, tel: 09-979
2333; www.aucklandnz.com.
Arataki Visitors Centre, daily 9am–
5pm summer; 10am–4pm winter; tel:
09-817 4941. The place to plan
explorations of the Waitakere Ranges
and west-coast beaches.

Waitomo
Waitomo i-site Visitors Centre, 21
Caves Road, Waitomo Caves, tel:
07-878 7640, 0800-474 839; www.
waitomodiscovery.co.nz.

Wanganui
Wanganui i-site Visitors Centre,
101 Guyton Street, tel: 06-349 0508;
www.wanganuinz.com.

Warkworth Area
Warkworth i-site Visitors Centre, 1
Baxter Street, Warkworth, tel: 09-425
9081; www.warkworth-information.co.nz. A
good website for the area is www.
matakanacoast.com.

Wellington
Wellington i-site Visitors Centre,
corner Wakefield Street and Civic
Square, tel: 04-802 4860; www.
wellingtonnz.com.

BELOW: the Shotover Jet.

Whakapapa Village/National Park
Whakapapa Visitors Centre at DOC,
Whakapapa Village, tel: 07-892 3729;
www.doc.govt.nz. Open 8am–6pm.

Whangamata
Whangamata i-site Visitors Centre,
616 Port Road, tel: 07 865 8340;
www.whangamatainfo.co.nz.

Whangarei
Whangarei i-site Visitors Centre,
SH1, tel: 09-438 1079; www.
whangareinz.org.nz.

Whitianga
Whitianga i-site Visitors Centre,
Albert Street and Blacksmith Lane,
tel: 07-866 5555; www.whitianga.co.nz.

Tourist Information Offices: South Island

Akaroa
Akaroa Information Centre, 80 Rue
Lavaud, tel: 03-304 8600; www.akaroa.
com.

Aoraki Mount Cook National Park
Aoraki Mount Cook Visitors Centre,
Bowen Drive, Mount Cook, tel: 03-435
1186; www.doc.govt.nz.

Arrowtown
Arrowtown Promotion and Business
Association, 49 Buckingham Street;
www.arrowtown.org.nz.
The Lakes District Museum operates
the local Information Centre, tel:
03-442 1824; www.museumqueenstown.
com.

Arthur's Pass
Arthur's Pass Visitor Information
Centre, tel: 03-318 9211; www.apinfo.
co.nz.

Blenheim
Blenheim i-site Visitors Centre,
Railway Station, SH1, tel: 03-577
8080; www.destinationmarlborough.com.

Christchurch
Christchurch and Canterbury i-site
Visitors Centre, Cathedral Square,
tel: 03-379 9629; www.akaroa.com.

Dunedin
Dunedin i-site Visitors Centre, 48
The Octagon, tel: 03-474 3300; www.
cityofdunedin.com.

Fox Glacier
Fox Glacier Visitors Centre,
Department of Conservation, SH6,
tel: 03-751 0807; www.west-coast.co.nz;
www.glaciercountry.co.nz.

Franz Josef Glacier
Franz Josef Glacier Visitors Centre, Department of Conservation, SH6, tel: 03-752 0796; www.west-coast.co.nz; www.glaciercountry.co.nz.

Greymouth
Greymouth i-site Visitors Centre, corner Mackay and Herbert streets, tel: 03-768 5101, 0800-767 080; www.west-coast.co.nz.

Haast
Haast Visitors Centre, Department of Conservation, Haast Junction, tel: 03-750 0809; www.doc.govt.nz.

Hanmer Springs
Hurunui i-site Visitors Centre, 42 Amuri Avenue, tel: 03-315 7128; www.hurunui.com.

Hokitika
Westland i-site Visitors Centre, Carnegie Building, Hamilton Street, tel: 03-755 6166; www.west-coast.co.nz.

Invercargill
Invercargill i-site Visitors Centre, 108 Gala Street, tel: 03-214 6243; www.invercargill.org.nz.
Venture Southland Tourism, 143 Spey Street, Invercargill, tel: 03-211 1429; www.southlandnz.com.

Kaikoura
Kaikoura i-site Visitors Centre, West End, tel: 03-319 5641; www.kaikoura.co.nz.

Lake Tekapo
Lake Tekapo Information Centre, Main Highway next to Lake Tekapo Scenic Resort, tel: 03-680 6686; www.laketekapountouched.co.nz.

Methven
Methven i-site Visitors Centre, 121 Main Street, tel: 03-302 8955; www.methveninfo.co.nz.

Nelson
Nelson i-site Visitors Centre, Millers Acres Centre, 77 Trafalgar Street, tel: 03-548 2304; www.i-SITENelsonNZ.com.

Picton and the Sounds
Picton i-site Visitors Centre, Foreshore, Picton, tel: 03-520 3113; www.destinationmarlborough.com.

Queenstown
Queenstown i-site Visitors Centre, Clock Tower Building, corner Shotover and Camp streets, tel: 03-442 4100, 0800-668 888; www.queenstownz.co.nz.

Stewart Island
Rakiura National Park Visitors Centre, Main Road, tel: 03-219 0002; www.doc.govt.nz is an indispensable source of information on how to make the most of this conservationists' paradise.
Stewart Island i-site Visitors Centre, Main Road, Halfmoon Bay, tel: 03-219 0009; www.stewartisland.co.nz.

Te Anau
Fiordland i-site Visitors Centre, Lakefront Drive (next to Real Journeys Office), tel: 03-249 8900.

Wanaka
Lake Wanaka i-site Visitors Centre, Waterfront Log Cabin, 100 Ardmore Street, tel: 03-443 1233; www.lakewanaka.co.nz.

V isas and Passports

Visa requirements differ, depending on nationality, purpose of visit and length of stay. Visitors must produce an onward or return ticket and sufficient funds to support themselves during their stay. Check with the New Zealand diplomatic or consular office in your country of residence (see page 379) or on www.immigration.govt.nz. All visitors to New Zealand require passports, which must be valid for at least three months beyond the date you intend leaving the country. See also Customs Regulations, page 378.

The following classes of people are prohibited by law from entering, either as tourists or immigrants, regardless of country of origin:
• Those suffering from tuberculosis, syphilis, leprosy, or mental disorders.
• Those convicted of an offence which drew a sentence of imprisonment of over one year.
• Those who have previously been deported from New Zealand.

BELOW: rural mailbox.

W eights and Measures

New Zealand uses the metric system to record weights and measurements, and has done so for more than 30 years. This decision was based on the requirements of the country's trading and export partners, and although the movement towards metric began in 1969, it wasn't until 14th December 1976 that it was fully integrated.

Women Travellers

New Zealand is a relatively safe country to travel around as a female, but, as always when travelling, it pays to heed a few basic precautions.

Projecting confidence and looking busy – or as if you know where you are going – is one of the best ways to stay safe and avoid being hassled. Consider carrying a mobile phone as it provides a little extra security and travelling with as little luggage as possible. When you are overburdened, you become an easy target for thieves.

Avoid doing things at night that can be done in the light of day, like withdrawing money from an ATM. As elsewhere in the world, it is best not to walk alone at night in areas that are dimly lit. Catch a taxi back to your accommodation instead. Your accommodation can provide the name and phone number for a local taxi company they trust. Hitch-hiking alone at any time of day or night, or in isolated places, is also not advisable.

Accommodation-wise, staying in a busy hotel in the heart of town is a lot less inconspicuous than a cottage on the outskirts.

Always put your safety first and remember that it's not all bad news: travelling alone as a woman makes you approachable.

FURTHER READING

History

The Penguin History of New Zealand by Michael King. This is the definitive New Zealand history.

Being Pakeha Now: Reflections and Recollections of a White Native by Michael King. The first serious analysis of what it means to be a non-Maori New Zealander. While recognising the place of Maori in New Zealand, King argues that Pakeha, too, belong inescapably to this country and have no other home. A topical and very popular book.

Moko by Michael King and Marti Friedlander. An iconic Kiwi book, with photos by one of the country's most eminent photographers – Moko features portraits of Maori tattooing in the 20th century and the women who wore it.

Healing Our History – the Challenge of the Treaty of Waitangi by Robert Consedine and Joanna Consedine. Expands upon critical treaty issues: the foreshore and seabed debate, Maori access to political power, the Maori economy, Maori education and the Treaty settlement process.

Heartlands: New Zealand Historians write about Where History Happened edited by Gavin McLean and Kyman Gentry. New Zealand's leading historians write about their favourite historic places, linking special moments in New Zealand history with personal memories.

Hongi Hika by D. Urlich-Clother. Biography of the great northern chief Hongi Hika, whose Ngapuhi tribe conquered large parts of the North Island of New Zealand during the Musket Wars of the early 1800s.

Literature/Fiction

The Bone People by Keri Hulme. Winner of the British McConnell Prize for fiction.

Dogside Story by Patricia Grace. Internationally acclaimed novel explores the strength and conflicts of the whanau (family), the power of the land, and the aroha (love) and humour of the community.

Landings by Jenny Patrick. Set on the Whanganui River at the turn of the 20th century, this historical novel weaves together the lives of the people who have made it their home.

Edwin + Matilda by Laurence Fearnley. Runner-up in the Montana 2008 Awards, this novel describes the unusual bond formed between a 62-two-year-old photographer and a 22-year-old girl.

Behind Closed Doors by Ngaire Thomas. This first-hand account tells of one family's experience in New Zealand's exclusive Brethren community.

The Denniston Rose by Jenny Pattrick. A bestseller, set in the 1880s, this is a story of isolation and survival, as spirited child Rose fends for herself in the bleak coal-mining settlement of Denniston, located high above New Zealand's west coast.

Opportunity by Charlotte Grimshaw. Individual stories of brilliantly drawn characters are interwoven in this novel about storytelling and opportunism.

Katherine Mansfield New Zealand Stories edited by V. O'Sullivan. A collection of the New Zealand stories of New Zealand's most celebrated writer, and one of the key figures in the history of the short story in English.

Kitty by Deborah Challinor. In the untamed Bay of Islands, missionaries struggle to establish Victorian England across the harbour from the infamous whaling port of Kororareka, hell-hole of the Pacific.

Once Were Warriors by Alan Duff. Over 85,000 copies in circulation in New Zealand, this is one of the most talked-about books ever published in this country, and is the basis of a powerful film.

Sky Dancer by Witi Ihimaera. This roller-coaster adventure ride of a read provides new ways of exploring Maori myth. Skylark O'Shea is on holiday with her mother at a town on the coast. Soon it becomes clear that Tuapa is not as it seems, and strange things begin to happen.

The Whale Rider by Witi Ihimaera. The story follows eight-year-old Kahu and her struggle to gain recognition as heir to chiefdom of Ngati Konohi – and her inherited ability to communicate with the whales. Made into a popular film.

Tu, A Novel by Patricia Grace. This is the story of three brothers who fought with the Maori Battalion in WWII. Only one returns home. Grace is one of New Zealand's greatest living novelists.

Plants/Animals/Natural History/Environment

Birds of Aotearoa – A Natural and Cultural History by Margaret Orbel. New Zealand's native birds are described through scientific references and an account of the ways they have been understood in Maori traditions, song and artefacts.

New Zealand Frogs and Reptiles by Gill and Whitaker. Identify 59 species of frogs, tuataras, geckos, skinks, turtles and sea snakes.

New Zealand Fishes by L. Paul. Identification of fishes in New Zealand waters. Species are described, with notes on distribution, life history and population.

From Weta to Kauri Janet Hunt and Rob Lucas. All-in-one guide to the New Zealand forest covering over 300 species of insects, birds and plants, with pictures and photographs to help with identification. A great book to take tramping.

A Field Guide to the Alpine Plants of New Zealand by John Salmon. Ideal field companion for walkers. Detailed descriptions and photographs.

Nature Guide to the New Zealand Forest by J. Dawson and R. Lucas. A comprehensive guide, detailed descriptions and photographs.

Back from the Brink: the Fight to Save Our Endangered Birds by Gerard Hutching. Back from the Brink celebrates the continued efforts of scientists to save New Zealand's endangered bird species. Over the past three decades, these groups have effectively saved a significant proportion of the most endangered bird populations.

Deer : The New Zealand Story by David Yerex. Red deer were introduced to New Zealand in the 1850s – this is the history of deer as trophies, noxious pest, wild resource and farm animal.

Our Islands, Our Selves by David Young. How a conservation ethic emerged in New Zealand, including photographs of conservation reserves throughout the country.
The Living Reef – The Ecology of New Zealand's Rocky Reefs by Andrew N, Francis M. Focuses on key species of fish, animal and plant life, while also profiling New Zealand's most important marine ecosystems, from the Kermadec Islands to Fiordland and Antarctica.
The Penguin Natural World of New Zealand by Gerard Hutching. Covers all aspects of New Zealand's natural history.

Geology

A Canoe in the Mist by Elsie Locke. Set in a volcanic wonderland, *A Canoe in the Mist* tells the true story of the destruction of the famous Pink and White Terraces over 100 years ago.
New Zealand Minerals and Rocks for Beginners by P.J. Forsyth and J.J. Aitken. Details of the minerals and rocks found in New Zealand, how they were formed and where you find them.

Sport

All Black Magic – 100 Years of New Zealand Test Rugby by Bob Howitt and Dianne Haworth. A celebration of New Zealand's national game.
The Book of Fame by L. Jones. Novel retelling the story of the 1905 All Blacks tour.
100 Years of Motoring in New Zealand by John McCrystal. A fascinating trip through a century of the Kiwi love affair with the private motor car.
101 Great Tramps of New Zealand by Mark Pickering and Rodney Smith. Now in its sixth edition, and with over 30,000 copies sold since its first release in 1988; includes new photos and regional maps. It also includes the new Hump Ridge circuit.
Te Araroa – The New Zealand Trail; The Long Pathway through New Zealand by Geoff Chapple. This is the story of an individual who pursued a dream, a walking trail from the far north of New Zealand to the far south, some 2,600km (1,600 miles).
The Complete NZ Fisherman – Saltwater and Freshwater Fishing by G. Thomas. Everything you need to know about fishing. Geoff Thomas, one of New Zealand's best-known fishermen, has written this comprehensive fishing guide specifically for New Zealand conditions.

Food and Wine

Kiwi Favourites by Simon and Alison Holst. Two of New Zealand's favourite cookbook writers provide over 100 popular Kiwi tried-and-true family recipes.
Country New Zealand by Ian Baker. Unique combination of scenic photography and recipes represents a special culinary journey around the rural heartlands of New Zealand.
2009 Buyer's Guide to NZ Wine by Michael Cooper. This "bible" of wines, now in its 17th year of publication, is firmly established as the most authoritative and sought-after guide to New Zealand wines.

Art and Culture

Into the Wider World: A Back Country Miscellany by Brian Turner. Brian Turner is one of New Zealand's best-known and best-loved poets, and most determined conservationists. In this beautifully illustrated anthology he brings together both old and new essays, columns, articles and poetry.
Native Wit by Hamish Keith. Legendary art commentator Hamish Keith's witty, revealing memoir gives readers an insight into his rich and immensely varied life.

Send Us Your Thoughts

We do our best to ensure the information in our books is as accurate and up-to-date as possible. The books are updated on a regular basis using local contacts, who painstakingly add, amend and correct as required. However, some details (such as telephone numbers and opening times) are liable to change, and we are ultimately reliant on our readers to put us in the picture.

We welcome your feedback, especially your experience of using the book "on the road". Maybe we recommended a hotel that you liked (or another that you didn't), or you came across a great bar or new attraction we missed.

We will acknowledge all contributions, and we'll offer an Insight Guide to the best letters received.

Please write to us at:
Insight Guides
PO Box 7910
London SE1 1WE
Or email us at:
insight@apaguide.co.uk

Rita Angus: An Artist's Life by Jill Trevelyan. In this revelatory and subtle book, Jill Trevelyan traces Angus's entire life, from her childhood in Napier and Palmerston North to her death in Wellington in 1970. Drawing on a wealth of newly available archives and letters, she brings Rita Angus to life, her attitudes and emotions, pacifist and feminist beliefs and her dedication, above all, to life as an artist.
Mana Pounamu – New Zealand Jade by Russell Beck. New Zealand jade, has always played an important role in New Zealand being pivotal to the development of Maori culture, traditionally serving as tool, weapon, adornment and currency.

Other Insight Guides

Insight Guides publish several other titles on the Australasian region:

Insight Guide: Australia, a superbly illustrated guide covering the island continent in detail.

Insight Guide: Tasmania is the complete guide to this magnificently scenic island.

Insight Step By Step Guide: New Zealand offers eighteen tailor-made itineraries to guide you around the country.

Insight Smart Guide: Sydney, a detailed look at the city in a handy A–Z format.

Insight Fleximap: New Zealand, a durable and practical laminated map, with a list of recommended sights.

ART AND PHOTO CREDITS

Agrodome 183
Alamy 136, 137, 259, 274, 317
APA 87R, 93, 239T
AP Photo 316T
Julian Apse/photonewzealand 264/265
Auckland Institute and Museum 30, 35, 36, 130, 216
Auckland Public Library Photograph Collection 34
Bay Of Plenty Images 4B, 6BR, 14/15, 185T, 188T, 358, 371
Warren Bayliss/photonewzealand 68
Andy Belcher/APA 6T, 7TR, CBL&CR, 17T, 21, 69L, 99, 118/119, 123BR, 126, 131&T, 132, 133, 134&T, 138, 153, 155T, 159T, 162T, 166, 172T, 173, 175T, 176/177, 178, 181T, 191&T, 195T, 201T, 202T, 204, 206, 207R, 210, 216T, 232, 235, 237T, 240T, 242T, 248T, 251, 261&T, 262, 266, 267, 268&T, 270BL, 273&T, 274T, 275, 278, 279, 280, 282, 285, 286, 287, 289, 294, 297&T, 299&T, 305, 307T, 321, 325, 326T, 336, 342, 363, 374, 382, 385, 386, 387
Harley Betts/photonewzealand 190
Rob Brown/Tourism New Zealand 7BR, 314T
Dennis Buurman/photonewzealand 236T
Chris Cameron/ Tourism New Zealand 127
Jocelyn Carlin/photonewzealand 85, 315
Richard Casswell/photonewzealand 253
Graham Charles/photonewzealand 171
CHCH 260T, 263T
Christchurch and Canterbury Marketing 71
Christchurch Art Gallery 62, 248
ClearwaterNZ 252
Ben Crawford/Tourism New Zealand 142, 148/149, 174
Gerald Cubitt 8BL
Sonya Cullimore/Tourism New Zealand 290
Stan Daniels/photonewzealand 256, 288
Jerry Dennis 244, 245, 247T
Destination Queenstown 284
Destination Rotorua 8C, 368
Darroch Donald/photonewzealand 65
Francis Dorai/APA 252T, 258, 270R, 281T, 302
Craig Dowling 256T
Driving Creek Railway and Potteries 169T
Mary Evans Picture Library 28, 29, 33, 39, 55
Gareth Eyres/Tourism New Zealand 313
Fat Tyre Adventures 322
Fotopress News Picture Agency 56, 132T
Arno Gasteiger/photonewzealand 86, 150, 170, 181, 185, 211, 306
Clive Gee/Reuters 43
Govett-Brewster Art Gallery 205
Simon Grosset 32
A.J. Hackett 285T
Hawke's Bay Tourism 198T, 199, 203
James Heremaia/Tourism New Zealand 8BR, 48/49, 53, 209T, 380

Miles Holden/Tourism New Zealand 2/3
Maarten Holl 76
Peter Hutton Collection 26, 31
iStockphoto.com 4T, 5, 8T, 16, 18, 20, 22B, 67, 69R, 82/83, 87L, 90, 91, 95, 104, 120, 135, 164, 182, 186, 187, 198, 213, 219&T, 247, 255, 257, 263, 271, 291, 298, 327, 334, 346, 357, 377, 384
Karori Sanctuary Trust/PA Wire 101
Richard King/photonewzealand 109
Hans Klüche 137T
The Kobal Collection 78
Lake Taupo Lodge/Tourism New Zealand 379
Ross Land/Getty 23B
Landsdown–Rigby 50, 169
Max Lawrence 217, 225, 236, 239, 251, 259T
Leonardo 326C
Rob Lile/photonewzealand 110, 140, 186T, 249, 292
Lodestone Press 22T, 38
Fay Looney/Tourism New Zealand 129, 208
Holger Leue/Tourism New Zealand 124/125, 154T, 310T
Nigel Marple/Reuters 23T
Sarah Masters/photonewzealand 269
Bob McCree/Tourism New Zealand 96/97, 168, 288T
Chris McLennan/photonewzealand 188, 189, 237, 254
Chris McLennan/Tourism New Zealand 7TL, CTL&BL, 98, 100, 103, 129T, 155, 157, 160, 164T, 179, 184, 231BR, 309, 331
Peter Morath/Tourism New Zealand 170T
New Line Studios 74, 79
The New Zealand Herald and Weekly News 44, 45, 200
New Zealand Tourist Board 59, 88, 108, 111, 141
Stewart Nimmo/photonewzealand 272
Northland Tourism 123TR&BL, 142T, 151, 156&T, 158, 159, 320, 330
Mark Orbell/photonewzealand 281, 308T
Mustafa Ozer/AFP/Getty 42
Penguin Place 102
Photobank New Zealand 316B
photonewzealand 58, 283
Axel Poignant Archive 24, 25, 27
Mike Powell/Getty 47
Neil Rabinowitz/Corbis 46
Andy Radka/photonewzealand 222
Rainbow Spring Nature Park184T
Gilbert van Reenen/Tourism New Zealand 303
M Ross/photonewzealand 260
Kieran Scott/Tourism New Zealand 17B, 57L, 89, 154, 231TR, 294T
Nick Servian/photonewzealand 92, 161, 162
Nick Servian/Tourism New Zealand 40, 145, 353
The Spire Hotel/Tourism New Zealand 351
Tony Stewart/photonewzealand 84, 201
Rob Suisted/Tourism New Zealand

10/11, 121L&BR, 145T, 163, 197, 228/229, 231L
Wayne Tait/photonewzealand 172
N.Tepper/Arcaid/Rex Features 212
Julia Thorne/photonewzealand 314
Topfoto 1, 54
Darryl Torckler/photonewzealand 106
Tourism Auckland 144, 146, 341, 355
Tourism Dunedin 9T, 293&T, 295
Tourism Eastland 194, 195
Tourism Leisure Group 165
Tourism Rotorua 19, 183T
Tourism West Coast 270T
Ian Trafford/photonewzealand 57R, 233, 240, 242, 243, 312
Ian Trafford/Tourism New Zealand 63, 94, 116/117, 202, 203T, 206T, 207L, 209, 221T, 224T, 225&T, 324, 366
Treble Cone Ski 107
Darryl Torckler/photonewzealand 241
Alexander Turnbull Library 37, 41
Scott Venning/Tourism New Zealand 3B, 60, 61, 70, 136T, 143, 147, 167, 222T, 223&T, 361
Venture Southland 307, 308, 310
Holly Wademan/Tourism New Zealand 12/13
David Wall/Tourism New Zealand 6BL, 175, 226/227, 311
Waitakere Estate 349
Miz Watanabe/photonewzealand 52
WellingtonNZ.com 51, 64, 121TR, 215&T, 218, 220, 221
Mick Wheeler/Tourism New Zealand 114/115
World of Wearable Art and Classic Cars Museum 238
Angela Wong/APA 250
Josh Woskett/Tourism New Zealand 210T
Zorb Rotorua 105

PICTURE SPREADS

72/73: Blaine Harrington 72/73; Hans Klüche 73TR; Axel Poignant Archive 72BL&BR, 73ML&BR
80/81: Arno Gasteiger/Tourism New Zealand 80TL; The Kobal Collection 80/81, 80C&BL; Rob Suisted/Tourism New Zealand 81TR
112/113: Simon Grosset/FSP 112/113, 112BR, 113TR&BR; Hans Klüche 113CL; Tourism Rotorua 112BL
192/193: Jerry Dennis 192BL, 193TR; Blaine Harrington 192/193, 192BR, 193CL; Chris McLennan/Tourism New Zealand 193BR
276/277: Andy Belcher/APA 277BR; Wolfgang Bittmann 277BR; Craig Dowling 276BR; iStockphoto.com 276TR; NHPA/ANT 276/277, 277CL

Map Production:
Polyglott Kartographie

© 2009 Apa Publications GmbH & Co. Verlag KG (Singapore branch)

Production: Linton Donaldson

INDEX

Numbers in bold refer to principal entries